Vital Records of Lyme and Dorchester New Hampshire 1887-2004

Richard P. Roberts

HERITAGE BOOKS
2006

HERITAGE BOOKS
AN IMPRINT OF HERITAGE BOOKS, INC.

Books, CDs, and more   Worldwide

For our listing of thousands of titles see our website
at
www.HeritageBooks.com

Published 2006 by
HERITAGE BOOKS, INC.
Publishing Division
65 East Main Street
Westminster, Maryland 21157-5026

Copyright ' 2006 Richard P. Roberts

All rights reserved. No part of this book may be reproduced or transmitted in any form or by any means, electronic or mechanical, including photocopying, recording or by any information storage and retrieval system without written permission from the author, except for the inclusion of brief quotations in a review.

International Standard Book Number: 978-0-7884-4119-1

TABLE OF CONTENTS

Introduction 1

Lyme Births 5

Lyme Marriages 155

Lyme Deaths 349

Dorchester Births 485

Dorchester Marriages 511

Dorchester Deaths 549

INTRODUCTION

Early vital records of many New Hampshire towns can be located either through the State's Vital Records Department or on microfilms made available through LDS Family History Centers. Some, however, have been lost or are inaccessible for various reasons. A valuable, but labor intensive, source of information for events occurring in 1887 and thereafter is the vital statistics which are provided in a section of the Annual Town Reports of many New Hampshire towns. Many of these town reports have been collected at the New Hampshire State Library in Concord, as well as more local repositories.

The amount of information published in these Annual Town Reports varies tremendously over time. Early records are far more detailed and comprehensive. Recent records are rather cursory, but issues of confidentiality and sensitivity to the privacy of those residents still living offsets the lack of information of genealogical value.

While the information provided is often very helpful, one must remember that it is not fool-proof or universally accurate, nor is it the primary source or the actual vital record itself. The fact that much of the data is self-reported suggests that it is reliable. However, errors in transcription, spelling (particularly with respect to French-Canadian and European families), and printing often are obvious. In addition, there may be, for example, two children listed as the third child of a particular couple, or the mother's maiden name, age or place of birth may differ or may be inconsistent from one entry to another. It is also important to note that a birth, marriage or death may have been reported in another town although the subject resided in Lyme or Dorchester, or the entry may not have been made in the first place.

Despite these shortcomings, the information contained in the Annual Town Reports can be a valuable tool for the genealogist. Marriage and death records from the late 1800's often identify parents who were married nearly a century before. Finally, those families that have remained in Lyme, Dorchester or adjacent towns for several generations can be traced and connected to the present.

Births - To the extent the information is available, the entries in the list of births are given as follows: child's name; date of birth; place of birth (where provided); the number of children in the family; father's name, place of birth, age and occupation; and the mother's maiden name, age and place of birth. As noted above, the amount of information in earlier records is substantially greater than in more recent years.

At times, the given names of many children are missing from the early reports. In this case, the sex of the child is given and they are listed chronologically at the beginning of the surname heading. On occasion, the child's name can be determined from marriage or death records, as well as secondary sources. These names are shown in brackets where available.

Marriages - To the extent the information is available, the entries in the list of marriages follow this format: groom's name; groom's residence; bride's name; bride's residence; date of marriage; place of marriage (where provided); H, signifying husband's information, and W, signifying wife's information, each in the following order - age, occupation, number of the marriage (if other than first), father's name, father's place of birth, father's occupation, mother's name, mother's place of birth, and mother's occupation. The name of the official conducting the marriage has been omitted but is generally provided in the original document. A separate listing of brides in alphabetical order follows this section in order to allow for cross-referencing.

Deaths - To the extent available, the entries in the list of deaths contain the following information: name of decedent; place of death; date of death; age at death; cause of death; marital status; birthplace; father's name; father's place of birth; mother's name; and mother's place of birth. Most of the entries listing a cause of death are self-explanatory.

Missing Years - There are several years during which Dorchester failed to publish the vital statistics as part of the annual report, perhaps because no such events occurred. In addition, the quality and completeness of the information in some years is questionable and, as always, an original source should be consulted.

LYME
BIRTHS

ABBOTT,
stillborn son, b. 5/17/1892; first; E. C. Abbott (farmer, 41, Fairlee, VT) and Hattie W. Robbins (31, Dorchester)
son, b. 7/16/1929 in Lyme; second; Freeman H. Abbott (laborer, 28, Sandwich) and Sadie M. Hanaford (25, Sanbornton)

ACKERMAN,
Emery William, b. 1/6/1908 in Lyme; seventh; William Ackerman (farmer, 38, St. Albans, VT) and Esther Emery (39, St. Albans, VT)
Fred Charles, b, 1/25/1940 in Hanover; third; Scott H. Ackerman (truck driver, 26, Chelsea, VT) and Flora B. Gray (19, Sutton, VT)
Golda Norris, b. 8/26/1905 in Lyme; sixth; William H. Ackerman (farmer, 36, St. Albans, VT) and Esther Francis Emery (36, St. Albans, VT)
Roger Jessie, b. 4/24/1942 in Hanover; fourth; Scott H. Ackerman (fillet cutter, 28, Chelsea, VT) and Flora B. Gray (21, Sutton, VT)

ACKERSON,
Eric Fernald, b. 11/2/1979 in Hanover; Richard Ackerson and Margaret Fernald
Kate West, b. 3/20/1982 in Hanover; Richard A. Ackerson and Margaret B. Fernald

ADAMS,
Bruce Barton, b. 3/8/1917; first; Harold L. Adams (farming, 22, Morrisville, VT) and Mildred Boyce (23, Fairfax, VT)

ALBERTS,
Jill Lorraine, b. 6/21/1966 in Lebanon; first; James Alberts (grad. student, Chicago, IL) and Lora E. Mayer (Berwyn, IL)

ALDEN,
F. Gertrude, b. 7/29/1891; first; R. Seabury Alden (farm supt., 33, Halifax, MA) and F. Gertrude Sawyer (24, Lyme); residence - Concord

ALDRICH,
Ralph, b. 11/8/1895 in Lyme; second; Clarence C. Aldrich (laborer,

35, Orford, PQ) and Addie Merrill (28, Dorchester)

ALLEN,
John Patrick, b. 12/16/1978 in Hanover; Norman Bruce Allen and
 Roberta A. Cook
Lise Margrethe, b. 11/17/1971 in Hanover; John Allen and Else
 Hyllested

AM[M]ELL,
Dorothy M., b. 9/12/1907 in Lyme; eleventh; Albert Amell, Jr.
 (section man, 37, Barnet) and Mary J. Cheney (34, Barnet, VT)
Gladys Solma, b. 9/7/1906 in Lyme; tenth; Albert Ammell, Jr.
 (section hand, 38, Barnet, VT) and Mary Cheney (32, Barnet,
 VT)
May E., b. 4/10/1901; second; Nelson Amell (laborer, 30, Barnet,
 VT) and Viola Stebbins (27, N. Hadley, PQ)

ANDREWS,
Barbara F., b. 12/6/1907 in Lyme; first; Lee C. Andrews (merchant,
 30, Lyme) and Alberta G. Cheney (31, Hyde Park, VT)

ANSELL,
stillborn son, b. 1/10/1921 in Lyme; first; Ray Ansell (clerk, 21,
 Manchester) and Margaret Gray (21, Bradford, VT)

ARMS,
Mary Ann, b. 2/6/1943 in Hanover; first; George Arms (US Navy, 28,
 CT) and Marion F. Sanborn (22, Gorham); resdience – New
 Rochelle, NY

ARMSTRONG,
Timothy James, b. 2/3/1986 in Hanover; Ted A. Armstrong and
 Patricia A. James

ASH,
Brandi Lee, b. 4/12/1981 in Hanover; Duane F. Ash and Kim L.
 Robertson
Kalen Marie, b. 1/26/1984 in Hanover; Duane F. Ash and Kim L.
 Robertson

ASHLINE,
daughter, b. 9/15/1968 in Hanover; Edward Ashline and Inez M. Reed
Christie Lynn, b. 6/5/1967 in Hanover; third; Edward Ashline, Jr. (mechanic, Hartland, VT) and Inez M. Reed (Hanover)
Lisa Marie, b. 4/7/1965 in Hanover; second; Edward F. Ashline (laborer, Hartland, VT) and Inez Reed (Hanover)
Wendy Anne, b. 12/31/1962 in Hanover; Edward Ashlie, Jr. (Hartland, VT) and Inez M. Reed (23, Hanover)

AUBUT,
Meaghan Michelle, b. 6/13/1997 in Laconia; Tracy Edward Aubut and Michelle Claire Beaudry

AULIS,
Dana Richard, b. 5/14/1963 in Lebanon; Richard E. Aulis (laborer, Hanover) and Elizabeth A. Clogston (31, Hanover)
Douglas Edward, b. 9/18/1965 in Hanover; second; Richard E. Aulis (truck driver, Hanover) and Elizabeth Clogston (Hanover)

AUSTIN,
stillborn daughter, b. 12/9/1907 in Lyme; first; Chauncey G. Austin (farmer, 28, Fairlee, VT) and Ida A. Smith (27, Lyme)
daughter, b. 2/22/1914; second; Alfred A. Austin (sawyer, 30, Canaan) and Mary A. Haskins (20, Enfield)

AVERILL,
Paul, b. 3/2/1888; second; Fred Averill (painter, 29, Barton, VT) and Lizzie O. ----- (29, Hanover, NY)

AVERY,
Christian Lee Quinton, b. 2/13/1994 in Lebanon; David Avery and Hebe Quinton
Cora Lovejoy, b. 9/3/1910 in Lyme; second; William Avery (laborer, 30, Chatham, NB) and Cora H. Lovejoy (32, Lyme)
Meade Rose Quinton, b. 9/11/1997 in Lebanon; David Leonard Avery and Hebe Bate Quinton

BACON,
daughter, b. 1/15/1933 in Lyme; second; George W. Bacon (laborer, 22, Thetford, VT) and Mina H. Hill (19, Danville, PQ)

Daryl Carlton, b. 10/9/1959 in Hanover; Carlton Bacon (electrician, 28, Norwich, VT) and Ruth M. Emerson (29, Piermont, VT)

Jane A., b. 5/6/1935 in Lyme; fourth; George W. Bacon (laborer, 25, Thetford, VT) and Mina Hill (21, Quebec)

Justin David, b. 5/1/1988 in Lebanon; Thomas C. Husband and Vicki Bacon

Laurie Lynn, b. 4/18/1963 in Hanover; Talbert W. Bacon (Lyme) and Priscilla A. LaMott (20, Hanover)

Neil William, b. 6/2/1970 in Hanover; Carlton G. Bacon and Ruth M. Emerson

Pamela Jean, b. 2/22/1948 in Hanover; sixth; George W. Bacon (foreman, 37, E. Thetford, VT) and Mina H. Hill (34, Danville, PQ)

Stewart Bruce, b. 2/2/1934 in Lyme; third; George W. Bacon (laborer, 24, Thetford, VT) and Nina H. Hill (20, Danville, PQ)

Susan Marie, b. 9/5/1956 in Hanover; Carlton G. Bacon (electrician, 25, Norwich, VT) and Ruth M. Emmerson (26, Piermont)

Talbert W., b. 7/2/1937 in Lyme; fifth; George Bacon (RR hand, 27, Thetford, VT) and Mina Hill (23, Quebec)

Vicki Lee, b. 10/16/1961 in Lebanon; Talbert W. Bacon (laborer, Lyme) and Priscilla LaMott (19, Hanover)

BADGER,
Elmer Edward, b. 1/20/1914; first; Carroll E. Badger (farmer, 24, Lyme) and Sadie F. Pellecer (24, FL)

Marion, b. 6/22/1892; seventh; Henry M. Badger (farmer, 46, Lowell, MA) and Clara H. Post (40, Lyme)

Mary, b. 7/26/1894 in Lyme; eighth; Henry M. Badger (farmer, 48, Lowell, MA) and Clara H. Post (42, Lyme)

Walter Edwin, b. 6/1/1917; second; Carroll E. Badger (farming, 27, Lyme) and Sadie Pellecer (28, Moultrie, FL)

BAILEY,
son, b. 4/16/1952 in Hanover; second; Morton Bailey (farmer, 41, Lyme) and Myrtle Russ (40, W. Fairlee, VT)

Barbara Jean, b. 4/18/1935 in Hanover; second; Henry A. Bailey (foreman, 41, Lyme) and Ida M. Hall (34, Canaan)

Beverly Ann, b. 12/13/1929 in Hanover; first; Henry A. Bailey (farmer, 36, Lyme) and Ida M. Hall (28, Canaan)

Dean Ackerman, b. 12/15/1916; third; Frank H. Bailey (farming, 41, Lyme) and Mary J. Ackerman (38, Chelsea, VT)

Deborah Jean, b. 9/15/1953 in Hanover; Morton Bailey (farmer, 42, Lyme) and Myrtle Russ (41, W. Fairlee, VT)
Della Myrtle, b. 8/6/1933 in Lyme; first; Henry J. Bailey (laborer, 27, Bradford, VT) and Margaret T. Wilmot (19, Lyme)
Elizabeth Myrtle, b. 7/19/1979 in Hanover; Morton R. Bailey and Katherine Gogg
Henry A., b. 9/1/1893 in Lyme; fifth; Henry A. Bailey (farmer, 45, Lyme) and Augusta M. Howard (46, Lyme)
Justin Edward, b. 5/8/1995 in Lebanon; Rebecca Florence Bailey
Laurence F., b. 7/23/1907 in Lyme; first; Frank H. Bailey (farmer, 32, Lyme) and Mary J. Ackerman (29, Chelsea, VT)
Morton A., b. 3/29/1911 in Lyme; second; Frank H. Bailey (farmer, 36, Lyme) and Mary J. Ackerman (32, Chelsea, VT)
Morton Frank, b. 12/27/1982 in Hanover; Morton R. Bailey and Katherine M. Fogg
Morton Russ, b. 12/10/1939 in Hanover; first; Morton B. Bailey (farmer, 28, Lyme) and Myrtle M. Russ (27, W. Fairlee, VT)
Rebecca Florence, b. 7/22/1974 in Hanover; Morton Russ Bailey and Katherine Mary Fogg
Russell Earl, b. 5/22/1918 in Lyme; first; Henry A. Bailey (farming, 24, Lyme) and Ethel D. Dimick (18, Lyme)
Tammy Rene, b. 3/27/1972 in Lebanon; Daniel R. Bailey and Mildred M. Movelle

BAKER,
Barbra Ann, b. 3/17/1970 in Haverhill; Ronald Roy Baker and Janet Ann Bradley

BALCH,
son, b. 10/25/1910 in Lyme; fourth; Harvey H. Balch (laborer, 40, Hartland, VT) and Josie Morrill (25, Hartford, VT)
stillborn son, b. 8/8/1925 in Lyme; eleventh; Harvey H. Balch (laborer, 57, Hartland, VT) and Lillian J. Morrow (36, Pomfret, VT)
son, b. 5/26/1928 in Lyme; tenth; Harvey H. Balch (laborer, 60, Hartland, VT) and Lillian J. Morrow (43, Hartford, VT)
daughter, b. 7/30/1933 in Lyme; second; Roy E. Balch (laborer, 27, Hartland, VT) and Olive W. Blanchard (20, Orford)
Alfred James, b. 12/26/1943 in Hanover; third; Raymond H. Balch (lumberman, 27, Lyme) and Esther E. Smith (25, Dorchester, MA)

Anthony Michael, b. 1/20/1962 in Lebanon; Raymond J. Balch (mechanic, Lyme) and Beverly J. Frost (18, Lyme)

Benjamin Allen, b. 4/26/1982 in Lebanon; Brett A. Balch and Connie L. Howland

Brenda Lee, b. 4/13/1948 in Dover; first; Donald J. Balch (student, 24, Hanover) and Mary A. Sawyer (26, Haverhill); residence – Durham

Brett Allen, b. 12/12/1959 in Lebanon; Raymond J. Balch (laborer, 22, Lyme) and Beverly J. Frost (16, Lyme)

Bruce Roger, b. 8/21/1947 in Lebanon; fourth; John C. Balch (emp. p. co., 24, Lyme) and Marian L. Gerue (26, Hanover)

Charles Russell, b. 10/16/1918 in Lyme; first; Ralph W. Balch (farming, 24, Lyme) and Mareta J. Smalley (27, Easton)

Charlotte Hilda, b. 9/14/1921 in Lyme; eighth; Harvey H. Balch (laborer, 52, Hartland, VT) and Josie L. Morrill (33, Hartford, VT)

Cindy Lillian, b. 8/24/1957 in Hanover; Ellery Balch (tree surg., Lebanon) and Christine A. Fish (Bradford, VT)

Donald James, b. 7/15/1922 in Hanover; second; Ralph W. Balch (farmer, 28, Lyme) and Mareta J. Smalley (30, Easton)

Dora Edna, b. 9/13/1919 in Lyme; eighth; Harvey H. Balch (laborer, 50, Hartland, VT) and Josie L. Morrill (31, Hartford, VT)

Douglas Grant, b. 2/5/1962 in Lebanon; Ronald J. A. Balch (unemployed, Hanover) and Barbara J. Evans (19, Hanover)

Frank James, b. 2/16/1938 in Haverhill; first; Grant P. Balch (farmer, 31, Mexico, ME) and Margaret Houston (32, Bath)

Harvey R., b. 11/30/1935 in Lyme; third; Roy E. Balch (laborer, 30, Hartland, VT) and Olive W. Blanchard (23, Orford)

Heather Grace, b. 7/7/1990 in Hanover; Russell R. Balch and Sandra G. Wood

James Nelson, b. 8/20/1923 in Lyme; tenth; Harvey H. Balch (laborer, 55, Hartland, VT) and Josie L. Morrow (35, Hartland, VT)

Janet Eva, b. 5/27/1938 in Hanover; first; John C. Balch (waiter, 20, Lyme) and Marion Gerue (17, Hanover)

John Carlton, b. 5/6/1918 in Lyme; seventh; Harvey H. Balch (laborer, 49, Hartland, VT) and Lillian J. Morrill (28, Hartford, VT)

John David, b. 2/4/1942 in Hanover; third; Roy E. Balch (farmer, 41, Cohasset, MA) and Helen A. Wioncek (33, Waterbury, CT)

John Francis, b. 7/19/1950 in Lebanon; fifth; John Balch (janitor, 32,

Lyme) and Marion Gerue (29, Hanover)
Julia Mae, b. 4/8/1939 in Haverhill; second; Grant P. Balch (farmer, 32, Mexico, ME) and Margaret L. Houston (35, Bath)
Justin Charles, b. 7/7/1990 in Hanover; Russell R. Balch and Sandra G. Wood
Kathleen Piper, b. 6/26/1972 in Lebanon; Ronald J. A. Balch and Barbara J. Evans
Kendra Joy, b. 7/3/1953 in Hanover; James N. Balch (delivery man, 29, Lyme) and Elizabeth Hardtke (28, Corinth, VT)
Kerry Lee, b. 4/14/1958 in Hanover; James N. Balch (dry cleaning, 34, Lyme) and Elizabeth Hardtke (33, Corinth, VT)
Kevin Ronald, b. 7/30/1964 in Lebanon; Ronald J. Balch (laborer, Hanover) and Barbara Evans (22, Hanover)
Lindy Ann, b. 3/24/1960 in Hanover; Ellery L. Balch (tree surgeon, 49, Lyme) and Christine A. Fish (24, Bradford, VT)
Mason E., Jr., b. 12/6/1935 in Hanover; second; Mason E. Balch (laborer, 21, Lyme) and Bertha L. Hart (19, Canaan)
Mason Elwin, b. 4/1/1914; fifth; Harvey H. Balch (farmer, 42, Hartland, VT) and Josie L. Merrill (27, Hartland, VT)
Merilyn Ann, b. 1/13/1941 in Hanover; first; Raymond H. Balch (laborer, 24, Lyme) and Esther E. Smith (22, Dorchester, MA)
Michael Evans, b. 4/5/1960 in Lebanon; Ronald J. Balch (laborer, 19, Hanover) and Barbara J. Evans (18, Hanover)
Paula Rae, b. 7/18/1964 in Lebanon; Alfred J. Balch (maintenance man, Hanover) and Barbara A. Moore (18, Hanover)
Penny Marie, b. 6/5/1967 in Hanover; second; Alfred J. Balch (appr. printer, Hanover) and Barbara A. Moore (Hanover)
Ralph West, b. 3/15/1894 in Lyme; first; West S. Balch (farmer, 45, Lyme) and Julia F. Pushee (29, Lyme)
Ramona Jane, b. 3/8/1939 in Hanover; second; Mason E. Balch (laborer, 24, Lyme) and Bertha L. Hart (22, Canaan)
Raymond Harvey, b. 5/29/1916; sixth; Harvey H. Balch (section, 47, Hartland, VT) and Lillian Morrill (28, Hartford, VT)
Raymond J., b. 6/2/1937 in Lyme; fourth; Roy E. Balch (laborer, 31, Hartland, VT) and Olive Blanchard (26, Orford)
Ronald John A., b. 2/14/1941 in Hanover; second; John C. Balch (truck helper, 22, Lyme) and Marion L. Gerue (19, Hanover)
Russell Ralph, b. 3/22/1949 in Hanover; Charles R. Balch and Mertie Uline
Ruth Margaret, b. 11/19/1948 in Haverhill; fourth; Grant P. Balch (farmer, 42, Mexico, ME) and Margaret L. Houston (42, Bath)

Sally Ann, b. 1/4/1939 in Lyme; second; Ellery L. Balch (tree surgeon, 29, Lyme) and Mildred L. Vachon (19, E. Broughton, PQ)

Sarah Louise, b. 10/13/1979 in Hanover; Russell Balch and JoAnn Strathmeyer

Sharon Doreen, b. 8/4/1948 in Hanover; sixth; Roy E. Balch (lumberman, 41, Hartford, VT) and Olive W. Blanchard (35, Orford)

Stephen Mark, b. 7/6/1959 in Lebanon; Mason F. Balch, Jr. (green's keeper, 23, Hanover) and Carol E. LaBombard (21, Norwich, VT)

Sylvia Fay, b. 12/30/1947 in Lebanon; fourth; Raymond H. Balch (lumberman, 31, Lyme Ctr.) and Esther E. Smith (29, Dorchester, MA)

Theresa May, b. 3/26/1963 in Lebanon; Raymond J. Balch (mechanic, Lyme) and Beverly J. Frost (19, Lyme)

Virginia Ann, b. 12/29/1944 in Haverhill; stillborn; third; Grant P. Balch (farmer, 38, Mexico, ME) and Margaret Houston (38, Bath)

Wanita Gail, b. 10/4/1942 in Hanover; second; Raymond H. Balch (truck driv., 26, Lyme) and Esther B. Smith (23, Dorchester, MA)

BALL,
Alexandra, b. 4/24/1989 in Hanover; Thomas W. Ball and Jean Olszewski

Caitlin, b. 10/7/1983 in Hanover; Thomas W. Ball and Jean M. Olszewski

Danielle, b. 6/16/1985 in Hanover; Thomas Ball and Jean Olszewski

Ethan Edward, b. 3/19/1991 in Hanover; Thomas W. Ball and Jean M. Olszewski

Kristin, b. 11/11/1980 in Hanover; Thomas W. Ball and Jean M. Olszewski

Rebecca, b. 5/23/1982 in Hanover; Thomas W. Ball and Jean M. Olszewski

Trevor James, b. 6/22/1987 in Hanover; Thomas W. Ball and Jean Olszewski

BANKER,
Jean Carol, b. 9/9/1945 in Lyme; fourth; Charles F. Banker (copper min., 36, Thetford Ctr., VT) and Hilda P. Smith (31, Thetford,

VT); residence – Thetford Ctr., VT

BANN,
William Stetson, b. 9/12/1993 in Lebanon; David Bann and Donna McCobb

BARBER,
Emily E., b. 11/29/1895 in Lyme; first; Thomas Barber (laborer, 21, Suffolk Co., England) and Clementine Clampet (21, Richmond, PQ)

BARDOS,
Laszlo Joseph, b. 2/9/1997 in Lebanon; Laszlo Christopher Bardos and Carolyn Marie Maher

BARKER,
Jonathan Paul, b. 6/11/1981 in Hanover; Paul H. Barker and Judith Fulton
Joshua Thomas, b. 1/29/1987 in Hanover; Paul H. Barker and Judith Fulton

BARNES,
daughter, b. 5/12/1900; third; Henry R. Barnes (creamery, 32, Richmond, VT) and Cora May Huntley (28, N. Troy, VT)
George Washington, b. 3/18/1866 in Lyme; Hiram Barnes and Esther B. Gillett (1948)

BARNUM,
Douglas Grant, b. 10/27/1971 in Hanover; Robert G. Barnum, III and Sarah E. Bryant

BARRETT,
Kathy Ann, b. 6/9/1955 in Hanover; third; Selby Barrett (salesman, Lyme) and Leila Willmott (Lyme)
Shirley Mae, b. 1/12/1950 in Hanover; second; Selby Barrett (farmer, 23, Newfoundland) and Leila Wilmot (29, Lyme)

BARRON,
Rupert Fraser, b. 10/11/1966 in Lebanon; first; Mortimer B. Barron (teacher, Orange, NJ) and Juliet S. Frey (Westport, CT)

BARTHOL,
Joanne Emily, b. 8/31/1992 in Lebanon; Walter Barthol and Joan Crane

BARTHOLD,
Eric Crane, b. 1/4/1990 in Hanover; W. Scott Barthold and Joan Crane

BARTON,
Edith Maria, b. 11/30/1892; second; George E. Barton (farmer, 41, Concord) and Mary E. Howland (29, Webster)

BASTIANELLI,
Christine Mattea, b. 4/2/1970 in Lyme; Pierre Bastianelli and Judith C. Putnam
Irene Francoise, b. 8/3/1968 in Lyme; Pierre Bastianelli and Judith C. Putnam

BATES,
Lillian May, b. 10/14/1906 in Lyme; third; Ernest G. Bates (laborer, 27, Ellenburgh, NY) and Minnie May Stark (25, Moores, NY)
Wayne P., b. 7/10/1936 in Lebanon; first; Zelma H. Bates (road agent, 33, Lebanon) and Sara E. Pushee (30, Lyme)

BATTAT,
James Benjamin, b. 6/7/1980 in Hanover; Joseph Y. Battat and Brenda E. J. Weare

BAUGHMAN,
Eric DeWeese, b. 6/15/1965 in Hanover; third; Richard Baughman (doctor, Greensburg, PA) and Amelia Noyes (New London, CT)

BAUMGARTNER,
Jonathan David, b. 6/6/1971 in Hanover; James Baumgartner and Yolanda Loo

BEACH,
Maximillian Murray, b. 4/27/1984 in Lebanon; Murray M. Beach and Mary K. Walkush

BEAN,
Barbara Louise, b. 11/18/1939 in Lyme; first; Norman C. Bean (laborer, 21, Orford) and Dorothy L. Lewis (25, W. Barrington, RI)
Danny Jamie, b. 2/18/1951 in Lebanon; second; Richard Bean (roller, 19, W. Rumney, ME) and Rita H. Pratt (21, Auburn, ME)
Laurie Elaine, b. 6/17/1969 in Hanover; Warren L. Bean and Shirley L. Gray
Mary Leanne, b. 10/17/1965 in Lebanon; first; Warren L. Bean (apprentice, Hanover) and Kathryn A. Larocque (Woodsville)
Nicole Lee, b. 12/17/1973 in Hanover; Warren Bean and Shirley L. Gray
William Warren, b. 1/30/1967 in Lebanon; second; Warren L. Bean (appr. printer, Hanover) and Kathryn A. Larocque (Woodsville)

BEANE,
David Lee, Jr., b. 9/28/1989 in Hanover; David L. Beane and Michelle Sanborn

BEAUPRE,
Angela Marie, b. 5/13/1979 in Lebanon; Peter Beaupre and Patricia Goodrich

BELYEA,
Joshua Dean, b. 5/26/1989 in Lebanon; Jay L. Belyea and Judith A. Pushee

BERGER,
Cynthia, b. 4/24/1968 in Hanover; Roger H. Berger and Christine Berkey
Kathleen, b. 12/28/1971 in Hanover; Roger H. Berger and Christine Berkey

BERNHARD,
Damarise Margare, b. 6/7/1957 in Hanover; Manfred Bernhard (artist, Berlin, Germany) and Joan B. Edgar (New York City)
Eugen Edgar, b. 9/25/1948 in Lebanon; first; Man. E. Bernhard (artist, 31, Berlin, Germany) and Joan B. Edgar (23, NY City)
Lucienne, b. 11/26/1949 in Lebanon; Manfred E. Bernhard and Joan Edgar
Mercedes, b. 8/28/1952 in Lyme; third; Manfred Bernhard (artist, 35,

Berlin, Germany) and Joan Edgar (27, New York City)
Robert Beaufort, b. 7/20/1962 in Hanover; Manfred E. Bernhard (advertising, Berlin, Germany) and Joan B. Edgar (37, New York, NY)

BERRY,
Allen Delma, b. 10/7/1954 in Lebanon; seventh; David R. Berry (laborer, 32, Wheelock, VT) and Barbara Snelling (30, Lyndonville, VT)
Beverly Ann, b. 6/17/1951 in Lyme; sixth; David Berry (farmer, 29, Wheelock, VT) and Barbara Snelling (27, Lyndonville, VT)
Rachel Lee, b. 9/18/1949 in Lebanon; David R. Berry and Barbara Snelling

BERTHIAUME,
John Arthur, b. 6/21/1943 in Lyme; second; John A. Berthiaume (truck driver, 26, Attleboro, MA) and Lenore M. Chadwick (21, Barnard, VT)

BESSO,
Alexandra Nina, b. 10/27/1986 in Hanover; George J. P. Besso and Sharon E. Regula
John Joseph Richard, b. 7/23/1989 in Hanover; John P. Besso and Sharon Regula
Susan Mathilde, b. 10/27/1986 in Hanover; George J. P. Besso and Sharon E. Regula

BILLINGHAM,
stillborn son, b. 2/17/1917; sixth; James Billingham (laborer, 37, England) and Julia V. Perrin (27, Island Pond, VT)
Charles Henry, b. 1/5/1912 in Lyme; fourth; James Billingham (laborer, 32, England) and Julia V. Perrin (22, Island Pond, VT)
Edith Viola M., b. 8/24/1914; fifth; James Billingham (laborer, 35, England) and Julia Perrin (24, Island Pond, VT)

BIRCHER,
Cynthia Mary, b. 5/5/1957 in Lebanon; Ralph J. Bircher (meat cut., Wilder, VT) and Lillian M. White (Hanover)

BIXBY,
daughter, b. 10/9/1892; second; Eugene S. Bixby (farmer, 30, Lyme)

and Sarah D. Spaulding (31, Fletcher, VT)
Florence M., b. 9/17/1896 in Lyme; fourth; Eugene S. Bixby (farmer, 35, Lyme) and Sarah D. Spaulding (34, Fairfield, VT)

BLANCHARD,
Betsy Ann, b. 3/7/1954 in Haverhill; first; Charles A. Blanchard (miner, 25, Strafford, VT) and Barbara I. Drew (19, Charlestown)

BLAU,
Ingrid Jane, b. 6/11/2002 in Lebanon; Christopher Blau and Wendy Blau
Lulu Bayne, b. 8/21/2000 in Lebanon; Christopher Blau and Wendy Blau

BOLINGER,
Elsa Sylvia, b. 12/25/2003 in Lebanon; Mark Bolinger and Ursula Slate

BOMBARD,
daughter, b. 1/27/1910 in Lyme; first; Charles W. Bombard (laborer, 25, Burlington, VT) and Myrtle Lillian Coates (20, Cornhill, NB)
stillborn daughter, b. 11/12/1913 in Lyme; third; Charles W. Bombard (laborer, 28, Burlington, VT) and Myrtle Coates (23, Corn Hill, NB)
Leon Charles, b. 4/26/1912 in Lyme; second; Charles W. Bombard (laborer, 27, Burlington, VT) and Myrtle L. Coates (22, Corn Hill, NB)
M. G. [female], b. 12/7/1903 in Lyme; first; Frank J. Bombard (laborer, 25, S. Vernon, MA) and Dora E. Jewell (23, Canada)
Ray Wendell, b. 7/28/1941 in Hanover; third; Leon C. Bombard (janitor, 29, Lyme) and Lucia Willard (27, Wareham, MA)
Robert W., b. 10/8/1937 in Lyme; first; Leon Bombard (laborer, 25, Lyme) and Lucia Willard (22, Wareham, MA)
Shirley Ann, b. 11/11/1939 in Hanover; second; Leon C. Bombard (laborer, 27, Lyme) and Lucia W. Willard (25, Wareham, MA)

BOND,
Margaret Viola, b. 11/5/1919 in Lyme; fourth; James A. Bond (laborer, 29, Saginaw, MI) and Cassie P. Cutting (27, Lyme)
Olive Myrle, b. 12/21/1919 in Lyme; first; Alden W. Bond (laborer,

26) and Beatrice E. Young (26, Burke, NJ); residence - Thetford, VT

BONNETT,
Robert Wilcox, b. 8/3/1924 in Hanover; third; Frank E. Bonnett (farmer, 30, Orford) and Rose C. Wilcox (30, Thetford, VT)

BOURNE,
Cameron James, b. 12/30/1982 in Hanover; Steven R. Bourne and Elizabeth S. Burrill
Molly Elizabeth, b. 9/26/1986 in Hanover; Steven R. Bourne and Elizabeth S. Burrill

BOWEN,
stillborn daughter, b. 3/28/1898; second; Clarence S. Bowen (laborer, 43, Corinth, VT) and Jennie Gammell (26, Barnet, VT)
Christopher Terry, b. 9/29/2000 in Lebanon; Terry Bowen and Jocelyn Bowen
Ida, b. 11/27/1891; first; C. S. Bowen (laborer, 32, Corinth, VT) and Jennie Gammell (20, Barnet, VT)
Ray Louis, b. 9/6/1900; third; Clarence S. Bowen (farmer, 46, Corinth, VT) and Jennie L. Gammell (29, Barnet, VT)
Theresa Viola, b. 2/15/1938 in Lyme; fourth; Edward A. Bowen (mechanic, 29, Groton, VT) and Florence M. Yon (23, Lewiston, ME)

BOZUWA,
Johanna Mary, b. 9/6/1991 in Hanover; Gijsbert P. Bozuwa and Colleen T. Barr

BRAASCH,
William Frederick, Jr., b. 12/4/1988 in Hanover; William F. Braasch and Eugenia Frey

BRACKEN,
Emily Lynne, b. 11/28/1975 in Hanover; Theodore Lane Bracken and Nancy Joan Lieblich

BRAGG,
Irena Alice, b. 6/17/1946 in Lyme; third; Kenneth C. Bragg (lumberman, 33, W. Fairlee, VT) and Alice E. LaMontagne (28,

Southboro, MA); residence – Thetford, VT
Sally Ann, b. 12/24/1944 in Lyme; second; Kenneth C. Bragg (lumberman, 31, Fairlee, VT) and Alice LaMontagne (27, Southboro, MA); residence – Thetford, VT

BRALEY,
Charles, b. 7/9/1895 in Lyme; first; Charles Braley (laborer, 21) and Flora A. Dunbar (21, Potter, Canada)
Leah Irene, b. 3/30/1919 in Lyme; second; Harry A. Braley (P.O. clerk, 22, Hartford, VT) and Maude E. Perkins (24, Lyme); residence - White River Jct.

BRESSETT,
son, b. 1/16/1895 in Lyme; tenth; Andrew Bressett (laborer, 54, Canada) and Julia Phillips (40, Highgate, VT)

BREWSTER,
Ariel Elizabeth, b. 5/4/1983 in Hanover; Raymond W. Brewster and Jan-Roberta Tarjan
Emma Brianne, b. 5/25/1988 in Hanover; Raymond W. Brewster and Jan-Roberta Tarjan

BRISTOL,
Katrina Sophia, b. 9/27/1999 in Lebanon; Adam Bristol and Deborah Bristol

BROCKETT,
Travis Clancy, b. 9/29/1976 in Lebanon; Bruce Edward Brockett and Suzanne Ellen Lorenz

BROCKWAY,
Ada M., b. 7/10/1901; sixth; George A. Brockway (laborer, 41, Waterbury, VT) and Nellie E. Dimick (35, Iron Hill, Canada)
Earl D., b. 1/31/1907 in Lyme; eighth; George A. Brockway (laborer, 47, Waterbury, VT) and Nellie E. Dimick (41, Iron Hill, Canada)
Florence May, b. 11/15/1887; first; George A. Brockway (laborer, 27, Waterbury, VT) and Nellie E. Brockway (21, PQ)
Guy Carlton, b. 1/15/1892; third; George A. Brockway (laborer, 31, Waterbury, VT) and Nellie E. Dimick (25, Iron Hill, PQ)
Janette Elizabeth, b. 1/29/1928 in Lyme; third; Guy C. Brockway (farmer, 36, Lyme) and Mary E. Lund (32, Norwich, VT)

Mabel Alice, b. 5/11/1908 in Lyme; ninth; George Brockway (laborer, 48, Waterbury, VT) and Nellie E. Dimick (42, Canada)
Margaret Louise, b. 11/6/1925 in Lyme; second; Guy C. Brockway (farmer, 33, Lyme) and Mary E. Lund (29, Norwich, VT)
Marjorie, b. 1/27/1904 in Lyme; seventh; George A. Brockway (laborer, 44, Dorchester) and Nellie E. Dimick (38, Iron Hill, Canada)
Nellie Margaret, b. 7/22/1889; second; George A. Brockway (laborer, Waterbury, VT) and Nellie E. Dimick (Iron Hill, PQ)
Rachel Ellen, b. 9/27/1924 in Lyme; first; Guy C. Brockway (farmer, 32, Lyme) and Mary E. Lund (28, Norwich, VT)

BROWN,
Asher Whiting, b. 4/17/1997 in Lyme; Matthew Whiting Brown and Elizabeth Page
Elizabeth Weatherby, b. 3/15/1958 in Hanover; Thomas S. Brown (physician, 31, Philadelphia, PA) and Nancy C. S. Jones (22, Mt. Crawford, VA)
Forest Walter, b. 4/12/1905 in Lyme; third; Fred W. Brown (laborer, 42, Warren) and Grace D. Goosh (23, W. Fairlee, VT)
Leon F., b. 11/29/1937 in Hanover; first; Kenneth C. Brown (carpenter, 28, Canada) and Dolores C. Jacques (24, Canada)
Leona F., b. 11/29/1937 in Hanover; second; Kenneth C. Brown (carpenter, 28, Canada) and Dolores C. Jacques (24, Canada)
Lindsay Young, b. 9/26/1975 in Hanover; Jerry Elijah Brown and Elizabeth A. Wheeler
Nathaniel Otis, b. 10/8/1992 in Lebanon; Mathew Brown and Elizabeth Page

BRYAN,
son, b. 7/6/1910 in Lyme; fifth; Richard E. Bryan (laborer, 41, Canaan) and Mary L. Jenks (30, Lyme)
Edith V., b. 6/22/1906 in Lyme; third; Richard E. Bryan (painter, 37, Canaan, VT) and Mary L. Jenks (32, Lyme)
Hugh Boyd, b. 4/8/1902; third; Richard E. Brian (sic) (painteer, 37, Canaan, VT) and Mary L. Jenks (27, Lyme)

BRYANT,
daughter, b. 1/17/1901; first; Fred J. Bryant (farmer, 23, Lyme) and Florence M. Henry (19, Thetford, VT)
Arthur William, b. 6/13/1902; second; Fred John Bryant (farmer, 24,

Lyme) and Florence M. Henry (26, Thetford, VT)
Della E., b. 9/24/1907 in Lyme; third; Fred J. Bryant (farmer, 29, Lyme) and Florence M. Henry (25, Thetford, VT)
Ellen-Louise, b. 4/27/1959 in Hanover; Sterle H. Bryant (truck driver, 29, Lyme) and Lorraine A. Wing (28, Orford)
Esther C., b. 4/26/1937 in Hanover; second; George H. Bryant (farmer, 33, Lyme) and Ruth E. Dimick (34, Lyme)
Esther Jane, b. 7/6/1961 in Hanover; Sterle H. Bryant (equip. operator, Lyme) and Lorraine Wing (29, Orford)
Eunice Arlene, b. 7/4/1923 in Lyme; first; Arthur Bryant (laborer, 21, Lyme) and Theda Sanborn (21, Lyme)
Forrest, b. 6/23/1948 in Hanover; second; Loren E. Bryant (woodsman, 32, Morgan, VT) and Beulah P. Marryfield (26, Ctr. Sandwich)
George H., b. 3/13/1904 in Lyme; third; Fred J. Bryant (farmer, 26, Lyme) and Florence M. Henry (22, Thetford, VT)
Leona Esther, b. 8/8/1930 in Lyme; third; Arthur W. Bryant (laborer, 28, Lyme) and Theda M. Sanborn (28, Lyme)
Randy Sterle, b. 8/30/1965 in Lebanon; fourth; Sterle H. Bryant (equip. operator, Lyme) and Lorraine A. Wing (Orford)
Sterle Henry, b. 7/1/1929 in Lyme; first; George H. Bryant (farmer, 25, Lyme) and Ruth E. Dimick (26, Lyme)
Verne Iro, b. 6/28/1924 in Lyme; second; Arthur W. Bryant (laborer, 22, Lyme) and Theda M. Sanborn (22, Lyme)

BUFFUM,
daughter, b. 1/13/1909 in Lyme; second; J. Arthur Buffum (farmer, 26, Somerville, MA) and Nettie E. Wing (25, Chateaugay, NY)
daughter, b. 7/15/1910 in Lyme; third; Arthur J. Buffum (carpenter, 27, Somerville, MA) and Nettie E. Wing (27, Chateaugay, NY)
Neal Arthur, b. 1/2/1913 in Lyme; fourth; Jabez A. Buffum (b. carpenter, 30, Somerville, MA) and Nettie Wing (29, Chateaugay, NY)

BUGBEE,
stillborn son, b. 1/16/1891; first; W. S. Bugbee (laborer, 24, Burke, VT) and Cynthia F. Weeks (25, Danville, VT)

BUNKER,
Kenneth Gordon, b. 3/3/1934 in Hanover; third; Kenneth C. Bunker (clergyman, 35, South Africa) and Alma Asted (28, Denmark)

BURGESS,
Barbara Ann, b. 8/31/1964 in Hanover; Donald E. Burgess (teacher, St. Johnsbury, VT) and Geraldine Burgess (22, Hanover)

BURNHAM,
R. E. [male], b. 5/14/1903 in Lyme; second; Clarence E. Burnham (farmer, 48, Hartland, VT) and Ruth H. Stark (31, Lyme)

BURTON,
Shirley Ann, b. 3/31/1931 in Lyme; third; Richard A. Burton (laborer, 26, Temple) and Maud L. Morrow (27, Taftsville, VT)

BUSKEY,
Eliza Hess, b. 5/11/1993 in Lebanon; Wilton Buskey and Shannon Daley

BUTMAN,
daughter, b. 8/24/1922 in Lyme; fifth; Oscar F. Butman (laborer, 30, Canaan) and Nellie Beaton (27, NS)
Anthony Zane, b. 5/8/1963 in Hanover; Herbert Butnam (Orford) and Elizabeth A. Clogston (16, Lebanon)
Catherine, b. 6/11/1967 in Lebanon; second; Herbert Butman (driller, Orfordville) and Suzanne Pushee (Hanover)
Elizabeth, b. 9/28/1969 in Haverhill; Herbert C. Butman and Suzanne Pushee
Gladys, b. 11/13/1898; first; Luelin C. Butman (laborer, 17, Orford) and Belle A. Smith (24, Lyme)
Lesley Ann, b. 7/27/1965 in Lebanon; first; Herbert C. Butman (driller, Orfordville) and Suzanne Pushee (Hanover)

BUZZELL,
Lewis Glen, b. 1/3/1949 in Lebanon; Glen R. Buzzell and Marion Harris
Max Harris, b. 4/19/1943 in Lebanon; second; Glen R. Buzzell (sawyer, 32, Waitsfield, VT) and Marion E. Harris (21, Wallingford, VT)

BYNUM,
Benjamin Robert, b. 5/20/1982 in Hanover; Robert D. Bynum and Barbara E. Spycher
Christopher David, b. 4/11/1980 in Hanover; Robert David Bynum

and Barbara E. Spycher
Priscilla Antoinette, b. 3/15/1978 in Hanover; Robert D. Bynum and Barbara Spycher

CADWELL,
Patricia Doris, b. 8/11/1944 in Lyme; sixth; Louis H. Cadwell (farmer, 41, E. Thetford, VT) and Nellie D. Harlow (36, E. Boston, MA); residence – E. Thetford, VT

CADY,
Natalie Fiona, b. 8/3/1996 in Lebanon; Stuart Cady, Jr. and Sara Nowicki

CALDWELL,
Heide Waters, b. 2/29/1992 in Lebanon; Timothy Caldwell and Margaret Waters
Lucy Waters, b. 9/10/1989 in Hanover; Timothy J. Caldwell and Margaret Waters
Patrick Fitzgerald Waters, b. 2/18/1994 in Lebanon; Timothy Caldwell and Margaret Waters

CALLAGHAN,
Grace Celia, b. 6/17/1999 in Lebanon; Timothy Callaghan and Eleanor Goode
Ryan James, b. 7/24/2004 in Lebanon; Timothy Callaghan and Eleanor Goode

CAMBER,
Harry Edward, Jr., b. 9/8/1947 in Lebanon; second; Harry E. Camber (farmer, 20, Lyndonville, VT) and Marion V. Stark (24, W. Canaan); residence – Hanover

CAMEAU,
Geneva May, b. 10/10/1930 in Lyme; fourth; Andrew J. Cameau (laborer, 27, Chatham, NB) and Lena M. Wood (25, Haverhill)

CAMP,
son, b. 8/10/1890; first; Willie E. Camp (laborer, 23, Orford) and Oliva M. Stark (Springfield, IL)
son, b. 6/22/1894 in Lyme; third; Willie E. Camp (laborer, 25, Orford) and Olivia M. Stark (27, Springfield, IL)

Gould Jason, b. 10/5/1893 in Lyme; second; Frank L. Camp (laborer, 25, Lyme) and Anna A. Alden (26, Lyme)
J. Edward, b. 7/7/1894 in Lyme; first; Edward M. Camp (laborer, 31, Morristown, PQ) and Martha L. Bowker (26, Bolton Center, PQ)
Martin A., b. 5/24/1904 in Lyme; fourth; Frank L. Camp (farmer, 35, Lyme) and Anna A. Alden (37, Lyme)
Newton Frank, b. 5/19/1892; second; Will E. Camp (laborer, 25, Orford) and Olivia M. Stark (23, Springfield, IL)
Pollie, b. 7/6/1892; first; Frank L. Camp (laborer, 23, Lyme) and Anna A. Alden (25, Lyme)
Rose L., b. 3/6/1895 in Lyme; third; Frank L. Camp (farmer, 26, Lyme) and Anna A. Alden (28, Lyme)

CAMPBELL,
daughter, b. 10/22/1948 in Lyme; third; Zane E. Campbell (clerical, 24, Post Mills, VT) and Delores W. Piper (19, Chicago, IL)
Carol Janice, b. 11/26/1946 in Lebanon; first; Zane Campbell (chopper, 22, Post Mills, VT) and Dolores Piper (17, Chicago, IL)
Christie Jean, b. 12/31/1947 in Hanover; second; Zane E. Campbell (lumbering, 24, Thetford Ctr., VT) and Dolores W. Piper (18, Chicago, IL)
Julie, b. 5/29/1964 in Hanover; Zane E. Campbell (truck driver, Post Mills, VT) and Dolores W. Piper (35, Chicago, IL)

CANFIELD,
daughter, b. 11/30/1890; second; Charles W. Canfield (laborer, 31, Lyme) and Susie E. Strong (21, Meriden)
Lucy Ellen, b. 5/7/1897 in Lyme; fourth; Charles W. Canfield (blacksmith, 38, Lyme) and Susie E. Strong (28, Meriden)
Maude Esther, b. 12/10/1893 in Lyme; third; Charles W. Canfield (blacksmith, 34, Lyme) and Susie Strong (24, Meriden)

CANNON,
Philip John, b. 4/10/1996 in Lebanon; David Caffry and Margaret Cannon

CAPSIS,
Nicholas Alexander, b. 6/14/1985 in Hanover; Steven Ligett and Daniela Capsis

CARNEY,
Brendan Timothy, b. 2/24/1980 in Lebanon; Timothy W. Carney and Stephanie Sacksteder

CARR,
daughter, b. 2/23/1891; first; Lewis P. Carr (salesman, 22, Plainfield) and Sadie R. Muchmore (18, Piermont)
daughter, b. 7/20/1902; second; Charles J. Carr (laborer, 28, Albany, NY) and Daisy E. Day (21, Waits River, VT)
son, b. 8/4/1906 in Lyme; third; Charles J. Carr (farmer, 32, Albany, NY) and Daisy E. Carr (25, Waits River, VT)
stillborn son, b. 3/25/1924 in Lyme; first; Lewis F. Carr (laborer, 24, Fairlee, VT) and Della F. Rowel (18, Corinth, VT)
Barbara Pauline, b. 6/5/1931 in Hanover; fifth; Lewis F. Carr (laborer, 32, Fairlee, VT) and Stella M. Rowell (25, Corinth, VT)
Charles Horace, b. 1/27/1914; first; Charles J. Carr (laborer, 40, Albany, NY) and Eva J. Rowell (16, Strafford, VT)
David Paul, b. 4/20/1938 in Haverhill; ninth; Lewis F. Carr (laborer, 38, Fairlee, VT) and Stella M. Rowell (30, Corinth, VT)
Edna Joyce, b. 4/19/1934 in Lyme; seventh; Lewis F. Carr (laborer, 35, Fairlee, VT) and Stella M. Rowell (26, Corinth, VT)
Ernest J., b. 8/20/1936 in Lyme; ninth; Lewis F. Carr (laborer, 36, Fairlee, VT) and Stella M. Rowell (28, Corinth, VT)
Jessie Ann, b. 5/9/1927 in Hartford, VT; third; Lewis F. Carr (farmer, 27, Fairlee, VT) and Stella M. Rowell (22, Corinth, VT)
Louise May, b. 10/24/1929 in Lyme; fourth; Lewis F. Carr (laborer, 29, Lyme) and Stella M. Rowell (23, Corinth, VT)
Robert Lewis, b. 8/11/1925 in Lyme; second; Lewis F. Carr (laborer, 26, Fairlee, VT) and Stella M. Rowell (20, Corinth, VT)

CARTER,
Carl Richard, b. 3/18/1947 in Hanover; first; Roscoe F. Carter (dairyman, 22, Norwich, VT) and Anne DeGoosh (21, Hanover)
Caroline Jean, b. 7/1/2003 in Lebanon; Andrew Carter and Jodi Carter
David Jeffers, b. 2/17/1948 in Hanover; second; Roscoe F. Carter (dairyman, 23, Norwich, VT) and Anne DeGoosh (22, Hanover)
James Ivan, b. 3/22/1981 in Lebanon; Lawrence Carter, Jr. and Rebecca A. Wheeler
Jean Keniston, b. 6/11/1971 in Lebanon; Carl R. Carter and Elizabeth Keniston

Joanne Keniston, b. 9/4/1977 in Hanover; Carl R. Carter and
    Elizabeth J. Keniston
Karen Sue, b. 7/23/1955 in Lebanon; fourth; Roscoe F. Carter
    (farmer, Norwich, VT) and Anne DeGoosh (Hanover)
Paul Fred, b. 9/4/1977 in Hanover; Carl R. Carter and Elizabeth J.
    Keniston
Roxanne Julia, b. 6/10/1953 in Lebanon; Roscoe F. Carter
    (dairyman, 29, Norwich, VT) and Ann DeGoosh (27, Hanover)
Violet Anne, b. 7/18/1978 in Lebanon; Lawrence Carter, Jr. and
    Rebecca A. Wheeler

CATHERON,
Lloyd Scott, b. 2/6/1960 in Haverhill; Allison Catheron, 2nd (forester,
    35, Boston, MA) and Shirley J. Flint (39, Milan)

CHAFFEE,
Sara, b. 9/21/1952 in Hanover; fifth; Robert Chaffee (geologist, 38,
    Rutland, VT) and Dorcas Dixon (37, Portsmouth)

CHAMBERLIN,
Edward Lee, b. 8/6/1955 in Hanover; first; Richard Chamberlin
    (miner, Newport, VT) and June Manning (Randolph, VT)
Elizabeth Greenwood, b. 12/12/1990 in Hanover; Robert M.
    Chamberlin and Katherine Emlen
Timothy Simons, b. 5/21/1993 in Lebanon; Robert Chamberlin and
    Katherine Emlen

CHAPIN,
Orrin Keyes, b. 1/19/1916; first; Orrin S. Chapin (farming, 22,
    Charlemont, MA) and Alice H. DeGoosh (26, Hartland, VT)

CHASE,
daughter, b. 11/4/1889; third; Edwin S. Chase (farmer, Piermont)
    and Emma C. Churchill (Lyme)
daughter, b. 11/4/1890; third; Edwin L. Chase (farmer, 39, Piermont)
    and Emma C. Churchill (Lyme)
son, b. 1/10/1891; third; Edwin S. Chase (farmer, 40, Piermont) and
    Emma F. Churchill (29, Lyme)
Nancy Jane, b. 9/30/1938 in Lebanon; second; William F. Chase
    (salesman, 33, Lyme) and Mildred B. Fey (34, Schroon Lake,
    NY)

Sally Ann, b. 10/5/1935 in Lebanon; first; William F. Chase (salesman, 30, Lyme) and Mildred B. Fey (31, Schroon Lake, NY)

William Francis, b. 7/21/1905 in Lyme; first; William Little Chase (farmer, 45, New Haven, CT) and Mary Andra Place (36, St. Albans, VT)

CHESLEY,
Annie Mabel, b. 10/27/1911 in Lyme; second; Arthur B. Chesley (farmer, 29, W. Fairlee, VT) and Geraldine M. Thompson (22, Canada)

Beth Gertrude, b. 5/22/1922 in Lyme; eighth; Arthur B. Chesley (farmer, 39, W. Fairlee, VT) and Geraldine Thompson (32, S. Ham, PQ)

Boyd Jerome, b. 3/30/1914; third; Edward H. Chesley (35) and Flora Huntley (22)

Carolyn Mary, b. 8/4/1949 in Hanover; Harold M. Chesley and Frances Ashley

Edith Pauline, b. 8/13/1929 in Hanover; eleventh; Arthur B. Chesley (farmer, 46, W. Fairlee, VT) and Monte Thompson (39, S. Ham, PQ)

Frank Arthur, b. 10/26/1909 in Lyme; first; Arthur Benjamin Chesley (farmer, 27, W. Fairlee, VT) and Monte Geraldine Thompson (19, Thetford, VT)

George Joseph, b. 1/18/1926 in Lyme; tenth; Arthur B. Chesley (farmer, 43, W. Fairlee, VT) and Monte Thompson (36, S. Ham, PQ)

Gladys, b. 8/28/1896 in Lyme; fifth; Frank A. Chesley (farmer, 38, W. Fairlee, VT) and Louisa H. Morey (37, W. Fairlee, VT)

Guy Osborne, b. 1/25/1932 in Hanover; twelfth; Arthur B. Chesley (mail carrier, 49, W. Fairlee, VT) and Mont Thompson (42, Canada)

Harold Merton, b. 4/26/1913 in Lyme; third; Arthur B. Chesley (farmer, 30, W. Fairlee, VT) and Monte G. Thompson (23, S. Ham, Canada)

Hermon Thompson, b. 11/26/1916; fifth; Arthur B. Chesley (farming, 34, W. Fairlee, VT) and G. M. Thompson (27, S. Ham, Canada)

Janet Lillian, b. 2/21/1946 in Lyme; third; Harold M. Chesley (farmer, 32, Lyme) and Frances S. Ashley (31, Rumney)

Lena May, b. 5/22/1920 in Lyme; seventh; Arthur Chesley (farmer, 37, W. Fairlee, VT) and Monte Thompson (30, S. Ham,

Canada)
Marion Devey, b. 5/27/1924 in Lyme; ninth; Arthur B. Chesley
(farmer, 41, W. Fairlee, VT) and Monte Thompson (34, S. Ham,
PQ)
Nellie M., b. 9/9/1892; fourth; F. E. Chesley (farmer, 34, W. Fairlee,
VT) and Louisa Morey (33, W. Fairlee, VT)
Ruth Louisa, b. 1/10/1915; fourth; Arthur B. Chesley (farmer, 32, W.
Fairlee, VT) and Monte G. Thompson (25, S. Ham, PQ)
Scarlet Virginia, b. 4/26/1942 in Hanover; first; Frank A. Chesley
(farmer, 33, NH) and Elsie E. Johnson (32, Norwich, VT)
Sharon Lee, b. 2/27/1951 in Lebanon; third; Herman Chesley
(carpenter, 35, Lyme) and Virginia Bowen (26, Rutland, VT)
Shelia Mae, b. 1/18/1954 in Lebanon; fourth; Herman T. Chesley
(carpenter, 36, Lyme) and Virginia Mae Bowen (30, Burlington,
VT)
Vera Geraldine, b. 2/11/1919 in Lyme; sixth; Arthur B. Chesley
(farming, 36, W. Fairlee, VT) and Monte G. Thompson (29, S.
Ham, PQ)

CLAESSENS,
Elizabeth Hannah, b. 1/7/1995 in Lebanon; Michael Thomas
Claessens and Jeana Marilyn Webster
Sarah Grace, b. 3/7/1997 in Lebanon; Michael Thomas Claessens
and Jeana Marilyn Webster

CLAFLIN,
son, b. 1/14/1890; third; Preston N. A. Claflin (tailor, 33, Auburn) and
Eva May Turner (Hebron, ME)
Edwin Loomis, b. 8/21/1888; first; Preston Claflin (farmer, 55, Lyme)
and Harriet Loomis (41, Colebrook)
H. Clayton, b. 5/19/1900; sixth; Preston H. A. Claflin (postmaster,
44, Auburn) and Eva M. Turner (41, Hebron, ME)
Hazen Southard, b. 12/19/1893 in Lyme; fourth; Preston H. A. Claflin
(postmaster, 37, Auburn) and Eva M. Turner (34, Hebron, ME)
Norma, b. 4/7/1932 in Lyme; first; Willis B. Claflin (laborer, 26,
Corinth, VT) and Florence E. Dike (19, Lyme)
Raymond E., b. 10/31/1897 in Lyme; fifth; Preston H. A. Claflin
(postmaster, 41, Auburn) and Eva May Turner (36, Hebron,
ME)
Willis B., Jr., b. 8/25/1933 in Lyme; second; Willis B. Claflin (laborer,
28, Corinth, VT) and Florence E. Dike (21, Lyme)

CLARK,
Alice R., b. 8/29/1935 in Lyme; first; Charles W. Clark (farming, 30, Thetford, VT) and Ruth A. Bean (19, Orford)
Forrest Sidney, b. 3/17/1944 in Lyme; third; Forrest S. Clark (farmer, 40, Littleton) and Lulu M. Tattersall (29, Lyme)
George Stanley, b. 5/–/1922 in Hanover; stillborn; eighth; Alexander G. Clark (farmer, 42, Thetford, VT) and Harriet R. Houston (36, Strafford, VT)
Vera Ellen, b. 12/27/1953 in Lebanon; Charles Clark (farmer, 48, Thetford, VT) and Mildred Underhill (39, Canaan)
Wilbur Gordon, b. 2/16/1947 in Lebanon; fourth; Charles Clark (farmer, 41, Thetford, VT) and Mildred Underhill (32, Canaan)

CLAUSON,
Karl Robert, b. 9/9/1973 in Hanover; Karl W. Clauson and Helen F. McColough
Sean Thomas, b. 2/23/1976 in Hanover; Karl William Clauson and Helen Frances McColough

CLAYTON,
Geoffrey Arthur, b. 7/18/2000 in Randolph; Geoffrey W. Clayton and Joanna Laro
Jin Maylee, b. 12/16/2004 in Randolph, VT; Geoffrey Clayton and Joanna Laro

CLOGSTON,
son, b. 10/9/1902; second; William M. Clogston (laborer, 22, Lyme) and Ada A. Patch (17, Orford)
Walter Lee, b. 3/13/1906 in Lyme; fourth; William Clogston (laborer, 26, Dorchester) and Ada A. Patch (20, Orford); residence - Piermont
William, b. 12/17/1903 in Lyme; third; William M. Clogston (laborer, 24, Dorchester) and Ada A. Patch (18, Orford)

CLOUD,
Thomas Gordon, b. 9/12/1949 in Hanover; Harold L. Cloud and Dorothy Hazen

COATES,
Ammie Alice, b. 2/15/1914; first; Thomas D. Coates (laborer, 31, Corn Hill, NB) and Christena F. Nelson (23, Wakefield)

George Barnes, b. 8/23/1922 in Lyme; second; Thomas D. Coates (trackman, 42, Corn Hill, NB) and Christina F. Nelson (32, Wakefield)

COBURN,
daughter, b. 3/16/1891; first; Alvin S. Coburn (farmer, 26, Enosburg, VT) and Lula F. Coburn (24, Berkshire, VT)
daughter, b. 8/31/1900; first; Lewis W. Coburn (farming, 24, Berkshire, VT) and Minnie A. Runnels (19, Wentworth)
Alvah W., b. 10/8/1906 in Lyme; fourth; Lewis W. Coburn (farmer, 25, E. Berkshire, VT) and Minnie A. Runnels (25, Wentworth)
George D., b. 5/31/1903 in Lyme; second; Lewis W. Coburn (farmer, 27, Berkshire, VT) and Minnie A. Runnels (22, Wentworth)
Helen Lizzie, b. 2/6/1905 in Lyme; third; Lewis W. Coburn (farmer, 28, E. Berkshire, VT) and Minnie A. Runnels (23, Wentworth)
Martha Louise, b. 1/11/1916; fifth; Lewis W. Coburn (farming, 39, E. Berkshire, VT) and Minnie A. Runnels (34, Wentworth)

COLE,
Albert Allen, b. 10/28/1942 in Hanover; second; Allen L. Cole (clerk, 31, Bethlehem) and Beth L. Pushee (32, Lyme)
Auburn Dorothy, b. 10/1/1974 in Hanover; Albert Allen Cole and Luane Carole Trottier
James Leslie, b. 6/23/1987 in Hanover; David M. Cole and Karen S. Henry
Judith Louise, b. 7/9/1939 in Hanover; first; A;;en L. Cole (clerk, 28, Bethlehem) and Beth L. Pushee (29, Lyme)
Tiffany Beth, b. 2/3/1973 in Hanover; Albert A. Cole and Luane C. Trottier
Virginia Lea, b. 8/14/1948 in Hanover; third; Allen L. Cole (carpenter, 37, Bethlehem) and Beth L. Pushee (38, Lyme)

COLLINS,
Tara Ruby, b. 5/29/1996 in Lebanon; Gary Collins and Ammie Thompson

COLUMBIA,
son, b. 4/22/1928 in Lyme; fourth; Fred R. Columbia (laborer, 32, Lebanon) and Lottie M. Smith (22, Hanover)
Irene Beverly, b. 7/15/1933 in Lyme; fifth; Fred R. Columbia (janitor, 37, Lebanon) and Lottie M. Smith (28, Hanover)

Richard O., b. 7/5/1935 in Hanover; sixth; Frederick R. Columbia (janitor, 39, Lebanon) and Lottie M. Smith (30, Hanover)

COMBES,
Andrea Walbridge, b. 6/23/1966 in Hanover; first; Abbott Combes IV (student, Chicago, IL) and Alice C. Schwab (Cold Springs, NY)

CONNOLLY,
Elias Rafferty, b. 11/16/1993 in Lebanon; John Connolly and Leslie Kasprzak
Sawyer Ian, b. 3/3/1992 in Lebanon; John Connolly and Leslie Kasprzak

CONNOR,
Deborah Jean, b. 10/27/1975 in Hanover; Paul R. Connor and Carol Jean Gallup

CONRAD,
Bonnie Irene, b. 3/11/1949 in Hanover; Franklyn K. Conrad and Sheila Silloway
David Leland, b. 10/14/1951 in Hanover; fourth; Franklyn Conrad (mechanic, 27, Rutland, VT) and Sheila Silloway (26, Morrisville, VT)
Timothy John, b. 6/22/1955 in Lebanon; fifth; Franklyn K. Conrad (auto mechanic, Rutland, VT) and Sheila G. Silloway (Morrisville, VT)

COOK,
Abigail Teresa, b. 12/9/1999 in Lebanon; Brian Cook and Kathryn Cook
Mary Finn, b. 12/19/2003 in Lebanon; Brian Cook and Kathryn Cook
Michael Rodney, b. 10/26/1963 in Hanover; Rodney M. W. Cook (doctor, London, England) and Agnes P. Wilson (32, Hanover)
Stacy Andrews, b. 8/31/1975 in Hanover; Gregory Joseph Cook and Gail Patricia Walker
Wesley Homer, b. 4/30/1924 in Lyme; first; Homer A. Cook (laborer, 36, Norwich, VT) and Gertrude Dugdale (18, Bradford, VT)

COOKE,
Emily Johnston, b. 3/22/1982 in Lyme; Donald F. Cooke and Jennifer Johnston

COPELAND,
Sarah Andrews, b. 6/10/1988 in Hanover; Manton Copeland and Nancy L. Krause
Tyler Manton, b. 6/27/1990 in Hanover; Manton Copeland and Nancy Lee Krause

CORNWELL,
Katherine Elizabeth, b. 7/7/1988 in Hanover; Gibbons G. Cornwell IV and Katherine Kennedy

CORY,
son, b. 12/25/1893 in Lyme; third; Carlton L. Cory (miller, 38, Chelsea, VT) and De– (33, Lyme)

COUGHLIN,
Claire Marie, b. 5/29/1951 in Hanover; tenth; Urban Coughlin (salesman, 48, Canada) and Catherine Gallant (37, Canada)
Maureen Helen, b. 3/23/1950 in Lyme; ninth; Urban Coughlin (carpenter, 47, Canada) and Catherine Gallant (36, Canada)

COURSER,
Beryl Eileen, b. 12/13/1915; second; Rodney C. Courser (creamery work, 36, Stockholm, NY) and Jessie M. Holmes (33, N. Lawrence, NY)
Muriel Holmes, b. 6/10/1913 in Lyme; first; Rodney C. Courser (butter maker, 33, Stockholm, NY) and Jessie M. Holmes (31, N. Lawrence, NY)

COUTERMARSH,
David L., b. 12/4/1941 in Hanover; fourth; Lawrence Coutermarsh (truck driver, 42, Lebanon) and Vivian Wilmot (30, Lyme)
Everett Laurance, b. 12/1/1930 in Lyme; first; L. J. Coutemarsh (laborer, 30, Lebanon) and Vivian Wilmot (20, Lyme)
Leroy Arthur, b. 11/17/1938 in Hanover; third; L. J. Coutermarsh (janitor, 39, Lebanon) and Vivian H. Wilmot (28, Lyme)
Ralph Henry, b. 6/3/1933 in Lyme; second; L. J. Coutermarsh (laborer, 33, Lebanon) and Vivian H. Wilmot (23, Lyme)

COUTURE,
Courtney Marie, b. 4/30/1998 in Lebanon; Robert N. Couture, Jr. and Michelle E. Cucuel

Matthew Robert, b. 12/22/1994 in Lebanon; Robert Norman
Couture, Jr. and Michelle Elizabeth Cucuel

COX,
Brian Norman Raymond, b. 4/19/1983 in Hanover; Gordon F. N. Cox
and Patricia A. Lewis
Callie Lynn, b. 6/22/1994 in Lebanon; John Cox and Betty Henry

COYLE,
Elizabeth Anna, b. 5/6/2003 in Lebanon; Robert Coyle and Denby
Coyle
Jackson Andrew, b. 10/25/1998 in Lebanon; Robert Harold Coyle
and Denby Allen Stowe
Samuel Allen, b. 6/9/2000 in Lebanon; Robert Coyle and Denby
Coyle

CRAIG,
Charles H., b. 12/1/1907 in Lyme; first; John W. Craig (farmer, 27,
Fredericton, NB) and Mary J. Hoag (27, Forestdale, VT);
residence - Laconia

CREASER,
son, b. 8/24/1893 in Lyme; sixth; Samuel H. Creaser (laborer, 35,
NS) and Ma– Ritchie (31, NS)

CREIGHTON,
Alexander Louis, b. 4/26/1988 in Hanover; Thomas W. Creighton
and Karen J. Silverang
Nicholas Scott, b. 5/9/1983 in Hanover; Robert P. Smith, Jr. and
Margaret S. Creighton
Ryan Humphrey, b. 4/21/1985 in Hanover; Thomas Creighton and
Karen Silverang

CRICHTON,
Molly Star, b. 8/10/1971 in Lyme; Robert Crichton and Ruth Roper

CRIMMINS,
Ian Curtis, b. 2/6/1992 in Lebanon; Curtis Crimmins and Heide
Heisel

CROOKER,
Carol Elizabeth, b. 12/10/1943 in Lyme; second; Charles W. Crooker (minister, 24, Malden, MA) and Elizabeth McGregor (24, Reading, MA)

CROSS,
June Irene, b. 12/4/1926 in Lyme; second; Frank G. Cross (lumber mill, 43, Meredith) and Doris H. Dennis (22, Lyme); residence - Northwood

CULLENBERG,
Travis, b. 6/3/1985 in Hanover; David Cullenberg and Christine Leavens

CUMMINGS,
daughter, b. 8/28/1890; second; Carl Cummings (farmer, 40, Bethlehem) and Electa A. Burnham (Windsor, VT)
Lynnie May, b. 5/8/1900; first; Harland H. Cummings (farmer, 22, Lyme) and Florence M. Lund (20, Alstead)
Norma Jane, b. 12/28/1943 in Lyme; sixth; Clyde A. Cummings (truck driv., 35, Thetford Ctr., VT) and Rosie E. Tallman (33, Orfordville); residence – Orford

CUNNINGHAM,
Charles Russell, b. 9/9/1997 in Lebanon; Leslie Doyle Cunningham and Barbara Ann Varnum
Erin Elizabeth, b. 7/14/1999 in Lebanon; Leslie Cunningham and Barbara Cunningham

CURRIER,
Oren Nathaniel, b. 5/25/1989 in Hanover; David H. Currier and Cecily Wilson

CURRY,
daughter, b. 12/7/1899; second; James Curry (laborer, 45) and Hattie M. L. Dunbar (18, Canada)

CUTTING,
son, b. 8/5/1890; second; Frank W. Cutting (carpenter, 34, Broome, Canada) and Lizzie C. Cole (Canaan)
daughter, b. 10/27/1890; first; Edd M. Cutting (laborer, 27, Lyme)

and Jennie A. Runnells (Lyme)
Barbara Ruth, b. 7/18/1931 in Lyme; sixth; Lee W. Cutting (laborer, 41, Lyme) and Alice M. Hobart (41, Lyme)
Caroline E., b. 12/15/1897 in Lyme; sixth; Frank W. Cutting (laborer, 42, Broome, PQ) and Lizzie C. Cole (30, Canaan)
Cassie, b. 11/15/1893 in Lyme; fourth; Frank W. Cutting (carpenter, 38, Canada) and Lizzie C. Cole (26, Canaan)
Clyde Allen, b. 9/7/1928 in Lyme; fifth; Lee W. Cutting (laborer, 38, Lyme) and Alice M. Hobart (38, Lyme)
Cole William, b. 4/17/1983 in Hanover; Frank A. Cutting, Jr. and Dina D. Hawthorne
Elinor Louise, b. 12/21/1923 in Lyme; third; Lee W. Cutting (laborer, 33, Lyme) and Alice M. Hobart (34, Lyme)
Elmer F., b. 12/21/1895 in Lyme; fifth; Frank W. Cutting (mechanic, 40, Browne, PQ) and Lizzie C. Cole (28, Canaan)
Frank Albert, b. 11/26/1926 in Lyme; fourth; Lee W. Cutting (laborer, 36, Lyme) and Alice M. Hobart (37, Lyme)
Harold Glen, b. 3/25/1918 in Lyme; first; Lee W. Cutting (laborer, 27, Lyme) and Alice M. Hobart (28, Lyme)
Jesse Smith, b. 9/1/1995 in Lebanon; Donald Wayne Cutting and Tracy Deborah Morrissette
Lee Weymouth, b. 8/18/1921 in Lyme; second; Lee W. Cutting (laborer, 31, Lyme) and Alice M. Hobert (31, Lyme)
MacKenzie Graham, b. 7/20/1998 in Lebanon; Donald W. Cutting and Tracy D. Morrissette
Paul Allen, b. 1/13/1962 in Lebanon; Clyde A. Cutting (engineer, Lyme) and Virginia Pushee (21, Hanover)
Rhonda Lee, b. 7/23/1959 in Lebanon; Clyde A. Cutting (laborer, 30, Lyme) and Virginia L. Pushee (19, Hanover)
Roy, b. 2/26/1892; third; Frank W. Cutting (laborer, 35, Broome, PQ) and Lizzie C. Cole (24, Canaan)
Viola May, b. 5/21/1888; first; Frank W. Cutting (carpenter, 32, Canada) and Lizzie Cole (20, Canaan)

DALEY,
Sara, b. 6/5/1968 in Hanover; Ford A. Daley and Gloria J. Beaulieu

DALL,
Barbara Susan, b. 5/25/1974 in Lebanon; Henry Appleton Dall and Susan Bridget Brown

DALVANO,
Nicholas James, Jr., b. 2/26/1945 in Lyme; first; Nicholas J. Dalvano (truck driver, 34, Long Island City, NY) and Rose H. McFarlane (22, Post Mills, VT); residence – NY

DANNA,
Morgan Paige, b. 10/21/1994 in Lebanon; Joseph Danna, Jr. and Judith Cohen

DAVAUX,
Charles William, b. 11/14/1981 in Hanover; David M. Davaux and Vera E. Clark

DAVIDSON,
Nicholas Bradley, b. 1/20/1984 in Hanover; George H. Davidson III and Laura Bradley

DAVIS,
son, b. 12/24/1891; first; Herbert S. Davis (20, Plainfield) and Mary F. Woodward (22, Plainfield)
son, b. 6/11/1899; third; Charles Davis (laborer, 37, Canada) and Rosa F. Gilbert (21, Lyme)
daughter, b. 3/3/1901; fourth; Charles Davis (laborer, 37, Canada) and Rosa Gilbert (23, Lyme)
Ava Christine, b. 9/20/1930 in Lyme; second; Gerald W. Davis (farmer, 28, Groton) and Hattie E. Davis (Canaan)
Clare Warren, b. 2/2/1921 in Lyme; second; Alfred T. Davis (trainman, 30, Stanstead, PQ) and Vera M. Warren (25, Thetford, VT); residence - Springfield, MA
David E., b. 12/1/1937 in Lyme; stillborn; first; Perry A. Davis (farmer, 41, Thetford, VT) and Elisbeth Schneyer (39, Danbury, CT)
Doris H., b. 3/17/1936 in Lyme; fifth; Gerald W. Davis (farmer, 34, Groton) and Hattie K. Davis (28, Canada)
Eileen Warren, b. 11/24/1917; first; Alfred T. Davis (trainman, 27, Stanstead, PQ) and Vera M. Warren (22, Thetford, VT)
Hazel Beth, b. 10/29/1938 in Lyme; sixth; Gerald W. Davis (farmer, 31, Groton) and Hattie K. Davis (30, Beebe Jct., Canada)
Irene May, b. 12/2/1932 in Lyme; third; Gerald W. Davis (farmer, 30, Groton, VT) and Hattie K. Davis (25, Beebe Jct., PQ)
Louise Myrtle, b. 2/15/1934 in Lyme; fourth; Gerald W. Davis

(farmer, 32, Groton) and Hattie K. Davis (26, Beebe, PQ)
Marjorie Ruth, b. 5/16/1941 in Lyme; seventh; Gerald W. Davis
(farmer, 39, Groton) and Hattie K. Davis (33, Beebe Jct., Canada)
Norris Sanborn, b. 10/30/1920 in Lyme; first; Perry A. Davis (farmer, 24, Thetford, VT) and Gladys Sanborn (22, Plymouth)

DAVISON,
Lewis Arthur, b. 2/28/1871 in Lyme; first; Levi W. Davison (farmer, 39, Lyme) and Susan E. Patch (22, Orford) (1929)

DAY,
stillborn son, b. 1/5/1907 in Lyme; third; Ethan A. Day (laborer, 26, Corinth, VT) and Eva B. Seavey (25, Andover)
Arlene May, b. 6/7/1927 in Lyme; third; William W. Day (farmer, 39, Bradford, VT) and Mary E. Webster (31, Lyme)
Brenda Marie, b. 2/4/1957 in Hanover; Roy W. Day (carpenter, Lyme) and Mary E. Hadlock (Norwich, VT)
Cameron Ross, b. 4/29/1998 in Lebanon; Robb Richard Day and Sara E. Stanhope
Cindy May, b. 9/17/1960 in Hanover; Roy W. Day (carpenter, 29, Lyme) and Mary E. Hadlock (29, Norwich, VT)
Dorothy Margaret, b. 7/26/1912 in Lyme; first; William W. Day (laborer, 23, Bradford, VT) and Ida Belle Stafford (22, Waterloo, VT)
Dusti Ann, b. 7/21/1975 in Haverhill; Daniel Arthur Day and Deann Kae Sanborn
Elizabeth Connie, b. 3/16/1951 in Lebanon; second; Jasper J. Day (lumberman, 29, Lyme) and Jeanette Brockway (23, Lyme)
Jasper John, b. 9/2/1921 in Lyme; second; William W. Day (farmer, 32, Bradford, VT) and Mary E. Webster (24, Lyme)
Regenna Ann, b. 9/8/1951 in Lebanon; first; Roy W. Day (lumberman, 20, Lyme) and Mary Etta Hadlock (20, Norwich, VT)
Roy William, b. 10/23/1930 in Lyme; fourth; William W. Day (farmer, 42, Bradford, VT) and Mary E. Webster (34, Lyme)
Ruth Alfretta, b. 10/10/1918 in Lyme; first; William W. Day (farming, 30, Bradford, VT) and Mary E. Webster (21, Lyme)
Sandra Jean, b. 10/5/1948 in Lebanon; first; Jasper J. Day (lumberman, 27, Lyme) and Jeanette E. Brockway (20, Lyme)

DEGOOSH,
Anne, b. 9/9/1925 in Lyme; fourth; Howard DeGoosh (farmer, 33, Cornish) and Nettie M. Pushee (31, Lyme)
Carroll Albert, b. 3/1/1914; eleventh; Elmer E. DeGoosh (farmer, 55, W. Fairlee, VT) and Belle Keyes (46, Reading, VT)
Coburn Pushee, b. 10/6/1919 in Lyme; first; Howard E. DeGoosh (farming, 27, Cornish) and Nettie M. Pushee (25, Lyme)
David Pushee, b. 8/25/1940 in Lyme; thirteenth; Howard E. DeGoosh (farmer, 48, Cornish) and Nettie M. Pushee (46, Lyme)
Ellsworth J., b. 5/30/1924 in Lyme; third; Howard DeGoosh (farmer, 32, Corinth, VT) and Nettie M. Pushee (30, Lyme)
Howard Elmer, Jr., b. 1/21/1934 in Lyme; ninth; Howard E. DeGoosh (laborer, 41, Cornish) and Nettie M. Pushee (40, Lyme)
Jane, b. 6/26/1929 in Hanover; sixth; Howard E. DeGoosh (farmer, 37, Cornish) and Nettie M. Pushee (35, Lyme)
John Sylvester, b. 7/10/1932 in Hanover; eighth; Howard E. DeGoosh (farmer, 40, Cornish) and Nettie M. Pushee (38, Lyme)
Kent K., b. 12/30/1936 in Lyme; eleventh; Howard E. DeGoosh (farmer, 44, Cornish) and Nettie M. Pushee (43, Lyme)
Mary, b. 9/25/1927 in Hanover; fifth; Howard DeGoosh (farmer, 35, Cornish) and Nettie Pushee (33, Lyme)
Nancy, b. 8/19/1938 in Hanover; twelfth; Howard E. DeGoosh (farmer, 46, Cornish) and Nettie M. Pushee (44, Lyme)
Nettie, b. 5/19/1935 in Hanover; tenth; Howard E. DeGoosh (farmer, 43, Cornish) and Nettie M. Pushee (41, Lyme)
Richard Howard, b. 12/29/1921 in Lyme; second; Howard DeGoosh (farmer, 29, Cornish) and Nettie M. Pushee (28, Lyme)
Ruth Gertrude, b. 2/3/1912 in Lyme; tenth; Elmer E. DeGoosh (farmer, 53, W. Fairlee, VT) and Belle Keyes (44, Reading, VT)
Sue, b. 9/20/1930 in Hanover; seventh; Howard E. DeGoosh (farmer, 38, Cornish) and Nettie M. Pushee (36, Lyme)
Timothy Allen, b. 11/15/1960 in Ruislip, England; Howard E. DeGoosh and Velma M. Nutting (1963)

DENNIS,
stillborn daughter, b. 7/10/1894 in Lyme; second; Myron Dennis (farmer, 33, Stratford) and Agnes L. Warren (28, Lyme)
son, b. 5/10/1897 in Lyme; third; George W. Dennis (farmer, 34, Stratford) and Carrie F. Church (30, Vershire, VT)

Doris Hazel, b. 8/11/1904 in Lyme; second; Albert Dennis (laborer, 22, Stratford) and Bertha M. Flint (20, Lyme)
George, Jr., b. 7/1/1904 in Lyme; fourth; George W. Dennis (farmer, 41, Stratford) and Carrie F. Church (36, Vershire, VT)
Josephine May, b. 9/13/1911 in Lyme; third; Albert B. Dennis (farmer, 28, Stratford) and Maude A. Piper (26, Lyme)
Larry Alan, b. 2/4/1955 in Hanover; second; Wendell L. Dennis (farmer, Lyme) and Myrtle I. Gibson (Newbury, VT)
Marion Gertrude, b. 8/29/1924 in Lyme; first; Alger E. Dennis (laborer, 27, Stratford) and Freda G. Smith (19, Lyme)
Steven Wendell, b. 11/6/1953 in Lebanon; Wendell Dennis (farmer, 33, Lyme) and Myrtle Gibson (24, Newbury, VT)
Wendall Leroy, b. 6/15/1919 in Lyme; first; Leroy E. Dennis (farming, 32, Stratford) and Effie Gage (27, Orford)

DERBY,
daughter, b. 5/4/1891; second; Lewis S. Derby (farmer, 54, Lyme) and Anna M. Smith (25, Hanover)
son, b. 8/15/1908 in Lyme; D. A. Derby (blacksmith, 42, Lyme) and Mary E. Thatcher (39, Dupont, OH)
Clinton Harris, b. 11/22/1888; first; Lewis S. Derby (farmer, 51, Lyme) and Annie M. Smith (22, Hanover)
Clyde A., b. 8/10/1903 in Lyme; eighth; Dana A. Derby (laborer, 38, Lyme) and Mary E. Thatcher (35, Dupont, OH)
Dana, Jr., b. 4/15/1928 in Lyme; sixth; Alvin H. Derby (laborer, 36, Hanover) and Josephine Brown (32, Searsmont, ME)
Emme Elizabeth, b. 6/27/1926 in Lyme; fifth; Alvin H. Derby (laborer, 34, Hanover) and Josephine Brown (30, Searsmont, ME)
Katie May, b. 9/7/1894 in Lyme; fourth; Dana A. Derby (laborer, 29, Lyme) and Mary E. Thatcher (26, Dupont, OH)
Weymouth Vinson, b. 4/23/1924 in Lyme; fourth; Alvin H. Derby (laborer, 32, Hanover) and Josephine Brown (28, Searmont, ME)

DEREGO,
Dakota Downing, b. 6/5/1990 in Lebanon; Edward C. DeRego and Kelly Downing
Dylan, b. 4/28/1996 in Lebanon; Edward DeRego and Kelly Downing

DEVAUX,
Amanda Ellen, b. 11/28/1983 in Hanover; David M. DeVaux and

Vera E. Clark

DEWITT,
son, b. 7/6/1907 in Lyme; sixth; Melvin Dewitt (laborer, 46, NB) and Melvina Byron (37, Littleton)
daughter, b. 1/27/1909 in Lyme; second; Melvin Dewitt (laborer, 47, NB) and Melvina E. Byron (38, Littleton)
Gladys L., b. 6/22/1906 in Lyme; fifth; Melvin E. DeWitt (lumberman, 44, NB) and Melvina E. Byron (35, Littleton)

DICKINSON,
Elizabeth, b. 11/29/1952 in Lyme; seventh; Edwards Dickinson (minister, 52, Holliston, MA) and Marjory Stocking (45, Keokuk, IA)

DIKE,
daughter, b. 1/21/1909 in Lyme; second; Frank S. Dike (laborer, 36, Lyme) and Ora Rich (21, Stratford)
Celia N., b. 1/25/1906 in Lyme; first; Frank S. Dike (laborer, 32, Lyme) and Ora E. Rich (19, Stratford)
Edna May, b. 4/14/1911 in Lyme; first; Charles E. Dike (laborer, 25, Lyme) and Jennie B. Perry (25, PEI)
Florence Emma, b. 5/29/1912 in Lyme; first; Leslie H. Dike (laborer, 35, Lyme) and Florence L. Johnson (20, Lyme)
Frank David, b. 11/4/1913 in Lyme; second; Charles E. Dike (laborer, 28, Lyme) and Jennie B. Perry (28, PEI)
Jessie Belle, b. 1/3/1911 in Lyme; third; Frank S. Dike (laborer, 39, Lyme) and Ora E. Rich (24, Stratford)
Leon F., b. 3/22/1903 in Lyme; second; Fred V. Dike (laborer, 24, Lyme) and Emma S. Tattersall (23, Lyme)

DIMICK,
Alice M., b. 9/24/1895 in Lyme; first; Edson L. Dimick (laborer, 22, Lyme) and Delia Wright (18, Lyme)
Eleanor H., b. 2/28/1907 in Lyme; first; Thomas E. Dimick (farmer, 32, Lyme) and Addie V. Jewell (27, Lyme)
Esther C., b. 1/18/1911 in Lyme; second; Thomas E. Dimick (farmer, 36, Lyme) and Addie V. Jewell (31, Newbury, VT)
Ethel, b. 2/14/1900; third; Charles P. Dimick (laborer, 35, Lyme) and Florence Carpenter (24, Littleton)
Eva May, b. 5/23/1898; second; Charles P. Dimick (laborer, 33,

Lyme) and Florence J. Carpenter (22, Littleton)
Gary Michael, b. 10/2/1954 in Lebanon; second; Kenneth C. Dimick (farmer, 36, Lyme) and Verla M. Perkins (28, Lyme)
Gregory Forrest, b. 8/13/1948 in Hanover; first; Kenneth C. Dimick (farmer, 30, Lyme) and Verla M. Perkins (22, Lyme)
Kenneth Charles, b. 1/21/1918 in Lyme; sixth; Charles P. Dimick (farming, 53, Lyme) and Florence Carpenter (41, Littleton)
Mabel Latora, b. 4/25/1909 in Lyme; fifth; Charles Pushee Dimick (farmer, 44, Lyme) and Florence J'n'te Carpenter (33, Littleton)
Pearl May, b. 5/9/1894 in Lyme; first; Edwin P. Dimick (farmer, 30, Lyme) and Hattie C. Gilbert (31, Lyme)
Ruth Elizabeth, b. 9/13/1902; fourth; Charles P. Dimick (laborer, 37, Lyme) and Florence J. Carpenter (26, Littleton)

DIMOND,
Kennith C., b. 8/14/1899; fourth; Willie L. Dimond (fireman, 33, Orange) and Julia E. Claflin (33, Auburn)

DISTLER,
Alexandra Lael, b. 12/16/1976 in Hanover; John Alan Distler and Jean Elizabeth Dickerman

DOE,
Joyce Elizabeth, b. 6/13/1943 in Lyme; sixth; Albert L. Doe (woodsman, 43, Canaan) and Eugenia F. Shaw (30, Scituate, MA)

DONNELLY,
William Jay, b. 9/12/1947 in Hanover; second; Robert J. Donnelly (painter, 31, Lisbon) and Nellie M. Cummings (22, Thetford, VT)

DOUGLAS,
John E., b. 7/29/1935 in Hanover; sixth; Elmer J. Douglas (farmer, 30, S. Reading, VT) and Julia M. Hammond (34, W. Windsor, VT)

DOWD,
Duncan Charles, b. 2/20/1992 in Lebanon; Leo Dowd III and Tami Pike
Killian Michael, b. 4/5/2000 in Lebanon; Leo Dowd and Darcy Dowd
Michaela Marie, b. 11/25/2001 in Lebanon; Leo Dowd and Darcy

Dowd
Patrick Wayne, b. 4/19/1990 in Hanover; Leon B. Dowd III and Tami Pike

DOWNING,
Robert E., b. 6/17/1926 in Lyme; fifth; Walter Downing (fireman, 38, Campton) and Mabel G. Parker (21, Plainfield); residence - Plainfield

DOYON,
Joseph Raoul Roger, b. 12/17/1938 in Lyme; second; Davila Doyon (woodsman, 30, Canada) and Simone Poulin (20, Canada)
Mary T. B., b. 8/24/1937 in Lyme; first; Davila Doyon (woodsman, 29, St. Rose, PQ) and Simone Poulin (19, St. Just., PQ)

DRAKE,
Casey Frances, b. 6/6/1989 in Hanover; Francis G. Drake and Tina Letourneau

DREW,
Carol Ann, b. 1/14/1937 in Lyme; third; Leslie P. Drew (farmer, 51, Fairhaven, MA) and Irene Blake (24, Claremont)
David Leslie, b. 8/11/1971 in Haverhill; Richard Drew and Delores Fillian
Emily Gertrude, b. 8/3/1938 in Haverhill; fourth; Leslie P. Drew (farmer, 52, Fairhaven, MA) and Irene B. Blake (24, Claremont)
Marjorie Ann, b. 4/15/1971 in Hanover; William Drew and Marilyn Toner
Richard Albert, b. 9/1/1979 in Lebanon; Richard Drew and Delores Fillian
Richard Henry, b. 11/17/1945 in Lyme; sixth; Leslie P. Drew (farmer, 60, Fairhaven, MA) and Irene B. Blake (32, Claremont)
William Leslie, b. 3/22/1940 in Lyme; fifth; Leslie P. Drew (farmer, 54, Fairhaven, MA) and Irene B. Blake (35, Claremont)

DRUHL,
Kevin Allen, b. 4/20/1988 in Lebanon; Michael D. Druhl and Jill A. King

DUBUQUE,
Terry Patrick, b. 11/21/1962 in Hanover; James Dubuque (proof

reader, Lebanon) and Sheila L. McEwan (25, Woodsville)

DUKE,
Murray Cameron, b. 6/17/1947 in Lebanon; third; George F. Duke (clergyman, 40, Kewanee, IL) and Evelyn Murray (38, Malden, MA)

DUNBAR,
son, b. 4/3/1903 in Lyme; first; Robert A. Dunbar (laborer, 23, Canada) and Edith May Simpson (26, Bradford, VT)
son, b. 3/30/1908 in Lyme; fourth; Robert A. Dunbar (farmer, 28, Canada) and Edith May Simpson (22, Bradford, VT)
stillborn daughter, b. 11/23/1921 in Lyme; colored; Robert Dunbar (laborer, 43, Canada) and Edith M. Simpson (35, Bradford, VT)
stillborn son, b. 11/16/1923 in Lyme; thirteenth; black; Robert A. Dunbar (laborer, 44, Canada) and Edith Simpson (37, Bradford, VT)
daughter, b. 3/29/1915; eighth; Robert A. Dunbar (laborer, 37, black, Canada) and Edith M. Simpson (30, Bradford, VT)
Carlie Roy, b. 7/18/1910 in Lyme; fourth; Robert A. Dunbar (farmer, 31, Canada) and Edith M. Simpson (24)
Ernest E., b. 4/6/1914; sixth; black; Robert A. Dunbar (farmer, 35, Canada) and Edith M. Simpson (28, Bradford, VT)
Frederick, b. 3/9/1898; first; Hattie M. S. Dunbar (16, Pottam, Canada, black)
John Ray, b. 2/12/1906; third; colored; Robert A. Dunbar (farming, 27, Canada) and Edith Simpson (20, Bradford, VT) (1916)
Lavina Hattie, b. 6/14/1917; ninth; colored; Robert Dunbar (farming, 38, Canada) and Edith Simpson (31, Bradford, VT)
Mabel Emma, b. 4/17/1912 in Lyme; fifth; Robert A. Dunben (farmer, 33, Canada) and Edith M. Simpson (26, Bradford, VT)
Pearl M., b. 6/2/1904 in Lyme; second; Robert A. Dunbar (farmer, 24, Canada) and Edith M. Simpson (21, Bradford, VT)

DURGIN,
Lawrence Mark, b. 7/5/1949 in Lebanon; Matthew A. Durgin and Shirley Laurent

DUROSS,
Jonathon Sloan, b. 10/23/1976 in Hanover; David Jonathon DuRoss and Mary Helene Greller

DYKE,
Craig Timothy, b. 4/9/1975 in Lebanon; Robert Leon Dyke and Nancy Carol Small
William Perry, b. 7/25/1946 in Hanover; second; Perry E. Dyke (mechanic, 26, Union Village, VT) and Bertice D. White (26, Haverhill)

EASTWICK,
Lorraine, b. 6/27/1947 in Hanover; third; John Eastwick (civil engineer, 36, Winchester, MA) and Dorothea L. Mason (34, S. Tamworth)

EATON,
Matthew Stuart, b. 10/6/1968 in Lebanon; John S. Eaton and Diane E. Vaughan

ELDER,
stillborn son, b. 12/31/1916; third; Burton W. G. Elder (farming, 23, Nashua) and Cora L. Blackman (20, Huntington, CT)
stillborn daughter, b. 12/31/1916; fourth; Burton W. G. Elder (farming, 23, Nashua) and Cora L. Blackman (20, Huntington, CT)
Anna Rose, b. 6/11/1930 in Thetford, VT; fourth; George B. Elder (farmer, 41, Hanover) and Rose L. Camp (35, Lyme)
Arthur Roy, b. 8/28/1945 in Lyme; third; Roger B. Elder (lumbering, 24, Hanover) and Loretta M. Nareau (24, Hanover)
Bruce Carl, b. 2/23/1967 in Lebanon; third; Don E. Elder (mechanic, Lyme) and Julia M. Balch (Woodsville)
Don Edward, b. 7/19/1938 in Lyme; second; Kenneth E. Elder (laborer, 24, Hanover) and Mildred E. Underhill (24, Canaan)
Ethel Louise, b. 12/28/1915; second; Burton W. G. Elder (farmer, 22, Nashua) and Cora L. Blackman (19, Shelton, CT)
Gail Marie, b. 10/15/1962 in Hanover; Don E. Elder (mechanic, Lyme) and Julia M. Balch (23, Woodsville)
Gordon Lee, b. 10/17/1952 in Lebanon; second; Kenneth Elder (farmer, 38, Hanover) and Ruth Bean (36, Orford); res. – Lyme Ctr.
Guy George, b. 5/27/1923 in Lyme; sixth; Burton Elder (laborer, 30, Nashua) and Cora Blackman (27, Huntington, CT)
Helen Louise, b. 4/29/1934 in Lyme; first; Kenneth E. Elder (laborer, 19, Hanover) and Mildred E. Underhill (18, Canaan)

Judith Sue, b. 2/8/1965 in Hanover; second; Don E. Elder (mechanic, Lyme) and Julia M. Balch (Woodsville)
Marguerite R., b. 9/16/1907 in Lyme; fourth; John Elder (laborer, 36, Canada) and Martha N. Harwood (36, Vitton, Canada); residence - Hanover
Marie Ann, b. 7/15/1943 in Hanover; second; Roger B. Elder (farming, 22, Hanover) and Loretta M. Nareau (22, Hanover)
Mark Alan, b. 8/31/1960 in Lebanon; Philip E. Elder (farming, 19, Lyme) and Joyce E. Mack (16, Windsor, VT)
Mary Beth, b. 1/18/1969 in Hanover; Don E. Elder and Julia M. Balch
Nancy Ann, b. 11/19/1959 in Hanover; Kenneth E. Elder (farmer, 45, Hanover) and Ruth A. Bean (43, Orford)
Philip Earl, b. 6/6/1941 in Lyme; third; Kenneth Elder (farmer, 27, Hanover) and Mildred Underhill (26, Canaan)
Saralee Jean, b. 3/10/1964 in Lebanon; Philip E. Elder (woodsman, Lyme) and Joyce E. Mack (19, Windsor, VT)
Thea Mae, b. 3/9/1921 in Lyme; fifth; Berton W. Elder (lumberman, 28, Nashua) and Cora Blackman (24, Huntington, CT)

ELLIOTT,
son, b. 7/15/1888; seventh; John F. Elliott (farmer, 37, Campton) and Kate Hewes (31, Lyme)
son, b. 10/7/1890; eighth; John F. Elliott (farmer, 40, Campton) and Kate Hewes (Lyme)
son, b. 4/12/1903 in Lyme; second; Harry A. Elliott (laborer, 21, Lyme) and Susan A. Carr (21, Orange, VT)
daughter, b. 5/14/1939 in Haverhill; first; Harry A. Willey, Jr. (20, Haverhill) and Doris E. Elliott (15, Lisbon)
Ethel S., b. 12/5/1902; first; David Elliott (butcher, 38, Mills Isle, PQ) and Sophronia B. Doxie (27, Hastings, ON)
Lena, b. 10/25/1897 in Lyme; tenth; John F. Elliott (farmer, 47, Campton) and Kate Hewes (41, Lyme)
Leslie, b. 8/19/1892; John F. Elliott (farmer, 42, Campton) and Kate Hewes (36, Lyme)
Stanley Carr, b. 6/28/1902; first; Harry A. Elliott (laborer, 20, Lyme) and Susan A. Carr (20, Orange, VT)
Stanley Carr, b. 8/8/1926 in Lyme; second; Stanley C. Elliott (laborer, 24, Lyme) and Lula B. Baker (20, Orford)

ELLIS,
Anthony, b. 10/15/1966 in Hanover; third; John W. Ellis (asst. principal, Portsmouth) and Elaine Chicaderis (Manchester)
Jonathan Michael, b. 10/5/1988 in Hanover; Robert P. Ellis and Michele Ann LaBelle
Lane Patrick, b. 5/31/1983 in Hanover; Robert P. Ellis and Michele A. LaBelle
Maria, b. 4/20/1965 in Hanover; second; John W. Ellis (sch. principal, Portsmouth) and Elaine Chicaderis (Manchester)

ELLSWORTH,
Dean Henry, b. 5/22/1896 in Lyme; first; Joseph Ellsworth (butcher, 42, Wentworth) and Jennie R. Glines (26, Haverhill)

EMERSON,
Bertha L., b. 10/27/1902; second; Andrew Emerson (farmer, 39, Newbury, VT) and Mary L. Bowen (18, Greenfield); residence - Bradford, VT

EMERY,
Erma Alice, b. 4/19/1917 in Lyme; Fay S. Emery (farmer, Piermont) and Gladys Chesley (20, Lyme) (1961)

EPPERSON,
Laura Marie, b. 10/19/1963 in Lyme; Larry D. Epperson (teaching asst., Memphis, TN) and Letitia Reams (21, Columbus, OH)

EREL,
Alon Yaarov, b. 8/4/1993 in Lebanon; Yigal Erel and Osnat Shoshani

ESTES,
Gail Lyn, b. 1/14/1963 in Hanover; Leo W. Estes (Hanover) and Sally Ann Chase (27, Lebanon)
Hailey Madison, b. 6/28/1996 in Lebanon; Timothy Estes and Michele Boutin
Linda Lee, b. 10/11/1947 in Hanover; sixth; Leonard R. Estes (farming, 29, Norwich, VT) and Evelyn D. Powers (22, Norwich, VT)
Nicholas Leonard, b. 3/17/1969 in Hanover; Russell G. Estes and Noreen E. Gallup
Patti Ann, b. 12/22/1960 in Hanover; Leo W. Estes (teacher, 23,

Hanover) and Sally A. Chase (25, Lebanon)
Pauline May, b. 5/24/1946 in Hanover; fifth; Leonard R. Estes (farmer, 28, Norwich, VT) and Evelyn D. Powers (20, Norwich, VT)
Roberta Ann, b. 5/22/1945 in Hanover; fourth; Leonard R. Estes (farmer, 27, Norwich, VT) and Evelyn D. Powers (19, Norwich, VT)
Timothy Russell, b. 7/24/1965 in Hanover; first; Russell G. Estes (carpenter, Hanover) and Noreen E. Gallup (Lebanon)

EVANS,
Barbara Jean, b. 3/26/1942 in Hanover; first; Harold B. Evans (trucking, 28, Hudson, NY) and Janet Piper (22, Lyme)
Brian Timothy, b. 3/2/1981 in Lebanon; James E. Evans, Sr. and Toni L. White
George Elwin, b. 5/4/1895 in Lyme; William H. Evans and Almyra B. Gilbert (1962)
James Edsel, b. 11/11/1978 in Lebanon; James E. Evans and Toni L. White
Lois Elizabeth, b. 12/10/1917; eighth; Charles S. Evans (farming, 40, Sanbornton) and Lois Mortimer (35, Troy)

EVARTS,
Adelaide Vestal, b. 8/17/1993 in Lebanon; George Evarts and Pamela French
Gibson Marshall, b. 6/24/1996 in Lebanon; George Evarts and Pamela French

EVERETT,
Ernest H., b. 1/26/1939 in Hanover; fourth; Earle D. Everett (laborer, 26, Four Falls, Canada) and Alice B. Brown (24, Quebec)

FAIRCLOTH,
Catherine Ann, b. 5/17/1947 in Hanover; second; Obediah Faircloth (stu. farmer, 27, Valdosta, GA) and Elizabeth A. Land (24, Brooklyn, NY)

FAY,
Nancy Ann, b. 11/5/1937 in Hanover; first; George H. Fay (con'ti'n man, 24, Danbury) and Frances H. Watts (18, W. Lebanon)
Sally Ann, b. 9/18/1944 in Lyme; first; Elmer L. Fay (taxi driver, 25,

Grafton) and Mercy J. Adams (19, Fairlee, VT); residence – Fairlee, VT

FERENCHAK,
Brett Peter, b. 10/6/1972 in Hanover; Ralph P. Ferenchak, M.D. and Pamela Alexson

FIELDS,
Bruce Benjamin, b. 10/10/1950 in Hanover; sixth; John Fields (carpenter, 37, Lebanon) and Meda Roberts (37, Lyme)
Carol Edna, b. 3/16/1942 in Hanover; fifth; John E. Fields (laborer, 29, Lebanon) and Meda P. Roberts (28, Lyme)
Dale Robert, b. 2/16/1954 in Hanover; eighth; John E. Fields (laborer, 41, Lebanon) and Meda P. Roberts (40, Lyme)
James Edward, b. 7/18/1943 in Hanover; fifth; John E. Fields (lumber man, 30, Lebanon) and Meda P. Roberts (29, Lyme)
Jayne Ann, b. 2/3/1940 in Lebanon; fourth; John E. Fields (truck driver, 27, Lebanon) and Meda P. Roberts (26, Lyme)
Joan F., b. 7/6/1936 in Hanover; second; John E. Fields (laborer, 23, Lebanon) and Meda P. Roberts (22, Lyme)
Mary Jane, b. 4/26/1938 in Etna; second; John Fields (laborer, 25, Lebanon) and Meda Roberts (25, Lyme)
Rebecca Jane, b. 4/5/1971 in Plymouth; James Fields and Patricia A. Olsen

FIFIELD,
Derrick Allen, b. 7/11/1943 in Lyme; third; Everett A. Fifield (laborer, 27, Thetford, VT) and Evelyn A. Estes (23, Norwich, VT); residence – Thetford Ctr., VT
Sandra May, b. 5/14/1946 in Lyme; fourth; Everett A. Fifield (electrician, 31, Thetford, VT) and Evelyn A. Estes (25, Norwich, VT); residence – Thetford Ctr., VT

FINLEY,
Alexandra Stokes, b. 11/15/1989 in Hanover; Rodrick J. Finley and Laurel Lehmann
Jessica Clare, b. 4/17/1987 in Hanover; Roderick J. Finley and Laurel Lehmann
Margaret Ann Marie, b. 7/23/2001 in Lebanon; Greg Finley and J. Marie Pippin
Ryan Aquila Scott, b. 7/25/1999 in Lebanon; Gregory Finley and J.

Marie Pippin
Samuel Russell, b. 7/22/1994 in Lebanon; Rodrick Finley and Laurel Lehmann

FISHER,
Oliver Justin, b. 7/21/1984 in Hanover; Timothy F. Fisher and Prudence B. Curtis

FISK,
Robert Arthur, b. 11/14/1919 in Lyme; second; Herbert A. Fisk (farming, 33, Hampton) and Olive S. Ellis (29, Cambridge, MA)

FITZGERALD,
John David, III, b. 10/17/1985 in Hanover; John D. Fitzgerald, Jr. and Kelly J. Pecor
Stefanie Mary-Elizabeth, b. 6/10/1988 in Hanover; John D. Fitzgerald, Jr. and Kelly J. Pecor

FLICKINGER,
Andrew Earl, b. 1/26/1991 in Hanover; Henry S. Flickinger and Tracy Strout
Cole Hudson, b. 11/3/1993 in Lebanon; Henry Flickinger, Jr. and Tracy Strout

FLINT,
Elizabeth J., b. 12/30/1911 in Lyme; second; Walter M. Flint (farmer, 34, Boston, MA) and Elizabeth H. Marston (36, Sandwich Ctr.)

FOLLANSBEE,
son, b. 10/28/1909 in Lyme; first; Grace E. Follansbee (22, Hartland, VT)

FORWARD,
Amanda Ashley, b. 3/17/1992 in Lebanon; Thomas Forward III and Barbara Burgess
Megan Elizabeth, b. 5/11/1994 in Lebanon; Thomas Forward III and Barbara Burgess
Thomas Chesley, IV, b. 10/4/1988 in Hanover; Thomas C. Forward III and Barbara A. Burgess

FOWLER,
David G., b. 11/20/1936 in Lyme; third; David G. Fowler (farmer, 35, Newport) and Olive Greenwood (24, Norwich, VT)
Donna Jean, b. 3/25/1944 in Lyme; sixth; David G. Fowler (dyer, 42, Newport) and Olive L. Greenwood (31, Norwich, VT)
Julia Mae, b. 6/7/1941 in Lyme; sixth; David G. Fowler (laborer, 39, Newport) and Olive Greenwood (28, Norwich, VT)
Linda Marie, b. 8/22/1951 in Lebanon; ninth; David Fowler (truck driver, 49, Newport) and Olive Greenwood (38, Norwich, VT)
Louis J., b. 5/16/1935 in Lyme; first; David C. Fowler (farmer, 34, Newport) and Olive L. Greenwood (22, Norwich, VT)
Luvie Ann, b. 4/1/1939 in Lyme; third; David G. Fowler (laborer, 37, Newport) and Olive L. Greenwood (26, Norwich, VT)
Mabel Louise, b. 8/29/1947 in Hanover; seventh; David G. Fowler (truck driver, 45, Newport) and Olive L. Greenwood (34, Norwich, VT)
Ruth Janice, b. 7/3/1949 in Lebanon; David G. Fowler and Olive Greenwood

FRANKLIN,
son, b. 6/25/1909 in Lyme; second; Harry Foster Franklin (farmer, 32, Lyme) and Clara Flavilla Piper (36, Lyme)
son, b. 10/18/1910 in Lyme; third; Harry Foster Franklin (farmer, 33, Lyme) and Clara F. Piper (37, Lyme)
Eva Betsey, b. 12/22/1902; first; George E. Franklin (farmer, 29, Waterbury, VT) and Gertrude G. Palmer (16, Pittsfield, VT)
Harold Shattuck, b. 5/23/1913 in Lyme; fourth; Harry F. Franklin (farmer, 35, Lyme) and Clara F. Piper (40, Lyme)
John D., b. 4/20/1937 in Hanover; first; Harry P. Franklin (truck driver, 27, Lyme) and Viola L. Davis (29, Groton)
Lisa Marie, b. 8/7/1969 in Hanover; John D. Franklin and Rebecca E. Taylor
Pearl, b. 8/3/1907 in Lyme; first; Henry Foster Franklin (mail carrier, 29, Lyme) and Clara F. Piper (34, Lyme)

FRAWLEY,
Taylor Lauren, b. 7/25/1994 in Lebanon; Thomas Frawley and Denise LeBlanc

FREIHOFER,
Samuel Gray, b. 8/29/1991 in Hanover; Daniel S. Freihofer and Dale

P. Breed
William Breed, b. 5/17/1986 in Hanover; Daniel S. Freihofer and Dale P. Breed

FROST,
Beverley Jean, b. 8/2/1943 in Lyme; second; Cadis E. Frost (trackman, 31, Topsham, VT) and Pearl R. Gardner (29, Enfield)
Patricia Ann, b. 10/30/1963 in Lebanon; Robert E. Frost (Lyme) and Muriel A. Webb (21, E. Barnet, VT)
Robert Edward, b. 12/23/1940 in Lyme; first; Cadie E. Frost (tracksman, 28, Topsham, VT) and Pearl R. Gardner (26, Enfield)
Robert Edward, Jr., b. 1/31/1961 in Lebanon; Robert E. Frost (laborer, Lyme) and Muriel A. Webb (19, E. Barnet, VT)
Tammy Jean, b. 4/14/1962 in Lebanon; Robert E. Frost, Jr. (laborer, Lyme) and Muriel A. Webb (20, E. Barnet, VT)

FULLER,
Jean Marie, b. 2/12/1946 in Lyme; third; Arthur A. Fuller (truck driver, 45, Wheelock, VT) and Martha C. Chase (38, Hillsboro); residence – Piermont

FULTON,
John Stark, b. 12/14/1957 in Hanover; Elmer B. Fulton (HS prin., Goshen) and Effie G. Thompson (Hanover)
Judith, b. 11/18/1948 in Hanover; first; Elmer B. Fulton (headmaster, 36, Goshen) and Effie G. Thompson (27, Hanover)
Thomas Bryant, b. 12/3/1953 in Hanover; Elmer Fulton (HS principal, 41, NH) and Effie Thompson (32, Hanover)

GALES,
Theodore Dean, b. 7/30/1994 in Lebanon; John Gales and Robin Checani

GALLA,
Angela Lesley, b. 11/20/1971 in Hanover; John P. Galla and Susan Kiefer
Mary Kiefer, b. 5/27/1974 in Hanover; John Paul Galla and Susan Mary Kiefer

GALLUP,
William Henry, b. 6/8/1954 in Lyme; fourth; Harley G. Gallup
(carpenter, 38, Montpelier) and Ella C. Johnson (33, Minneapolis, MN)

GAMAGE,
Marilyn Louise, b. 11/28/1940 in Lyme; second; Harold W. Gamage
(farmer, 26, Greene, ME) and Louise M. Briggs (28, Minot, ME)
Nelson Elroy, b. 2/22/1938 in Lyme; first; Harold W. Gamage
(farmer, 24, Greene, ME) and Louise M. Briggs (25, Minot, ME)
Rachel Irene, b. 10/14/1949 in Hanover; Russell W. Gamage and Irene Briggs

GAMBLE,
Lucy May, b. 9/18/1993 in Lebanon; Thomas Gamble and Anne Conway

GARDNER,
Wendall R., b. 10/9/1937 in Lyme; sixth; Glen Gardner (laborer, 35, Orford) and Nellie A. Gage (33, Orford)

GARRITY-HANCHETT,
Hazel Rose, b. 5/21/2000 in Lebanon; Michael Hanchett and Elise Garrity
Olivia Iris, b. 2/23/1994 in Lebanon; Michael Hanchett and Elisa Garrity

GAYLOR,
Nicole Elizabeth, b. 8/9/1992 in Lebanon; Peter Gaylor and Rebecca Cunningham

GEILICH,
Benjamin Mahler, b. 4/27/1990 in Hanover; Micharl M. Geilich and Cynthia Mahler
Jared Mahler, b. 5/29/1993 in Lebanon; Michael Geilich and Cynthia Mahler

GEORGE,
David Lee, b. 8/11/1952 in Hanover; second; Ronald George (laborer, 22, Hanover) and Ruth Lewis (21, Nashua)
Donald Wayne, b. 3/12/1950 in Hanover; first; Ronald H. George

(creamery worker, 20, Hanover) and Ruth Lewis (19, Nashua)
Edith Ethel, b. 11/1/1940 in Hanover; first; Earl F. George (carpenter, 28, Hanover) and Freda M. Johnson (27, S. Vershire, VT)
John Patrick, b. 7/22/1965 in Lebanon; sixth; Walter L. George (truck driver, W. Fairlee, VT) and Lodie M. Wilmot (Lyme)
Judy May, b. 2/22/1947 in Lebanon; first; Walter L. George (laborer, 17, W. Fairlee, VT) and Addie M. Wilmot (23, Lyme)
Walter Leroy, Jr., b. 8/8/1952 in Lebanon; fourth; Walter George (laborer, 23, W. Fairlee, VT) and Addie Wilmot (29, Lyme)

GERLING,
Megan Jeanne, b. 10/18/1992 in Lebanon; Michael Gerling and Barbara Rackow

GERNHARD,
Christopher Richard, b. 9/15/1959 in Hanover; Frederick C. Gernhard (clerk, 23, Norwich, CT) and Irene D. Pushee (20, Lyme)
Douglas Robert, b. 10/25/1960 in Hanover; Frederick Gernhard (machinist, 24, Norwich, CT) and Irene D. Pushee (21, Lyme)
Jerry James, b. 5/7/1963 in Hanover; Frederick C. Gernhard (machinist, Norwich, CT) and Irene D. Pushee (23, Lyme)
Jordan Elliot, b. 7/11/1988 in Hanover; Jerry J. Gernhard and Robin L. Fisher
Timothy Scott, b. 10/5/1964 in Hanover; Frederick C. Gernhard (machinist, Norwich, CT) and Irene D. Pushee (25, Lyme)
Tucker James, b. 10/16/1986 in Hanover; Jerry J. Gernhard and Robin L. Fisher

GIBSON,
Marion Estelle, b. 12/15/1900; first; Frederick L. Gibson (music teacher, 40, Ryegate, VT) and Cynthia Ann Wilson (19, Lyme)
Velma A., b. 10/22/1903 in Lyme; second; Frederic L. Gibson (piano tuner, 43, Ryegate, VT) and Cynthia A. Wilson (22, Lyme)

GILBERT,
son, b. 5/29/1899; first; David E. Gilbert (laborer, 32, Lyme) and Nettie Flanders (16, Corinth, VT)
stillborn son, b. 3/31/1932 in Concord; first; C. A. Gilbert (carpenter, 62, E. Barnet, VT) and Doris Pease (30, Orford)

Arthur Ansel, b. 6/9/1889; first; Henry L. Gilbert (farmer, Lyme) and Mary Ella Gardine (Scotland)

Arthur Ansel, b. 10/7/1894 in Lyme; third; Henry L. Gilbert (horse car cond., 36, Lyme) and Mary E. Jordan (36, Edinburgh, Scotland); residence - Charlestown, MA

Jacqueline Elyse, b. 9/13/1993 in Lebanon; Robert Gilbert and Karen Hoy

Marjorie Blanch, b. 6/9/1921 in Lyme; first; Arthur A. Gilbert (carpenter, 26, Lyme) and Blanch N. Rowe (21, Rochester)

Mildred M., d. 2/6/1897 in Lyme; fourth; Henry L. Gilbert (farmer, 38, Lyme) and Mary Jordan (34, Edinburgh, Scotland)

Susie May, b. 3/18/1902; second; David E. Gilbert (laborer, 36, Lyme) and Nettie Flanders (18, Corinth, VT)

GILMAN,
Roger Lee, b. 6/23/1926 in Hanover; second; Bert L. Gilman (farmer, 28, W. Fairlee, VT) and Florence S. Clark (24, Bradford, VT)

GIRARDIN,
Laurier Joseph, Jr., b. 7/19/1938 in Lyme; second; Laurier J. Girardin (woodsman, 28, Chisholm, ME) and Phyllis Boutin (27, Canada)

GLOVER,
Cecelia Elizabeth, b. 6/20/1975 in Hanover; John B. Glover and Kendra J. Balch

GODFREY,
Bruce Allan, b. 10/11/1956 in Lebanon; Franklin G. Godfrey (mason, 22, Thetford, VT) and Margaret H. Leonard (21, Lebanon)

Ethel May, b. 3/7/1892; third; Edward G. Godfrey (laborer, 28, Waterbury, VT) and Mary Farrell (23, Shipton, PQ)

Forrest E., b. 6/26/1893 in Lyme; fourth; Edwin J. Godfrey (laborer, 29, Waterbury, VT) and May Farrell (24, Shipton, PQ)

Henry M., b. 7/5/1899; seventh; Edward J. Godfrey (laborer, 36, Stowe, VT) and May Farrell (30, Shipton, PQ)

Janice Marion, b. 7/19/1945 in Lyme; fourth; Floyd L. Godfrey (farmer, 35, W. Fairlee, VT) and Marion H. Barker (34, Thetford, VT); residence – W. Fairlee, VT

Ruth Ellen, b. 1/8/1926 in Lyme; first; Roy Godfrey (farmer, 32, Fairlee, VT) and Della E. Marsh (21, Orford)

Sarah M., b. 4/18/1895 in Lyme; fifth; Edward J. Godfrey (laborer, 30, Waterbury, VT) and Mary Farrell (25, Shipton, PQ)

GOODALE,
Susan Cabot, b. 5/30/1958 in Hanover; Fairfield Goodale (physician, 40, Boston, MA) and Mary M. Lyman (31, Westwood, MA)
Timothy Pickering, b. 9/9/1959 in Hanover; Fairfield Goodale (pathologist, 36, Boston, MA) and Mary Margaret Lyman (32, Westwood, MA)

GOODELL,
son, b. 3/2/1891; second; Alvin Goodell (farmer, 39, Lyme) and Jennie M. P. Kimball (29, Windham)
daughter, b. 1/12/1901; third; Alvin Goodell (farmer, 49, Lyme) and Jennie M. P. Kimball (39, Windham)
Carrol Wesley, b. 5/29/1887; first; John Wesley Goodell (laborer, 21, Lyme) and Ida Goodell (28, Lyme)
Dorothy May, b. 9/24/1907 in Lyme; first; Charles N. Goodell (farmer, 34, Lyme) and Lizzie F. Southworth (31, Fairlee, VT)
Harold L., b. 8/23/1903 in Lyme; eighth; George F. Goodell (farmer, 32, Montpelier, VT) and Ada M. Colburn (30, Braintree, VT)

GOODHUE,
Susan Jean, b. 2/17/1946 in Hanover; third; E. Sargent Goodhue (farmer, 35, Corinth, VT) and Ruth E. Cook (35, Thetford Ctr., VT)

GOODRICH,
Bonnie Marie, b. 11/4/1961 in Hanover; Robert L. Goodrich (carpenter, Grantham) and Marion Dennis (37, Lyme)
Brian Wayne, b. 2/3/1973 in Lebanon; Wayne Goodrich and Marjorie Linda Sayers
Dennis Lee, b. 4/21/1949 in Hanover; Robert L. Goodrich and Marian Dennis
Lisa Marie, b. 4/19/1971 in Lebanon; Wayne R. Goodrich and Marjorie L. Sayers
Muriel Jean, b. 4/30/1947 in Hanover; second; Robert L. Goodrich (sawyer, 32, Grantham) and Marion G. Dennis (23, Lyme)
Patricia Ann, b. 5/18/1959 in Hanover; Robert L. Goodrich (truck operator, 42, Grantham) and Marion G. Dennis (35, Lyme)
Steven Bruce, b. 5/5/1955 in Hanover; fourth; Robert L. Goodrich

(truck driver, Grantham) and Masrion G. Dennis (Lyme)
Wayne Robert, b. 5/24/1946 in Hanover; first; Robert L. Goodrich (sawyer, 31, Grantham) and Marion G. Dennis (21, Lyme)

GOODSPEED,
William Bruce, b. 9/28/1982 in Hanover; Richard C. Goodspeed, Jr. and Sheila R. Harriman

GORDON,
Theodore Keyes, b. 5/8/1917; first; Edwin R. Gordon (clergyman, 34, Salisbury) and Ruth C. Rowley (30, Westford, MA)

GOSS,
son, b. 3/27/1900; first; Wesley R. Goss (laborer, 22, Hanover) and Mary Gelo (22, Bradford, VT)

GOSZ,
Stephanie Lee, b. 5/1/1969 in Lebanon; James R. Gosz and Mary Jane O'Reilly

GRAF,
Jake Alan, b. 2/22/1990 in Hanover; Kevin L. Graf and Jodi Hager

GRAINGER,
Amy Lynn, b. 4/7/1982 in Hanover; Michael J. Grainger and Lynn A. Francoeur

GRANGER,
Charlotte, b. 12/29/1932 in Hanover; first; Ira N. Granger (farmer, 38, Elgin, PQ) and Verna L. Smith (32, Norwich, VT)

GRANT,
son, b. 1/14/1909 in Lyme; first; John Erastus Grant (laborer, 27, Lyme) and Sarah Jane Wilson (15, Lyme)
son, b. 2/20/1909 in Lyme; first; George P. Grant (farmer, 23, Lyme) and Ethel M. Pushee (18, Lyme)
Alanson Ware, b. 3/21/1911 in Lyme; first; Fred W. Grant (farmer, 30, Lyme) and Viola E. Ware (33, Thetford, VT)
Bernice May, b. 12/2/1917; fourth; George P. Grant (laborer, 32, Lyme) and Ethel M. Pushee (26, Lyme)
Clyde Forest, b. 2/26/1918 in Lyme; second; Fred W. Grant

(farming, 37, Lyme) and Viola E. Ware (39, Thetford, VT)
Elizabeth Viola, b. 3/31/1939 in Hanover; second; Alanson W. Grant (trucking, 28, Lyme) and Evelyn V. Marsh (23, Orford)
George Wayne, b. 8/23/1912 in Lyme; second; George P. Grant (laborer, 26, Lyme) and Ethel Pushee (21, Lyme)
Muriel J., b. 9/14/1936 in Lyme; first; Alanson W. Grant (laborer, 25, Lyme) and Evelyn V. Marsh (21, Orford)
Robert Palmer, b. 4/12/1915; third; George P. Grant (laborer, 29, Lyme) and Ethel M. Pushee (24, Lyme)

GRAY,
daughter, b. 7/29/1893 in Lyme; second; Wilbur Gray (section man, 26, Sheffield, VT) and ----- (26, Barre, VT); residence - Barton, VT
daughter, b. 8/29/1895 in Lyme; seventh; Orren Gray (laborer, 25, Sheffield, VT) and Effie E. Lazott (21, Nashua)
son, b. 7/31/1910 in Lyme; second; Jesse Gray (laborer, 23, Sheffield, VT) and Emily C. Perron (30, Belfast, ME)
son, b. 9/14/1911 in Lyme; fourth; Jesse G. Gray (laborer, 25, Strafford, VT) and Emily L. Perron (31, Belfast, ME)
stillborn child, b. 4/30/1913 in Lyme; Jessie G. Gray (laborer, 27, Sheffield, VT) and Emily C. Farrell (33, Belfast, ME)
daughter, b. 3/29/1934 in Lyme; sixth; Harry N. Gray (laborer, 41, Plymouth, ME) and Hazel E. Staples (39, Athens, ME)
son, b. 7/13/1968 in Lebanon; Richard Gray and Norine A. Dyke
Aurilla, b. 6/7/1909 in Lyme; first; Jesse Gilbert Gray (laborer, 22, Sheffield, VT) and Emily Gorima Ferrall (29, Belfast, ME)
Beatrice Hazel, b. 11/14/1931 in Lyme; fourth; Harry M. Gray (laborer, 39, Plymouth, ME) and Hazel Staples (33, Athens, ME)
Benjamin Troy, b. 8/24/1971 in Hanover; Richard C. Gray and Norine A. Dyke
Beth-Anne Jenks, b. 10/9/1976 in Haverhill; Edmund George Gray and Linda Marie Jenks
Beverly Ann, b. 8/18/1938 in Lyme; seventh; Harley H. Gray (foreman, 42, Lyme) and Hattie M. Pike (35, Lyme)
Bruce Elton, b. 6/2/1971 in Haverhill; Bruce R. Gray and Linda P. Brown
Bruce Richard, b. 8/10/1952 in Lebanon; third; Harley Gray, Jr. (laborer, 20, Lyme) and Joyce Greer (19, Bradford, VT); res. – Lyme Ctr.

Dale Edward, b. 8/12/1950 in Lebanon; third; Richard Gray (fireman,
    28, Lyme) and Olive Thompson (32, Lyme)
Deborah Elaine, b. 2/15/1973 in Haverhill; William A. Gray and
    Beverly E. Fisher
Donna Lee, b. 4/18/1964 in Hanover; Harley Gray, Jr. (laborer,
    Lyme) and Alice E. Greer (31, Bradford, VT)
Dorothy Jean, b. 7/7/1954 in Lebanon; fifth; Richard H. Gray
    (fireman, 32, Lyme) and Olive Thompson (36, Lyme)
Edmund George, b. 6/10/1973 in Haverhill; Edmund G. Gray and
    Linda M. Jenks
Frances Edna, b. 1/14/1929 in Lyme; ninth; Herbert L. Gray (laborer,
    40, Plymouth, ME) and Edna Cornforth (37, Unity, ME)
George Edward, b. 7/6/1922 in Lyme; second; Jesse G. Gray
    (farmer, 36, Sheffield, VT) and Florence Larvey (19, Craftsbury,
    VT)
Gile Russell, b. 3/20/1928 in Lyme; fifth; Harley Gray (farmer, 32,
    Lyme) and Hattie M. Pike (26, Lyme)
Gregory Charles, b. 6/6/1968 in Lebanon; Wallace R. Gray and
    Anna L. Longley
Harley, Jr., b. 3/6/1932 in Lyme; sixth; Harley Gray (laborer, 36,
    Lyme) and Hattie May Pike (30, Lyme)
Harley Estes, b. 9/10/1974 in Lebanon; Samuel Allen Gray and
    Pauline M. Estes
Harlie, b. 3/12/1896 in Lyme; first; A. J. C. Gray (laborer, 30,
    Sheffield, VT) and Etta Muzzey (26, Bradford, VT)
Kevin Edward, b. 7/28/1975 in Lebanon; Dale Edward Gray and
    Barbara Ann Dyke
Kimberly Lucille, b. 12/19/1966 in Lebanon; first; Samuel A. Gray
    (carpenter, Lyme) and Pauline M. Estes (Hanover)
Lawrence Harley, Jr., b. 8/23/1946 in Hanover; second; Lawrence H.
    Gray (logger, 26, Haverhill) and Jenny A. Stelmach (26, N.
    Tonawanda, NY)
Leonard Richard, b. 9/11/1970 in Lebanon; Samuel A. Gray and
    Pauline M. Estes
Mark Hildreth, b. 6/2/1969 in Hanover; David H. M. Gray and Sally J.
    Skillman
Ray John Aaron, b. 7/23/1891; second; Andrew J. C. Gray (laborer,
    26, Sheffield, VT) and Lovina Buchanan (26, St. Giles, Canada)
Richard Charles, b. 5/8/1948 in Lebanon; second; Richard H. Gray
    (logger, 26, Lyme) and Olive A. Thompson (29, Lyme)
Richard Horace, b. 7/8/1922 in Lyme; Harley Gray (farmer, 25,

Lyme) and Hattie M. Pike (20, Lyme)
Ruth, b. 2/15/1930 in Hanover; third; Harry Gray (mill worker, 37, Plymouth, ME) and Hazel Staples (31, Athens, ME)
Samuel Allen, b. 10/7/1941 in Lyme; first; Richard H. Gray (laborer, 19, Lyme) and Olive Thompson (23, Lyme)
Scott Matthew, b. 10/27/1971 in Haverhill; William Gray and Beverly Fisher
Shirley Louise, b. 6/30/1951 in Lebanon; second; Harley Gray, Jr. (laborer, 19, Lyme) and Joyce Greer (18, Bradford, VT)
Stephanie Christine, b. 1/11/1992 in Lebanon; Todd Gray and Brenda Glesing
Terry Raymond, b. 4/10/1964 in Lebanon; Wallace R. Gray (maintenance man, S. Ryegate, VT) and Anna L. Longley (26, Pomfret, VT)
Timothy John, b. 6/4/1952 in Lebanon; fourth; Richard Gray (fireman, 30, Lyme) and Olive Thompson (34, Lyme)
Todd Christopher, b. 4/1/1970 in Haverhill; William A. Gray and Beverly Kaye Fisher
Toni Lee, b. 7/22/1971 in Haverhill; Dale Gray and Barbara A. Dyke
William Arthur, b. 8/30/1950 in Lebanon; first; Harley Gray, Jr. (laborer, 18, Lyme) and Joyce Greer (18, Bradford, VT)

GREATOREX,
Travis Regan, b. 8/16/1974 in Hanover; Alan R. Greatorex and Sharon Doreen Balch

GREELEY,
Mariya Helene, b. 7/31/1993 in Lebanon; Harold Greeley and Nancy Humiston
Patrick Harold, b. 7/9/1990 in Hanover; Harold P. Greeley and Nancy Humiston

GREEN,
Kathryn Lee, b. 12/27/1958 in Lebanon; William E. Green III (laborer, 21, Orford) and Donna Lee Morris (23, Massillon, OH)
Leona A., b. 4/22/1904 in Lyme; first; Henry G. Green (laborer, 21, Lyme) and Emma F. Piper (21, Hanover)
William Edgar, IV, b. 11/18/1959 in Lebanon; William E. Green III (laborer, 22, Orford) and Donna L. Morris (24, Massillon, OH)

GREENWOOD,
Corliss Clement, b. 3/29/1926 in Lyme; first; Corliss C. Greenwood (laborer, 25, Troy, VT) and Edith R. Morrisette (19, Hanover)
Josephene May, b. 8/26/1930 in Lyme; first; Olive L. Greenwood (17, Thetford, VT)

GREER,
Mary Marcella, b. 9/15/1970 in Hanover; Freddie L. Greer and Judy M. Vandevender

GREGORY,
Dorothy Mildred, b. 6/19/1915; second; Frank P. Gregory (farmer, 31, Grantham) and Sadie M. Porter (29, S. Ham, PQ)
Edith, b. 9/1/1921 in Hanover; fourth; Frank T. Gregory (farmer, 37, Grantham) and Sadie M. Porter (36, S. Ham, PQ)
Lillian Barbara, b. 6/7/1911 in Lyme; first; Frank T. Gregory (farmer, 26, Grantham) and Sadie M. Porter (25, Canada)
Mildred, b. 4/23/1925 in Hanover; fifth; Frank T. Gregory (farmer, 40, Grantham) and Sadie M. Porter (39, S. Ham, PQ)
Vivian May, b. 8/24/1918 in Lyme; third; F. T. Gregory (farming, 34, Grantham) and Sadie M. Porter (33, S. Ham, PQ)

GRIFFITHS,
Catherine Clark, b. 3/5/1968 in Hanover; James W. Griffiths and Martha W. Steele

GUENETTE,
Joseph P., b. 2/20/1939 in Hanover; second; Joseph H. Guenette (truck driver, 27, Jay, VT) and Mary D. Robillard (20, S. Troy, VT)

GUITAR,
stillborn child, b. 3/28/1925 in Lyme; first; Harry E. Guitar (26, Fredericktown, ME) and Margaret Gray (25, Bradford, VT)
son, b. 1/22/1955 in Hanover; second; Phineas Guitar (mechanic, Lyme) and Kiyoko I. Shigaki (Yokohama, Japan)
Gale Brenda, b. 12/15/1952 in Hanover; first; Phineas Guitar (garage worker, 26, NH) and Kiyoko ------ (18, Japan); res. – Lyme Ctr.
Linda Sue, b. 10/15/1956 in Hanover; Daniel M. Guitar (mechanic, 26, Thetford, VT) and Phyllis G. Hayden (24, Missoula, MT)

Phineas Jackson, b. 5/12/1926 in Lyme; third; Harry E. Guitar (laborer, 26, Morrisville, NB) and Marguerite Gray (26, Bradford, VT)
Wilford Orrin, b. 9/17/1931 in Lyme; fifth; Harry E. Guitar (laborer, 32, Fredericton, NB) and Marguerite Gray (31, Bradford, VT); residence - N. Thetford, VT

HADLEY,
Jeffrey Morgan, b. 8/28/1960 in Hanover; David Hadley, Jr. (US Navy, 19, Concord) and Myrna E. Record (23, Hanover)

HAESSLER,
Alexandra, b. 9/29/1971 in Hanover; Walter Haessler and Barbara Overton
Lara Caroline, b. 10/24/1973 in Hanover; W. Theodore Haessler and Barbara A. Overton

HALL,
son, b. 1/12/1903 in Lyme; second; Fred Parker Hall (farmer, 36) and Mary L. Chandler (31, Orford)
stillborn son, b. 12/18/1914; Ora P. Hall (farmer, 33, Orford) and Minnie Clark (28, Worcester, MA)
Charles Warren, b. 8/23/1928 in Lyme; fifth; Ora P. Hall (farmer, 47, Orford) and Minnie Clark (42, Worcester, MA)
Gordin Leon, b. 7/4/1922 in Lyme; first; Everett A. S. Hall (laborer, 29, Lancaster) and Pearl A. Wing (22, Orford)
Ray Everett, b. 5/19/1929 in Lyme; fourth; Everett A. L. Hall (laborer, 36, Lancaster) and Pearl A. Wing (29, Orford)
Richard Lane, b. 9/20/1924 in Lyme; second; Everett A. L. Hall (laborer, 31, Lancaster) and Pearl A. Wing (24, Orford)
Roger Courtney, b. 4/22/1932 in Lyme; first; Everett A. L. Hall (laborer, 39, Lancaster) and Pearl A. Wing (32, Orford)

HAMBLETON,
Kathleen Lorraine, b. 7/20/1975 in Hanover; James Thomas Hambleton and Mary Ann Movelle

HAMMOND,
Seth Willard, b. 12/4/1918 in Lyme; third; W. F. Hammond (farming, 46, Winchester) and Maude E. Cotton (41, Sullivan)

HAMPSON,
Stanley H., b. 3/4/1939 in Lyme; second; Floyd A. Hampson (painter, 36, Hanover) and Rachel M. Bassett (33, Lebanon)

HANCHETT,
son, b. 7/26/1903 in Lyme; second; Ivan D. Hanchett (farmer, 31, Plainfield) and Florence P. Clark (24, Orange)
Delia Sophronia, b. 8/31/1887 in Lyme; Dennis Hanchett (farmer, Hartland, VT) and Elizabeth C. Read (Plainfield)
Errold Frederick, b. 4/10/1917; third; Fred B. Hanchett (farming, 28, Lyme) and Bernice L. Homan (24, Lebanon)
Helen Luella, b. 2/28/1891 in Lyme; Dennis A. Hanchett and Lizzie C. Reed (1955)
Marion Elizabeth, b. 6/17/1912 in Lyme; first; Fred B. Hanchett (farmer, 24, Lyme) and Bernice I. Homan (19, Lebanon)
Pearl Lillian, b. 10/4/1914; second; Fred B. Hanchet (farmer, 25, Lyme) and Bernice L. Homan (21, Lebanon)
Ronald Ward, b. 1/28/1941 in Lyme; fourth; Ralph J. Hanchett (farmer, 39, Hanover) and Ethel Ward (29, Strafford, VT); residence – Strafford, VT

HANNETT,
Gordon Earl, Jr., b. 1/15/1966 in Lebanon; first; Gordon E. Hannett (unemployed, Plymouth) and Evelyn V. Macomber (White Plains, NY)
Mark Robert, b. 4/24/1968 in Hanover; Gordon E. Hannett and Evelyn Macomber

HARDY,
son, b. 9/5/1901; first; Charles H. Hardy (farmer, 36, Clarksville) and Angie L. Turner (36, Portsmouth)
daughter, b. 7/2/1914; second; Solon B. Hardy (laborer, 24, Enfield) and Eliza A. Johnson (26, St. Sebastian, PQ); residence - Enfield
Herbert Westley, b. 11/4/1915; third; Solon B. Hardy (laborer, Enfield) and Eliza A. Johnson (Canada)

HARRIMAN,
Anna Louise, b. 2/21/1925 in Lyme; first; William Harriman (laborer, 21, N. Haverhill) and Elizabeth Pike (19, Lyme); residence - N. Haverhill

William Bert, b. 12/24/1932 in Lyme; second; William B. Harriman (laborer, 27, Haverhill) and Elizabeth A. Pike (25, Lyme)

HARRIS,
Preston Randall, b. 12/26/1988 in Hanover; John L. Harris and Charlene R. Maxey

HART,
Barbara Ann, b. 4/9/1946 in Hanover; fifth; Lawrence F. Hart (laborer, 34, Canaan) and Esther M. Young (28, Lyme)
Franklin C., b. 3/19/1888; first; Lyman Hart (laborer, 67, Chelsea, VT) and Minnie J. Columbia (24, Chelsea, VT)
James William, b. 4/24/1947 in Hanover; sixth; Lawrence F. Hart (laborer, 35, Canaan) and Esther M. Young (29, Lyme)
Larry Douglas, b. 1/24/1951 in Hanover; seventh; Lawrence F. Hart (laborer, 38, Canaan) and Esther M. Young (33, Lyme)
Nancy Lee, b. 1/6/1940 in Hanover; second; Lawrence F. Hart (laborer, 27, Canaan) and Esther M. Young (21, Lyme)
Robert Lawrence, b. 5/15/1938 in Hanover; first; Lawrence F. Hart (laborer, 26, Canaan) and Esther M. Young (20, Lyme)

HARVEY,
Lillian Xenia, b. 8/6/1994 in Lebanon; Jonathan Harvey and Victoria Kahan

HASPERG,
Keith Stuart, b. 11/5/1982 in Hanover; Keith S. Hasperg and Sharon A. Patterson

HASTINGS,
stillborn son, b. 2/19/1944 in Lyme; sixth; Elwin C. Hastings (farmer, 29, Corinth, VT) and Viola M. Tyler (31, E. Barnet, VT); residence – Corinth, VT

HAWKINS,
Velma S., b. 10/3/1895 in Lyme; second; Max Hawkins (clerk, 23, Bath) and Alice V. Mousley (21, Orford)

HAWTHORNE,
Devin Marie, b. 9/21/1994 in Lebanon; Jarrett Hawthorne and Connie Smith

HAZEN,
stillborn son, b. 4/21/1892; first; Ada Hazen (housekeeper, 17, N. Era, VT)
daughter, b. 4/14/1902; first; Robert D. Hazen (pattern maker, 22, Manchester) and Mary A. Bailey (20, Lyme); residence - Manchester

HEFLIN,
daughter, b. 8/31/1890; sixth; Carlos Heflin (miller, 35, Johnson, VT) and Jennie Johnson (Franklin)

HEITZMAN,
Peili Rollins, b. 12/3/2002 in Liuzhou, China; Tom Heitzman and Andrea Heitzman

HENDERSON,
Joseph Vanwirt III, b. 7/3/1989 in Hanover; Joseph V. Henderson, Jr. and Anna Stein

HENRIQUES,
Alois Moore, b. 8/31/1994 in Lebanon; Horace Henriques and Kathleen Rosenauer
Horace Fuller, IV, b. 10/2/1992 in Lebanon; Horace Henriques III and Kathleen Rosenauer

HENRY,
daughter, b. 7/16/1902; second; Ora M. Henry (laborer, 21, E. Thetford, VT) and Bessie M. Mayo (23, Lyme)
daughter, b. 4/19/1908 in Lyme; fifth; Ora M. Henry (laborer, 26, Thetford, VT) and Bessie M. Mayo (28, Cabot, VT)
Mark L., b. 1/10/1906 in Lyme; fourth; Ora M. Henry (laborer, 24, Thetford, VT) and Bessie M. Mayo (26, Lyme)
Ray L., b. 8/30/1903 in Lyme; third; Ora M. Henry (laborer, 21, Thetford, VT) and Bessie M. Mayo (23, Lyme)

HETHERINGTON,
son, b. 6/11/1898; first; James Hetherington (dyer, Glasgow, Scotland) and Sarah J. Muzzy (32, Piermont)

HEWES,
daughter, b. 8/6/1887; fourth; Michael J. Hewes (farmer, 55, Lyme)

and Fannie Hewes (36, New York City)
daughter, b. 9/10/1900; first; Fred C. Hewes (farmer, 24, Lyme) and
   Lena M. Chesley (20, W. Fairlee, VT)
daughter, b. 9/11/1902; second; Fred C. Hewes (farmer, 26, Lyme)
   and Lena Chesley (22, W. Fairlee, VT)
Daniel Charles, b. 3/24/1957 in Hanover; Charles A. Hewes (farmer,
   Etna) and Louise A. Cutting (Hancock, MA)
Ethel Marion, b. 12/11/1902; first; Frank S. Hewes (farmer, 31,
   Lyme) and Addie M. Elliott (25, Lyme)
Grace Theda, b. 9/16/1912 in Lyme; second; Fred C. Hewes
   (farmer, 36, Lyme) and Ethel G. Spencer (29, Hanover)
Hattie Lucille, b. 3/31/1887; first; Frederick L. Hewes (bookkeeper,
   25, Lyme) and Hattie A. Hewes (26, Hanover); residence -
   Springfield, MA
Jo Elizabeth, b. 8/12/1968 in Hanover; Charles A. Hewes and Louise
   A. Cutting
Julie Elnora, b. 4/13/1902; third; Herbert G. Hewes (laborer, 31,
   Delhi, NY) and Alice L. Wilkie (32, Bramington, NY)
Keri Ann, b. 7/13/1981 in Hanover; Stephen C. Hewes and Rose M.
   Clark
Lena May, b. 11/29/1909 in Lyme; first; Fred Chester Hewes
   (farmer, 33, Lyme) and Ethel Grace Spencer (26, Hanover)
Michael Willard, b. 3/26/1960 in Hanover; Charles A. Hewes (farmer,
   39, Etna) and Louise A. Cutting (31, Hancock, MA)
Nancy Minette, b. 3/12/1947 in Hanover; first; Gerald F. Hewes
   (farmer, 25, Hanover) and Margaret A. Pierce (25, Hanover)
Peggy Anne, b. 1/20/1953 in Hanover; Charles A. Hewes (farmer,
   32, Hanover) and Louise A. Cutting (23, Hancock, MA)
Ralph Wright, b. 10/17/1905 in Lyme; second; Frank S. Hewes
   (farmer, 34, Lyme) and Addie M. Elliott (27, Lyme)
Roy Francis, b. 2/7/1948 in Hanover; second; Gerald F. Hewes
   (farming, 26, Hanover) and Margaret A. Pierce (26, Hanover)
Stacey Ann, b. 1/6/1986 in Lebanon; Mark K. Hewes and Dorothea
   Kingsbury
Stephen Corbett, b. 3/9/1954 in Hanover; second; Charles A. Hewes
   (farmer, 34, Hanover) and Louise A. Cutting (25, Hancock, MA)

HEWITT,
Courtney Powers, b. 8/10/1975 in Hanover; David C. Hewitt and
   Katharine Powers Lamb
Julie Chandler, b. 12/1/1988 in Hanover; Alan D. Hewitt and Susan

C. Nickerson
Meghan Lakin, b. 4/23/1984 in Hanover; Alan D. Hewitt and Susan C. Nickerson

HIBBARD,
Verna Maude, b. 9/20/1914 in Lyme; Clarence George Hibbard and Maude McCloskey (1974)

HIBLER,
Elizabeth Louise, b. 10/22/1973 in Hanover; William D. Hibler, III and Betty M. Behrendes
William David, b. 7/20/1975 in Hanover; William David Hibler, III and Betty M. Behrendes

HIGGINS,
Clayton Arthur, b. 11/17/1929 in Lyme; third; Clayton A. Higgins (laborer, 26, Thetford, VT) and Arlene M. Crane (27, Springfield, MA)

HIKORY,
Emmet Lyman, b. 5/10/1974 in Lyme; John Hikory and Julia M. Ingersoll

HILL,
Aurora Borealis, b. 3/11/1985 in Lyme Ctr.; Douglas P. Hilll and Ingrid L. Curtis
Brenda, b. 3/17/1949 in Hanover; Loyd D. Hill and Nadine George
Joshua Alan, b. 4/21/1981 in Lebanon; Alan H. Hill and Roberta K. Pike
Richard Harvey, b. 6/22/1946 in Hanover; fourth; Maurice H. Hill (yard boss, 32, Bristol) and Goldie M. Jones (27, Etna)
Tressa D., b. 6/13/1894 in Lyme; eighth; Enock Hill (farmer, 40, Chateaugay, NY) and Mina M. Young (33, Clarenceville, Canada)

HINSLEY,
Aidan Lewis Meagher, b. 7/25/1998 in Lebanon; Michael C. Hinsley and Barbara A. O'Mara
Connor Andrew, b. 12/11/1994 in Lebanon; Michael Hinsley and Barbara Anne O'Mara
Liam David, b. 6/6/1996 in Lebanon; Michael Hinsley and Barbara

O'Mara

HOBART,
daughter, b. 10/11/1889; first; Albert Hobart (farmer, Hebron) and Nellie H. Phelps (Lowell, MA)
Jennie Maud, b. 10/19/1891; second; Albert Hobart (farmer, 46, Hebron) and Nellie H. Phelps (34, Lowell, MA)

HOBBS,
Carlos O., b. 11/3/1894 in Lyme; fourth; Carlos Hobbs (farmer, 47, Wentworth) and Mary A. Ellsworth (33, Wentworth)
Diane, b. 1/17/1947 in Hanover; first; George B. Hobbs (trucking, 24, Lyme) and Marion V. Pushee (20, Lyme)
George Barnes, b. 9/11/1922 in Lyme; second; Hervey H. Hobbs (laborer, 42, Wentworth) and Jessie Waterman (35, Thetford, VT)
Jarene, b. 8/2/1955 in Hanover; third; George Hobbs (salesman, Lyme) and Marion Pushee (Lyme)
Morris Earle, b. 4/19/1910 in Lyme; first; Hervey Herbert Hobbs (30, Lyme) and Jesse D. Waterman (23, Thetford, VT)
Verne Algia, b. 8/5/1897 in Lyme; fifth; Carlos Hobbs (farmer, 50, Wentworth) and Mary Ann Ellsworth (36, Wentworth)

HOFFMAN,
Esther Elizabeth, b. 5/2/2004 in Lebanon; Michael Hoffman and Camarie Hoffman

HOLLIS,
James Eugene, Jr., b. 2/18/1938 in Lyme; second; James E. Hollis (laborer, 26, Roxbury, MA) and Edith MacLeod (18, Scotstown, PQ)

HOLMES,
Karen Williams, b. 1/15/1969 in Hanover; Richard T. Holmes and Deborah C. Williams
Richard John, b. 9/25/1925 in Hanover; second; John S. Holmes (laborer, 29, Lynn, MA) and Estabelle Braley (26, Washington)

HOOD,
stillborn son, b. 7/25/1927 in Lyme; third; Nelson Hood (laborer, 24, Newbury, VT) and Ida M. Philbrick (34, Springfield)

Nelson Robert, b. 4/16/1929 in Lyme; fourth; Nelson Hood (laborer, 26, Newbury, VT) and Ida Philbrick (36, Springfield)

HORTON,
son, b. 7/5/1907 in Lyme; sixth; Charles H. Horton (farmer, 48, Enfield) and Fannie B. Kempton (Everett, MO)
daughter, b. 4/21/1909 in Lyme; sixth; Charles Herbert Horton (farmer, 52, Enfield) and Frances Belle Kempton (31, Everett, MO)
Audrey Lane, b. 3/27/1997 in Lebanon; Sammy Joe Horton and LaDonna Ranee Porter
Charles Ira, b. 12/3/1913 in Lyme; sixth; Charles H. Horton (farmer, 55, Enfield) and Frances B. Kempton (Everitt, MO)
George Edward, b. 5/2/1915; seventh; Charles H. Horton (farmer, 55, Enfield) and Frances Kempton (37, Everett, MO)
Zelma Beatrice, b. 7/12/1916; eighth; C. H. Horton (farming, 56, Enfield) and Frances B. Kempton (38, Everett, MO)

HOSKING[S],
Bernard Henry, b. 1/13/1911 in Lyme; first; William J. Hoskins (laborer, 22, NS) and Ida Belle Lamott (17, Lyme)
Mildred Lorain, b. 9/15/1914; second; William J. Hosking (laborer, 26, NS) and Ida B. Lamott (22, Lyme)

HOSMER,
Robert D., b. 5/19/1903 in Lyme; third; Josiah D. Hosmer (laborer, 24, Groton, VT) and Clymene H. Braley (23, Rumney)

HOUSE,
daughter, b. 12/12/1899; fourth; Clinton E. House (laborer, 36, Newport, VT) and Lottie D. Gilbert (26, Lyme)
son, b. 12/24/1902; fifth; Clinton E. House (laborer, 39, Newport, VT) and Lottie D. Gilbert (29, Lyme)
Dorothy G., b. 7/1/1904 in Lyme; sixth; Clinton E. House (laborer, 42) and Lottie Gilbert (32, Lyme)
Helen Ruby, b. 12/7/1897 in Lyme; third; Clinton E. House (laborer, 24, Newport, VT) and Lottie D. Gilbert (24, Lyme)
Merle H., b. 3/20/1895 in Lyme; first; Clinton E. House (laborer, 31, Newport, VT) and Lottie D. Gilbert (22, Lyme)

HOWE,
Randy Orin, b. 10/22/1972 in Hanover; Orin C. Howe and Linda J. Chapley

HOWELL,
Caroline Marie, b. 11/12/1995 in Lebanon; Scott Kirk Howell and Alexandra Lucia Levintow

HOYT,
Clara Isa, b. 12/14/1884 in Lyme; Caleb Hoyt and Arvilla Ellsworth (1950)

HUBBARD,
son, b. 4/7/1890; first; Charles A. Hubbard (roll coverer, 27, Brookfield) and Alice M. Goodrich (Hanover); residence - Manchester
Dawn Lisa, b. 3/7/1963 in Hanover; Fred W. Hubbard (Topeka, KS) and Carol S. Waite (23, Hanover)

HUDSON,
Kathaleen June, b. 9/30/1930 in Lyme; first; Albert Hudson (farmer, 21, NB) and Ethel Wheelock (21, E. Fairfield, VT); residence - Thetford, VT

HUMISTON,
son, b. 2/2/1898; fifth; John A. Humiston (farmer, 27, Canada) and Mabel Small (27, Rockburn, PQ)
daughter, b. 1/22/1899; sixth; John A. Humiston (farmer, 28, Canada) and Mabel Small (28, Rockburn, PQ)
Amos Frank, b. 4/28/1929 in Lyme; second; Frank Huminston (farmer, 34, Jaffrey) and Sylvia Wilmot (20, Lyme)
Kenneth John, b. 8/18/1934 in Lyme; third; Frank Humiston (farmer, 39, E. Jaffrey) and Sylvia J. Wilmot (25, Lyme)

HUNTINGTON,
stillborn son, b. 4/27/1924 in Lyme; first; J. H. Huntington (Thetford, VT) and Eva L. Granger (Chateaugay, NY); residence - Thetford, VT

HURD,
daughter, b. 2/4/1908 in Lyme; fourth; Frank P. Hurd (laborer, 35,

Clintonville, WI) and D. Etta Carpenter (25, Pierre, SD)
Deette, b. 2/22/1910 in Lyme; fifth; Frank P. Hurd (laborer, 38, Floyd, MI) and Deette Carpenter (28, Pierre, SD)
Howard Leroy, b. 9/14/1898; third; Charles T. Hurd (mechanic, 26, Wallace, NS) and Lillian J. Ramsey (27, Barton, VT); residence - Worcester, MA
Vance V., b. 4/29/1911 in Lyme; sixth; Frank P. Hurd (laborer, 38, Clintonville, WI) and Deette Carpenter (25, Pierre, SD)

HUTCHINS,
Brenda Lee, b. 3/15/1967 in Lebanon; first; John J. Hutchins, Jr. (laborer, Hanover) and Priscilla M. Haskins (Lebanon)
Donald Lee, b. 7/24/1963 in Hanover; Wilbur B. Hutchins (farmer, Hanover) and Lois A. Cook (27, Hanover)
Gary Lee, b. 5/26/1955 in Hanover; second; Joseph Hutchins (truck driver, Rochester) and Rose T. Roman (Lebanon)
Hazel Ann, b. 5/11/1947 in Hanover; seventh; John J. Hutchins (truck driver, 37, Hanover) and Ruth A. Beard (37, Manchester)
Kerene Lillie, b. 9/12/1966 in Hanover; fourth; Wilbur B. Hutchins (laborer, Hanover) and Lois A. Cook (Hanover)
Laurence, b. 6/10/1899; first; Charles H. Hutchins (laborer, 25, Hanover) and Elsie M. King (20, Lyme)
Mary Ann, b. 10/6/1964 in Hanover; Wilbur B. Hutchins (laborer, Hanover) and Lois A. Cook (28, Hanover)
Rosemarie Ann, b. 12/21/1956 in Hanover; Joseph D. Hutchins (truck driver, 23, Rochester) and Rose T. Roman (22, Lebanon)

HYERLE,
Alexander Goodman, b. 9/21/1993 in Lebanon; David Hyerle and Sara Goodman

INGALLS,
stillborn son, b. 12/5/1921 in Lyme; first; Fred E. Ingalls (laborer, Chester, MA) and Ray Sherwood (40, NJ)

IVES,
Sybil M., b. 8/27/1897 in Lyme; fifth; George G. Ives (farmer, 37, Chateaugay, NY) and Ada S. Young (33, Burke, NY)

JENKINS,
Arlene Rita, b. 11/13/1957 in Hanover; Lincoln W. Jenkins (laborer,

Thetford, VT) and Marjorie Woodward (Hanover)
Darlene Elise, b. 11/13/1957 in Hanover; Lincoln W. Jenkins (laborer, Thetford, VT) and Marjorie Woodward (Hanover)
Holly Ivis, b. 12/25/1954 in Hanover; third; Lincoln W. Jenkins (laborer, 29, Thetford, VT) and Marjorie Woodward (28, Hanover)

JENKS,
son, b. 9/12/1894 in Lyme; first; Will F. Jenks (laborer, 23, Lyme) and Emma D. Smith (15, Lyme)
son, b. 4/30/1907 in Lyme; second; Edward E. Jenks (laborer, 32, Lyme) and May C. Lamott (23, Lyme)
son, b. 5/23/1957 in Hanover; Thomas E. Jenks (bindery, Lyme) and Doris H. Balch (Lyme)
son, b. 5/23/1957 in Hanover; Thomas E. Jenks (bindery, Lyme) and Doris H. Balch (Lyme)
Carol Ann, b. 5/24/1953 in Lyme; Roger C. Jenks (power shovel op., 25, Hanover) and Ruth E. Godfrey (24, Bradford, VT)
Christopher Peter, b. 11/16/1954 in Lebanon; fourth; Edward F. Jenks (truck driver, 24, Hanover) and Edith M. Record (22, Hanover)
David Allen, b. 5/12/1956 in Lebanon; Edward F. Jenks (truck driver, 25, Hanover) and Edith M. Record (23, Hanover)
Deborah Mae, b. 11/28/1958 in Hanover; Thomas E. Jenks (bindery work, 27, Woodsville) and Doris H. Balch (25, Lyme)
Dorothy Edith, b. 12/29/1943 in Hanover; first; Merton A. Jenks (farmer, 32, Belchertown, MA) and Florence E. Wilmot (25, Lyme)
Douglas Edward, b. 10/28/1955 in CO; Thomas E. Jenks (airman, NH) and Doris H. Balch (NH)
Edward Burton, b. 12/27/1917; third; Andrew B. Jenks (laborer, 29, Albany, VT) and Amy M. Guyer (24, Lebanon)
Edward Donald, b. 12/10/1950 in Lebanon; first; Edward Jenks (laborer, 20, Hanover) and Edith Record (18, Hanover)
Edward Lee, b. 3/14/1952 in Lebanon; second; Edward Jenks (laborer, 21, Hanover) and Edith Record (19, Hanover)
Edwin El'ridge, b. 2/26/1909 in Lyme; third; Edward Elias Jenks (laborer, 37, Lyme) and May C. LaMott (24, Lyme) (see following entry)
Edwin Elbridge, b. 2/26/1909 in Lyme; Edward E. Jenks (laborer, Lyme) and May C. LaMott (Lyme) (1966) (see preceding entry)

Esther May, b. 4/26/1917; fourth; Edward E. Jenks (sec. hand, 47, Lyme) and May C. LaMott (34, Lyme)

Gregory Allen, b. 8/5/1954 in Texas; second; Thomas E. Jenks (USAF, 23, NH) and Doris H. Balch (21, NH); residence – Burkburnett, Texas

Holly Janette, b. 5/16/1975 in Hanover; James L. Jenks and Patricia A. Grant

James Lee, b. 1/18/1952 in Lyme; first; Roger Jenks (power shovel op., 23, Hanover) and Ruth Godfrey (23, Bradford, VT)

Jennifer Lynn, b. 4/18/1975 in Lebanon; Douglas Edward Jenks and Sharon Ann Kuehn

Jonathan Chester, b. 2/25/1980 in Hanover; James L. Jenks and Patricia A. Grant

Kathleen, b. 8/22/1961 in Hanover; Edward F. Jenks (road agent, Hanover) and Edith Record (28, Hanover)

Katrina Leigh, b. 1/2/1972 in Lebanon; James L. Jenks and Patricia A. Grant

Megan Amory, b. 10/16/1977 in Hanover; Ronald Jenks and Teresa Pearson

Melanie, b. 12/19/1958 in Hanover; Edward F. Jenks (road agent, 28, Hanover) and Edith M. Record (26, Hanover)

Michael Steven, b. 8/27/1953 in Lebanon; Edward E. Jenks (truck driver, 22, Hanover) and Edith Record (20, Hanover)

Norma Dorothy, b. 3/28/1934 in Hanover; second; Elbridge E. Jenks (laborer, 25, Lyme) and Lillian Gregory (22, Lyme)

Peter Scott, b. 9/25/1961 in Hanover; Roger C. Jenks (heavy equip., Hanover) and Ruth Godfrey (33, Bradford, VT)

Richard Ernest, b. 6/19/1962 in Lebanon; Richard F. Jenks (truck driver, Hanover) and Anne E. Grenon (29, Hanover)

Robert Elbridge, b. 1/7/1945 in Lyme; third; Elbridge E. Jenks (farmer, 35, Lyme) and Lillian B. Gregory (33, Lyme)

Robyn Lynn, b. 4/20/1980 in Hanover; Robert Elbridge Jenks and Annette L. Henry

Roger Chester, b. 2/27/1928 in Hanover; first; Chester Jenks (farmer, 21, Lyme) and Marion Hanchett (16, Lyme)

Samantha Lee, b. 1/31/1976 in Lackland AFB, San Antonio, Texas; Ronald H. Jenks and Theresa W. Pearson

Sherwin Arthur, b. 11/17/1932 in Hanover; second; Leo Jenks (lumberman, 32, Dwight, MA) and Ethel Carrier (23, Bradford, VT)

Steven Roy, b. 3/1/1953 in Hanover; Thomas E. Jenks (USAF, 22,

Woodsville) and Doris H. Balch (19, Lyme)
Susan Edna, b. 10/16/1950 in Hanover; fourth; Elbridge Jenks (farmer, 41, Lyme) and Lillian Gregory (39, Lyme)
Thomas Edward, b. 6/7/1931 in Woodsville; first; Elbridge E. Jenks (laborer, 22, Lyme) and Lillian M. Gregory (20, Lyme)
Veronica Raven, b. 3/15/1980 in Hanover; Ronald H. Jenks and Teresa Pearson

JENKYN,
Amanda Katherine, b. 1/21/1977 in Hanover; Lawrence R. Jenkyn and Geraldine L. McLaughlin

JOHNSON,
stillborn child, b. 1/12/1888; first; Wilson D. Johnson (laborer, 26, Hanover) and Alice S. Woodward (26, Hanover)
daughter, b. 8/6/1889; second; Wilson D. Johnson (laborer, Hanover) and Alice S. Woodward (Hanover)
son, b. 1/5/1891; third; Wilson D. Johnson (laborer, 29, Hanover) and Alice L. Woodward (29, Hanover)
daughter, b. 11/17/1892; fourth; Wilson D. Johnson (farmer, 31, Hanover) and Alice S. Woodward (31, Hanover)
son, b. 12/21/1894 in Lyme; fourth; Wilson D. Johnson (laborer, Hanover) and Alice S. Woodward (Hanover)
daughter, b. 2/2/1905 in Lyme; first; Harry D. Johnson (farmer, 37, Salisbury) and Martha E. Brown (22, Troy, NY); residence - Troy, NY
daughter, b. 1/8/1908 in Lyme; first; Carl Johnson (lumberman, 30, Windsor, VT) and Ethel Hardy (31, Manchester)
Amos Stoumen, b. 10/27/1979 in Lebanon; James Johnson and Cathy Stoumen
Carl Edward, b. 7/17/1910 in Lyme; third; Carl W. Johnson (laborer, 33, W. Windsor, VT) and Ethel R. Parker (34, Manchester)
Ida M., b. 9/11/1901; first; Haynes E. Johnson (farmer, 22, Bradford, VT) and Grace Frost (21, Lyme)
Janice Ellen, b. 12/9/1947 in Hanover; second; John H. Johnson (farming, 55, Malden, MA) and Mildred P. Mahan (31, Chatham, VA)
Joyce Ann, b. 4/19/1944 in Lyme; second; Walter H. Johnson (laborer, 34, Thetford, VT) and Mary E. Johnson (30, Deerfield)
Kimberly Heather, b. 11/9/1971 in Worcester, MA; Philip Johnson and Judith King

Mildred Alida, b. 7/3/1949 in Hanover; John H. Johnson and Mildred Mahan
Nathan Paul, b. 9/19/2000 in Lebanon; Melvin Johnson and Nancy Johnson
Sandra Lee, b. 2/19/1953 in Lebanon; Walter H. Johnson (truck driver, 42, Thetford, VT) and Mary E. Lewis (39, Deerfield)
Sylvia Marie, b. 8/10/1939 in Lyme; first; Walter H. Johnson (laborer, 28, Thetford, VT) and Mary E. Lewis (25, Deerfield)
Zoe Stoumen, b. 5/22/1978 in Lebanon; James A. Johnson and Cathy Stoumen

JONES,
Ella Tyler, b. 10/19/2001 in Lebanon; Perrin Jones and Laura Jones

JUDD,
Anita Ida, b. 8/8/1920 in Lyme; first; Carlos S. Judd (26, Franconia) and Edith M. Mativia (20, Lyme); residence - Bradford, VT

KARON,
Holden Wenger, b. 3/18/2002 in Lebanon; Stuart Karon and Jodi Wenger

KEELER,
Holly, b. 12/17/1965 in Hanover; first; Charles M. Keeler (geologist, Plattsburg, NY) and Elaine S. Evans (Boston, MA)
Kathleen, b. 3/31/1967 in Hanover; second; Charles M. Keeler (geologist, Plattsburg, NY) and Elaine S. Evans (Boston, MA)

KELSEY,
Carter George, b. 11/22/1990 in Hanover; Curt M. Vinson and Alison A. Kelsey
Casey Virginia, b. 12/13/1987 in Hanover; James V. Kelsey and Ann Bracken
Gray Alexandra, b. 8/17/1990 in Hanover; James V. Kelsey and Ann C. Bracken
Preston Jerome, b. 2/23/1993 in Lebanon; James Kelsey and Ann Bracken

KENDRICK,
Willie, b. 2/19/1894 in Lyme; third; William H. Kendrick (farmer, 31, Newbury, VT) and Nellie M. Bowen (25, Piermont)

KENNARD,
  Margaret Utley, b. 12/12/1960 in Hanover; Delano Q. Kennard (store owner, 26, Boston, MA) and Kay Lois Robinson (25, Rhinebeck, NY)
  Richard Munroe, b. 4/3/1962 in Hanover; Delano Q. Kennard (store owner, Boston, MA) and Kay L. Robinson (26, Rhinebeck, NY)

KENNEY,
  Crete Mabel, b. 3/25/1887; first; Charles H. Kenney (clerk, 24, Hanover) and Alice M. Kenney (21, Lyme)

KENNISTON,
  Jesse Irvin, b. 6/13/1926 in Lyme; third; Jesse O. Kenniston (laborer, 41, Gilead, ME) and Nellie R. Hood (26, Newbury, VT)

KENT,
  Hazel, b. 10/17/1986 in Hanover; Thomas W. Kent and Janet W. Reed

KERN,
  Benjamin David, b. 1/30/1992 in Lebanon; David Kern and Mary Weidler

KIMBALL,
  daughter, b. 11/16/1890; fourth; Wyman Kimball (laborer, 33, Potsdam, NY) and Nora King (26, Granville, VT)
  son, b. 3/31/1892; fifth; Wyman W. Kimball (laborer, 35, Potsdam, NY) and Mary M. King (27, Granville, VT)
  child, b. 12/24/1893 in Lyme; sixth; Wyman W. Kimball (laborer, 47, NY) and Nora King (29, Granville, VT)
  Grace, d. 2/22/1896 in Lyme; seventh; Wyman W. Kimball (laborer, 40, Potsdam, NY) and Nora King (32, Granville, VT)

KING,
  son, b. 5/20/1887; third; Frank King (farmer, 32, Lyme) and Bessie King (23, Lyme)
  daughter, b. 10/17/1887; second; John King (farmer, 35, Ephiah, NS) and Matilda King (31, PQ)
  daughter, b. 10/6/1889; fourth; Frank King (farmer, Lyme) and Betsey King (Lyme)
  daughter, b. 1/28/1890; third; Walter H. King (farmer, 40, Groton)

and Ida L. Norris (Dorchester)
Andrea Lynn, b. 11/8/1972 in Lebanon; Lloyd F. King and Erma E. Kingsbury
Coleen Beth, b. 8/26/1953 in Lebanon; Frederick King (carpenter, 31, Barton, VT) and Catherine Doyle (33, Strafford, VT)
Daniel William, b. 3/1/1956 in Enfield; Charles H. King (laborer, 26, Newport) and Florence L. Howland (24, Enfield)
Garnet Winona, b. 9/21/1920 in Lyme; first; John A. King (farmer, 39, Dorchester) and Clara A. Chesley (29, W. Fairlee, VT)
Ida N., b. 3/13/1895 in Lyme; fourth; Walter E. King (farmer, 45, Groton) and Ida L. Norris (36, Dorchester)
Lucy M., b. 8/24/1896 in Lyme; third; John King (farmer, 43, Euphrates, NY) and Matilda Suitor (40, Broughton, PQ)
Sandra Gail, b. 12/24/1951 in Hanover; fourth; Frederick W. King (carpenter, 30, Barton, VT) and Catherine M. Doyle (32, Strafford, VT)
Stephen Dawson, b. 12/24/1951 in Hanover; fifth; Frederick W. King (carpenter, 30, Barton, VT) and Catherine M. Doyle (32, Strafford, VT)
Steven Anthony, b. 8/26/1959 in Hanover; Charles H. King, Jr. (truck driver, 29, Newport) and Florence L. Howland (27, Enfield)
Susan Doris, b. 1/9/1955 in Lebanon; seventh; Frederic W. King (carpenter, Barton, VT) and Catherine Doyle (Strafford, VT)
Theresa Marie, b. 6/13/1973 in Hanover; Bruce H. King and Sylvia M. Stearns

KINLAW,
William Brissenden, b. 5/10/1980 in Hanover; William B. Kinlaw and Sarah H. Brissenden

KINNEY,
Charles Melvin, b. 1/18/1917; second; Ralph H. Kinney (farming, 26, Cornish) and Emma B. St. Mary (28, Easton, NY)

KNAPP,
Anna Marie, b. 10/11/1985 in Hanover; David Knapp and Marcia Anderson
Sarah Jean, b. 3/25/1967 in Lyme; first; Anthony W. Knapp (instructor, Morristown, NJ) and Susan E. Hayward (New London)

KNIGHT,
Anne, b. 9/9/1925 in Lyme; first; Frank Knight (farmer, 26, Hastings, FL) and Jennie M. Temple (18, Lyme); residence - Hastings, FL

KNIGHTS,
Kristian Peter, b. 3/5/1981 in Hanover; Calvin R. Knights and Ellen K. Engelstad

KOCH,
Sarah Page, b. 3/23/1983 in Hanover; Michael O. Koch and Hannah B. Page

KOLTYS,
Drew Marek, b. 2/11/1987 in Hanover; Henry Koltys and Laurel Fisher

KONINGS-SHEFFIELD,
Eleanor, b. 12/8/2004 in Lebanon; Elke Konings-Sheffield and Rhonda Konings-Sheffield

KOTZ,
Andrew Quante, b. 6/2/2001 in Lebanon; David Kotz and Pamela Jenkins
Margaret Katherine, b. 2/6/1999 in Lebanon; David Kotz and Pamela Jenkins

KOVATSH,
Henry R., b. 11/23/1907 in Lyme; first; Henry Kovatsh (farmer, 38, Hungary) and Rosa Fresli (24, Hungary)

KRCMARIK,
John Paul, Jr., b. 1/29/1997 in Lebanon; John Paul Krcmarik and Kellie Marie Luke

KRESS,
Clay Emerson, b. 7/22/2003 in Lebanon; Brian Kress and Nancy Kress

LABBIE,
Todd Timothy, b. 10/10/1975 in Hanover; Timothy Gerard Labbie and Rosemarie A. Hutchins

LABOMBARD,
Adrienne Marie, b. 12/14/1982 in Hanover; Anthony G. LaBombard
 and Florence C. Mullan
Donna Carol, b. 1/29/1953 in Hanover; Willis LaBombard, Jr.
 (student, 19, Lebanon) and Ruth C. Braman (16, Marlboro, MA)

LACOUR,
David Paul, b. 3/3/1998 in Lebanon; Charles Hilliard LaCour and
 Lynda J. Kosubinsky
Russell Charles, b. 6/14/1996 in Lebanon; Charles LaCour and
 Lynda Kosubinsky

LADD,
Sarah Elizabeth, b. 9/3/2003 in Lebanon; Robert Ladd and Rebecca
 Ladd

LADEAU,
Hilda Mae, b. 3/14/1918 in Lyme; third; Levi J. Ladeau (farming, 40,
 Hyde Park, VT) and Dora C. Smith (32, Orford)

LAHR-PASTOR,
Katerina, b. 3/15/1995 in Lebanon; Charles Dwight Lahr and Beatriz
 Pastor

LAMONTAGNE,
Gloria Jean, b. 1/13/1963 in Haverhill; Gilbert LaMontagne
 (Concord, VT) and Margaret J. Lamotte (26, Lunenburg, VT)

LAMOTT,
stillborn son, b. 1/30/1898; ninth; David Lamott (laborer, 39, Quebec)
 and Lavina S. Jenks (42, Lyme)
son, b. 6/1/1909 in Lyme; fourth; George J. Lamott (laborer, 32,
 Lyme) and Alice Martha Chaffee (28, Wilton, ME)
Elwin A., b. 7/19/1895 in Lyme; first; Albert M. Lamott (farmer, 23,
 Dorchester) and Bertha L. Cutting (17, Lowell, MA)
Evan Clair, b. 6/26/1912 in Lyme; fifth; George J. Lamott (farmer, 36,
 Lyme) and Georgia B. Russell (31, Wilton, ME)
Frank Henry, b. 12/13/1892; seventh; David LaMott (laborer, 35,
 Canada) and Lavina Jenks (37, Lyme)
Irving Earl, b. 1/28/1897 in Lyme; second; Albert M. Lamott (farmer,
 24, Dorchester) and Bertha L. Cutting (18, Lowell, MA)

Irving Earl, b. 8/1/1926 in Lyme; stillborn; first; Irving E. LaMott (laborer, 29, Lyme) and Hazel F. Young (30, Burke, NY)

Lavina Ellen, b. 11/12/1911 in Lyme; first; Owen B. Lamott (laborer, 23, Lyme) and Nora May Andrews (23, Wolfsboro, NY)

Marjorie L., b. 3/26/1906 in Lyme; second; James I. Lamott (lumberman, 25, Dorchester) and Pearl M. Wing (25, Burke, NY)

Nelson Edward, b. 2/4/1947 in Hanover; second; Dean E. LaMott (highway dept., 27, Orford) and Charlotte H. Balch (25, Lyme Ctr.)

Priscilla Anne, b. 8/28/1942 in Hanover; first; Dean E. LaMott (laborer, 23, Orford) and Charlotte H. Balch (20, Lyme)

Ralph Elrie, b. 7/31/1913 in Lyme; sixth; George J. LaMott (laborer, 36, Lyme) and Georgia B. Russell (32, Wilton, ME)

Verde E., b. 2/23/1906 in Lyme; third; George J. Lamott (laborer, 25, Lyme) and Georgia B. Russell (25, Wilton, ME)

LAMOTTE,
Clara Mae, b. 2/3/1886 in Lyme; David LaMotte and Lavina Jenks (1950)

LAMPHERE,
son, b. 3/1/1947 in Hanover; second; Walter R. Lamphere (farmer, 45, Lyme) and Helen I. Gotler (38, Wolcott, VT)

Allen Eugene, b. 10/23/1928 in Hanover; second; Walter Lamphere (farmer, 26, Lyme) and Helen Cutler (20, Wolcott, VT)

Maud, b. 2/1/1891; first; Charles O. Lamphere (farmer, 29, Lyme) and Nellie S. Quiver (26, Strafford, VT)

Ralph Albert, b. 6/30/1892; second; C. O. Lamphere (farmer, 29, Lyme) and Nellie S. Turner (27, Thetford, VT)

Walter R., b. 1/31/1902; third; Charles O. Lamphere (farmer, 39, Lyme) and Nellie S. Turner (38, Thetford, VT)

LANDERS,
stillborn son, b. 10/10/1891; second; William K. Landers (laborer, 25, Concord) and Georgia Wilson (23, Onondager Hill)

LANGMAID,
son, b. 1/21/1910 in Lyme; twelfth; George Langmaid (teamster, 42, Brockton, MA) and Josie Goodell (34, Worcester, VT)

son, b. 1/21/1910 in Lyme; thirteenth; George Langmaid (teamster,

42, Brockton, MA) and Josie Goodell (34, Worcester, VT) stillborn daughter, b. 6/29/1912 in Lyme; twelfth; George B. Langmaid (laborer, 42, Weymouth, MA) and Josie Goodell (38, Woodstock)

Adeline Mae, b. 4/8/1898 in Lyme; George Langmaid (London, England) and Josephine Goodell (Montpelier, VT)(1954)

Edgar E., b. 4/25/1906 in Lyme; thirteenth; George B. Langmaid (teamster, 38, Brockton, MA) and Josie M. Goodell (32, Worcester, VT)

F. F. [male], b. 6/2/1903 in Lyme; sixth; George B. Langmaid (farmer, 35, Brockton, MA) and Josie M. Goodell (30, Duxbury, VT)

Florence May, b. 1/11/1905 in Lyme; twelfth; George B. Langmaid (farmer, 35, Brockton, MA) and Josie M. Goodell (32, Calais, VT)

Gladys Belle, b. 9/20/1900; fourth; George B. Langmaid (farmer, 34, Weymouth, MA) and Josie May Goodell (28, Waterbury, VT)

Martha A., b. 1/12/1902; fifth; George B. Langmaid (farmer, 33, Brockton, MA) and Josie M. Goodell (28, Waterbury, VT)

LANGWAY,
Jo Anne Katherine, b. 4/28/1964 in Hanover; Chester C. Langway, Jr. (research glaciologist, Worcester, MA) and Rosemary Vovesny (36, Chicago, IL)

Mary Elizabeth, b. 11/1/1961 in Hanover; Chester C. Langway, Jr. (geologist, Worcester, MA) and Rosemary Vovesny (34, Chicago, IL)

Thomas Joseph, b. 4/11/1967 in Hanover; fourth; Chester Langway (geologist, Worcester, MA) and Rosemary H. Vovesny (Chicago, IL)

LARDNER,
Henry Semler, b. 10/23/1996 in Lebanon; Samuel Lardner and Katherine Semler

LARO,
Jessica Lynn Hei Eun, b. 11/24/1987 in Jeisu-do, S. Korea; Arthur E. Laro and Donna L. Pushee

Lisa Marie, b. 10/9/1963 in Hanover; Arthur E. Laro (Lebanon) and Donna L. Pushee (21, Hanover)

LAROCQUE,
David Scott, b. 8/12/1967 in Lebanon; third; Raymond Larocque, Jr. (printer, Woodsville) and Anita LaFlam (N. Troy, VT)
Douglas Raymond, b. 10/13/1970 in Lebanon; Raymond A. Larocque, Jr. and Anita V. LaFlam
Michael Arthur, b. 9/15/1964 in Hanover; Raymond A. Larocque, Jr. (printer, Woodsville) and Anita V. LaFlam (20, N. Troy, VT)
Richard Earl, b. 8/27/1970 in Hanover; Richard A. Larocque and Arlene C. Stone
Tina Louise, b. 4/2/1966 in Lebanon; second; Raymond Larocque (printer, Woodsville) and Anita V. LaFlam (N. Troy, VT)

LAWSON,
Doris Ann, b. 8/19/1949 in Hanover; George M. Lawson and Joanne Brady
George Martin, b. 6/29/1928 in Hanover; second; John W. Lawson (farmer, 33, Barre, VT) and Mary E. Martin (29, Barre, VT)
Michelle Ethel, b. 10/14/1958 in Hanover; George M. Lawson (maintenance, 30, Hanover) and Joanne D. Brady (26, Norwich, VT)
Terry George, b. 1/11/1955 in Hanover; second; George M. Lawson (garage man, Hanover) and Joanne D. Bailey (Norwich, VT)

LAYCOCK,
Eliza Mayor, b. 5/18/1998 in Lebanon; William S. Laycock, III and Kathryn A. Zug

LEA,
Creston Arkin, b. 12/15/1971 in Hanover; Sydney L. Lea, Jr. and Carole Bradford
Erika Anne, b. 4/25/1977 in Hanover; Sydney Lea, Jr. and Carola Bradford

LEATHERS,
Ruth Jeanette, b. 5/31/1891; first; Fred S. Leathers (minister, 28, Brooks, ME) and Jennie Steele (32, Wolfeboro)

LEAVITT,
Louise Violet, b. 2/15/1950 in Hanover; second; George C. Leavitt (dist. mgr., 43, NE) and Violet Dusenbury (41, FL)

LEE,
Jane Shih Mei, b. 11/26/1990 in Hanover; John K. Lee and Celia Y. Chen

LEGGETT,
Ariel Victoria, b. 10/23/1985 in Lebanon; Daniel Leggett and Alison Murray

LEONARD,
Benjamin John, b. 11/11/1978 in Hanover; Thomas M. Leonard and Joann M. Colinski
Jeremiah Ross, b. 5/28/1996 in Lebanon; Thomas Leonard, Jr. and Robin Model
Krista Elizabeth, b. 6/19/1980 in Hanover; Thomas M. Leonard and Joann M. Golinski
Patrick Eric, b. 8/23/1985 in Hanover; Thomas Leonard and Joann Golinski
Raine Lee McCrea, b. 3/10/1999 in Lebanon; Susan Leonard
Thomas Carl, III, b. 2/1/1993 in Lebanon; Thomas Leonard, Jr. and Robin Model
Thomas Patrick, b. 7/15/1982 in Hanover; Thomas M. Leonard and Joann M. Golinski

LERNER,
Ross Matthew, b. 8/30/1979 in Hanover; Elliot Lerner and Maxine Chertok
Seth Alden, b. 10/8/1982 in Hanover; Elliot D. Lerner and Maxine B. Chertok

LESLIE,
Carrie Emma, b. 9/12/1895 in Lyme; first; Charles P. Leslie (laborer, 33, Greenwood, ME) and Emma J. Tyrrell (27, Hebron)

LEVEY,
Mary Iris Thomas, b. 7/20/2004 in Lebanon; Samuel Levey and Christine Thomas

LEWIS,
Jennifer Kumike, b. 1/28/1982 in Hanover; Jonathan N. Lewis and Angela N. Watanabe

LIMLAW,
Robyn Renee, b. 3/3/1969 in Hanover; Gardner L. Limlaw and Velma C. Armstrong
Vicki Lynn, b. 1/12/1955 in Lebanon; fifth; Gardner L. Limlaw (carpenter, Brownington, VT) and Velma C. Armstrong (Newport, VT)

LITTLE,
Chelsea Jean, b. 7/5/1987 in Hanover; Geoffrey O. Little and M. Jean McIntyre

LOCKWOOD,
Vesta May, b. 9/27/1922 in Hanover; first; Charles Lockwood (laborer, 38, Meriden) and Ellen Lamott (36, Lyme)

LOEW,
Jennifer Ann, b. 11/8/1963 in Hanover; Donald E. Loew (med. student, Detroit, MI) and Nancy E. Lonsbury (25, Boston, MA)

LOEWE,
Bianca, b. 8/14/1987 in Hanover; Peter Loewe and Elke Loewe

LORD,
Edwin P., b. 5/0/1935 (sic) in Hanover; second; Edwin C. Lord (farmer, 34, Cohassett, MA) and Helen A. Wionck (26, Waterbury, CT)
Sarah Marie, b. 3/7/1942 in Lyme; sixth; Edwin C. Lord (teamster, 36, W. Hartford, VT) and Olive W. Balch (29, Orford)

LOVEJOY,
daughter, b. 1/4/1891; third; Lewis P. Lovejoy (farmer, 48, Orford) and Hattie Perkins (32, Dorchester)

LUCE,
daughter, b. 7/30/1911 in Lyme; seventh; Leslie Luce (laborer, 42, Tunbridge, VT) and Rosie Hubbard (33, Canada)

LUDWIG,
John David, b. 3/14/1962 in Hanover; Frank A. Ludwig (contractor, Tolland, CT) and Barbara L. Sherry (41, St. Johnsbury, VT)

LUMLEY,
Emma Russell, b. 1/29/1992 in Lebanon; Andrew Lumley and Judith Russell
Jane Patricia, b. 3/31/1998 in Lebanon; Andrew Edward Lumley and Judith Gale Russell

LUND,
Pauline Lois, b. 11/11/1943 in Lyme; first; Paul R. Lund (laborer, 22, Waterford, VT) and Arlene I. Maxfield (16, N. Thetford, VT); residence – Post Mills, VT

LYNCH,
Benjamin Thompson, b. 5/25/1997 in Lebanon; Daniel Thompson Lynch and Barbara Ann Brysh
John Middlebrook, b. 3/20/2001 in Lebanon; Daniel Lynch and Barbara Lynch

LYONS,
Gerald Jonathan Alden, b. 10/9/1971 in Hanover; Dana Lyons and Marilyn Chappell
Jonathan Prescott, b. 8/15/1967 in Hanover; first; Dana H. Lyons (engineer, Newton, MA) and Marilyn J. Chappell (Clarksville)

MACHT,
Alexander Daniel, b. 2/20/1971 in Hanover; Richard M. Macht and Christa Guenther

MACLEAN,
Theodore E., b. 12/28/1904 in Lyme; second; Elwin G. Maclean (farmer, 26, Pictou, NS) and Abbie V. Dimick (27, Lyme)

MADDEN,
Evan Christopher, b. 7/19/1991 in Hanover; Christopher R. Madden and Melissa A. Paton

MALCOLM,
Allison Zoe, b. 5/24/1983 in Hanover; Allen F. Malcolm and Jacqueline A. Doucette
Elissa Fraser, b. 11/7/1976 in Hanover; William Fraser Malcolm, Jr. and Miriam Pearl Bauer
James Foster, b. 5/26/1985 in Hanover; Allen Malcolm and

Jacqueline Doucette
John Fraker, b. 4/24/1980 in Hanover; William F. Malcolm, Jr. and
Miriam Bauer

MANCHESTER,
Sara Ann, b. 5/2/1975 in Hanover; Robert D. Manchester and
Shirley Ann Adams

MANN,
Aiden Myles, b. 6/25/2002 in Lebanon; Richard Mann and Lisa
Cohen
Maxfield Spenser, b. 6/25/2002 in Lebanon; Richard Mann and Lisa
Cohen

MARCOTTE,
Karl Willis, b. 9/13/1919 in Lyme; first; Eugene F. Marcotte (laborer,
19) and Pearl A. Wing (19, Lyme)

MARK,
Lauren Renee, b. 8/8/1982 in Hanover; Leighton P. Mark and Karen
A. Stowe

MARKS,
Emma Claire, b. 3/9/2002 in Lebanon; Jeffrey Marks and Karen
Marks

MARSH,
Lisa Marie, b. 2/16/1969 in Lebanon; Henry Marsh, Jr. and Wanita
G. Balch

MARSHALL,
daughter, b. 7/5/1887; Dudley Marshall (farmer, 27, Canaan) and
Frances A. Marshall (22, Lyme)
son, b. 9/9/1889; first; Bry Marshall (blacksmith, Auburn) and Hattie
J. Balch (Orford)
son, b. 10/15/1970 in Hanover; Richard D. Marshall and Sharon L.
Parvin
daughter, b. 10/15/1970 in Hanover; Richard D. Marshall and
Sharon L. Parvin
Hazel, b. 12/22/1893 in Lyme; third; Bry Marshall (blacksmith, 35,
Goffstown) and Hattie Balch (27, Orford)

Jennifer Paige, b. 10/19/1971 in Hanover; Richard D. Marshall and Sharon Parvin

MARTIN,
John Stephen, b. 4/17/1965 in Hanover; second; Thurman Martin, Jr. (maintenance, Hanover) and Maureen D. Grayson (Charlestown, SC)

MARTZ,
Dianne, b. 7/19/1960 in Lyme; Richard E. Martz (executive aid, 24, Detroit, MI) and Lee Graves (23, New York City)

MASON,
Brandon James, b. 2/16/1983 in Hanover; James E. Mason and Dayle A. Drescher
Kate Elizabeth, b. 2/16/1983 in Hanover; James E. Mason and Dayle A. Drescher
Sarah Ingalil, b. 1/27/1981 in Hanover; James E. Mason and Dayle A. Drescher

MASTERS,
Mabel E., b. 10/1/1898; first; William J. Masters (laborer, 25, Richford, VT) and Eva G. Woodward (33, Hanover)
Robert Arthur, b. 7/12/1900; second; William J. Masters (laborer, 28, Bedford, Canada) and Eva G. Woodward (35, Hanover)

MASURE,
Lawrence Roland, b. 7/12/1944 in Lyme; first; Basel C. Masure (farm lab., 17, Lyndon, VT) and Marguerite Blodgett (19, Wheelock, VT); residence – N. Thetford, VT

MATIVIA,
daughter, b. 8/7/1887; third; Henry J. Mativia (farmer, 31, Corinth, VT) and Hattie C. Mativia (25, Fairlee, VT)
Darius Roswell, b. 10/27/1945 in Lyme; first; Roswell L. Mativia (farmer, 51, Lyme) and Ina Squires (38, Sharon, VT)
Esther Mir'da, b. 2/16/1900; second; Darius R. Mativia (horse dealer, 37, N. Hartland, VT) and Ida A. Stark (31, Lyme)
Perry M., b. 2/17/1896 in Lyme; fourth; Henry J. Mativia (farmer, 41, Corinth, VT) and Hattie C. Stickney (36, Fairfax, VT)
Roswell Louis, b. 12/30/1894 in Lyme; first; Darius R. Mativia

(laborer, 30, Hartford, VT) and Ida A. Stark (26, Lyme)

MAY,
Spencer Vance, b. 12/6/2003 in Lebanon; Bennett May and Vicki May

MAYERS,
Courtney Lynne, b. 3/16/1993 in Lebanon; James Mayers and Debra Goodrum

MAYETTE,
Francis E., b. 11/9/1901; second; Francis B. Mayette (laborer, 26, N. Monroe) and Catherine M. Fleming (29, Halifax, NS)
James, b. 2/5/1898; first; Francis B. Mayette (laborer, 25, Monroe) and Catherine M. Fleming (26, Halifax, NS)

MAYO,
Ralph, b. 3/24/1891; first; George S. Mayo (farmer, 48, Lyme) and Alma N. Converse (42, Lyme)

McCABE,
Colin Edward, b. 3/27/1984 in Hanover; Donald R. McCabe and Elizabeth C. Broderick

McCARTHY,
Padhrig Thomas, b. 12/25/1966 in Lebanon; third; Lawrence McCarthy (research asst., Rochester, NY) and Elsie A. Dickens (Rochester, NY)

McCONNELL,
Betty Ann, b. 7/16/1939 in Lyme; third; Forrest F. McConnell (farmer, 31, Whitefield) and Althea E. Nelson (25, Haverhill)
Doris Fay, b. 1/3/1941 in Lyme; fifth; Forrest M. McConnell (farm laborer, 36, Whitefield) and Althea E. Nelson (27, Haverhill)
Elinor I., b. 8/13/1937 in Lyme; third; Forrest McConnell (farmer, 30, Whitefield) and Althea Nelson (22, Haverhill)

McCOY,
Phyllis Ann, b. 10/2/1937 in Lyme; second; Frank McCoy (poultryman, 28, Jefferson) and Lulu Tattersall (22, Lyme)

McEWAN,
son, b. 5/6/1902; fifth; John Leslie McEwan (farmer, 39, Pleasant Valley, ON) and Diantha Rattway (30, Wolf Island)
Aurlie, b. 1/19/1933 in Hanover; second; Leslie McEwan (gas salesman, 31, Lyme) and Marcia A. Simmons (21, Piermont)
Donald Leslie, b. 1/1/1932 in Hanover; first; Leslie G. McEwan (pump mech., 29, Lyme) and Marcia Simmons (20, Piermont)
Lorna, b. 10/11/1926 in Lyme; second; Harry McEwan (carpenter, 27, Canada) and Alice Clark (32, Plainfield)

McINTYRE,
Elizabeth Geary, b. 4/5/1965 in Hanover; third; Oswald R. McIntyre (doctor, Chicago, IL) and Lisa Geary (Newark, NJ)

McLEOD,
Alexander A., b. 5/15/1901; second; Murdo A. McLeod (laborer, 30, Norton, VT) and Ina A. White (23, Windsor, PQ)

McMANN,
daughter, b. 3/20/1896 in Lyme; first; Henry McMann (laborer, 23, Groveton) and Mary E. Moore (22, Lyme)
Leon H., b. 10/29/1896 in Lyme; first; James McMann (laborer, 28, Groveton) and Nellie L. Gilbert (19, Lyme)
Maurice Henry, b. 3/9/1909 in Lyme; first; Henry McMann (laborer, 36, Groveton) and Mabel Alice Cutting (25, Lyme)
Nellie M., b. 1/28/1895 in Lyme; first; John L. McMann (laborer, 27, Johnstown, NY) and Rosa F. Gilbert (17, Lyme)

McMANUS,
Mary Margaret, b. 11/14/1957 in Hanover; Richard A. McManus (physician, Elizabeth, NJ) and Kathleen J. O'Neill (New York City)

MEAGHER,
Benjamin David, b. 5/21/2000 in Lebanon; Matthew Meagher and Jennifer Meagher
Caleb John, b. 1/16/2002 in Lebanon; Matthew Meagher and Jennifer Meagher
Jacob Patrick, b. 7/29/1998 in Lebanon; Matthew K. Meagher and Jennifer L. Scanlon

MELENDY,
son, b. 3/12/1900; third; Albert P. Melendy (farmer, 50, Croydon) and Eva L. Biathrow (25, Hanover)
Don Lee, b. 10/4/1905 in Lyme; fourth; Albert P. Melendy (laborer, 55, Lebanon) and Eva L. Biathrow (30, Lebanon)
Heidi, b. 9/21/1962 in Hanover; Robert H. Melendy (clerk, Norwich, VT) and Elizabeth R. Wing (38, Hanover)
Nancy Lee, b. 8/31/1954 in Haverhill; third; Raymond A. Melendy (laborer, 27, Hanover) and Etta M. Pike (23, Lyme)
Shirley Mae, b. 1/30/1951 in Lebanon; first; Raymond Melendy (lumberman, 23, Hanover) and Etta Mae Pike (20, Lyme)

MELVIN,
Theda Mae, b. 3/10/1904 in Lyme; first; Leon O. Melvin (clerk, 22, Lyme) and Florence M. Wells (23, Lyme)
Thelma G., b. 9/15/1907 in Lyme; second; Leon O. Melvin (brakeman, 26, Lyme) and Florence M. Wells (27, Lyme)

MENARD,
Deborah Sue, b. 1/30/1964 in Hanover; Gerard J. Menard (carpenter, Island Pond, VT) and Margaret L. Uline (26, Lyme)
Loralie Louise, b. 4/9/1969 in Hanover; Gerard J. Menard and Margaret L. Uline

MENGE,
Karen Louise, b. 11/5/1956 in Hanover; John A. Menge (teacher, 29, Milwaukee, WI) and Geneva R. Ferguson (30, Vandalia, MO)
Mellissa Ann, b. 2/22/1966 in Hanover; third; John A. Menge (professor, Milwaukee, WI) and Geneva R. Ferguson (Vandalia, MO)
Susan Lorraine, b. 7/16/1958 in Hanover; John A. Menge (asst. professor, 31, Milwaukee, WI) and Geneva R. Ferguson (31, Vandalia, MO)

MESSER,
Crystal Jayne, b. 5/21/1980 in Lebanon; Paul B. Messer, Jr. and Ellen L. Bryant

MESSIER,
Beth Louise, b. 1/3/1916; third; Ernest M. Messier (laborer, 29, Thetford, VT) and Bessie Gilbert (25, Monroe)

Gilbert George, b. 1/16/1914; second; Ernest M. Messier (laborer, 28, Thetford, VT) and Bessie E. Gilbert (23, Monroe)

Hazel May, b. 5/17/1911 in Lyme; first; Ernest M. Messier (laborer, 25, Thetford, VT) and Bessie E. Gilbert (21, Monroe)

METZ,
Luke Cyrus, b. 12/24/1968 in Hanover; Donald A. Metz and Cora V. Brooks

MEYER,
Jasper Baton, b. 10/29/1999 in Lebanon; Robert Meyer and Jane Stevenson Meyer

Tristan Steele, b. 4/16/2002 in Lebanon; Robert Meyer and Jane Meyer

MILLER,
Wanda Marie, b. 1/26/1962 in Hanover; Caryl W. Miller (laborer, Woodsville) and Margaret Reeves (24, Mars Hill, ME)

MILLIMAN,
Annika Elizabeth, b. 3/10/2003 in Lebanon; Christopher Milliman and Kimberly Milliman

Silke Margretta, b. 11/19/2000 in Lebanon; Christopher Milliman and Kimberly Milliman

MOEN,
Pierce Harding, b. 9/28/2000 in Lebanon; Glenn Moen and Kathleen Moen

MOFFATT,
Elizabeth Emerson, b. 12/5/1991 in Texarkana, TX; Sterling Moffatt

MOHR,
Jack Harrison, b. 11/7/1996 in Lebanon; Jack Mohr and Julie Johnson

MOORE,
Linda Marie, b. 5/30/1948 in Hanover; third; James E. Moore (laborer, 25, Cambridgeport, VT) and Heiliene E. Austin (25, Hartland, VT)

MORAN,
James Edmund, b. 7/2/1917; second; D. James Moran (ct. foreman, 32, New Haven, CT) and Vera S. Wilson (22, Fletcher, VT)
Richard Wilson, b. 2/16/1916; first; James D. Moran (laborer, 31, Ireland) and Vera S. Wilson (20, Fletcher, VT)
Rufus Harvey, b. 12/21/1918 in Lyme; third; Dennis J. Moran (33, N. Haven, CT) and Vera S. Wilson (22, Fletcher, VT)

MOREY,
Adrienne Aline, b. 12/21/1960 in Hanover; Charles T. Morey (asst. professor, 33, Cumington, MA) and Eleanore F. Wronowska (36, Detroit, MI)
Drew Linden, b. 7/23/1959 in Lyme; Charles T. Morey (artist-teacher, 32, Cummington, MA) and Eleanore F. Wronowska (35, Detroit, MI)
Gladys Arlene, b. 6/15/1955 in TX; Richard A. Morey (US Army, VT) and Helen L. Elder (NH)
Paul Richard, b. 11/17/1956 in ME; Richard A. Morey (USAF, Ludlow, VT) and Helen L. Elder (Lyme)

MORGAN,
Amy Patchett, b. 11/14/1975 in Hanover; G. James Morgan and Linda J. Patchett

MORIARTY,
Arthur, b. 11/1/1895 in Lyme; first; Daniel Moriarty (com. traveler, 24, Springfield, MA) and Alice E. Keep (24, Brooklyn, LI); residence - Newark, NJ

MORRIS,
son, b. –/–/1890; first; Fred W. Morris (merchant, 35, IA) and Ruth A. Hadlock (18, Lyme); residence - Olcott, VT

MORRISON,
Marjorie Gray, b. 12/27/1895 in Lyme; fourth; Roland M. Morrison (farmer, 46, Fairlee, VT) and Lizzie G. Chaffie (33, E. Providence, RI)

MORSE,
Timothy Latherop, b. 6/5/1967 in Hanover; first; Robert E. Morse (US Army, N. Conway) and Sylvia F. Balch (Lebanon)

MOULTON,
Theodore Michael, b. 12/4/1986 in Hanover; Steven Moulton and Susan Newhouse

MOUSLEY,
son, b. 9/3/1900; ninth; George W. Mousley (farmer, 38, Lyme) and Julia E. Dike (37, Lyme); residence - Orford
Bessie May, b. 8/7/1892; second; Orton Mousley (laborer, 23, Lyme) and Hattie B. Fales (20, Lyme)
Ila M., b. 9/30/1896 in Lyme; fourth; Orton M. Mousley (laborer, 30, Lyme) and Hattie B. Fales (24, Lyme)
William Carroll, b. 8/15/1890; first; Orton M. Mousley (laborer, 21, Lyme) and Hattie B. Fales (Lyme)

MOVELLE,
Alfred Lyman, b. 11/19/1925 in Lyme; third; William J. Movelle (carpenter, 39, New Bedford, MA) and Mildred Gilbert (27, Lyme)
Gerald James, b. 3/14/1952 in Hanover; fifth; William Movelle (carpenter, 30, Lyme) and Esther Gray (27, Lyme); res – Lyme Ctr.
Gloria Jean, b. 9/10/1947 in Hanover; fourth; William Movelle (carpenter, 25, Lyme) and Esther L. Gray (23, Lyme)
James Arthur, b. 1/23/1932 in Lyme; fourth; William J. Movelle (carpenter, 46, New Bedford, MA) and Mildred M. Gilbert (34, Lyme)
Mary Ann, b. 5/28/1943 in Hanover; second; William J. Movelle (mill worker, 21, Lyme) and Esther L. Gray (18, Lyme)
Mildred May, b. 11/11/1953 in Hanover; William Movelle (carpenter, 31, Lyme) and Esther Gray (29, Lyme)
Morgan Bryant, b. 10/24/1993 in Lebanon; Paul Movelle and Jane Bryant
Nancy Lee, b. 10/23/1945 in Hanover; third; William Movelle (US Army, 24, Lyme) and Esther L. Gray (21, Lyme Ctr.)
Paul Allen, b. 10/15/1956 in Hanover; William J. Movelle (deceased, 35, Lyme) and Esther L. Gray (32, Lyme)
Rose Marie, b. 1/13/1942 in Hanover; first; William J. Movelle (lumberman, 21, Lyme) and Esther L. Gray (17, Lyme)
Vera Agnes, b. 10/5/1919 in Lyme; first; William J. Movelle (carpenter, 33, New Bedford, MA) and Mildred M. Gilbert (22, Lyme)

William Joseph, Jr., b. 8/28/1921 in Lyme; second; William J. Movelle (farmer, 34, New Bedford, MA) and Mildred M. Gilbert (23, Lyme)
William Joseph, Jr., b. 5/4/1955 in Hanover; seventh; William J. Movelle (carpenter, Lyme) and Esther L. Gray (Lyme)

MULVIHILL,
Madeline Jane, b. 2/5/1996 in Lebanon; Peter Mulvihill and Ellen Henderson

MUNN,
daughter, b. 8/6/1910 in Lyme; eighth; Charles H. Munn (farmer, 41, Canterbury) and Katherine Ordway (36, Northfield, MN)
Robert, b. 7/4/1905 in Lyme; sixth; Charles H. Munn (farmer, 35, Canterbury, VT) and Kathleen Ordway (31, Stanton, MN)
Robert Ordway, b. 4/13/1913 in Lyme; ninth; Charles H. Munn (farmer, 43, Canterbury) and Kathrine Ordway (39, Northfield, MN)
Rosina T., b. 11/8/1907 in Lyme; seventh; Charles H. Munn (farmer, 37, Canterbury, VT) and Kathleen Ordway (33, Stanton, MN)

MURPHY,
Abigail, b. 6/24/1966 in Hanover; second; William N. Murphy (teacher, Erie, PA) and Karen Obermayer (Boston, MA)
Gabrielle, b. 4/7/1970 in Hanover; William N. Murphy and Karen Obermayer

NELSON,
Florence E., b. 6/15/1892; first; George W. Nelson (farmer, 22, Newbury, VT) and Hattie S. Webster (21, Lyme); residence - Haverhill
Raymond Arthur, b. 10/26/1945 in Lyme; second; Alvie H. Nelson (copper min., 36, Bridgewater, CT) and Claire J. Thibodeau (24, Newport, VT); residence – S. Strafford, VT

NEMATOLAHI,
Negar Ellen, b. 1/13/1969 in Hanover; Heidar Nematolahi and Ellen C. Urban

NEVEL,
Douglas Clifford, b. 7/14/1964 in Hanover; Donald E. Nevel

(research engineer, Williamsport, PA) and Susette W. Elder
(Peoria, IL)
Valerie Jean, b. 8/10/1963 in Hanover; Donald E. Nevel (research
eng., Williamsport, PA) and Susette W. Elder (23, Peoria, IL)

NEWHALL,
Donald J., Jr., b. 6/2/1940 in Hanover; third; Donald J. Newhall
(farmer, 25, Royalton, MA) and Mabel V. Chadwick (21, N.
Sutton)
Pauline Ann, b. 6/21/1938 in Hanover; second; Donald J. Newhall
(farmer, 23, Royalton, MA) and Mabel V. Chadwick (19, N.
Sutton)

NICHOLS,
Amara Ashley, b. 2/24/1997 in Lebanon; Benjamin Jay Nichols and
Amy Christina DeCato
Benjamin Jay, b. 10/28/1968 in Lebanon; William R. Nichols and
Srimalai Karnruksa
Cassandra Mary, b. 5/4/2001 in Lebanon; Scott Nichols and Heidi
Nichols
Evan James, b. 9/7/2003 in Lebanon; Scott Nichols and Heidi
Nichols
James Edward, b. 10/13/1945 in Lyme; third; Guy E. Nichols
(hardware, 32, Enosburg Falls, VT) and Esther E. Chaffee (27,
Enosburg Falls, VT)
Jill Elizabeth, b. 3/19/1974 in Lebanon; James E. Nichols and Vera
Katherine August
Lloyd George, b. 2/11/1944 in Lyme; third; Guy E. Nichols (sawmill
op., 30, Enosburg Falls, VT) and Esther E. Chaffee (25,
Enosburg Falls, VT)
Rain Lee, b. 3/7/1971 in Lyme; Robert G. Nichols and Gloria Liedke
Timothy Ryan, b. 3/28/1995 in Lebanon; Benjamin Jay Nichols and
Amy Christina DeCato
William Richard, b. 10/13/1945 in Lyme; fourth; Guy E. Nichols
(hardware, 32, Enosburg Falls, VT) and Esther E. Chaffee (27,
Enosburg Falls, VT)

NICKELS,
Amanda Leigh, b. 3/19/1986 in Hanover; Kirby L. Nickels and
Kathleen J. Boley

NOYES,
Eva May, b. 3/28/1889; first; Frank W. Noyes (laborer, Dorchester) and Anna M. Dunbar (Lyme)

NUNES,
Jennifer Ann, b. 12/6/1969 in Lebanon; Melvyn D. Nunes and Barbara Burk

O'BRIEN,
Sarah Margaret, b. 9/28/1963 in Hanover; Harold W. O'Brien (physicist, Sangerville, ME) and Dolores A. Rowe (34, Old Town, ME)
Sheri Arlene, b. 11/20/1964 in Hanover; Harold W. O'Brien (physicist, Sangerville, ME) and Dolores A. Rowe (35, Old Town, ME)

O'CONNOR,
Kathleen Ann, b. 12/7/1976 in Hanover; James Joseph O'Connor and Colleen Ann Condon

O'DONNELL,
Hugh Blanchard, III, b. 8/9/1953 in Hanover; Hugh O'Donnell, Jr. (carpenter, 26, Vershire, VT) and Joan Pushee (20, Lyme)
Katherine Ann, b. 1/10/1976 in Hanover; Joseph F. O'Donnell and Janice M. Atkinson
Linda Belle, b. 9/22/1954 in Hanover; second; Hugh B. O'Donnell (carpenter, 27, Vershire, VT) and Joan Pushee (21, Lyme)
Michael Roger, b. 1/31/1959 in Hanover; Hugh B. O'Donnell (carpenter, 31, Vershire, VT) and Joan Pushee (26, Lyme)
Patricia Irene, b. 9/20/1962 in Hanover; Hugh B. O'Donnell (carpenter, Vershire, VT) and Joan Pushee (29, Lyme)
Phillip Dale, b. 7/18/1961 in Hanover; Hugh O'Donnell, Jr. (carpenter, Vershire, VT) and Joan Pushee (28, Lyme)
Rebecca Ann, b. 11/26/1955 in Barre, VT; Leo W. O'Donnell (lumberman, 22, Vershire, VT) and Lila E. Covey (18, Bradford, VT)
Thelma Jane, b. 10/30/1957 in Hanover; Hugh B. O'Donnell (carpenter, Vershire, VT) and Joan Pushee (Lyme)

O'HARA,
Ann, b. 11/9/1972 in Hanover; Daniel O'Hara and Julia A.

Briggerman
Mary, b. 12/20/1967 in Hanover; first; Daniel O'Hara (engineer, Waltham, MA) and Julia A. Briggerman (Peoria, IL)
Timothy Ezra, d. 2/12/1974 in Hanover; Daniel O'Hara and Julia Ann Briggerman

O'KEEFE,
Kaleb Hawthorne, b. 2/27/1998 in Lebanon; Shaun James O'Keefe and Marci D. Hawthorne

OFFICER,
Andrew Lewis, b. 1/4/1989 in Lebanon; Thomas C. Officer and Ashley Lewis
Thomas Chandler, b. 4/19/1987 in Lebanon; Thomas C. Officer and Ashley Lewis

OLENEC,
Meredith Ellen, b. 3/2/2003 in Lebanon; Christopher Olenec and Kristina Olenec

OLMSTE[A]D,
Andrew Moody, b. 1/10/1968 in Hanover; Richard W. Olmsted and Emily R. Heck
James Nicolas, b. 1/13/1964 in Hanover; Richard W. Olmsted (business manager, NY) and Emily R. Heck (30, Shelby, OH)
Peter David, b. 11/7/1962 in Hanover; Richard W. Olmstead (business manager, Pleasantville, NY) and Emily R. Heck (29, Shelby, OH)

OLSEN,
Diana Susan, b. 8/12/1949 in Hanover; Edward T. Olsen and Elizabeth Davis
Douglas Edward, b. 11/4/1953 in Lyme; Edward Olsen (farmer, 30, Strafford, VT) and Elizabeth Davis (26, Manchester)
Douglas Scott, b. 6/23/1985 in Lebanon; Timothy Olsen and Deborah Menard
Edward Thomas, Jr., b. 9/15/1950 in Lyme; second; Edward Olsen (carpenter, 27, Strafford, VT) and Elizabeth Davis (23, Manchester)
Jarrett Joseph, b. 3/10/1987 in Lebanon; Timothy S. Olsen and Deborah Menard

Jessie Renee, b. 5/8/1996 in Lebanon; Peter Olsen and Shawn
    Hamilton
Joel Thomas, b. 2/11/1955 in Lyme; fifth; Edward T. Olsen (farmer,
    Strafford, VT) and Elizabeth Davis (Manchester)
Kaitlin Elizabeth, b. 4/18/1995 in Lebanon; Timothy Scott Olsen and
    Deborah Sue Menard
Samantha Sue, b. 5/30/1990 in Lebanon; Timothy S. Olsen and
    Deborah Menard
Sandra Gail, b. 12/4/1951 in Lyme; third; Edward T. Olsen (farmer,
    28, Strafford, VT) and Elizabteh Davis (24, Manchester)
Zachary Scott, b. 6/19/1994 in Lebanon; Peter Olsen and Shawn
    Hamilton

OREM,
Daniel Radcliffe, b. 8/25/2000 in Lebanon; Nicholas Orem and Laura
    Scott

OSBORN,
Emilia Axelina, b. 7/17/2004 in Lebanon; Frederick Osborn and
    Krista Osborn
Maya Zena Schieffelin, b. 7/17/2004 in Lebanon; Frederick Osborn
    and Krista Osborn

OSBORNE,
Elizabeth M., b. 1/25/1906 in Lyme; first; James P. Osborne
    (contractor, 36, Lancaster) and Margaret Stokes (33, Dublin,
    Ireland); residence - W. Lebanon

OSHER,
Jordan Elena, b. 9/21/1985 in Hanover; Fred Osher and Catharine
    Klebes

OSTLER,
John Boyer, b. 5/14/1993 in Lebanon; David Ostler and Rachelle
    Taylor
Joseph Richards, b. 4/23/1986 in Lebanon; David B. Ostler and
    Rachelle Taylor
Leslie Jane, b. 10/30/1990 in Hanover; David B. Ostler and Rachelle
    Taylor

PACKARD,
Ashlie Nichole, b. 6/12/1992 in Lebanon; Jeffrey Packard and Tina Thurston
Jessica Ann, b. 9/26/1994 in Lebanon; Jeffrey Packard and Tina Thurston

PAGE,
Luceil Evelyn, b. 5/28/1908 in Lyme; ninth; Charles W. Page (laborer, 41, Orfordville) and Emma J. Dyke (42, Lyme)

PAIGE,
Sarah Bell, b. 9/29/1888; first; Charles W. Paige (laborer, 21, Orford) and Emma J. Dike (22, Lyme)

PALMER,
K. D. [male], b. 11/28/1903 in Lyme; second; Charles E. Palmer (farmer, 33, Kent Co., NB) and Sallie M. Chase (33, Lyme)
Kathleen Rose, b. 10/7/1999 in Lebanon; James Palmer and Ellen Palmer
Sally M., b. 9/22/1896 in Lyme; first; Charles E. Palmer (farmer, 28, Rend Co., NB) and Sally M. Chase (26, Lyme)
Suzanne, b. 12/4/1944 in Lyme; seventh; Charles C. Palmer (farmer, 41, Thetford, VT) and Eileen B. Blodgett (38, Hebron)

PANTEL,
Haddon Jacob, b. 5/16/1985 in Hanover; Robert Pantel and Mona Todras

PARRIS,
daughter, b. 7/22/1932 in Lyme; third; August L. Parris (laborer, 31, France) and Eva May Cameau (25, Plymouth)

PATCH,
daughter, b. 9/25/1901; first; Ada A. Patch (16, Orford)

PATTISON,
Elizabeth Skye Aimi, b. 12/22/1991 in Hanover; David G. Pattison and Julia Misun Chung
Ian Grange Hyugk, b. 5/5/1993 in Lebanon; David Pattison and Julia Chung

PELL,
Tripler, b. 4/10/1974 in Hanover; Christopher T. H. Pell and Janet Alexander

PELLETIER,
Alline Marie, b. 2/6/1938 in Lyme; fifth; Zephire Pelletier (woodsman, 33, Quebec) and Alma Douillard (32, Quebec)

PERKINS,
child, b. 1/19/1888; third; Adna Perkins (farmer, 39, Lyme) and Mary C. Clement (33, Dorchester)
son, b. 10/22/1902; seventh; Adna Perkins (farmer, 53, Lyme) and Margaret Hazen (28, N. Hero, VT)
Archie Allen, b. 11/10/1900 in Lyme; Adna Perkins and Margaret Hazen (1965)
Charles Dean, b. 11/11/1891; first; Edwin H. Perkins (clerk in market, 32, Lyme) and Kate G. Perkins (34, Lyme)
Forrest Ryder, b. 2/19/1908 in Lyme; Adna Perkins and Margaret Hazen (1958)
George, b. 4/30/1893 in Lyme; second; Adna Perkins (farmer, 44, Lyme) and Addie M. Hazen (19, N. Hero, VT)
Herbert J., b. 2/13/1905 in Lyme; seventh; Adna Perkins (stage driver, 56, Lyme) and Margaret A. Hazen (30, N. Hero, VT)
James Vernon, b. 4/24/1911 in Lyme; ninth; Adna Perkins (stage driver, 60, Lyme) and Addie M. Hazen (36, N. Hero, VT)
Jaunita Marie, b. 1/29/1943 in Lebanon; first; Harry W. Perkins (farmer, 40, Lyme) and Martha E. Hardy (21, Londonderry)
Maude Emma, b. 4/19/1895 in Lyme; third; Adna Perkins (stage driver, 47, Lyme) and Addie M. Hazen (20, N. Hero, VT)
Robert Edmond, b. 9/26/1951 in Lebanon; first; Robert Perkins (farmer, 21, Hartford, CT) and Alice Blake (19, Pittsfield, MA)
Ruth Evelyn, b. 1/29/1913 in Lyme; tenth; Adna Perkins (stage driver, 62, Lyme) and Ada M. Hazen (38, N. Hero, VT)
Shirley Yvonne, b. 3/16/1947 in Lebanon; second; Harry W. Perkins (farmer, 44, Lyme) and Martha E. Hardy (25, Londonderry)
Verla Maxine, b. 5/23/1926 in Lyme; first; Forest R. Perkins (laborer, 18, Lyme) and Charlotte M. Webb (23, Lyme)

PERRY,
Angela Christina, b. 8/2/1977 in Warzburg, Germany; David William Perry and Kathryn Green (1978)

Nicole Shannon, b. 11/18/1970 in Hanover; Anthony W. Perry and Carole A. Chesley

Shiloh Anthony, b. 11/2/1976 in Hanover; Anthony Wayne Perry and Carol Ann Chesley

PETERS,
Edward Lee, b. 4/5/1945 in Lyme; first; William A. Peters (teacher, 30, Bradford, VT) and Pauline E. Hunt (28, Cobleskill, NY); residence – Thetford Hill, VT

PETERSON,
Else Riley, b. 5/16/1994 in Lebanon; Kevin Peterson and Victoria Smith

Miles Baker, b. 8/3/1991 in Hanover; Kevin A. Peterson and Victoria L. Smith

Samuel Adams, b. 11/6/1989 in Hanover; Kevin A. Peterson and Victoria Smith

PFISTER,
Benjamin Edward, b. 10/28/1991 in Hanover; John F. Pfister and Catherine P. Cramer

Noah Christopher Cramer, b. 10/26/1989 in Hanover; John F. Pfister and Catherine Cramer

PICKARD,
Holly Ann, b. 10/15/1984 in Hanover; Bruce J. Pickard and Constance L. Avery

PIEHLER,
Britton Worth, b. 6/12/1975 in Hanover; Jeffrey M. Piehler and Kristina L. Lund

PIERCE,
Kristen Kelly, b. 11/26/1969 in Hanover; John B. Pierce, Jr. and Robin L. Boak

PIERSON,
Sheila Mae, b. 5/14/1948 in Lyme; third; Wallace H. Pierson (road labor, 40, Topsham, VT) and Evelyn N. Weeks (26, Fairlee, VT); residence – Orford

PIKE,
son, b. 7/19/1889; first; Fred L. Pike (farmer, Lyme) and Anna Bell Roberts (Lyme)
son, b. 10/29/1890; second; Charles D. Pike (farmer, 39, Hanover) and Ida A. Baily (Lyme)
son, b. 8/5/1891; second; Fred L. Pike (laborer, 32, Lyme) and Anna B. Roberts (24, Lyme)
daughter, b. 11/9/1892; third; C. D. Pike (farmer, 41, Hanover) and Ida Alice Bailey (36, Lyme)
son, b. 12/7/1893 in Lyme; fourth; Charles D. Pike (farmer, 42, Hanover) and Ida Bailey (37, Lyme)
son, b. 4/19/1899; sixth; Charles D. Pike (farmer, 47, Hanover) and Ida Bailey (42, Lyme)
son, b. 5/8/1899; third; Henry M. Pike (farmer, 33, Lyme) and Anna P. Gilbert (24, Orford)
daughter, b. 12/20/1899; sixth; Fred L. Pike (farmer, 41, Lyme) and Anna B. Roberts (32, Lyme)
daughter, b. 9/5/1901; fourth; Henry M. D. Pike (farmer, 36, Hanover) and Anna P. Gilbert (26, Lyme)
daughter, b. 4/28/1907 in Lyme; fifth; Henry M. D. Pike (farmer, 40, Lyme) and Annie P. Gilbert (30, Orford)
daughter, b. 7/22/1907 in Lyme; ninth; Fred L. Pike (farmer, 48, Lyme) and Anna B. Roberts (40, Lyme)
stillborn son, b. 6/11/1948 in Lyme; second; Horace E. Pike (laborer, 27, Lyme) and Maxine Heath (21, Littleton); residence – Orford
son, b. 6/11/1948 in Lyme; third; Horace E. Pike (laborer, 27, Lyme) and Maxine Heath (21, Littleton); residence – Orford
daughter, b. 9/21/1952 in Hanover; third; Herbert Pike (lumberman, 26, Lyme) and Jessie Storms (23, Belgium); res. – Lyme Ctr.
Allie Chester, b. 2/1/1923 in Lyme; second; Earl H. Pike (laborer, 23, Lyme) and Myrtle L. Coates (31, Corn Hill, NB)
Allie Wayne, b. 7/31/1943 in Lyme; first; Allie C. Pike (farmer, 20, Lyme) and Marjorie M. Heath (18, Littleton)
Arthur Dwight, b. 8/31/1949 in Lebanon; Charles C. Pike and Betty Schwotzer
Beatrice Annie, b. 1/29/1925 in Lyme; fourth; Earl H. Pike (farmer, 25, Lyme) and Myrtle Coates (34, Corn Hill, NB)
Bertram Earl, b. 1/29/1925 in Lyme; fifth; Earl H. Pike (farmer, 25, Lyme) and Myrtle Coates (34, Corn Hill, NB)
Bonnie Lee, b. 2/21/1953 in Hanover; Weymouth H. Pike (truck driver, 25, Lyme) and Helen Marsh (20, Wentworth)

Brenda Lee, b. 2/3/1962 in Hanover; Horace E. Pike (lumberman, Lyme) and Maxine L. Heath (35, Littleton)

Carrie Lill, b. 9/21/1897 in Lyme; fifth; Fred L. Pike (farmer, 38, Hanover) and Annie Belle Roberts (29, Lyme)

Charles Chester, b. 10/29/1920 in Lyme; first; Chester D. Pike (farmer, 26, Lyme) and Polly C. Camp (28, Lyme)

Clarence Clayton, b. 12/22/1902; seventh; Fred L. Pike (farmer, 44, Lyme) and Anna B. Roberts (34, Lyme)

Darlene Annette, b. 6/16/1969 in Hanover; Arthur D. Pike and Linda A. Johns

David Carleton, b. 10/2/1920 in Lyme; fifth; Carlton E. Pike (teacher, 43, Boston, MA) and Blanche Pushee (30, Lyme)

David Michael, b. 10/6/1956 in gx; Lon J. Pike (road worker, 36, Lyme) and Susan J. Waterbury (26, Norwalk, CT)

Donna Lee, b. 12/17/1945 in Hanover; second; Allie C. Pike (farmer, 22, Lyme) and Marjorie M. Heath (20, Littleton)

Dorothy May, b. 4/20/1915; first; Lon C. Pike (farmer, 25, Lyme) and Lucy E. Jewell (29, Canada)

Earl Francis, b. 2/16/1932 in Lyme; ninth; Earl H. Pike (farmer, 32, Lyme) and Myrtle L. Coates (40, Corn Hill, NB)

Earl Francis, Jr., b. 3/21/1957 in Hanover; Earl F. Pike (woodsman, Lyme) and Janet E. Bradley (Concord, MA)

Ella L., b. 1/20/1895 in Lyme; fourth; Fred L. Pike (farmer, 34, Lyme) and Anna P. Roberts (27, Lyme)

Ethel Rose, b. 2/4/1919 in Lyme; fourth; Lon C. Pike (farming, 29, Lyme) and Lucy E. Jewell (35, Canada)

Etta May, b. 2/3/1897 in Lyme; second; Henry M. Pike (laborer, 32, Lyme) and Annie P. Gilbert (22, Orford)

Etta May, b. 1/5/1931 in Lyme; eighth; Earl H. Pike (farmer, 31, Lyme) and Myrtle L. Coates (39, Corn Hill, NB)

Faye Ann, b. 7/13/1955 in Hanover; fifth; Weymouth H. Pike (lumberman, Lyme) and Helen M. Marsh (Wentworth)

Forrest Carlton, b. 1/17/1917; second; Lon C. Pike (farming, 27, Lyme) and Lucy E. Jewell (33, Canada)

Foster Melrose, b. 1/17/1917; third; Lon C. Pike (farming, 27, Lyme) and Lucy E. Jewell (33, Canada)

George W., b. 8/24/1896 in Lyme; fifth; Charles D. Pike (farmer, 45, Hanover) and Ida I. Bailey (40, Lyme)

Gerald Clayton, b. 12/5/1912 in Lyme; first; Ray Flanders (21, Norwich, VT) and Ella L. Pike (18, Lyme)

Gladys Evelyn, b. 3/17/1905 in Lyme; eighth; Fred L. Pike (farmer,

46, Hanover) and Belle Anna Roberts (37, Lyme)
Herbert Edward, b. 3/11/1926 in Lyme; sixth; Earl H. Pike (laborer, 27, Lyme) and Myrtle L. Coates (35, Corn Hill, NS)
Holly Norma, b. 8/7/1926 in Hanover; stillborn; third; Weymouth Pike (patrolman, 27, Lyme) and Dora Taylor (28, Thetford, VT)
Holly Wilder, b. 2/5/1923 in Hanover; stillborn; second; G. Weymouth Pike (laborer, 26, Lyme) and Dora D. Taylor (25, Thetford, VT)
Horace Earle, b. 11/8/1920 in Lyme; fourth; Earl H. Pike (farmer, 21, Lyme) and Myrtle L. Coates (29, Corn Hill, NB)
Ida Josephene, b. 10/29/1925 in Lyme; third; Chester D. Pike (laborer, 31, Lyme) and Polly C. Camp (33, Lyme)
James Ernest, b. 4/17/1954 in Haverhill; fourth; Weymouth H. Pike (laborer, 26, Lyme) and Helen M. Marsh (21, Wentworth)
Jessie Lorraine, b. 3/4/1922 in Lyme; second; Earl H. Pike (farmer, 21, Lyme) and Myrtle L. Coates (31, Corn Hill, NB)
Jessie Winona, b. 1/29/1919 in Lyme; first; G. Weymouth Pike (farming, 22, Lyme) and Dora D. Taylor (21, Thetford, VT)
John William, b. 2/18/1959 in Hanover; Lon J. Pike (laborer, 37, Lyme) and Susan J. Waterbury (28, Norwalk, CT)
Judy Marie, b. 9/4/1956 in Hanover; Weymouth H. Pike (woodsman, 28, Lyme) and Helen M. Marsh (23, Wentworth)
Laura Bell, b. 1/10/1889; third; Henry M. Pike (farmer, Lyme) and Eva G. Woodward (Hanover)
Laura Blanch, b. 12/6/1921 in Lyme; second; Chester D. Pike (mail carrier, 28, Lyme) and Corinne P. Camp (29, Lyme)
Lawrence Franklin, b. 4/23/1944 in Lyme; second; Charles C. Pike (farmer, 23, Lyme) and Betty C. Schwotzer (21, Manchester)
Linda Carol, b. 12/22/1946 in Hanover; first; Horace E. Pike (lumberman, 26, Lyme) and Maxine L. Heath (20, Littleton)
Lon Jewell, b. 4/14/1921 in Lyme; fifth; Lon C. Pike (farmer, 31, Lyme) and Lucy E. Jewell (37, Canada)
Martha Mary, b. 10/28/1955 in Hanover; first; Lon J. Pike (road work, Lyme) and Susan J. Waterbury (Norwalk, CT)
Michael Earl, b. 8/30/1959 in Hanover; Horace E. Pike (lumberman, 39, Lyme) and Maxine L. Heath (33, Littleton)
Nellie, b. 9/2/1892; fourth; Fred L. Pike (laborer, 33, Lyme) and Anna B. Roberts (24, Lyme)
Patricia Anne, b. 7/10/1951 in Haverhill; fifth; Horace E. Pike (laborer, 30, Lyme) and Maxine Heath (24, Littleton)
Peggy Ellen, b. 10/28/1962 in Lebanon; Lon J. Pike (laborer, Lyme)

and Susan J. Waterbury (32, Norwalk, CT)
Rachel, b. 7/9/1914; second; Carlton E. Pike (teacher, 37, Boston, MA) and Blanch Pushee (23, Lyme); residence - Stonington, CT
Ralph Charles, b. 6/18/1942 in Hanover; first; Charles C. Pike (farmer, 21, Lyme) and Betty C. Schwotzer (19, Manchester)
Roberta Kathryn, b. 3/4/1959 in Hanover; Earl F. Pike (woodsman, 27, Lyme) and Janet E. Bradley (20, MA)
Sally Jane, b. 8/9/1948 in Lebanon; second; Herbert E. Pike (lumberman, 22, Lyme) and Jessie J. Storms (19, Antwerp, Belgium)
Sharon Marie, b. 7/10/1953 in Hanover; Horace E. Pike (lumberman, 32, Lyme) and Maxine Heath (26, Littleton)
Tami Marie, b. 6/29/1966 in Lebanon; second; Allie Wayne Pike (farmer, Lyme) and Roberta A. Estes (Hanover)
Weymouth Henry, b. 2/21/1928 in Lyme; seventh; Earl H. Pike (laborer, 29, Lyme) and Myrtle Coates (Cornhill, NB)
William C., b. 2/11/1937 in Lyme; first; Verne Hobbs (garage, 39, Lyme) and Carrie Pike (39, Lyme)

PINDELL,
Gabriella Mia, b. 9/6/1992 in Ft. Worth, TX; James Pindell and Alison Hobbs

PIPER,
son, b. 9/11/1890; third; Walter G. Piper (carpenter, 31, Pembroke) and Hattie E. Esty (Troy, VT)
Allen E., b. 11/14/1894 in Lyme; fourth; Walter G. Piper (lumber mfr., 35, Lyme) and Hattie E. Estey (28, Lyme)
Anna Maria, b. 12/6/1949 in Lebanon; John D. Piper and Fedorka Kurelmeyer
Arthur H., b. 10/4/1936 in Lyme; fifth; William C. Piper (laborer, 40, Chicago, IL) and Dorothy B. Henry (28, Lyme)
Beryl Ruth, b. 1/15/1915; first; Allen E. Piper (farmer, 20, Lyme) and Nina R. Wing (19, Lyme)
Devey Allen, b. 2/9/1940 in Hanover; second; Walter J. Piper (carpenter, 23, Lyme) and Vivian M. Gregory (21, Hanover)
Ellen Edna, b. 1/2/1946 in Hanover; fourth; Walter J. Piper (farmer, 28, Lyme) and Vivian M. Gregory (26, Hanover)
Gerald Walter, b. 9/23/1887; second; Walter G. Piper (carpenter, 28, Pembroke) and Hattie E. Piper (21, Troy, VT)

Herman Dean, b. 9/20/1933 in Lyme; third; William C. Piper (laborer, 38, Chicago, IL) and Dorothy R. Henry (25, Lyme)

James Mason, b. 10/26/1970 in Lebanon; William C. Piper and Beverly M. Balch

Janet, d. 12/23/1919 in Lyme; second; Frank A. Piper (teamster, 28, Orford) and Vivian F. French (25, Orford)

John Devy, b. 5/13/1919 in Lyme; second; Lee W. Piper (carpenter, 29, Lyme) and Annie K. Thompson (26, S. Ham, PQ)

John Patrick, b. 12/16/1978 in Hanover; William R. Piper and Janet L. Pease

Katherine Mildred, b. 4/5/1948 in Hanover; fifth; Walter J. Piper (laborer, 32, Lyme) and Vivian Gregory (29, Hanover)

Kyle Thomas, b. 8/18/1992 in Lebanon; Neil Piper and Ann Reynolds

Linda Vivian, b. 10/15/1941 in Hanover; third; Walter J. Piper (laborer, 26, Lyme) and Vivian M. Gregory (23, Hanover)

Lisa Maureen, b. 11/28/1967 in Hanover; first; Devey A. Piper (laborer, Lyme) and Beverly M. Hickey (Rumford, ME)

Olive Kay, b. 4/23/1970 in Hanover; Devey A. Piper and Beverly M. Hickey

Pamela Jane, b. 8/31/1953 in Hanover; William C. Piper (laborer, 22, Lyme) and Beverly Balch (19, Piermont)

Patricia Lee, b. 9/7/1953 in Lebanon; John Piper (carpenter, 34, Lyme) and Fedorka Kurelmeyer (24, St. Louis, MO)

Patty Dolores, b. 5/8/1959 in Lyme; William C. Piper (farm laborer, 27, Lyme) and Beverly Balch (25, Piermont)

Rebecca Joyce, b. 12/24/1938 in Hanover; first; Walter J. Piper (laborer, 23, Lyme) and Vivian M. Gregory (20, Hanover)

Ronald A., b. 4/8/1935 in Hanover; fourth; William C. Piper (farmer, 39, Chicago, IL) and Dorothy B. Henry (26, Lyme)

Virginia, b. 8/20/1917; first; Frank A. Piper (farming, 26, Orford) and Vivian F. French (23, Orford)

Walter Joseph, b. 11/11/1915; first; Lee W. Piper (carpenter, 25, Lyme) and Annie K. Thompson (23, S. Ham, PQ)

William Converse, b. 8/8/1931 in Lyme; second; William C. Piper (laborer, 38, Chicago, IL) and Dorothy B. Henry (22, Lyme)

William Reginald, b. 12/2/1955 in Lebanon; second; William C. Piper (laborer, Lyme) and Beverly Balch (Piermont)

PIPPIN,
Caitlyn Emily, b. 5/4/1994 in Lebanon; Richard Pippin, Jr. and

Tammy Bailey
Molly Elizabeth, b. 4/12/1996 in Lebanon; Richard Anthony Pippin, Jr. and Tammy Bailey
Richard Anthony, b. 5/19/2001 in Lebanon; Richard Pippin and Tammy Pippin

POND,
Richard Charles, Jr., b. 10/19/1947 in Hanover; first; Richard C. Pond (clerk, 23, Lunenburg, VT) and Charlotte Cowles (25, Lunenburg, VT)
Stuart Gordon, b. 1/10/1955 in Lebanon; second; Richard C. Pond, Sr. (merchant, Lunenburg, VT) and Charlotte Cowles (Lunenburg, VT)

POULTER,
Thaddeus Kendric, b. 2/9/1976 in Lebanon; William Douglas Poulter and Patricia H. Hodgkin

PRATT,
Irene Ann, b. 2/21/1939 in Haverhill; seventh; Joseph A. M. Pratt (weaver, 32, Lebanon) and Emma M. B. Tremblay (27, Lebanon)

PRESCOTT,
daughter, b. 5/23/1893 in Lyme; first; Joseph Prescott (laborer) and Flo– —an (30, Vershire, VT)
daughter, b. 10/13/1920 in Lyme; third; Earle N. Prescott (laborer, 21, Bradford, VT) and Viola Hutchinson (23, Lisbon)

PUSHEE,
daughter, b. 3/7/1891; fourth; Clarence S. Pushee (farmer, 42, Lyme) and Fannie C. Post (30, Lyme)
stillborn son, b. 6/15/1896 in Lyme; first; George A. Pushee (farmer, 20, Lyme) and Emma B. Cline (22, Manchester)
stillborn daughter, b. 5/14/1898; second; George A. Pushee (farmer, 22, Lyme) and Emma B. Cline (25, Manchester)
stillborn daughter, b. 5/14/1898; third; George A. Pushee (farmer, 22, Lyme) and Emma B. Cline (25, Manchester)
son, b. 8/5/1909 in Lyme; sixth; David J. Pushee (farmer, 43, Lyme) and Mary M. Gilbert (37, St. Johnsbury, VT)
daughter, b. 11/20/1958 in Hanover; Donald E. Pushee (carpenter,

29, Hanover) and Mabel C. O'Donnell (29, Vershire, VT)
Albert William, b. 6/16/1927 in Hanover; fourth; Harris A. Pushee (mechanic, 35, Lyme) and Inez Clark (35, Plainfield)
Alfred Max, b. 7/19/1902; first; George A. Pushee (farmer, 26, Lyme) and Mabel Agnez Gilbert (25, Lyme)
Arnold George, b. 12/11/1953 in Lebanon; Albert Pushee (bookkeeper, 26, NH) and Minnie Small (22, NH)
Augusta F., b. 8/16/1907 in Lyme; fifth; David J. Pushee (farmer, 41, Lyme) and Mary M. Gilbert (35, St. Johnsbury, VT)
Barbara Jane, b. 1/11/1956 in Lebanon; Clarence L. Pushee, Jr. (painter, 17, Orford) and Hazel B. Davis (17, Lyme)
Beth Louise, b. 5/29/1910 in Lyme; third; George Alfred Pushee (farmer, 34, Lyme) and Mabel Agnes Gilbert (33, Lyme)
Blanch May, b. 10/23/1890; first; David J. Pushee (laborer, 24, Lyme) and Mary M. Gilbert (St. Johnsbury, VT)
Bruce Arthur, b. 8/24/1950 in Hanover; third; Dean Pushee (woodchopper, 29, Fairlee, VT) and Vera Movelle (30, Lyme)
Clarence Leslie, b. 3/29/1897 in Lyme; fifth; Clarence S. Pushee (farmer, 48, Lyme) and Fannie C. Post (36, Lyme)
Dale Frank, b. 6/28/1969 in Lebanon; Frank A. Pushee and Marcia L. Bedor
David J., Jr., b. 6/1/1905 in Lyme; fourth; David J. Pushee (farmer, 39, Lyme) and Mary Gilbert (33, St. Johnsbury, VT)
David Jeffers, b. 3/7/1962 in Hanover; Frank A. Pushee (carpenter, Hanover) and Marcia L. Bedor (19, Hanover)
David Miles, b. 5/12/1947 in Hanover; second; Harris C. Pushee (clerk, 28, Hanover) and Louise A. Miles (25, Hartford, CT)
Donald Elmer, b. 12/3/1927 in Hanover; first; David J. Pushee, Jr. (laborer, 22, Lyme) and Florence DeGoosh (20, Unity)
Donald Elmer, Jr., b. 9/26/1955 in Hanover; fourth; Donald E. Pushee (carpenter, Hanover) and Mabel O'Donnell (Vershire, VT)
Donna Louise, b. 1/12/1942 in Hanover; second; Roger C. Pushee (laborer, 24, Hanover) and Isabelle S. Uline (24, Lyme)
Ellen, b. 12/31/1924 in Lyme; third; Harris A. Pushee (carpenter, 32, Lyme) and Inez A. Clark (33, Plainfield)
Eric Albert, b. 1/4/1978 in Hanover; William A. Pushee and Cheryl Carpenter
Fawn Marie, b. 7/7/1960 in Lebanon; Clarence Pushee, Jr. (painter, 22, Orfordville) and Hazel B. Davis (21, Lyme)
Frank Albert, b. 8/17/1930 in Hanover; third; David J. Pushee, Jr.

(farmer, 25, Lyme) and Florence DeGoosh (23, Unity)
Gladys May, b. 11/4/1915; first; Walter S. Pushee (farmer, 29, Lyme) and Addie M. Langmaid (17, Lyme)
Harris Albert, b. 4/10/1892; second; David J. Pushee (laborer, 26, Lyme) and Mary M. Gilbert (20, St. Johnsbury, VT)
Harris Clark, b. 7/17/1918 in Hanover; first; Harris A. Pushee (carpenter, 26, Lyme) and Inez A. Clark (26, Plainfield)
Ian Harris, b. 8/23/1978 in Lebanon; Wayne A. Pushee and Faith Kimball
Irene Dorothy, b. 7/26/1939 in Lyme; seventh; David J. Pushee, Jr. (farmer, 34, Lyme) and Florence B. DeGoosh (32, Lyme)
James Alfred, b. 3/23/1954 in Lyme; fifth; Dean S. Pushee (lumberman, 34, Fairlee, VT) and Vera A. Movelle (35, Lyme)
Jean, b. 3/5/1934 in Lyme; fifth; David J. Pushee, Jr. (laborer, 29, Lyme) and Florence B. DeGoosh (26, Unity)
Jean Marie, b. 2/23/1953 in Hanover; Dean S. Pushee (lumberman, 31, Fairlee, VT) and Vera A. Movelle (32, Lyme)
Jessie George, b. 7/23/1922 in Hanover; fourth; George A. Pushee (farmer, 46, Lyme) and M. Agnes Gilbert (45, Lyme)
Joan, b. 11/5/1932 in Lyme; fourth; David J. Pushee, Jr. (laborer, 27, Lyme) and Florence B. DeGoosh (25, Unity)
Judith Ann, b. 10/12/1958 in Lebanon; Dean S. Pushee (painter, 39, Fairlee, VT) and Vera A. Movelle (39, Lyme)
Julia Edna, b. 6/2/1906 in Lyme; second; George A. Pushee (farmer, 30, Lyme) and Mabel Agnes Gilbert (29, Lyme)
Julie Anne, b. 9/20/1966 in Hanover; second; Peter R. Pushee (carpenter, Hanover) and Donna L. Pike (Hanover)
Kevin Arnold, b. 10/19/1981 in Hanover; Wayne A. Pushee and Faith C. Kimball
Lucinda Lee, b. 8/22/1959 in Lebanon; Frank A. Pushee (truck driver, 29, Hanover) and Marcia L. Bedor (17, Hanover)
Mae Esther, b. 8/30/1945 in Hanover; seventh; David J. Pushee (farmer, 40, Lyme) and Florence DeGoosh (38, Unity)
Marion Viola, b. 3/6/1926 in Lyme; second; Frank A. Pushee (farmer, 50, Lyme) and Viola M. Cutting (38, Lyme)
Mary Bell, b. 4/4/1957 in Hanover; Donald E. Pushee (carpenter, Hanover) and Mabel O'Donnell (Vershire, VT)
Michael Peter, b. 7/9/1968 in Hanover; Peter R. Pushee and Donna L. Pike
Mirinda Lee, b. 8/3/1989 in Lebanon; Timothy J. Pushee and Brenda L. Ragan

Nettie Maude, b. 11/8/1893 in Lyme; third; David J. Pushee (laborer, 27, Lyme) and Mary Gilbert (21, St. Johnsbury, VT)

Paul B., b. 8/10/1939 in Hanover; second; Olyph A. Pushee (carpenter, 30, Lyme) and Doris E. Johnson (23, Thetford, VT)

Paul Ralph, b. 8/14/1944 in Hanover; third; Olyph Pushee (carpenter, 35, Lyme) and Doris E. Johnson (28, Thetford, VT)

Pauline, b. 8/15/1920 in Lyme; second; Harris A. Pushee (carpenter, 28, Lyme) and Inez Clark (28, Plainfield)

Peter Roger, b. 10/6/1944 in Hanover; third; Roger C. Pushee (US Marines, 26, Lyme) and Isabelle S. Uline (27, Lyme)

Richard W., b. 7/4/1936 in Hanover; first; Olyph A. Pushee (laborer, 26, Lyme) and Dorris Johnson (19, Thetford, VT)

Robert David, b. 9/12/1943 in Hanover; second; Olyph A. Pushee (carpenter, 34, Lyme) and Doris E. Johnson (27, Thetford, VT)

Robert Dean, b. 5/4/1947 in Lebanon; first; Dean S. Pushee (const. wkr., 26, Fairlee, VT) and Vera Movelle (27, Lyme)

Ronald Harris, b. 5/1/1943 in Hanover; first; Harris C. Pushee (US Army, 24, Hanover) and Louise A. Miles (21, Hartford, CT)

Ruth M., b. 10/19/1906 in Lyme; first; Henry S. Pushee (farmer, 28, Lyme) and Nellie J. Mativia (24, Lyme)

Sally Ann, b. 5/13/1953 in Hanover; Donald E. Pushee (carpenter, 26, Lyme) and Mabel O'Donnell (24, Vershire, VT)

Sarah Elizabeth, b. 9/25/1905 in Lyme; first; Frank A. Pushee (farmer, 30, Lyme) and Viola M. Cutting (17, Lyme)

Scott William, b. 2/13/1977 in Hanover; William Albert Pushee and Cheryl Ann Carpenter

Sharon Lee, b. 6/6/1958 in Lebanon; Clarence L. Pushee, Jr. (painter, 20, Orford) and Hazel B. Davis (19, Lyme)

Shirley Belle, b. 8/5/1929 in Hanover; second; David Pushee, Jr. (farmer, 24, Lyme) and Florence DeGoosh (22, Unity)

Shirley Marie, b. 4/12/1951 in Hanover; second; Donald Pushee (lumberman, 23, Hanover) and Mabel O'Donnell (21, Vershire, VT)

Stanley D., b. 4/15/1936 in Lyme; sixth; David J. Pushee, Jr. (farmer, 30, Lyme) and Florence B. DeGoosh (28, Unity)

Steven Bruce, b. 3/6/1965 in Hanover; first; Peter R. Pushee (carpenter, Hanover) and Donna L. Pike (Hanover)

Susan Jean, b. 6/22/1949 in Hanover; Donald E. Pushee and Mabel O'Donnell

Suzanna, b. 6/8/1946 in Hanover; fourth; Roger C. Pushee (disabled vet., 28, Hanover) and Isabelle S. Uline (29, Lyme)

Tammy Lynn, b. 11/7/1966 in Hanover; third; Frank A. Pushee (carpenter, Hanover) and Marcia L. Bedor (Hanover)

Thomas John, b. 6/1/1967 in Lebanon; fourth; Albert W. Pushee (man. bkkpng., Hanover) and Verla M. Clogston (Hanover)

Timothy James, b. 11/10/1963 in Lebanon; Albert W. Pushee (bookkeeping supv., Hanover) and Verla M. Clogston (34, Hanover)

Virginia Lee, b. 6/13/1940 in Hanover; first; Roger C. Pushee (laborer, 22, Lyme) and Isabel S. Uline (23, Lyme)

Walter S., Jr., b. 6/22/1918 in Lyme; second; Walter S. Pushee (farming, 32, Lyme) and Addie M. Langmaid (20, Lyme)

Wayne Alan, b. 5/9/1953 in Hanover; Harris C. Pushee (bank teller, 34, Hanover) and Louise A. Miles (31, Hartford, CT)

William Albert, b. 5/30/1950 in Lebanon; first; Albert Pushee (bookkeeper, 22, Hanover) and Minnie Small (19, Hanover)

William Joseph, b. 12/1/1948 in Lebanon; second; Dean S. Pushee (lumberman, 28, Fairlee, VT) and Vera A. Movelle (29, Lyme)

PUTNAM,

Constance Elizabeth, b. 3/2/1943 in Hanover; third; William F. Putnam (physician, 33, Stanford, CT) and Mildred M. Best (33, LaGrange, IL)

Craig Stewart, b. 9/12/1950 in Lyme; sixth; William F. Putnam (physician, 41, Stamford, CT) and Mildred Best (40, LaGrange, IL)

Judith Choat, b. 4/23/1940 in Hanover; second; William F. Putnam (physician, 30, Stamford, CT) and Mildred M. Best (30, LaGrange, IL)

Kendrick William, b. 8/21/1938 in Hanover; first; William F. Putnam (physician, 29, Stamford, CT) and Mildred Best (28, LaGrange, IL)

Michael Glennie, b. 5/28/1965 in Plymouth, MA; Kendrick W. Putnam and Eleanor J. G. Holmes (1969)

Ross Worcester, b. 4/13/1948 in Lyme; fifth; William F. Putnam (physician, 38, Stamford, CT) and Mildred M. Best (38, LaGrange, IL)

Spencer Cole, b. 12/11/1945 in Lyme; fourth; William F. Putnam (physician, 36, Stamford, CT) and Mildred M. Best (35, LaGrange, IL)

PUTNEY,
daughter, b. 9/13/1908 in Lyme; fourth; Eli J. Putney (mason, 38, Bridgewater) and May L. Pellerin (33, Lyme)
Pansy Isabel, b. 6/8/1913 in Lyme; sixth; Eli J. Putney (laborer, 42, Lebanon) and Mary L. Pellerin (38, Lyme)
Vera Inez, b. 3/1/1911 in Lyme; fifth; Eli J. Putney (laborer, 41, Bridgewater) and Mary L. Pellerin (36, Lyme)

RAGAN,
Brenda Lee, b. 6/2/1964 in Lebanon; Wallace E. Ragan (garage, self emp., Hanover) and Barbara Scirocco (Brooklyn, NY)
Charles Ray, b. 8/10/1961 in Lebanon; Wallace E. Ragan (mechanic, Hanover) and Barbara Scirocco (22, Brooklyn, NY)
Michaela Lynn, b. 6/19/1994 in Lebanon; Charles Ragan and Terri Truell
Pamela Carolyn Mildred, b. 8/22/1959 in Hanover; Wallace E. Ragan (mechanic, 24, Lyme) and Barbara L. Scirocco (20, Brooklyn, NY)
Wallace Elmore, b. 10/14/1934 in Hanover; first; Laurence Ragan (laborer, 24, Lebanon) and Carolyn Jackman (20, Lisbon)

RAMSDEL,
Gardiner Cassius, b. 10/18/1867 in Lyme; first; James G. Ramsdel (retired, E. Rindge) and Julia A. Carter (22, Winterport, ME); residence - Philadelphia, PA (1913)

RAMSEY,
Albert Carleton, b. 2/3/1891; second; Ulric A. Ramsey (laborer, 27, Piermont) and Ruth E. Tallman (24, Orford)
Merva Emma, b. 8/22/1889; first; Ulric A. Ramsey (laborer, Piermont) and Ruth E. Tallman (Orford)

RANDALL,
Patricia Ann, b. 3/1/1955 in Haverhill; fifth; Thomas Randall (laborer, N. Easton, MA) and Esther Lord (Boston, MA)
Robert John, b. 1/23/1954 in Haverhill; fourth; Thomas R. Randall (mill worker, 33, N. Easton, MA) and Esther Lord (32, Boston, MA)

RAY,
Vicki Ann, b. 9/30/1961 in Hanover; Robert E. Ray (grad. student,

Exeter) and Olga S. Skovron (24, Lawrence, MA)

READ,
Albert Cushing, b. 4/29/1887; third; Joseph B. Read (clergyman, 57, Dighton, MA) and Mary E. Read (40, Lyme)

REED,
Matthew Kent, b. 9/5/1973 in Lebanon; Allen G. Reed and Shirley Y. Perkins

REEVES,
Jason Otis, b. 9/6/1984 in Lebanon; William R. Reeves and Debra Rathburn
Joel Aaron, b. 11/29/1985 in Lebanon; William Reeves and Debra Rathburn

REINHARD,
James Adam Kenneth, b. 8/31/1985 in Hanover; James Reinhard and Stella Kaufmann

REYNOLDS,
Sherry Lee, b. 8/26/1944 in Lyme; second; Kenneth Reynolds (mill hand, 28, Strafford, VT) and Ruth M. Morse (18, W. Brookfield, MA); residence – Thetford, VT

RICE,
Freda Raymond, b. 6/29/1922 in Lyme; first; Freda R. Rice (loco eng., 43, Winthrop, NY) and Laura Simmons (33, Lyme); residence - Woodsville

RICH,
daughter, b. 4/14/1899; eighth; Fred Rich (farmer, 39, Groveton) and Ada S. Swift (32, Stratford)
Aaron Winslow, b. 2/26/1979 in Hanover; Brian E. Rich and Josephine Davies
Alexis Winona, b. 6/4/2000 in Lebanon; Tyler E. Rich and Rachel L. Pierson
Brian Everett, b. 6/19/1947 in Hanover; second; Everett B. Rich (merchant, 30, Lyme Ctr.) and Verna W. Simmons (25, Union, ME)
Everett Bradbury, b. 8/24/1916; second; John S. Rich (mail carrier,

N. Stratford) and Ida N. King (21, Lyme)
Jessie B., b. 12/18/1894 in Lyme; sixth; Fred Rich (farmer, 36, Groveton) and Ada F. Swift (28, Stratford)
Kaydence Lynn, b. 8/14/2004 in Lebanon; Tyler Rich and Rachel Pearson
Lena May, b. 9/22/1897 in Lyme; seventh; Fred Rich (farmer, 39, Northumberland) and Ada F. Swift (31, Stratford)
Roger King, b. 8/22/1915; first; John S. Rich (farmer, 26, Stratford) and Ida N. King (20, Lyme)
Tyler Everett, b. 12/27/1980 in Hanover; Brian E. Rich and Josephine M. Davies
Verna E., b. 1/8/1906 in Lyme; ninth; Fred Rich (farmer, 47, Northumberland) and Ada F. Swift (39, Stratford)

RICHARDSON,
son, b. 9/14/1899; fourth; Fred A. Richardson (peddler, 42, Goshen, MA) and Amy L. Cleasby (35, Bradford, VT)
Augustus Lee, b. 10/26/1897 in Lyme; third; Fred A. Richardson (laborer, 40, Goshen, MA) and Amy L. Cleasby (33, Bradford, VT)
Leona Winifred, b. 4/5/1913 in Lyme; first; Leon W. Richardson (farmer, 26, W. Fairlee, VT) and Nellie M. Bedelle (20, Danvers, MA); residence - Orford
Lisa Mae, b. 11/14/1972 in Hanover; Donald Richardson and Elizabeth Bickford

RICKER,
Jodi Ann, b. 6/14/1956 in Hanover; Lawrence R. Ricker (bulldozer op., 29, Norwich, VT) and Beverly A. Record (23, Hanover)
Lillian Sarah D'ty, b. 1/13/1912 in Lyme; third; Eugene Ricker (laborer, 40, E. Haven, VT) and Laura Towne (23, Kirby, VT)

RIOS,
Anna, b. 11/14/1946 in Hanover; fifth; Anselmo Rios (farmer, 27, Dorado, PR) and Aleja Rodriquez (26, Dorado, PR)
Anselmo, b. 12/5/1944 in Lyme; fourth; Anselmo Rios Baez (farmer, 26, Dorado, PR) and Aleja Morales (24, Dorado, PR)
Pablo, b. 1/9/1945 in Lyme; third; Anselmo Rios Baez (farmer, 25, Dorado, PR) and Aleja M. Rivera (23, Dorado, PR)

RIVES,
Vickie Sharlyn, b. 7/14/1952 in Hanover; second; Arthur Rives (US Navy, 27, Dupo, IL) and Beth Chesley (30, Lyme); res – Lyme Ctr.

ROBERTS,
daughter, b. 11/3/1890; third; Harris A. Roberts (farmer, 30, Lyme) and Emma L. Wells (Johnson, VT)
daughter, b. 8/28/1900; fifth; Thomas W. Roberts (farmer, 43, Dorchester) and Ella M. White (43, Orford)
Alfonzo, b. 6/11/1897 in Lyme; third; T. W. Roberts (farmer, 40, Dorchester) and Ella M. White (40, Orford)
Evelyn Rose, b. 12/18/1919 in Lyme; fifth; Guy A. Roberts (laborer, 31, Bradford, VT) and Jennie M. Hobart (27, Lyme)
Harry Albert, b. 10/13/1911 in Lyme; first; Guy A. Roberts (farmer, 24, Bradford, VT) and Jennie M. Hobart (20, Lyme)
Harry Albert, II, b. 7/12/1944 in Hanover; first; Harry A. Roberts (US Army, 32, Lyme) and Mary L. Morrill (33, Pike)
Jessie Lestor, b. 1/27/1918 in Lyme; fourth; Guy A. Roberts (farming, 29, Bradford, VT) and Jennie M. Hobart (27, Lyme)
John Keith, b. 1/29/1933 in Lyme; first; John P. Mara (20, Portsmouth) and Meda P. Roberts (19, Lyme)
John Philip, b. 7/23/1917; first; Cyrus L. Roberts (farming, 27, Orford) and Annabelle Beaton (20, Florence, NS)
Leroy, b. 4/28/1903 in Lyme; twelfth; Thomas W. Roberts (farmer, 46, Dorchester) and Ella White (46, Orford)
Louise Belle, b. 7/17/1891; first; Thomas W. Roberts (farmer, 34, Dorchester) and Minnie Belle Stone (17, Orford)
Meda Pauline, b. 10/4/1913 in Lyme; second; Guy A. Roberts (laborer, 26, Lyme) and Jennie M. Hobart (22, Lyme)
Ray Carroll, b. 7/3/1916; third; Guy A. Roberts (laborer, 28, Bradford, VT) and Jennie M. Hobart (24, Lyme)
Rosa L., b. 10/8/1898; fourth; Thomas W. Roberts (farmer, 41, Dorchester) and Ella M. White (41, Orford)
Thomas F., b. 5/6/1896 in Lyme; second; T. Will Roberts (farmer, 39, Dorchester) and Ella M. White (39, Orford)

ROBINSON,
Erin Margaret Ann, b. 9/15/1994 in Lebanon; Colin Robinson and Mary Louise Reynolds
Galen Christian, b. 5/17/1993 in Lebanon; Colin Robinson and Mary

Reynolds
Robert Willis, b. 2/12/1963 in Hanover; Robert A. Robinson (truck driver, Windsor, VT) and Ruby M. Hutchins (21, Hanover)

RODI,
Alice Campbell, b. 5/29/2003 in Lebanon; Scott Rodi and Emily Rodi
Elizabeth Freeman, b. 12/27/2000 in Lebanon; Scott Rodi and Emily Rodi

ROGERS,
Barbara Jane, b. 12/26/1934 in Hanover; first; Robert D. Rogers (baker, 25, Wells River, VT) and Ruth Pushee (28, Lyme)
Cora A., b. 1/2/1898; second; George R. Rogers (laborer, 23, Lone Valley, Canada) and Hattie M. McDonald (23, Peacham, VT)
Lois May, b. 8/28/1925 in Hanover; first; George G. Rogers (fur buyer, 38, Thetford, VT) and Hazel Hutchinson (19, W. Fairlee, VT)
Philip Ashley, b. 5/4/1922 in Lyme; first; Fred A. Rogers (farmer, 24, Hartland, VT) and Doris Cartee (22, Thetford, VT)
Reginald, b. 7/24/1943 in Hanover; second; Robert D. Rogers (US Army, 36, Wells River, VT) and Ruth M. Pushee (36, Lyme)

ROLLINS,
Sandra Lea, b. 4/7/1943 in Lyme; first; Leon C. Rollins (foreman, 31, Newport) and Elinor L. Cutting (19, Lyme)

RONDEAU,
Molly Jane, b. 5/27/1989 in Lebanon; David G. Rondeau and Lois Pushee
Samuel George, b. 3/11/1992 in Lebanon; David Rondeau and Lois Pushee

ROSE,
Anya, b. 1/28/1991 in Hanover; Robert J. Rose and Heidi J. Root

ROTH,
Alexander Richard, b. 5/27/2002 in Lebanon; Bryan Roth and Kristin Roth
Amelia Helene, b. 2/8/2000 in Lebanon; Bryan Roth and Kristin Roth
James Edward, b. 5/27/2002 in Lebanon; Bryan Roth and Kristin Roth

ROUSSEAU,
Joan Edna, b. 7/7/1925 in Hanover; first; Ludovic Rousseau (laborer, 21, Franklin) and Edna L. Wheeler (19, Franklin)

ROWE,
Bertha E., b. 6/19/1903 in Lyme; first; George E. Rowe (farmer, 45, Auburn, ME) and Mary A. Mulhearn (39, Elgin, PQ)
Nathon Garrett, b. 12/24/1969 in Hanover; Garrett B. Rowe and Sandra Limlaw

ROWELL,
son, b. 2/19/1913 in Lyme; eleventh; Harry H. Rowell (laborer, 39, W. Fairlee, VT) and Maggie A. Bailey (29, Bradford, VT)
stillborn son, b. 6/24/1916; fourteenth; Harry H. Rowell (farming, 41, W. Fairlee, VT) and Marguerite A. Bailey (32, Bradford, VT)
Gladys Ethel, b. 8/19/1915; thirteenth; Harry H. Rowell (farmer, 40, W. Fairlee, VT) and Marguerite A. Bailey (31, Bradford, VT)
Rosa Hannah, b. 7/20/1914; twelfth; Harry H. Rowell (laborer, 39, W. Fairlee, VT) and Margarett A. Bailey (30, Bradford, VT)

RUSH,
Jason Rudolph, b. 5/22/2003 in Lebanon; John Rush and Hope Rush

RUSSELL,
Carrie Elizabeth, b. 4/26/1982 in Lebanon; Daniel J. Russell and Renee J. Chenard
Jennie Beth, b. 11/5/1990 in Lebanon; Daniel J. Russell and Renee Chenard

RYAN,
Corina Estelle, b. 3/16/1990 in Lebanon; R. Bret Ryan and Ellen C. Wagner
Jennifer Lynn, b. 9/17/1988 in Lebanon; R. Bret Ryan and Ellen C. Wagner
Luke Williams, b. 6/10/2002 in Lebanon; Philip Ryan and Gwendolyn Ryan

ST. JAMES,
Nastasya Leigh, b. 12/14/1980 in Hanover; Robert A. St. James and Jennifer A. Smith

Nicole Grace, b. 11/27/1981 in Hanover; Robert A. St. James and Jennifer A. Smith

Silas Matthew, b. 10/5/1984 in Hanover; Robert A. St. James and Jennifer A. Smith

Tiana Elizabeth, b. 5/24/1986 in Lebanon; Robert A. St. James and Jennifer A. Smith

SABIN,
Edward, b. 7/14/1927 in Lyme; fifth; Wilmot Sabin (mechanic, 37, NS) and Amelia Cary (27, Bridgeport, CT)

SAFFORD,
Nephi Charles, b. 9/18/1981 in Hanover; Charles R. Safford and Patricia J. Woodward

Owen Arthur, b. 6/22/1986 in Lebanon; Charles R. Safford and Patricia J. Woodward

Sariah Ruth, b. 9/5/1984 in Lebanon; Charles R. Safford and Patricia J. Woodward

SAMUELS,
Robert Thomas, b. 8/22/1971 in Hanover; Henry Samuels and Diana Olsen

SAMWICK,
Aidan Lucas, b. 1/10/2002 in Lebanon; Andrew Samwick and Maria-Teresa Samwick

SANBORN,
son, b. 5/21/1890; first; Charles A. Sanborn (carpenter, 29, Lyme) and Carrie D. Clark (Canaan)

stillborn daughter, b. 6/11/1896 in Lyme; first; Newton F. Sanborn (farmer, 28, Lyme) and Eliza Welch (22, Lyme)

Arleen Elizabeth, b. 3/6/1925 in Lyme; first; Ora R. Sanborn (laborer, 35, Orford) and Minnie Patterson (30, Woodstock); residence - Orford

Gail Harriet, b. 8/20/1943 in Lyme; third; Richard H. Sanborn (31, Bath) and Cora H. Blake (29, Plymouth)

Helen Pauline, b. 1/30/1933 in Lyme; twelfth; Otis M. Sanborn (laborer, 52, Dummer) and Grace Perkins (42, Gorham)

Lawrence, b. 8/3/1921 in Lyme; third; Cornelius Sanborn (carpenter, 30, Fairlee, VT) and Lillian Ackerman (23, St. Albans, VT)

Marcy Lynn, b. 7/5/1974 in Hanover; Robert Earle Sanborn and
   Hazel Ann Hutchins
Michelle Ann, b. 8/10/1971 in Hanover; Robert Sanborn and Hazel
   Hutchins
Neal Alden, b. 3/21/1918 in Lyme; first; C. R. Sanborn (laborer, 26,
   Fairlee, VT) and Lillian Ackerman (19, St. Albans, VT)
Philip W., b. 7/25/1937 in Lyme; second; Ralph Sanborn (laborer,
   27, Gorham) and Mildred Merrihew (23, Lebanon)
Robert Earle, b. 3/14/1943 in Hanover; first; Harry E. Sanborn
   (laborer, 28, Gorham) and Dora E. Balch (23, Lyme)
Roberta Jean, b. 12/10/1946 in Hanover; second; Harry E. Sanborn
   (foreman, 32, Gorham) and Dora E. Balch (27, Lyme)
Terrill David, b. 4/14/1946 in Lyme; fifth; Paul D. Sanborn (carpenter,
   38, Thetford, VT) and Elva M. Brown (35, Dallas, TX);
   residence – Thetford Ctr., VT
Theda M., b. 9/29/1901; second; Newton F. Sanborn (laborer, 33,
   Lyme) and Eliza Welch (27, Lyme)
Troy Heath, b. 1/23/1946 in Lyme; fourth; Richard H. Sanborn
   (machinist, 33, Bath) and Cora H. Blake (31, Plymouth);
   residence – Wentworth
William Ransom, b. 9/15/1919 in Lyme; second; Cornelius R.
   Sanborn (carpenter, 29, Fairlee, VT) and Lillian M. Ackerman
   (21, St. Albans, VT); residence - Fairlee, VT

SANDALL,
Devon Joan, b. 5/30/1994 in Lebanon; Scott Sandall and Joan
   Campbell

SANDERS,
Edward R., b. 12/10/1956 in Hanover; Richard M. Sanders (student,
   23, St. Paul, MN) and Barbara J. Rogers (21, Hanover)

SANGER,
John McGilvray, b. 8/17/1965 in Hanover; first; Joseph W. Sanger
   (grad. student, New York, NY) and Jean M. McGilvray (New
   York, NY)

SANSBURY,
Gail Margaret, b. 2/13/1948 in Lebanon; third; John W. Sansbury
   (chef, 42, Daleville, AL) and Dorothy M. Gregory (32, Lyme)
Jeanne Rosa, b. 7/13/1940 in Hanover; first; John W. Sansbury

(chef, 35, Dalaville, AL) and Dorothy M. Gregory (25, Lyme)

SARGENT,
Tonya Jean, b. 8/12/1979 in Hanover; Lawrence Sargent and Lois Horton

SAUNDERS,
Olivia Erica, b. 7/9/1986 in Hanover; James F. G. Saunders and Eileen Moynihan
Shannon Elizabeth, b. 1/19/1990 in Hanover; James F. Saunders and Eileen Moynihan

SCHAUER,
Roy William, b. 9/23/1970 in Lebanon; Laverne H. Schauer, Jr. and Regenna A. Day

SCHIFFMAN,
Eva Sage, b. 2/7/2002 in Lebanon; Mark Schiffman and Jennifer Schiffman
Zane David, b. 8/27/2004 in Lebanon; Mark Schiffman and Jennifer Schiffman

SCHLENKER,
Lela Sylvia, b. 7/23/1986 in Hanover; Thomas C. Schlenker and Constance E. Filbin
Skyler Christian, b. 1/6/1990 in Lebanon; Thomas C. Schlenker and Constance Filibin

SCHNEIDER,
Emma Marie, b. 7/5/1997 in Lebanon; Donald Scott Schneider and Miriam Guadalupe Colon

SCHWEER,
Donald James, b. 1/20/1929 in Lyme; fourth; Robert H. Schweer (farmer, 37, Bloomfield, NJ) and Jennie Copperwhite (40, Newark, NJ)
Howard William, b. 2/12/1924 in Lyme; fourth; Robert H. Schweer (farmer, 31, Broomfield, NJ) and Jennie Cooperwhite (35, Newark, NJ)
Mortin Edward, b. 3/25/1926 in Lyme; third; Robert H. Schweer (farmer, 34, Bloomfield, NJ) and Jennie Cooperwhite (37,

Newark, NJ)
Weymouth George, b. 4/5/1931 in Lyme; fifth; Robert H. Schweer (farmer, 39, Bromfield, VT) and Jennie Cooperwhite (42, Newark, NJ)

SCRUGGS,
Alaina Jane, b. 2/6/2002 in Lebanon; Michael Scruggs and Hilary Scruggs

SEACE,
Russell Chester, Jr., b. 3/18/1970 in Hanover; Russell Seace and Carol Lee Noury

SEIBERT,
Kirsten Ann, b. 2/27/1962 in Hanover; Dean J. Seibert (physician, Hartford, CT) and Ann Strunk (28, Jamestown, NY)

SEMPREBON,
Andrew Paul, b. 3/28/1961 in Hanover; Louis Sembrebon (eng. research, Barre, VT) and Ann Messinger (27, Los Angeles, CA)

SHATTUCK,
George Henry, b. 5/31/1905 in Lyme; first; Warren J. Shattuck (farmer, 43, Hanover) and Ada Emma Muzzey (36, Orford)
Madelyn Jean, b. 12/25/1979 in Lebanon; George Shattuck and Cathlene Webster

SHAW,
Alayne E., b. 5/6/1935 in Lyme; third; Norman E. Shaw (farmer, 31, St. Johnsbury, VT) and Ara Wentworth (29, Lunenburg, VT)
Thelma Joy, b. 3/18/1932 in Lyme; second; Norman Shaw (farmer, 28, St. Johnsbury, VT) and Ara Wentworth (28, Lunenburg)

SHEPARD,
Emily Pearl, b. 8/23/1998 in Lebanon; Curtis J. Shepard and Caryn A. Crump

SILLOWAY,
Una Grace, b. 9/6/1920 in Lyme; second; Mark Silloway (laborer, 33, Fairlee, VT) and Grace Follansbee (33, Hartland, VT)

SIMMONS,
Carrie E., b. 9/16/1894 in Lyme; fourth; Auburn L. Simmons (farmer, 34, Lyme) and May B. Clement (29, Benton)
Fairie E., b. 9/16/1894 in Lyme; fifth; Auburn L. Simmons (farmer, 34, Lyme) and May B. Clement (29, Benton)

SIMONDS,
Benjamin Woodward, b. 4/24/1987 in Hanover; Spencer W. Simonds and Debra Astles

SIMPSON,
Marguerite Lois, b. 6/22/1931 in Lyme; first; Sheldon Simpson (farm hand, 17, Corinth, VT) and Evelyn Mather (17, Brushton, NY)

SKINNER,
stillborn son, b. 11/7/1887; fourth; Brewster P. Skinner (farmer, 36, Lyme) and Carrie P. Skinner (25, Plymouth)
daughter, b. 11/4/1890; sixth; Brewster P. Skinner (farmer, 39, Lyme) and Carrie B. Farnam (Plymouth)
stillborn son, b. 7/24/1897 in Lyme; ninth; Brewster P. Skinner (laborer, 46, Lyme) and Carrie P. Farnham (35, Plymouth)
Anna L., b. 5/16/1893 in Lyme; seventh; Brewster P. Skinner (laborer, 43, Lyme) and Carrie P. Farnham (41, Plymouth)
Fannie Bell, b. 12/12/1888; fifth; Brewster P. Skinner (farmer, 37, Lyme) and Carrie P. Farnham (26, Plymouth)
Harold G., b. 3/7/1900; second; Grant G. Skinner (merchant, 34, Lowell, VT) and Jennie A. Corley (34, Craftsbury, VT)
Nellie L., b. 10/15/1894 in Lyme; eighth; Brewster P. Skinner (laborer, 43, Lyme) and Carrie P. Farnham (32, Plymouth)
Theda I., b. 8/5/1896 in Lyme; first; Grant G. Skinner (storekeeper, 31, Lowell, VT) and Jennie A. Carlie (31, Craftsbury, VT)

SLACK,
Genevieve Gertrude, b. 2/10/1925 in Hanover; second; James P. Slack (laborer, 23, Boston, MA) and Gertrude I. Braley (20, Antrim)
Leola Alice, b. 12/11/1923 in Lyme; first; James P. Slack (laborer, 22, Boston, MA) and Gertrude Braley (19, Antrim)

SMALL,
son, b. 7/17/1909 in Lyme; sixth; Duane Walter Small (miller, 37,

Brownsville, VT) and Lucy Minnetta Lobdell (37, Pierrepont, NY)
son, b. 6/1/1935 in Lyme; third; Harry Small (laborer, 25, Lyme) and Daisy B. Melendy (23, W. Fairlee, VT)
Duane Walker, b. 4/1/1933 in Lyme; second; Ralph D. Small (miller, 32, Cornish) and Ida Young (32, Burke, NY)
Eugene Scott, b. 2/18/1964 in Lebanon; Duane W. Small (laborer, Lyme) and Alice R. Clark (28, Lyme)
Evelyn M., b. 3/3/1937 in Etna; fourth; Harry Small (truck driver, 27, Lyme) and Daisy Melendy (24, W. Fairlee, VT)
Jean Marion, b. 12/2/1925 in Lyme; first; Ralph D. Small (grain dealer, 25, Cornish) and Ida V. Young (25, Burke, NY)
Jeffrey Arnold, b. 9/18/1960 in Lebanon; Duane Small (laborer, 27, Lyme) and Alice R. Clark (25, Lyme)
Kenneth Clayton, b. 2/9/1943 in Lebanon; seventh; Harry A. Small (fireman, 38, Lyme) and Daisy B. Melendy (30, Fairlee, VT)
Larry John, b. 11/6/1941 in Lebanon; sixth; Harry A. Small (truck driver, 32, Lyme) and Daisy B. Melendy (29, Fairlee, VT)
Mary Jane, b. 11/28/1946 in Lebanon; eighth; Harry Small (carpenter, 37, Lyme) and Daisy Melendy (34, W. Fairlee, VT)
Minnie Alberta, b. 5/19/1931 in Lyme; first; Harry A. Small (laborer, 21, Lyme) and Daisy B. Mellendy (19, W. Fairlee, VT)
Nancy Carol, b. 12/23/1949 in Lyme; Harry A. Small and Daisy Melendy
Reta Belle, b. 5/15/1934 in Lyme; second; Harry A. Small (laborer, 24, Lyme) and Daisy B. Melendy (22, W. Fairlee, VT)
Richard J., b. 9/26/1939 in Lebanon; fifth; Harry A. Small (trucking, 30, Lyme) and Daisy B. Melendy (27, W. Fairlee, VT)
Robert George, b. 9/6/1952 in Lyme; tenth; Harry Small (carpenter, 43, Lyme) and Daisy Melendy (40, W. Fairlee, VT)
Wesley Lee, b. 12/2/1970 in Lebanon; Duane W. Small and Alice R. Clark

SMALLIDGE,
Emelia Ann, b. 1/1/1982 in Lebanon; Peter D. Smallidge and Elisabeth R. Cole
Rebecca Grace, b. 8/30/1985 in Lebanon; Peter Smallidge and Elisabeth Cole
Samuel Cole, b. 9/6/1983 in Lebanon; Peter D. Smallidge and Elisabeth R. Cole

SMARSIK,
Samantha Marion, b. 1/7/1989 in Lebanon; Richard D. Smarsik and Janice Chapman

SMILEY,
Carlton Carlisle, b. 8/20/1933 in Lyme; second; James A. Smiley (truck driver, 27, St. Augustine, FL) and Ethel A. Temple (21, Lyme); residence - Hastings, FL

SMITH,
daughter, b. 6/23/1895 in Lyme; first; George B. Smith (hotel keeper, 31, Littleton) and Fannie M. Pelton (26, Lyme)
stillborn son, b. 2/5/1897 in Lyme; third; Charles S. Smith (laborer, 22, Corinth, VT) and Annie R. Flanders (20, W. Fairlee, VT)
daughter, b. 6/8/1897 in Lyme; second; Carl Smith (laborer, 19, Lyme) and Rosa F. Gilbert (20, Lyme)
stillborn son, b. 10/18/1898; second; Bion Smith (mechanic, 26, Mount Vernon) and Esther M. Sanborn (22, Lyme)
daughter, b. 12/7/1908 in Lyme; fourth; C. Alonzo Smith (laborer, 34, Lyme) and Ida Bressett (24, Hanover)
son, b. 1/15/1911 in Lyme; fifth; Carlton P. Smith (farmer, 36, Lyme) and Ida M. Bressett (25, Hanover)
son, b. 12/20/1921 in Lyme; ninth; Carlton A. Smith (farmer, 48, Lyme) and Ida A. Bressette (37, Hanover)
Alaina Kathleen, b. 10/27/1988 in Hanover; Bruce G. Smith and Lynn R. Richmond
Albert Lee, b. 3/30/1893 in Lyme; fourth; Edgar Smith (farmer, 41, Manchester) and Clara Spaulding (32, Hancock, VT)
Barbara, b. 11/6/1932 in Lyme; fourth; Dennis C. Smith (laborer, 26, Lyme) and Margaret Billingham (23, Bradford, VT)
Benjamin W., b. 3/16/1904 in Lyme; first; Carlton A. Smith (laborer, 30, Lyme) and Ida M. Bressett (19, Hanover)
Bessie Alice, b. 4/1/1889; third; Edgar Smith (laborer, Manchester) and Clara L. Smith (Hancock, VT)
Charles Henry, b. 5/15/1887; second; Edgar Smith (laborer, 35, Manchester) and Clara L. Smith (27, Hancock, VT)
Chauncey Austin, b. 10/20/1915; sixth; Carlton A. Smith (farmer, 41, Lyme) and Ida M. Bressett (31, Hanover)
Clayton, b. 5/8/1895 in Lyme; fifth; Scott Smith (laborer, 34, Holderness) and Minnie D. Delno (25, Montreal, Canada)
Daisy Rose, b. 2/23/1917; seventh; Carlton A. Smith (farming, 42,

Lyme) and Ida M. Bressett (32, Hanover)
Dennie C., Jr., b. 1/14/1935 in Lyme; fifth; Dennie C. Smith (laborer, 29, Lyme) and Margaret E. Billingham (27, Bradford, VT)
Dennis C., b. 10/7/1906 in Lyme; third; Carlton A. Smith (farmer, 33, Lyme) and Ida M. Bressett (22, Hanover)
Dorothy, b. 11/26/1930 in Lyme; third; Dennie C. Smith (farmer, 24, Lyme) and Marg'te Billingham (21, Bradford, VT)
Earl Milton, b. 11/19/1898; first; Ezra M. Smith (butcher, 26, Hanover) and Bertha M. Flint (20, Lyme)
Eathan Allen, b. 6/3/1894 in Lyme; first; Byron R. Smith (22, Amherst) and Esther M. Sanborn (18, Lyme); residence - New Boston
Freda G., b. 8/17/1904 in Lyme; third; Ezra M. Smith (butcher, 32, Hanover) and Bertha M. Flint (26, Lyme)
Helen Sun, b. 10/7/1928 in Hanover; second; Dennie Smith (woodsman, 22, Lyme) and Margaret Bellingham (19, Bradford, VT)
Ian MacIntyre, b. 8/29/1986 in Hanover; Bruce G. Smith and Lynn R. Richmond
Katie C., b. 5/8/1895 in Lyme; fourth; Scott Smith (laborer, 34, Holderness) and Minnie D. Delno (25, Montreal, Canada)
Leon Albert, b. 5/27/1912 in Lyme; first; Robert L. Smith (farmer, 21, Sullivan) and Inez M. Porter (20, Alstead)
Leon Earl, b. 10/14/1928 in Lyme; second; Joel Smith (laborer, 27, Orford) and Elizabeth Howe (21, Cornish Flat)
Lonnie S., b. 12/19/1939 in Lyme; fifth; Joel C. Smith (farmer, 38, Orford) and Elizabeth J. Howe (32, Cornish)
Madeline M., b. 3/19/1927 in Hanover; first; Dennie C. Smith (farmer, 21, Lyme) and Marguerite Billingham (17, Bradford, VT)
Mitchel Robert, b. 11/14/1943 in Hanover; first; Robert A. Smith (US Army, 21, Quebec) and Marion D. Chesley (19, Lyme)
Pansie Hattie, b. 2/23/1920 in Lyme; eighth; Carlton A. Smith (farmer, 46, Lyme) and Ida M. Bressett (35, Hanover)
Robert Freeman, b. 9/24/1938 in Lyme; fifth; Carlton A. Smith, Jr. (farmer, 31, Rumney) and Theda M. Sanborn (34, Lyme)
Stanley Richard, b. 7/7/1927 in Lyme; first; Benjamin W. Smith (laborer, 23, Lyme) and Josephine Dennis (16, Lyme); residence - Lebanon
Verna Louise, b. 4/2/1929 in Lyme; second; Benjamin W. Smith (laborer, 24, Lyme) and Josephine M. Dennis (18, Lyme)

Walter Francis, b. 10/22/1902; second; Ezra M. Smith (laborer, 31, Hanover) and Bertha M. Flint (24, Lyme)

SNELLING,
Brenda Lee, b. 10/23/1949 in Lebanon; second; Wilbur Snelling (farmer, 23, Sheffield, VT) and Lorraine LaTouche (19, Island Pond, VT) (1950)
Chelsea Lynn, b. 11/24/1987 in Lebanon; Jeffrey B. Snelling and Deborah Raynes
Elijah Soll, b. 12/8/1998 in Lebanon; Kenneth Byron Snelling and Stephanie Carver
Hope Renee, b. 8/29/1968 in Hanover; Kenneth Snelling and Beverly A. Gray
Isaiah Carver, b. 3/13/1996 in Lebanon; Kenneth Snelling and Stephanie Carver
Jeffrey Byron, Jr., b. 11/20/1990 in Lebanon; Jeffrey B. Snelling and Deborah A. Raynes
Randy Bryant, b. 4/12/1996 in Lebanon; Jeffrey Snelling and Deborah Raynes

SNITKO,
Walter Joseph, b. 8/1/1950 in Lebanon; fourth; Theodore Snitko (meat cutter, 27, Berlin) and Margaret Fitzgerald (33, E. Jaffrey)

SOPER,
Ila E., b. 8/6/1901; second; A. A. Soper (farmer, 43, Marblehead, MA) and Alice M. Morey (23, Lyme)
Iris May, b. 2/24/1896 in Lyme; first; Ambrose A. Soper (laborer, 35, Danvers, MA) and Alice M. Morey (18, Lyme)

SOUTHWORTH,
Gary Alan, b. 5/17/1975 in Lebanon; Howard E. Southworth, Jr. and Linda B. O'Donnell
Howard Earl, Jr., b. 10/9/1952 in Haverhill; first; Howard Southworth (20, W. Fairlee, VT) and Dorothy Drew (19, Charlestown)
Mara G., b. 5/7/1999 in Lebanon; Gary Southworth and Lisa Southworth
Sarah Joan, b. 9/21/1981 in Lebanon; Howard E. Southworth and Linda B. O'Donnell
Steven Earl, b. 6/16/1978 in Lebanon; Howard E. Southworth and Linda B. O'Donnell

SPITZ,
Ruby Kathryn Brown, b. 8/16/1999 in Lebanon; Gregory Spitz and Audrey Brown

SPLINE,
Isabel Lilla, b. 6/6/1905 in Lyme; first; Claude J. Spline (shoemaker, 21, Canada) and Amelia M. Brown (19, Canada)

SPRAGUE,
Dale Robert, b. 6/26/1952 in Lebanon; second; Harry Sprague (truck driver, 38, Lincoln, VT) and Barbara Hood (20, Haverhill)
Lucinda Mae, b. 5/3/1955 in Lyme; second; Harry Sprague (truck driver, Lincoln, VT) and Barbara M. Hood (Piermont)

STARK,
daughter, b. 1/7/1901; first; John L. Stark (teamster, 46, Lyme) and Edna L. Dike (34, Lyme)
son, b. 1/9/1901; sixth; George E. Stark (laborer, 34, Lyme) and Alice M. Chaffee (31, Newport)
son, b. 4/29/1903 in Lyme; seventh; George E. Stark (farmer, 37, Lyme) and Alice M. Chaffee (34, Newport)
stillborn son, b. 6/17/1908 in Lyme; ninth; George C. Stark (laborer, 41, Lyme) and Alice M. Chaffee (39, Newport)
son, b. 6/2/1909 in Lyme; tenth; George Eprihum Stark (farmer, 41, Lyme) and Alice Martha Chaffee (39, Newport)
Chester A., b. 10/27/1904 in Lyme; eighth; George E. Stark (farmer, 37, Lyme) and Alice M. Chaffee (34, Newport) (see following entry)
Chester Anson, b. 10/27/1904 in Lyme; eighth; George E. Stark (farmer, Lyme) and Alice M. Chaffin (Newport) (1967) (see preceding entry)
Dorris Belle, b. 10/18/1902; first; Loren G. Stark (laborer, 22, Lyme) and Florence A. Dike (20, Lyme)
Herald, b. 7/9/1897 in Lyme; second; Lillian May Stark (23, Lyme)
Marion E., b. 11/7/1896 in Lyme; fourth; George E. Stark (farmer, 30, Lyme) and Alice M. Chaffin (27, Newport)
Maude Alice, b. 4/16/1894 in Lyme; third; George E. Stark (farmer, 27, Lyme) and Alice M. Chaffin (24, Newport)
Reginald Chester, b. 1/19/1928 in Lyme; first; Chester A. Stark (farmer, 23, Lyme) and Margaret Bliss (19, Danbury)
Verne C., b. 3/10/1895 in Lyme; first; Clarence E. Burnham (Lyme)

and Lilla May Stark (23, Lyme)
Walter E., b. 5/15/1899; fifth; George E. Stark (farmer, 33, Lyme) and Alice M. Chaffin (30, Newport)
Wendell Anderson, b. 3/8/1930 in Lyme; second; Chester A. Stark (farmer, 24, Lyme) and Margaret L. Bliss (21, Danbury) (see following entry)
Wendell Anson, b. 3/8/1930 in Lyme; second; Chester A. Stark (laborer, Lyme) and Margaret L. Bliss (Danbury) (1967) (see preceding entry)

STEARNS,
Benjamin Russell, b. 8/10/1992 in San Antonio, TX; Russell Stearns and Diane Berard
Brent Ernest, b. 7/30/1971 in Lebanon; Reginald Stearns and Pauline LaDeau
Candace Lynn, b. 1/12/1981 in Hanover; Denzil C. Stearns and Wendy M. Guerin
Cassandra Jean, b. 3/7/1983 in Hanover; Denzil C. Stearns and Wendy M. Guerin
Crystal Gail, b. 3/6/1982 in Hanover; Denzil C. Stearns and Wendy M. Guerin
Daisy Lynn, b. 1/17/1977 in Hanover; Fred Stearns III and Elizabeth G. Sunn
David Richard, b. 6/17/1949 in Lebanon; Fred O. Stearns, Jr. and Edna Hutchins
Denzil Charles, b. 11/19/1958 in Hanover; Fred O. Stearns, Jr. (trucker, 29, Lebanon) and Edna R. Hutchins (28, E. Pepperill, MA)
Doris Lillian, b. 4/12/1979 in Hanover; Fred Stearns III and Elizabeth Sunn
Elaine Fern, b. 1/4/1968 in Hanover; Fred Stearns and Edna R. Hutchins
Fabienne Inez, b. 9/17/1983 in Hanover; Fred O. Stearns III and Elizabeth G. Sunn
Fred Orren, III, b. 12/19/1956 in Hanover; Fred O. Stearns, Jr. (truck driver, 27, Lebanon) and Edna R. Hutchins (26, E. Pepperell, MA)
Raymond Alonzo, b. 4/3/1971 in Hanover; David Stearns and Anah M. Race
Reginald E., b. 7/15/1940 in Lyme; thirteenth; Fred O. Stearns (teamster, 40, Plainfield) and Doris L. Hazelton (38, Bristol)

Rita Mae, b. 8/12/1955 in Haverhill; second; Eli R. Stearns (lumberman, Etna) and Ramona LaDeau (Fairlee, VT)

Russell Ralph, b. 2/15/1965 in Hanover; sixth; Fred O. Stearns, Jr. (truck driver, Lebanon) and Edna R. Hutchins (E. Pepperell, MA)

Ruth Ann, b. 7/9/1953 in Hanover; Fred Stearns, Jr. (truck driver, 24, Lebanon) and Edna Hutchins (22, E. Pepperell, MA)

STEPHENSON,

Walter Clarke, b. 1/19/1983 in Hanover; William Stephenson and Polly Clarke

STETSON,

daughter, b. 6/15/1887; third; Charles F. Stetson (farmer, 30, Lyme) and Hattie E. Stetson (28, Lyme)

STEVENS,

son, b. 5/8/1892; first; Henry E. Stevens (27, Ludlow, VT) and Ida J. Rash (25, Piermont)

Daniel Fred, b. 2/17/1946 in Lyme; first; Fred H. Stevens (mechanic, 29, E. Charleston, VT) and Dorothy C. Hilt (20, Lewiston, ME)

Ira H., Jr., b. 1/16/1939 in Hanover; first; Ira H. Stevens (steam fitter, 24, Newport, VT) and Eleanor F. Swasey (21, Hartford, VT)

James H. M., b. 4/23/1895 in Lyme; first; James T. M. Stevens (minister, 26, Wilkes-Barre, PA) and Flora B. Hadlock (19, Lyme); residence - Coventry, VT

Laura Mabel, b. 5/27/1946 in Lyme; fourth; William H. Stevens (carpenter, 36, Conway Ctr.) and Melba E. Martin (38, Groveton)

Mildred Sadie, b. 7/10/1908 in Lyme; third; George M. Stevens (farmer, 37, Fryeburg, ME) and Etta B. Allen (37, Gilmanton)

Sarah Lois, b. 6/26/1934 in Gorham; first; William H. Stevens (pulp worker, 24, Conway Ctr.) and Melba E. Martin (26, Gorham)

Stanley Walter G., b. 12/20/1948 in Lebanon; second; Fred H. Stevens (laborer, 32, E. Charlestown, VT) and Dorothy C. Hilt (23, Lewiston, ME)

STICKNEY,

stillborn daughter, b. 5/29/1889; first; Charles L. Stickney (farmer, Westford, VT) and Inez L. Hadlock (Monroe)

Thelma P., b. 6/6/1896 in Lyme; eighth; Charles L. Stickney (laborer,

49, Westford, VT) and Inez L. Hadlock (31, Monroe)
Willa Dale, b. 11/12/1897 in Lyme; ninth; Charles L. Stickney (laborer, 49, Westford, VT) and Inez L. Hadlock (32, Monroe)
Winthrop, b. 2/13/1893 in Lyme; fifth; Charles L. Stickney (laborer, 44, Westfield, VT) and Inez L. Hadlock (29, Bath)

STILL,
daughter, b. 3/30/1908 in Lyme; third; Charles E. Still (carpenter, 28, Newport) and Maggie M. Shea (32, Manchester)
son, b. 9/15/1909 in Lyme; first; Grover C. Still (farmer, 23, Claremont) and Bessie E. Judd (19, Thetford, VT)
Horace E., b., 9/17/1906 in Lyme; second; Charles E. Still (carpenter, 28, Newport) and Maggie M. Shea (29, Manchester)
Lelia May, b. 7/6/1905 in Lyme; first; Charles E. Still (farmer, 26, Newport) and Margaret M. Shea (28, Manchester); residence - Orford
Roland Victor, b. 3/5/1911 in Lyme; fourth; Charles E. Still (farmer, 31, Newport) and Maggie Shea (34, Manchester)

STRAIGHT,
Richard Edward, b. 6/26/1956 in Hanover; Robert F. Straight (farmer, 37, Providence, RI) and Genevieve Makowski (35, Douglass, MA)
Ronald Eugene, b. 5/15/1959 in Lyme; Robert F. Straight (farmer, 39, RI) and Genevieve E. Makowski (38, MA)

STRAW,
daughter, b. 6/30/1891; first; Charles L. Straw (farmer, 31, Lyme) and Emma F. Stevens (28, Thetford, VT)
Lean E., b. 9/5/1894 in Lyme; second; Charles L. Straw (farmer, 34, Lyme) and Emma F. Stevens (32, Thetford, VT)

STRENTA,
Alexander Thomas, b. 2/7/1992 in Lebanon; Angelo Strenta and Alice Feola
Stephanie Alice, b. 11/24/1988 in Hanover; Angelo C. Strenta and Alice C. Feola

STROUT,
Bonnie Jean, b. 8/28/1971 in Haverhill; James D. Strout and Ruth Fero

Francis G., b. 4/23/1939 in Lyme; first; Gerald G. Strout (laborer, 24, Alton, ME) and Elizabeth R. Wilmot (19, Lyme)
Gene Arnold, b. 2/7/1957 in Lebanon; Gerald G. Strout (fireman, Alton, ME) and Elizabeth R. Wilmot (Lyme)
Harley Nello, b. 8/18/1943 in Hanover; third; Gerald G. Strout (mill hand, 28, Alton, ME) and Elizabeth R. Wilmot (24, Lyme)
James Dale, b. 7/3/1946 in Lebanon; fifth; Gerald G. Strout (laborer, 31, Alton, ME) and Elizabeth R. Wilmot (27, Lyme)
Leslie Jackson, b. 11/11/1944 in Hanover; fourth; Gerald G. Strout (millhand, 30, Alton, ME) and Elizabeth R. Wilmot (25, Lyme)
Marion Evalyn, b. 8/3/1951 in Lyme; sixth; Gerald Strout (laborer, 36, Alton, ME) and Elizabeth Wilmot (32, Lyme)
Rose Lyndia, b. 4/19/1941 in Lyme; second; Gerald G. Strout (millhand, 26, Alton, ME) and Elizabeth Wilmot (21, Lyme)
Steven Lee, b. 11/3/1972 in Haverhill; James D. Strout and Ruth O. Pero

STRUCKHOFF,
Ian Charles, b. 7/19/1978 in Hanover; Eugene C. Struckhoff, III and Dolores Crate

STRUE,
daughter, b. 9/23/1898; first; Will E. Strue (laborer) and Cora H. Lovejoy (20, Lyme)

SULLIVAN,
Erin Elizabeth, b. 1/23/1980 in Hanover; John Sullivan and Elizabeth A. DiMaina

SUNDQUIST,
Patrick Dennis, b. 6/3/1993 in Lebanon; Thomas Sundquist and Katherine Andrada

SWART,
Scott Phillip, b. 2/17/1987 in Hanover; Peter D. Swart and Cynthia C. Supplee

SWEENEY,
John Christopher, b. 4/21/1995 in Lebanon; John Francis Sweeney and Kristen Anne Farley

SWEITZER,
Christopher, b. 5/12/1991 in Hanover; Robert J. Sweitzer and
  Elizabeth R. Hoffmeister
Melissa Anne, b. 8/17/1981 in Hanover; James R. Sweitzer and
  Karyn A. MacCaulley
Michael James, b. 3/10/1983 in Hanover; James R. Sweitzer and
  Karyn A. MacCaulley
Paul Alexander, b. 2/14/1986 in Hanover; James R. Sweitzer and
  Karyn A. MacCaulley

SYMONDS,
Lee Guy, b. 6/15/1893 in Lyme; second; Frank W. Symonds
  (laborer, 23, Boston, MA) and Harriet Henry (19, Thetford, VT)

TATTERSALL,
son, b. 9/6/1903 in Lyme; second; George E. Tattersall, Jr. (laborer,
  25, Lyme) and Hattie G. Merrill (19, Orford)
son, b. 10/11/1907 in Lyme; fourth; George E. Tattersall, Jr. (laborer,
  30, Orford) and Hattie G. Merrill (23, Orford)
daughter, b. 9/13/1926 in Lyme; fifth; George E. Tattersall (laborer,
  49, Orford) and Emily A. Mousley (31, Thetford, VT)
Albert Edward, b. 2/21/1917; second; George E. Tattersall
  (carpenter, 38, Orford) and Emily A. Mousley (21, Thetford, VT)
Emily Louise, b. 7/14/1954 in Hanover; sixth; George Tattersall
  (unemployed, 29, Lyme) and Bertha Wells (27, Littleton)
Ernest A., b. 4/3/1902; first; George E. Tattersall (laborer, 24,
  Orford) and Hattie G. Merrill (18, Orford)
Evelyn Thelma, b. 5/27/1919 in Lyme; third; George E. Tattersall
  (farming, 41, Orford) and Emily A. Mousley (24, Thetford, VT)
George Eaton, b. 9/11/1924 in Lyme; fourth; George E. Tattersall
  (laborer, 46, Orford) and Emily A. Mousley (29, Thetford, VT)
Gloria Jean, b. 12/4/1940 in Concord; sixth; Ernest A. Tattersall
  (laborer, 38, Lyme) and Evelyn M. Cox (30, Concord)
James L., b. 7/20/1939 in Concord; third; Ernest A. Tattersall
  (laborer, 36, Lyme) and Evelyn M. Cox (29, Concord)
Leona Lulu, b. 11/17/1905 in Lyme; third; George E. Tattersall, Jr.
  (laborer, 27, Orford) and Hattie E. Merrill (21, Orford)
Linda Marie, b. 1/3/1950 in Haverhill; fourth; George Tattersall, Jr.
  (laborer, 24, NH) and Bertha Wells (23, NH)
Lula May, b. 2/28/1915; first; George E. Tattersall (laborer, 36,
  Orford) and Emily A. Mousley (19, Lyme)

Marion Esther, b. 7/1/1930 in Lyme; sixth; George E. Tattersall (mechanic, 53, Orford) and Emily A. Mouseley (35, Thetford, VT)

Robert Franklin, b. 7/5/1932 in Lyme; second; Ernest Tattersall (laborer, 30, Lyme) and Evelyn Cox (22, Concord)

TAYLOR,

Emilie Anne, b. 1/9/1998 in Lebanon; Brian Allen Taylor and Holly Janette Jenks

Jessica Ann, b. 10/8/1985 in Hanover; Richard Taylor and Vickie Carson

Olivia Grace, b. 8/18/2000 in Lebanon; Brian Taylor and Holly Taylor

Susan Cooksey, b. 12/16/1986 in Hanover; John Taylor, Jr. and Christine Ann Place

TECCA,

Grace Alexander, b. 8/30/1996 in Lebanon; Mark Tecca and Martha Boyd

TEMPLE,

Ethel Amy, b. 12/19/1911 in Lyme; third; Leslie J. Temple (farmer, 40, Bakersfield, VT) and Amy L. Pushee (32, Lyme)

F. A. [female], b. 4/29/1903 in Lyme; first; Leslie J. Temple (farmer, 31, Blakesfield, VT) and Amy L. Pushee (23, Lyme)

Jennie M., b. 8/15/1907 in Lyme; second; Leslie J. Temple (farmer, 36, Bakersfield) and Amy L. Pushee (27, Lyme)

TENSEN,

Arend Jacob Balch, b. 1/14/2001 in Lebanon; Arend Tensen and Paula Balch

THAYER,

Whitney Fellows, b. 6/2/1977 in Lebanon; Jeffrey Craig Thayer and Anne Whitney Fellows

THEBODO,

John William, b. 6/20/1979 in Hanover; Robert Thebedo and Honora Garvey

Matthew Garvey, b. 9/21/1984 in Hanover; Robert E. Thebedo and Honora M. Garvey

Robert Edward, b. 10/2/1981 in Hanover; Robert E. Thebedo and

Honora M. Garvey

THOMAS,
son, b. 11/1/1889; second; Schuyler W. Thomas (engineer, Lunenburg, VT) and Luvia Bugbee (Burke, VT)
Herbert George, b. 6/4/1897 in Lyme; sixth; George W. Thomas (farmer, 47, Lyme) and Lizzie V. George (35, Knowlton)
Robert George, b. 12/25/1917; first; Herbert G. Thomas (laborer, 20, Lyme) and Lavina E. Ormsby (21, Peru, NY)
Scott Edward, b. 10/8/1888; fourth; George W. Thomas (mechanic, 38, Lyme) and Lizzie George (26, Knowlton, Canada)

THOMPSON,
Allan James, b. 4/15/1948 in Hanover; first; Charles A. Thompson (mill hand, 21, Lyme) and Ruby A. Watson (20, Newbury, VT)
Ammie Leigh, b. 3/13/1973 in Lebanon; Wayne J. Thompson and Ruth M. Hook
Arlene D., b. 3/19/1936 in Lyme; fifth; William H. Thompson (farmer, 48, Quebec) and Della E. Bryant (28, Lyme)
Arlene Ethel, b. 11/25/1924 in Lyme; third; Joseph A. Thompson (farmer, 34, S. Ham, PQ) and Grace H. Archer (34, Colebrook)
Arthur W., b. 3/19/1936 in Lyme; fourth; William H. Thompson (farmer, 48, Quebec) and Della E. Bryant (28, Lyme)
Bertha May, b. 9/27/1922 in Lyme; second; Joseph A. Thompson (farmer, 32, S. Ham, PQ) and Grace H. Archer (32, Colebrook)
Brandy Lynn, b. 7/29/1977 in Lebanon; Wayne Thompson and Ruth Marian Hook
Charles Allen, b. 8/12/1926 in Lyme; fourth; Joseph A. Thompson (farmer, 36, S. Ham, PQ) and Grace H. Archer (36, Colebrook)
Christina Anne, b. 1/1/1978 in Lebanon; Allen J. Thompson and Ellen Yurek
Daisy Evelyn, b. 1/27/1925 in Lyme; first; William H. Thompson (laborer, 37, S. Ham, PQ) and Della E. Bryant (17, Lyme)
Daniel M., b. 4/5/1905 in Lyme; eleventh; Joseph G. Thompson (farmer, 43, Southam, PQ) and Annie Mary Devey (43, Danville, PQ)
Daniel Moses, b. 8/21/1926 in Lyme; second; William H. Thompson (farmer, 38, S. Ham, PQ) and Della E. Bryant (18, Lyme)
Elizabeth Annie, b. 7/24/1930 in Lyme; third; William H. Thompson (farmer, 42, S. Ham, PQ) and Della E. Bryant (22, Lyme)
Henry Anthony, b. 3/18/1909 in Lyme; ninth; William W. Thompson

(farmer, 44, Ham, PQ) and Lilly Frances Dewey (43, Danville, PQ)
Janice W., b. 4/12/1937 in Lyme; fourth; George W. Thompson (carpenter, 41, Quebec) and Josephene Dennis (25, Lyme)
Joseph William, b. 9/3/1985 in Lebanon; Allen Thompson and Ellen Yurek
Nelson Enough, b. 3/29/1887; ninth; Henry P. Thompson (laborer, 44, Queensburg, NY) and Lucinda D. Thompson (31, Canada)
Olive Annie, b. 5/13/1918 in Lyme; first; J. A. Thompson (farming, 27, S. Ham, PQ) and Grace Archer (27, Colebrook)
Patricia A., b. 4/18/1936 in Lyme; third; George W. Thompson (carpenter, 40, Canada) and Josephine M. Dennis (24, Lyme)
Scott Allen, b. 10/4/1979 in Lebanon; Allen Thompson and Ellen Yurek
Shirley Inez, b. 2/17/1923 in Lyme; first; George P. Thompson (laborer, 27, Canada) and Doris H. Dennis (18, Lyme)
Wayne Joseph, b. 4/15/1948 in Hanover; second; Charles A. Thompson (mill hand, 21, Lyme) and Ruby A. Watson (20, Newbury, VT)

THORBURN,
Richard Michael, b. 6/16/1969 in Lyme; Alexander J. Thorburn and Carolyn C. Rauh

THORNTON,
Graeme Wheeler, b. 6/3/1990 in Lebanon; Geoffrey G. Thornton and Bonnie McCouch
Kelsea McCouch, b. 7/15/1987 in Hanover; Geoffrey G. Thornton and Bonnie M. Thornton

THURSBY,
Richard Van B., b. 8/30/1940 in Hanover; first; Irvin G. Thursby (clergyman, 26, Brooklyn, NY) and Ruth L. Hartman (27, Tyrone, PA)

THURSTON,
Carlos Humphrey, b. 1/5/1934 in Lyme; first; Lyle H. Thurston (laborer, 29, Bradford, VT) and Sibyl P. Wilmot (16, Lyme)
Christopher Carl, b. 12/29/1976 in Hanover; Weldon Palmer Thurston and Debra Lee King
Claude E., b. 3/26/1935 in Lyme; second; Lyle H. Thurston (laborer,

30, Bradford, VT) and Sibyl P. Wilmot (17, Lyme)
Cynthia Lee, b. 11/17/1958 in Woodsville; Carlos H. Thurston (mechanic, 24, Lyme) and Marvel K. Guyer (27, Vershire, VT)
Elwood E., b. 7/7/1937 in Lyme; third; Lyle Thurston (laborer, 32, Bradford, VT) and Sybil P. Wilmot (19, Lyme)
Justin Lyle, b. 9/19/1938 in Lyme; fourth; Lyle Thurston (laborer, 34, Bradford, VT) and Sibyl P. Wilmot (21, Lyme)
Kathy Marie, b. 7/1/1956 in Lyme; Carlos H. Thurston (mill worker, 22, Lyme) and Marvel K. Guyer (25, Vershire, VT)
Weldon Palmer, b. 8/25/1951 in Lebanon; first; Carlos Thurston (laborer, 17, Lyme) and Marvel Palmer (20, Vershire, VT)

TIBBITS,
Constance, b. 1/12/1978 in Hanover; Richard Tibbits and Katherine LaRocque
Doris B., b. 8/10/1936 in Lyme; second; Ralph Tibbitts (laborer, 23, VT) and Irene Maxwell (19, VT)

TILDEN,
Kathryn Sylvia, b. 7/1/1930 in Lyme; fifth; Weymouth Tilden (laborer, 26, Norwich, VT) and Helen W. Keene (25, Gardner, ME)

TODOROVICH,
James, b. 9/8/1935 in Lyme; fourth; Dewey Todorovich (showman, 22, Kansas City, MO) and Poarieh Adams (27, Shawnee, OK); residence - Kansas City, MO

TONER,
Charles Stephen, III, b. 7/17/1975 in Hanover; Charles S. Toner, Jr. and Claire E. Gallant
Travis Joseph, b. 1/7/1979 in Hanover; Charles Toner, Jr. and Claire Gallant

TOWLE,
Claire Beth, b. 3/7/1968 in Hanover; David W. Towle and Helen Ingram

TOWNSEND,
Jeffrey Peter, b. 11/11/1991 in Lyme; Charles L. Townsend and Jean Helburn
Kaitlyn Elizabeth, b. 3/27/1997 in Lebanon; Jerremy Scott Townsend

and Hilary Jane Wilcox
Lauren Katherine, b. 10/17/1999 in Lebanon; Jerremy Townsend and Hilary Wilcox Townsend

TRACY,
Anne Sheridan, b. 10/2/1993 in Lebanon; Brian Tracy and Nancee Errion

TRAVIS,
Jared Mark, b. 4/26/1974 in Hanover; Peter Warren Travis and Valerine June Mooney
Matthew Jeremy, b. 6/4/1976 in Hanover; Peter Warren Travis and Valerie June Mooney

TROTTIER,
Donna Mae, b. 5/19/1939 in Lebanon; third; Rudolph J. Trottier (janitor, 28, Bradford, VT) and Olive D. Goodell (25, Laconia)
Ellen Christine, b. 8/11/1957 in Hanover; Douglas R. Trottier (student, Lebanon) and Corinne E. Gamage (Litchfield, ME)
Luane Carole, b. 7/3/1943 in Lebanon; fourth; Rodolphe Trottier (janitor, 32, Hartford, VT) and Olive D. Goodwll (29, Laconia)

TRUE,
Mary Jean, b. 10/6/1944 in Hanover; fourth; Rowley N. True (US Army, 24, Fremont) and Leora M. Camber (23, Newark, VT)

TULLAR,
Jeramie, b. 11/16/1974 in Hanover; Bernard Wayne Tullar, Jr. and Shirley M. LaMountain
Patrick Wayne, b. 8/30/1971 in Hanover; Bernard Wayne Tullar, Jr. and Shirley LaMountain

TURKINGTON,
Brian Callahan, b. 6/26/2001 in Lebanon; Thomas Turkington and Nancy Turkington

TURNER,
Richard Clarence, b. 9/11/1930 in Hanover; fifth; Hazen B. Turner (mechanic, 36, Lyme) and Christine M. Lake (34, Keene)
Robert Henry, b. 9/11/1930 in Hanover; fourth; Hazen B. Turner (mechanic, 36, Lyme) and Christine M. Lake (34, Keene)

Virginia Susan, b. 3/18/1925 in Lyme; second; Hazen E. Turner (garage, 31, Columbia) and Christine M. Lake (30, Keene)

TWERDOWSKY,
Rachel Yvonne, b. 2/5/1998 in Lebanon; Paul Shawn Twerdowsky and Cheryl Light

TYLER,
Joan Margaret, b. 9/15/1942 in Haverhill; second; Donald L. Tyler (chef, 28, Haverhill) and Marion C. Bonnett (21, Fairlee, VT)

ULINE,
daughter, b. 1/30/1889; second; Hiram Uline (laborer, Canaan) and Addie L. Lamphere (Lyme)
daughter, b. 9/17/1890; third; Hiram Uline (farmer, 39, Canaan) and Addie L. Lamphere (Lyme)
Alberta May, b. 2/21/1914; third; Hiram Uline, Jr. (laborer, 30, Albany, NY) and Grace M. Gilbert (26, Littleton)
Betsy, b. 8/22/1952 in Hanover; second; Kenneth Uline (carpenter, 25, Hanover) and Ruth Bull (30, Ashland, ME)
Cheryl Joyce, b. 12/31/1944 in Hanover; second; Ray A. Uline (mechanic, 24, Lyme) and Lena F. Brown (21, Newbury, VT)
Connie Jean, b. 10/27/1950 in Hanover; third; Ray Uline (welder, 30, Lyme) and Lena Brown (27, Newbury, VT)
Gerald G., b. 11/30/1903 in Lyme; first; Hiram Uline, Jr. (laborer, 20, Lyme) and Grace M. Gilbert (16, Littleton)
Harry Martin, b. 11/22/1894 in Lyme; fourth; Hiram Uline (barber, 43, Canaan) and Addie L. Lamphere (34, Lyme)
Isabel Shirley, b. 4/16/1917; fourth; Hiram Uline, Jr. (laborer, 33, Lyme) and Grace M. Gilbert (29, Littleton)
Margaret Louise, b. 1/26/1938 in Lyme; third; Millard R. Uline (carpenter, 30, Lyme) and Susie E. B. Cadwell (32, Thetford, VT)
Mertie Louise, b. 10/25/1923 in Lyme; sixth; Hiram Uline, Jr. (laborer, 40, Lyme) and Grace M. Gilbert (36, Littleton)
Millard R., b. 5/4/1907 in Lyme; second; Hiram Uline, Jr. (laborer, 23, Lyme) and Grace M. Gilbert (20, Littleton)
Nancy Ann, b. 6/24/1948 in Hanover; first; Kenneth H. Uline (carpenter, 21, Hanover) and Ruth M. Bull (26, Ashland, ME)
Pauline Elizabeth, b. 8/11/1934 in Lyme; second; Millard R. Uline (carpenter, 27, Lyme) and Susie E. B. Cadwell (29, Thetford,

VT)
Ray Allen, b. 2/28/1920 in Lyme; fifth; Hiram Uline, Jr. (laborer, 36, Lyme) and Grace M. Gilbert (32, Littleton)
Shirley Irene, b. 2/7/1931 in Lyme; first; Millard R. Uline (laborer, 23, Lyme) and Susie E. B. Cadwell (25, Thetford, VT)

UNDERHILL,
stillborn son, b. 9/8/1899; first; L. G. Underhill (farmer, 24, Orange) and Augusta A. Welch (22, Lyme)

URRIBARRI,
Bennett James, b. 2/4/2004 in Boston, MA; James Urribarri and Kristen Garfield

VALLEY,
Garland Cliff, b. 11/12/1965 in Hanover; second; Clifton Valley (stoneman, Akron, OH) and Marilyn A. Balch (Hanover)
Sherry Sue, b. 2/25/1962 in Hanover; Clifton H. Valley (apprentice, Akron, OH) and Marilyn A. Balch (21, Hanover)

VAN VLECK,
Harriet Evelyn, b. 4/20/1979 in Hanover; Roy Van Vleck and Emily Trevor
Tielman, b. 6/11/1976 in Hanover; Roy Tomlinson Van Vleck and Emily Norwood Trevor

VAUGHAN,
Jason Allie, b. 11/15/1987 in Hanover; Robert D. Vaughan and Lynn A. Pike
Shirley Louise, b. 4/26/1945 in Lyme; sixth; Robert C. Vaughan (farmer, 36, Thetford, VT) and Lillian M. Hill (34, Danville, PQ); residence – Thetford, VT

VEEDER,
Carlton Orrin, b. 3/8/1921 in Lyme; first; Carlton S. Veeder (fisherman, 23, Bedford, MA) and Frances Ackerman (18, Orford); residence - Bedford, MA

VENTI,
Brian Moore, b. 7/9/1983 in Hanover; Steven F. Venti and Nancy J. Moore

Leah Moore, b. 9/6/1984 in Hanover; Steven F. Venti and Nancy J. Moore

VERALLI,
Ian Joseph, b. 9/23/1976 in Hanover; Paul Joseph Veralli and Linda Margaret Chase

VESCUSO,
Daniel Robert, b. 5/12/1987 in Hanover; Peter A. Vescuso and Ellen DiPaola

VINSON,
Henry Adams, b. 5/13/1987 in Hanover; Curt M. Vinson and Alison Kelsey

VOGT,
Lydia Rose, b. 12/5/1994 in Lebanon; Douglas Vogt and Mary Mia Arnold
Mason Andrew, b. 3/29/1993 in Lebanon; Douglas Vogt and Mary Arnold

WAGNER,
Anne Duncan, b. 8/1/1960 in Hanover; Frederick E. Wagner (timberland oper., 43, Milwaukee, WI) and Creigh O. Collins (40, Chicago, IL)
Ellen Creigh, b. 10/1/1956 in Hanover; Frederick E. Wagner (lumber business, 39, Milwaukee, WI) and Creigh O. Collins (36, Chicago, IL)
Laura Oliphant, b. 10/16/1957 in Hanover; Frederick E. Wagner (businessman, Milwaukee, WI) and Creigh O. Collins (Chicago, IL)

WALLACE,
Harper Oklahoma Weeks, b. 11/30/1999 in Lebanon; William Weeks and Amy Wallace
Joplin Maycomb Weeks, b. 9/16/1997 in Lebanon; William Brinson Weeks and Amy Elizabeth Wallace
Scott Tecumseh Weeks, b. 5/15/1993 in Lebanon; William Weeks and Amy Wallace

WALLIS,
Sadie Mae, b. 12/24/2001 in Lebanon; Peter Wallis and Patti Wallis

WALSH,
Catherine Mary, b. 6/5/1969 in Newport; William P. Walsh and Joyce
E. Pashowsky

WARE,
daughter, b. 5/23/1910 in Lyme; second; Edgar Russell Ware (clerk,
25, Lyme) and Edith M. Morrison (26, Lyme)
Lois Priscilla, b. 6/7/1912 in Lyme; third; Edgar R. Ware (clerk, 27,
Thetford, VT) and Edith M. Morrison (28, Somerville, MA)
Roland Russell, b. 1/5/1908 in Lyme; first; Edgar R. Ware (farmer,
23, Lyme) and Edith M. Morrison (21, Somerville, MA)
Virginia Yvonne, b. 2/7/1926 in Lyme; third; Samuel P. Ware
(farmer, 34, Elkins, WV) and Effie E. Gray (22, Willoughby, VT);
residence - Willoughby, VT

WARREN,
son, b. 4/1/1887; second; Charles H. Warren (farmer, 25, Lyme) and
Emma L. Warren (29, Lyme)
stillborn child, b. 4/1/1887; third; Charles H. Warren (farmer, 25,
Lyme) and Emma L. Warren (29, Lyme)
son, b. 4/1/1888; second; Charles H. Warren (farmer, 25, Lyme) and
Emma L. Gilbert (29, Lyme)
Amanda Trow, b. 6/22/1978 in Hanover; Thomas S. Warren and
Martha Sylvester
Clyde Stearns, b. 2/14/188; first; Arad J. Warren (merchant, 31,
Lyme) and Myra L. Warren (28, Starksboro, VT)
Grace May, b. 6/15/1908 in Lyme; third; Fred M. Warren (farmer, 50,
Lyme) and Jennie M. Camp (42, Hanover)
Kelsey Nathan, b. 9/11/1974 in Hanover; Thomas Stuart Warren and
Martha Jean Sylvester
Lee West, b. 1/4/1893 in Lyme; second; Arad J. Warren
(storekeeper, 36, Lyme) and ----- (34, Starksboro, VT)
Lewis J., b. 6/4/1899; second; Fred N. Warren (farmer, 41, Lyme)
and Jennie N. Camp (33, Hanover)
Minnie Jane, b. 9/13/1897 in Lyme; first; Fred N. Warren (farmer, 40,
Lyme) and Jennie M. Camp (31, Hanover)
Tilea Elizabeth, b. 5/15/1977 in Hanover; Thomas S. Warren and
Martha J. Sylvester

Travis Sumner, b. 9/14/1972 in Hanover; Thomas S. Warren and Martha J. Sylvester

WASHBURN,
David Bradley, b. 2/16/1944 in Lyme; first; Carroll H. Washburn (farmer, 35, Colebrook) and Ruth E. Reed (35, Bath)

WASTE,
David William, b. 8/3/1993 in Lebanon; William Waste and Kathleen Dryden
Elizabeth Anne, b. 9/10/1984 in Hanover; William H. Waste and Kathleen L. Dryden

WATERMAN,
daughter, b. 7/13/1903 in Lyme; ninth; Charles H. Waterman (bd. sawyer, 47, Springfield, MA) and Emma J. Baker (42, Springfield, MA)
Mylo George, b. 9/2/1889; second; Melville A. Waterman (farmer, Barnet, VT) and Rosa M. Balch (Lincoln, VT)
Ray Wesley, b. 1/1/1921 in Lyme; fourth; Leon Waterman (farmer, 42, Lyme) and Lennie Flanders (32, Enfield)
Ruby Ethel, b. 5/3/1916; third; Leon O. Waterman (farming, 37, Lyme) and Ethel L. Flanders (28, Enfield)

WATERS,
Denorah Rose, b. 9/11/1957 in Hanover; Francis L. Waters (farm mgr., Hague, NY) and Marjorie Sanderson (Woodstock, VT)

WATSON,
daughter, b. 1/28/1909 in Lyme; first; John Watson (laborer, NY) and Laulein Wilson (18, Lyme)
Arthur, b. 1/19/1904 in Lyme; third; John R. Watson (laborer, 33, Franklin, PQ) and Anna L. Hennigan (33, Moores, NY)
David R., b. 2/21/1898; second; John R. Watson (laborer, 28, Hinshinbrook, PQ) and Laura A. Hennigan (27, Moores, NY)
Edith, b. 2/2/1907 in Lyme; fourth; John R. Watson (laborer, 35, Rockburn, Canada) and Laura A. Hennigan (35, Moore, NY)
Jennifer Kristi, b. 11/23/1983 in Hanover; James J. Watson and Eileen C. Wheeler
Ruth Elmira, b. 6/5/1900; third; John R. Watson (laborer, 29, Rockburn, Canada) and Anna Laura Hennigan (29, Moores,

NY)

WATTS,
Richard Alan, b. 4/15/1938 in Lyme; fourth; Donald Watts (laborer, 23, Canaan) and Mildred M. Hill (29, Strafford, VT)

WEAVER,
Eleanor Olivia, b. 1/6/1986 in Hanover; John B. Weaver and Sharon L. Ramey

WEBB,
Bertha May, b. 10/12/1893 in Lyme; first; Charles Benjamin Webb (painter, farmer, 33, Lyme) and Rhoda Smith (26, Hanover)
Betty Lucille, b. 7/4/1930 in Orford; first; Charles D. Webb (laborer, 24, Lyme) and Nera M. Bean (20, Orford)
C. M. [female], b. 5/11/1903 in Lyme; second; Charles B. Webb (farmer, 43, Lyme) and Lucy M. Conant (23, Lyme)
Charlotte Elizabeth, b. 3/25/1985 in Hanover; Leon Webb and Karen Wetterhahn
Eddie Garfield, b. 10/3/1888 in Lyme; Henry O. Webb and Mary Cline (1948)
Edith V., b. 6/22/1906 in Lyme; third; Charles B. Webb (farmer, 46, Lyme) and Lucy M. Conant (26, Lyme)
Harold Conant, b. 11/13/1914; fourth; Charles B. Webb (painter, 54, Lyme) and Lucy M. Conant (34, Lyme)
John Lawrence, b. 4/11/1992 in Lebanon; Gary Webb and Karen Muirhead
Leon Ashley, b. 1/11/1983 in Hanover; Leon H. Webb and Karen E. Wetterhahn
Madelyn Louise, b. 11/3/1995 in Lebanon; Gary Edward Webb and Karen Lynn Muirhead
Rhoda M., b. 9/6/1901; first; Charles B. Webb (farmer, 41, Lyme) and Lucy M. Conant (22, Lyme)
Valerie Jeanne, b. 1/25/1947 in Hanover; first; Harold C. Webb (creamery, 32, Lyme) and Dorothy W. George (26, Hanover)

WEBSTER,
David Brinton, b. 6/29/1908 in Lyme; fourth; Brinton M. Webster (clergyman, 43, Cambridge, MA) and Lizzie H. Smith (42, Cabot, ME)
Mary E., b. 11/22/1896 in Lyme; first; John H. Webster (farmer, 26,

Lyme) and Abbie M. Coates (25, Corn Hill, NB)

WEEDEN,
John Jewett, b. 7/29/1948 in Lebanon; second; John S. Weeden (student, 24, Lebanon) and Betty L. Moller (23, Manchester)
Patricia Lee, b. 6/17/1948 in Hanover; first; Stanley J. Weeden (store clerk, 20, Bridgewater, VT) and Jean E. Smith (20, Hanover)
Thomas Royal, b. 8/12/1947 in Hanover; first; John S. Weeden (laborer, 22, Lebanon) and Betty L. Moller (21, Manchester)

WEEKS,
Atticus Collins, b. 4/2/1990 in Hanover; William B. Weeks and Amy E. Wallace
Savannah Boone, b. 7/26/1991 in Hanover; William B. Weeks and Amy E. Wallace

WELCH,
Harold Edward, III, b. 2/17/1963 in Hanover; Harold E. Welch, Jr. (student, Boston, MA) and Catherine M. MacKenzie (21, Concord)
Mary F., b. 2/5/1894 in Lyme; fourth; George A. Welch (laborer, 28, York, ME) and Lucy L. Parsons (30, York, ME)

WEST,
Edwin Allyn, b. 10/27/1909 in Lyme; first; Frank Edwin West (merchant, 29, Orford) and Jennie Florence Blood (31, Orford)
Samuel Dalton, b. 2/13/1990 in Hanover; Ralph T. West, Jr. and Lesley Slosser

WETHERELL,
Erin Marie, b. 6/8/1986 in Hanover; Walter D. Wetherell and Celeste M. Tousignant
Mathew David, b. 5/23/1990 in Hanover; Walter D. Wetherell and Celeste Tousignant

WEYMOUTH,
son, b. 8/11/1890; second; George W. Weymouth (physician, 34, Andover) and Minnie E. Morgan (Sacramento, CA)
Forrest Mann, b. 5/20/1892; third; G. W. Weymouth (physician, 36, Andover) and Minnie T. Morgan (30, Sacramento, CA)

WHEELER,
son, b. 2/16/1900; sixth; Horace A. Wheeler (farmer, 44, Haverhill) and Clara A. Winchester (32, Haverhill)
daughter, b. 12/3/1901; seventh; Horace A. Wheeler (laborer, 46, Haverhill) and Clara D. Winchester (34, Haverhill)
Daniel Walton, b. 5/27/1952 in Lebanon; fourth; Ernest Wheeler (car man RR, 26, Barnard, VT) and Hazel Campbell (28, Pomfret, VT); res – Lyme Ctr.
Isabelle Hopkins, b. 9/28/1994 in Lebanon; Mark Wheeler and Elizabeth Hopkins
Jack Lester, b. 2/26/1958 in Lebanon; Ermest W. Wheeler (RR car inspector, 31, Barnard, VT) and Hazel P. Campbell (33, Pomfret, VT)
Terry Martin, b. 5/5/1953 in Lebanon; Ernest W. Wheeler (coach cleaner, 27, Barnard, VT) and Hazel Campbell (29, Pomfret, VT)

WHEELOCK,
Beverly June, b. 7/10/1931 in Hanover; third; Dorman Wheelock (farmer, 26, E. Fairfield, VT) and Christabel Druge (22, Strafford, VT)
Dorman O'Honory, b. 4/12/1930 in Lyme; second; Dorman Wheelock (farmer, 24, E. Fairfield, VT) and Christabel Druge (21, Strafford, VT)
Katherine Rose, b. 3/7/1929 in Hanover; first; Dorman G. Wheelock (farmer, 23, Fairfield, VT) and Christabel Druge (20, Strafford, VT)
Ruth Louise, b. 11/27/1932 in Hanover; fourth; Dorman C. Wheelock (farmer, 26, Fairfield, VT) and Christobel Druge (24, Strafford, VT)

WHITCHER,
daughter, b. 8/9/1914; first; Howard Whitcher (laborer, 20, Wentworth) and Florence Muzzey (20, Dorchester)
Raymond Calvin, b. 3/15/1897 in Lyme; fourth; William W. Whitcher (carpenter, 38, Hendrick, VT) and Fannie C. Strong (40, Norwich, VT)
Wesley John, b. 4/4/1925 in Lyme; second; Howard Whitcher (laborer, 31, Rumney) and Doris B. Jenks (19, Lyme)

WHITCOMB,
Eleanor Towle, b. 7/8/1985 in Hanover; Michel Whitcomb and Susan Blodgett

WHITE,
son, b. 12/11/1891; eighth; Ira C. White (farmer, 37, Fairlee, VT) and Ada F. Waterman (39, Helena, NY)
Martha, b. 7/20/1889; seventh; Ira C. White (farmer, Fairlee, VT) and Addie F. Waterman (Helena, NY)
Olivia Warrington, b. 5/2/2003 in Lebanon; Brent White and Sarah White

WHITEHILL,
Connie Marie, b. 11/19/1965 in Lebanon; fourth; Alton I. Whitehill (farmer, Newbury, VT) and Pearl L. Sayers (Ryegate, VT)
Nancy Lee, b. 2/20/1962 in Haverhill; Alton I. Whitehill (farming, Newbury, VT) and Pearl L. Sayers (34, Ryegate, VT)

WHITMAN,
Alec Bridgham, b. 12/7/1986 in Hanover; Michael C. Whitman and Lynn B. McRae
Tobin McRae, b. 3/22/1982 in Lebanon; Michael C. Whitman and Lynn B. McRae

WHITTEMORE,
daughter, b. 2/3/1909 in Lyme; third; Luther L. Whittemore (farmer, 34, Plymouth) and Carrie W. Washburn (37, Lyme)
Pauline E., b. 2/8/1906 in Lyme; second; Luther J. Whittemore (clerk, 31, Plymouth) and Carrie W. Washburn (34, Lyme)
Stella May, b. 6/8/1891; second; Frank G. Whittemore (farmer, 43, Manchester) and Roxie M. Stetson (36, Lyme)

WHITTINGTON,
Marc, b. 10/17/1990 in Hanover; William E. Whittington, IV and Christiane E. Hipp
Miriam Louise, b. 1/2/1994 in Lebanon; William Whittington and Christiane Hipp
Rebecca, b. 10/17/1990 in Hanover; William E. Whittington, IV and Christiane E. Hipp

WIGGINS,
Leon Joseph, b. 10/18/1928 in Hanover; second; Clayton Wiggins (farmer, 35, Thetford, VT) and Adeline M. Crane (25, Springfield, MA)

WILCOX,
Hilary Jane, b. 12/29/1972 in Lebanon; Robert Wilcox and Pamela J. Bacon
Mina Beth, b. 7/12/1970 in Lebanon; Robert T. Wilcox and Pamela J. Bacon
Ryan David, b. 4/28/1974 in Lebanon; Robert Thomas Wilcox and Pamela Jean Bacon

WILDES,
Nathaniel Sherman Bond, b. 4/27/1990 in Hanover; Bruce S. Wildes and Nancy Jane Seamans

WILKIE,
stillborn daughter, b. 11/24/1912 in Lyme; first; Herbert M. Wilkie (laborer, 33, Barton, VT) and Marion E. Chapin (22, S. Boston, MA)

WILLEY,
stillborn child, b. 5/8/1897 in Lyme; third; Bertram E. Willey (physician, 33, Hinsdale) and Mary A. Ramsey (28, Barton, VT)

WILLIAMS,
daughter, b. 11/24/1887; first; Frank H. Williams (laborer, 21, Plainfield) and Hattie A. Williams (20, Lyme)
daughter, b. 3/28/1892; second; Frank H. Williams (laborer, 25, Plainfield) and Hattie A. Davison (24, Lyme)
Alexis Charlotte, b. 9/12/1994 in Lebanon; Ian Williams and Annette Breed
Cole Jacob, b. 4/24/1993 in Lebanon; Steven Williams and Tiffany Cole
Reid Gordon, b. 4/23/1997 in Lebanon; Ian Reid Williams and Annette Augusta Breed

WILLIGAR,
daughter, b. 9/28/1910 in Lyme; second; Stephen A. Willigar (farmer, 37, West Bay, NS) and Hattie Dell Dustin (32,

Wentworth)
Flora Mertie, b. 10/19/1904 in Lyme; first; Albert Willigar (farmer, 31, West Bay, NS) and Delia Dustin (27, Wentworth)

WILMOT,
son, b. 9/2/1887; fifth; Erni F. Wilmot (farmer, 32, Thetford) and Minnie E. Wilmot (36, Barnard, VT)
stillborn son, b. 9/7/1896 in Lyme; seventh; Harry C. H. Wilmot (laborer, 30, Thetford, VT) and Jennie R. Lamphrey (18, Lyme)
daughter, b. 11/17/1910 in Lyme; second; Elbur E. Wilmot (laborer, 30, Strafford, VT) and Myrtle P. Cummings (20, Lyme)
daughter, b. 7/14/1915; fifth; Elber E. Wilmot (laborer, 37, Lyme) and Myrtle P. Cummings (24, Lyme)
daughter, b. 7/14/1915; sixth; Elber E. Wilmot (laborer, 37, Lyme) and Myrtle P. Cummings (24, Lyme)
stillborn daughter, b. 9/18/1916; fifth; Leo A. Wilmot (farming, 31, Lyme) and Fannie M. Chapin (27, Boston, MA)
son, b. 12/8/1917; sixth; Leo A. Wilmot (farming, 32, Lyme) and Fannie M. Chapin (28, Boston, MA)
son, b. 12/8/1917; seventh; Leo A. Wilmot (farming, 32, Lyme) and Fannie M. Chapin (28, Boston, MA)
stillborn son, b. 3/8/1918 in Lyme; first; Irvin A. Wilmot (laborer, 30, Lyme) and Lillian D. Sayre (22, Thetford, VT)
stillborn daughter, b. 10/25/1919 in Lyme; second; Leamon F. Wilmot (farming, 38, Thetford, VT) and Goldia L. Oliver (34, Bradford, VT)
stillborn son, b. 12/14/1921 in Lyme; tenth; Leo A. Wilmot (farmer, 35, Lyme) and Fannie M. Chapin (32, Boston, MA)
stillborn daughter, b. 3/12/1923 in Lyme; eleventh; Leo A. Wilmot (farmer, 36, Lyme) and Fannie M. Chapin (33, S. Boston, MA)
Ada May, b. 7/4/1923 in Lyme; fourth; Irving A. Wilmot (farmer, 35, Lyme) and Lillian D. Sayre (28, Thetford, VT)
Archie Frank, b. 1/16/1924 in Lyme; fifth; Homer D. Wilmot (farmer, 31, Lyme) and Flora M. Wing (25, Lyme)
Asa Earl, b. 1/6/1922 in Lyme; fourth; Homer D. Wilmot (farmer, 29, Lyme) and Flora M. Wing (23, Lyme)
Betty Jane, b. 7/4/1942 in Hanover; fourth; Earl R. Wilmot (laborer, 30, Lyme) and Florence G. Covill (24, Charleston, VT)
Chester Homer, b. 12/17/1925 in Lyme; sixth; Homer D. Wilmot (laborer, 33, Lyme) and Flora M. Wing (27, Lyme)
Dorothy Ruth, b. 5/2/1932 in Lyme; eighth; Irven A. Wilmot (farmer,

44, Lyme) and Lillian Sayre (36, Thetford, VT)

Elizabeth Rose, b. 5/2/1919 in Lyme; second; Irvin A. Wilmot (farming, 32, Lyme) and Lillian D. Sayre (23, Thetford, VT)

Florence Ethel, b. 12/22/1918 in Lyme; eighth; Leo A. Wilmot (farming, 32, Lyme) and Fannie M. Chapin (29, S. Boston, MA)

Florine Marguerite, b. 7/26/1934 in Lyme; eleventh; Homer D. Wilmot (farmer, 42, Lyme) and Flora M. Wing (35)

Gladys Mildred, b. 4/–/1914; fourth; Leo A. Wilmot (farmer, 29, Lyme) and Fannie M. Chapin (25, S. Boston, MA)

Harold Elmer, b. 2/20/1913 in Lyme; third; Leo A. Wilmot (farmer, 27, Lyme) and Fannie M. Chapin (24, Boston, MA)

Helen Alice, b. 12/16/1931 in Lyme; ninth; Homer D. Wilmot (laborer, 39, Lyme) and Flora M. Wing (33, Lyme)

Homer, b. 4/14/1892; sixth; Ervin F. Wilmot (farmer, 36, Thetford, VT) and Minnie E. Packard (41, Barnard, VT)

Hope Oliver, b. 10/21/1916; first; Leamon F. Wilmot (farming, 35, Strafford, VT) and Goldia L. Oliver (31, Bradford, VT)

Irene Edna, b. 4/12/1921 in Lyme; third; Irvin A. Wilmot (laborer, 32, Lyme) and Lillian D. Sayre (25, Thetford, VT)

Irven Atwell, b. 8/29/1927 in Lyme; sixth; Irven A. Wilmot (laborer, 29, Lyme) and Lillian D. Sayre (22, Thetford, VT)

Jean Allen, b. 5/14/1933 in Lyme; tenth; Homer D. Wilmot (laborer, 41, Lyme) and Flora M. Wing (35, Lyme)

Joyce Elaine, b. 11/19/1940 in Hanover; third; Kenneth I. Wilmot (laborer, 27, Lyme) and Hannah M. Donna (30, Westmore, VT)

June Esther, b. 6/25/1934 in Hanover; second; Leamon F. Wilmot (farmer, 53, Strafford, VT) and Ida J. Smith (25, Lyme)

Kenneth Ira, b. 4/12/1913 in Lyme; third; Elber E. Wilmot (laborer, 35, Lyme) and Myrtle P. Cummings (23, Lyme)

Leila Roxanna, b. 8/4/1920 in Lyme; ninth; Leo A. Wilmot (farmer, 34, Lyme) and Fannie M. Chapin (31, S. Boston, MA)

Lenwood, b. 8/11/1918 in Lyme; second; Homer D. Wilmot (farming, 26, Lyme) and Flora M. Wing (20, Lyme)

Lillian D., b. 3/24/1936 in Lyme; ninth; Irving A. Wilmot (farmer, 48, Lyme) and Lillian D. Sayre (40, Thetford, VT)

Lloyd Edgar, b. 2/9/1917; first; Homer D. Wilmot (farming, 24, Lyme) and Flora M. Wing (18, Lyme)

Margaret Theckla, b. 3/31/1914; fourth; Elber E. Wilmot (laborer, 35, Lyme) and Myrtle P. Cumming (24, Lyme)

Marion Evelyn, b. 8/3/1925 in Lyme; fifth; Ervin A. Wilmot (farmer, 37, Lyme) and Lillian D. Sayre (30, Thetford, VT)

Marjorie Edith, b. 5/3/1927 in Lyme; twelfth; Leo A. Wilmot (farmer, 42, Lyme) and Fannie M. Chapin (38, S. Boston, MA)
Maurice Lester, b. 7/28/1909 in Lyme; first; Leo Alfred Wilmot (laborer, 24, Lyme) and Fanny May Chapin (20, S. Boston, MA)
Merle Kenneth, b. 8/28/1942 in Lyme; third; Kenneth I. Wilmot (farm labor, 29, Lyme) and Hannah M. Downs (32, Westmore, VT)
Mildred F., b. 3/28/1936 in Lyme; twelfth; Homer D. Wilmot (farmer, 43, Lyme) and Flora M. Wing (37, Lyme)
Nancy Ann, b. 2/21/1945 in Lyme; fourth; Earl R. Wilmot (farmer, 34, Lyme) and Florence G. Covill (26, Charleston, VT)
Nina Mynetta, b. 2/17/1928 in Lyme; seventh; Homer Wilmot (laborer, 35, Lyme) and Flora M. Wing (27, Lyme)
Ray Alanson, b. 12/24/1920 in Lyme; third; Homer D. Wilmot (farmer, 28, Lyme) and Flora M. Wing (22, Lyme)
Roscoe Earle, b. 9/10/1911 in Lyme; second; Leo A. Wilmot (farmer, 25, Lyme) and Fannie M. Chapin (22, Boston, MA)
Roscoe Earl, b. 8/8/1933 in Lyme; first; Earl R. Wilmot (laborer, 21, Lyme) and Florence G. Covell (16, Charlestown, VT)
Russell E., b. 9/1/1937 in Lyme; thirteenth; Homer D. Wilmot (farmer, 44, Lyme) and Flora M. Wing (39, Lyme)
Sibyl Phoebe, b. 9/7/1917; seventh; Elber E. Wilmot (laborer, 40, Strafford, VT) and Myrtle B. Cummings (26, Lyme)
Stanley Henry, b. 3/7/1930 in Lyme; seventh; Irven A. Wilmot (farmer, 42, Lyme) and Lillian D. Sayre (34, Thetford, VT)
Sylvia Judith, b. 4/19/1909 in Lyme; second; Elber Erni Wilmot (laborer, 32, Strafford, VT) and Myrtle Phebe Cummings (18, Lyme)
Virginia Rose, b. 1/15/1930 in Lyme; first; Leamon F. Wilmot (farmer, 49, Strafford, VT) and Ida J. Smith (21, Lyme)
Wayne Wilber, b. 12/25/1929 in Lyme; eighth; Homer D. Wilmot (farmer, 37, Lyme) and Flora M. Wing (31, Lyme)

WILMOTT,
Alan Scott, b. 8/14/1965 in Hanover; second; Wayne W. Wilmot (US mailman, Lyme) and Violet P. Howe (Lebanon)
Bradley Alan, b. 8/21/1964 in Hanover; Jess A. Wilmott (construction, Lyme) and Vera Howe (25, Meriden)
David Lee, b. 3/17/1948 in Lebanon; second; Len. R. Wilmott (farmer, 29, Lyme) and Viola B. LaFlore (22, E. Thetford, VT)
Dean Ronald, b. 2/23/1946 in Lyme; first; Lenwood R. Wilmott (lumbering, 27, Lyme) and Viola Merryfield (20, Thetford, VT)

Debra Ann, b. 10/2/1961 in Hanover; Jess A. Wilmott (mechanic, Lyme) and Vera Howe (22, Meriden)
Diana Lee, b. 10/2/1961 in Hanover; Jess A. Wilmott (mechanic, Lyme) and Vera Howe (22, Meriden)
Eugene Alan, b. 7/18/1949 in Lebanon; Lenwood R. Wilmott and Viola Laflore
Gerald Frank, b. 7/25/1950 in Lebanon; second; Archie Wilmott (carpenter, 26, Lyme) and Dorothy Brady (20, Newport)
Isabella DaJung, b. 6/23/1999 in S. Korea; Michael Wilmott and Vanora Wilmott
Jack San-Ah, b. 11/7/1995 in Korea; Michael Wilmott and Van Taylor
Stuart Milton, b. 8/11/1946 in Lyme; first; Archie F. Wilmott (farm laborer, 23, Lyme) and Dorothy M. Brady (17, Newport)
Wayne Wilbur, Jr., b. 9/26/1963 in Hanover; Wayne W. Wilmott (laborer, Lyme) and Violet P. Howe (25, Lyme)

WILSON,
son, b. 9/13/1888; fourth; Henry Wilson (farmer, 41, Jackson, OH) and Georgianna Flanders (30, Concord)
son, b. 9/5/1899; seventh; Henry Wilson (farmer, 52, Jackson, OH) and Georgia A. Flanders (40, Concord)
son, b. 10/15/1908 in Lyme; first; Henry Wilson (sawyer, 24, Lyme) and Sarah B. Paige (20, Lyme)
Gerald H., b. 1/25/1898; fifth; Rufus H. Wilson (farmer, 39, Glensutton, Canada) and Nancy E. Huntley (35, Troy, VT)
Herald D., b. 8/9/1894 in Lyme; sixth; Henry Wilson (farmer, 47, Jackson, OH) and Georgia A. Flanders (36, Concord)
Sarah Jane, b. 6/12/1893 in Lyme; fifth; Henry Wilson (farmer, 44, Jackson, OH) and Georgia A. Flanders (35, Concord)

WING,
Albert E., b. 9/4/1899; eleventh; Nathan L. Wing (farmer, 44, Berkshire, VT) and Flora A. Hill (42, Chateaugay, NY)
Cassie M., b. 3/31/1895 in Lyme; ninth; Nathan L. Wing (farmer, 40, Berkshire, VT) and Flora A. Hill (38, Chateaugay, NY)
Clifton Leonard, b. 3/18/1909 in Lyme; second; Leonard T. Wing (farmer, 24, Burne, NY) and Florence May Rattery (22, Wolf Is., ON)
Harold Clinton, b. 2/28/1912 in Lyme; sixth; Milton L. Wing (farmer, 38, Burke, NY) and Nina H. Courtney (33, Rochester, VT)

Joan Ruth, b. 9/5/1937 in Hanover; first; Harold C. Wing (farmer, 25, Lyme) and Liullian A. Thompson (22, Orange)
John Henry, b. 5/10/1943 in Hanover; second; Harold C. Wing (farmer, 31, Lyme) and Lillian A. Thompson (28, Orange)
Leonard John, b. 4/22/1925 in Lyme; first; Albert E. Wing (farmer, 24, Lyme) and Ester M. Small (19, Cornish)
Mildred Flora, b. 8/5/1898 first; Milton L. Wing (farmer, 25, Burke, NY) and Nina H. Courtney (19, Rochester, VT)
Nina Ruth, b. 9/16/1896 in Lyme; tenth; Nathan L. Wing (farmer, 41, Berkshire, VT) and Flora Ann Hill (39, Chateaugay, NY)
Vera E., b. 11/29/1907 in Lyme; first; Leonard T. Wing (laborer, 21, Burke, NY) and Florence M. Rattray (21, Wolf Island, Canada)

WINSLOW,
daughter, b. 9/–/1890; second; George G. Winslow (farmer, 32, Lyme) and Jane Post (Lyme)
Banks Bronson, b. 1/19/1887; first; William B. Winslow (farmer, 26, Lyme) and Addie L. Winslow (22, Thetford, VT)
Susan Johanne, b. 9/4/1947 in Hanover; third; W. Winslow, Jr. (farming, 29, Chicago, IL) and Jeanette Anderson (27, Boston, MA)
Theda Blanche, b. 6/20/1894 in Lyme; second; William B. Winslow (farmer, 34, Lyme) and Addie Ladd (29, Thetford, VT)

WISE,
daughter, b. 10/13/1901; second; Willie F. Wise (farmer, 34, Thetford, VT) and Helen S. Goulett (27, Norwich, VT)
George William, b. 5/11/1897 in Lyme; first; William F. Wise (farmer, 30, Thetford, VT) and Helen S. Goulett (23, Norwich, VT)
Hattie May, b. 11/28/1888; first; Theodore W. Wise (farmer, 34, Lyme) and Mary L. Bragg (22, Fairlee, VT)

WOLFORD,
Heather, b. 9/8/1972 in Hanover; George L. Wolford and Phyllis A. Young
Wendy, b. 10/22/1970 in Hanover; George L. Wolford and Phyllis A. Young

WOMER,
Scott Christian, b. 4/20/1994 in Lebanon; Geoffrey Womer and Christina Barreiro

WOODARD,
Cally Mary, b. 5/7/1979 in Lebanon; Michael Woodard and Barbara Simon
Chelsea Simon, b. 3/19/1982 in Lebanon; Michael S. Woodard and Barbara A. Simon
Dawson James, b. 11/15/1983 in Lebanon; Michael S. Woodard and Barbara A. Simon

WOODBURY,
David Balch, b. 9/12/1957 in Lebanon; William D. Woodbury (geologist, New Haven, CT) and Janet E. Balch (Hanover)

WOODWARD,
son, b. 12/17/1904 in Lyme; fifth; Herbert E. Woodward (farmer, 46, Montgomery, VT) and Jennie E. Coburn (43, Berkshire, VT)
Dawn Marie, b. 7/29/1966 in Haverhill; first; Wendell Woodward (student, Lebanon) and Linda L. Estes (Hanover)
Debra Ann, b. 1/4/1963 in Hanover; Melvin L. Woodward (maintenance, Roxbury, MA) and Ethel F. Gould (41, Rutland, VT)
James Melvin, b. 11/23/1960 in Hanover; Melvin L. Woodward (maintenance, 41, Roxbury, MA) and Ethel F. Gould (39, Rutland, VT)
Jordan Michael, b. 5/8/1999 in Lebanon; Michael Woodward and Nicole Perry Woodward
Laura Katherine, b. 9/21/1971 in Lebanon; Michael Woodward and Carol L. Mackie
Michael Lewis, b. 11/4/1950 in Hanover; first; Melvin Woodward (plumber, 31, Roxbury, MA) and Ethel Gould (29, Rutland, VT)
Minta M., b. 1/1/1895 in Lyme; fourth; Herbert E. Woodward (farmer, 36, Montgomery, VT) and Jennie Coburn (33, Berkshire, VT)
Richard Emerson, b. 2/19/1950 in Haverhill; first; Emerson Woodward (laborer, 22, Hanover) and Ruth Gray (20, Hanover)
Robert Alan, b. 9/10/1958 in Lyme; Emerson Woodward (trucker, 31, NH) and Ruth Gray (28, NH)
Ronald Lee, b. 12/15/1954 in Lyme; second; Emerson G. Woodward (trucking, 27, Hanover) and Ruth Gray (24, Hanover)

WU,
Daniel Xiu, b. 3/12/2003 in Lebanon; Yong Wu and Jun Shao

YOUNG,
Esther May, b. 3/27/1918 in Lyme; third; Leon F. Young (laborer, 30, Burke, NY) and Louise Columbia (25, St. Albans, VT)
Francis Earle, b. 8/8/1913 in Lyme; first; Joseph W. Young (farmer, 30, Burke, NY) and Clara E. Marlowe (24, Malone, NY)
Hazel Louise, b. 2/24/1933 in Hanover; ninth; Leon F. Young (laborer, 45, Chateaugay, NY) and Louise M. Columbia (40, St. Albans, VT)
Hilda Ann, b. 10/1/1945 in Hanover; sixth; Stanley C. Young (farmer, 29, Thetford, VT) and Alice L. Moses (29, Dorchester)
Howard Cr'fton, b. 11/27/1913 in Lyme; first; Harold C. Young (farmer, 27, Chateaugay, NY) and Nellie M. Brockway (24, Lyme)
Ira Morris, b. 6/29/1914; first; Leon F. Young (laborer, 26, Chateaugay, NY) and Louisa M. Columbia (21, St. Albans, VT)
James Hamilton, b. 3/26/1920 in Lyme; fourth; Leon F. Young (laborer, 32, Burke, NY) and Louise Columbia (26, St. Albans, VT)
Janice Barbara, b. 3/10/1930 in Hanover; second; Joseph W. Young (laborer, 46, Burke, NY) and Edith Hood (40, FL)
Lawrence Malcomb, b. 12/21/1922 in Lyme; fifth; Leon F. Young (laborer, 35, Chateaugay, NY) and Louise Columbia (30, St. Albans, VT)
Leon Francis, b. 8/29/1929 in Lyme; seventh; Leon F. Young (laborer, 41, Chateaugay, NY) and Louise M. Columbia (36, St. Albans, VT)
Patricia Ann, b. 1/25/1931 in Hanover; eighth; Leon F. Young (carpenter, 38, Chateaugay, NY) and Louise Columbia (38, St. Albans)
Ralph Carlton, b. 4/25/1917; third; Harold C. Young (farming, 31, Burke, NY) and Nellie M. Brockway (27, Lyme)
Robert Crawford, b. 4/25/1917; second; Harold C. Young (farming, 31, Burke, NY) and Nellie M. Brockway (27, Lyme)
Sylvia Mae, b. 9/9/1944 in Hanover; fifth; Stanley C. Young (laborer, 28, Thetford, VT) and Alice L. Moses (28, Dorchester)

ZEILINGER,
Dana Esther, b. 8/29/1975 in Lyme; Harry Zeilinger and Penelope J. Bliss

ZUCKERMAN,
Alexander Porter, b. 1/15/1995 in Lebanon; Randall Scott
Zuckerman and Jennifer Brett Bentley

LYME MARRIAGES

ABBOTT,
Forrest L. of Montclair, NJ m. Ruth E. **Putnam** of Lyme 11/20/1937 in Lyme; H - 30, teacher, b. Linneus, MO, s/o James C. Abbott (Linneus, MO, mechanic) and Ethel L. McCormick (Linneus, MO, housewife); W - 23, c. shopper, b. Montclair, NJ, d/o George W. Putnam (Nashua, asst. princ.) and Bertha M. Cole (Lebanon, housewife)

ABORJALLY,
Richard V. m. Cynthia **Loring** 7/29/1977 in Lyme

ACKERMAN,
Glen E. of Fairlee, VT m. Nettie **DeGoosh** of Lyme 9/15/1956 in Lyme; H – 21, carpenter, s/o Lewis Ackerman and Esther R. Sanborn, res. – Fairlee, VT; W – 21, secretary, d/o Howard DeGoosh and Nettie Pushee, res. – Lyme
Joseph C. of Lyme m. Alice M. **Merrill** of Post Mills, VT 12/7/1901 in Lyme; H - 20, farmer, b. Chelsea, VT, s/o Joseph C. Ackerman (Alexandria, farmer) and Lizzie Currier (Chelsea, VT, housewife); W - 18, housework, b. Post Mills, VT, d/o Cyrus Merrill (Canada, farmer) and Eliza Atkins (Brainington, VT, housewife)

ADAMS,
Aldrich L. of Fairlee, VT m. Violetta L. **Smith** of Lyme 4/2/1888 in Lyme; H - 25, lumberman, b. Corinth, VT, s/o J. L. Adams (Salem, MA) and Mary J. Willis (Enosburgh, VT); W - 20, housekeeper, b. Lyme, d/o Benjamin Smith (Lyme) and Angelina Worthen (Lyme)

ALBERTINI,
Ralph S. of Lyme m. Katharine A. **Phillips** of Lyme 7/28/1984 in Hanover

ALDEN,
Ezra B. of Lyme m. Luella P. **Ames** of Piermont 9/5/1893 in Piermont; H - 38, farmer, b. Lyme, s/o Amos B. Alden (Lyme, farmer) and Lydia M. Hall (Newbury, VT); W - 24, teacher, b. Orford, d/o Asa A. Ames (Orford, farmer) and Mary W. Runnels (Piermont)
R. Seabury of Lyme m. F. Gertrude **Sawyer** of Lyme 2/1/1891 in

Thetford; H - 32, farmer, b. Halifax, MA, s/o Ruel T. Alden (Middleboro, MA, farmer) and Isabella Warren (Lyme, housekeeper); W - 23, tel. operator, b. Lyme, d/o Albert E. Sawyer (Lyme, farmer) and Gracie A. Carpenter (Strafford, VT, housekeeper)

Stephen Bruce of Lyme m. Carol Ann **Vredenburgh** of Lyme 12/2/2000

ALDRICH,

Almon F. of Thetford, VT m. Ethel M. **Hewes** of Lyme 11/8/1924 in Thetford, VT; H - 38, mechanic, b. Strafford, VT, s/o Almon Aldrich and Ida L. Thompson (Topsham, VT); W - 23, at home, b. Lyme, d/o Frank S. Hewes (Lyme, laborer) and Addie Elliott (Lyme, housewife)

George M. of Plainfield m. Joyce E. **Wilmot** of Lyme Ctr. 7/27/1962 in Plainfield; H – 23, s/o George M. Aldrich and Helen B. Russell of Plainfield; W – 21, d/o Kenneth I. Wilmot and Hannah M. Donna, res. – Lyme Ctr.

George W. of Lyme m. Della Viola **LeDoux** of Hanover 6/12/1930 in Lyme; H - 29, electrician, 2nd - D, b. Canaan, VT, s/o Henry Aldrich (Pittsburgh, mechanic) and Hattie Stevens (Newport, VT, housewife); W - 18, at home, b. Cabot, VT, d/o Walter LeDoux (Bakersfield, VT, farmer) and Lena D. Coffran (Hydepark, VT, housewife)

George W. of Lyme m. Gerda E. **Pruneau** of Lyme –/21/1938 in Fairlee, VT; H - 37, electric eng., 3rd - D, b. Canaan, VT, s/o Henry Aldrich (Pittsburgh) and Hattie Everett (Coventry, VT); W - 29, 2nd - D, b. Denmark, d/o Andrew Rasmussen (Denmark) and Eleanor Sorsen (Denmark)

Lucian C. of Chelsea, VT m. Lida A. **Smith** of Chelsea, VT 5/23/1899 in Lyme; H - 55, painter, 3rd, b. Vershire, VT, s/o Irving Aldrich (farmer) and Diana West (houswork); W - 40, housework, 2nd, b. McIndoes Falls, VT, d/o ----- Roberts (shoemaker) and ----- Grant (housewife)

ALFIERI,

Anthony V. of New York, NY m. Ellen B. **Grant** of New York, NY 7/30/1988 in Lyme

ALLEN,

Philip A., Jr. of Conway m. Sylvia F. **Morse** of Lyme Ctr. 9/21/1973 in Lyme; H – 35, b. NH, s/o Philip Allen and Arlene Mills; W – 26, b. NH, d/o Raymond H. Balch and Esther Smith

ALLIS,
George W. of Whately, MA m. Ruth M. **Stevens** of Lyme 11/15/1922 in Lyme; H - 32, carpenter, 2nd - W, b. Whately, MA, s/o Irving Allis (Whately, MA, retired) and Augusta M. Hawes (Ashfield, MA, housewife); W - 26, house keeper, b. Windham, VT, d/o Frank A. Stevens (Brookline, VT, farmer) and Laura P. Allbee (Cambridgeport, VT, deceased)

ALVARADO,
Francisco A. of Brooklyn, NY m. Julie L. **Farrar** of Brooklyn, NY 7/11/1987 in Lyme

ANDERSON,
Carl E. m. Heidi R. **Roliz** 3/1/1981 in Lyme
Glen David of Lyme m. Laura Julie **Cooper** of Lyme 5/21/1999

ANDREWS,
J. Earl of Lyme m. Annie M. **Lamott** of Dorchester 1/14/1903 in Lebanon; H - 23, farmer, b. Lyme, s/o Nelson H. Andrews (Dorchester, farmer) and Minnie L. Cook (Lyme, housewife); W - 26, housework, b. Dorchester, d/o James Lamott (Canada, lumber mfr.) and Catherine McBain (Canada, housewife)

ANSELL,
Ray H. of Lyme m. Alice S. **Collins** of Norwich, VT 8/30/1945 in Lyme; H – 47, clerk, 2nd – W, b. Manchester, b. Everett Ansell (machinist) and Margaret Gallagher (Ireland, housewife); W – 47, housewife, 3rd – W, b. Thetford, VT, d/o Nelson Sawyer (Thetford, VT, butcher) and Roxy Avery (Thetford, VT, housewife)

ANTHONISEN,
Niels L. of Hanover m. Vernone S. **Mitchell** of Lyme 6/27/1975 in Hanover; H – b. 1/19/1898 in Norway, s/o Claus Anthonisen and Dorothea Landmark; W – b. 4/3/1905 in Canada, d/o ----- Sillig and ----- Harkness

ASHLINE,
Edward F., Jr. of Hanover m. Inez M. **Reed** of Lyme Ctr. 3/ 23/1/1962 in Lyme; H – 20, s/o Edward F. Asgline of Hanover and Violet A. Ladeau of Richford, VT; W – 22, d/o Jessie M. Reed of Newport

ASHTON,
Norman W. of Lyme m. June M. **Varney** of S. Strafford, VT 10/28/1974 in Lyme; H – b. 3/8/1922 in MA, s/o Carl Ashton and Claire Millner; W – b. 6/1/1927 in England, d/o Norman Matthews and Mary Kemp

ASPINWALL,
Dwight Channing of Tempe, AZ m. Catherine Ann **Knapp** of Lyme --/--/1991

ASSOURAMOU,
Eleuthere G. of Cotonou, Benin m. Mary E. **Daschbach** of Lyme 10/13/2002

AUDETTE,
Paul, Jr. of Lebanon m. Carol Ann **Jenks** of Lyme 5/26/1973 in Lyme; H – 21, b. NH, s/o Paul Audette and Kathleen Herrin; W – 20, b. NH, d/o Roger Jenks and Ruth Godfrey

AVERY,
David Leonard of Lyme m. Hebe Bate **Quinton** of Lyme --/--/1991
Harry E. of Lyme m. Myrtle P. **Wilmott** of Lyme 4/25/1953 in Lyme; H – 62, watchmaker, 5th – D, b. Canaan, s/o Frederick F. Avery (RI) and Lizzie M. Warner (Orford); W – 62, housewife, 2nd – W, b. Lyme, d/o Carlos Cummings (Thetford, VT) and Electa A. Buhns (Windsor, VT)
William of Lyme m. Cora **Lovejoy** of Chatham, NB 8/4/1909 in Lyme; H - 26, cook, b. Chatham, NB, s/o William Avery (Calais, ME, captain st'b) and Mary Fairman (Chatham, NB, housewife); W - 28, housework, 2nd, b. Lyme, d/o Lewis P. Lovejoy (Orford, farmer) and Hattie Perkins (Lyme, housework)

BACON,
Carlton G. of Lyme m. Ruth M. **Emerson** of Thetford, VT 6/6/1954 in Thetford, VT; H – 23, Air Force, b. Norwich, VT, s/o George W.

Bacon (VT) and Mina H. Hill (Quebec); W – 24, clerk, b.
Piermont, d/o Frank Emerson (Bradford, VT) and Edith
Blanchard (Piermont)

Frank A. of Thetford, VT m. Stella M. **Randall** of Thetford, VT
10/30/1901 in Lyme; H - 21, laborer, b. Strafford, VT, s/o
Charles E. Bacon (Pomfret, VT, farmer) and Lucy A. Terry
(Canada, housewife); W - 17, housework, b. Wentworth, d/o
Barnard J. Randall (Ellsworth, farmer) and Rosa C. Simpson
(Orford, housewife)

Stuart B. of Lyme m. Bettina L. **Austin** of W. Fairlee, VT 8/18/1952
in Lyme; H – 18, plumber, b. Lyme, s/o George Bacon (VT) and
Mina Hill (Canada); W – 18, hostess, b. VT, d/o George Austin
(VT) and Pearl Morrison (VT)

Stuart Bruce, II m. Melanie **Jenks** 12/23/1978 in Lyme

Talbert W. of Lyme m. Priscilla A. **LaMott** of Lyme 9/4/1960 in Lyme;
H – s/o George W. Bacon and Vina H. Hill, res. – Lyme; W –
d/o ----- E. LaMott and Charlotte H. Balch, res. – Lyme Ctr.

BADGER,

Charles H. of Lyme m. Nettie M. **Sawyer** of Thetford, VT 11/14/1900
in Lyme; H - 29, laborer, b. Lyme, s/o Henry M. Badger (Lowell,
MA, farmer) and Clara H. Post (Lyme, housewife); W - 21,
teacher, b. Thetford, VT, d/o Richard Sawyer (Thetford, VT,
farmer) and Mary A. Colby (Thetford, VT, housewife)

BAER,

Eric R. of Meriden, CT m. Rebecca D. **Smith** of Meriden, CT
6/21/1986 in Lyme

BAILEY,

Daniel R. of Lyme m. Mildred M. **Movelle** of Lyme 11/20/1971 in
Lyme; H – 19, b. NH, s/o Morton R. Bailey and Myrtle Russ; W
– 17, b. NH, d/o William Movelle and Esther Gray

Forrest E. of Thetford, VT m. Cassie May **Wing** of Lyme 10/19/1914
in Lyme; H - 20, tel. oper., b. Bath, s/o Clarence E. Bailey
(Bath, farmer) and Lillian Chamberlain (Ryegate, VT,
housewife); W - 19, housework, b. Lyme, d/o Nathan L. Wing
(Berkshire, VT, farmer) and Anna F. Hill (Chateaugay, NY,
housewife)

Frank H. of Lyme m. Mary J. **Ackerman** of Lyme 12/21/1904 in
Lyme; H - 29, farmer, b. Lyme, s/o Henry A. Bailey (Lyme,

farmer) and Augusta Howard (Lyme, housewife); W - 26, nurse, b. Lyme, d/o Joseph Ackerman (Alexandria, farmer) and Elizabeth Currier (Charlestown, VT, housewife)

Henry A. of Lyme m. Ethel I. **Dimick** of Lyme 12/4/1916 in Lyme; H - 23, farming, b. Lyme, s/o Henry A. Bailey (Lyme, farming) and Augusta B. Howard (Lyme, housewife); W - 16, at home, b. Lyme, d/o Charles P. Dimick (Lyme, farming) and Florence J. Carpenter (Littleton, housewife)

Henry A. of Lyme m. Ida M. **Hall** of Lyme 7/3/1926 in Hanover; H - 32, laborer, 2nd - W, b. Lyme, s/o Henry A. Bailey (Lyme) and Augusta Howard (Lyme); W - 25, at home, b. Canaan, d/o Hiland G. Hall (Maidstone, VT, farmer) and Agnes Dunham (St. George, NB, housewife)

James R. m. Tammy Etta **Mason** 6/10/1979 in Lyme

John T. B. of Lyme m. Myra J. **Winslow** of Lyme 11/25/1908 in Lyme; H - 62, farmer, 2nd, b. Lowell, MA, s/o John Trull Bailey (Andover, MA, farmer) and Orilla Norcross (Woodbury, VT, housewife); W - 50, housewife, 2nd, b. Lyme, d/o Winthrop Post (Lyme, farmer) and Laura Wise (Groton, housewife)

Laurence F. of Lyme m. Katie M. **Strout** of Fairlee, VT 8/4/1928 in Haverhill; H - 21, garage man, b. Lyme, s/o Frank H. Bailey (Lyme, farmer) and Mary J. Ackerman (Orford, housewife); W - 38, waitress, 2nd - W, b. Alton, ME, d/o John Hatch (Alton, ME, paymaster) and Cora Moore (Alton, ME, housewife)

Morris A. of Newbury, VT m. Eva M. **Lapine** of Newbury, VT 7/4/1891 in Lyme; H - 29, farmer, b. Newbury, VT, s/o Harrison Bailey (Newbury, VT, farmer) and Abigail Paro (Ryegate, VT); W - 16, housekeeper, b. Newbury, VT, d/o Lapoleur Lapine (Canada, farmer) and M. Rowe

Morton B. of Lyme m. Myrtle M. **Russ** of Lyme 12/7/1935 in W. Fairlee, VT; H - 24, farming, b. Lyme, s/o Frank H. Bailey (Lyme, farmer) and Mary J. Ackerman (Chelsea, VT, housewife); W - 23, domestic, b. W. Fairlee, VT, d/o Daniel C. Russ (W. Fairlee, VT, farmer) and Harriet Boyd (Chateaugay, NY, housewife)

Morton R. of Lyme m. Katherine M. **Fogg** of Wilder, VT 8/11/1973 in Orford; H – 34, b. NH, s/o Morton B. Bailey and Myrtle Russ; W – 25, b. VT, d/o Frank Fogg and Florence Whitcomb

Russell E. of Lyme m. Mildred V. **Withington** of Wilder, VT 6/20/1941 in Wilder, VT; H – 23, carpenter, b. Lyme, s/o Henry A. Bailey (Lyme) and Ethel Dimick (Lyme); W – 23, b. Enfield, d/o Eben Withington (Hubbardston, MA) and Alice Labbie (Hanover)

BAKER,
Ronald of Orfordville m. Janet **Pike** of Lyme 12/8/1969 in Enfield; H – 33, b. NH, s/o Maurice Baker and Hattie Streeter; W – 31, b. MA, d/o Leo Bradley and Florence Mayro

BALCH,
Alfred J. of Lyme m. Carolyn **Dole** of Lyme 9/22/1988 in Lyme
Alfred James of Lyme m. Beverly Ann **Snelling** of Lyme 10/11/1997
Charles R. of Lyme m. Mertie L. **Uline** of Lyme 7/1/1943 in Lyme; H – 24, farmer, b. Lyme, s/o Ralph W. Balch (Lyme, farmer) and Mareta J. Smalley (Easton, housewife); W – 19, at home, b. Lyme, d/o Hiram Uline (Lyme, carpenter) and Grace Gilbert (Littleton, housewife)
Donald J. of Lyme m. Mary A. **Sawyer** of N. Haverhill 4/21/1946 in Haverhill; H – 23, student, b. Hanover, s/o Ralph W. Balch (Lyme, farmer) and Mareta Smalley (Easton, housewife); W – 25, teacher, b. Haverhill, d/o Clyde Sawyer (Haverhill, farmer) and Lilly Ward (Monroe, housewife)
Ellery L. of Lyme m. Mildred **Vachon** of Lyme 5/15/1937 in Lyme; H – 26, laborer, b. Lyme, s/o Harvey H. Balch (Taftsville, VT, farmer) and Josephine L. Morrill (Taftsville, VT, housewife); W – 18, housework, b. E. Broton, PQ, d/o Ernest Vachon (Rochester, laborer) and Mary Fornia (St. Johnsbury, VT, housewife)
Frank F. of Lyme m. Harriet A. **Pushee** of Lyme 11/28/1901 in Lyme; H - 25, carpenter, b. Lyme, s/o West S. Balch (Lyme, farmer) and Mary W. Grant (Lyme); W - 27, teacher, b. Lyme, d/o Alfred W. Pushee (Lyme, farmer) and Edna Steele (Lyme, housework)
Grant P. of Lyme m. Margaret L. **Houston** of Bath 11/29/1936 in Bath; H - 30, laborer, b. Mexico, ME, s/o Frank F. Balch (Lyme, carpenter) and Harriet A. Pushee (Lyme, housewife); W - 30, at home, b. Bath, d/o Alfred E. Houston (New Ipswich, farmer) and Florence L. Johnson (Fairlee, VT, housewife)
Harvey H. of Lyme m. Josie **Morrill** of Hartford, VT 5/25/1910 in Lebanon; H - 39, laborer, 2nd, b. Hartland, VT, s/o Lowell L. Balch (farmer) and Hulda Whiting; W - 25, housework, 2nd, b. Pomfret, VT, d/o William Morrill and Lillian Chamberlain

(housewife)

Harvey R. of Lyme m. Beverly M. **Jenks** of Lyme 4/3/1955 in Lyme; H – 19, clerk, b. Lyme, s/o Roy E. Balch (Hartford, VT) and Olive Blanchard (Orford); W – 20, typist, b. Hanover, d/o Chester Jenks (Lyme) and Marion Hanchett (Lyme)

James N. of Lyme m. Elizabeth **Hardtke** of Bakersfield, VT 6/7/1947 in Orford; H – 23, tree surgeon, b. Lyme, s/o Harvey H. Balch (Hartland, VT, retired) and Josephine Morrow (Woodstock, VT, housewife); W – 22, teacher, b. Corinth, VT, d/o Hugo Hardtke (Hammerstein, Germany, farmer) and Aurelia Azabal (Presburg, Hungary, housewife)

Jeffrey A. of Hanover m. Beverly A. **Breed** of Hanover 6/25/1983 in Lyme

John C. of Lyme m. Marion L. **Gerue** of Lebanon 6/29/1937 in Lyme; H - 19, laborer, b. Lyme, s/o Harvey H. Balch (Hartland, VT, laborer) and Josephine L. Morrill (Taftsville, VT, housewife); W - 16, b. Hanover, d/o Arthur C. Gerue (Ellenburg, NY, carpenter) and Hazel Hall (Canaan, housewife)

Kevin R. of Lyme m. Michelle D. **Plaisted** of Lyme 7/26/2003

Mason of Lyme m. Bertha **Hart** of Piermont 2/10/1934 in Orford; H - 19, laborer, b. Lyme, s/o Harvey H. Balch (Taftsville, VT, laborer) and Lillian Morrill (Taftsville, VT, housewife); W - 17, at home, b. Canaan, d/o Frank Hart (Lyme, laborer) and Julia Buckley (Ireland, housewife)

Mason E., Jr. of Lyme m. Carol **LaBombard** of Hanover 5/25/1957 in Lyme; H – 21, s/o Mason E. Balch of Lyme and Bertha Hart of Windsor, VT; W – 19, d/o Clarence LaBombard of Lebanon and Alice LaDeau of Woodsville

Mason E., III of Lyme m. Vivian Lynn **Lefebvre** of Fairlee, VT 6/12/1982 in Lyme

Ralph W. of Lyme m. Mareta J. **Smalley** of Littleton 11/29/1917 in Littleton; H - 23, farming, b. Lyme, s/o West S. Balch (Lyme, farming) and Julia F. Pushee (Lyme, housewife); W - 26, teaching, b. Easton, d/o James A. Smalley (Littleton, farming) and Helen Langmaid (S. Ryegate, VT, teaching)

Raymond H. of Lyme m. Ester E. **Smith** of Thetford, VT 10/5/1940 in Hanover; H – 24, laborer, b. Lyme, s/o Harvey H. Balch (Hartland, VT, laborer) and Lillian J. Morrill (Pomfret, VT, housewife); W – 21, nurse, b. Dorchester, MA, d/o Dennis B. Smith (Halifax, NS, carpenter) and Annie E. Ketty (NS, housewife)

Raymond John of Lyme m. Beverly Jean **Frost** of Lyme 8/16/1959 in Norwich, VT; H – s/o Roy E. Balch and Olive Blanchard, res. – Lyme; W – d/o Cadis E. Frost and Pearl R. Gardner, res. – Lyme

Ronald J. A. of Lyme m. Barbara Jean **Evans** of Lyme 8/21/1959 in Orford; H – s/o John C. Balch and Marion L. Gerue, res. – Lyme Ctr.; W – d/o Harold B. Evans of Wellesley, MA and Janet F. Piper of Lyme

Russell R. of Lyme m. Sandra G. **Sweeney** of W. Lebanon 7/31/1988 in Lyme

Stephen M. of Lyme Ctr. m. Kandi K. **Downs** of Meriden 6/10/1989 in Lyme

West S. of Lyme m. Julia F. **Pushee** of Lyme 6/2/1888 in Lyme; H - 39, farmer, 2nd, b. Lyme, s/o Samuel W. Balch (Lyme) and Joanna Perkins (Hanover); W - 23, housekeeper, b. Lyme, d/o Alfred W. Pushee (Lyme) and Edna Steele (Lyme)

BARGMANN,
Brian Christopher of Lyme m. Lauren Corinne **Sutula** of W. Lebanon 10/28/1995

BARNES,
Earl F. of Lyme m. Florence L. F. **Dayton** of Lyme 6/16/1903 in Lyme; H - 26, painter, b. Richmond, VT, s/o Henry L. Barnes (Shilott, VT, butter maker) and Mary E. Bryant (Richmond, VT, housewife); W - 25, teacher, b. Newark, NJ, d/o James L. Dayton (New York City, real estate agent) and Sarah F. Foster (Brockton, MA, housework)

George W. of Lyme m. Laura A. **Smith** of Hanover 12/25/1897 in Hanover; H - 31, farmer, b. Lyme, s/o Hiram Barnes (Lebanon, farmer) and Esther B. Gillette (Thetford, VT, housework); W - 28, teacher, b. Hanover, d/o Chandler P. Smith (Hanover, farmer) and Sarah J. Camp (Hanover, housewife)

Russell Lee of Lyme m. Beth **Taylor** of Lyme 5/4/1996

BARNETT,
Wallace, Jr. of Plainfield m. Shelly **Thurston** of Lyme 8/22/1992

BARRELL,
Fred A. of White River Jct. m. Doris M. **Rogers** of White River Jct. 9/12/1946 in Lyme; H – 69, optometrist, 3rd – D, b. Turner, ME,

s/o William Barrell (Turner, ME, farmer) and Mary Parker (Auburn, ME, housewife); W – 43, at home, 2nd – W, b. Graniteville, VT, d/o Angus Morrison (Scotland, supt.) and Mary Murray (Stornaway, PQ, housewife)

BARRETT,
Charles Keith of PA m. MaryAnn **D'Esopo** of Lyme Ctr. 7/5/1975 in Lyme; H – b. 12/12/1926 in NC, s/o George William Barrett and Ann Mary Jenkins; W – b. 12/8/1943 in NH, d/o Joseph Albert D'Esopo and Beatrice Fraser Thomas

Frank Joseph, Jr. of Ely, VT m. Teresa Mavis **Leavitt** of White River Jct. 6/4/1994

Selby of N. Thetford, VT m. Leila E. **Wilmot** of Lyme 8/4/1946 in Lyme; H – 20, farming, b. New Melbourne, NF, s/o William Barrett (NF, farmer) and Bessie Pynn (Canada, housewife); W – 25, housework, b. Lyme, d/o Leo Wilmot (Lyme, farmer) and Fannie Chapin (New Boston, MA, housewife)

BARROWS,
Kenneth P. of Lyme m. Brenda J. **Lahaye** of Lebanon 4/17/1971 in Lebanon; H – 23, b. NH, s/o Philip Barrows and Naomi Trottier; W – 30, b. NH, d/o William Lahaye and Winifred Corpieri

BARTON,
Weston C. of Lyme m. Rose **Oliver** of Lyme 3/10/1897 in Lyme; H - 20, laborer, b. Woodbury, VT, s/o John Barton, Jr. (Washington, VT, farmer) and Martha M. Clark (Alburgh, NY, housewife); W - 16, housework, b. Lyme, d/o Henry Oliver (England) and Lillian Roberts (Lyme, housewife)

BATCHELDER,
Verne C. of Lyme m. Kathryn A. **George** of Gardner, MA 7/3/1942 in Lyme; H - --, farmer, D, b. Morgan, VT, s/o Elmer Batchelder (Morgan, VT, farmer) and Della Batchelder (Bloomfield, VT, housewife); W – 23, nurse, b. Fairlee, VT, d/o Ami George (Ely, VT, farmer) and Jennie Holtham (Barton, VT, housewife)

BATES,
R. W. of Lyme m. E. B. **Brockway** of Lyme 9/13/1919 in Lyme; H - 24, machinist, b. Lebanon, s/o S. W. Bates (W. Fairlee, VT, farming) and H. G. Hanchett (Lyme, housewife); W - 18,

housework, b. Lyme, d/o G. A. Brockway (Waterbury, VT, farming) and N. E. Dimick (Iron Hill, Canada, housewife)

Zelma H. of Lyme m. Sarah E. **Pushee** of Lyme 10/15/1929 in Lyme; H - 26, carpenter, b. Lebanon, s/o Sidney W. Bates (W. Fairlee, VT, farmer) and Gertrude Hanchett (Lyme, housewife); W - 24, housekeeper, b. Lyme, d/o Frank A. Pushee (Lyme, lumberman) and Viola M. Cutting (Lyme, housewife)

Zelma H. of Lyme m. Dor. B. **Goodwin** of Lyme 11/25/1948 in Lyme; H – 45, trucking, D, b. Lebanon, s/o Sidney Bates (W. Fairlee, VT, farmer) and Gertrude Hanchett (Plainfield, housewife); W – 43, at home, W, b. Hanover, d/o William Hart (Hanover, farmer) and May Glode (Bristol, housewife)

BEANE,

Charles A. of Orford m. Tammy A. **Dickey** of Lyme 3/14/1986 in Lyme

David L. of Lyme Ctr. m. Michelle A. **Sanborn** of Lyme Ctr. 8/5/1989 in Lyme

BEAUPRE,

Peter L. m. Patricia A. **Goodrich** 9/3/1977 in Lyme

BEEDE,

Earl J., Jr. of Post Mills, VT m. Patricia J. **Doyle** of W. Fairlee, VT 9/23/1961 in Lyme; H – 22, s/o Earl J. Beede, Sr. and Dorothy Clark, res. – Post Mills, VT; W – 18, d/o William J. Doyle and Irene Preston, res. – W. Fairlee, VT

Gilman F. of Lyme m. Albin A. **Webster** of Lyme 4/8/1912 in Lyme; H - 45, farmer, b. Orange, VT, s/o John Beede (farmer) and Melissa Thompson (Orange, VT, housewife); W - 42, housewife, 2nd, b. Corn Hill, NB, d/o Thomas S. Coates (Corn Hill, NB, farmer) and Mary E. Perry (New Canaan, NB, housewife)

BELL,

Robert C. of Valley Stream, NY m. Jeanne R. **Sansbury** of Lyme 7/1/1961 in Lyme; H – 20, s/o Robert H. Bell and Cora R. Tilton, res. – Valley Stream, NY; W – 20, d/o John W. Sansbury and Dorothy Gregory, res. – Lyme

BELLOWS,
Eugene R. of Brighton, MA m. Barbara L. **Bowden** of Lyme 9/12/1965 in Holderness; H – 27, retail, b. Newfoundland, s/o Paul Bellows and Margaret Abbott; W – 21, student, b. Tarrytown, NY, d/o John W. Bowden and Mary Sharples

BENT,
C. Colby m. Marguerite A. **Strohbehn** 12/29/1977 in Lyme Ctr.

BERNSTEIN,
Charles K. m. Susan B. **Laufer** 8/17/1977 in Lyme

BERQUIST,
Allen E. m. Paula R. **Seace** 9/24/1977 in Lyme

BERRY,
Solon K. of Thetford, VT m. Augusta A. **Holt** of Lyme 11/12/1888 in Lyme; H - 60, farmer, 3rd, b. Meredith, s/o Jazeb B. Berry (Lyme, CT) and N. Ranstead (Lyme); W - 58, housekeeper, 2nd, b. Lyme, d/o John Hall and Ester Smith (Thetford, VT)

BETHEL,
Mark Leslie of Lyme m. Christine Macleod **Wiggin** of Lyme 5/17/1975 in Lyme; H – b. 2/3/1950 in OH, s/o Jack Leslie Bethel and Phyllis Lehner; W – b. 3/1/1951 in MA, d/o Roy M. Wiggin and Margaret Deane

BETTIS,
Harley R. of Hartford, VT m. Roxanne J. **Carter** of Lyme 7/4/1970 in Thetford, VT; H – 22, b. NH, s/o Raymond H. Bettis and Anna M. Navish; W – 17, d/o Roscoe F. Carter and Anne DeGoosh
Raymond H. of Hartford, VT m. Velma L. **Hackett** of Hartford, VT 5/5/1934 in Lyme; H - 20, trucking, b. Hartford, VT, s/o John M. Bettis (Stowe, VT, RR man) and Rubie Ploof (Stowe, VT, housewife); W - 19, at home, b. Springfield, MA, d/o Earnest Hackett (Hartford, VT, RR man) and Jennie Shaltra (Westfield, VT, housewife)

BEZARA,
Alfredo Enrique of Hollis Hills, NY m. Petra Johanna **Fette** of Hollis Hills, NY 8/17/1996

BICKFORD,
Ronald G. of Lyme m. Della M. **Tibbetts** of Lyme 7/2/1966 in Lyme; H – 34, carpenter, b. Vershire, VT, s/o Harry Bickford and Gertrude Tibbetts; W – 32, sewing, b. Lyme, d/o Henry J. Bailey and Margaret Wilmot

BIRCH,
Richard W. of Lyme m. Rose Marie **McNamara** of Lyme 3/13/1976 in Lyme; H – b. 1/15/1955 in MA, s/o Warren Birch and Lucille A. Merrill; W – b. 9/15/1955 in TX, d/o Reginald McNamara and Lawrencia Dashnei

BISCUTI,
Paul of CT m. Katherine **Geisler** of CT 7/17/1976 in Lyme; H – b. 2/15/1953 in VA, s/o Philip Biscuti and ----- Margarella; W – b. 5/18/1951 in NY, d/o William Zartun and Katherine Schiess

BISHOP,
Myron of Bradford, VT m. Nancy **Hart** of Lyme 5/4/1963 in Hanover; H – s/o ----- Bishop and ----- Cheney, res. – Bradford, VT; W – d/o Lawrence Hart and ----- Young, res. – Lyme Ctr.

BIX,
Rendall of Lyme m. Thelma **Race** of Lyme 10/14/1933 in Lyme; H - 22, farmer, b. Stockbridge, VT, s/o Angus Bix (Potsdam, NY, farmer) and Tammie Harlow (E. Bethel, VT, housewife); W - 19, at home, b. Stockbridge, VT, d/o Henry Race (Hancock, VT, carpenter) and Flora LaCount (Sherburne, VT, housewife)

BLACK,
Harry A. of Hartford, VT m. Leslie G. **Morse** of Lyme 1/18/1969 in Hartford, VT; H – 31, b. NH, s/o Henry F. Black and Beatrice Skinner; W – 27, b. NY, d/o David Gibson and Kitty Canvet

BLAIR,
Donald Robert of Lyme m. Christine Mary **Turino** of Cos Cob, CT 9/24/1994

BLAKE,
Charles H. of Indianapolis, IN m. Constance B. **McDowell** of Lyme 9/24/1983 in Hanover

Mark D. of Lyme m. Georgia A. **Sanborn** of Canaan 3/3/1907 in Lyme; H - 57, farmer, 2nd, b. Dorchester, s/o Charles D. Blake (Dorchester, farmer) and Jerusha Elliott (Boscawen, housewife); W - 52, housework, 2nd, b. Canaan, d/o Charles D. Washburn (Woodstock, VT, farmer) and Harriet M. Richardson (Canaan, housewife)

BLANCHARD,
Charles A. of W. Fairlee, VT m. Barbara I. **Drew** of Lyme 3/5/1954 in Vershire, VT; H – 25, miner, b. W. Fairlee, VT, s/o Charles Blanchard (Norwich, VT) and Hazel Rogers (Tunbridge, VT); W – 19, unemployed, b. Charlestown, d/o Leslie Drew (Fairhaven, MA) and Irene Blake (Claremont)

Edwin L. of Lyme m. Jennie A. **Bailey** of Lyme 1/15/1902 in Lyme; H - 33, farming, b. W. Corinth, VT, s/o Simeon Blanchard (Groton, shoemaker) and Cynthia Leach (W. Corinth, VT, housewife); W - 32, teacher, b. Lyme, d/o Henry A. Bailey (Lyme, farmer) and Augusta A. Howard (Lyme, housewife)

BLANFORD,
Franklin C. of Lyme m. Roberta J. **Thurston** of W. Fairlee, VT 9/16/1989 in Lyme

BLAU,
Christopher of Manhattan, NY m. Wendy **Stevenson** of Lyme 8/1/1992

BLISS,
Fred G. of Lyme m. S. Louise **Merrill** of Enfield 8/28/1891 in Lyme; H - 26, farmer, b. Lyme, s/o George R. Bliss (Lyme, farmer) and Dolly Goodell (Lyme, housekeeper); W - 26, school teacher, b. Enfield, d/o H. N. Merrill (Hanover, farmer) and A. C. Paige (Barnard, VT, housekeeper)

BLIVEN,
David Christopher of Bradford, VT m. Paula Cowell **Reynolds** of Bradford, VT 9/5/1999

BLOOD,
Elmer A. of Lyme m. Hattie C. **Lincoln** of Lyme 1/1/1902 in Lyme; H - 20, butcher, b. Orford, s/o Daniel A. Blood (Orford, butcher)

and Mercy A. Merrill (Groton); W - 25, housework, b. Lyme, d/o
Gardner H. Lincoln (Chelsea, VT, tinsmith) and Sarah F.
Sanborn (Topsham, VT, housewife)
George G. of Lyme m. Farrie L. **Jones** of E. Thetford, VT
10/16/1892; H - 24, station agent, b. Lyme, s/o Edwin Blood
(Thetford, VT, wheelwright) and Louisa J. Jewell (Dorchester,
housewife); W - 20, dress-maker, b. Newbury, VT, d/o Frank M.
Jones (Newbury, VT, merchant) and Claribelle Fleming
(Newbury, VT, dress-maker)
Sidney A. of Lyme m. Ella M. **Seavey** of Manchester 7/14/1923 in
Lyme; H - 74, farmer, 3rd - W, b. Lyme, s/o Abel Blood
(Windsor, VT, farmer) and Susan Bixby (Lyme, housewife); W -
50, forelady, b. Lyme, d/o Horace Seavy (Fairfax, VT,
carpenter) and Julia A. Smith (Beekmanton, NY, housewife)

BLUM,
Steven G. of Lyme m. Suzie H. **Long** of Swarthmore, PA 7/6/2002

BOHUS,
Robert W. of Lyme Ctr. m. Betti Jo **Horshfield** of Lyme Ctr.
12/12/1986 in Lyme

BOMBARD,
Charles W. of Lyme m. Myrtle L. **Coates** of Lyme 12/14/1907 in
Lyme; H - 23, laborer, b. Burlington, VT, s/o Phillip Bombard
(Burlington, VT, laborer) and Ellen Welch (S. Vernon, MA,
housework); W - 17, housework, b. Corn Hill, NB, d/o Thomas
S. Coates (Corn Hill, NB, farmer) and Mary E. Perry (New
Canaan, NB, housework)
Frank J. of Lyme m. Dora E. **Jewell** of Lyme 8/8/1903 in Lyme; H -
25, laborer, b. Northfield, MA, s/o Philip Bombard (Burlington,
VT, laborer) and Nellie Welch (S. Vernon, MA, housewife); W -
22, housework, b. Canada, d/o Frank Jewell (Dorchester,
laborer) and Eliza Jewell (Canada, housework)
Leon C. of Lyme m. Lucia **Willard** of Haverhill 7/6/1936 in Orford; H
- 24, farmer, b. Lyme, s/o Charles W. Bombard (Burlington, VT,
mason) and Myrtle L. Coates (Corn Hill, NB, housewife); W -
21, at home, b. Wareham, MA, d/o Leonard Willard (Brooklyn,
NY, merchant) and Jennie Buck (Haverhill, housewife)

BOMHOWER,
Harold W. of Lyme m. Jean E. **Cutting** of Lyme 5/17/1970 in Lyme; H – 42, b. VT, s/o John L. Bomhower and Martha Stone; W – 42, b. NH, d/o Winslow Smith and Gladys Burnham

BOND,
Alden W. of Lyme m. Gladys B. **Reynolds** of Hanover 9/26/1923 in Hanover; H - 29, painter, b. Newbury, VT, s/o Daniel M. Bond (Topsham, VT, retired) and Julia E. Bailey (Corinth, VT, housewife); W - 30, nurse, b. Abbott's Cor., d/o Albert Reynolds (St. Armand, PQ, retired) and Mary J. Krans (Dunham, PQ, housewife)

Charles H. of Thetford, VT m. Edna H. **Sargent** of Fairlee, VT 8/27/1952 in Lyme; H – 37, bookkeeper, b. VT, s/o William Bond (VT) and Sadie Houston (VT); W - 35, nurse, 2nd – D, b. Canada, d/o Talbert Hill (NY) and Lila Leet (Canada)

Otis D. of N. Thetford, VT m. Jessie M. **Cook** of Lyme 7/17/1906 in Lyme; H - 21, clerk, b. Corinth, VT, s/o Daniel M. Bond (Topsham, VT, merchant) and Julia E. Bailey (Chateaugay, NY, farmer); W - 23, teacher, b. Burke, NY, d/o Hiram Cook (Chateaugay, NY, farmer) and Ellen Small (Canada, housewife)

BORGER,
Richard F. of Wentworth m. Mae E. **Pushee** of Lyme 11/16/1961 in Lyme; H – 17, s/o Francis A. Borger of Waltham, MA and Elizabeth Winkle of Jamaica, NY; W – 16, d/o David J. Pushee and Florence DeGoosh, res. – Lyme

BORGSTROM,
Keith Cornell of Lyme m. Karen Joy **Creighton** of Lyme 5/29/1994

BORNE,
Albert of Montpelier, VT m. Alberta **Courchesne** of Montpelier, VT 9/14/1946 in Lyme; H – 24, carpenter, b. Ireland, s/o Alfred Borne (England, supt.) and Florence M'Grenahan (Ireland, housewife); W – 20, secretary, b. Walden, VT, d/o Albert Courchesne (Canada, farmer) and Lillian Lee (Elmore, VT, housewife)

BOSWORTH,
Hazen W. m. Pamela J. **Sirois** 8/26/1980 in Lyme

BOUCHIER,
Lester J., Jr. of Lebanon m. Bernice A. **Howe** of Lyme 5/5/1962 in Lebanon; H – 24, s/o Lester J. Bouchier, Sr. and Beatrice Sanborn, res. – Lebanon; W – d/o Edward C. Howe and Hazel A. Martin, res. - Meriden

BOUDREAU,
Raymond Alfred of Malden, MA m. Kathleen Piper **Balch** of Malden, MA 10/4/1997

BOURASSA,
Christopher M. of Lyme m. Paula J. **Corriveau** of Lyme 6/10/1984 on Lake Winnipesaukee

BOURNE,
Steven R. m. Elizabeth S. **Phillips** 11/11/1980 in Lyme

BOWKER,
James F. of Lyme m. Carole A. **Lavoie** of Orford 9/13/1946 in Lebanon; H – 31, truck driver, b. Lunenburg, VT, s/o Edward Bowker (Lunenburg, VT, mfg.) and Mattie Vance (Lunenburg, VT, housewife); W – 36, teacher, b. E. Haverhill, d/o Henry Lavoie (Benton, farmer) and Nellie Dearborn (E. Haverhill, housewife)

BOYNTON,
Fred A. of Lyme m. Minnie E. **Lewis** of Piermont 5/21/1933 in Orford; H - 66, retired, 3rd - W, b. Ballston Spa, NY, s/o John T. Boynton (Mercier, ME, iron worker) and Sarah J. Coombs (Utica, NY, housewife); W - 52, housekeeper, 3rd - W, b. Vershire, VT, d/o George A. Church (Vershire, VT, board sawyer) and Sarah F. Aldrich (Corinth, VT, housewife)

BRADLEY,
Hiel of Norwich, VT m. Elizabeth J. **Bean** of Lyme 6/30/1897 in Lyme; H - 63, farmer, 2nd, b. Norwich, VT, s/o Ranna Bradley (Newport, farmer) and Mehitabel Mathews (Bristol, CT, housework); W - 43, nurse, 2nd, b. Lyme, d/o William Thomas (England, wheelwright) and Nancy Cook (Lyme)
Ransom L. of Norwich, VT m. Caroline F. **Bean** of Lyme 5/25/1899 in Lyme; H - 35, farmer, b. Norwich, VT, s/o Hial Bradley

(Norwich, VT, farmer) and Harriet Gilkey (Sharon, VT); W - 24, housework, b. Piermont, d/o Fred Bean (Piermont) and Elizabeth Thomas (Lyme, housewife)

William A. of Greensboro, VT m. Gail **Sanford** of Greensboro, VT 11/5/1983 in Lyme

BRALEY,

Charles L. of Lyme m. Etta **Batchelder** of Post Mills, VT 4/14/1896 in Lyme; H - 22, laborer, b. Grafton, s/o Charles G. Braley (France, blacksmith) and Lizzie Spiller (Concord); W - 21, housework, b. Hillsboro, d/o Harry Batchelder (Post Mills, VT, farmer) and Eliza Bowles (Post Mills, VT, housewife)

Charles L. of Lyme m. Julia **Billingham** of Lyme 10/4/1921 in Lyme; H - 29, farmer, b. Lyme, s/o Charles L. Braley (Danbury) and Flora Dunbar (Canada); W - 32, housework, 2nd, b. Island Pond, VT, d/o William H. Perrin (England) and Sarah LaFrance (Quebec, housewife)

Chester A. of Plainfield m. Linda M. **Bickford** of Lyme 9/16/1965 in Hartford, VT; H – 19, caretaker, b. Plainfield, s/o Roy S. Braley and Mildred Clarke; W – 16, asst. gardener, b. Hanover, d/o Henry Bickford and Lillian Gould

BRAMAN,

Lawrence F. of Lyme m. Margaret R. **Boyd** of Hanover 11/15/1954 in Hanover; H – 42, farmer, b. MA, s/o Clarence Braman (MA) and Eva Lawrence (MA); W – 39, home, b. NH, d/o William Boyd (NY) and Henrietta Rennie (Canada)

BRANDIS,

Durward Porter of Lyme m. Nancy Murray **Ashton** of Lyme 7/11/1975 in Lyme

BRECK,

David L. of Manchester m. Gail M. **Elder** of Lyme 6/9/1984 in Lyme

BREWSTER,

Raymond W. of Lyme m. Jan-Roberta **Tarjan** of Lyme 9/26/1982 in Hanover

BRIGGS,

Frank S. of Littleton m. Bessie E. **Marden** of Lyme 5/9/1918 in

Littleton; H - 26, farmer, b. Littleton, s/o Orrin S. Briggs (Littleton, farmer) and Lizzie Defossie (Littleton, housewife); W - 36, housework, 2nd - D, b. Lyme, d/o George Page (farmer) and Annie Page (Lyme, housewife)

Hoyt A. of Thetford, VT m. Lena M. **Chesley** of Lyme 5/21/1940 in Windsor, VT; H – 22, laborer, b. Colebrook, s/o Cassius O. Briggs (Holland, VT) and Mildred Markwell (Canada); W – 19, waitress, b. Lyme, d/o Arthur B. Chesley (W. Fairlee, VT) and Geraldine Thompson (Canada)

BRITCH,
Cecil Jay of Lyme m. Lisa M. **Avery** of Lyme 3/16/1996

BRITTON,
Douglas G. of Norwich, VT m. Katherine **Fisher** of Norwich, VT 8/20/1994

BROCKETT,
Bruce Edward of Lyme m. Suzanne Ellen **Lorenz** of Lyme 4/27/1974 in Lyme; H – b. 5/18/1944 in CT, s/o Edward Brockett and Anne Morgowicz; W – b. 1/19/1952 in NY, d/o Lloyd Lorenz and Gertrude Brunton

BROCKWAY,
Guy C. of Lyme m. Mary E. **Lund** of Norwich, VT 6/30/1920 in Thetford, VT; H - 28, farmer, b. Lyme, s/o George A. Brockway (Waterbury, VT, farmer) and Ada E. Wells (Iron Hill, PQ, housewife); W - 24, b. Norwich, VT, d/o George R. Lund (E. Haven, VT) and Sarah Ricker (Tingwick, Canada, housewife)

BROG,
Timothy Edward of NY m. Jennifer Alyce **Knight** of NY 8/21/1999

BROOKS,
Wilbur E. of Lyme m. Sadie E. **Robie** of Bradford, VT 8/11/1891 in Lyme; H - 30, insurance agent, b. Lyme, s/o David B. Brooks (Post Mills, VT, farmer) and A. Mutchmore (Post Mills, VT, housekeeper); W - 26, housekeeper, b. Bradford, VT, d/o Nathaniel Robie (Bradford, VT, farmer) and Frances Freeman (Fairlee, VT, housekeeper)

BROTMAN,
Harvey I. of Lyme m. Judith L. Shelnutt **Hilbert** of Lebanon 8/5/1984 in Hanover
Harvey Irvin m. Martha Elizabeth **Adams** 2/11/1978 in Lyme

BROWN,
Charles H. of Strafford, VT m. Ellen E. **Piper** of Lyme 6/6/1970 in S. Strafford, VT; H – 37, b. VT, s/o Frank H. Brown and Marjorie Sheldon; W – 24, b. NH, d/o Walter J. Piper and Vivian Gregory
Everett B. of Hanover m. Frances **Hart** of Lyme 12/25/1931 in Etna; H - 19, laborer, b. Graniteville, s/o Charles Brown (Newport, VT, laborer) and Flora Allen (Newport, VT, housekeeper); W - 18, at home, b. Canaan, d/o Frank Hart (Lyme, farmer) and Julia Buckley (Ireland, housewife)
Fred F. of Bradford, VT m. Bernice A. **Bagley** of Bradford, VT 11/4/1945 in Lyme; H – 45, telephone, 2nd – W, b. Strafford, VT, s/o Alvin E. Brown (Strafford, VT, carpenter) and Anna Kimball (W. Lebanon, housewife); W – 24, housework, b. Bradford, VT, d/o Carl Bagley (Bradford, VT, mail carrier) and Gertrude Worthen (Bradford, VT, housewife)
Jeffery L. of Lyme m. Carmella **Santorelli** of Lyme 7/23/1988 in W. Newbury, VT
Matthew Whiting of Lyme m. Elizabeth **Page** of Lyme 8/25/1990 in Lyme

BROWNLOW,
Frank W. of Bangor, Ireland m. Jeanne B. **Piazza** of Lyme 6/24/1961 in Thetford, VT; H – 26, s/o Frank Brownlow and Katherine Darroch, res. – Bolton, England; W – 26, d/o Joseph Piazza and Helen M. Geiger, res. – Lyme

BRUMSTED,
John Robert m. Nicole Yvette **Versyp** 12/10/1977 in Hanover

BRYAN,
Jeffrey N. of Lyme m. Ellen **Rieger** of Dumont, NJ 11/29/1975 in Durham; H – b. 1/19/1951 in NH, s/o Neal R. Bryan and Helen Goddard; W – b. 3/17/1950 in NJ, d/o John Rieger and Gene Hoover
Richard E. of Canaan, VT m. May L. **Jenks** of Lyme 4/9/1892; H - 22, painter, b. Canaan, VT, s/o Edward Bryan (Ireland, farmer)

and Elizabeth Hervey (Canada, housewife); W - 19, b. Lyme, d/o Marshall Jenks (Lyme, laborer) and Sarah Meader (Thetford, VT, housekeeper)

BRYANT,
Arthur W. of Lyme m. Theda M. **Sanborn** of Lyme 9/20/1922 in Lyme; H - 20, laborer, b. Lyme, s/o Fred J. Bryant (Lyme, farmer) and Florence Henry (Thetford, VT, housewife); W - 20, at home, b. Lyme, d/o Newton Sanborn (Lyme, mill man) and Eliza E. Welch (Lyme, housewife)
Fred J. of Lyme m. Florence M. **Henry** of Hanover 5/1/1900 in Hanover; H - 22, farmer, b. Lyme, s/o Horace M. Bryant (Hanover, farmer) and Clara Chesley (Canada); W - 18, housework, b. Thetford, VT, d/o William H. Henry (Derby, VT, farmer) and Elizabeth E. Emery (Thetford, VT, housewife)
Fred J. of Lyme m. Katherine **Keniston** of Lyme 6/9/1946 in Lyme; H – 68, farmer, 2nd – W, b. Lyme, s/o Horace Bryant (Hanover, farmer) and Clara Chesley (Canada, housewife); W – 31, teacher, b. Plymouth, d/o Everett Keniston (Plymouth, merchant) and Martha Savage (Orford, teacher)
George H. of Lyme m. Ruth E. **Dimick** of Lyme 5/1/1926 in Lyme; H - 22, laborer, b. Lyme, s/o Fred J. Bryant (Lyme, farmer) and Florence Henry (Thetford, VT, housewife); W - 23, domestic, b. Lyme, d/o Charles P. Dimick (Lyme, farmer) and Florence Carpenter (Littleton, housewife)
Horace M. of Lyme m. Sarah F. **Lincoln** of Lyme 5/30/1900 in Lyme; H - 46, farmer, 2nd, b. Hanover, s/o John Bryant (Hanover, farmer) and Sally Ellsworth (Wentworth, housework); W - 56, housework, 2nd, b. Topsham, VT, d/o Ebenezer Sanborn (Warren, blacksmith) and Ruth Haywood (Topsham, VT, housework)
Sterle H. of Lyme m. Lorraine A. **Wing** of Lyme 2/11/1957 in Orford; H – 27, s/o George H. Bryant and Ruth Dimick, res. – Lyme; W – 24, d/o Albert E. Wing and Esther Small, res. – Lyme

BUCKLEY,
James E. of Unity, ME m. Denise Eileen **Beach** of Unity, ME 9/9/1995

BUEDDEMAN,
N. L. of Bradford m. Mil. G. **Greenwood** of Lyme 4/30/1948 in Lyme;

H – 23, hotel work, b. Danbury, CT, s/o Lester Bueddeman (Patterson, NJ, manager) and Vera Wilmott (Stratford-on-Avon, housewife); W – 24, student, b.. Hanover, d/o John Greenwood and Eva McGill (Canada, housewife)

BUFFUM,
Jabos Arthur of Dorchester m. Nettie E. **Wing** of Lyme 11/28/1903 in Lyme; H - 20, farming, b. Somerville, MA, s/o Charles P. Buffum (Melrose, MA, farmer) and Alice Greene (Malden, MA, housewife); W - 20, teacher, b. Chateaugay, NY, d/o Nathan L. Wing (Berkshire, VT, farmer) and Anna F. Hill (Chateaugay, NY, housewife)

BURELLE,
Timothy James of Lyme m. Patricia Mary **Redman** of Lyme 9/18/1999

BURKE,
John F. of Wilton m. Nina I. **Thompson** of Lyme 12/19/1925 in Lyme; H - 34, mill opr., b. Lancaster, MA, s/o John R. Burke (Lancaster, MA, mill opr.) and Bertha Raymond (S. Lyndeboro, housewife); W - 24, nursing, 2nd - W, b. S. Ham, PQ, d/o Joseph Thompson (S. Ham, PQ, farmer) and Mary A. Devy (S. Ham, PQ, housewife)

BUSHAW,
Fred E. of Bradford, VT m. Edna B. **Messier** of Lyme 3/17/1917 in Lyme; H - 22, laborer, b. Corinth, VT, s/o Oliver Bushaw (Canada, laborer) and Sophia Surrell (Canada, housewife); W - 26, housework, 2nd, b. Monroe, d/o George C. Gilbert (England, laborer) and Malvina E. Byron (Littleton, housewife)

BUSKA,
Olan J. of Middlesex, VT m. Barbara A. **Willey** of Berlin, VT 9/25/1951 in Lyme; H – 21, truck driver, b. Burlington, VT, s/o John Buska (Malone, NY) and Alice Santamore (NY); W – 18, at home, b. Westminster, VT, d/o Harold Willey (Berlin, VT) and Ruth Chatfield (Montpelier, VT)

BUSKEY,
Wilton L. of Lyme m. Mary Jane Shannon **Daley** of Lyme 11/3/1990

in Hanover

BUTMAN,
Herbert C. of Orford m. Carol J. **Campbell** of Lyme 10/20/1962 in Lyme; H – 20, s/o Richard C. Butman and Marion Streeter, res. – Orford; W – 15, d/o Zane E. Campbell and Dolores Piper, res. – Lyme

Herbert C. of Orford m. Suzanne **Pushee** of Lyme 1/22/1965 in Orford; J – 22, construction, 2nd, b. Orford, s/o Richard C. Butman and Marion Streeter; W – 18, at home, b. Hanover, d/o Roger C. Pushee and Isabelle Uline

BUZZELL,
George L. of Lyme m. Doris A. **Dudley** of Gilmanton 9/10/1960 in Gilmanton; H – s/o Olin R. Buzzell and Marion E. Harris, res. – Lyme; W – d/o Irving D. Dudley, Jr. and Dorothy A. Hurlbutt, res. – Gilmanton

Max H. of Lyme m. Jean C. **Banker** of Thetford Ctr., VT 8/11/1963 in Thetford, VT; H – s/o Olin R. Buzzell and Marion Harris, res. – Lyme; W – d/o Welles F. Banker and ----- Smith, res. – Thetford, VT

BYRD,
Harry Flood, II of Westwood, MA m. Nancy Lynn **Bliss** of Lyme 10/14/1995

CADWELL,
Benjamin T. of Thetford, VT m. Donna J. **Fowler** of Lyme 12/2/1961 in Thetford, VT; H – 19, s/o Harvey L. Cadwell and Nellie Harlow, res. – Thetford, VT; W – 17, d/o David G. Fowler and Olive Greenwood, res. – Lyme

CAMBER,
Harry E. of Hanover m. Marion V. **Rogers** of Lyme 11/11/1946 in Lyme; H – 19, farmer, b. Lyndonville, VT, s/o Charles Camber (Newark, VT, farmer) and Hannah Donna (Westmore, VT, housewife); W – 23, housework, 2nd – D, b. Canaan, d/o Robert Stark (Lyme, sawyer) and Mattie Blake (Orange, housewife)

CAMP,
Edward M. of Lyme m. Martha L. **Bowker** of Piermont 3/21/1893 in

Lyme; H - 29, farmer, b. Hyde Park, VT, s/o Bushrod W. Camp (Morrisville, VT, laborer) and Ellen L. Spiller (Chelsea, VT); W - 25, domestic, d/o S. Bowker (Parishville, NY) and Maria P. Brown (Stanstead, PQ)

Frank L. of Lyme m. Anna A. **Alden** of Lyme 1/16/1892; H - 23, farmer, b. Lyme, s/o Bushrod W. Camp (Morrisville, VT, laborer) and Ellen L. Spiller (Chelsea, VT, housekeeper); W - 24, housekeeper, b. Lyme, d/o Amos B. Alden

Willie E. of Lyme m. Olivia M. **Stark** of Lyme 6/8/1889 in Lyme Ctr.; H - 22, laborer, b. Orford, s/o Bushrod W. Camp (Morristown, VT, laborer) and Ellen L. Spiller (Chelsea, VT, housekeeper); W - 20, housekeeper, b. Lyme, d/o David C. Stark (Lyme, laborer) and Mary Runnells (Lyme, housekeeper)

CAMPBELL,

Paul Jason of Tunbridge, VT m. Jenni Marie **Mongeur** of Tunbridge, VT 6/26/2004

Willard L. of Hartford, VT m. Marion G. **Rogers** of Hartford, VT 7/27/1963 in Piermont; H – s/o Charles Campbell and ----- E. Elliott of Hartford, VT; W – d/o George Lyford of Chelsea, VT and ----- Goulette

William Bruce of Wellesley, MA m. Eltiena Johanna **Sample** of Wellesley, MA 8/14/1993

CAMPION,

Brian Walsh of Lyme m. Kristen Colleen **Gaughan** of Lyme 7/10/1993

CAPRON,

Glenn C. of Newton Falls, NY m. Barbara I. **Lockwood** of Springfield, VT 8/4/1951 in Lyme; H – 33, mason, b. Braintree, VT, s/o Floyd Capron (VT) and Mary Morse (VT); W – 20, student, b. Springfield, VT, d/o Arthur Lockwood (VT) and Gertrude Eagan (VT)

CARCHIA,

Antonio of Abington, MA m. Susan M. **Williams** of Abington, MA 5/26/1984 in Lyme

CARES,

Charles C. m. Eleanor W. **Mudge** 6/25/1977 in Lyme

CARGILL,
Leland A. of Lyme m. Carrie L. **Pike** of Lyme 7/24/1947 in W. Lebanon; H – 39, carpenter, 2nd – D, b. Washington, ME, s/o Alton J. Cargill (Washington, ME, farmer) and Ethel O'Leary (Kingston Sta., NS, housewife); W – 49. domestic, 2nd – D, b. Lyme, d/o Fred L. Pike (Lyme, retired) and Anna Roberts (Lyme, housewife)

CARON,
Joseph Albert of Lyme m. Lucinda Marie **Kolo** of Lyme 5/31/1997

CARPENTER,
Seth Maxwell of N. Grafton, MA m. Emily Ann **Richmond** of N. Grafton, MA 10/3/2004

CARR,
Charles J. of Lyme m. Daisy E. **Day** of Plymouth 11/2/1897 in Haverhill; H - 23, farmer, b. Alburgh, NY, s/o Horace F. Carr (Grantham, farmer) and Ellen Jeffers (Royalton, VT, housewife); W - 16, housework, d/o ----- Day (farmer)
Charles J. of Lyme m. Eva Jane **Rowell** of Lyme 6/15/1913 in Fairlee, VT; H - 39, farmer, 2nd, b. Albany, NY, s/o Horace F. Carr (Haverhill) and Ellen Jeffers (S. Royalton, VT); W - 18, b. Strafford, VT, d/o Harry H. Rowell (W. Fairlee, VT) and Margaret Bailey (Bradford, VT)
Lewis F. of Lyme m. Della M. **Rowell** of Thetford, VT 3/24/1924 in Lyme; H - 24, lumberman, b. Fairlee, VT, s/o Charles J. Carr (Albany, NY, blacksmith) and Daisy E. Day (Corinth, VT, housewife); W - 18, at home, b. Corinth, VT, d/o Harry H. Rowell (Fairlee, VT, farmer) and Margaret Bailey (Bradford, VT)

CARTER,
Carl R. of Lyme m. Elizabeth J. **Keniston** of Lyme 9/4/1970 in Lyme; H – 23, b. NH, s/o Roscoe Carter and Anne DeGoosh; W – 25, b. NH, d/o Fred Plaisted and Marjorie Keniston
Carl Richard of Lyme m. Vera Ellen **Devaux** of Lyme 6/30/1990 in Lyme
Dusty C. of Bradford, VT m. Laurie E. **Bean** of Bradford, VT 9/9/1989 in Lyme
Lawrence, Jr. of Lyme Ctr. m. Rebecca A. **Wheeler** of Lyme Ctr. 10/6/1973 in Hanover; H – 20, b. VT, s/o Lawrence Carter and

Vivian Wilmot; W – 18, b. VT, d/o Ernest Wheeler and Hazel Campbell

Roscoe F. of Lyme m. Anne **DeGoosh** of Lyme 7/30/1946 in Lyme; H – 22, farmer, b. Norwich, VT, s/o Frank Carter (Canada, janitor) and Julia Bailey (W. Fairlee, VT, housewife); W – 20, secretary, b. Hanover, d/o Howard DeGoosh (Cornish, farmer) and Nettie Pushee (Lyme, housewife)

CARTISSER,
John James of MA m. Deborah Dressel **North** of MA 9/9/2000

CASSIDY,
Bruce P. of Bristol, VT m. Mary E. **Hanson** of Monkton, VT 4/24/1971 in Lyme; H – 20, b. VT, s/o Bernard Cassidy and Peggy Murphy; W – 20, b. VT, d/o William Hanson and Gladys Watson

CHAMBERLIN,
Robert M. of Plainfield m. Katherine P. **Emlen** of Lyme 8/26/1989 in Lyme

CHAPIN,
Orrin H. of Lyme m. Alice H. **DeGoosh** of Lyme 4/2/1915 in Lyme; H – 21, laborer, b. Charlemont, MA, s/o Elmer G. Chapin (Ludlow, MA, laborer) and Fannie M. Deveau (Salmon River, NS, housewife); W – 25, housework, b. Hartland, VT, d/o Elmer E. DeGoosh (W. Fairlee, VT, farmer) and Belle M. Keyes (Reading, VT, housewife)

CHASE,
Robin A. m. Karen **Wynkoop** 6/14/1977 in Lyme Ctr.

William F. of Lyme m. Mildred **Fey** of Lebanon 2/14/1931 in Claremont; H - 25, salesman, b. Lyme, s/o William L. Chase (New Haven, CT, salesman) and Mary A. Place (St. Albans, VT, housewife); W - 26, milliner, b. Schroon Lake, NY, d/o George Fey (Schroon Lake, NY, retired) and Catherine Hall (Schroon Lake, NY, housekeeper)

William L. of Lyme m. Mary A. **Place** of Highgate, VT 12/18/1901 in Highgate, VT; H - 41, drummer, b. New Haven, CT, s/o Hannibal Chase (Bristol, farmer) and Marinda Jeffers (Lyme, housewife); W - 32, teacher, b. St. Albans, VT, d/o Miles E.

Place (St. Albans, VT, merchant) and Mary E. Barr (housewife)

CHENEY,
Alan V. m. Joyce **Currie** 7/10/1981 in Lyme

CHESLEY,
Arthur B. of Lyme m. Geraldine M. **Thompson** of Lyme 2/17/1909 in Hanover; H - 26, farmer, b. W. Fairlee, VT, s/o Frank A. Chesley (W. Fairlee, VT, farmer) and Louise Morey (W. Fairlee, VT, housewife); W - 19, housework, b. S. Ham, PQ, d/o Joseph G. Thompson (S. Ham, PQ, farmer) and Annie May Dency (S. Ham, PQ, housewife)
Frank A. of Lyme m. Elsie E. **Johnson** of Norwich, VT 8/25/1940 in Lyme; H – 30, farmer, b. Lyme, s/o Arthur B. Chesley (W. Fairlee, VT, RFD carrier) and Monte G. Thompson (Canada, housewife); W – 30, domestic, b. Norwich, VT, d/o Stuart Johnson (Thetford, VT, carpenter) and Alice Jenkins (Thetford, VT, housewife)
George H. of Lyme m. Janet M. **Arachikavitz** of Worcester, MA 1/30/1952 in Lyme; H – 26, US Army, b. Lyme, s/o Arthur Chesley (VT) and Monte Thompson (Canada); W – 19, at home, b. Worcester, MA, d/o Henry Arachikavitz (MA) and Janet Brown (MA)
Harold M. of Lyme m. Frances S. **Ashley** of Rumney 9/29/1938 in Pittsfield; H - 25, farmer, b. Lyme, s/o Arthur B. Chesley (W. Fairlee, VT, mail carrier) and Monte G. Thompson (Canada, housewife); W - 23, waitress, b. Rumney, d/o Gordon Ashley (PEI) and Lillian M. French (Rumney, housewife)

CHILD,
Stephen T. of Lyme m. Stephanie A. **Merrill** of Lebanon 6/15/1986 in Hanover

CHILDS,
Preston E. of N. Attleboro, MA m. Mabel E. **Donnelly** of N. Attleboro, MA 9/1/1957 in Lyme; H – 26, s/o Francis B. Childs and Edith M. Bearisto, res. – N. Attleboro, MA; W – 34, d/o Jay W. Donnelly and Della A. Pease of N. Attleboro, MA

CHIVERS,
Roland W. of Hanover m. Evelyn M. **Wolfe** of Lyme 9/11/1948 in

Lyme; H – 30, hotel mgr., b. Hanover, s/o Arthur H. Chivers (Amesbury, MA, professor) and Helen W. Warren (Keene, housewife); W – 30, at home, b. Bridgeton, ME, d/o Gurdon C. Wolfe (Lawton, MA, salesman) and Ruth P. Hubbard (Rochester, NY, farmer)

CHOW,
Timothy of Norwich, VT m. Lynne Barbara **Casey** of Norwich, VT 7/15/1995

CHRISTIANSEN,
Martin of Lyme m. Emma M. **Hanson** of Concord 3/2/1929 in Lyme; H - 52, mill, 2nd - W, b. Norway, s/o Christen Christiansen (Norway, farmer) and Elizabeth Anderson (Norway, housewife); W - 46, housekeeper, 2nd - W, b. Concord, d/o George E. Drew (Allenstown, mason) and Orissa Baker (Pembroke, housewife)

CHRISTIE,
Kent F. of White Plains, NY m. Helen B. **Gottschaldt** of White Plains, NY 6/1/1946 in Lyme; H – 23, as. main eng., b. Brooklyn, NY, s/o George Christie (Brooklyn, NY, advertising) and Mildred Fleming (Brooklyn, NY, housewife); W – 21, at home, b. Atlanta, GA, d/o Allan Gottschaldt (New York, NY, advertising) and Rebecca Walker (Atlanta, GA, housewife)

CLAFLIN,
Clayton H. of Lyme m. Gladys J. **Fellows** of Hanover 10/20/1920 in Meriden; H - 20, laborer, b. Lyme, s/o P. H. A. Claflin (Auburn, postmaster) and Eva M. Turner (Hebron, ME, housewife); W - 18, at home, b. Hanover, d/o Fred A. Fellows (Hanover, weaver) and Nina A. Camp (Hanover, housewife)
E. L. of Lyme m. J. G. **Hibbard** of Woodsville 2/10/1919 in Lyme; H - 30, teamster, b. Lyme, s/o P. Claflin (farming) and H. I. Loomis (Lyme, housewife); W - 36, housekeeper, 2nd - W, b. Lunenburg, VT, d/o J. Powers (Colbrook, farming) and L. Phillips (Lunenburg, VT, housewife)
Preston L. of Lyme m. Anna C. **Fairfield** of Lyme 6/12/1907 in Lyme; H - 24, watchmaker, b. Lyme, s/o Preston H. A. Claflin (Auburn, P.M.) and Eva M. Turner (Hebron, ME, housewife); W - 23, teacher, b. Lyme, d/o Payson E. Fairfield (Lyme, clerk) and Caroline C. Churchill (Lyme, housewife)

Willis B. of Lyme m. Florence E. **Dike** of Lyme 5/6/1931 in Newbury, VT; H - 26, laborer, b. Corinth, VT, s/o Herbert W. Claflin (Corinth, VT, farmer) and Emma E. Avery (Haverhill, housewife); W - 18, at home, b. Lyme, d/o Leslie H. Dike (Lyme, laborer) and Florence S. Johnson (Lyme, housewife)

Willis B., Jr. of Lyme m. Barbara R. **Walker** of White River Jct. 10/25/1952 in White River Jct.; H – 19, painter, b. Lyme, s/o Willis B. Claflin (VT) and Florance Dyke (Lyme); W - 18, at home, b. Winsted, CT, d/o Archie Walker (VT) and Ruth Baker (VT)

CLARK,

Charles W. of Lyme m. Mildred E. **Elder** of Lyme 6/30/1945 in Orford; H – 39, farmer, 2nd – D, b. Thetford, VT, s/o Gilman A. Clark (Thetford, VT, farmer) and Harriett Houston (Strafford, VT, housewife); W – 30, housewife, 2nd – D, b. Canaan, d/o Lancelot Underhill (Orange, retired) and Augusta Welch (Lyme, housewife)

Charley W. of Lyme m. Ruth A. **Bean** of Orford 9/3/1934 in Lyme; H - 29, farming, b. Thetford, VT, s/o Gilman A. Clark (Thetford, VT, farmer) and Harriett R. Houston (Strafford, VT, housewife); W - 18, at home, b. Orford, d/o Edwin J. Bean (Orford, farmer) and Alice M. Marsh (Orford, housewife)

Dean L. of N. Haverhill m. Linda V. **Piper** of Lyme 3/20/1971 in Weare; H – 33, b. NH, s/o Robert Clark and Hazel Masure; W – 30, b. NH, d/o Walter J. Piper and Vivian Gregory

Forest E. of Fairlee, VT m. Lulu M. **McCoy** of Pelham, NY 5/2/1942 in Rochester; H – 38, farmer, b. Littleton, s/o Sidney L. Cook (Littleton, farmer) and Belle Stone (Piermont, housewife); W – 27, housekeeper, W, b. Lyme, d/o George Tattersall (Orford, carpenter) and Emily Mousley (Thetford, VT, housewife)

Wilbur Gordon m. Joan D. **Nadeau** 3/3/1978 in Lyme

CLOGSTON,

Gordon R. of VT m. Leona **Melendy** of NH 9/9/1972 in Lyme; H – 21, b. NH, s/o Walter C. Clogston and Betty Godfrey; W – 21, b. NH, d/o Robert Melendy and Elizabeth Wing

CLOUD,

Norman D., Jr. of E. Thetford, VT m. Theresa **Forward** of Lyme Ctr. 5/5/1982 in Lyme

COATES,

Arthur M. of Lyme m. Susan E. **Cowie** of Lyme 9/5/1904 in Lyme; H - 21, laborer, b. Corn Hill, Canada, s/o Thomas S. Cotes (Corn Hill, Canada) and Mary E. Perry (New Canaan, Canada, housework); W - 19, housework, b. MD, d/o David Cowie (Scotland) and Avogle Phillips (MD)

Thomas D. of Lyme m. Christina **Nelson** of Lyme 8/10/1908 in Lyme; H - 26, laborer, b. Corn Hill, NB, s/o Thomas S. Coates (Corn Hill, NB, farmer) and Mary E. Perry (New Canaan, NB, housework); W - 18, housework, b. Wakefield, d/o F. F. Nelson (Denmark, farmer) and Caroline Sorenson (Denmark, housework)

COBURN,

David of Lyme m. Anabel **Hutchinson** of W. Fairlee, VT 1/1/1917 in W. Fairlee, VT; H - 84, farming, 3rd, b. E. Berkshire, VT, s/o David Coburn (Cornish Flat, farming) and P. Jewett (CT, housewife); W - 62, nurse, 3rd, b. E. Corinth, VT, d/o H. M. Gates (Hanover, carriage maker) and Susan Gates (Scotland, housewife)

David E. of Lyme m. Mary A. **Pushee** of Lyme 5/23/1900 in Lyme; H - 26, farming, b. E. Berkshire, VT, s/o David Coburn (E. Berkshire, VT, farmer) and Lucy Smith (Enosburg, VT, housewife); W - 21, housework, b. Lyme, d/o Albert J. Pushee (Lyme) and Frances S. Jeffers (Lyme, housework)

Lewis W. of Lyme m. Minnie L. **Runnels** of Lyme 1/11/1900 in Orford; H - 23, farmer, b. E. Hardwick, VT, s/o David Coburn (E. Berkshire, VT, farmer) and Lucy Smith (Enosburg, VT, housewife); W - 18, housework, b. Wentworth, d/o George W. Runnels (Hanover, laborer) and Mary Tyler

Peter D. of Lyme m. Joanne M. **Guthrie** of Lyme 10/5/1987 in Lyme

COCKBURN,

Richard F. m. Scarlett V. C. **Forward** 12/3/1977 in Piermont

COLBY,

Ambrose of St. Johnsbury, VT m. Carolin A. **Shores** of St. Johnsbury, VT 10/6/1929 in Lyme; H - 42, foreman, 2nd - D, b. Topsham, VT, s/o Edwin R. Colby (Bradford, VT, retired) and Martha Eastman (Topsham, VT, housewife); W - 38, housekeeper, 2nd - D, b. Granby, VT, d/o Wilber Shores

(Granby, VT, farmer) and Flora ----- (retired)

Ambrose E. of Lyme Ctr. m. Edna M. **Hutchins** of Fairlee, VT 12/23/1909 in Lyme Ctr.; H - 22, teamster, b. Topsham, VT, s/o Edwin R. Colby (Bradford, VT, laborer) and Martha E. Eastman (Topsham, VT, housewife); W - 16, housework, b. Haverhill, d/o Edward Hutchins (ME) and Myrtle Woods (Haverhill, housework)

Howard of Bradford, VT m. Ruth **Clark** of Lyme 4/11/1964 in W. Fairlee, VT; H – s/o Walter Colby and Edith Blake; W – d/o William Clark and Ruth Callaghan, res. - Lyme

COLE,

Albert A. of Lyme m. Luane C. **Trottier** of Lyme 6/5/1966 in Lyme; H – 23, student, b. Hanover, s/o Allen L. Cole and Beth Pushee; W – 22, student, b. Lebanon, d/o Rudolph Trottier and Olive D. Goodell

Allen E. of Windsor, VT m. Beth L. **Pushee** of Lyme 9/4/1937 in Lyme; H - 26, hd. press op., b. Bethlehem, s/o John B. Cole (Littleton, shoemaker) and Beatrice McVety (Warren, housewife); W - 27, nurse, b. Lyme, d/o George A. Pushee (Lyme, farmer) and M. Agnes Gilbert (Lyme, housewife)

Allen Lee of Lyme m. Ruth Marion **Jenks** of Thetford, VT 8/16/1975 in Lyme Ctr.; H – b. 3/2/1911 in NH, s/o John B. Cole and Beatrice McVety; W – b. 9/20/1935 in MA, d/o Raymond W. Jenks and Edith S. Marsh

Fred A. of Lyme m. Flora B. **Shattuck** of Canaan 11/29/1890 in Lebanon; H - 20, carpenter, b. Dorchester, s/o Charles A. Cole and Alma J. Noyes; W - 19, housekeeper, b. Canaan, d/o Charles W. Shattuck and Lydia Bryant

COLEBURN,

William C. of Melrose, MA m. Eileen M. **Broderick** of Lyme Ctr. 9/25/1982 in Orford

COLTON,

Hial S. of Post Mills, VT m. Blanche W. **Cook** of Lyme 9/25/1903 in Thetford, VT; H - 18, clerk, b. Vershire, VT, s/o Arthur H. Colton (Vershire, VT, merchant) and Annie F. Darling (Vershire, VT, housewife); W - 18, housework, b. Burke, VT, d/o Hiram Cook (Chateaugay, NY, farmer) and Ellen Small (Canada, housewife)

COLUMBIA,
Charles of Canaan m. Mary **Graham** of N. Troy, VT 5/16/1887 in Lyme; H - 26, farmer, b. Canaan, s/o Lewis Columbia (Canada) and Clara Columbia (Canada); W - 30, b. N. Troy, VT, d/o Leonard P. Graham (Liverpool, England) and ----- (Richford, VT)

Fred of Enfield m. Lottie M. **Smith** of Lyme 1/1/1923 in Lyme; H - 26, spinner, b. Lebanon, s/o Peter Columbia (laborer) and Emma Greenwood; W - 17, at home, b. Hanover, d/o Carlton Smith (Lyme, farmer) and Ida Brissette (Hanover, housewife)

CONARD,
Nathaniel E. of Vershire, VT m. Brenda L. **Hamm** of Terryville, CT 7/10/1982 in Lyme

CONVERSE,
Sidney A. of Lyme m. Ila M. **Lincoln** of Lyme 10/7/1891 in Lyme; H - 33, butter maker, b. Lyme, s/o Benjamin P. Converse (Lyme, farmer) and Miranda Walker (housekeeper); W - 21, school teacher, b. Munbridge, VT, d/o Gardner H. Lincoln (Chelsea, VT, tinsmith) and Sarah F. Sanborn (Topsham, VT, housekeeper)

COOK,
Duane Stanley of Thetford, VT m. Andrea Lee **Grant** of Lyme Ctr. 6/21/1975 in Lyme; H – b. 7/22/1953 in NH, s/o Duane P. Cook and Virginia Stanley; W – b. 12/26/1956 in NH, d/o John Grant and Janet Piper

Guy M. of Corinth, VT m. Martha E. **Travis** of Corinth, VT 11/12/2004

Homer of Thetford, VT m. Gertrude **Dugdale** of Bradford, VT 12/2/1923 in Lyme; H - 26, lumber surv., 2nd - D, b. Norwich, VT, s/o George Cook (Norwich, VT, farmer) and Lily Ross (Pembroke, housewife); W - 18, household, b. Bradford, VT, d/o Samuel Dugdale (England, laborer) and Maude Gunter (Canada, housewife)

Samuel E. of Norwich, VT m. Inez K. **Hutchins** of Lyme 6/15/1957 in Lyme; H – 24, s/o Fred Cook and Wilma Stanley, res. – Norwich, VT; W – 18, d/o John Hutchins and Ruth Beard, res. – Lyme

Timothy R. of Lyme m. Carol Lynn **Willcock** of Lyme 8/25/1984 in

Lyme

COOPER,
Fred G. of Wells, VT m. Dorothy **Johnston** of Ira, VT 12/7/1921 in Lyme; H - 19, farmer, b. Wells, VT, s/o Rollin Cooper (Wells, VT, farmer) and Bernice White (N. Pawlet, VT, housewife); W - 19, housework, b. Ira, VT, d/o Harry Johnston (Canada, painter) and Mary Peak (Ira, VT, dressmaker)

COURSER,
Rodney C. of Lyme m. Jessie M. **Holmes** of Nashua 6/5/1912 in Nashua; H - 33, butter maker, b. Stockholm, NY, s/o Homer Courser (Parishville, NY, butter maker) and Ellen Thippen (Stockholm, NY, housewife); W - 30, forelady, b. Stockholm, NY, d/o Elmer E. Holmes (Lawrence, NY, restaurateur) and Abbie J. Merrill (Stockholm, NY, housewife)

COUTERMARSH,
Lawrence of Lyme m. Vivian H. **Wilmot** of Lyme 7/8/1926 in Thetford, VT; H - 26, laborer, b. Lebanon, s/o Alec Coutermarsh (Hartland, VT) and Rose Granger (VT); W - 16, b. Lyme, d/o Elber Wilmot (Strafford, VT, farmer) and Myrtle Cummings (Lyme, housewife)

COUTURE,
Gerald A. m. Susan **Dennis** 9/3/1977 in Lyme

CRAMER,
Reginald H. of Fairlee, VT m. Jane **DeGoosh** of Lyme 6/11/1950 in Lyme; H – 21, driver agt., b. Newport, VT, s/o Reginald Cramer (Quebec) and Edna Welsh (Holland, VT); W – 20, bookkeeper, b. Hanover, d/o Howard DeGoosh (Cornish) and Nettie Pushee (Lyme)

CRARY,
Jonathan K. of New York City, NY m. Suzanne L. **Jackson** of New York City, NY 8/9/1986 in Lyme

CRAWFORD,
Maurice J. of Lyme m. Arlene **Simonds** of Hartland, VT 11/30/1933 in Hartland, VT; H - 25, trucking, b. Thetford, VT, s/o Roy S.

Crawford (Lyndon, VT, salesman) and Sadie L. Pushee (Norwich, VT, housewife); W - 19, b. Hartford, VT, d/o Robert Simonds (Hartford, VT, laborer) and Annie Esdon (Bainsville, ON, housewife).

Ward H. of Lyme m. Eleanor **Antwiler** of Manchester 6/25/1932 in Lyme; H - 27, clergyman, b. Manchester, s/o Elmer H. Crawford (Hoosac Falls, NY, supt.) and Sarah F. Mann (Petersham, MA, housewife); W - 22, teacher, b. New Haven, CT, d/o Joseph Antwiler (New York, NY, cigar maker) and Eleanor Zimmer (New York, NY, housewife).

CROCKER,

Clarence A. of Lyme m. Anna M. **Balch** of Lyme 7/20/1904 in Lyme; H - 49, horse trainer, b. Hamden, ME, s/o Velorus Crocker (ME, farmer) and Sarah Floyd (ME, housewife); W - 51, housework, 2nd, b. Thetford, VT, d/o James R. Webster (farmer) and Charlotte Coburn (housewife).

CROSS,

Frank C. of Lyme m. Doris H. **Dennis** of Lyme 3/1/1926 in Orford; H - 43, millman, 2nd - D, b. Meredith Ctr., s/o Frank R. Cross (New Hampton, blacksmith) and Elizabeth Hatch (Guilford, retired); W - 21, at home, b. Lyme, d/o Albert B. Dennis (Stratford, farmer) and Maude A. Piper (Lyme, housewife).

CUMMINGS,

Harland of Lyme m. Florence M. **Lund** of Lyme 10/9/1897 in Lyme; H - 20, farmer, b. Lyme, s/o Daniel P. Cummings (Thetford, VT, farmer) and Orpha O. Holt (Lyme, housewife); W - 17, housework, b. Alstead, d/o Byron B. Lund (farmer) and Alice Wilder.

CUNNINGHAM,

Lucius F. of Etna m. Ruth L. **Chesley** of Lyme –/25/1938 in White River Jct.; H - 24, laborer, b. Big Timber, MT, s/o Lucius M. Cunningham (Belfast, ME) and Marie Rose (Spring Valley, MT); W - 23, nurse, b. Lyme, d/o Arthur B. Chesley (W. Fairlee, VT) and Monte G. Thompson (Canada).

CUSHMAN,

David Orin of Canaan m. Carole Agnes **Bircher** of Fairlee, VT

9/12/1976 in Lyme; H – b. 2/4/1953 in NH, s/o Philip Cushman and Inez M. Cushman; W – b. 3/14/1945 in NH, d/o Ralph Bircher and Lillian White

CUTTING,
Clyde A. of Lyme m. Virginia L. **Pushee** of Lyme 12/13/1958 in Lyme; H – 30, s/o Lee W. Cutting and Alice M. Hobart, res. – Lyme; W – 18, d/o Roger C. Pushee and Isabel Uline, res. – Lyme

Donald of Lyme m. Tracy **Morrissette** of Lyme 9/19/1992

Edd M. of Lyme m. Jennie W. **Runnels** of Lyme 8/13/1887 in Lyme; H - 24, farmer, b. Lyme, s/o Ezra F. Cutting (Lyme) and Fannie P. Meade (Piermont); W - 16, housekeeper, b. Lyme, d/o George W. Runnels (Hanover) and May Tyler (Lyme)

Edd M. of Lyme m. Gracie L. **Reed** of Lyme 11/28/1906 in Lyme; H - 43, farming, 2nd, b. Lyme, s/o Ezra F. Cutting (Lyme, farmer) and Fannie P. Mead (Benton, housewife); W - 27, housework, b. Dorchester, d/o Henry T. Reed (Dorchester, farmer) and Lenora A. Merrill (Groton, housewife)

Elmer F. of Lyme m. Mildred E. **Dennis** of Haverhill 10/14/1921 in Lyme; H - 25, laborer, b. Lyme, s/o Frank Cutting (Broome, Canada) and Elizabeth M. Cole (Canaan); W - 17, at home, b. Piermont, d/o Byron H. Dennis (Orford) and Eva M. Spencer (Strafford, VT, housewife)

Frank A. of Lyme m. Jean S. **Weeden** of Hanover 3/26/1955 in Hanover; H – 28, US Marines, b. Lyme, s/o Lee W. Cutting (Lyme) and Alice Hobart (Lyme); W – 26, secretary, widow, b. Hanover, Winslow Smith (Hanover) and Gladys Burnham (Hanover)

Frank A. of Lyme m. Eleanor M. **LaBombard** of W. Lebanon 12/25/1982 in Lyme Ctr.

Frank A., Jr. of Lyme m. Dina D. **Hawthorne** of Lyme 7/17/1982 in Hanover

Lee W. of Lyme m. Alice M. **Hobart** of Lyme 12/30/1914 in Lyme; H - 24, laborer, b. Lyme, s/o Frank W. Cutting (Broom Woods, PQ, wheelwright) and Elizabeth Cole (Canaan, housewife); W - 25, bookkeeper, b. Lyme, d/o Albert Hobart (Hebron, farmer) and Harriet N. Phelps (Lowell, MA, housewife)

CYR,
Charles R. of Underhill, VT m. Abbie G. **Penfield** of Underhill, VT

9/6/1987 in Lyme

DALTON,
Norman T. of Lyme m. Jean K. **Molloy** of Lebanon 7/28/2001

DANETRA,
Leonard Daniel of Lyme m. Barbi-Jo **Harden** of Lyme 6/23/1975 in Portsmouth; H – b. 1/12/1949 in NY, s/o Leonard Danetra and Gloria Magrini; W – b. 4/4/1950 in NH, d/o Robert Conrad Harden and Barbara McAulay

DAVIDSON,
Harry of Bradford, VT m. June **Godfrey** of Thetford, VT 6/28/1969 in Lyme; H – 27, b. VT, s/o Ralph Davidson and Katherine Hutchinson; W – 22, b. NH, d/o Bernard Godfrey and Jean Rhodes

Paul H. of Farmington m. Nancy J. **Chase** of Lyme 9/7/1957 in Lyme; H – 25, s/o Walter Davidson of Dover and Corinne Thurston of Albertson, NY; W – 18, d/o William F. Chase and Mildred B. Fey, res. – Lyme

DAVIS,
Alfred T. of Newport, VT m. Vera M. **Warren** of Lyme 10/3/1916 in Lyme; H - 26, trainman, b. Boynton, PQ, s/o Titus A. Davis (Boynton, PQ, farming) and Leila Lincoln (Fairfax, PQ, housewife); W - 21, at home, b. Thetford, VT, d/o Arad J. Warren (Lyme, ins. agent) and Myra L. Stearns (Starksboro, VT, housewife)

Bruce H. of Lyme m. Sharon L. **Davidson** of Lyme 10/4/1986 in Lyme

Charles E. of Lyme m. Mina E. **Davis** of Canaan 1/1/1924 in Lyme; H – 45, farmer, 2nd - W, b. Groton, s/o Daniel C. Davis (Chelsea, VT, shoemaker) and Louisa Quimby (Hooksett, housewife); W - 48, housekeeper, 2nd - W, b. Canaan, d/o Frank P. Clark (Canaan, farmer) and Nellie B. Gray (Alexandria, housewife)

Gerald W. of Lyme m. Hattie K. **Davis** of Cornish 3/27/1927 in Grantham; H - 25, teamster, b. Groton, s/o Charles A. Davis (Groton, farmer) and Alva Wheet (Groton, housewife); W - 19, housework, b. Canada, d/o Alah H. Davis (N. Troy, VT, bus driver) and Mertie B. Woodard (Holland, VT, housewife)

P. A. of Lyme m. G. M. **Sanborn** of Orford 1/1/1919 in Lyme; H - 22, farming, b. Thetford, VT, s/o W. E. Davis (England, engineer) and A. E. Lines (England, housewife); W - 20, at home, b. Plymouth, d/o J. Sanborn (Rumney, farming) and F. M. Hutchins (Rumney, housewife)

Perry A. of Lyme m. Elsbeth S. **Davis** of Waterbury, CT 9/7/1935 in Orford; H - 38, farmer, 2nd - D, b. Thetford, VT, s/o William E. Davis (England, engineer) and Annie E. Lines (England, housewife); W - 37, domestic, 2nd - W, b. Danbury, CT, d/o Herman Schneyer (Germany, milk dealer) and Anna Scherzle (Germany, invalid)

Roger Martin, Jr. of Lyme m. Suzanne M. **Rousseau** of Claremont 11/15/1985 in Hanover

DAY,
Jasper J. of Lyme m. J. E. **Brockway** of Lyme 10/3/1948 in Lyme; H – 27, lumberman, b. Lyme, s/o William W. Day (Corinth, VT, retired) and Mary E. Webster (Lyme, housewife); W – 20, teacher, b. Lyme, d/o Guy C. Brockway (Lyme, farmer) and Mary Lund (Norwich, VT, housewife)

Michael W. m. Elizabeth A. **Fisk** 12/26/1981 in Lyme

Roy W. of Lyme m. Mary E. **Hadlock** of Hanover 5/19/1950 in Hanover; H – 19, carpenter, b. Lyme, s/o William W. Day (Bradford, VT) and Mary E. Webster (Lyme); W – 18, secretary, b. Norwich, VT, d/o Clayton Hadlock (Troy, VT) and Jeanette Williams (Montpelier, VT)

William W. of Lyme m. Mary E. **Webster** of Lyme 5/30/1917 in Lyme; H - 28, farming, 2nd, b. Bradford, VT, s/o Jasper Day (Haverhill, MA, farming) and Alfretta Simpson (W. Topsham, VT, housewife); W - 20, housework, b. Lyme, d/o John H. Webster (Lyme, farming) and Abbie Coates (Corn Hill, NB, housewife)

DEBAUN,
Roger W. of W. Fairlee, VT m. Margaret R. **Doscher** of W. Fairlee, VT 1/2/1951 in Lebanon; H – 54, farmer, b. Bloomingdale, NJ, s/o David DeBaun (NJ) and Cora Freeland (NJ); W – 58, at home, 2nd – D, b. Jersey City, NJ, d/o Frederick Ruddle (England) and Ida Miles (NJ)

DECKER,
Rand A. of Hanover m. Tracy E. **Penfield** of Lyme 9/27/1975 in

Lyme; H – b. 4/18/1954 in IL, s/o Robert W. Decker and Joann Stabley; W – b. 5/22/1956 in IL, d/o Donald W. Penfield and Abbie Emmons

DEGOOSH,
E. J. of Lyme m. Ida J. **Pike** of Lyme 9/26/1948 in Lyme; H – 24, shipper, b. Lyme, s/o Howard DeGoosh (Cornish, farmer) and Nettie Pushee (Lyme, housewife); W – 22, reg. nurse, b. Lyme, d/o Chester D. Pike (Lyme, farmer) and Polly C. Camp (Lyme, housewife)

Edward A. of Lyme m. Gail F. **Turcotte** of N. Haverhill 9/27/1975 in Manchester; H – b. 2/20/1954 in NH, s/o Richard DeGoosh and Laura B. Pike; W – b. 4/26/1946 in NH, d/o Romel Turcotte and Geraldine Jackson

Howard E. of Lyme m. Nettie M. **Pushee** of Lyme 10/18/1916 in Lyme; H - 24, laborer, b. Cornish, s/o Elmer E. DeGoosh (W. Fairlee, VT, farming) and Minnie B. Keyes (Reading, VT, housewife); W - 22, teacher, b. Lyme, d/o David J. Pushee (Lyme, laborer) and Mary M. Gilbert (St. Johnsbury, VT, housewife)

John S. of Lyme m. Dorothy J. **Kendall** of White River Jct. 12/20/1952 in Hanover; H – 20, US Navy, b. Hanover, s/o Howard DeGoosh (Cornish) and Nettie Pushee (Lyme); W – 19, factory worker, b. Woodstock, VT, d/o Merton Kendall (Hanover) and Bernice Churchill

Richard of Lyme m. Laura B. **Pike** of Lyme 6/23/1946 in Lyme; H – 24, mechanic, b. Lyme, s/o Howard DeGoosh (Cornish, farmer) and Nettie Pushee (Lyme, housewife); W – 24, teacher, b. Lyme, d/o Chester D. Pike (Lyme, farmer) and Polly Camp (Lyme, housewife)

DELONG,
John D. of Grantham m. Susan Mary **Dubois** of Somerset, MA 7/29/1995

DEMASSE,
Raymond C., Jr. of Hanover m. Jane E. **Mace** of Lyme 2/14/1975 in Hanover; H – b. 8/26/1948 in NH, s/o Raymond C. DeMasse, Sr. and Lucy Magnano; W – b. 11/25/1950 in VT, d/o Fred John and Florence LaBelle

DEMERS,
Alphonse E. of Lebanon m. Esther V. **Elder** of Lyme 11/12/1938 in Lebanon; H - 23, cook, b. Canada, s/o Ludger Demers and Jenophe Boisvert; W - 19, waitress, b. Hanover Ctr., d/o George B. Elder (Canada, farmer) and Rose L. Camp (Lyme, housewife)

DENNIS,
Alger E. of Lyme m. Freda G. **Smith** of Lyme 2/19/1922 in Lyme; H - 24, farmer, b. Lyme, s/o George W. Dennis (Stratford, farmer) and Caroline F. Church (Vershire, VT, housewife); W - 17, housework, b. Lyme, d/o Ezra M. Smith (Hanover, deceased) and Bertha M. Flint (Lyme, housewife)
David E., II of NH m. Susan **Grosjean** of NH 8/22/1972 in Hanover; H – 17, b. MA, s/o David E. Dennis and Nancy Eason; W – 18, b. NH, d/o William Grosjean and Joan Davis
David Emerson, II m. Karen Jeane **Estes** 5/5/1978 in Lyme
Wendell L. of Lyme m. Myrtle I. **Gibson** of Newbury, VT 4/26/1950 in Lyme; H – 30, farmer, b. Lyme, s/o Leroy Dennis (N. Stratford) and Effie Gage (Orford); W – 20, at home, b. Newbury, VT, d/o George Gibson (Newton Mills, VT) and Gladys Keyes (Orange, MA)
Ralph E. of Orford m. Ramona J. **Wing** of Lyme 11/3/1950 in Manchester; H – 24, farmer, b. Hanover, s/o Walter Dennis (Piermont) and Theresa Rugg (Fairlee, VT); W – 21, at home, b. Orford, d/o Albert Wing (Lyme) and Esther Small (Cornish)

DERBY,
Arthur E. of Lyme m. Blanche A. **Mosher** of Brooklyn, NY 7/11/1917 in Concord; H - 34, farming, b. Lyme, s/o John H. Derby (Troy, VT, farming) and Ruhannah E. Gordon (Dorchester, housewife); W - 36, pastor's asst., b. Gold River, NS, d/o William Mosher (Gold Rivers, NS, farming) and Sophy Keddy (Gold River, NS, housewife)
Herbert F. of Lyme m. Jennie M. **Derby** of Hanover 5/20/1908 in Hanover; H – 38, ladder mfg., b. Lebanon, s/o Alvin H. Derby (Canaan, farmer) and Catherine E. Nay (Hanover, housewife); W - 34, housework, 2nd, b. Canada, d/o Joseph Sloan (Canada, carpenter) and Jessie Small (Canada, housewife)
Lewis S. of Lyme m. Annie M. **Smith** of Hanover 9/21/1887 in Lyme; H - 50, farmer, 2nd, b. Lyme, s/o Harris Derby (Lyme) and

Hannah Avery (Orford); W - 22, housekeeper, b. Hanover, d/o
Alonzo Smith (Langdon) and Julia Heath (Stewartstown, VT)

DEREGO,
Edward C. of Lyme m. Margo E. **Farnham** of Lyme 8/4/1984 in
Lyme
Edward C. of Lyme m. Kelly **Downing** of Lyme 7/1/1989 in Canaan

DEVAUX,
David M. m. Vera E. **Clark** 9/24/1977 in Lyme

DICKEY,
Thomas R. of Provincetown, MA m. Lynne K. **Newton** of
Provincetown, MA 8/12/1989 in Lyme

DIKE,
Charles E. of Lyme m. Jennie **Perry** of Lawrence, MA 11/9/1910 in
Lyme; H - 24, laborer, b. Lyme, s/o Edna L. Dike (Lyme,
housework); W - 24, housework, b. PEI, d/o Joseph Perry (PEI,
farmer) and Mary Clare (PEI, housework)
Frederick V. of Lyme m. Emma S. **Tattersall** of Lyme 12/6/1904 in
Lyme; H - 26, laborer, b. Lyme, s/o Volney R. Dike (Lyme,
laborer) and Lizzie S. Nash (Plainfield, housewife); W - 25,
housework, 2nd, b. Lyme, d/o George E. Tattersall (England,
farmer) and Mary H. Sweet (Plainfield, housewife)

DILLON,
John Francis, Jr. of Berkeley, CA m. Elizabeth Margot **Maddock** of
Berkeley, CA 7/28/1990 in Lyme

DIMICK,
Charles H. of Lyme m. Cordelia H. **Flint** of Lyme 7/19/1888 in Lyme;
H - 44, farmer, 2nd, b. Lyme, s/o James P. Dimick (Lyme) and
Pametia Blanchard (Vershire, VT); W - 43, housekeeper, 2nd, b.
Gilford, VT, d/o Edward H. Smith (Conway) and Hanna Field
(Chester, VT)
Edson L. of Lyme m. Delia **Wright** of Lyme 3/31/1894 in Lyme; H -
21, laborer, b. Lyme, s/o Lewis Dimick (Canada, farmer) and
Hannah E. Welch (Groton, VT, housekeeper); W - 17,
housework, b. Lyme, d/o James Wright (Groton, farmer) and
Almira S. Fox (Strafford, VT, housekeeper)

Edwin P. of Lyme m. Hattie E. **Gilbert** of Orford 3/26/1890 in Lebanon; H - 26, farmer, b. Lyme, s/o William H. Dimick and Delia R. Ames; W - 27, housekeeper, b. Lyme, d/o Israel H. Gilbert and Manerva Cutting

Kenneth C. of Lyme m. Verla M. **Perkins** of Lyme 1/20/1946 in Lyme; H – 27, laborer, b. Lyme, s/o Charles Dimick (Lyme, farmer) and Florence Carpenter (Littleton, housewife); W – 19, at home, b. Lyme, d/o Forrest Perkins (Lyme, mail carrier) and Charlotte Webb (Lyme, clerk)

Lawrence F. of Windsor, VT m. Louise M. **Martin** of Windsor, VT –/14/1938 in Lyme; H - 21, truck driver, b. W. Windsor, VT, s/o Floyd F. Dimick (W. Windsor, VT, foreman) and Nellie Chase (Hartland, VT, housewife); W - 19, domestic, b. W. Windsor, VT, d/o George W. Martin (Windsor, VT, painter) and Pearl L. Marcotte (Lebanon, housewife)

Thomas E. of Lyme m. Addie V. **Jewell** of W. Newbury, VT 6/27/1902 in Lyme Ctr.; H - 27, farmer, b. Lyme, s/o Charles H. Dimick (Lyme, farmer) and Viola C. Cook (Lyme, housewife); W - 22, teacher, b. W. Newbury, VT, d/o George Jewell (W. Newbury, VT, farmer) and Elizabeth Brock (W. Newbury, VT, housework)

DINGMAN,
Stanley L. of kx m. Ruth Jane Brower **Van Zandt** of Lyme 2/2/1974 in Lyme Ctr; H – b. 1/31/1939 in NH, s/o Stanley T. Dingman and Beatrice Zullo; W – b. 1/5/1931 in NJ, d/o Arthur Van Zandt and Ruth Baker

DIX,
Chester F. of Hanover m. Dora A. **Balch** of Lyme 5/23/1953 in Lyme; H – 26, printer, b. Brattleboro, VT, s/o Justin H. Dix (VT) and Myrtle Briggs (NH); W – 22, sales clerk, b. Haverhill, d/o Roy E. Balch (VT) and Olive Blanchard (NH)

George A. of Plainfield, VT m. Bernice **Rothney** of Somerville, MA 9/19/1954 in Lyme; H – 38, road comm., b. VT, s/o Arthur L. Dix (VT) and Dorothy Bancroft (VT); W – 48, waitress, b. Quebec, d/o Alexander Rotheney (Canada) and Mary Ross (Canada)

DOHERTY,
Edward J. of Lyme Ctr. m. Patricia Barnes **Detar** of Lyme Ctr. 6/19/1976 in Hanover; H – b. 1/21/1933 in MA, s/o Neil Doherty

and Mary E. McHugh; W – b. 10/18/1937 in PA, d/o Kirkworth Barnes and Lillian Ringhoffer

DONAHUE,
Paul A. of Lyme m. Bobbye B. **Taylor** of Lyme 11/15/1986 in Lyme

DOTY,
F. E. of Winchester m. M. O. **Roberts** of Lyme 12/29/1919 in Lyme; H - 52, boxmaker, 2nd - W, b. Tinmouth, VT, s/o A. Doty (Wallingford, VT, retired) and Helen Cook (Danby, VT, housewife); W - 49, domestic, 2nd - W, b. Littleton, d/o Harry Dyke (Littleton, shoemaker) and S. E. Tucker (Strafford, VT, housewife)

DOWD,
Jonathan O. of Lyme m. Tamaura L. **Demasse** of Lyme 8/14/2001
Leo B., III of Lyme m. Darcy M. **Guerin** of Lyme 4/11/1999

DOWNING,
Everett H. of W. Thornton m. Augusta E. **Cook** of Lyme 9/17/1912 in Lyme; H - 21, farming, b. W. Thornton, s/o Benjamin P. Downing (Ellsworth, farming) and M. W. Magnuson (Gothenburg, Sweden, housewife); W - 22, housework, b. Burke, NY, d/o Hiram Cook (Chateaugay, NY, farming) and Ellen Smith (Rockburn, Canada, housewife)

DOYLE,
Richard D. of Strafford, VT m. Nancy **DeGoosh** of Lyme 12/22/1957 in Lyme; H – 20, s/o James W. Doyle and Mildred Judd, res. – Strafford, VT; W – 19, d/o Howard DeGoosh and Nettie Pushee, res. – Lyme

DOYON,
Davila of Lyme m. Simone **Poulin** of Lyme 5/6/1936 in Hanover; H - 28, lumberman, b. St. Rose, PQ, s/o Leon Doyon (St. Victor, Canada, farmer) and Mary Turcotte (St. Rose, Canada, housewife); W - 18, bookkeeper, b. St. Just, PQ, d/o Joseph A. Poulin (St. Everiste, Canada, jobber) and Anna Boutin (Shinly, PQ, housewife)

DRAKE,
Francis G. of Lyme m. Tina M. **Letourneau** of Lyme 4/19/1986 in Lyme

DREW,
William of Lyme m. Marilyn **Toner** of Lyme 6/20/1970 in Orford; H – 30, b. NH, s/o Leslie Drew and Irene Blake; W – 27, b. NY, d/o Charles Toner and Beulah Willette

DRISCOLL,
Kenneth F. of W. Fairlee, VT m. Dorothy M. **Colby** of W. Fairlee, VT 2/11/1950 in Haverhill; H – 31, auto mech., 2nd – D, b. Canada, s/o Roland O. Driscoll (Jersey Is.) and Hazel Wright (Canada); W – 31, housework, 2nd – D, b. W. Fairlee, VT, d/o Fred Brown (W. Fairlee, VT) and Marion Blake (W. Fairlee, VT)

DRUHL,
Michael D. of W. Lebanon m. Jill A. **King** of Lyme 9/26/1987 in Meriden

DUBE,
Ferdinand of Lyme m. Ruth E. **LeClair** of Norwich, VT 7/25/1935 in Lyme; H - 29, lumberman, b. Canada, s/o Alfred Dube (Canada, retired) and Jeorjina Blanchard (Salem, MA, housewife); W - 27, domestic, 2nd - D, b. Sutton, VT, d/o Joe LaClair (Glover, VT, farmer) and Della C. Foster (Albany, VT, housewife)

DUMAIS,
Thomas of Somersworth m. Mary A. **Morrill** of Lyme 6/12/1971 in Hanover; H – 24, b. NH, s/o George Dumais and Blanche Labrie; W – 21, b. NH, d/o Jack Morrill and Helen Eanchuck

DUNBAR,
Frank H. of Lyme m. Eva L. **Melendy** of Lyme 1/4/1915 in Lyme; H - 36, farmer, b. Canada, s/o George E. Dunbar (Guildhall, VT, farmer) and Sophia E. Clough (Lyme, housewife); W - 39, housewife, 2nd, b. Lebanon, d/o Soloman Biathrow (Barton, VT, farmer) and Clara Lord (Barton, VT, housewife)
Frederick of Woodstock, VT m. Hattie M. **Dunbar** of Lyme 6/25/1900 in Lyme; H - 21, farming, black, b. Woodstock, VT, s/o John H.

Dunbar (Woodstock, VT, job team) and Elizabeth H. Rowe (Pomfret, VT, housewife); W - 19, housework, black, b. Canada, d/o George E. Dunbar (Chelsea, VT, farmer) and Sophia E. Clough (Washington, VT, housewife)

Robert A. of Lyme m. Edith M. **Simpson** of Lyme 6/24/1902 in Lyme; H - 22, farmer, black, b. Canada, s/o George E. Dunbar (Guildhall, VT, farmer) and Sophia E. Clough (Washington, VT, housewife); W - 16, housework, b. Bradford, VT, d/o Herman L. Simpson (Orford, farmer) and Ella M. Hackett (Orford, housewife)

DUNKLING,
Paul R. of Sharon, VT m. Ruth A. **Holmes** of Sharon, VT 7/16/1988 in Lyme

DUNN,
John M. of Lyme m. Teresa **Cioffredi** of Lyme 9/28/1984 in Lyme

DURKEE,
Gary James m. Rebecca Lee **Carpenter** 7/15/1978 in Lyme
Leonard of Union Village, VT m. Joan F. **Fields** of Lyme 9/29/1956 in Orford; H – 26, cook, s/o Ralph Durkee and Beatrice Goodrich, res. – Union Village, VT; W – 20, salesgirl, d/o John Fields and Meda Roberts, res. – Lyme

DWYER,
John A. of Thetford, VT m. Ruth E. **Cook** of Thetford, VT 10/18/1984 in Lyme

DYKE,
John F. of Lyme m. Patty D. **Piper** of Lyme 11/21/1987 in Orford
Leslie of Lyme m. Florence **Johnson** of Lyme 10/3/1908 in Lyme; H - 30, carpenter, b. Lyme, s/o Henry Dyke (Lyme, carpenter) and Addie Wilmot (Thetford, VT, housework); W - 16, housework, b. Lyme, d/o Wilson D. Johnson (Hanover, blacksmith) and Alice B. Woodward (Hanover, housework)

EASTBURN,
Jimmie J. of Lyme m. Catherine **Butman** of Lyme 7/23/1994

EASTMAN,
Brian Gene of Fairlee, VT m. Crystal Rene **Pike** of Fairlee, VT
--/--/1991

EATON,
George B. of Lyme m. Lucie A. **Morey** of Lyme 12/29/1898 in Lyme; H - 60, farmer, 3rd, b. Grantham, s/o Jacob Eaton (Grantham, farmer) and Mehitable Garland (housewife); W - 52, music teacher, 2nd, b. Lyme, d/o William P. Morey (Norway, ME, house painter) and Annie W. Hall (Lyme, housekeeper)

Maurice of Lyme m. Margaret **Southworth** of Fairfield, CT 9/26/1941 in W. Fairlee, VT; H – 22, laborer, b. Thetford, VT, s/o Don A. Eaton (Lisbon) and Margaret Boyd (Chataugay, NY); W – 22, b. W. Fairlee, VT, d/o Arthur Southworth (N. Bradford, VT) and Maud Kidder (Bradford, VT)

Ray B. of W. Fairlee, VT m. Bertha M. **Webb** of Lyme 5/15/1917 in W. Fairlee, VT; H - 25, farming, b. Bradford, VT, s/o Henry Eaton (Landaff) and Eliza J. Brown (St. Johnsbury, VT); W - 23, b. Lyme, d/o Charles B. Webb (Lyme, painter) and Rhoda E. Smith (Hanover, housewife)

Russell B. of Lyme m. Elspeth **Powell** of Thetford, VT 8/5/1937 in Lyme; H – 22, mechanic, b. Bradford, VT, s/o Don A. Eaton (Bradford, VT, carpenter) and Margaret Boyd (Thetford, VT, housewife); W - 22, teacher, b. Thetford, VT, d/o Ray Powell (Thetford, VT, salesman) and Harriet Burr (Roxbury, MA, housewife)

EGGLESTON,
Eric David of Lyme m. Terry Lea **Beckett** of Amherst, MA 8/8/1993

ELDER,
Don E. of Lyme m. Julia M. **Balch** of Lyme 10/15/1961 in N. Thetford, VT; H – 23, s/o Kenneth Elder and Mildred Underhill, res. – Lyme; W – 22, s/o Grant Balch and Margaret Houston, res. – Lyme

Kenneth E. of Lyme m. Mildred **Underhill** of Lyme 7/1/1933 in Fairlee, VT; H - 19, farmer, b. Hanover, s/o George B. Elder (Canada, farmer) and Rose Camp (Lyme, housewife); W - housework, b. Canaan, d/o Alanacelot Underhill (Canaan) and Augusta Welch (Lyme, housewife)

Kenneth E. of Lyme m. Ruth A. **Clark** of Lyme 6/30/1945 in

Piermont; H – 31, farmer, 2nd – D, b. Hanover, s/o George B. Elder (Ormstown, PQ, mill worker) and Rose Camp (Lyme, housewife); W – 28, housewife, 2nd – D, b. Orford, d/o Edwin Bean (Orford, farmer) and Alice Marsh (Orford, housewife)

Philip E. of Lyme Ctr. m. Beatrice A. **Ryan** of Lyme Ctr. 12/21/1973 in Lyme; H – 32, b. NH, s/o Kenneth E. Elder and Mildred Underhill; W – 37, b. NY, d/o Allen Tobey and Beatrice Carter

Philip Earl of Lyme m. Joyce Elaine **Mack** of Post Mills, VT 12/23/1959 in Thetford, VT; H – s/o Kenneth E. Elder of Lyme and Mildred Underhill; W – d/o Delbert W. Mack and Pearl MacFarlane, res. – Post Mills, VT

Roger B. of Lyme m. Loretta M. **Nareau** of Lebanon 5/25/1941 in Lebanon; H – 20, chef, b. Hanover, s/o George B. Elder (Canada, woodsman) and Rose L. Camp (Lyme, housewife); W – 20, waitress, b. Hanover, d/o Albert J. Mareau (Chataguay, NY, carder, mill) and Me'ra E. Builbrault (Biddeford, ME, housewife)

ELKOUH,

Nabil Abdel-Fattah of Enfield m. Sheila Kay **Cragg** of Enfield 12/6/1997

ELLIOTT,

Harry A. of Lyme m. Susan A. **Carr** of Lyme 6/28/1902 in Lyme; H - 20, laborer, b. Lyme, s/o John F. Elliott (Campton, miller) and Kate V. Hewes (Lyme, housewife); W - 20, teacher, b. Orange, VT, d/o Robert Carr (Corinth, VT, farmer) and Ella Lawrence (Fairlee, VT, housework)

Thomas Earl m. Sandra Jean **Hibbard** 7/20/1979 in W. Fairlee Ctr., VT

ELLSWORTH,

Isaac N. of Lyme m. Clara E. **Waldron** of Concord 4/5/1914 in Lyme; H - 58, farmer, 2nd, b. Wentworth, s/o Benjamin Ellsworth (Wentworth, farmer) and Hannah Davis (Wentworth, housewife); W - 44, nurse, 2nd, b. Rockport, MA, d/o Henry Baily (Bingham, ME, brakeman) and Elsena M. Kimball (Wentworth, housewife)

Joseph of Lyme m. Jennie R. **Glines** of Lyme 1/22/1895 in Haverhill; H - 43, butcher, b. Wentworth, s/o Benjamin Ellsworth (Wentworth, farmer) and Hannah Davis (Wentworth, housekeeper); W - 25, milliner, b. Haverhill, d/o Henry Glines (Haverhill, farmer) and Ellen C. Dean (Haverhill, housewife)

EMERSON,
Andrew of Bradford, VT m. Mary L. **Bowen** of Lyme 5/5/1900 in Lyme; H - 35, farming, 2nd, b. Bradford, VT, s/o Dan Emerson (Newbury, VT, farmer) and Hannah Corliss (Topsham, VT, housework); W - 17, housework, b. Greenfield, d/o Clarence S. Bowen (Corinth, VT, laborer) and Ida Hall (Greenfield)

EMERY,
Fay S. of Piermont m. Gladys C. **Chesley** of Lyme 7/24/1915 in Lyme; H - 27, farmer, b. Piermont, s/o George S. Emery (Suncook, farmer) and Hannah E. Sargent (Wentworth, housewife); W - 18, teacher, b. Lyme, d/o Frank A. Chesley (W. Fairlee, VT, farmer) and Louise R. Morey (W. Fairlee, VT, housewife)
Leroy W. of Lyme m. Winifred Ida **Cummings** of Lyme 1/2/1911 in Lyme; H - 62, farmer, 2nd, b. Thetford, VT, s/o Addison A. Emery and Miranda B. Downer; W - 25, at home, b. Thetford, VT, d/o H. P. Cummings (Thetford, VT, farmer) and Ida Colburn (Norwich, VT, housewife)

EMLEN,
Robert P. of Orford m. Julia Ellen **Seeley** of Lyme 7/3/1971 in Hanover; H – 24, b. PA, s/o Robert L. Emlen and Cora W. Peabody; W – 24, b. NY, d/o Lewis Seeley and Helen Quinn

ERWIN,
Wayne A. of Bradford, VT m. Anne **Chatellier** of Lyme 4/5/1952 in Lyme; H – 18, student, b. VT, s/o Hayward Erwin (VT) and Alice Cunningham (VT); W – 17, student, b. NJ, d/o Richard Chatellier (NJ) and Miriam Townley (NJ)

ESTES,
Gary Lee m. Cindy May **Day** 8/14/1978 in Lyme
Leo W. of Hanover m. Sally A. **Chase** of Lyme 12/23/1955 in Lyme; H – 18, student, b. Hanover, s/o George W. Estes (VT) and Helen N. Sayah (VT); W – 20, bank clerk, b. Lebanon, d/o William F. Chase (Lyme) and Mildred Fey (NY)
Russell G. of Lyme m. Noreen E. **Gallup** of Orford 6/6/1964 in

Orford; H – s/o Leonard Estes and Evelyn Powers, res. – Lyme; W – d/o Harley Gallup and Ella Johnson, res. – Orford
Timothy of Lyme m. Michele **Boutin** of Concord 8/29/1992

EVANS,
James E. of Lyme m. Toni L. **White** of Lyme 8/21/1976 in Lyme; H – b. 9/7/1957 in NH, s/o Robert Evans and Marjorie Wilmot; W – b. 12/1/1957 in NH, d/o Roger White and Thelma Fisher
Robert W. of Weathersfield, VT m. Marjorie E. **Wilmot** of Lyme 5/18/1953 in Weathersfield, VT; H – 27, machinist, 3rd – D, b. Enfield, s/o Walter E. Evans (Canaan) and Georgiana M. Bordeau (Concord); W – 26, shop help, b. Lyme, d/o Leo A. Wilmot (Lyme) and Fannie M. Chapin (S. Boston, MA)

EWELL,
Michael G. m. Melissa J. **Massicotte** 6/25/1977 in Lyme

FAIRBROTHER,
Lawrence W. of Lyme m. Betty J. **Ordway** of Lyme 7/8/1967 in Lyme; H – 41, truck driver, b. Vershire, VT, s/o Ernest Fairbrother and Julia F. Ward; W – 34, IBM operator, b. Barre, VT, d/o Merton C. Huntley and Elsie Chandler

FAY,
George H. of Lyme m. Frances J. H. **Watts** of Lyme 11/26/1936 in Danbury; H - 23, farmer, b. Danbury, s/o George H. Fay (Danbury, laborer) and Alvina Locke (Concord, housewife); W - 18, at home, b. Lebanon, d/o Ned E. Watts (Hanover, farmer) and Barbara Thompson (Canada, housewife)

FEICK,
Matthew F. of New York, NY m. Karen L. **Menge** of Lyme 8/1/1987 in Lyme

FELLERS,
Gregory E. of Hartford, VT m. Carol A. **Walker** of Lyme Ctr. 6/21/1969 in Hartford, VT; H – 26, b. OH, s/o Allison Fellers and Mary Jackson; W – 25, b. NH, d/o Harris Walker and Mary Gunderson

FELLOWS,
Harold A. of Hanover m. Saidee A. **Sprague** of Lyme 8/3/1951 in Lyme; H – 48, plumber, 2nd – D, b. Hanover, s/o Fred Fellows (Hanover) and Nina Camp (Hanover); W – 38, housewife, 2nd – D, b. Albany, VT, d/o Harry Duckless (Albany, VT) and Winifred Hyde (Albany, VT)
Thomas E. of Hanover m. Nancy J. **King** of Lyme 2/1/1964 in Hanover; H – s/o Robert E. Fellows and Arlene E. Beliveau, res. – Etna; W – d/o Frederick W. King and Catherine M. Doyle, res. – Lyme

FERGUSON,
Paul D. m. Elizabeth S. **Rawnsley** 3/28/1981 in Hanover

FERLAND,
Scott M. of Enfield m. Stephanie L. **White** of Lyme 7/17/2002

FERRY,
Robert G. of Lyme m. Anita **Beloin** of Lyme 4/4/2002

FERSCH,
Emer. C. of Hamilton, NY m. Pat. A. **Woerner** of New York, NY 6/22/1948 in Lebanon; H – 23, student, b. Greene, NY, s/o Cornelius Fersch (Jersey City, NJ, clergyman) and Hazel Butters (New York, NY); W – 20, student, b. Bronx, NY, d/o Wil. Woerner, Sr. (New York, NY, rest'r'nteur) and Gertrude Jaeger (New York, NY, person'l clerk)

FICHTER,
Joseph F. of Bellows Falls, VT m. Laurie E. **Penfield** of Lyme 8/5/1989 in Lyme

FIELDMAN,
Richard P. m. Elizabeth R. **Pickett** 11/25/1977 in Lyme

FIELDS,
Dale R. m. Patricia L. **Van Ells** 8/18/1979 in Orford
James E. of Lyme m. Patricia A. **Olsen** of Lyme 11/28/1970 in Lyme; H – 27, b. NH, s/o John Fields and Meda Roberts; W – 19, b. NH, d/o Edward Olsen and Elizabeth Davis
John E. of Lyme m. Meda P. **Roberts** of Lyme 6/26/1935 in Lyme; H

– 22, cook, b. Lebanon, s/o Benjamin B. Fields (Port Henry, NY, laborer) and Fannie F. Crossin (Ireland, housewife); W - 21, waitress, b. Lyme, d/o Guy A. Roberts (Bradford, VT, rd. foreman) and Jennie M. Hobart (Lyme, housewife)

FIFIELD,
Gary Bernard of Thetford Ctr., VT m. Colleen Beth **King** of Lyme 8/3/1974 in Lyme Ctr.; H – b. 11/22/1952 in NH, s/o Bernard Fifield and Priscilla Caswell; W – b. 8/26/1953 in NH, d/o Frederick King and Catherine Doyle

FILLIAN,
Douglas Steven m. Patty D. **Piper** 10/14/1978 in Lyme
Gary L. of Lyme m. Rhonda L. **Cutting** of Lyme 8/23/1986 in Lyme
Richard M. of Lyme m. Karen S. **Carter** of Lyme 9/20/1975 in Lyme; H – b. 1/22/1952 in DE, s/o Richard Fillian and Sara Holland; W – b. 7/23/1955 in NH, d/o Roscoe F. Carter and Anne DeGoosh

FINLEY,
Gregory Scott of Lyme m. J. Marie **Pippin** of Lyme 10/8/1994

FISHER,
Edmond C. of Hartford, VT m. Augusta F. **Hutchins** of Lyme 8/28/1932 in Lyme; H - 27, trucking, 2nd - D, b. Hartford, VT, s/o Harley Fisher (Whitefield, laborer) and Clara A. Kenyon (Quechee, VT, hosuewife); W - 52, housework, 2nd - D, b. Lyme, d/o David J. Pushee (Lyme, farmer) and Mary M. Gilbert (St. Johnsbury, VT, housewife)
Floyd E. of Lunenburg, VT m. Imogene **Miller** of Northampton 8/21/1928 in Lyme; H - 22, farmer, b. Lunenburg, VT, s/o Goodell Fisher (Lunenburg, VT, farmer) and Mary Valley (Lunenburg, VT, housewife); W - 19, at home, b. Northampton, d/o Herbert Miller (Kingston, Canada, salesman) and Mary F. Cole (Northampton, MA, housewife)
Richard Kaye of Lyme m. Margaret Ann **Schurman** of Conway 2/21/1959 in Conway; H – s/o Ralph K. Fisher and Rosalee R. Nusbaum, res. – New York, NY; W – d/o David B. Schurman and Elizabeth M. Headley, res. – Conway

FITZGERALD,
Gary J. of Charlestown, MA m. Donna M. **Hansen** of Charlestown,

MA 6/17/1995

FLANDERS,
Carl L. of Lyme m. Dorothy B. **Piper** of Lyme 10/25/1942 in W. Lebanon; H – 40, lumberman, D, b. Warren, s/o Leonard Flanders (Warren, lumberman) and Ellen Dowse (Newbury, VT, housewife); W – 34, housewife, W, b. Lyme, d/o Orry Henry (N. Thetford, VT, painter) and Bessie Mayo (VT, housewife)

FLICKINGER,
Henry S., Jr. of Windsor, CT m. Tracy E. **Strout** of Lyme 6/5/1982 in Lyme

FLINN,
Frank L. of Lyme m. Anna A. **Flint** of Lyme 6/11/1926 in Lyme; H - 54, painter, 2nd - W, b. Guildhall, VT, s/o Frank Flinn (Guildhall, VT, retired) and Maria Lewis (Danville, VT); W - 53, postmistress, b. Lyme, d/o Francis Flint (Lyme) and Cordelia Smith (Gilford, VT, housewife)

FLINT,
Berton M. of Lyme m. Ella L. **Horton** of Piermont 10/3/1895 in Lyme; H - 23, farmer, b. Lyme, s/o Wesley S. Flint (Lyme) and Olivia M. Cook (Canaan, housekeeper); W - 19, school teacher, b. Orford, d/o William H. Horton (Barnard, VT, farmer) and Mary Chesley (Compton, PQ, housekeeper)
Charles H. of Lyme m. Annie F. **Jesseman** of Lyme 8/27/1893 in Canaan; H - 24, laborer, b. Lyme, s/o Francis F. Flint (Lyme, farmer) and Cordelia Smith (Guilford, VT); W - 29, domestic, 2nd, b. Nashua, d/o Willard Dodge (New Boston, farmer)
Herbert L. of Lyme m. Lulie K. **Cole** of Randolph, VT 9/9/1891 in Lyme; H - 19, laborer, b. Williamstown, VT, s/o Edward Flint (painter) and Fannie O. Bennett (Randolph, VT); W - 18, housekeeper, b. Braintree, VT, d/o Van Cole (Highgate, VT, farmer) and Ora Annies (Winchester)

FOLLANSBEE,
E. J. of Lyme m. L. E. **Hutchinson** of W. Fairlee, VT 10/20/1908 in Lyme; H - 29, farmer, b. W. Fairlee, VT, s/o John H. Follansbee (Manchester, farmer) and Mary G. DeGoosh (W. Fairlee, VT, housewife); W - 23, nurse, 2nd, b. Barnard, VT, d/o Edgar H.

Harlow (Woodstock, VT, farmer) and Mariah E. Grey (Barnard, VT, nurse)

Perley A. of Lyme m. Pearle N. **Biathrow** of Dorchester, MA 12/29/1920 in Nashua; H - 22, machinist, b. W. Fairlee, VT, s/o John Follansbee (Manchester, farmer) and Mary E. DeGoosh (W. Fairlee, VT, housewife); W - 18, household, b. Hanover, d/o Harry Biathrow (Hanover, farmer) and ----- (Lebanon, housewife)

FORWARD,

Thomas C., III of Lyme m. Barbara A. **Burgess** of Salisbury 9/28/1985 in Salisbury

FOSTER,

Anthony of N. Dartmouth, MA m. June D. **White** of N. Dartmouth, MA 4/17/1948 in Lyme; H – 36, farmer, b. N. Dartmouth, MA, s/o Manuel Foster (Azores, Portugal, farmer) and Mary Isabella (Azores, Portugal, housewife); W – 38, at home, D, b. N. Dartmouth, MA, d/o Herbert Davenport (New Bedford, MA, manager) and Elsie E. Stowell (New Bedford, MA, housewife)

Anthony, Jr. m. Marit Kristin **Kikals** 11/18/1978 in Lyme

Richard W. m. Michele **Squeo** 12/21/1980 in Lyme

FOWLER,

Charles E. of Lyme m. Lillian C. **Gilbert** of Lyme 1/25/1922 in Lyme; H - 48, farmer, 2nd - D, b. Newport, s/o David G. Fowler (Colchester, VT, farmer) and Lucy Patten (Croydon, housewife); W - 55, housewife, 3rd - W, b. Lyme, d/o Thomas W. Roberts (Raymond, deceased) and Caroline Smith (Wentworth, deceased)

Charles E. of Lyme m. Clara **Nelligan** of Unity 2/19/1930 in Lyme; H - 58, farmer, 3rd - W, b. Newport, s/o David G. Fowler (Colchester, VT, millman) and Lucy Patten (Croydon, housewife); W - 57, housewife, 3rd - W, b. Unity, d/o Nathaniel Thurber (Unity, blacksmith) and Madelia Eastman (Corinth, VT, housewife)

David G. of Lyme m. Olive L. **Greenwood** of Lyme 11/28/1934 in Lyme; H - 34, farmer, b. Newport, s/o Charles E. Fowler (Newport, farmer) and Clara L. Thurber (Unity, housewife); W - 22, at home, b. Norwich, VT, d/o John L. Greenwood (Knowlton, Canada, farmer) and Eva M. McGill (Belvidere, VT, laundress)

FRACCHIA,
John R. of Ithaca, NY m. Elizabeth Ann **Pomeroy** of Ithaca, NY 6/17/1995

FRAIN,
Richard F. of Manchester m. Virginia L. **Cole** of Lyme 6/28/1968 in Manchester; H – 21, b. NH, s/o Thomas F. Frain and Charlotte Reagan; W – 20, b. NH, d/o Allen L. Cole and Beth Pushee

FRANKLIN,
Harry F. of Lyme m. Clara F. **Piper** of Manchester 6/27/1906 in Manchester; H - 28, mail carrier, b. Lyme, s/o Harry O. Franklin (Lyme, farmer) and Lizzie S. Shattuck (Dorchester, housewife); W - 33, housework, b. Lyme, d/o William B. Piper (Dorchester, harness maker) and Harriet E. Gilbert (Lyme, housework)
Harry P. of Lyme m. Erville D. **Mativia** of Lyme 2/14/1969 in Hanover; H – 60, b. NH, s/o H. Foster Franklin and Clara Piper; W – 66, b. NH, d/o Charles A. Davis and Ava Wheet

FRASCA,
Salv. of Lynn, MA m. Barbara **Mason** of Lynn, MA 5/1/1948 in Lyme; H – 23, contractor, b. Lynn, MA, s/o Michael Frasca (Italy, contractor) and Mary Jordan (Italy, housewife); W – 20, at home, b. Lynn, MA, d/o Edward Mason (Chicago, IL, electrician) and Ida Paige (Fitchburg, MA, housewife)

FREEMAN,
Edward Bicknell of Toronto, Canada m. Priscilla Devitt **Hinchcliffe** of Lyme 9/26/1959 in Lyme; H – s/o Bruce C. Freeman and Helen E. Bicknell of E. Aurora, NY; W – d/o George F. Hinchcliffe and Rachelle Shacklette, res. – Lyme

FREIHOFER,
Daniel S. of Hanover m. Sarah Swift **Barnes** of Lyme 5/15/2004

FRENCH,
Ervin of Lebanon m. Doris M. **Bryll** of Lyme 1/18/1927 in Lyme; H - 34, automobiles, 2nd - W, b. Weston, VT, s/o William French (Weston, VT, carpenter) and Julia Snow (Ludlow, VT,

housewife); W - 26, nurse, b. Hyde Park, VT, d/o George E. Bryll (Franklin, VT, station agent) and Anna J. Soule (Fairfield, VT, housewife)

Walter, Jr. of Lyme m. Abbie C. **Greenwood** of Hanover 4/11/1925 in Lyme; H - 20, laborer, b. Orford, s/o Walter H. French (Orford, dep. sheriff) and Nellie F. Knight (Hartland, VT, housewife); W - 18, at home, b. Tunbridge, VT, d/o Edd Greenwood (Wells River, VT, chauffeur) and Della Sanborn (Vershire, VT, housewife)

FROST,
Robert Edward of Lyme m. Muriel Augusta **Webb** of St. Albans, VT 12/12/1959 in Lyme; H – s/o Cadis E. Frost and Pearl Gardner, res. – Lyme; W – d/o Wendell A. Webb, Sr. and Madine M. Flinn, res. – St. Albans, VT

FULTON,
Elmer E. m. Marion E. **Guyer** 9/8/1979 in Lyme

GAMBLE,
J. R. Peter m. Pamela J. **Gile** 5/30/1981 in Lyme Ctr.

GAMINS,
Albert of Boston, MA m. Florence C. **Shea** of Boston, MA 7/4/1936 in Lyme; H - 30, salesman, b. Russia, s/o Jacob Gamins (Russia, farmer) and Bessie Pollack (England, retired); W - 25, at home, 2nd - D, b. Boston, MA, d/o Jeremiah Twomey (Ireland, laborer) and Catherine McPherson (Canada, housewife)

GARBERSON,
James Whitney of Newton, MA m. Kathryn Elizabeth **Thomas** of Watertown, MA 6/3/1995

GARDNER,
Daren T. of San Diego, CA m. Peggy E. **Pike** of San Diego, CA 6/27/1987 in Lyme

Glen F. of Lyme m. Nellie P. **LaFountaine** of Lyme 8/14/1938 in Bradford, VT; H - 36, laborer, b. Orford, s/o Ned F. Gardner (Orford) and Carrie B. Brown (Orford); W - 2nd - D, b. Orford, d/o Everett Gage (Orford) and Hattie Coolidge

GAUDETTE,
Lawrence Bernard of Lyme m. Vera **Andronova** of Lyme 8/1/1998

GAYLOR,
Michael S. m. Elaine F. **Shamos** 9/25/1977 in Hanover
Peter J. of Lyme m. Rebecca A. **Cunningham** of Lyme 5/15/1982 in Hanover

GENZER,
Scott Jacob of NY m. Kim Eliza **Goodman** of NY 8/23/1998

GEORGE,
Harry E. of Lyme m. Amy M. **Chase** of Derry 7/6/1940 in Lebanon; H – 23, carpenter, 2nd – D, b. Woodsville, s/o William E. George (Fairlee, VT, carpenter) and Ethel M. Sanborn (Fairlee, VT, housewife); W – 18, at home, b. Derry, d/o Perley Chase (Derry, shoemaker) and Marjorie M. Stark (Norwich, VT, housekeeper)

GEREAU,
A. C. of Hanover m. H. H. **Hall** of Lyme 9/13/1919 in Lyme; H - 23, carpenter, b. Ellenburg, NY, s/o C. B. Gereau (Ellenburg, NY, farming) and L. Tourville (Chateaugay, NY, housewife); W - 20, dressmaker, b. Canaan, d/o H. Hall (Maidstone, VT, farming) and A. Dunham (St. George, NB, housewife)

GERNHARD,
Frederick C. of Norwich, CT m. Irene D. **Pushee** of Lyme 9/2/1957 in Lyme; H – 21, s/o Joseph Gernhard and Dorothy Kendall, res. – Norwich, CT; W – 18, d/o David Pushee and Florence DeGoosh, res. – Lyme
Jerry J. m. Robin L. **Staszewski** of Lyme 2/22/1986 in Lyme Ctr.

GESSAY,
Richard Stephen of Orford m. Deborah Ann **Williams** of Orford 10/9/1999

GIBSON,
Frederick L. of Ryegate, VT m. Cynthia A. **Wilson** of Lyme 1/16/1900 in Lyme; H - 39, musician, b. Ryegate, VT, s/o William F. Gibson (farmer) and Phebe Somers (Barnet, VT,

housework); W - 18, housework, b. Lyme, d/o Henry Wilson (farmer) and Georgia Wells (housewife)

William M. of Barnet, VT m. Mary L. **Pearsons** of Barnet, VT 9/27/1925 in Lyme; H - 34, farmer, b. Ryegate, VT, s/o Martin H. Gibson (Ryegate, VT, lumberman) and Mary Clark (Peacham, VT, housewife); W - 29, domestic, 2nd - D, b. Monroe, d/o Elmer Goodwin (Littleton, farmer) and Hattie B. Emery (Haverhill, housewife)

GILBERT,

Austin J. of Lyme m. Edith **Dunbar** of Lyme 5/20/1890 in Lyme; H - 28, laborer, b. Lyme, s/o John A. Gilbert and Elizabeth Post; W - 16, laborer, b. Lyme, d/o George E. Dunbar and Sophia Clough

Charles A. of Lyme m. May L. **Marshall** of Lyme 2/28/1893 in Lyme; H - 23, laborer, b. Barnet, VT, s/o Harris A. Gilbert (Orford, farmer) and Augusta Chamberlin (Newbury, VT); W - 25, domestic, b. Lyme, d/o George C. Marshall (Lyme, farmer) and Sarah J. Blaisdell (Dorchester)

Charles A. of Lyme m. Ada D. **Ellis** of Lyme 8/23/1917 in Lyme; H - 47, farming, 2nd, b. Barnet, VT, s/o Harris A. Gilbert (Orford, farming) and A. A. Chamberlin (Newbury, VT, housewife); W - 50, domestic, 2nd, b. Danville, PQ, d/o Levi Stevens (Island Pond, VT, farming) and Priscilla Barlow (Island Pond, VT, housewife)

David E. of Lyme m. Nettie L. **Flanders** of Orford 5/18/1897 in Lyme; H - 30, laborer, b. Lyme, s/o John A. Gilbert (Lyme, farmer) and Elizabeth Post (Vershire, VT, housewife); W - 17, housework, b. Corinth, VT, d/o Albert Flanders (Corinth, VT, farmer) and Susan Danforth (Corinth, VT, housewife)

Jessie G. of Lyme m. Della S. **Bailey** of Bradford, VT 8/26/1916 in Lyme; H - 22, laborer, b. Monroe, s/o George C. Gilbert (England, laborer) and Melvina E. Byron (Littleton, housewife); W - 29, housework, 2nd, b. Orford, d/o Frank Biathrow (Newport, VT, farming) and Nellie Hurlburt (Hanover, housewife)

Senior P. of Lyme m. Lillian **Oliver** of Lyme 5/7/1887 in Lyme; H - 38, farmer, 2nd, b. Lyme, s/o Israel H. Gilbert (Lyme) and Minerva Cutting (Lyme); W - 25, housekeeper, 2nd, b. Thomas W. Roberts (Lyme) and Caroline Smith (Lyme)

GILE,
Amos W. of Lyme m. Lorna C. **Gile** of Lyme 12/14/1990 in Lyme

GILTINAN,
Garvan Michael of MA m. Heather Shawn **Nathans** of MA 6/18/2000

GLAVICKAS,
John L. of Easthampton, MA m. Rose Marie **Movelle** of Lyme 6/30/1966 in Hanover; H – 32, roofer, b. Easthampton, MA, s/o John Glavickas and Josephine Szary; W – 24, typist, b. Hanover, d/o William J. Movelle and Esther L. Gray

GLOVER,
John Blandin of Hanover m. Kendra J. **Balch** of Lyme 12/5/1970 in Lyme; H – 19, b. NY, s/o Paul W. Glover and Diane Rose; W – 17, b. NH, d/o James Balch and Elizabeth Hartdke

GODFREY,
Roy B. of Lyme m. Helena L. **Ware** of Goshen, VT 1/1/1930 in Goshen, VT; H - 36, farmer, 2nd - W, b. W. Fairlee, VT, s/o William L. Godfrey (W. Fairlee, VT, farmer) and Ada Dennison (Washington, VT, housewife); W - 39, housekeeper, 2nd - W, b. Topsham, VT, d/o Henry Leete (Newbury, VT, retired) and Mary Lambert (Georgia, VT, housewife)
Roy B. of Fairlee, VT m. Ella M. **Wilson** of Lyme 5/31/1952 in Springfield, VT; H – 59, laborer, 3rd – D, b. W. Fairlee, VT, s/o William Godfrey (VT) and Ada Dennison (VT); W – 64, housework, 3rd – W, b. Canaan, d/o Elmore J. Dodge (NY) and Hattie E. Brown (MA)

GOODELL,
Charles N. of Lyme m. Lizzie F. **Southworth** of Lyme 2/5/1898 in W. Fairlee, VT; H - 25, farmer, b. Lyme, s/o John S. Goodell (Lyme, farmer) and Anna L. Carr (ME, housewife); W - 22, housework, b. W. Fairlee, VT, d/o Frank Southworth (W. Fairlee, VT, farmer) and Anna Hurst (housework)
John Wesly of Lyme m. Ida Anna **Webb** of Lyme 1/25/1887 in Lyme; H - 20, farmer, b. Lyme, s/o John S. Goodell (Lyme) and Anna C. Carr (Lebanon, ME); W - 27, teacher, b. Lyme, d/o Charles C. Webb (Newbury, VT) and Mahala Jackson (Lyme)

GORDON,
Edwin R. of Lyme m. Ruth C. **Rowley** of Craftsbury, VT 8/16/1916 in Craftsbury, VT; H - 33, clergyman, b. Salisbury, s/o Charles E. Gordon (Lawrence, MA, clergyman) and Amy A. Keyes (Eastford, CT, housewife); W - 29, at home, b. Westford, MA, d/o Charles H. Rowley (Moriah, NY, clergyman) and Martha C. Brown (Sheldon, VT, housewife)

GOULD,
Clarence F. of Lyme m. Patricia **Hosmer** of Grantham 9/16/1969 in Grantham; H – 22, b. NH; W – 17, b. VT, d/o Ralph Hosmer and Mabel Nelson

GRADY,
John R. of Lyme m. Bonnie M. **Rice** of Lyme 10/7/1989 in Lyme
John Richard, Sr. of Lyme m. Cherylann **L'Esperance** of Lyme --/--/1991

GRAF,
Kevin L. of Lyme m. Jodi L. **Scott** of Lyme 5/29/1989 in Lyme

GRAHAM,
Fred R. of Lyme m. Mary M. **Chase** of Lyme 9/14/1898 in Lyme; H - 24, farmer, b. Putnam, NY, s/o Robert P. Graham (Putnam, NY, farmer) and Maggie Ledgerwood (Putnam, NY, housewife); W - 26, housework, b. Lyme, d/o Hannibal Chase (farmer) and Marinda Jeffers (housewife)

GRANGER,
Ira N. of Thetford, VT m. Verna L. **Smith** of Lyme 11/17/1931 in Lyme; H - 36, clerk, b. Elgin, PQ, s/o John Granger (New York, NY, laborer) and Charlotte Cann (Elgin, PQ, housewife); W - 31, at home, b. Norwich, VT, d/o Charles N. Smith (Hanover, merchant) and Anna Foss (Lebanon, housewife)

GRANT,
Alanson W. of Lyme m. Evelyn V. **Marsh** of Lyme 5/31/1935 in Lyme; H - 24, laborer, b. Lyme, s/o Fred W. Grant (Lyme, farmer) and Viola E. Ware (Thetford, VT, housewife); W - 20, at home, b. Lyme, d/o David Marsh (Orford, farmer) and Delia Smith (Topsham, VT, housewife)

Clyde F. of Lyme m. Janice M. **Garrity** of Hanover 8/4/1984 in Lyme
Fred W. of Lyme m. Viola E. **Ware** of Lyme 11/15/1905 in Lyme; H - 25, farmer, b. Lyme, s/o David A. Grant (Lyme, farmer) and Phebe L. Whipple (Lyme, housewife); W - 27, housework, b. Thetford, VT, d/o Daniel A. Ware (Thetford, VT, farmer) and Luella Morey (Manchester, housewife)
George H. of Lyme m. Ethel M. **Pushee** of Lyme 2/5/1908 in Lyme; H - 22, hotel, b. Lyme, s/o John H. Grant (Lyme, farmer) and Cina Pelton (Lyme, housework); W - 17, housework, b. Lyme, d/o Clarence Pushee (Lyme, farmer) and Fannie Post (Lyme, housework)
James M. of Lyme m. Patricia A. **Train** of Cornish 8/26/1967 in Lyme; H – 26, barber, b. Boston, MA, s/o Elliott M. Grant and Evelyn Nay; W – 24, secretary, b. Hartford, CT, d/o Ralph Train and Viola Ludwig
John E. of Lyme m. Sarah J. **Wilson** of Lyme 1/14/1909 in Lyme; H - 27, laborer, b. Lyme, s/o John H. Grant (Lyme, farmer) and Cina A. Pelton (Lyme, housewife); W - 15, at home, b. Lyme, d/o Henry Wilson (Lyme, farmer) and Georgia A. Flanders (Concord, housewife)

GRAY,
Andrew J. C. of Lyme m. Etta **Muzzey** of Orford 7/4/1894 in Fairlee, VT; H - 28, laborer, 2nd, b. Sheffield, VT, s/o Aaron H. Gray (Sheffield, VT, farmer) and Sarah Simpson (Sheffield, VT, domestic); W - 24, housekeeper, b. Bradford, VT, d/o George Muzzy (Bradford, VT, farmer) and Anna Colby (Bradford, VT, domestic)
Bruce R. of Lyme m. Linda P. **Brown** of Lyme 9/4/1970 in Fairlee, VT; H – 18, b. NH, s/o Harley Gray, Jr. and Joyce Woodward; W – 20, b. NY, d/o Clifton Brown and Paulette LeBlanc
Clarence K. of Lebanon m. Sarah E. **Bates** of Lyme 8/17/1947 in Lyme; H – 43, lumber dlr., 2nd – D, b. Lebanon, s/o Arthur Gray (Lebanon, farmer) and Lilla Tenney (Lebanon, housewife); W – 41, household, 2nd – D, b. Lyme, d/o Frank A. Pushee (Lyme, farmer) and Viola M. Cutting (Lyme, housewife)
Dale Edward of Lyme m. Barbara Ann **Dyke** of Orford 1/9/1971 in Orford; H – 20, b. NH, s/o Richard H. Gray and Olive A. Thompson; W – 21, b. NH, d/o George C. Dyke and Beulah Bockus
Edmund of Lyme m. Linda **Jenks** of Lyme 9/4/1971 in Hanover; H –

23, b. NH, s/o W. Raymond Gray and Irene Page; W – 18, b. NH, d/o Richard Jenks and Anne Grenon

Gerald of Lyme m. Sylvia **Streeter** of Hanover 9/5/1953 in Lyme; H – 25, truck driver, b. Lyme, s/o Harlie Gray (Lyme) and Hattie Pike (Lyme); W – 18, clerk, b. VT, d/o Charles Streeter (NH) and Sybil Potter (NH)

Harley, Jr. of Lyme m. Joyce E. **Greer** of Orford 6/30/1950 in Lyme; H – 18, laborer, b. Lyme, s/o Harley Gray (Lyme) and Hattie Pike (Lyme); W – 17, at home, b. Bradford, VT, d/o Nelson R. Greer (Littleton) and Dorothy Sanborn (Bradford, VT)

Irving D. of Lyme m. Ola S. **Ricketts** of White River Jct. 8/24/1948 in St. Johnsbury, VT; H – 31, bus driver, b. Hartland, ME, s/o Harry Gray (Hartland, ME) and Hazel Staples (Athens, ME); W – 29, mfg. worker, D, b. St. Johnsbury, VT, d/o George Simpson (St. Johnsbury, VT) and Kittie Parker (Tampico, VT)

Lawrence H. of Lyme m. Daune M. **Chicoine** of Thetford, VT 11/15/1968 in Woodsville; H – 22, b. NH, s/o Lawrence H. Gray and Eugenia Stelmach; W – 19, b. VT, d/o Raymond Chicoine and Betty Brown

Lester E. of Orford m. Nellie M. **Chesley** of Lyme 5/21/1925 in Orford; H - 39, laborer, b. Orford, s/o Hiram Gray (Canada, laborer) and Sarah Simpson (Rumney, housewife); W - 32, domestic, b. Lyme, d/o Frank Chesley (W. Fairlee, VT, farmer) and Louise Morey (W. Fairlee, VT, housewife)

Lester E. of Orford m. Alice C. **King** of Lyme 11/2/1930 in Lyme; H - 44, laborer, 2nd - W, b. Orford, s/o Hiram Gray (Canada, laborer) and Sarah Simpson (Orford, housewife); W - 39, housewife, 2nd - W, b. W. Fairlee, VT, d/o Frank A. Chesley (W. Fairlee, VT, farmer) and Louisa Morey (W. Fairlee, VT, housewife)

Michael Shawn of Lyme m. Laura Ingrid **Taylor** of Lyme 9/23/1995

Richard of White River Jct. m. Karen **Maurice** of White River Jct. 10/10/1992

Richard C. of Lyme m. Norine A. **Dyke** of Orfordville 9/16/1967 in Hanover; H – 19, laborer, b. Lebanon, s/o Richard H. Gray and Olive Thompson; W – 15, student, b. Orford, d/o Benjamin Dyke, Jr. and Dorothy Alice

Richard H. of Lyme m. Olive A. **Thompson** of Lyme 6/29/1941 in Orford; H – 18, laborer, b. Lyme, s/o Harlie Gray (Lyme, laborer) and Hattie Pike (Lyme, housewife); W – 23, domestic, b. Lyme, d/o Joseph Thompson (S. Ham, PQ, laborer) and

Grace Archer (Colebrook, housewife)
Samuel A. of Lyme m. Pauline M. **Estes** of Lyme 4/29/1966 in Lyme; H – 24, carpenter, b. Lyme, s/o Richard H. Gray and Olive Thompson; W – 19, at home, b. Hanover, d/o Leonard Estes and Evelyn Powers
Wallace R. of Lyme m. Anna L. **Vincent** of Lyme 2/7/1964 in Lebanon; H – s/o Wallace W. Gray and Vira J. Thurston, res. Wells River, VT; W – d/o Arthur S. Longley and Susan E. Boyd, res. N. Pomfret, VT
William A. of Lyme m. Beverly K. **Fisher** of Lyme 12/6/1968 in Lyme; H – 18, b. NH, s/o Harlie Gray, Jr. and Joyce Greer; W – 18, b. NY, d/o Ralph K. Fisher and Rosa Lee Nusbaum
William A. m. Beverly K. **Gray** 8/13/1977 in Lyme Ctr.

GREATOREX,
Alan R. of Lebanon m. Sharon D. **Balch** of Lyme 12/14/1968 in Lyme; H – 25, b. NH, s/o Harold W. Greatorex and Irena Frost; W – 20, b. NH, d/o Roy E. Balch and Olive Blanchard

GREEN,
Thomas D. of Lyme m. Rhonda Y. **Pillsbury** of Hanover --/--/1991
Thomas Daniel of Lyme m. Tracy Lee **Larabee** of Lyme 1/18/1997
William E., III of Orford m. Donna L. **Morris** of Lyme 8/1/1958 in Orford; H – 21, s/o William E. Green of Fairlee, VT and Phyllis Boyer of Orford; W – 23, d/o Samuel T. Morris and Helen Kaylor, res. – Lyme
William M. of Lyme m. Thelma H. **Wright** of Ludlow, VT 10/3/1936 in Ludlow, VT; H - 21, clerk, b. Perkinsville, VT, s/o George Green (Reading, VT) and Julia Millen (Weathersfield, VT); W - 19, b. Westminster, VT, d/o Harry Wright (Saxtons River, VT) and Vera Simonds (Westboro, VT)

GREENWOOD,
Harry W. of Lyme m. Evelyn L. **Cook** of Norwich, VT 11/26/1940 in Lyme; H – 30, truck driver, b. Thetford, VT, s/o John L. Greenwood (Canada, laborer) and Eva M. McGill (Canada, housekeeper); W – 18, housework, b. Thetford, VT, d/o Homer E. Cook (truck driver) and Marion J. Waterman (Thetford, VT, postmistress)
Lionel H. of Westport, MA m. Elinore L. **Reed** of Westport, MA 10/16/1971 in Lyme; H – 44, b. MA, s/o George Greenwood

and Nellie Tripp; W – 29, b. MA, d/o William Allen and Dorothea Gallop

Paul F. of Hanover m. Marion E. **Wilmot** of Lyme 8/3/1944 in Orford; H – 18, chef, b. Hanover, s/o Edward Greenwood (Woodsville, salesman) and Della Sanborn (Bradford, VT, unemployed); W – 18, laundry emp., b. Lyme, d/o Irvin Wilmot (Lyme, farmer) and Lillian Sayre (Thetford, VT, housewife)

GREGORY,

Frank T. of Lyme m. Sadie May **Porter** of Lyme 3/16/1910 in Lyme; H - 25, farmer, b. Grantham, s/o Lewis Gregory (W. Canaan, farmer); W - 23, housework, b. Canada, d/o ----- Porter and Margaret Thompson

Frank T. of Lyme m. Mattie M. **Mason** of Lisbon 4/9/1932 in Lyme; H - 47, farmer, 2nd - W, b. Grantham, s/o Lewis Gregory (Canada, farmer); W - 41, housekeeper, 3rd - W, b. Lunenburg, VT, d/o Fred L. Vance (Lunenburg, VT, real estate) and Mattie M. Woodworth (Lunenburg, VT, housewife)

GREY,

Gilbert of Lyme m. Emily J. **Perron** of Lyme 7/17/1908 in Lyme; H - 22, laborer, b. Sheffield, VT, s/o Aaron H. Grey (Sheffield, VT, farmer) and Sarah Simpson (Lyme, housewife); W - 30, housework, 2nd, b. Belfast, ME, d/o John Farrell (Bath, ME, farmer) and Ella Keith (Bath, ME, housewife)

GROVE,

Murphy E. m. Jean L. **Elliott** 8/26/1979 in Lyme

GUITAR,

Wilfred O. of Lyme m. Theresa L. **Dube** of Lebanon 9/17/1954 in Lyme; H – 22, plumbing, b. Lyme, s/o Harry Guitar (Canada) and Margaret Gray (Lyme); W – 20, clerk, b. Lebanon, d/o Merrill Dube (Canada) and Yvonne Dion (VT)

GUNN,

Ghyler, Jr. m. Katherine A. **Fanelli** 11/4/1977 in Hanover

GUYER,

Richard M. of Hanover m. Diane **Hobbs** of Lyme 6/25/1966 in Lyme; H – 23, student, b. Hanover, s/o Raymond Guyer and Marion E.

Thompson; W – 19, student, d/o George B. Hobbs and Marion V. Pushee

HACKETT,
Benjamin F. of Lyme m. Bertha L. **Bowen** of Lyme 11/24/1893 in Lyme; H - 42, farmer, 2nd, b. Haverhill, s/o Moses D. Hackett (Lyman, farmer) and Martha Hutton (England); W - 14, domestic, b. Greenfield, d/o Clarence S. Bowen (Corinth, VT, farmer) and Ida Hall (Greenfield)

HADLEY,
David Carroll, Jr. of Pittsylvania, VA m. Donna Estelle **Record** of Lyme 7/18/1959 in Lyme; H – s/o David C. Hadley of Danville, VA and Olive S. Gerry of Nashua; W – d/o Donald L. Record and Ada O. Olsen, res. – Lyme

HADLOCK,
Roger H. m. Deborah A. **Marsh** 10/17/1981 in Lyme Ctr.

HAGERMAN,
David S. of Lyme m. Brooke **Giddings** of Lyme 5/23/2004

HAGGARD,
Alfred K. of Lyme m. Marie L. **Morin** of Lyme 1/6/2001

HAGGERTY,
Hugh C. of Lyme m. Elizabeth E. **Sargent** of Northfield, VT 7/9/1966 in Northfield, VT; H – 28, teacher, b. Richford, VT, s/o Francis Haggerty and Ethel Sherrer; W – 22, student, b. Northfield, VT, d/o Edward H. Sargent and Emma Slack

HALL,
Everett A. of Lyme m. Pearle A. **Wing** of Lyme 11/5/1921 in Lebanon; H - 28, farmer, b. Lancaster, s/o Hiland G. Hall (Maidstone, VT, farmer) and Agnes Dunham (St. George, NB, housewife); W - 21, housework, b. Orford, d/o Milton L. Wing (Chateaugay, NY, farmer) and Nina Courtney (Rochester, VT, housewife)
Frank H. of Lyme m. Josephine **Hall** of Lyme 5/7/1890 in Lyme; H - 48, laborer, b. Lyme, s/o Joel Hall and Joannah Ferbush; W - 36, housekeeper, black, b. Piermont

Frank W. of Orford m. Bessie M. **Dennis** of Lyme 6/30/1909 in Lyme; H - 20, laborer, b. Easton, s/o William B. Hall (Manchester, farmer) and Adra J. Kibbey (Tunbridge, VT, housewife); W - 20, school teacher, b. Piermont, d/o George W. Dennis (Stratford, farmer) and Carrie Church (Vershire, VT, housewife)

Glenn B. of E. Thetford, VT m. Carla A. **Costes** of E. Thetford, VT 8/31/1985 in Lyme

Thord T., Jr. of Lyme m. Christina J. **Kinnett** of Lyme 8/14/2004

HAMBLETON,

James Thomas of Barrington m. Mary Ann **Movelle** of Lyme 8/25/1974 in Barrington; H – b. 2/14/1942 in NH, s/o Kenneth Allan Hambleton and Kathleen Margaret Fox; W – b. 2/28/1943 in NH, d/o William Joseph Movelle and Esther L. Gray

HAMEL,

Joseph T. of Lebanon m. Evelyn M. **Small** of Lyme 10/20/1956 in Lebanon; H – 20, tree surgeon, s/o Victor Hamel and Lucille St. Lawrence, res. – Lebanon; W – 19, secretary, d/o Harry Small and Daisy Melendy, res. – Lyme

HANCHETT,

Merlyn I. of Lyme m. Doris L. **Bartlett** of Northfield 10/13/1930 in Piermont; H - 27, farmer, b. Lyme, s/o Ivan D. Hanchett (Plainfield, farmer) and Florence P. Clark (Grafton, housewife); W - 21, bank clerk, b. Northfield, d/o Charles Bartlett (Bath, weaver) and Maude Haywood (Northfield, housewife)

Merlyn I. of Lyme m. Elizabeth A. **Harriman** of Lyme 6/2/1945 in Lyme; H – 41, janitor, 2nd – D, b. Lyme, s/o Ivan Hanchett (Plainfield, farmer) and Florence Clark (Orange, housewife); W – 38, clerk, 2nd – D, b. Lyme, d/o Henry Pike (Lyme, farmer) and Annie Gilbert (Lyme, housewife)

HANNETT,

Gordon E. of Haverhill m. Evelyn V. **Macomber** of Lyme 9/11/1965 in Lyme; H – 20, debarker op., b. Plymouth, s/o Frank Hannett and Thelma Roberts; W – 17, at home, b. White Plains, NY, d/o Harry Macomber and Mildred Eastwood

HANO,
George David of Lyme m. Diane Rose **Crowley** of Lyme 11/30/1996

HAREL,
Uri of Thetford Ctr., VT m. Virginia Lee **Wallis** of Thetford Ctr., VT 8/24/1996

HARLOW,
Kenneth C. of Thetford Ctr., VT m. Bonnie M. **Goodrich** of Bradford, VT 8/21/1982 in Lyme Ctr.
Robert D. of N. Thetford, VT m. Candie J. **Osgood** of N. Thetford, VT 11/17/1984 in Lyme

HARNISH,
Stephen N. of Lyme m. Marsha M. **Reed** of Lyme 11/13/1983 in Gilford

HARRIMAN,
William B. of Lyme m. Dora D. **Taylor** of Orford 10/31/1936 in Bellows Falls, VT; H - 32, truck driver, 2nd - D, b. Haverhill, s/o Henry D. Harriman (Littleton) and Alice Cox (Holderness); W - 38, 2nd - D, b. Thetford, VT, d/o Fred J. Taylor (Thetford, VT, farmer) and Daisy C. Wilder
William B., Jr. of Lyme m. Ethel **Luce** of Hartford, VT 9/1/1956 in Hartford, VT; H – 23, garage attendant, s/o William Harriman of Lebanon and Elizabeth Pike of Lyme; W – 24, beautician, d/o Fred Luce and Fidelia Murray, res. – Lincoln, VT

HARRINGTON,
C. T. of Lyme m. L. C. **Ackerman** of Lyme –/2/1919 in Lyme; H - 34, farming, b. New Bedford, MA, s/o J. A. Harrington (New Bedford, MA, baker) and A. Fuller (New Bedford, MA, housewife); W - 19, at home, b. St. Albans, VT, d/o J. Ackerman (St. Albans, VT, farming) and E. E. Emery (St. Albans, VT, housewife)

HART,
Jeffrey of Lyme m. Nancy K. **Nakano** of Lyme 6/29/1984 in Hanover
Lawrence F. of Lyme m. Esther M. **Young** of Lyme 3/31/1937 in Lyme; H - 25, farmer, b. Canaan, s/o Frank Hart (Lyme, laborer) and Julia Buckley (Ireland, housewife); W - 19,

domestic, b. Lyme, d/o Leon F. Young (Chateaugay, NY, laborer) and Louise Columbia (St. Albans, VT, housewife)

Lawrence G. of Lyme Ctr. m. Susan E. **Sanborn** of Orford 6/27/1959 in Orford; H – s/o Earl W. Hart and Dorothy L. Knickerbocker, res. – Lyme Ctr.; W – d/o Robert B. Sanborn and Evelyn Blake, res. – Orford

HARTT,
Wayne P. of Westboro, MA m. Linda J. **Owen** of Lyme 6/28/1986 in Lyme

HARWOOD,
George G. of Lyme m. Julia A. **Bassett** of Lyme 8/17/1905 in Lyme; H - 44, farmer, 2nd, b. England, s/o Joel Harwood (England, farmer) and Julia A. Gay (England, housewife); W - 41, housework, 2nd, b. NY, d/o Edson M. French (NY, M.D.) and Catherine Bradley (New Haven, CT, housewife)

HATHAWAY,
Ernest F. of W. Springfield m. Marjorie E. **Evans** of Lyme 7/8/1965 in Sutton; H – 44, textile, 2nd, b. Washington, VT, s/o William Hathaway and Blanche Braman; W – 38, at home, 2nd, b. Lyme, d/o Leo Wilmot and Fannie Chapin

Shaun Willard of Unity m. Wendy Sue **French** of Lyme 12/31/1993

HAWTHORNE,
Daryle L. of Jewett City, CT m. Elise A. **Garrity** of Lyme 11/2/1985 in Lyme

James of Lyme m. Helen **Bond** of Norwich, VT 10/31/1931 in Orford; H - 21, painter, b. Penacook, s/o James H. Hawthorne (Franklin, paper maker) and Josie Chase (Bath, housewife); W - 19, at home, b. Orford, d/o William Bond (Norwich, VT, farmer) and Elizabeth Hall (Hanover, housewife)

HAYES,
A. Reed of Lyme m. Sheila M. **Gladney** of Lyme 7/4/1987 in Lyme
Kenneth Ronald of Lyme m. Lisa Marie **Franklin** of Lyme 6/30/1995

HAZEN,
Robert D. of Manchester m. Mary A. **Bailey** of Lyme 9/13/1900 in Lyme; H - 20, pattern maker, b. Manchester, s/o Herman D.

Hazen (N. Hero, VT) and Maria I. Merriam (Lowell, MA, housewife); W - 20, housework, b. Lyme, d/o Henry A. Bailey (Lyme, farmer) and Augusta A. Howard (Lyme, housewife)

HEATH,
Norman E. of Landaff m. Esther C. **Bryant** of Lyme 9/7/1958 in Lyme; H – 30, s/o Harrison M. Heath and Mary F. McKenzie, res. – Landaff; W – 21, d/o George H. Bryant and Ruth E. Dimick, res. – Lyme

HEITZMAN,
Tom Craig of Lyme m. Andrea Beth **Lieberman** of Lyme 9/16/1995

HENDERSON,
James M. of Lyme m. Leslie H. **Graham** of Lyme 8/19/1989 in Lyme

HENDRICK,
Robert N. of Lyme m. Margaret **Swift** of Thetford, VT 9/14/1935 in Orford; H - 25, farming, b. Lancaster, s/o Levi W. Hendrick (Lancaster, farmer) and Cora M. Hodgdon (Lancaster, housewife); W - 18, at home, b. Strafford, VT, d/o Kenneth J. Swift (Thetford, VT, farmer) and Carrie Boot (Strafford, VT, housewife)
Shirley I. of Lyme m. Ethel R. **Elliott** of Newport, VT –/7/1938 in Lyme; H - 23, farming, b. Lunenburg, VT, s/o William D. Hendrick (Lancaster, farmer) and Cora Hodgdon (Lancaster, housewife); W - 22, domestic, b. Newport, VT, d/o Herbert Elliott and Nellie Gray

HEWES,
Berton F. of Lyme m. E. Addie **Blood** of W. Windsor, VT 9/25/1895 in Lyme; H - 29, laborer, b. Lyme, s/o Eleazer W. Hewes (Lyme, farmer) and Ruth Leonard (Orford, housewife); W - 22, housework, b. W. Windsor, VT, d/o Aretus B. Blood (W. Windsor, VT, farmer) and Nancy D. Oakes (W. Windsor, VT, housewife)
Charles A. of Lyme m. Louise A. **Cutting** of Fryeburg, ME 6/24/1950 in Fryeburg, ME; H – 30, farmer, b. Etna; W – 21, stud. nurse, b. Fryeburg, ME
Frank S. of Lyme m. Addie M. **Elliott** of Lyme 12/13/1899 in Lyme; H - 28, farmer, b. Lyme, s/o Nathan W. Hewes (Lyme, farmer)

and Lucy W. Cobb (Hardwick, VT); W - 22, housework, b. Lyme, d/o John F. Elliott (Campton, miller) and Kate V. Hewes (Lyme, housewife)

Fred C. of Lyme m. Lena M. **Chesley** of Lyme 8/3/1898 in Lyme; H - 22, farmer, b. Lyme, s/o Nathan W. Hewes (Lyme, farmer) and Lucy Cobb (Hardwick, VT); W - 18, teacher, b. W. Fairlee, VT, d/o Frank A. Chesley (W. Fairlee, VT, farmer) and Louisa M. Morey (housewife)

Fred C. of Lyme m. Ethel **Spencer** of Hanover 4/19/1908 in Lyme; H - 31, farmer, 2nd, b. Lyme, s/o Nathan W. Hewes (Lyme, farmer) and Lucy Cobb (Hardwick, VT, housework); W - 25, housework, d/o Willie Spencer (postmaster) and ----- Newton (housework)

Fred C. of Lebanon m. I. Estella **Angel** of Lyme 5/3/1915 in Claremont; H - 38, farmer, 3rd, b. Lyme, s/o Nathan W. Hewes (Lyme, farmer) and Lucia Cobb (Hardwick, VT, housewife); W - 19, housework, b. RI

Ralph W. of Lyme m. Goldie **Ackerman** of Lyme 9/29/1926 in Orford; H - 20, laborer, b. Lyme, s/o Frank S. Hewes (Lyme, laborer) and Addie E. Elliott (Lyme, housewife); W - 21, at home, b. Lyme, d/o William J. Ackerman (St. Albans, VT, carpenter) and Esther F. Emery (St. Albans, VT, housewife)

HEWETT,

Charles E. m. Jacqueline A. **Kennedy** 6/6/1981 in Lyme

Charles W. of Evanston, IL m. Barbara P. **Brown** of Lyme 11/19/1967 in Lyme; H – 24, U. S. Navy, b. Evanston, IL, s/o Ernest J. Hewitt and Ruth Burns; W – 25, secretary, b. Washington, DC, d/o Aaron S. Brown and Dorothy I. Park

HILL,

Alan H. m. Roberta K. **Pike** 8/16/1980 in Lyme

Arnold R. of Lyme m. Eldora M. **Page** of W. Rumnet 9/3/1945 in Lyme; H – 33, carpenter, b. Danville, PQ, s/o Talbert W. Hill (Chateaugay, NY, farmer) and Lila M. Leet (Danville, PQ, housewife); W – 22, typist, b. W. Rumney, d/o Herbert E. Page (Campton, farmer) and Doris A. Colburn (S. Wentworth, housewife)

David Bradley of NC m. Kelly Ann **Currier** of NC 8/7/1999

Douglas P. of Lyme m. Ingrid L. **Curtis** of Lyme 5/18/1984 in Lyme

Lloyd D. of Thetford, VT m. Nadine E. **George** of Fairlee, VT 5/24/1944 in Lebanon; H – 20, carpenter, b. Thetford, VT, s/o

Max F. Hill (Thetford, VT, machinist) and Carrie L. Cook (Chateaugay, NY, housewife); W – 18, at home, b. Hanover, d/o Wilbur A. George (St. Albans, VT, carpenter) and Ethel M. Sanborn (Fairlee, VT, housewife)

Oscar B. of W. Fairlee, VT m. Eleanor D. **O'Keefe** of Lyme 10/20/1953 in Lyme; H – 46, laborer, b. NH, s/o Oliver Hill (NH) and Viola -----; W – 21, housewife, b. NH, d/o Joseph O'Keefe (NH) and Thelma Olyer (NH)

Parker S. of Ely, VT m. Esther C. **Sanborn** of W. Fairlee, VT 9/5/1958 in Hinsdale; H – 62, s/o Lyndon J. Hill and Mary E. Scott, res. – Chauteaugay, NY; W – 45, d/o Hart E. Crandall and Flora M. Hadley, res. – Lebanon

Ransom D. of Lyme m. Joan D. **Grosjean** of Lyme 8/1/1967 in Hanover; H – 35, plumber, b. Morrisville, VT, s/o Glen Hill and Hazel Perry; W – 36, secretary, b. Rutland, VT, d/o Floyd E. Davis and Elizabeth Barriere

Richard H. of Norwich, VT m. Kathy L. **King** of Lyme 7/19/1969 in Lyme; H – 23, b. NH, s/o Maurice Hill and Goldie May Jones; W – 19, b. NH, d/o Charles King and Bessie Severance

Van Scott of Andover m. Julie Ann **Gray** of Andover 7/10/1998

HILLNER,
H. Randall of Fairfield, IA m. Jane I. **Wickware** of Lyme 7/11/1982 in Lyme

HIMOT,
Peter of Brighton, MA m. Jain **Bowden** of Lyme 8/22/1970 in Lyme; H – 34, b. NY, s/o Jacob Himot and Sadye Fox; W – 23, b. NY, d/o John W. Bowden and Mary Sharples

HINSLEY,
Michael Cagney of Lyme m. Barbara Ann **O;Mara** of Lyme 6/5/1993

HOAG,
Kenneth V. of Pittsfield, MA m. Frances M. **Delmolino** of Pittsfield, MA 3/14/1953 in Lyme; H – 31, stock clerk, b. MA, s/o Raymond Hoag (MA) and Laura Chase (MA); W – 21, inspector, 2nd – D, b. MA, d/o Armand Beliveau (MA) and Evelyn Fountain (MA)

HOBART,
Albert of Hebron m. Nellie H. **Phelps** of Lyme 4/23/1887 in Lyme; H - 42, farmer, 2nd, b. Hebron, s/o David Hobart (Hebron) and Mary Frye (Melham, MA); W - 30, housekeeper, b. Lyme, d/o Timothy B. Phelps (Orford) and Harriet N. Dicky (Windham)

HOBBS,
George B. of Lyme m. Marion V. **Pushee** of Lyme 9/30/1944 in Lyme; H – 22, US Navy, b. Lyme, s/o Hervey H. Hobbs (Wentworth, coal dealer) and Jessie Waterman (Thetford, VT, housewife); W – 18, defense work, b. Lyme, s/o Frank Pushee (Lyme, farmer) and Viola Cutting (Lyme Ctr., housewife)

HODSON,
David Thomas of Brooklyn, NY m. Esther **Shatavsky** of Brooklyn, NY 8/7/1993

HOEMANN,
Andrew Ramiro of NY m. Cynthia Ellen **Carroll** of NY 8/12/2000

HOLFORD,
Fred Dewitt of Lyme m. Doris Hadley **Hill** of Lyme --/--/1991

HOLMAN,
Hugh F. of Baltimore, MD m. Gail M. **Sansbury** of Lyme 12/22/1968 in Hanover; H – 21, b. NY, s/o Y. R. Holman and Emily Brown; W – 20, b. NH, d/o John Sansbury and Dorothy Gregory

HOLT,
Herbert H. of Lyme m. Emma L. **Barnes** of Lyme 11/15/1890 in Thetford, VT; H - 33, farmer, b. Lyme, s/o Isaac P. Holt and Emily Mallard; W - 26, school teacher, b. Lyme, d/o Hiram Barnes and Esther Gillett

HORTON,
Bradley of Lyme Ctr. m. Pamela **Phillips** of Lyme Ctr. 12/30/1972 in Hanover; H – 21, b. NH, s/o George Horton and Esther Gerue; W – 19, b. OH, d/o Paul Phillips and Dorothy Baker

Charles E. of Lyme m. Shirley T. **Veverka** of Hanover 5/25/1963 in Hanover; H – s/o ----- W. Horton and ----- G. Tracy, res. – Lyme; W – d/o ----- T. Tanzi and ----- E. Patterson of Hanover

George E. of Lyme m. Esther L. **Gerue** of Lyme 6/14/1941 in Hanover; H – 26, mill worker, b. Lyme, s/o Charles Horton (Enfield, farmer) and Frances Kempton (Everett, MO, housewife); W – 18, beauty parlor o., b. Hanover, d/o Arthur C. Gerue (Elenburg, NY, carpenter) and Hazel H. Hall (Canaan, housewife)

L. C. of Lyme m. C. G. **Jones** of Hanover –/15/1919 in Lyme; H - 22, farming, b. Springfield, s/o C. H. Horton (Enfield, farming) and F. D. Kempton (Everett, MA, housewife); W - 18, at home, b. Hanover, d/o W. Jones (Canaan, farming) and E. Simpson (Sheffield, VT, housewife)

HOSMER,

Ralph of Marlboro, CT m. Lillian **Pommer** of Marlboro, CT 11/22/1968 in Lyme; H – 61, b. VT, s/o Darlean Hosmer and Clemenie Worth; W – 48, b. NY, d/o Philip Traynor and Bridget McConnell

HOUSE,

Clinton E. of Newport, VT m. Lottie D. **Gilbert** of Lyme 10/17/1894 in Lyme; H – 30, laborer, b. Newport, VT, s/o Timothy J. House (Stanstead, PQ, carpenter) and Charlotte C. Martin (Stanstead, PQ, housekeeper); W - 21, housework, b. Lyme, d/o Elam Gilbert (Lyme, harness maker)

HOUSTON,

Gregory R. of E. Thetford, VT m. Dorothy E. **Curran** of Fairlee, VT 8/1/1987 in Lyme

HOWE,

Orin of Lyme m. Linda **Chapley** of Franklin 7/17/1971 in Franklin; H – 24, b. NH, s/o Edward Howe and Hazel Martin; W – 24, b. NH, d/o Frank Chapley and Louise Allen

HUBBARD,

Charles H., Jr. of Lyme m. Eugenia **Emery** of St. Albans, VT 5/30/1903 in Lyme Ctr.; H - 20, laborer, b. Sherbrook, PQ, s/o Charles H. Hubbard (ME, farmer) and Mary Perry (Orford, housewife); W - 23, housework, b. St. Albans, VT, d/o Charles Emery (St. Albans, VT, farmer)

F. Alden of Lebanon m. Shirley I. **Uline** of Lyme 8/2/1958 in Lyme; H

– 39, s/o J. Fred Hubbard and Josephine Flint, res. – Lebanon; W – 27, d/o Millard H. Uline and Susie Cadwell, res. – Lyme

HUDSON,
Edward J. of Woodsville m. Etta Mae **Melendy** of Lyme 12/17/1954 in Haverhill; H – 32, laborer, 3rd - D, b. VT, s/o Alfred Hudson (VT) and Mattie Dunn (VT); W – 23, housewife, 2nd – D, b. Lyme, d/o Earl H. Pike (Lyme) and Myrtle Coates (Canada)

HUGHES,
Thomas W. of Lyme m. Maureen H. **Byrne** of Lyme 10/1/1999

HUMISTON,
Frank of Lyme m. Sylvia **Wilmot** of Lyme 7/17/1926 in Thetford, VT; H - 31, farmer, b. E. Jaffrey, s/o Frank Humiston (NY) and Carrie B. Tarbel (W. Groton, VT); W - 18, b. Lyme, d/o Elber Wilmot (Strafford, VT, farmer) and Myrtle Cummings (Lyme, housewife)

HUNT,
Walter C. of White River Jct. m. Bernice V. **Watson** of White River Jct. 9/29/1934 in Lyme; H - 28, truck driver, b. Rochester, VT, s/o George F. Hunt (Bedford, PQ, carpenter) and Lelia M. Green (Hereford, PQ, housewife); W - 28, bookkeeper, b. Hartford, VT, d/o George W. Watson (Canton, NY, laborer) and Viola M. Hackett (Hartford, VT, housewife)

HUNTINGTON,
Harold L. of Orford m. Mary Jane **Fields** of Lyme 1/13/1958 in Hanover; H – 30, s/o Harold K. Huntington and Laura LeLane, res. – Orford; W – 19, d/o John Fields and Meda Roberts, res. – Lyme

HUNTLEY,
Thomas R. m. Doris A. **O'Donnell** 10/15/1977 in Lyme

HUSBAND,
Thomas C. of Windsor, VT m. Vicki L. **Bacon** of Lyme 8/25/1984 in Lyme

HUTCHINS,
Charles H. of Lyme m. Elsie **King** of Lyme 8/27/1895 in Lyme; H - 22, laborer, b. Lyme, s/o John W. Hutchins (Boltonville, CT, laborer) and Eliza Webb (Hanover, housewife); W - 17, housework, b. Lyme, d/o Samuel King (farmer)
George of Lyme m. Edna **Dike** of Lyme 5/2/1888 in Lyme; H - 20, laborer, b. Lyme, s/o John Hutchins (Hanover) and Eliza Webb (Lyme); W - 22, housekeeper, b. Lyme, d/o David Dike (Lyme)
John J., Sr. of NH m. Alta **Holmes** of ME 8/31/1972 in Lyme; H – 62, b. NH, s/o Joseph D. Hutchins and Corinne K. Johnson; W – 54, b. NH, d/o Arthur Cushing and Esther C. Marston
John Joseph, Jr. of Lyme m. Priscilla M. **Haskins** of Hanover 5/7/1966 in Lyme; H – 20, laborer, b. Hanover, s/o John J. Hutchins and Ruth Beard; W – 18, student, b. Lebanon, d/o Robert Haskins, Sr. and Alice Thurston
Joseph D. of Hanover m. Jennie **Farrington** of Lebanon 6/11/1887 in Lyme; H - 20, laborer, b. Hanover, s/o Haven K. Hutchins (Hanover) and Pamelia Danniels (Lebanon); W - 18, housekeeper, b. Methuen, MA, d/o Horace Farrington (Methuen, MA) and Ellen Brochen (Quebec, Canada)
Joseph D. of Lyme m. Rose **Roman** of Lebanon 6/21/1952 in Lyme; H – 19, truck driver, b. Rochester, s/o John Hutchins (Hanover) and Ruth Beard (Manchester); W – 18, at home, b. Lebanon, d/o Frank Roman (Poland) and Lydia Rancourt (Canada)
Joseph D., Jr. of NH m. Mary T. **Kendall** of VT 6/10/1972 in S. Strafford, VT; H – 20, b. NH, s/o Joseph D. Hutchins and Rose Roman; W – 17, b. VT, d/o Watson Kendall and Margaret Jones
Lawrence of Lyme m. Augusta F. **Pushee** of Lyme 6/5/1926 in Plainfield; H - 23, farmer, b. Lyme, s/o Charles H. Hutchins (Hanover, laborer) and Elsa M. King (Lyme, housewife); W - 18, student, b. Lyme, d/o David J. Pushee (Lyme, laborer) and Mary M. Gilbert (St. Johnsbury, VT, housewife)

INGALLS,
Nelson P. of Worcester, MA m. Florence **Mayberry** of Lyme 7/13/1925 in Lyme; H - 29, manager, b. Newburyport, MA, s/o Edward Ingalls (Wentworth, garage) and Ida. Littlefield (Newburyport, MA, housewife); W - 27, teacher, b. Manchester, d/o John Mayberry (Cumberland, ME, farmer) and Augusta Stearns (Haverhill, housewife)

IRVING,
John P. of Newton m. Marguerite **Genereaux** of Lyme 5/3/1958 in Lebanon; H – 53, s/o John P. Irving and Willa D. Cairns; W – 57, d/o Michael Maskill and Margaret Connery

ISENBERG,
William A. of Camden, NJ m. Elizabeth H. **Partridge** of Camden, NJ 7/6/1940 in Lyme; H – 28, ind. engineer, b. Harrisburg, PA, s/o Alfred P. Isenberg (Houtzdale, PA, physician) and Fame Ford (Houtzdale, PA, housewife); W – 29, teacher, b. Camden, NJ, d/o Harvey K. Partridge (Camden, NJ, sales manager) and Emma Hires (Bridgeton, NJ. housewife)

JACKMAN,
Charles R. of Bradford, VT m. Ruth **Dennis** of Lyme 3/8/1910 in Orford; H - 19, farmer, b. Lisbon, s/o Charles Jackman (Lisbon, farmer) and Nettie Noyes (Lyman, housewife); W - 19, at home, b. Piermont, d/o George W. Dennis (Stratford, farmer) and Carrie Church (Vershire, VT, housewife)

JACKSON,
Christopher of Lyme m. Karen Lee **Sapp** of Lyme 6/21/1975 in Hanover; H – b. 6/11/1946 in NH, s/o David Jackson and Maisie Cowper; W – b. 12/10/1945 in ME, d/o John Sapp and Dorothy Mercer
Leon D. of Ft. Devens, MA m. Nancy A. **Elder** of Lyme 11/3/1984 in Lyme

JARVIS,
Kevin Gordon m. Marilyn S. **Archamnbeault** 10/25/1980 in Manchester

JENKS,
Alan A. of Lyme m. Vea M. **Palmer** of Hanover 11/11/1966 in Lyme; H – 36, laborer, b. Ware, MA, s/o Leo A. Jenks and Ethel Carrier; W – 25, messenger aide, b. Hanover, d/o Vernon E. Palmer and Eunice Preston
Arthur L. of Lyme m. Thelma P. **Bonds** of Lyme 11/12/1950 in Lyme; H – 82, retired, 2nd – W, b. Ludlow, MA, s/o Lucien Jenks (Belchertown, MA) and Almeda Bartlett (Belchertown, MA); W – 54, factory worker, 2nd – D, b. Lyme, d/o Charles Stickney

(Danville, VT) and Inez Hadlock (Lyme)
Berton A. of Hartford, VT m. Grace L. **Rowe** of Hartford, VT 6/26/1907 in Lyme; H - 25, laborer, b. Hanover, s/o George J. Jenks (Lyme, laborer) and Etta Packard (housewife); W - 17, housework, b. Lebanon, d/o George E. Rowe (Auburn, ME, farmer) and Sarah P. Sanborn (Hanover, housework)
Charles C. of Lyme m. Edna **Sturtevant** of Bradford, VT 12/9/1887 in Lyme; H - 28, farmer, b. Lyme, s/o Dexter Jenks (Lyme) and Betsy Fox (Strafford, VT); W - 18, housekeeper, b. Orford, d/o Hiram Sturtevant (Claremont) and Mary Maria Wards (Bradford, VT)
Chester of Lyme Ctr. m. Marion **Hanchett** of Lyme 10/17/1927 in N. Thetford, VT; H - 21, laborer, b. Lyme, s/o Edward E. Jenks (Lyme, laborer) and Mae E. LaMott (Lyme, housekeeper); W - 16, student, b. Lyme, d/o Fred Hanchett (Lyme, farmer) and Bernice Homan (Lebanon, housekeeper)
Chester C. of Lyme m. Ouida N. **Rines** of Lebanon 1/26/1958 in Lebanon; H – 50, s/o Edward Jenks and Mae LaMott, res. – Lyme; W – 46, d/o Ralph Nichols and Emma Morrill, res. – Lebanon
Edward F. of Lyme m. Edith M. **Record** of Lyme 9/3/1950 in Springfield, VT; H – 19, laborer, b. Hanover, s/o Chester Jenks (Lyme) and Marion Hanchett (Lyme); W – 17, at home, b. Hanover, d/o Donald Record (Hanover) and Ada Olsen (Stoughton, MA)
Gregory Allen of Lyme m. Patricia Lee **Jenks** of Lyme 9/19/2004
James of Lyme m. Patricia **Grant** of Lyme 6/26/1971 in Lyme; H – 19, b. NH, s/o Roger Jenks and Ruth Godfrey; W – 16, b. NH, d/o John Grant and Janet Piper
John E. of Lyme m. Lucy **Lord** of Norwich, VT 9/7/1887 in Lyme; H - 40, laborer, 2nd, b. Lyme, s/o Dexter Jenks (Lyme) and Betsey Fox (Strafford, VT); W - 24, housekeeper, b. Norwich, VT, d/o David Lord (Norwich, VT) and Elizabeth Lord (Norwich, VT)
Merton A. of Lyme m. Florence E. **Wilmot** of Lyme 8/13/1941 in Lyme; H – 29, lumberman, b. Belchertown, MA, s/o Arthur L. Jenks (Ludlow, MA, farmer) and Edith Arnold (Granby, MA, housewife); W – 20, at home, b. Lyme, d/o Leo A. Wilmot (Lyme, farmer) and Fannie Chapin (S. Boston, MA, housewife)
Richard F. of Lyme m. Lori L. **Durkee** of E. Thetford, VT 8/16/1986 in Hanover
Robert E. of Lyme m. Brenda J. **Phelps** of Thetford, VT 11/23/1968

in Lyme; H – 23, b. NH, s/o Elbridge Jenks and Lillian Gregory; W – 18, b. VT, d/o George Phelps and Gloria Morrill

Robert Elbridge m. Annette Louise **Henry** 7/8/1978 in Lyme

Roger C. of Lyme m. Ruth E. **Godfrey** of E. Thetford, VT 11/27/1949

Ronald Harvey of Lyme m. Teresa W. **Pearson** of W. Fairlee, VT 7/26/1975 in Lyme; H – b. 5/23/1957 in NH, s/o Thomas Jenks and Doris Balch; W – b. 11/5/1957 in NH, d/o John Pearson and Lorraine White

Sherwin A. of Lyme m. Ann **Longworth** of Hanover 12/22/1951 in Hanover; H – 19, US Army, b. NH, s/o Leo A. Jenks (MA) and Ethel Carrier (MA); W – 19, secretary, b. NH, d/o Percy Longworth (England) and Winifred Caine (England)

Stanley of Lyme m. Margaret **Courtemanche** of Lebanon 5/27/1950 in Lebanon; H – 21, carpenter, b. Lyme, s/o Chester Jenks (Lyme) and Marion Hanchett (Lyme); W – 20, stitcher, b. NH, d/o Joseph Courtemanche (VT) and Merilda Lessard (Canada)

Steven R. of NH m. Katherine M. **Paskus** of NH 10/10/1972 in Hanover; H – 19, b. NH, s/o Thomas Jenks and Doris Balch; W – 18, b. NY, d/o Garrison Paskus and Gertrude Weinheimer

Thomas E. of Lyme m. Doris H. **Balch** of Lyme 8/4/1951 in Lyme; H – 20, carpenter, b. Lyme, s/o Elbridge Jenks (Lyme) and Lillian Gregory (Lyme); W – 18, at home, b. Lyme, d/o Roy E. Balch (Hartland, VT) and Olive Blanchard (Orford)

William F. of Lyme m. Emma D. **Smith** of Lyme 8/16/1894 in Lyme; H - 22, farmer, b. Lyme, s/o Elias Jenks (Lyme, laborer) and Martha Decatur (Lyme, housekeeper); W - 15, housekeeper, b. Lyme, d/o Edgar Smith (Manchester, farmer) and Delia S. Worthen (Lyme, housekeeper)

JEWELL,

Carrol of Lyme m. Rosa E. **Wilder** of Lyme 5/2/1894 in Lyme; H - 28, laborer, b. Lyme, s/o John Jewell (NY, farmer) and Caroline Whitcher (Wentworth, housekeeper); W - 26, housework, b. Thetford, VT, d/o George E. Wilder (barber) and Caroline Barrett (Thetford, VT, housekeeper)

John of Lyme m. Jane **Breck** of Lyme 5/28/1891 in Lyme; H - 74, farmer, 3rd, b. Lyme, s/o Mark Jewell (NY) and Mabel Hall (NY); W - 46, housekeeper, b. Lyme, d/o Melvin C. Breck (Lyme, farmer) and Matilda Andrews (housekeeper)

John L. of Lyme m. Daisy E. **Carr** of Lyme 5/30/1917 in Lyme; H - 31, farming, b. Canada, s/o Frank Jewell (Dorchester, laborer)

and Eliza Jewell (housewife); W - 34, housework, 2nd, b. Waits River, VT, d/o Jasper Day (Haverhill, MA, farming) and Alfretta Simpson (W. Topsham, VT, housewife)

JOHNS,
Dirk Alexander of Chesterfield, MO m. Jennifer Moore **Hayes** of Chesterfield, MO 8/21/1993

JOHNSON,
Arthur Herbert, II of FL m. Carol H. **Gillen** of FL 8/13/2000

Carl of Lyme m. Ethel **Hardy** of Lyme 1/6/1908 in Lyme; H - 30, teamster, 2nd, b. W. Windsor, VT, s/o Reuben Johnson (Claremont, teamster) and May Whittemore (W. Lebanon, housework); W - 31, housework, 2nd, b. Manchester, d/o John H. Parker (Franconia, farmer) and Henrietta Miller (Lebanon, household)

Curtis R. of Montpelier, VT m. Emma A. **Lund** of Vershire, VT 6/6/1946 in Lyme; H – 64, auto dealer, 3rd – D, b. Shapleigh, ME, Herbert Johnson (Machese, ME, carpenter) and Suzanna Ham (Acton, ME, housewife); W – 45, mail carrier, 2nd – W, b. Windsor Mills, PQ, d/o Thomas Cousineau (Vantekil, ON, retired) and Christian Francis (Vantekil, ON, housewife)

Fred H. of Lyme m. Laura B. **Huckins** of Lyme 10/7/1905 in Hanover; H - 41, farmer, b. Norwich, VT, s/o John H. Johnson (Underhill, VT, farmer) and Harriet Fox (Hanover, housewife); W - 28, housework, 2nd, b. Lyme, d/o Henry O. Webb (Hanover, farmer) and Mary Cline (Lyme, housewife)

Fred H. of Lyme m. Bertha M. **Smith** of Lyme 11/7/1929 in Lyme; H - 65, farmer, 2nd - D, b. Norwich, VT, s/o John H. Johnson (Underhill, VT, retired) and Harriet Fox (Hanover, housewife); W - 51, housekeeper, 2nd - W, b. Lyme, d/o Francis F. Flint (Lyme, farmer) and Cordelia Smith (Guilford, VT, housewife)

Haynes E. of Lyme m. Grace D. **Frost** of Lyme 8/24/1899 in Lyme; H - 20, farmer, b. Bradford, VT, s/o Arthur F. Johnson (Bradford, VT, farmer) and Ida M. Carlton (Newbury, VT, housewife); W - 19, housework, b. Lyme, s/o Frank Frost (Topsham, VT, farmer) and Delia Mativia (Hartford, VT, housewife)

Irving J. of Norwich, VT m. Zippie L. **Rogers** of Norwich, VT 3/15/1887 in Lyme; H - 21, student, b. Canada, s/o Jackson D. Johnson (Underhill, VT) and May W. Hatch (Norwich, VT); W -

19, teacher, b. Norwich, VT, d/o George F. Rogers (Norwich, VT) and Lydia Roberts (Norwich, VT)

J. P. R. of Milford, MA m. Georgia **Flanders** of Lyme 10/10/1908 in Milford, MA; H - 52, engineer, 2nd, b. Sweden, s/o John E. Johnson and Anna C. Galdell; W - 49, at home, 2nd, b. Concord, d/o Samuel E. Flanders and Jane Nelson

Philip of Holden, MA m. Judith A. **King** of Lyme 8/24/1968 in Lyme; H – 22, b. MA, s/o Dr. Robert Johnson and Margaret Chesley; W – 19, b. NH, d/o Everett R. King and Priscilla Hazleton

Walter H. of Lyme m. Mary E. **Lewis** of Deerfield –/8/1938 in Etna; H - 27, laborer, b. Thetford, VT, s/o Herbert H. Johnson (Norwich, VT, farmer) and Mabel E. Roberts (Thetford, VT, housewife); W - 24, cook, b. Deerfield, d/o Willis A. Lewis (Allenstown, carpenter) and Ernestine G. Small (Cornish, ME, housewife)

JOHNSTON,

Richard H. of Lyme m. Frances A. **Borovick** of Lyme 11/15/1986 in Lyme

JONES,

Benjamin Parker of CA m. Pamela Ann **Zachar** of IL 4/18/1998

Matthew of Gainesville, FL m. Ginny **Eckert** of Gainesville, FL 8/17/1992

Maynard A. of Lyme m. Frances F. **Hill** of Noank, CT 9/11/1931 in Noank, CT; H - 25, camp work, b. Joplin, MO, s/o Samuel F. Jones and Olive Gammell; W - 25, at home, b. Noank, CT, d/o William M. Hill and Anna Squires

JOY,

Gailon Arthur of Lyme m. Ann Marie **Camire** of W. Lebanon 6/16/1974 in Lyme; H – b. 5/14/1952 in ME, s/o Clayton A. Joy and Mildred Farmer; W – b. 2/12/1951 in VT, d/o Ona Nelson Camire and Cecile Benoit

JOYCE,

Roy Thomas m. Marion Evelyn **Northrup** 7/29/1978 in Lyme

JUDD,

Carlos S. of Bradford, VT m. Edith M. **Mativia** of Lyme 4/6/1918 in Lyme; H - 24, electrician, b. Franconia, s/o Benjamin S. Judd (Lisbon, blacksmith) and Linda J. Streeter (Lisbon, housewife);

W - 18, at home, b. Lyme, d/o Darius R. Mativia (N. Hartland, VT, mail carrier) and Ida A. Stark (Lyme, housewife)

KATZ,
Jason Stephan of CO m. Christina Marie **Perry** of CO 6/3/2000

KAUFMAN,
Michael of Quechee, VT m. Deborah **Hopkins** of Quechee, VT 11/14/1992

KEARNEY,
Patrick of E. Thetford, VT m. Ann L. **Lutjen** of Lyme Ctr. 4/19/1986 in Hanover

KEEFE,
John Joseph m. Eleanor C. **Lull** 1/5/1980 in Lyme

KEGAN,
Robert C. of Lyme m. Carolyn C. **Roth** of Lyme 9/12/1971 in Lyme; H – 25, b. MN, s/o Bernard Kegan and Saralee Rosenberg; W – 29, b. MN, d/o Everett Coultier and Marilyn Jenne

KENDALL,
Eugene Franklin of Lebanon m. Regenna Ann **Lyster** of Lebanon 12/17/1976 in Lyme; H – b. 2/26/1948 in VT, s/o Watson Kendall and Margaret Jones; W – b. 9/8/1951 in NH, d/o Roy William Day and Maryetta Hadlock

KENNEDY,
John Willard of NJ m. Jerene **Hobbs** of NJ 5/17/1975 in Lyme; H – b. 9/21/1952 in NJ, s/o John William Kennedy and Doris Mayhew; W – b. 8/2/1955 in NH, d/o George Hobbs and Marion Pushee

KENT,
Thomas W. of Lyme m. Ruth C. **Dwyer** of Thetford, VT 7/4/2002

KIBBEE,
Edmund M. of Lyme m. Rosa D. **Burnor** of Wilder, VT 12/6/1902 in Lyme; H - 22, laborer, b. Orfordville, s/o George W. Kibbee (farmer) and Lucy J. Mackintire (housewife); W - 18, housewife,

d/o John Burnor

George W. of Lyme m. Annie **Masiah** of Haverhill 10/16/1900 in Lyme; H - 60, farmer, 3rd, b. Cabot, VT, s/o James Kibbee (Morristown, VT, farmer) and Sarah Hudson; W - 55, housework, 2nd

KIBLING,

Charles A. of Hanover m. Jennie M. **Dyke** of Lyme 10/22/1887 in Lyme; H - 19, hotel keeper, b. Norwich, VT, s/o George F. Kibling (Ashburnham, MA) and Emma Reynolds (Norwich, VT); W - 18, housekeeper, b. Lyme, d/o David K. Dyke (Hanover) and Lucinda Roberts (Strafford, VT)

KIDDER,

Stephen F. m. Dorothy J. **Gray** 4/16/1977 in Lyme

KILBURN,

Gilbert G. of Hartford, VT m. Emma F. **Straw** of Lyme 9/30/1903 in Lyme; H - 38, carpenter, 2nd, b. Thetford, VT, s/o Nathaniel Kilburn (Thetford, VT, farmer) and Melissa E. Gove (Thetford, VT, housewife); W - 39, housework, 2nd, b. Thetford, VT, d/o Edwin B. Stevens (farmer) and Mary Pike (housewife)

KILHAM,

Benjamin of Lyme m. Debra Ann **Dawnorowitz** of Lyme 6/28/1986 in Lyme

KIMBALL,

Scott B. of Lyme m. Paula C. **Bradford** of Lyme 7/13/1985 in Lebanon

KING,

Howard A. of Burlington, VT m. Doris A. **Lawson** of Lyme 8/22/1970 in Hanover; H – 21, b. VT, s/o Arthur King and Betty Rounsefell; W – 21, b. NH, d/o George Lawson and Joanne Brady

John Adams of Lyme m. Alice C. **Chesley** of Lyme 11/20/1908 in Lyme; H - 27, farmer, b. Dorchester, s/o Walter E. King (Groton, mail carrier) and Ida L. Norris (Dorchester, housewife); W - 17, teacher, b. W. Fairlee, VT, d/o Frank A. Chesley (Lyme, farmer) and Louise Morey (W. Fairlee, VT, housewife)

Lloyd F. of Lyme m. Erma E. **Kingsbury** of Lebanon 6/29/1968 in

Lyme; H – 20, b. NH, s/o Charles H. King, Sr. and Bessie O. Severance; W – 18, b. VT, d/o Leroy Kingsbury and Mary Brown

KINGSBURY,
Dennis D. m. Florence A. **Kendall** 6/4/1977 in Lyme
Karlton K. m. Dorothea C. **Shattuck** 6/23/1979 in Lyme

KIRK,
Christopher George of NY m. Breanna Comolli **Powers** of NY 12/12/1998

KIRWAN,
Robert J. of Hanover m. Katharine H. **Stephenson** of Lyme 8/13/1982 in Lyme

KIVINIEMI,
Jan A. of Lyme m. Barbara Carter **Clunie** of Lyme 3/22/1975 in Hanover; H – b. 1/1/1943 in OH, s/o Aimo J. Kiviniemi and Viola A. Schrulocke; W – b. 3/27/1950 in ME, d/o Frederick B. Clunie and Myra S. Simmons

KNIGHT,
Raymond J. of Tupper Lake, NY m. Wenda M. **Howard** of Tupper Lake, NY 3/27/1967 in Lyme; H – 39, construction, b. Shandaken, NY, s/o Audrey Knight; W – 31, sales clerk, b. W. Stockholm, NY, d/o Lawrence Sabre and Sadie Trade

KNOOP,
Jeshard W. of Boston, MA m. Addie L. **Benson** of Manchester, VT 8/23/1930 in Hanover; H - 36, salesman, 2nd - D, b. Germany, s/o William Knoop (Germany, German officer) and Emma Rehrens (Germany, retired); W - 24, teacher, b. ND, d/o Earl C. Benson (Winhall, VT, farmer) and Ola Kendall (Winhall, VT, housewife)

KOBOKOVICH,
William J. of MD m. Linda J. **White** of Lyme 6/26/1976 in Hanover; H – b. 3/9/1954 in MD, s/o William J. Kobokovich, Sr. and Mary Ann Boney; W – b. 12/30/1953 in NH, d/o Roland A. White and Barbara Gray

KONYA,
John A. of Lyme m. Betty M. **Thurston** of E. Thetford, VT 8/7/1985 in Lyme Ctr.

KRAMER,
George S. of Ashland m. Gladys M. **Wilmot** of Lyme 6/9/1932 in Ashland; H - 27, farmer, b. Winchester, MA, s/o Watts S. Kramer (Cambridge, MA, importer) and E. Alice Plummer (Detroit, MI, housewife); W - 18, at home, b. Lyme, d/o Leo A. Wilmot (Lyme, farmer) and Fannie M. Chapin (S. Boston, MA, housewife)

KRESS,
Brian T. of Lyme m. Nancy C. **Emerson** of Lyme 7/20/2002

KRUEGER,
Myron W., II of Short Hills, NJ m. Susan K. **Tippit** of Cleveland, OH 3/9/1964 in Lyme; H – s/o Myron Krueger and Dorothy B. Sterrett, res. – Short Hills, NJ; W – d/o Clifford Tippit and Elsie J. MacGregor, res. – Cleveland, OH

KUHN,
Scott D. of Houston, TX m. Angela Claire **Dayton** of Austin, TX 7/5/1986 in Lyme

LABBIE,
Timothy Gerard of Lebanon m. Rosemarie Ann **Hutchins** of Lyme 9/28/1974 in Lyme; H – b. 3/1/1957 in NH, s/o Gerard Labbie and Doris Odom; W – b. 12/24/1956 in NH, d/o Joseph Hutchins and Rose Roman

LABOMBARD,
William H. of Hanover m. Gloria J. **Movelle** of Lyme 3/26/1971 in Lyme; H – 28, b. NH, s/o Richard LaBombard and Helen Conoroy; W – 23, b. NH, d/o William Movelle and Esther Gray
Willis H. of Norwich, VT m. Ruth C. **Braman** of Lyme 9/7/1952 in Lyme; H – 19, laborer, b. Lebanon, s/o Willis LaBombard (NY) and Norma Sanborn (Gorham); W – 16, student, b. Marlboro, MA, d/o Clarence Braman (MA) and Eva Lawrence (MA)

LACKEY,
Douglas R. of Orford m. Eleanor **Pruneau** of Lyme 6/30/1951 in Lyme; H – 19, milk tester, b. Fairlee, VT, s/o Louis Lackey (VT) and Elizabeth Bard (W. Fairlee, VT); W – 19, secretary, b. New Britain, CT, d/o Ernest J. Pruneau (Websterville, VT) and Gerda Rasmussen (Copenhagen, Denmark)

LACOSS,
Dorrance R. of Lyme m. Anna M. **Walker** of Randolph, VT 6/30/1934 in Randolph, VT; H - 27, painter, b. VT, s/o William LaCoss (NY) and Grace Wilson (VT); W - 23, b. Ontario, Canada, d/o Aloysius Walker (Canada) and Elizabeth Keon (MI)
Neal C. of Lyme m. Virginia P. **Cutting** of Lyme 1/26/1974 in Lyme; H – b. 12/8/1935 in NH, s/o Richard LaCoss and Blanche Chapin; W – b. 6/13/1940 in NH, d/o Roger Pushee and Isabel Uline
Paul R. of Hanover m. Janet E. **Balch** of Hanover 2/18/1956 in Orford; H – 20, USMC, s/op Richard E. Lacoss of Hanover and Blanche M. Chapin of VT; W – 17, student, d/o John C. Balch of Lyme and Marion L. Gerue of NH

LACOUNT,
Ralph T. of Lyme m. Rose E. **Paquette** of Bethel, VT 12/24/1931 in Randolph, VT; H - 26, lumber, b. Bridgewater, VT, s/o Will E. LaCount (Brookfield, VT) and Mahala B. Briggs (Plymouth, VT); W - 20, b. Shrewsbury, MA, d/o Elissee Paquette (St. Alexander, PQ) and Theodora L. Pecard (Shrewsbury, MA)

LADD,
Horace F. of Lyme m. Carlie M. **Poor** of Lyme 4/17/1890 in Lebanon; H - 22, laborer, b. Waterford, VT, s/o Wallace W. Ladd and Almeda P. Gilbert; W - 20, housekeeper, b. Danville, VT, d/o ----- Poor and ----- Chandler

LADEAU,
Alfred H., Sr. m. Bonnie L. **Boyce** 8/29/1980 in Lyme
Kenneth J. of Fairlee, VT m. Arlene W. **Trussell** of Fairlee, VT 7/16/1936 in Lyme; H - 26, barber, b. Hartford, VT, s/o Levi J. LaDeau (Morrisville, VT, barber) and Dora C. Smith (Orford, housewife); W - 20, tel. operator, b. Fairlee, VT, d/o George F. Trussell (Orford, mill wright) and Grace H. Tilton (Bristol,

housewife)

LAFLAM,
Eddie of Lyme Ctr. m. Diane **Pelton** of Etna 3/7/1969 in Lyme; H – 23, b. VT, s/o Edmond LaFlam and Margaret Bell; W – 28, b. NH, d/o Kenneth Pelton and Barbara Hill

LAIRD,
Francis R. of Chelsea, VT m. H. Minnie **McIntyre** of Tyler Hill, PA 7/10/1890 in Lyme; H - 34, farmer, b. Washington, VT, s/o William Laird and Elizabeth Houghton; W - 21, housekeeper, b. Tyler Hill, PA, d/o Alexander McIntyre and Sarah McIntyre

LAMERE,
James A., Jr. m. Lavona J. K. **Burns** 9/4/1981 in Sharon, VT

LAMOTT,
Albert M. of Lyme m. Bertha L. **Cutting** of Lyme 9/26/1894 in Lyme; H - 22, laborer, b. Dorchester, s/o James LaMott (Canada, lumber dealer) and Catherine McBain (Canada, housekeeper); W - 16, housework, b. Lowell, MA, d/o E. Dimick Cutting (Canada, laborer) and Lillie J. Rugg (housekeeper)
Charles W. of Lyme m. Minnie M. **Robinson** of Meriden 7/20/1898 in Lyme; H - 19, laborer, b. Lyme, s/o David Lamott (Canada, laborer) and Lavina Jenks (Lyme, housewife); W - 20, housework, d/o David A. Robinson and Clara E. Stearns
Dean E. of Lyme m. Charlotte H. **Balch** of Lyme 9/20/1940 in Hanover; H – 21, laborer, b. Orford, s/o Elwin A. LaMott (Lyme, meat cutter) and Lela M. Willis (Orford, housewife); W – 18, domestic, b. Lyme, d/o Harvey H. Balch (Hartland, VT, laborer) and Lillian J. Morrill (Pomfret, VT, housewife)
George J. of Lyme m. Georgia B. **Russell** of Hanover 8/22/1900 in Lyme; H - 24, laborer, b. Lyme, s/o David LaMott (Canada, laborer) and Lavina Jenks (Lyme, housewife); W - 19, teacher, b. Milton, ME, d/o George Russell and Angie Smith (housewife)
Irving of Lyme m. Hazel **Young** of Lyme 11/3/1921 in Lyme; H - 24, laborer, b. Lyme, s/o Albert LaMott (Dorchester, mill) and Bertha Cutting (Lowell, MA, housewife); W - 25, at home, b. Burke, NY, d/o Ira Young (Clarenceville, PQ, farmer) and Barbara Carr (Elgne, Canada)
James I. of Dorchester m. Pearl M. **Wing** of Lyme 6/26/1901 in

Lyme; H - 22, laborer, b. Dorchester, s/o James LaMott
(Canada, lumber dlr.) and Catherine McBain (Canada,
housewife); W - 22, housework, b. Burke, NY, d/o Nathan L.
Wing (Chateaugay, NY, farmer) and Anna Hill (Chateaugay,
NY, housewife)

Nelson E. of Lyme m. Susan A. **Fondry** of Barre, VT 6/13/1970 in
Barre, VT; H – 23, b. NH, s/o Dean E. LaMott and Charlotte
Balch; W – 21, b. VT, d/o John C. Fondry and Constance
Eastman

Owen B. of Lyme m. Nora M. **Andrews** of Vershire, VT 2/22/1911 in
Lyme Ctr.; H - 22, laborer, b. Lyme, s/o David Lamott (Canada,
laborer) and Lavina Jenks (Lyme); W - 18, housework, b.
Willsboro, NY, d/o Orin H. Andrews (Willsboro, NY, farmer) and
Maggie J. Bobare (Willsboro, NY, housewife)

Paul I. of Lyme m. Muriel I. **Spooner** of Haverhill 11/23/1938 in
Newbury, VT; H - 21, surveyor, b. Lyme, s/o Elwin A. LaMott
(Lyme, meat cutter) and Lela M. Willis (Orford, housewife); W -
22, nurse, b. Haverhill, d/o Edwin A. Spooner (Haverhill, farmer)
and Hazel T. Brown (Haverhill, housewife)

LAMPHERE,
Abizio P. of Lyme m. Nell **Humphrey** of Lyme 10/26/1887 in Lyme;
H - 60, laborer, 3rd, b. Hartland, VT, s/o David Lamphere
(Hartland, VT) and Sarah Lamphere (Hartland, VT); W - 48,
housekeeper, 4th, b. Plainfield, d/o Salmond Corey (Plainfield)
and Caroline Corey (Plainfield)

Allen E. of Lyme m. Evelyn L. **Hackett** of Piermont 5/17/1952 in
Piermont; H – 23, salesman, b. Hanover, s/o Walter Lamphere
(Lyme) and Helen Cutler (VT); W – 19, salesgirl, b. Hanover,
d/o Harley Hackett (Orford) and Jeannae Everson (MA)

Charles N. of Barre, VT m. Lena M. **Celley** of Barre, VT 11/5/1938 in
Lyme; H - 50, quarry man, 2nd - W, b. Lyme, s/o Charles N.
Lamphere (Hartland, VT, laborer) and Emily Straw (Canada,
housewife); W - 29, b. Peacham, VT, d/o Stephen Celley
(laborer) and Gertrude Balow (Peacham, VT, housewife)

Charles O. of Lyme m. Nellie S. **Turner** of Lyme 5/4/1889 in Lyme;
H - 27, farmer, b. Lyme, s/o Albert A. Lamphere (Thetford, VT,
mason) and Sarah Lamphere (Hartland, VT, housekeeper); W -
24, milliner, b. Thetford, VT, d/o Allen O. Turner (farmer) and
Edna Gove (Thetford, VT, housekeeper)

Ralph A. of Lyme m. Martha J. **Emerson** of Lancaster 3/18/1918 in

Thetford, VT; H - 25, clerk, b. Lyme, s/o Charles O. Lamphere (Lyme, mason) and Nellie S. Turner (Thetford, VT, milliner); W - 25, teacher, b. Lancaster, d/o Charles Emerson (Newbury, VT, farmer) and Jeannette L. Morse (Guildhall, VT, housewife)

Thomas A. of Lyme m. Jennie M. **Fairbanks** of Hanover 5/12/1889 in Lebanon; H - 27, farmer, b. Lyme, s/o Albert A. Lamphere (Thetford, VT, mason) and Sarah Lamphere (Hartland, VT, housekeeper); W - 29, dressmaker, b. Lebanon, d/o Chester M. Fairbanks (Cornish, machinist) and Mary E. Leseur (Boston, MA, housekeeper)

Walter of Lyme m. Helen I. **Cutler** of Wolcott, VT 10/1/1927 in Plainfield; H - 25, farmer, b. Lyme, s/o Charles O. Lamphere (Lyme, farmer) and Nellie S. Turner (Thetford, VT, housewife); W - 19, domestic, b. Orleans, VT, d/o Fred E. Cutler (Hyde Park, VT, farmer) and Elsie E. Phillips (Underhill, VT, housewife)

LANG,
Roger of Hanover m. Hazel **Gerue** of Lyme 8/30/1930 in Lyme; H - 29, laborer, b. Cleveland, OH, s/o Louis Lang (Cleveland, OH, machinist) and Agnes Kluender (Russia, housewife); W - 31, domestic, 2nd - W, b. Canaan, d/o Hiland G. Hall (Maidstone, VT, farmer) and Agnes Dunham (St. George, NB, housewife)

LARO,
Arthur E. of Lebanon m. Donna L. **Pushee** of Lyme 2/20/1960 in Lebanon; H – s/o Ernest L. Laro and Dorothy Carlisle, res. – Lebanon; W – d/o Roger C. Pushee and Mabel Uline, res. – Lyme

LAROCQUE,
Raymond Arthur, Jr. of Lyme m. Anita V. **LaFlam** of Lebanon 1/18/1964 in Lyme; H – s/o Raymond A. Larocque and Louise G. Adams, res. – Lyme; W – d/o Edward LaFlam of Glover, VT and Marion H. Belle of Jay, VT

Richard A. of Lyme m. Arlene Corina **Stone** of Lebanon 12/6/1969 in Lyme; H – 18, b. NH, s/o Raymond Larocque, Sr. and Louise Adams; W – 18, b. NH, d/o Everett Stone and Mary Libby

LATHROP,
George A. of Montpelier, VT m. Mina **Coburn** of Lyme 2/1/1893 in

Lyme; H - 38, farmer, 2nd, b. Manchester, s/o A. D. Lathrop (VT, baker) and Harriet Hall (Montpelier, VT); W - 35, dressmaker, b. Berkshire, VT, d/o David Coburn (Berkshire, VT, farmer) and Lucy Smith (Enosburg, VT)

LAUGHLIN,
Herbert L., Jr. m. Elizabeth Ann **Sengstaken** 6/24/1978 in Sandwich

LAWSON,
George M. of Lyme m. Joanne D. **Brady** of Lyme 8/16/1949
Terry George m. Cynthia Lynn **Godfrey** 9/10/1977 in Orford

LAZAR,
Robert, II of S. Hadley, MA m. Heather **Hutchins** of Lyme 12/31/1992

LECUYER,
Peter D. m. Dianne **Barber** 8/25/1979 in Hanover

LEE,
Desmond of Lyme m. Phuong **Hang** of Worcester, MA 8/14/2004
Richard N. of W. Springfield, MA m. Valerie J. **Randall** of Danbury, CT 8/2/1986 in Lyme

LEHET,
John of Lyme m. Barbara J. **Hutchings** of Lyme 9/9/1984 in Cornish

LERNER,
Elliot D. m. Maxine B. **Chertok** 10/2/1977 in Lyme

LESTER,
Patrick S. m. Nancy H. **Alt** 1/27/1979 in Hanover

LEWIS,
Edwin M., IV of Columbus, OH m. Karen M. **Strout** of Lyme 7/21/1984 in Lyme
Jeffrey B. of Lyme m. Lynn **Vavreck** of Lyme 8/12/2000

LINCK,
Robert L. of Hanover m. Leanne **Klyza** of Lyme 6/28/1985 in W. Lebanon

LISA,
Joseph of Montpelier, VT m. Virginia **Francisco** of Ravena, NY 3/2/1957 in Lyme; H – 37, divorced, s/o Peter Lisa and Lena Romano of New York, NY; W – 19, d/o John Francisco and Jean Higginbotham, res. – Ravena, NY

LITTLE,
Arthur M. of Boston, MA m. Margaret M. **Watson** of Boston, MA 10/21/1908 in Lyme; H – 41, broker, 2nd, b. Boston, s/o Samuel Little (Hingham, MA, banking) and Elizabeth Malborn (Cohasset, MA, housewife); W - 30, at home, b. Cape Breton, NS, d/o Samuel Watson (Baddeck, NS, farmer) and Emma Sparling (Baddeck, NS, housewife)

LIVINGSTONE,
Alfred, III m. Renee M. **Gardner** 8/13/1978 in Lyme

LONGACRE,
Joseph M. of Plainfield m. Margo E. **Farnham** of Lyme 9/26/1998

LORD,
Edward C. of Ipswich, MA m. Annie L. **Deland** of Lyme 10/20/1897 in Lyme; H - 24, grocery clerk, b. Ipswich, MA, s/o John E. Lord (Ipswich, MA, shoe cutter) and Clara Combs (Lynn, MA, housework); W - 21, housework, b. Danvers, MA, d/o John Deland (Topsfield, MA) and Isabel Greenough (Salem, MA, housewife)

John C. of Lyme m. Kathleen H. **Campion** of Etna 10/25/1975 in Hanover; H – b. 3/27/1950 in CT, s/o Arthur Lord and ----- Curren; W – b. 3/7/1953 in NH, d/o James W. Campion, III and ----- O'Callaghan

John D. of Lyme m. Caroline J. **Peterson** of Lebanon 2/13/1964 in Claremont; H – s/o Edwin C. Lord and Helen Wioncek, res. – Hanover; W – d/o Frederick A. Peterson and Catherine Little, res. - Canaan

LORNITZO,
Steven F. of Lyme m. Robin A. **Leonard** of Lyme 11/23/2003

LOUZER,
Samuel of Wilder, VT m. Mary B. **Green** of Lyme 6/1/1915 in Lyme;

H - 25, laborer, b. Gentillis, PQ, s/o Adolph Louzer (Canada, laborer) and Zoe Mailhoit (Canada, housewife); W - 24, housewife, 2nd, b. Littleton, d/o Albert P. Mehan (Canada) and Lorinda Byron (Canada)

LUND,
Arthur R. of Lyme m. Florence M. **Roberts** of Thetford, VT 3/5/1956 in Lyme; H – 22, miner, s/o Chester A. Lund and Elizabeth Locke, res. – Hampstead; W – 18, at home, d/o Edwin G. Roberts and Stella M. Warren, res. – N. Thetford, VT
Burton G. of Lyme m. Mildred J. **Darbyson** of Hanover 10/22/1945 in Lyme; H – 29, US Army, b. Thetford, VT, s/o Loren Lund (Thetford, VT, laborer) and Maud Lambert (Thetford, VT, housewife); W – 28, waitress, b. Campbellton, NB, d/o Robert Darbyson (Springhill, NS, factory worker) and Nettie Young (Pt. Daniel, PQ, housewife)

LYSTER,
Randy Michael of Bradford, VT m. Brenda Marie **Day** of Lyme Ctr. 8/21/1975 in Lyme Ctr.; H – b. 6/7/1954 in NC, s/o Edward C. Lyster and Mary B. Wakefield; W – b. 2/4/1957 in NH, d/o Roy Day and Mary Etta Hadlock

MACK,
Brian Lewis m. Lori Ann **Wilmott** 10/1/1977 in Orfordville
Willie F. of Bradford, VT m. Ella **Smith** of Lyme 5/14/1887 in Lyme; H - 25, farmer, b. Bradford, VT, s/o Elijah Mack (Bradford, VT) and Jane Fuller (Bradford, VT); W - 16, b. Lyme, d/o Edgar Smith (Lyme) and Delia Smith (Lyme)

MACKLEAN,
E. G. of Worcester, MA m. Abbie V. **Dimick** of Lyme 9/10/1901 in Lyme; H - 23, conductor, b. Picton, NS, s/o T. H. Macklean (Picton, NS, watchman) and Margaret E. Grant (Picton, NS, housewife); W - 24, nurse, b. Lyme, d/o Charles H. Dimick (Lyme, farmer) and Viola C. Cook (Lyme)

MACLAY,
Roderick J. of Strafford, VT m. Janet J. **Bacon** of Lyme 4/12/1953 in S. Strafford, VT; H – 19, dairy farming, b. Bennington, VT, s/o Joseph T. Maclay (Scotland) and Jessie E. Sumner (Rutland,

VT); W – 20, clerk, b. Lyme, d/o George W. Bacon (Thetford, VT) and Mina H. Hill (Quebec)

MACMILLEN,
Robert Brooks of Lyme m. Jennifer Dewey **Lorin** of Quechee, VT --/--/1991

MACNAMEE,
Duncan B. m. Barbara **Johnson** 9/1/1979 in Lyme

MACOMBER,
Richard H. of Lyme m. Linda J. **Towle** of Vershire, VT 5/25/1963 in W. Fairlee, VT; H – s/o ----- T. Macomber and ----- Eastwood, res. – Lyme; W – d/o ----- S. Towle and ----- Felix, res. – Vershire, VT

MADDOCK,
Stephen J. of S. Berwick, ME m. Susan E. **Rackow** of S. Berwick, ME 10/3/1987 in Lyme

MALCOLM,
William F. of Lyme Ctr. m. Bonnie L. **Cornell** of Lyme Ctr. 9/7/1985 in Lyme

MALETZ,
Mark C. m. Ilana **Schager** 8/17/1980 in Lyme

MALONE,
Keith of Lyme m. Jelena **Pavljuk** of Hanover 9/16/2001

MANHARD,
Warren B., II of MA m. Patricia Y. **Bong** of MA 8/6/1972 in Lyme; H – 37, b. MI, s/o Warren Manhard and Ursula M. Hollander; W – 38, b. NY, d/o Claude Young and Martha Russell

MANN,
Richard K. of Lyme m. Lisa B. **Cohen** of Lyme 8/4/2001

MARINER,
Jessie L. of Silver Lane, CT m. Carrie E. **Simmons** of Lyme 9/22/1917 in Lyme; H - 26, mechanic, b. Atlantic, VA, s/o

William D. Mariner (Atlantic, VA, farming) and Charlotte Ailworth (Atlantic, VA, housewife); W - 23, bookkeeper, b. Lyme, d/o Auburn L. Simmons (Lyme, farming) and Belle Clement (Benton, housewife)

MARKHAM,
Burton L. of San Diego, CA m. Diane L. **Bentley** of San Diego, CA 5/20/1989 in Lyme

MARSH,
Elwin R. of Orford m. Janet E. **Marsh** of Lyme 6/26/1964 in Lyme; H – s/o Ralph E. Marsh and Gladys Cutler, res. – Orford; W – d/o John C. Balch and Marion L. Gerue, res. – Lyme

Frank D. of Orford m. Ina **Strue** of Lyme 3/4/1920 in Orford; H - 24, laborer, 2nd - D, b. Orford, s/o Daniel C. Marsh (W. Fairlee, VT, farmer) and Delia Smith (Corinth, VT, housewife); W - 21, domestic, b. Lyme, d/o William Strue (Lyme, laborer) and Cora Lovejoy (Lyme, housewife)

Henry G. of Orford m. Wanita G. **Balch** of Lyme 12/24/1960 in Orford; H – s/o Glenn G. Marsh and Verna M. Hibbard, res. – Orford; W – d/o Raymond H. Balch and Esther E. Smith, res – Lyme Ctr.

Peter C. of Lyme Ctr. m. Diane R. **Almon** of Lyme Ctr. 9/21/1985 in Lyme Ctr.

MARSHALL,
Bry of Lyme m. Hattie J. **Balch** of Lyme 2/1/1887 in Lyme; H - 28, blacksmith, b. Auburn, s/o Thomas S. Marshall (Alstead) and Dorothy A. Evans (Stoddard); W - 20, housekeeper, b. Lyme, d/o William W. Balch (Lyme) and Wealthy Flint (Lyme)

MARTIN,
Harry Fred of W. Fairlee, VT m. Arletta Lauraine **Beau** of Lyme 6/14/1997

Walter D. of Lebanon m. Juanita M. **Perkins** of Lyme Ctr. 7/7/1973 in Lyme; H – 31, b. MA, s/o Elizabeth W. Martin; W – 30, b. NH, d/o Harry W. Perkins and Martha Hardy

William Canavan of Chicago, IL m. Corrie Sue **Wolosin** of Chicago, IL 10/10/1993

MASON,
Frank, Jr. of Taunton, MA m. Helen G. **Costello** of Taunton, MA 11/19/1955 in Lyme; H – 56, foreman, b. Taunton, MA, s/o Frank Mason (Boston) and Katherine Curran (MA); W – 42, elect. worker, b. MA, d/o James Costello (MA) and Rose Phillips (MA)

MATHER,
David J. of Lyme m. Lindsay E. **Sawyer** of Lyme 9/25/1999

MATHIEU,
William of E. Thetford, VT m. Roberta Bailey **Levasseur** of E. Thetford, VT 7/27/1996

MATIVIA
Darius R. of Lyme m. Ida A. **Stark** of Lyme 5/17/1888 in Orford; H - 25, laborer, b. Hartland, VT, s/o Lewis Mativia and Maria Eastman (Corinth, VT); W - 21, dressmaker, b. Lyme, d/o John Stark (Lyme) and Emeline Warren (Lyme)

Darius R. of Lyme m. Nancy J. **Gunn** of White River Jct. 7/6/1968 in Lebanon; H – 23, b. NH, s/o Roswell Mativia and Ina Squires; W – 20, b. NH, d/o Wendell Gunn and Mercedes Potter

Perry M. of Lyme m. Ervill A. **Davis** of Hanover 6/9/1947 in Lyme; H – 51, fill sta. op., b. Lyme, s/o Henry Mativia (Corinth, VT, farmer) and Hattie Stickney (Greensboro, VT, housewife); W – 43, domestic, b. Groton, d/o Charles A. Davis (Groton, farmer) and Ava Wheat (Groton, housewife)

Roswell of Lyme m. Amelia V. **Jobling** of Hartford, VT 5/26/1918 in Lebanon; H - 23, farmer, b. Lyme, s/o Darius R. Mativia (N. Hartland, VT, mail carrier) and Ida A. Stark (Lyme, housewife); W - 21, tel. operator, b. Hartford, VT, d/o Joseph E. Jobling (London, England, railroad) and Jennie E. Bell (St'mst'd, PQ, housewife)

Roswell of Lyme m. Ina C. **Squires** of Hartford, VT 9/11/1926 in Thetford, VT; H - 31, carpenter, 2nd - W, b. Lyme, s/o Darius Mativia (N. Hartland, VT, mail carrier) and Ida Stark (Lyme, housewife); W - 19, b. Sharon, VT, d/o Lewis E. Squires (RI) and Florence Caswell (Pomfret, VT)

MAXFIELD,
Leslie E. of Lyme m. Bertha Virginia **Shepard** of Lyme 12/31/1959 in

Lebanon; H – divorced, s/o Dan A. Maxfield and Hattie I. Gorelet; W – divorced, d/o Seldon E. Miller and Pearl A. Miller, res. – Hartland, VT

MAY,
Earl E. of Lyme m. Bernita A. **Stearns** of Lyme 11/10/1940 in Lyme; H – 26, mill hand, 2nd – D, b. Sharon, VT, s/o Edgar E. May (Rochester, VT, laborer) and Ida L. Kimball (Lyme, housekeeper); W – 16, at home, b. E. Plainfield, d/o Fred G. Stearns (Meriden, mill man) and Doris L. Hazelton (Bristol, housewife)

MAYNARD,
Michael L. of Grand Forks, ND m. Nancy **Bowden** of Lyme 10/11/1975 in Holderness; H – b. 4/5/1949 in VT, s/o Kenneth Maynard and Mabel Dalrymple; W – b. 1/29/1950 in NY, d/o John W. Bowden and Mary Sharples

MAYO,
George S. of Lyme m. Florence N. **Morrill** of Orford 4/25/1911 in Orfordville; H - 69, farmer, 3rd, b. Lyme, s/o Hiram Mayo (Ludlow, VT, farmer) and Betsy Whipple (Lyme, housewife); W - 53, housework, b. Landaff, d/o Benjamin Morrill (Danville, VT, merchant) and Harriet N. Simonds (Landaff, housewife)
Lawrence R. of Littleton, CO m. Gail **O'Hara** of Lyme 8/21/1960 in Hanover; H – s/o Ralph Mayo and Margaret Oliver, res. – Littleton, CO; W – d/o Dwight O'Hara and Elvie M. Hopton, res. – Lyme

McASSEY,
Patrick M. m. Lydia C. **Smith** 7/22/1979 in Lyme

McCARTHY,
Dean Allan of Hartford, VT m. Sarah Barrelett **Winnett** of Hartford, VT 2/14/1993
Ian Aquinas of Lyme m. Heather Jean **Scholl** of Hanover 11/6/1993

McEWAN,
Bertram of Lyme m. Minnie A. **Bacon** of Fairlee, VT 6/19/1915 in Piermont; H - 18, laborer, b. ON, s/o John L. McEwan (Matilda, ON, farmer) and Dyanthia Rattray (Wolf Island, ON, housewife);

W - 20, teacher, b. Fairlee, VT, d/o Gilman G. Bacon (Strafford, VT, farmer) and Frances E. Green (Thetford, VT, housewife)
Harry A. of Lyme m. Alice E. **Clark** of Plainfield 6/29/1922 in Plainfield; H - 23, mechanic, b. Canada, s/o John McEwan (Canada, deceased) and Diantha Rattray (Canada, housewife); W - 28, teacher, b. Plainfield, d/o Samuel W. Clark (Plainfield, farmer) and Susan L. Pritchard (Green Garden, IL, housewife)

McGRANAHAN,
Ivan M. of S. Royalton, VT m. Evelyn S. **Tash** of S. Royalton, VT 12/29/1964 in Lyme; H – s/o Joseph McGranahan of Morristown, VT and Florence E. McGranahan; W – d/o Harold Sees and Selma Ness, res. – Montpelier, VT

McGUIRE,
Thomas H. of Hanover m. Esther May **Lowell** of Lyme 7/22/1929 in Wilder, VT; H - 41, farmer, W, b. Holton, ME, s/o Arthur McGuire (Scotland) and Maria Horn (Ireland); W - 17, b. St. Johnsbury, VT, d/o Harry Lowell (St. Johnsbury, VT) and Maude Dane (N. Troy, VT)

McINTYRE,
Michael Edward of Orford m. Maria Sue **Durso** of Orford 8/14/1999

McKEE,
Lindsay L. of Franklin m. Una G. **Silloway** of Lyme 6/20/1945 in Northfield; H – 36, machinist, b. Canada, s/o F. C. McKee (Canada, dentist) and L. A. Huntington (Canada, housewife); W – 24, teacher, b. Lyme, d/o Mark Silloway (W. Fairlee, VT, RR employee) and Grace Follansbee (Windsor, VT, housewife)

McKENNA,
Thomas P. m. Gail S. **Kurgan** 9/13/1981 in Lyme Ctr.

McKEOWN,
Stephan G. of Lyme m. Alice S. **Kitchell** of Barnet, VT 12/29/1970 in St. Johnsbury, VT; H – 23, b. CA, s/o Forrest McKeown and Betty L. Benz; W – 22, b. VT, d/o Douglas Kitchell and Sybil Beck

McMANN,
Henry of Lyme m. Mabel A. **Cutting** of Lyme 8/14/1902 in Lebanon; H - 29, laborer, 2nd, b. Groveton, s/o Michael McMann (Canada, farmer) and Margaret Sheridan (Canada, housewife); W - 18, housework, b. Lyme, d/o Frank Cutting (Lyme, farmer) and Ella F. Warren (Lyme, housewife)
James of Groveton m. Nellie L. **Gilbert** of Lyme 12/8/1894 in Lyme; H - 27, laborer, b. Groveton, s/o Michael McMann (Canada, farmer) and Margaret Sheridan (Canada, housekeeper); W - 17, housework, b. Lyme, d/o Elam Gilbert (Lyme, harness maker)
John S. of Lyme m. Rosa **Gilbert** of Lyme 1/5/1895 in Lyme; H - 28, laborer, b. Johnstown, NY, s/o James McMann (Indian Lake, NY, farmer) and Lucy McCray (St. John, NB, domestic); W - 17, housework, b. Lyme, d/o John A. Gilbert (Lyme) and Elizabeth Post (Boonville, NY, housework)

McNAIR,
Peter H. m. Sandra L. **Turgeon** 1/29/1977 in Lyme

McPHAIL,
Bruce G. of Cambridge, MA m. Deborah **Chaffee** of Lyme 6/24/1967 in Lyme; H – 26, harpsichord maker, b. Cambridge, MA, s/o Donald McPhail and Eleanor Glidden; W – 21, student, b. Rochester, d/o Robert G. Chaffee and Dorcas A. Dixon

McTAGUE,
William D. of Piermont m. Katherine M. **Piper** of Lyme 10/16/1965 in Lyme; H – 19, laborer, b. MA, s/o Robert McTague and Elizabeth Perry; W – 17, student, b. NH, d/o Walter J. Piper and Vivian Gregory

MELENDY,
Arthur H. of Lyme m. Sandra M. **Fitchett** of Vershire, VT 10/29/1966 in Lyme; H – 19, salad man, b. Hanover, s/o Robert Melendy and Elizabeth Wing; W – 18, waitress, b. St. Johnsbury, VT, d/o Herbert C. Fitchett and Florence E. Hugin
Jon David of Lyme m. Gloria Jean **Southworth** of Fairlee, VT 6/21/1975 in Fairlee, VT; H – b. 7/2/1953, s/o Robert Melendy and Elizabeth Wing; W – b. 9/16/1955, d/o Howard Southworth, Sr. and Dorothy Drew

Jon David of S. Strafford, VT m. Suzanne L. **Wright** of S. Strafford, VT 7/2/1990 in Lyme

Raymond A. of Lyme m. Etta Mae **Pike** of Lyme 8/20/1949

MELVIN,

Leon O. of Lyme m. Florence M. **Wells** of Lyme 2/19/1902 in Lyme; H - 20, clerk, b. Lyme, s/o George Melvin (E. Weare, merchant) and Mary D. Warren (Lyme, housewife); W - 21, housework, b. Lyme, d/o Rollin S. Wells (Underhill, VT, farmer) and Eliza Hall (Lyme, housewife)

Story of Lyme m. Anna M. **Smith** of Lyme 10/27/1894 in Haverhill; H - 35, clerk, b. Lyme, s/o Oscar Melvin (Weare, auctioneer) and Betsy J. Marshall (Weare, housekeeper); W - 40, dress maker, b. Haverhill, d/o Charles G. Smith (Washington, VT) and Ruth Morse (Haverhill, housekeeper)

MENARD,

Girard J. L. of Lyme m. Margaret L. **Uline** of Lyme 5/31/1958 in Hanover; H – 22, s/o Girard Menard and Mertie Bumps, res. – Unity; W – 20, d/o Millard B. Uline and Susie Cadwell, res. – Lyme

MENGE,

Richard B. of Lyme m. Jaqueline A. **Richter** of Lebanon 10/22/1983 in Hanover

MERRICK,

Keith Russell of Post Mills, VT m. Sherry Lynn **Seiter** of Post Mills, VT --/--/1991

MERRILL,

Robert S., Jr. of Lyme m. Donna L. **Gray** of Lyme 8/8/1982 in Lyme

Stillman of Lyme m. Mercy H. **Breck** of Lyme 8/22/1896 in Lyme; H - 64, carriage maker, 2nd, b. Groton, s/o Leonard M. Merrill (Newbury, farmer) and Susan Ray (Hillsboro, housewife); W - 49, housework, b. Lyme, d/o Melvin C. Breck (Lyme, farmer) and Matilda W. Andrews (Dorchester, housewife)

MESSER,

Ernest M. of Lyme m. Bessie E. **Gilbert** of Lyme 12/3/1910 in Lyme; H - 24, laborer, b. Thetford, VT, s/o Isaac H. Messer

(Charleston, Canada, farmer) and Abbie Ricker (Strafford, VT, housewife); W - 20, housework, b. Monroe, d/o George Gilbert and Melvina E. Byron (Littleton, housewife)
Paul B., Jr. m. Ellen L. **Bryant** 12/23/1978 in Lyme

MESSIER,
Mylon I. of Lyme m. Helen L. **Hanchett** of Lyme 8/18/1907 in Lyme; H - 23, laborer, b. Thetford, VT, s/o Isaac H. Messier (Canada, farmer) and Abbie H. Ricker (E. Haven, VT, housewife); W - 17, housework, b. Lyme, d/o Dennis A. Hanchett (Hartland, VT, farmer) and Elizabeth C. Reed (Plainfield, housewife)
Roland M. of Lyme m. Dorotha E. **Lanphere** of Franklin 6/29/1934 in Plymouth; H - 26, farming, b. Strafford, VT, s/o Mylon I. Messier (Thetford, VT, farmer) and Helen E. Hanchett (Lyme, housewife); W - 25, teacher, b. Tilton, d/o Homer R. Lanphere (St. Johnsbury, VT, salesman) and Minnie M. Pellerin (Lyme, housewife)

METZ,
Donald A. m. Keita **Colton** 12/19/1981 in Hanover
Donald A. of Lyme m. Melinda D. **Ashley** of Waltham, MA 6/29/2002

MEYER,
Robert Scott of Cape Elizabeth, ME m. Jane Bancroft **Stevenson** of Cape Elizabeth, ME 9/1/1996

MILLER,
Caryl W. of Orford m. Margaret L. **Reeves** of Lyme 11/28/1958 in Orford; H – 20, s/o Wayne C. Miller and Martha E. True, res. – Orford; W – 21, d/o Otto B. Reeves and Rose Raymond, res. – Lyme
John T. m. Betany J. **Blake** 7/18/1981 in Orford

MOREY,
Frederick A. of Enfield m. Theresa D. **Tatro** of N. Pomfret, VT 8/12/1988 in Lyme
Robert C. of Lyme m. Marjorie E. **Beal** of Lyme 8/12/1942 in Lyme; H – 35, farmer, b. W. Fairlee, VT, s/o William Morey (W. Fairlee, VT, farmer) and May Child (W. Fairlee, VT, housewife); W – 36, teacher, b. Ellensburg, WA, d/o Albert M. Beal (PA, retired) and Grace Clark (Jasper, IL, housewife)

MORGAN,
Millett Granger, II of Hanover m. Elizabeth Ann **Nichols** of Lyme 8/10/1963 in Lyme; H – s/o ----- G. Morgan and ----- Walbridge, res. – Hanover; W – d/o ----- E. Nichols and ----- E. Chaffee, res. – Lyme

MORISETTE,
Alfred J. of Lebanon m. Lizzie S. **Dike** of Lyme 7/12/1913 in Lyme; H - 42, carpenter, 3rd, b. Ormstown, PQ, s/o John B. Morisette (farmer) and Mary Ouimet (housewife); W - 54, housewife, 2nd, b. Plainfield, d/o Fields Nash (Rockingham, farmer) and Jane P. Walker (housewife)

MORRILL,
Elmer F. of Lyme m. Nettie M. **Rickard** of Montpelier, VT 2/16/1907 in Franklin; H - 45, farmer, 2nd, b. Boscawen, s/o Enoch L. Morrill (Boscawen, farmer) and Susanah Coffin (Boscawen, housewife); W - 40, teacher, b. S. Woodbury, VT, d/o Thomas Rickard (S. Woodbury, VT, farmer) and Harriet M. Richardson (S. Woodbury, VT, housewife)

MORRIS,
Fred W. of Hartford, VT m. Ruth A. **Hadlock** of Lyme 6/15/1889 in Thetford, VT; H - 30, merchant, b. Lawrence, MA, s/o James E. Morris (Fairlee, VT, merchant) and Masy A. Wyman (Chelsea, VT, housekeeper); W - 18, housekeeper, b. Lyme, d/o Charles P. Hadlock (Stanstead, PQ, carpenter) and Lucilla Hoover (Springfield, OH, housekeeper)

MORSE,
Emerson G. of Lyme m. Lois A. **Dunn** of Lock Haven, PA 9/7/1961 in Thetford, VT; H – 67, s/o Elijah G. Morse and Clara R. Jelly; W – 51, d/o Charles Dunn of New York, NY and Mabel L. Kitredge

Robert E. of Intervale m. Sylvia F. **Balch** of Lyme 12/17/1966 in Lyme; H – 20, road construction, b. N. Conway, s/o Roland L. Morse and Constance L. Walker; W – 18, at home, b. Lebanon, d/o Raymond H. Balch and Esther E. Smith

MOSES,
Jonathan of Lyme m. Lottie **Smith** of Tunbridge, VT 6/30/1913 in

Lyme; H - 38, basketmaker, 3rd, b. Tunbridge, VT, s/o Orra Moses (Lester, VT, basketmaker) and Margaret Barton (Lester, VT, housewife); W - 34, housework, 3rd, b. Sharon, VT, d/o Albert Preston (Sharon, VT, farmer) and Mary Ladd

MOTT,
Edward of Canaan m. Jane **Jewell** of Lyme 12/28/1895 in Lyme; H - 58, farmer, 2nd, b. Alburgh, VT, s/o Joseph M. Mott (Alburgh, VT, farmer) and Elizabeth Mix (S. Hero, VT, housewife); W - 51, housekeeper, 2nd, b. Lyme, d/o Melvin C. Breck (farmer) and Matilda Andrews (housewife)

MOULTROUP,
Terry B. of Richmond, VT m. Dawna S. **Jaquith** of Norwich, VT 6/12/1982 in Lyme

MOUSLEY,
John H. of Lyme m. May E. **Nickerson** of Lyme 11/6/1887 in Lyme; H - 21, laborer, b. Lyme, s/o William H. Mouseley (Canada) and Kathirine J. Quint (Orford); W - 33, teacher, 2nd, b. Canaan, d/o James Cook (Lyme) and Esther Richardson (Canaan)

MOVELLE,
Gerald J. of Newburyport, MA m. Ann T. **Robinson** of Newburyport, MA 7/20/1985 in Lyme
James A. of Lyme m. Beatrice H. **Gray** of Lyme 5/29/1954 in Lyme; H – 22, carpenter, b. Lyme, s/o William Movelle (MA) and Mildred Gilbert (Lyme); W – 22, sales clerk, b. Lyme, d/o Harry Gray (ME) and Hazel Staples (NH)
William J., Jr. of Lyme m. Esther L. **Gray** of Lyme 10/17/1941 in Orford; H – 20, laborer, b. Lyme, s/o William Movelle (New Bedford, MA, carpenter) and Mildred Gilbert (Lyme, domestic); W – 17, at home, b. Lyme, d/o Harlie Gray (Lyme, laborer) and Hattie M. Pike (Lyme, housewife)
William Joseph, Jr. of Lyme m. Denise Lynn **Barton** of Lebanon 10/6/1990 in Lyme

MUDGE,
Gilbert H. of Lyme m. Barbara F. **Jones** of New Canaan, CT 6/17/1967 in New Canaan, CT; H – 22, student, b. Cooperstown, NY, s/o Gilbert H. Mudge and Eleanor McKenzie;

W – 22, teacher, b. Madison, CT, d/o William F. Jones and Elinor MacBrayne

MURPHY,
Norman C. of Lyme m. Corrie L. **Toffoli** of Lebanon 7/13/1996

MURRAY,
Dennis J. of Mobile, AL m. Mamie D. **Hill** of Lyme 11/14/1921 in Lyme; H - 37, salesman, b. Mobile, AL, s/o William Murray (Ireland) and Mary A. Denne (Burke, NY); W - 41, housework, 2nd, b. Craftsbury, VT, d/o Myra A. Annis (Craftsbury, VT, laborer) and Julia Miles (Craftsbury, VT, housewife)

NAPIER,
James Maurice of Lyme m. Bridie Christin **Newman** of Lyme 5/1/1999

NAVARRO,
Julio Fernando of Somerville, MA m. Jennifer **Winthrop** of Somerville, MA 12/22/1990 in Lyme

NEHEI,
Taiichi of White River Jct. m. Donna M. **Trottier** of Lyme 11/12/1960 in Lyme; H – s/o Nakoto Nehei and Kimi Hashino, res. – Japan; W – d/o Rodolphe Trottier and Olive D. Goodell, res. – Lyme

NELSON,
David M. of Milwaukee, WI m. Sharon C. **LaFleur** of Lyme 3/21/1969 in Lyme; H – 23, b. WI, s/o Reginald Nelson and Jean Dinnen; W – 23, b. NH, d/o Robert LeFleur and Mary Yaquis

Waino of Fitchburg, MA m. Claire **Hastings** of Fitchburg, MA 12/25/1936 in Lyme; H - 25, laborer, b. Fitchburg, MA, s/o Victor Nelson (Finland, weaver) and Helena Lahti (Finland, housewife); W - 18, waitress, b. Fitchburg, MA, d/o Clarence Hastings (comb maker) and Rose Gendron (Canada, housewife)

NEWELL,
Benjamin C. of Lyme m. Margie L. **West** of Piermont 2/8/1893 in Piermont; H - 65, farmer, 3rd, b. Jaffrey, s/o Jacob Newell

(Jaffrey, carpenter) and Julia R. Comings (Cornish); W - 44, domestic, 2nd, b. Orford, d/o Nathan Ames (Orford, farmer) and Millie P. Howard (Campton)

NEWTON,
Arthur L., Jr. of Lyme Ctr. m. Tammy L. **Meyer** of Lyme Ctr. 8/8/1999

NICHOLS,
Benjamin Jay of Lyme m. Amy Christiana **Decato** of Lyme --/--/1991

NOBLE,
Ralph E. of Underhill, VT m. Bertha D. **Eddy** of Randolph, VT 6/25/1924 in Lyme; H - 24, teacher, b. Randolph, VT, s/o Henry J. Noble (Canada, farmer) and Bertha Deering (Bethel, VT, housewife); W - 28, nurse, b. Huntington, VT, d/o Will Eddy (Starksboro, VT, farmer) and Anna Ashline (Richmond, VT, housewife)

NORRIS,
Frank D. of Manchester m. Eunice M. **Rich** of Lyme 7/2/1916 in Lyme; H - 25, carpenter, b. Orford, s/o Elisha Norris (Williamstown, VT, teamster) and Emma D. French (Brattleboro, VT, housewife); W - 25, teacher, b. Stratford, d/o Dwight Rich (Northumberland, farming) and Sarah I. Claflin (Auburn, housewife)

NORTHUP,
Gilbert P. of Sharon, VT m. Evelyn **Strout** of Lyme 3/6/1971 in N. Thetford, VT; H – 22, b. VT, s/o Mildred Kratky; W – 19, b. NH, d/o Gerald Strout and Elizabeth Wilmot

NORTON,
Richard J. of Lyme m. Marie A. **Pike** of Lyme 5/21/1976 in Canaan; H – b. 6/9/1945 in NY, s/o Richard J. Norton and ----- Richardson; W – b. 9/10/1950 in VT, d/o Edward S. Humphery and Ruby M. Cheney

NOYES,
Frank W. of Lyme m. Anna M. **Dunbar** of Lyme 10/27/1888 in Lyme; H - 22, laborer, b. Dorchester, s/o Amos L. Noyes and Hanna Peaslee (Wilmot); W - 17, housekeeper, b. Canada, d/o George

Dunbar (Guildhall, VT) and Sophia Clough (Lyme)

Frank W. of Lyme m. Maude M. **Trask** of Hanover 3/7/1896 in Lyme; H – 28, laborer, 2nd, b. Dorchester, s/o Amos S. Noyes (Landaff, carpenter) and Anna Peaslee (Manchester); W – 17, housework, b. Lyme, d/o Edward Trask (Boston, MA) and Mary Green (Topsham, VT, housewife)

NUNN,

Paul R. of Claremont m. Olive M. **Goodhue** of Lyme 11/24/1954 in Hanover; H – 33, teacher, 3rd – D, b. MA, s/o Robert A. Nunn (ON) and Laura M. Jarvis (NY); W – 33, bank teller, b. Canada, d/o Frederick Goodhue (Canada) and Edith Pierce (MA)

O'DONNELL,

Hugh B. of Vershire, VT m. Joan **Pushee** of Lyme 6/14/1952 in Lyme; H – 25, US Army, b. VT, s/o Hugh O'Donnell (VT) and Claudia Button (VT); W – 19, housework, b. Lyme, d/o David Pushee and Florence DeGoosh

Hugh B., III of NH m. Genevieve M. **Butman** of NH 9/9/1972 in Lyme; H – 19, b. NH, s/o Hugh O'Donnell, Jr. and Joan Pushee; W – 18, b. ME, d/o Gerald Butman and Helena Gallagher

OATHOUT,

Douglas M. of Carrboro, NC m. Hope R. **Snelling** of Carrboro, NC 5/8/1993

ODELL,

Brian K. m. Cynthia **Bircher** 7/23/1977 in Lyme

Timothy P. of Lyme Ctr. m. Nancy A. **Papademas** of Lyme Ctr. 12/21/1985 in Lyme

OFFICER,

Thomas C. of Lyme m. Ashley **Lewis** of Lyme 10/4/1986 in Hanover

OGDEN,

Fred Lee of Ft. Collins, CO m. Michelle Denise **Marez** of Ft. Collins, CO 6/18/1990 in Lyme

OLMSTEAD,

Richard W. of W. Lebanon m. Mary S. **Bowden** of Lyme 3/18/1989 in Lyme

OLSEN,
Joel T. m. Fiona **Swift** 8/18/1979 in Hanover
Timothy S. of Lyme m. Deborah Sue **Menard** of Lyme 9/18/1982 in Lyme

ORF,
Walter Christian of Thetford, VT m. Emily G. **Drew** of Lyme 3/25/1961 in Thetford, VT; H – 18, s/o Walter Orf and Anna C. Blodgett, res. – Niagara Falls, NY; W – 22, d/o Leslie Drew and Irene Blake, res. – Lyme

OWENS,
Chester Raymond of Ft. Lyon, CO m. Ann Lee **Owens** of Burley, ID 1/20/1993

PACINI,
Augustine F. of Montpelier, VT m. Alberta R. **Borne** of Montpelier, VT 7/9/1955 in Lyme; H – 26, florist, b. VT, s/o Jack Pacini (Italy) and Florence Abbiti (Italy); W – 28, bookkeeper, divorced, b. VT, d/o Albert Borne (Elmore, VT) and Lillian Lee (Elmore, VT)

PACKARD,
Mark A. of S. Strafford, VT m. Joyce Marie **Benway** of S. Strafford, VT 5/21/1994

PAGEAU,
Mark G. m. Janet L. **Townsend** 1/2/1981 in Lyme

PAIGE,
Charles W. of Lyme m. Emma **Dyke** of Lyme 7/15/1887 in Lyme; H - 21, laborer, b. Orford, s/o Thomas J. Paige (Thornton) and Elizabeth J. Smith (Lyme); W - 20, housekeeper, b. Lyme, d/o Volney R. Dike (Lyme) and Sarah J. Hall (Lyme)

PALERMO,
Joseph R., Jr. of Lyme m. Jeanne C. **Houle** of Dracut, MA 10/24/1958 in Rutland, VT; H – 21, s/o Joseph R. Palermo, Sr. and Mildred A. Hall, res. – Lowell, MA; W – 20, d/o Emile A.

Houle and Gertrude Dozois, res. – Lowell, MA

PANTEL,
Robert Craig of Lyme m. Juliet Davenport **Gilbert** of Lyme --/--/1991

PAPAGEORGE,
Tod of New Haven, CT m. Deborah S. **Flomenhaft** of New York, NY 6/21/1987 in Lyme

PAQUIN,
Raymond Eugene of Lyme m. Drusilla **Williams** of Lyme 4/16/2004

PARE,
Alan J. of Sharon, VT m. Terri M. **Lewis** of Sharon, VT 8/21/1993

PARK,
Donald I. of Lyme m. Esther P. **Wakefield** of Concord 9/20/1948 in Concord; H – 23, student, b. Hackensack, NJ, s/o Isaac Park (Scotland, merchant) and Hazel Irvine (Hackensack, NJ, librarian); W – 21, clerk, b. Concord, d/o Harold Wakefield (Tilton, fireman) and Dorothy Morey (Andover, housewife)

PARKINGTON,
John K. of Lyme m. Priscilla **Hutchins** of Lebanon 6/21/1969 in Lyme; H – 21, b. CT, s/o Tom Parkington and Dorothy Crofts; W – 21, b. NH, d/o Robert Haskins and Alice Thurston

PARSHLEY,
Ronald C. of Lyme m. Patricia I. **Ulman** of Lyme 7/13/2002

PATTEN,
Dana D. of Enfield m. Penny M. **Balch** of Lyme 11/7/1987 in Lyme

PATTERSON,
Ronald F. of Windsor, VT m. Carol **Slayton** of Lyme 5/18/1968 in Lyme; H – 26, b. VT, s/o Fred Patterson and Esther W. St. Cyr; W – 22, b. NH, d/o Zane Campbell and Dolores Piper

PEARL,
Paul of Thetford, VT m. Carolyn **Olsen** of Thetford, VT 6/20/1992

PEAVEY,
Albert M. of Hartford, VT m. Elaine P. **Kimball** of Hartford, VT 9/5/1935 in Lyme; H - 20, restauranter, b. Hanover, s/o James M. Peavey (Lowell, MA, farmer) and Hattie E. Belware (Littleton, waitress); W - 18, at home, b. Hartford, VT, d/o Waverly O. Kimball (Manchester, police) and Armina Mason (Woodsville, housewife)

John P. m. Menta M. **Gray** 7/11/1981 in Lyme Ctr.

Larry M. of Hanover m. Christie J. **Campbell** of Lyme 9/3/1966 in Lebanon; H – 25, construction, b. Newbury, VT, s/o James Peavey and Pearl E. Green; W – 18, none, b. Hanover, d/o Zane E. Campbell and Dolores W. Piper

PELLERIN,
Lewis of Lyme m. Ethel A. **Clark** of Hanover 10/15/1901 in Canaan; H - 31, farmer, b. Lyme, s/o Jules Pellerin (Canada, farmer) and Thirzah McDonald (Canada, housewife); W - 17, housework, b. Andover, d/o Frank Clark (Andover, farmer) and Rebecca A. Williams (Canaan, housewife)

Pierre m. Tamara F. **Loring** 7/28/1979 in Lyme

PELLETIER,
Timothy of Wilton m. Barbara **Thompson** of Lyme 12/19/1925 in Hanover; H - 28, garage owner, b. Wilton, s/o Timothy Pelletier (Canada, laborer) and Mary L. Levesque (Canada, housewife); W - 30, housekeeper, b. S. Ham, PQ, d/o Joseph Thompson (S. Ham, PQ, farmer) and Mary A. Devy (S. Ham, PQ, housewife)

PENA,
Geigel Cecil of Concord m. Sheila Mary **Ross** of Lyme 6/13/1995

PERKINS,
Adna of Lyme m. Margaret A. **Hazen** of Lyme 3/15/1893 in Lyme; H - 43, farmer, 2nd, b. Lyme, s/o Apollos Perkins (Lyme, farmer) and Damaris W. Converse (Lyme); W - 19, domestic, b. N. Hero, VT, d/o Spellman Hazen (OH, farmer) and Phila Hazen (N. Hero, VT)

Archie A. of Lyme m. Bertha H. **Davis** of Hartford, VT 12/28/1928 in Wilder, VT; H - 28, truckman, b. Lyme, s/o Adna Perkins (Lyme, retired) and Margaret Hazen (N. Hero, VT, housewife); W - 24, teacher, b. Hartford, VT, d/o Newton O. Davis (W. Fairlee, VT, farmer) and Caroline George (Derry, housewife)

Calvin J. of Durham m. Katherine M. **Piper** of Lyme 12/2/1967 in Durham; H – 24, student, b. Plymouth, s/o Vernon J. Perkins and Marjorie Burnham; W – 19, student, b. Hanover, d/o Walter J. Piper and Vivian M. Gregory

Earl C. of Lyme m. Marion N. **Small** of Lyme 9/3/1938 in Etna; H - 53, painter, b. Lyme, s/o Adna Perkins (Lyme, farmer) and Mary C. Clement (Dorchester, housewife); W - 35, bookkeeper, b. Cornish, d/o Duane W. Small (W. Windsor, VT, grain dealer) and L. Minetta Lobdell (Pierrepont, NY, housewife)

Forest R. of Lyme m. Charlotte **Webb** of Lyme 6/20/1925 in Fairlee, VT; H - 19, laborer, b. Lyme, s/o Adna Perkins (Lyme, farmer) and Margaret Hazen (N. Hero, VT, housewife); W - 22, teacher, b. Lyme, d/o Charles B. Webb (Lyme, painter) and Lucy Conant (Lyme, housewife)

Harry W. of Lyme m. Martha E. **Hardy** of Lyme –/13/1938 in Fairlee, VT; H - 35, farmer, b. Lyme, s/o Adna Perkins (Lyme) and Margaret Hazen (N. Hero, VT); W - 16, b. Londonderry, d/o Frank Hardy (Londonderry) and Elizabeth Bocash (Fairfield, VT)

John J. of Claremont m. Anna M. **Pellerin** of Lyme 8/22/1900 in Lyme; H - 32, concreter, 2nd, b. Danville, PQ, s/o W. M. B. Perkins (Shipton, PQ) and Mary Fowler (Timoirck, PQ, housekeeper); W - 26, housework, b. Lyme, d/o Jules Pellerin (Canada, farmer) and Thirzah McDonald (Canada, housewife)

Robert E. of Lyme m. Alice E. **Blake** of Lyme 5/6/1950 in Lyme; H – 20, farmer, b. Hartford, CT, s/o Edmund Bass (Berlin) and Marjorie Perkins (Gorham); W – 18, housework, b. Pittsfield, MA, d/o Charles Blake (Stockbridge, MA) and Dorothy Toombs (Washington, DC)

Robert E. of Lyme m. Frances E. **Seace** of Hanover 9/12/1955 in W. Lebanon; H – 25, farmer, divorced, b. Hartford, CT, s/o Edwin --- (unknown) and Marjorie Perkins (Gorham); W – 18, at home, b. Hanover, d/o Arthur Seace (Bath) and Evelyn Pressey (Hanover)

Vernon W. of Lyme m. Marjorie M. **Burnham** of W. Rumney 4/4/1941 in Orford; H – 28, teacher, b. Lyme, s/o Adna Perkins (Lyme, stage driver) and Addie Hazen (N. Hero, VT, housewife); W – 20, at home, b. W. Rumney, d/o Berkley Burnham (Dorchester, laborer) and Vernie Pease (Lancaster,

housewife)

PERRONE,
Anthony Benedict of Lyme m. Margot E. **Poisson** of Lyme 7/20/1975 in Hanover; H – b. 6/15/1946 in MA, s/o Benedict Anthony and Josephine Fusco; W – b. 10/23/1946 in NY, d/o Joseph Richard Poisson and Elizabeth Brigham

PERRY,
Anthony W. of Orford m. Carol Ann **Chesley** of Lyme Ctr. 6/16/1963 in Glencliff; H – s/o ----- A. Perry and ----- Gilbert, res. – Orford; W – d/o ----- T. Chesley and ----- M. Bower, res. – Lyme Ctr.
Archie F. of Hanover m. Elizabeth **Greenwood** of Lyme 8/18/1927 in Hanover; H - 39, lumberman, 2nd - W, b. Highgate, VT, s/o Albert Perry (Highgate, VT, farmer) and Violet Sartwell (Highgate, VT, housewife); W - 19, housekeeper, b. Thetford, VT, d/o John Greenwood (Canada, lumberman) and Eva McGill (Canada, housewife)
David William m. Kathryn Lee **Green** 2/19/1977 in Lyme
Ranson W. of Lyme m. Sheila M. **Conley** of Lyme 5/10/1986 in Lyme

PETERSON,
Kevin A. of Lyme m. Victoria L. **Smith** of Lyme 8/27/1988 in Cornish

PHELPS,
William C. of Thetford, VT m. Carol Ann **Drew** of Lyme 5/6/1955 in Vershire, VT; H – 19, mechanic, b. Topsham, VT, s/o Ernest A. Phelps, Sr. (Topsham, VT) and Harriett F. Sweetser (Fayston, VT); W – 18, at home, b. Lyme, d/o Leslie P. Drew (Fairhaven, MA) and Irene Blake (Charlestown)

PHILLIPS,
Charles David of Lexington, KY m. Michelle Kei **Nihei** of Lexington, KY 7/3/1993
Jon F. of Alberta, Canada m. Lauren T. **Arffa** of Alberta, Canada 9/11/1982 in Lyme

PIKE,
Allie C. of Lyme m. Marjorie M. **Heath** of Orford 11/29/1941 in Orford; H – 18, farmer, b. Lyme, s/o Earl H. Pike (Lyme, farmer)

and Myrtle Coates (NB, housewife); W – 16, domestic, b. Littleton, d/o Max Heath (Littleton, laborer) and Irene Elliott (Littleton, housewife)

Allie W. of Lyme m. Roberta A. **Estes** of Lyme 9/14/1963 in Hanover; H – s/o Allie C. Pike and Marjorie Heath, res. – Lyme; W – d/o ----- R. Estes and ----- Power, res. – Lyme

Arthur D. of Lyme Ctr. m. Joyce L. **Weingart** of Fairlee, VT 5/8/1982 in Lyme Ctr.

C. D. of Lyme m. P. C. **Camp** of Lyme 11/15/1919 in Lyme; H - 25, laborer, b. Lyme, s/o C. D. Pike (Hanover, farming) and I. A. Bailey (Lyme, housewife); W - 27, housework, b. Lyme, d/o F. L. Camp (Lyme, farming) and A. Alden (Lyme, housewife)

Carlton E. of Boston, MA m. Blanche May **Pushee** of Lyme 11/16/1910 in Lyme; H - 33, teacher, b. Boston, MA, s/o Elbridge N. Pike (Southboro, MA, manufacturer) and Ella F. Fay (Framingham, MA); W - 20, teacher, b. Lyme, d/o David Pushee (Lyme, farmer) and Mary Gilbert (housewife)

Charles C. of Lyme m. Betty C. **Schwotzer** of Lyme 11/15/1941 in Lyme; H – 21, mechanic, b. Lyme, s/o Chester D. Pike (Lyme, farmer) and Polly C. Camp (Lyme, housewife); W – 18, domestic, b. Manchester, d/o Albert Schwotzer (Manchester, draftsman) and Violet Mead (Northwood, hairdresser)

Charles D. of Lyme m. Ida A. **Bailey** of Lyme 12/2/1888 in Lyme; H - 37, farmer, b. Hanover, s/o Horace Pike (Hebron) and Lizzie Trippe (New Bedford, MA); W - 32, housekeeper, b. Lyme, d/o Amos Bailey (Bath) and Mary A. Aiken (Chesterfield)

Charles D. of Lyme m. Angie C. **Hinckson** of Lyme 9/12/1903 in Lyme; H - 52, farmer, 2nd, b. Hanover, s/o Horace G. Pike (Hebron, farmer) and Elizabeth R. Tripp (New Bedford, MA, housework); W - 46, housework, 3rd, b. ME, d/o William B. Smith (blacksmith) and Susan N. Dow (Livermore, ME, housework)

Earl F. of Lyme m. Janet **Bradley** of Lyme 11/19/1956 in Orford; H – 25, woodsman, s/o Earl H. Pike and Myrtle Coates, res. – Lyme; W – 18, student, d/o Leo Bradley of Lyme and Florence Myro of E. Thetford, VT

Earl F., Jr. of Lyme m. Melissa J. **Powell** of Lyme 7/19/1997

Earl Francis, Jr. of Lyme Ctr. m. Janet L. **Tillotson** of Lyme Ctr. 8/14/1976 in Lyme Ctr.; H – b. 3/21/1957 in NH, s/o Earl Francis Pike, Sr. and Janet A. Bradley; W – b. 2/3/1956 in VT, d/o Lee M. Tillotson and Louise Laundry

Earl Francis, Jr. of Lyme m. Shelbie N. **Wing** of Lyme 5/28/1994
Earle H. of Lyme m. Myrtle L. **Bombard** of Lyme 10/16/1920 in Lyme; H - 21, farmer, b. Lyme, s/o Henry M. D. Pike (Lyme, laborer) and Anna Gilbert (Lyme, household); W - 29, household, 2nd - D, b. Corn Hill, NB, d/o Albion A. Coates (Corn Hill, NB, housewife)
Fred L. of Lyme m. Anna B. **Roberts** of Lyme 6/23/1888 in Lyme; H - 29, laborer, b. Lyme, s/o Horace Pike (Hanover) and Lizzie Tripp (New Bedford, MA); W - 21, housekeeper, b. Lyme, d/o Thomas W. Roberts (Raymond) and Caroline Smith (Lyme)
Gary C. of Lyme m. Marie A. **Humphrey** of E. Barnet, VT 6/12/1971 in Lyme; H – 22, b. NH, s/o Allie C. Pike and Marjorie Heath; W – 20, b. VT, d/o Edward Humphrey and Ruby Cheney
George W. of Lyme m. Dora D. **Taylor** of Lyme 9/5/1916 in Lyme; H - 20, farming, b. Lyme, s/o Charles D. Pike (Hanover, farming) and Ida M. Bailey (Lyme, housewife); W - 18, housework, b. Thetford, VT, d/o Fred J. Taylor (Thetford, VT, farming) and Daisy C. Wilder (Thetford, VT, housewife)
George W. of Lyme m. Lela M. **LaMott** of Lyme –/27/1938 in Etna; H - 41, road patrolman, 2nd - D, b. Lyme, s/o Charles D. Pike (Hanover, retired) and Ida A. Bailey (Lyme, housewife); W - 40, waitress, 2nd - D, b. Orford, d/o Eugene F. Willis (Warren, carpenter) and Nellie A. Flanders (Warren, housewife)
Herbert E. of Lyme m. Jessie J. **Storms** of Lyme 11/6/1947 in Lyme; H – 21, US Army, b. Lyme, s/o Earl H. Pike (Lyme, farmer) and Myrtle Coates (Corn Hill, NB, housewife); W – 18, housewife, b. Berchen, Belgium, d/o Jack Storms (Antwerp, Belgium, steel fac.) and Maria V. Hoboken (Antwerp, Belgium, housewife)
Horace E. of Lyme m. Maxine **Pike** of Orford 10/16/1946 in Orford; H – 25, lumbermand, 2nd – D, b. Lyme, s/o Earl Pike (Lyme, farmer) and Myrtle Coates (NB, housewife); W – 20, housewife, 2nd – D, b. Littleton, d/o Max Heath (painter) and Irene Elliott (Littleton, housewife)
Lon C. of Lyme m. Lucy E. **Jewell** of Lyme 6/23/1909 in Lyme Ctr.; H - 19, farmer, b. Lyme, s/o Charles D. Pike (Hanover, farmer) and Ida A. Bailey (Lyme, housework); W - 24, housework, b. Canada, d/o Frank R. Jewell (Dorchester, laborer) and Eliza Jewell (Lyndonville, VT, housework)
Lon J. of Lyme m. Susan J. **Waterbury** of Lyme 4/20/1952 in Lyme; H – 31, USAF, b. Lyme, s/o Lon C. Pike (Lyme) and Lucy Jewell (Canada); W – 21, at home, b. Norwalk, CT, d/o Leon

Waterbury (CT) and Elizabeth Litchfield (NY)

PINKUS,
Edward C. of Boston, MA m. Gail G. **Banks** of Boston, MA 2/23/1982 in Lyme

PIPER,
Allen E. of Lyme m. Nina Ruth **Wing** of Lyme 7/14/1914 in Lyme; H - 19, laborer, b. Lyme, s/o Walter G. Piper (Pembroke, carpenter) and Hattie E. Estey (Troy, NY, housewife); W - 17, schoolgirl, b. Lyme, d/o Nathan L. Wing (Berkshire, VT, farmer) and Anna F. Hill (Chateaugay, NY, housewife)

Devey A. of Lyme m. Beverly M. **Hickey** of Laconia 3/20/1965 in Lyme; H – 25, laborer, b. Lyme, s/o Walter J. Piper and Vivian Gregory; W – 19, at home, b. Rumford, ME, d/o Norman Hickey and Idella Cassaugh

Frank A. of Lyme m. Vivian F. **French** of Lyme 6/28/1916 in Lyme; H - 25, farming, b. Orford, s/o Charles Piper (Fairlee, VT, laborer) and Anna R. Robinson (Stratford, housewife); W - 22, tel. oper., b. Orford, d/o Walter H. French (Orford, dep. sheriff) and Nellie F. Knight (N. Hartland, VT, housewife)

Lee W. of Lyme m. Annie K. **Thompson** of Lyme 7/21/1915 in Portland, ME; H - 25, carpenter, b. Lyme, s/o Walter G. Piper (Pembroke, carpenter) and Hattie E. Estey (Troy, VT, housewife); W - 23, housework, b. S. Ham, PQ, d/o Joseph Thompson (S. Ham, PQ, farmer) and Annie M. Devey (Danville, PQ, housewife)

Walter G. of Lyme m. M. Jennie **Pelton** of Lyme 2/19/1898 in Lyme; H - 38, carpenter, 2nd, b. Pembrook, s/o John C. Piper (Dorchester, carpenter) and Sysan Baker; W - 37, dressmaker, b. Lyme, d/o Josiah C. Pelton (farmer)

Walter J. of Lyme m. Vivian M. **Gregory** of Lyme 10/14/1937 in Lyme; H - 21, laborer, b. Lyme, s/o Lee W. Piper (Lyme, farmer) and Annie K. Thompson (S. Ham, PQ, housewife); W - 19, domestic, b. Lyme, d/o Frank T. Gregory (Grantham, farmer) and Sadie M. Porter (S. Ham, PQ, housewife)

William C. of Lyme m. Beverly M. **Balch** of Lyme 5/14/1953 in Lyme; H – 21, laborer, b. Lyme, s/o William Piper (IL) and Dorothy Henry (NH); W – 19, at home, b. Piermont, d/o Mason Balch (NH) and Bertha Hart (NH)

William R. m. Janet Lee **Pease** 7/3/1978 in Lyme

PIPPIN,
Richard, Jr. of Lyme m. Tammy **Bailey** of Lyme 9/12/1992

PIXLEY,
Wendell I. of S. Strafford, VT m. Margaret L. **Brockway** of Lyme 6/12/1949

POITRAS,
Everett B. of Rumney m. Patricia A. **Young** of Lyme 2/4/1956 in Hanover; H – 24, technician, s/o Louis Poitras and Almina R. Demerrit, res. – Rumney; W – 24, clerk, d/o Leon F. Young of NY and Louise Columbia of VT

POND,
Richard C. of Lyme m. Charlotte H. **Cowles** of Lyndon Ctr., VT 6/16/1946 in Lyndon Ctr., VT; H – 21, merchant, b. Lunenburg, VT, s/o Dorsie Pond (Lunenburg, VT, merchant) and Grace Cole (Lunenburg, VT, housewife); W – 24, teacher, b. Lunenburg, VT, d/o Harley Cowles (Craftsbury, VT) and Susan Hale (Lunenburg, VT)
Richard C., Jr. of Lyme m. Susan M. **Beauford** of Lyme 10/31/1970 in Hanover; H – 23, b. NH, s/o Richard C. Pond and Charlotte Cowles; W – 22, b. ME, d/o Ralph Beauford and Melvina Bearor

POWER,
Samuel D. of Verdun, Quebec m. Priscilla A. **Balch** of Lyme 2/19/1966 in Hanover; H – 21, nursing asst., b. Charlottetown, PEI, s/o Walter Power and Mary A. Williams; W – 22, nurse, b. St. Petersburgh, FL, d/o Charles R. Balch and Mertie Uline

PRATT,
Augustus K. of Middleboro, MA m. Mary L. **Gottschaldt** of Lyme 5/1/1943 in Lyme; H – 22, student, b. Boston, MA, s/o Alton G. Pratt (Taunton, MA, in. tax as.) and Marion K. Tilson (Boston, MA, housewife); W – 21, clerk, b. Atlanta, GA, d/o Allan Gottschaldt (New York City, advertiser) and Rebecca Walker (Atlanta, GA, housewife)
H. O. of Claremont m. E. M. **Dimick** of Lyme 9/3/1919 in Lyme; H - 23, machinist, b. Williamstown, VT, s/o J. Pratt (Hyde Park, VT,

quarry man) and D. Courtemarsh (Swanton, VT, housewife); W – 21, housework, b. Lyme, d/o C. P. Dimick (Lyme, farming) and F. J. Carpenter (Littleton, housewife)

PREBLE,
Alfred A. of Waterbury, VT m. Louise E. **Pierce** of Montpelier, VT 6/29/1957 in Lyme; H – 50, divorced, s/o Arthur Preble of S. Weymouth, MA and Ada Morey of S. Vernon, MA; W – divorced, d/o Harry J. Hughes and Rose L. Loiselle of Montpelier, VT

PRESBY,
Frank B. of Lyme m. Flora **Childs** of N. Wolcott, VT 6/16/1895 in Lyme; H – 23, laborer, b. Bloomfield, VT, s/o Charles F. Presby (Lunenburg, VT, carpenter) and Amanda Jackman (Lisbon, housewife); W – 21, housework, b. N. Wolcott, VT, d/o Warren Childs (N. Wolcott, VT, farmer) and Frances Parker (N. Wolcott, VT, housewife)

PRILESON,
Jeffrey A. m. Jennifer **Grant** 8/5/1978 in Lyme

PRIOR,
Lyle W. of St. Johnsbury, VT m. Irene E. **Wilmot** of St. Johnsbury, VT 4/12/1942 in Woodsville; H – 24, brakeman, b. Burlington, VT, s/o William E. Prior (Essex, VT, retired) and Della Church (Underhill, VT, housewife); W – 20, housework, b. Lyme, d/o Irvin A. Wilmot (Lyme, farmer) and Lillian Sayre (E. Thetford, VT, housewife)

PROVOST,
David Alan of Post Mills, VT m. Alicia Lind **Miller** of Post Mills, VT 5/22/1993

PULLEN,
Michael C. m. Karen L. **Morris** of Brooklyn, NY 6/21/1986 in Cornish

PUSHEE,
Albert W. of Lyme m. Minnie A. **Small** of Lyme 8/6/1949
Albert W. of Lyme m. Verla C. **Howland** of Thetford, VT 8/14/1959 in Orford; H – divorced, s/o Harris A. Pushee and Inez A. Clark,

res. – Lyme; W – divorced, d/o John B. Clogston and Susie A. Preston, res. – Union Village, VT

Albert William of Lyme m. Mabel C. **Pushee** of Lyme 8/19/1994

Bruce A. m. Mable L. **Kane** 10/4/1980 in Lyme

Clarence L. of Lyme m. Emmerette E. **Rogers** of Fairlee, VT 11/25/1915 in Lyme; H - 18, farming, b. Lyme, s/o Clarence S. Pushee (Lyme, farmer) and Fannie C. Post (Lyme, housewife); W - 18, housework, b. Fairlee, VT, d/o Charles S. Rogers (Westmoreland, mail carrier) and Minnie A. Morris (Thetford, VT, housewife)

Clarence L. of Lyme m. Evelyn T. **Tattersall** of Lyme 6/30/1936 in Orford; H - 39, laborer, 2nd - D, b. Lyme, s/o Clarence S. Pushee (Thetford, VT, farmer) and Fannie C. Post (Lyme, housewife); W - 17, at home, b. Lyme, d/o George E. Tattersall (Orford, carpenter) and Emily A. Mousley (Lyme, housewife)

Clarence L., Jr. of Lyme m. Hazel B. **Davis** of Orford 7/17/1955 in Orford; H – 17, painter, b. Orford, s/o Clarence L. Pushee (Lyme) and Evelyn Tattersall (Derry); W – 16, at home, b. Lyme, d/o Gerald W. Davis (Groton) and Hattie K. Davis (Canada)

David J. of Lyme m. Mary M. **Gilbert** of Lyme 10/2/1889 in Piermont; H - 23, farmer, b. Lyme, s/o Albert J. Pushee (Lyme, farmer) and Sarah F. Jeffers (Lyme, housekeeper); W - 18, housekeeper, b. St. Johnsbury, VT, d/o Harris A. Gilbert (Lyme, farmer) and Ella A. Chamberlin (Newbury, VT, housekeeper)

David J., Jr. of Lyme m. Florence **DeGoosh** of Hanover 5/29/1927 in Lyme; H - 22, laborer, b. Lyme, s/o David J. Pushee (Lyme, farmer) and Mary M. Gilbert (St. Johnsbury, VT, housewife); W - 20, housework, b. Unity, d/o Elmer E. DeGoosh (W. Fairlee, VT, farmer) and Belle Keyes (Reading, VT, housewife)

Donald E. of Lyme m. Mabel C. **O'Donnell** of Vershire, VT 1/23/1949

Eugene C. of Lyme m. Minnie A. **Bombard** of Lyme 12/20/1913 in Lyme; H - 31, laborer, b. Lyme, s/o Clarence S. Pushee (Lyme, farmer) and Fannie C. Post (Lyme, housewife); W - 33, housework, b. Northfield, MA, d/o Philip Bombard (Burlington, VT) and Ellen Welch (Northfield, MA, housewife)

Frank A. of Lyme m. Viola M. **Cutting** of Lyme 8/23/1904 in Lyme; H - 28, farmer, b. Lyme, s/o Albert J. Pushee (Lyme, farmer) and Sarah F. Jeffers (Lyme, housework); W - 17, housework, b. Lyme, d/o Frank W. Cutting (Broom, Canada, carpenter) and

Lizzie Cole (Stanstead, Canada, housewife)

George A. of Lyme m. Emma B. **Cline** of Lyme 12/14/1895 in Lyme; H - 19, farmer, b. Lyme, s/o Alfred W. Pushee (Lyme, farmer) and Edna Steele (Lyme, housekeeper); W - 21, housekeeper, b. Manchester, d/o Benjamin Cline (Lyme, farmer) and Luthera Cook

George A. of Lyme m. Agnes M. **Gilbert** of Lyme 2/4/1900 in Lyme; H - 23, farmer, 2nd, b. Lyme, s/o A. W. Pushee (Lyme, farmer) and Edna Steele (Lyme, housekeeper); W - 23, school teacher, b. Lyme, d/o Zadok Gilbert (Lyme, farmer) and Horace M. Bryant (Lyme)

George A. of Lyme m. Blanche C. **George** of Manchester 1/1/1924 in Lyme; H - 47, farmer, 3rd - W, b. Lyme, s/o Alfred W. Pushee (Lyme, farmer) and Edna E. Steele (Lyme, housewife); W - 38, nurse, 3rd - W, d/o Albert F. Matthews (Wilmot) and Carrie E. Tucker (Salisbury)

Harris A. of Lyme m. Inez A. **Clark** of Plainfield 4/3/1917 in Plainfield; H - 25, carpenter, b. Lyme, s/o David J. Pushee (Lyme, laborer) and Mary M. Gilbert (St. Johnsbury, VT, housewife); W - 25, teacher, b. Plainfield, d/o Samuel W. Clark (Plainfield, farming) and Susan L. Prichard (Green Garden, IL, housewife)

Harris C. of Ely, VT m. Louise A. **Miles** of Boise, ID 5/29/1942 in Lyme; H – 23, bank teller, b. Hanover, s/o Harris A. Pushee (Lyme, carpenter) and Inez Clark (Plainfield, housewife); W – 20, bookkeeper, b. Hartford, CT, d/o Ralph Miles (Barton, VT, poultryman) and Alice Dexter (Glover, VT, housewife)

Henry S. of Lyme m. Nellie J. **Mativia** of Lyme 4/29/1903 in Lyme; H - 24, farmer, b. Lyme, s/o Alfred W. Pushee (Lyme, farmer) and Edna E. Steele (Lyme, housework); W - 20, housework, b. Lyme, d/o Henry J. Mativia (Corinth, VT, farmer) and Hattie Stickney (Fairlee, VT, housewife)

Michael P. of W. Fairlee, VT m. Wendy D. **Ricker** of W. Fairlee, VT 5/3/1989 in Lyme

Olyph of Lyme m. Doris **Johnson** of Lyme 12/11/1934 in Lebanon; H - 24, farmer, b. Lyme, s/o David J. Pushee (Lyme, farmer) and Mary M. Gilbert (Passumpsic, VT, housewife); W - 18, domestic, b. Lyme, d/o Edwin Johnson (carpenter) and Mildred Silloway (W. Fairlee, VT, housewife)

Robert D. of Lyme m. Germaine H. **Thibodeau** of Lebanon 7/12/1967 in Lebanon; H – 20, U. S. Army, b. Lebanon, s/o

Dean S. Pushee and Vera Movelle; W – 17, stitcher, b. Lebanon, d/o Onesime Thibodeau and Frances Noel

Roger C. of Lyme m. Isabel S. **Uline** of Lyme 2/4/1940 in Lyme; H – 22, laborer, b. Lyme, s/o Clarence L. Pushee (Lyme, laborer) and Emerette Rogers (W. Fairlee, VT, housewife); W – 22, at home, b. Lyme, d/o Hiram Uline (Lyme, carpenter) and Grace M. Gilbert (Littleton, housewife)

Ronald H. of Lyme m. Marian J. **Senter** of Pushee, CA 5/10/1963 in Lyme; H – s/o ----- Pushee and ----- A. Miles, res. – Lyme; W – d/o ----- P. Senter and ----- E. Frerichs, res. – Eureka, CA

Steven Bruce of Lyme m. Maria Gema **Mayo** of Spain 1/10/1998

Timothy J. of Lyme m. Brenda L. **Ragan** of Lyme 2/23/1985 in Lyme

Walter S. of Lyme m. Addie M. **Langmaid** of Lyme 8/7/1914 in Lyme; H - 28, farmer, b. Lyme, d/o Clarence S. Pushee (Lyme, farmer) and Fannie C. Post (Lyme, housewife); W - 16, housework, b. Lyme, d/o George B. Langmaid (Brockton, MA, farmer) and Josephine Goodell (Worcester, MA, housewife)

Wayne Alan of Lyme m. Faith Carol **Kimball** of Lyme 5/17/1975 in Lyme; H – b. 5/9/1953 in NH, s/o Harris C. Pushee and Louise Miles; W – b. 2/26/1953 in NY, d/o Arnold R. Kimball and Mildred Souliske

William Albert of Lyme m. Cheryl Ann **Carpenter** of Lyme Ctr. 7/12/1975 in Lyme; H – b. 5/30/1950 in NH, s/o Albert W. Pushee and Minnie Small; W – b. 6/5/1956 in VT, d/o Warren D. Carpenter and Eleanor M. Florucci

William Albert of Lyme m. Julie Ann **Pushee** of Lyme --/--/1991

William J. of Lyme m. Judith E. **Truman** of Lebanon 11/3/1967 in Lebanon; H – 18, U. S. Army, b. Lebanon, s/o Dean S. Pushee and Vera Movelle; W – 17, none, b. Lebanon, d/o Isaac T. Truman and Esther Goodwin

PUTNAM,

Ora D. of Lyme m. Alberta P. **Trask** of Orford 3/25/1939 in Warren; H - 23, laborer, b. Bradford, VT, s/o Harry Putnam (laborer) and Dera Bathrow (W. Fairlee, VT, housewife); W - 20, domestic, 2nd - W, b. Haverhill, d/o Charles A. Perry (Whitefield, laborer) and Inez C. Lindsey (Haverhill, housewife)

Spencer C. of Lyme m. Verena E. **Hostettler** of Yorktown, NY 6/25/1969 in Middlebury, VT; H – 24, b. NH, s/o William F. Putnam and M. Margaret Best; W – 22, b. Switzerland, d/o Ernst Hostettler and Agnes Freudenberg

QUINT,
Orrison D. of Lyme m. Mary E. **Webster** of Lyme 4/16/1911 in Lyme; H - 57, carpenter, 2nd, b. Orford, s/o Thomas W. Quint (Orford, farmer) and Mary Archer (Orford, housewife); W - 62, housewife, 2nd, b. Dorchester, d/o Samuel Fellows (Ipswich, MA) and Sarah Niles (England, housewife)

RAGAN,
Charles R. of Lyme m. Terri L. **Truell** of Lyme 6/21/1986 in Lyme
Laurence F. of Lyme m. Carolyn N. **Jackman** of Lyme 7/9/1932 in Haverhill; H - 22, laborer, b. Lebanon, s/o George W. Ragan (Plainfield, carpenter) and Ida M. Bramble (Yankton, SD, housewife); W - 18, housework, b. Lyman, d/o Charles R. Jackman (Lyman, mason) and Ruth S. Dennis (Piermont, housewife)
Wallace E. of Lyme m. Suzette **Keller** of Lebanon 2/12/1992

RAILA,
Paul M. of Somerville, MA m. Madaleine L. **Butler** of Somerville, MA 9/6/1986 in Lyme

RAJBALLIE,
Ramesh John of Canada m. Anna Grace Roberts **Bognolo** of Lyme 8/3/1996

RANDLETT,
George W. of Lyme m. Hannah W. **Sanborn** of Orford 6/28/1894 in Orford; H - 59, merchant, 2nd, b. Plymouth, s/o Jacob Randlett (Sanbornton, farmer) and Effie Wells (Bristol, domestic); W - 57, domestic, 2nd, b. Orford, d/o Stedman Willard (merchant) and Merial Wheeler (Orford, domestic)

RATHBON,
John W. of Mansfield, MA m. Henrietta C. **Tozier** of Lyme 12/23/1893 in Lyme; H - 22, bookkeeper, b. Washington, RI, s/o E. W. Rathbon (Griswold, CT, merchant) and Phebe A. Briggs (E. Greenwich, RI); W - 24, b. Woodstock, NB, d/o J. M. Tozier (N. Esk., NB, minister) and Rebecca Stoddard (Woodstock, NB)

RAY,
Michael D. of Mt. Herman, CA m. Shelda L. **Claflin** of Mt. Herman,

CA 8/27/1989 in Lyme

RAYMOND,
Alan J. of Lebanon m. Dianne M. **Goodrich** of Lyme 5/25/1986 in Lebanon

RECORD,
Walter L. of Lyme m. Amy Q. **Mintz** of Strafford, VT 8/24/1986 in Lyme Ctr.

REED,
Allen G. of Orford m. Shirley Y. **Perkins** of Lyme 2/24/1967 in Lyme; H – 19, machine operator, b. Hanover, s/o Donald Reed and Edna Gregory; W – 19, cosmetologist, b. Lebanon, d/o Harry W. Perkins and Martha E. Hardy

REEVES,
Richard of Lyme m. Sharon **Barker** of Thetford, VT 7/23/1971 in Lyme; H – 29, b. ME, s/o Otto Reeves and Rose Raymond; W – 19, b. NH, d/o Kenneth Barker and Barbara Kennedy
Roger D. of Lyme m. Bonnie Sue **Rollins** of Bradford, VT 12/26/1964 in Chelsea, VT; H – s/o Otto Reeves and Helen Raymond, res. – Lyme; W – d/o Henry Rollins of Newbury, VT and Gladys Padgett
William R. m. Debra **Rathburn** 11/1/1981 in Piermont

RENNIE,
Harold R. of Hanover m. Della **Hanchett** of Lyme 9/12/1906 in Lyme; H - 22, farming, b. Canada, s/o Alexander Rennie (Canada, farmer) and Mary Glasgon (Canada, housewife); W - 19, housework, b. Lyme, d/o Dennis A. Hanchett (Hartland, VT, farmer) and Elizabeth Reed (Plainfield, housewife)

RICE,
John T. of Lyme m. Marjorie A. **Barry** of Lyme 12/2/1988 in Lyme

RICH,
Aaron W. of Lyme m. Patience B. **Farnham** of Lyme 6/14/2003
Brian E. of Lyme Ctr. m. Josephine M. **Davies** of Berkeley, CA 7/14/1973 in Hanover; H – 26, b. NH, s/o Everett S. Rich and Verna Simmons; W – 18, b. OR, d/o William Davies and

Virginia Telford
Everett B. of Concord m. Verna W. **Simmons** of Lyme 12/26/1942 in Lyme; H – 26, US Army, b. Lyme, s/o John S. Rich (N. Stratford, merchant) and Ida N. King (Lyme, housewife); W - --, soda clerk, b. Union, ME, d/o Harold A. Simmons (Union, ME, blacksmith) and Beulah A. Rowell (Liberty, ME, housewife)

John S. of Lyme m. Ida N. **King** of Lyme 1/6/1915 in Lyme; H - 26, farmer, b. Stratford, s/o Dwight Rich (Groveton, farmer) and Sarah I. Claflin (Auburn, housewife); W - 19, housework, b. Lyme, d/o Walter E. King (Groton, mail carrier) and Ida L. Norris (Dorchester, housewife)

Perley M. of Lyme m. Marion F. **Prichard** of Somerville, MA 7/3/1905 in Lyme; H - 21, farmer, b. Stratford, s/o Dwight Rich (farmer) and Isabel Claflin (housewife); W - 18, d/o Charles Prichard (drummer) and Grace M. Fuller (housewife)

Preston W. of Hanover m. Rosie B. **King** of Lyme 7/7/1910 in Lyme Ctr.; H - 28, clerk carrier, b. Stratford, s/o Dwight Rich (Groveton, farmer) and Sarah I. Claflin (Auburn, housewife); W - 25, teacher, b. Lyme, d/o Walter E. King (Groton, mail carrier) and Ida Norris (Dorchester, housewife)

Ray B. of Lyme m. Lunie B. **Fowler** of Hanover 7/2/1916 in Lyme; H - 23, farming, b. Lyme, s/o Dwight Rich (Northumberland, farming) and Sarah I. Claflin (Auburn, housewife); W - 20, housework, b. Newport, d/o Charles E. Fowler (Newport, farming) and Clara Thurber (Unity, housewife)

Roger K. of Haverhill m. Arlene B. **Starkey** of Lyme 8/2/1942 in Lyme; H – 26, merchant, b. Lyme, s/o John S. Rich (N. Stratford, merchant) and Ida King (Lyme, housewife); W – 22, teacher, b. Keene, d/o Elmo D. Starkey (Roxbury, farmer) and Bertha Davis (Keene, housewife)

RICKER,

John W. of Vershire, VT m. Jean **Pushee** of Lyme 10/25/1953 in Lyme; H – 21, farmer, b. Vershire, VT, s/o George Ricker (NH) and Mabel Shearer (VT); W – 19, at home, b. Lyme, d/o David Pushee (Lyme) and Florence DeGoosh (NH)

Philip Jay m. Debra Marie **Carpenter** 7/15/1978 in Lyme

Roger Frederick of Post Mills, VT m. Susan Marie **Bacon** of Lyme 9/14/1974 in Lyme; H – b. 2/12/1953 in VT, s/o Floyd H. Ricker and Marjorie Andrews; W – b. 9/5/1956 in NH, d/o Carlton G. Bacon and Ruth Emerson

RIESS,
Peter of Lyme m. Heide **Kropp** of W. Lebanon 8/22/1987 in Cornish

RIVERA,
Valentin of Piermont m. Rose L. **Strout** of Lyme 12/16/1961 in Thetford, VT; H – 23, s/o Evangelista Rivera and Rosaura Rivera, res. – Puerto Rico; W – 20, d/o Gerald Strout and Elizabeth Wilmot, res. – Lyme

ROBERTS,
Daniel W. of N. Thetford, VT m. Verna M. **Clark** of Lyme 11/25/1961 in Thetford, VT; H – 24, s/o Edwin G. Roberts and Stella Warren; W – 20, d/o William G. Clark and Ruth Callahan, res. – Lyme

Ed. O. of Enfield m. Martha **Dike** of Lyme 7/4/1907 in Lyme; H - 40, laborer, b. Lyme, s/o Omer Roberts (Orford, laborer) and Elmina Rush (Piermont, laborer); W - 37, housework, 2nd, b. Littleton, d/o Harry Dike (Dalton, shoemaker) and Sarah E. Tucker (Strafford, VT, housewife)

Guy A. of Lyme m. Jennie M. **Hobart** of Lyme 9/30/1908 in Lyme; H - 20, laborer, b. Bradford, VT, s/o Harris P. Roberts (Lyme, laborer) and Emma Wells (Waterville, VT, housework); W - 17, housework, b. Lyme, d/o Albert Hobart (Hebron, farmer) and Nellie Phelps (Lowell, MA, housework)

Harry A. of Lyme m. Mary L. **Morrill** of Haverhill 5/31/1944 in Haverhill; H – 32, US Army, b. Lyme, s/o Guy Roberts (Lyme, patrolman) and Jennie Roberts (Lyme, housewife); W – 33, unemployed, b. Haverhill, d/o Lawrence Morrill (White Rock, RI, welder) and Annie Geroux (Bradford, England, housewife)

Jesse L. of Lyme m. Josephine M. **Thompson** of Hanover 3/26/1949

Thomas M. of Marion, OH m. Connie Lu **Seiter** of Marion, OH 10/3/1985 in Lyme Ctr.

Thomas W. of Lyme m. Minnie Bell **Strue** of Lyme 8/24/1889 in Vershire, VT; H - 31, farmer, b. Lyme, s/o Thomas F. Roberts (Raymond, farmer) and Caroline Smith (Lyme, housekeeper); W - 15, housekeeper, b. Lyme, d/o George E. Strue (Canada, laborer) and Alma A. Lamphere (Lyme, housekeeper)

ROBINSON,
Frank E. of Winooski, VT m. Marie **Reeve** of Burlington 9/7/1920 in

Lyme; H - 35, supt., 2nd - W, b. Colchester, VT, s/o Cassius Robinson (Rouses Point, NY, retired) and Hannah Merrill (Colchester, VT, housewife); W - 33, nurse, b. Williamston, Canada, d/o Thomas Reeve (Norfolk, England, watchman) and Isabel McKenzie (Scotland)

Harrie E. of S. Strafford, VT m. Patricia M. **Swift** of Lyme 11/5/1943 in Lebanon; H – 25, US Army, b. Hanover, s/o Justin Robinson (S. Strafford, VT, farmer) and Margaret Walsh (NS, housewife); W – 17, domestic, b. Thetford, VT, d/o Kenneth Swift (S. Strafford, VT, farmer) and Carrie I. Root (S. Strafford, VT, housewife)

ROCHE,
Harvey D. of Lyme m. Dorothy E. **Sanders** of Grantham 1/14/1949

ROEWER,
George E., Jr. of Cambridge, MA m. Margaret F. **Hudson** of Cambridge, MA 5/1/1937 in Lyme; H - 23, student, b. Boston, MA, s/o George E. Roewer (Syracuse, NY, lawyer) and Rose Heirven (Boston, MA, housewife); W - 22, clerk, b. NS, d/o Clifford G. Hudson (IN, contractor) and Irere Parker (NS, housewife)

ROGERS,
George G. of Lyme m. Hazel **Hutchinson** of Lyme 7/13/1924 in Lyme; H - 38, laborer, 2nd - D, b. Thetford, VT, s/o Alfred Rogers (Thetford, VT, retired) and Ellen Newcomb (Thetford, VT, housewife); W - 18, at home, b. W. Fairlee, VT, d/o Edward Hutchinson (laborer) and Lizzie E. Harlow (Windsor, VT, housewife)

Kenneth Shantz of Somerville, MA m. Gina Marie **Yarbrough** of Somerville, MA --/--/1991

ROLLINS,
Leon C. of Lyme m. Elinor L. **Cutting** of Lyme 6/5/1942 in Piermont; H – 20, foreman, D, b. Newport, s/o Charles Rollins (Grantham, carpenter) and Addie Goodhue (Croydon, housewife); W – 18, at home, b. Lyme, d/o Lee W. Cutting (Lyme, mail carrier) and Alice M. Hobart (Lyme, housewife)

RONDEAU,
David G. of Lyme m. Lois J. **Pushee** of Lyme 10/24/1987 in Orfordville

ROSE,
Martin W. of Thetford, VT m. Arlene D. **Thompson** of Lyme 6/21/1953 in Lyme; H – 20, mill worker, b. Oxbo, NY, s/o Benjamin Rose (NH) and Grace Pickens (VT); W – 17, student, b. Lyme, d/o William H. Thompson (Canada) and Della Bryant (NH)

Robert John of Lyme m. Heidi Joan **Root** of Lyme 6/16/1990 in Lyme

ROSEN,
Joseph M. of Lyme m. Stina L. **Kohnke** of Lyme 8/19/2000

ROSS,
John J. of Lyme m. Orissa M. **Armstrong** of Lyme 3/30/1929 in Lyme; H – 21, laborer, b. Minto, NB, s/o Fred Ross (Oak Point, NB, laborer) and Dorothy Lee (Glenwood, NB, housewife); W – 18, bookkeeper, b. Concord, d/o Oliver M. Armstrong (Brooklyn, NY, brakeman) and Cora S. Drew (Hopkinton, housewife)

ROTZ,
John Joseph of Needham, MA m. Roberta J. **Sanborn** of Lyme 9/18/1971 in Lyme; H – 28, b. PA, s/o John B. Rotz and Mabel Wagaman; W – 24, b. NH, d/o Harry Sanborn and Dora Balch

ROWE,
George E. of Lyme m. Susan A. **McAloney** of Cambridge, MA 3/19/1907 in Lyme; H - 50, laborer, 4th, b. Brunswick, ME, s/o William Rowe (Strafford, mechanic) and Alvira E. Marden (Lancaster, housewife); W – 53, housework, 2nd, b. Cambridge, MA, d/o Loderick Smith (England, laborer) and Sarah Godfrey (Halifax, NS, housewife)

George E. of Lyme m. Rosa M. **Waterman** of Lebanon 12/18/1924 in Lebanon; H - 68, farmer, 5th - D, b. Auburn, ME, s/o William Rowe (Stratford, wheelwright) and Alvira Marden (Lancaster, housewife); W - 68, domestic, 2nd - W, b. Lincoln, VT, d/o William W. Balch (Lyme, retired) and Wealtha Flint (Lyme, housewife)

ROWLINSON,
Matthew C. of Lyme m. Alexandra C. **Torres** of Lyme 7/13/2002

ROY,
Alan C. of Lyme m. Marlene S. **Crook** of Norwich, VT 9/3/1983 in Lyme

RUBEN,
George J. of Lyme m. Irene **Dolgin** of Lyme 7/31/1942 in Lyme; H – -9, salvage yard, b. Bangor, ME, s/o Isaac Ruben (Russia, junk yard) and Bessie Ames (Lithuania, housewife); W - -9, bookkeeper, b. Everett, MA, d/o Harry Dolgin (Kiev, Russia, auto salv.) and Francis Kichstein (Lynn, MA, housewife)

RUNNELS,
Arthur N. of Concord m. Julia E. **Pushee** of Lyme 3/28/1930 in Concord; H - 30, painter, b. Concord, s/o Ezra Runnels (Bradford, VT, retired) and Mary Hame (Concord, housewife); W - 23, teacher, b. Lyme, d/o George A. Pushee (Lyme, farmer) and Agnes Gilbert (Lyme, housewife)

RUSS,
Daniel C., Jr. of Lyme m. Doris **Esterbrooke** of Lyme 1/31/1952 in Haverhill; H – 37, lumbering, b. VT, s/o Daniel Russ (VT) and Harriet Boyd (NY); W – 43, at home, 2nd – D, b. Oakfield, ME, d/o Boardman Joslyn (ME) and Bertha Martin (ME)

RUSSELL,
David H. of W. Lebanon m. Ruth M. **Balch** of Lyme 7/5/1975 in N. Thetford, VT; H – b. 10/24/1943 in NH, s/o Esmond Russell and Norma Wing; W – b. 11/19/1948 in NH, d/o Grant P. Balch and Margaret Houston

RUTSTEIN,
Michael Howard of Brookline, MA m. Melissa Usher **Meyer** of Brookline, MA 10/16/1993

RYAN,
Anthony H. m. Marjorie J. **Gustin** 4/15/1978 in Hanover
Anthony H. of Lyme m. Marjorie **Schaub** of Northfield, VT 8/25/1992
Carlos of Lyme m. Fannie M. **Pelton** of Lyme 4/30/1901 in Lyme; H -

29, laborer, b. Richford, VT, s/o Isaac Ryan (Canada, farmer) and Juliaette Davis (Highgate, VT, housewife); W - 30, housework, b. Lyme, d/o Josiah C. Pelton (Plymouth, farmer) and Mary Roycroft (England, housework)
Richard Bret of Lyme m. Ellen Creigh **Wagner** of Lyme 7/19/1985 in Lyme

ST. PETER,
Lewis E. of Lyme m. Donna L. **Pushee** of Lyme 12/24/1984 in Lyme

SAILER,
Eric A. of Lyme Ctr. m. Nancy K. **Holschuh** of Lyme Ctr. 12/31/1982 in Lyme Ctr.

SALDIBAR,
Stephen R. of Ansonia, CT m. Ingrid E. **Malmstrom** of W. Haven, CT 6/18/1983 in Lyme

SAMUELS,
Henry of Hanover m. Diana S. **Olsen** of Lyme 8/15/1968 in Lebanon; H – 31, b. WA, s/o Louis Samuels and Susie Moses; W – 19, b. NH, d/o Edward Olsen and Elizabeth Davis

SANBORN,
Charles D. of Lyme m. Daisy C. **Taylor** of Lyme 12/11/1907 in Lyme; H - 45, mill man, b. Lyme, s/o Freeman P. Sanborn (Dorchester, farmer) and Mary A. Moore (Thetford, VT, housework); W - 36, housework, 2nd, b. Thetford, VT, d/o George E. Wilder (laborer) and Caroline O. Barrett (Thetford, VT, housework)

Clifford O. of Lyme m. Florence L. **Potter** of Stoneham, MA 3/19/1938 in Hanover; H - 24, laborer, b. Gorham, s/o Otis M. C. Sanborn (Dummer, farmer) and Grace E. Perkins (Gorham, housewife); W - 24, domestic, b. Kingman, ME, d/o Archibald C. Potter (Pembroke, ME) and Kitty L. Scott (Kingman, ME, housewife)

Fred J. of Orford m. Carrie L. **Pike** of Lyme 11/22/1938 in Haverhill; H - 58, veterinary, 2nd - D, b. Bradford, VT, s/o Charles A. Sanborn (Rumney, farmer) and Abbie Chase (Bradford, VT, housewife); W - 41, domestic, b. Lyme, d/o Fred L. Pike (Lyme, laborer) and Anna B. Roberts (Lyme, housewife)

Harry E. of Lyme m. Dora E. **Balch** of Lyme –/4/1938 in Etna; H - 23, laborer, b. Berlin, s/o Otis M. Sanborn (Dummer, laborer) and Edith G. Perkins (Gorham, housewife); W - 18, housework, b. Lyme, d/o Harvey H. Balch (Taftsville, VT, laborer) and Lillian J. Morrell (Taftsville, VT, housewife)

Newton F. of Lyme m. Eliza E. **Welch** of Lyme 8/8/1894 in Lyme; H - 26, laborer, b. Lyme, s/o Freeman F. Sanborn (Dorchester, farmer) and Mary A. Moore (Thetford, VT, domestic); W - 21, housekeeper, b. Lyme, d/o Joseph R. Welch (Canaan, wheelwright) and Zilpha Cutting (Canada)

Norman R. of Lyme m. Vina G. **Corliss** of Bradford, VT 8/1/1951 in Lyme; H – 33, laborer, 2nd – D, b. Gorham, s/o Otis Sanborn (Dummer) and Grace Perkins (Gorham); W – 18, waitress, b. Haverhill, d/o Milo Corliss (W. Fairlee, VT) and Ima Davis (Hyde Park, VT)

Robert B., Jr. of Orford m. Sarah N. **Hart** of Lyme 7/1/1961 in Lyme; H – 26, s/o Robert E. Sanborn, Sr. and Evelyn Blake, res. – Orford; W – 22, d/o Earl W. Hart and Dorothy Knickerbocker, res. – Lyme

Robert E. of Lyme m. Hazel A. **Hutchins** of Lyme 10/29/1966 in Lyme; H – 23, greenskeeper, b. Hanover, s/o Harry E. Sanborn and Dora E. Balch; W – 19, typist, b. Hanover, d/o John J. Hutchins, Sr. and Ruth Beard

Robert F. of Lyme m. Deborah L. **Caswell** of Lyme 6/20/1993

SANDERS,

Richard M. od Needham, MA m. Barbara J. **Rogers** of Hanover 2/18/1956 in Thetford, VT; H – 22, student, s/o Richard B. Sanders of St. Paul, MN and Martha Miller of White River Jct.; W – 21, student, d/o Robert D. Rogers of Berlin and Ruth Pushee of Lyme

SANSBURY,

John W. of Newton, AL m. Dorothy M. **Gregory** of Lyme 10/30/1939 in Lyme; H - 32, chef, b. Newton, AL, s/o Raymond D. Sansbury (Daleville, AL, laborer) and Anna R. Hall (Pine Grove, AL, housewife); W - 24, at home, b. Lyme, d/o Frank T. Gregory (Grantham, farmer) and Sadie M. Porter (S. Ham, PQ, housewife)

SANSONE,
Paul of White River Jct. m. Mary E. **Stevens** of White River Jct. 3/30/1996

SARGENT,
David B. of Fairlee, VT m. Mary R. **Fifield** of Thetford, VT 12/21/1957 in Lyme; H – 20, s/o Murray Sargent of Vero Beach, FL and Edna Hill of Fairlee, VT; W – 19, d/o Everett Fifield and Evelyn Estes, res. – Thetford, VT
Lawrence Henry m. Lois Jean **Martinson** 1/20/1978 in Lyme
Steven King of Lyme m. Avery Walker **Bross** of Lyme 8/15/1998

SAVERY,
Wendell H. of Williamstown, VT m. Evelyn G. **Barrett** of Norwich, VT 8/10/1938 in Lyme; H 0 26, farmer, b. Williamstown, VT, s/o Vernon B. Savery (Northfield, VT, farmer) and Nellie Pebbles (Williamstown, VT, housewife); W - 29, secretary, b. Norwich, VT, d/o Day T. Barrett (Thetford, VT, farmer) and Marcia H. Hutchinson (Vershire, VT, housewife)

SAWYER,
William F. of Boston, MA m. Annie **Bryant** of Upton, MA 10/11/1921 in Lyme; H - 73, druggist, 2nd, b. Charlestown, MA, s/o Seth Sawyer (Bolton, MA) and Susan P. Frost (Bolton, MA); W - 65, author, 2nd, b. Exeter, d/o John Burnham (Essex, MA) and Caroline A. Sweet (E. Kingston)

SCHIFFMAN,
Mark Lawrence of VT m. Jennifer Sage **Smith** of VT 8/8/1998

SCHILLHAMMER,
William Renold, III of Lyme m. Marion Woodward Atchley **Merrick** of Lyme 9/2/1995

SCHINE,
James D. of CT m. Penelope E. **Piggott** of IL 2/5/1972 in Lyme; H – 25, b. CT, s/o Harold Schine and Joan Goldwasser; W – 24, b. IL, d/o John C. Pigott and Eleanor Anderson

SCHMIDT,
Kurt W. of Lyme m. Barbara C. **Harrington** of Lyme 4/5/1999

SCHRIEVER,
Jack Richard of Lyme m. Doris Marie **Huberth** of Lyme 6/17/1975 in Hanover; H – b. 4/25/1906 in NY, s/o John C. Schriever and Marie Rebenklau; W – b. 11/8/1909 in NY, d/o George Rohmann and Martha Osmer

SCHUIRMANN,
Michael Lee of Lyme m. Beth Ann **McElreath** of Lyme 12/3/1994

SCOPPETTONE,
Peter N. m. Katherine L. **Gordon** 8/16/1980 in Lyme

SCOTT,
William E. of Lyme m. Sherry L. **Seiter** of Lyme 9/4/1982 in Lyme

SEACE,
Albert L. of Lyme m. Carol Ann **Dickey** of Lyme 3/17/1990 in Lyme

SECTOR,
Peter W. of Lyme m. Diane Murray **Hatch** of Lyme 5/27/1995

SENGPANYA,
Khanty of Essex Jct., VT m. Paphanh **Sithavady** of Lyme 5/29/1999

SHAMMA,
Shihab Ahmed of Washington, DC m. Gwendolen Marie **Kuendel** of MD 1/3/1998

SHANNON,
William B. of Winchester, MA m. Marilyn Kay **George** of Lyme 7/15/1995

SHATTUCK,
Amos E. m. Carlene J. **Webster** 4/12/1980 in Lyme
George F. of Lyme m. Annie B. **Cutting** of Lyme 4/8/1890 in Lyme; H - 23, carpenter, b. Hanover, s/o Charles W. Shattuck and Lydia M. Bryant; W - 24, housekeeper, b. Lyme, d/o Ezra F. Cutting and Fannie P. Mead
Warren J. of Lyme m. Addie E. **Muzzy** of Lyme 5/10/1904 in Lyme; H - 41, carpenter, b. Hanover, s/o Charles W. Shattuck (Bethlehem, carpenter) and Lydia M. Bryant (Hanover,

housework); W - 34, housework, d/o Jesse J. Muzzy (Corinth, VT, laborer) and Anna Batchelder (Deerfield, housework)

SHAW,
Scott Michael of Lyme m. Regan Vanessa **Shaw** of W. Lebanon 12/12/1997

SHEPARD,
Curtis Jay of Lyme m. Caryn May **Crump** of Lyme 9/30/1995
James W. of New York, NY m. Zelda G. **Spoll** of Lake Mohegan, NY 5/10/1958 in Lyme; H – 20, s/o Lee L. Shepard and Sylvia Wilson, res. – New York, NY; W – 20, d/o Harry Spoll and Frieda Abrams, res. – Lake Mohegan, NY

SHEPHERD,
Evan J. of Lyme m. Deborah F. **Fisher** of Lyme 6/14/1986 in Lyme

SHERRY,
Thomas W. m. Tracey K. **Werner** 8/21/1981 in Woodstock

SHINE,
John Francis of Lyme m. Nora Esperanza **Thompson** of Somerville, MA 10/2/2004

SILLOWAY,
Mark of Lyme m. Grace E. **Follansbee** of Lyme 11/15/1917 in Lyme; H - 30, laborer, b. Fairlee, VT, s/o Wells Silloway (Bradford, VT, laborer) and Lilla Moore (W. Fairlee, VT, housewife); W - 30, housework, b. Hartland, VT, d/o John H. Follansbee (Manchester, farming) and Ella DeGoosh (W. Fairlee, VT, housewife)

SIMKULET,
Michael W. of Skaneateles Falls, NY m. Sandra Gail **King** of Lyme 3/23/1974 in Lyme Ctr.; H – b. 2/22/1952 in NY, s/o William Simkulet and Martha Miles; W – b. 12/24/1951 in NH, d/o Fredric W. King and Cathrine Doyle

SIMONDS,
Spencer W. m. Debra A. **Astles** 7/25/1981 in Lyme

SKINNER,

Ephriam H. of Lyme m. Gertie **Woodward** of Lyme 4/27/1891 in Lyme; H - 28, laborer, b. Lyme, s/o Joshua G. Skinner (Lyme, farmer) and Paulina A. Chandler (Hanover, housekeeper); W - 18, housekeeper, b. Lyme, d/o Stephen Woodward (Woodstock, VT, farmer) and Jane Hadley (Plainfield, housekeeper)

SLACK,

Harold E. of Norwich, VT m. Katherine L. **Goodell** of Norwich, VT 10/17/1936 in Lyme; H - 32, laborer, 2nd - D, b. Chelsea, VT, s/o Carlton Slack (Norwich, VT, farmer) and Ernie B. Felch (Williamstown, VT, retired); W - 19, at home, b. Norwich, VT, d/o Perry F. Goodell (Lyme, lumberman) and Gladys Harmon (Plainfield, housewife)

James P. of Thetford, VT m. Gertrude **Braley** of Lyme 3/17/1923 in Lebanon; H - 21, laborer, b. Thetford, VT, s/o William P. Slack (Strafford, VT, farmer) and Alice Robinson (Thetford, VT, housewife); W - 19, laundress, b. Claremont, d/o Israel Braley (Rumney, laborer) and Mabel Vadney (Claremont, housewife)

Wilbur F. of Lyme m. Ida E. **Garey** of Lyme 9/2/1896 in Lyme; H - 46, laborer, b. Wells River, VT, s/o Fred S. Slack (Thetford, VT, farmer) and Angeline Goodnow (Montpelier, VT, housewife); W - 46, housework, 2nd, b. Akron, OH, d/o John S. Kent (Lyme, farmer) and Sophronia Perkins (Lyme, housewife)

SLAYTON,

Ray T. of Plainfield m. Carol J. **Butman** of Lyme 4/29/1967 in Lyme; H – 22, grinder, b. Windsor, VT, s/o Hayden Slayton and Bernice Barrop; W – 20, clerk, b. Lebanon, d/o Zane Campbell and Dolores Piper

SMALL,

Duane W. of Lyme m. Alice R. **Clark** of Lyme 11/1/1958 in Lyme; H – 25, s/o Ralph D. Small and Ida V. Young, res. – Lyme; W – 23, d/o Charles W. Clark and Ruth A. Bean, res. – Lyme

Harry R. of Lyme m. Daisy B. **Melendy** of W. Fairlee, VT 8/30/1930 in Piermont; H - 21, miller, b. Lyme, s/o Duane W. Small (Brownsville, VT, miller) and L. Minnie Lobdell (Pierpont, VT, housewife); W - 18, at home, b. W. Fairlee, VT, d/o Clinton A. Melendy (Fairlee, VT, merchant) and Effie B. Perkins (Newbury,

VT, housewife)
Ralph D. of Lyme m. Ida D. **Young** of Lyme 9/1/1920 in Meriden; H - 20, chauffeur, b. Corinish, s/o Duane M. Small (Brownsville, VT, miller) and Lucy M. Lobdell (Pierpont, NY, housewife); W - 19, at home, b. Burke, NY, d/o Ira Young (Clarenceville, PQ, farmer) and Barbara Carr (Elgone, Canada, housewife)
Richard of Lyme m. Priscilla **White** of Brattleboro, VT 3/17/1962 in Hanover; H – 22, s/o Harry A. Small and Daisy Melendy, res. – Lyme; W – 19, d/o Charles White of Brattleboro, VT and Nella Zolyniack of Hollywood, FL

SMALLIDGE,
Peter D. m. Elizabeth R. **Cole** 10/4/1980 in Lyme

SMITH,
Benjamin W. of Lyme m. Josephine **Dennis** of Lyme 3/7/1927 in White River Jct.; H - 23, laborer, b. Lyme, s/o Carlton A. Smith (Lyme, farmer) and Ida M. Brissett (Hanover, housewife); W - 18, at home, b. Lyme, d/o Albert B. Dennis (Piermont, farmer) and Maude Piper (Lyme, housewife)
Carlton A. of Lyme m. Ida M. **Bressett** of Hanover 7/19/1902 in Lyme; H - 28, laborer, b. Lyme, s/o Benjamin Smith (Wentworth, laborer) and Angeline Worthen (Orford, housewife); W - 18, housework, b. Hanover, d/o William E. Bressett (farmer) and Hattie Bill (housewife)
Chauncey of Lyme m. Mildred M. **Movelle** of Lyme 12/24/1941 in Lyme; H – 26, US Army, b. Lyme, s/o Carl Smith (Lyme, mill operator) and Ida Bassett (Hanover, mill operator); W – 44, housekeeper, 2nd – D, b. Lyme, d/o Henry Gilbert (Lyme, farmer) and Mary Jordan (Edinburgh, Scotland, cook)
Clayton R. m. Patricia **Quarti** 9/10/1981 in Enfield, CT
Dennie C. of Lyme m. Marguerite **Billingham** of Lyme 1/1/1927 in Fairlee, VT; H - 21, laborer, b. Lyme, s/o Carlton A. Smith (Lyme, farmer) and Ida Brissett (Hanover, housewife); W - 17, at home, b. Bradford, VT, d/o James Billingham (England) and Julia V. Perrin (Island Pond, VT)
Earle M. of Lyme m. Winnie J. **Anable** of N. Hadley, MA 9/18/1920 in Lyme; H - 21, lumberman, b. Lyme, s/o Ezra M. Smith (Canaan, laborer) and Bertha M. Flint (Lyme, housewife); W - 25, laundress, b. N. Hadley, MA, d/o Minnie Anable (N. Hadley, MA, housewife)

Ezra M. of Lyme m. Bertha M. **Flint** of Lyme 10/25/1898 in Lyme; H
- 26, butcher, b. Hanover, s/o Alonzo A. Smith (Hanover,
farmer) and Julia A. Heath (Colebrook, housewife); W - 20,
housework, b. Lyme, d/o Frances F. Flint (Lyme, farmer) and
Cordelia H. Smith (Gilford, VT, housewife)

Fenton H. of Lyme m. Alice M. **Welch** of Lyme 6/12/1912 in
Lebanon; H - 46, farmer, 2nd, b. Lyme, s/o Rodney V. Smith
(Hadley, MA, carpenter) and Deborah Claflin (Lyme,
housewife); W - 17, housework, b. W. Fairlee, VT, d/o John
Welch (farmer) and Lizzie Manion (Fayston, VT, housework)

Luther F. of Lyme m. Ellen M. **Bailey** of Fairlee, VT 9/1/1910 in
Lyme Ctr.; H - 26, laborer, b. Lyme, s/o Benjamin Smith
(Wentworth, farmer) and Angeline Worthen (Orford); W - 18,
housework, b. Strafford, VT, d/o Joseph Bailey (Providence, RI)
and Hattie M. Bushaw (Canada)

North Craig m. Marguerite J. **Haley** 9/15/1979 in Hanover

S. Dean of Brookfield, VT m. Emma A. **Johnson** of Brookfield, VT
11/28/1952 in Lyme; H – 70, engineer, 2nd – D, b. Hardwick, VT,
s/o Adolphus Smith (VT) and Hariett Magoon (VT); W – 51,
seamstress, 3rd – D, d/o Thomas Cousineau (ON) and Christy
Masieau (Canada) (see following entry)

Samuel D. of Springfield, MA m. Emma A. **Johnson** of Brookfield,
VT 6/1/1953 in Lyme; H – 71, steam engineer, 2nd – D, b. VT,
s/o Adolphus Smith (VT) and Harriet Magoon (VT); W – 51, at
home, 3rd – D, b. Quebec, d/o Thomas E. Cousineau (ON) and
Christie Massieau (ON) (see preceding entry)

SMOLINSKI,
Christopher Patric of MD m. Mina Beth **Wilcox** of MD 2/13/1999

SNELLING,
Michael A. of Lyme m. Ann N. **Murdoch** of Durham 6/22/1985 in
Durham

SONTHOFF,
Herbert G. of S't'more, PA m. Helen H. **Wolfe** of Lyme 10/15/1943 in
Lyme; H – 30, college ins., b. Berlin, Germany, s/o Anton
Sonthoff (Hothdorf, Germany, engineer) and Agnes Kessler
(Berlin, Germany, housewife); W – 27, secretary, b. Rochester,
NY, d/o Gordon C. Wolfe (Newton, MA, salesman) and Ruth P.
Hubbard (Rochester, NY, farmer)

SOPER,
Ambrose A. of Lyme m. Alice M. **Morey** of Lyme 6/6/1895 in Lyme; H - 34, laborer, b. Danvers, MA, s/o Ambrose A. Soper (Bath, ME, shoemaker) and Hannah E. Stone (Marblehead, MA, housework); W - 17, housework, b. Lyme, d/o William D. Morey (Londonderry, laborer) and Esther J. Rowe (Gray, ME, work in mill)

Joseph H. of Lyme m. Mary E. **Murphy** of Boston, MA 4/18/1897 in Boston, MA; H - 30, farmer, b. Danvers, MA, s/o Jeremiah S. Soper (Marblehead, MA, shoemaker) and Caroline C. Quint (Orford, housework); W - 32, housework, b. Cape Briton, NS, d/o Bernard Murphy (Cape Briton, NS, merchant) and Roseana O'Neil (Cape Briton, NS)

SOUTHWORTH,
Howard E., Jr. of Lyme m. Linda Belle **O'Donnell** of Lyme 4/6/1974 in Lyme; H – b. 10/9/1952 in NH, s/o Howard Southworth, Jr. and Dorothy Drew; W – b. 9/22/1954 in NH, d/o Hugh O'Donnell, Jr. and Joan Pushee

Kenneth B. of W. Fairlee, VT m. Virginia A. **Slack** of Thetford, VT 1/16/1952 in Lyme; H – 31, farmer, b. W. Fairlee, VT, s/o Lawrence Southworth (VT) and Vena Slack (NH); W – 29, telephone op., b. Thetford, VT, d/o Daniel Slack (VT) and Florence Hatch (VT)

SPAFFORD,
Jason A. of Minneapolis, MN m. Cynthia **Berger** of Minneapolis, MN 12/30/1994

SPAULDING,
Gary C. of Norwich, VT m. Paula R. **Balch** of Lyme 8/4/1984 in Lyme

SPITANLY,
Kenneth C. of S. Orange, NJ m. Lynne E. **Smith** of Pittsburgh, PA 5/23/1971 in Lyme; H – 21, b. NJ, s/o William Spitanly and Juanita Weisbrod; W – 21, b. PA, d/o Robert Smith and Stella Myers

STANHOPE,
David C. of Lyme m. Doris L. **Stearns** of Lyme 11/23/2003

STANLEY,
Keith Alan m. Barbara Jewette **Stanley** 12/10/1977 in Lyme Ctr.

STARK,
Chester A. of Lyme m. Margaret L. **Bliss** of S. Danbury 6/6/1927 in Lebanon; H - 22, laborer, b. Lyme, s/o George E. Stark (Lyme, farmer) and Alice Chaffin (Newport, housewife); W - 18, at home, b. Danbury, d/o Fred P. Bliss (Orange, laborer) and Florence Westcot (Canaan, housewife)

David C. of Lyme m. Lucinda A. **Sullivan** of Manchester 6/11/1903 in Lyme Ctr.; H - 63, laborer, 2nd, b. Lyme, s/o Anson Stark (Hanover, farmer) and Lydia Dodge (Lyme, housework); W - 51, housework, 3rd, b. Jay, ME, d/o Jackson Allen (Jay, ME, farmer) and Salome Bean (Jay, ME, housewife)

George E. of Lyme m. Nancy J. **Bellair** of Newport 8/6/1888 in Newport; H - 21, laborer, b. Lyme, s/o Anson Stark (Albany, VT) and Lucinda Clough (Champlain, NY); W - 21, housekeeper, b. Newport, d/o Philor Bellair (Fletcher, VT) and Nancy A. Lanssil (Westford, VT)

Gerry W. of Lyme m. Jill C. **Hood** of Lyme 9/5/1987 in W. Lebanon

John L. of Lyme m. Edna L. **Hutchins** of Lyme 12/16/1899 in Lebanon; H - 46, carpenter, b. Hanover, s/o John C. Stark and Emeline Warren (Lyme); W - 33, housework, b. Lyme, d/o David K. Dike (Lyme, laborer)

Loren G. of Lyme m. Augusta F. **Dike** of Lyme 8/14/1901 in Lyme; H - 20, laborer, b. Lyme, s/o John L. Stark (Hanover, laborer) and Jennie F. Gordon (Lyme); W - 19, housework, b. Lyme, d/o Volney R. Dike (Lyme, laborer) and Lizzie Nash (Plainfield, housewife)

Robert A. of Lyme m. Mattie **Blake** of Lyme 8/30/1915 in Lyme; H - 22, laborer, b. Newport, s/o George E. Stark (Lyme, farmer) and Alice M. Chaffin (Newport, housewife); W - 18, housework, b. Orange, d/o Alvin Blake (farmer) and Clara Flanders (Orange, housewife)

Thomas B. of Hanover m. Joyce E. **Elder** of Lyme 6/28/1968 in Hanover; H – 22, b. NH, s/o Chester A. Stark and Margaret L. Bliss; W – 24, b. VT, d/o Delbert Mack and Pearl McFarlane

Walter E. of Lyme m. Reine K. **Mooney** of Canaan 6/23/1920 in Lyme; H - 21, laborer, b. Lyme, s/o George E. Stark (Lyme, farmer) and Alice M. Chaffin (Newport, housewife); W - 23, at home, b. Canaan, d/o Arthur E. Mooney (Canaan, farmer) and

Ada E. Wells (Canaan, housewife)

STEARNS,
Brent Ernest of Lyme m. Lori Ann **Pierson** of Lyme --/--/1991
David R. of Lyme m. Anah M. **Race** of Strafford, VT 8/31/1968 in Norwich, VT; H – 19, b. NH, s/o Fred Stearns, Jr. and Edna Hutchins; W – 20, b. NH, d/o Wendell Race and Ada C. Manning
David R. of Lyme m. Glenna H. **Seaver** of Lyme 11/20/1988 in Lyme
Denzil Charles m. Wendy Mae **Guerine** 6/9/1979 in W. Lebanon
Eli Robert of Thetford, VT m. Ramona H. **LaDeau** of Thetford, VT 10/17/1953 in Lyme; H – 18, lumbering, b. Etna, s/o Fred O. Stearns (Meriden) and Doris L. Hazelton (Bristol); W – 16, student, b. Fairlee, VT, d/o Kenneth LaDeau (Hartford, VT) and Arline Trussell (Fairlee, VT)
Fred O., Jr. of Lebanon m. Edna R. **Hutchins** of Lyme 5/28/1949
Fred O., III of Lyme m. Elizabeth G. **Sunn** of Lyme Ctr. 6/26/1976 in Lyme Ctr.; H – b. 12/19/1956 in NH, s/o Fred O. Stearns, Jr. and Edna Hutchins; W – b. 7/20/1957 in NH, d/o George Sunn, Jr. and Daisy Guthrie

STEBBINS,
Jesse A. of Newbury, VT m. Elizabeth **Stone** of Newbury, VT 5/20/1950 in Lyme; H – 64, trackman, b. Newbury, VT, s/o Edward Stebbins (Newbury, VT) and Martha Townsend (Bethel, VT); W – 53, housewife, 2nd – W, b. Waterbury, VT, d/o Will Lovely (Plattsburgh, NY) and Harriet Stafford (Waterbury, VT)

STEELE,
Carl F. of Lyme m. Lena L. **Cutting** of Lyme 1/14/1903 in Lyme; H - 30, farmer, b. Lyme, s/o David C. Steele (Lyme, farmer) and Matilda M. Pushee (Lyme, housewife); W - 24, housework, b. Lyme, d/o Frank Cutting (Lyme, auctioneer) and Ella F. Warren (Lyme, housework)

STEPHENS,
James T. M. of Lyme m. Flora B. **Hadlock** of Lyme 4/26/1894 in Lyme; H - 24, minister, b. Rockaway, NJ, s/o James L. Stephens (Cornwall, England) and Mary Mayle (Cornwall, England); W - 18, d/o Charles P. Hadlock (Rock Island, builder) and Drucilla Hoover (Springfield, OH, housekeeper)

STERNBACH,
Yaron of Watertown, MA m. Katherine Eleanor **MacDonald** of Watertown, MA 6/25/1994

STEVENS,
Fred H. of Lyme m. Dorothy C. **Hilt** of Claremont 5/19/1945 in Lyme; H – 29, mechanic, b. E. Charleston, VT, s/o Walter Stevens (Newport Ctr., VT, farmer) and Annie Taylor (Island Pond, VT, housewife); W – 19, shoeworker, b. Lewiston, ME, d/o William Hilt (Lewiston, ME, machinist) and Dorothy Bradstreet (Bridgewater, ME, housewife)

Henry Wheeler of W. Lebanon m. Florence Dike **Claflin** of Lyme 11/25/1994

Ira H. of Lyme m. Eleanor F. **Swasey** of Norwich, VT 9/28/1935 in Lyme; H - 21, steam fitter, b. E. Charleston, VT, s/o Walter M. Stevens (Newport, VT, farmer) and Annie E. Taylor (E. Charleston, VT, housewife); W - 18, at home, b. Hartford, VT, d/o Harry E. Swasey (Norwich, VT, laborer) and Mildred Logan (Thetford, VT, housewife)

James Casey of Lyme m. Lorna M. **Craig** of Lyme 6/22/1985 in Orford

John A. of W. Burke, VT m. Eunice M. **Taylor** of W. Burke, VT 3/30/1932 in Lyme; H - 22, laborer, b. Westmore, VT, s/o Fred Stevens (Barton, VT, carpenter) and Mabel Uran (Lincoln, NE, housewife); W - 22, housework, 2nd - D, b. Barton, VT, d/o Fred Smith (laborer) and Ella Heath (housewife)

John T. of Brookville, PA m. Sarah D. **Sansbury** of Lyme 7/24/1965 in Lyme; H – 24, US Army, b. Pittsburgh, PA, s/o John Stevens and Sarah Ferguson; W – 23, teacher, b. Hanover, d/o John Sansbury and Dorothy Gregory

STEYN,
Mark David Henry of Lyme m. Ann Mary **Crookenden** of London, England 4/15/1993

STICKNEY,
Charles L. of Lyme m. Inese **Hadlock** of Lyme 9/15/1888 in Lyme; H - 40, farmer, 2nd, b. Westford, VT, s/o J. N. Stickney (Fletcher, VT) and H. McAdams (Westford, VT); W - 25, housekeeper, 2nd, b. Munroe, d/o James Hadlock (Bath) and Mary J. Fifield (Salisbury)

STILL,
George D. of Lyme m. Flora M. **Parker** of Marlboro, MA 9/18/1910 in Marlboro, MA; H - 33, farmer, b. S. Strafford, VT, d/o Benjamin Still (Claremont, farmer) and Mary Etta Bragg (S. Strafford, VT, housework); W - 35, stenographer, b. Berlin, MA, d/o Sylvanus H. Parker and Marietta Gates (sewing)

STOCKING,
Steven S. of Fairlee, VT m. Rachel I. **Gamage** of Lyme 9/5/1971 in Lyme; H – 22, b. CT, s/o Donald Stocking and Shirley Armstrong; W – 21, b. NH, d/o Russell Gamage and Irene Briggs

STOCKMAN,
Ralph R. of Bradford, VT m. Leomia O. **Covey** of Bradford, VT 3/31/1945 in Lyme; H – 23, farmer, b. Lowell, VT, s/o Harold Stockman (Stowe, VT) and Alice Coolbeth (Lowell, MA, housewife); W – 18, at home, b. Eltona, NY, d/o Harland Covey (Ellenburg, NY, lumberman) and Delia Clark (Ellenburg, NY, housewife)

STONE,
Harold S. of Lyme m. Violet M. **Sturtevant** of Lyme 8/25/1950 in Lyme; H – 21, carpenter, b. Hanover, s/o Herman Stone (Hanover) and Alleen Bates (Lebanon); W – 20, housework, b. Andover, d/o Carl Sturtevant (Canada)

Herman M. of Hanover m. Alleen E. **Bates** of Lyme 1/7/1921 in Lyme; H - 24, farmer, b. Hanover, s/o Charles W. Stone (Danbury) and Ida Marshall (Pittsfield, housewife); W - 21, housework, b. Lebanon, d/o Sidney W. Bates (W. Fairlee, VT, farmer) and Gertrude Hanchett (Plainfield, housewife)

STOWE,
Robert E. of Hartford, VT m. Barbara J. **Bailey** of Lyme 6/22/1957 in White River Jct.; H – 26, s/o Guy Stowe and Ernestine Roberts; W – 22, d/o Henry A. Bailey and Ida M. Hall, res. – Lyme

STRANGE,
William B. of Hanover m. Romona E. **Conant** of Lyme 6/29/1968 in Randolph, VT; H – 27, b. TX, s/o Lonnie B. Strange and Dovie L. Kyser; W – 26, b. VT, d/o Edward Conant and Doris Sargent

STRAW,
John F. of Lyme m. Gertrude M. **Whipple** of Lyme 2/10/1896 in Lyme; H - 33, laborer, b. Lyme, s/o Daniel M. Straw (Lyme, farmer) and Hannah H. Weed (Orford, housewife); W - 22, housework, b. Lyme, d/o Carroll C. Whipple (Lyme, laborer) and Mary E. Skinner (Lyme, housewife)

STRONG,
George F. of Lyme m. Hattie F. **Quint** of Lyme 1/1/1887 in Lyme; H - 21, farmer, b. Meriden, s/o Dillias D. Strong and Ellen Corey (Meriden); W - 21, housekeeper, b. Orford, d/o James Quint and Hattie Quint

STROUT,
Francis G. of Lyme m. Dorothy A. **Roberts** of N. Thetford, VT 8/27/1960 in Thetford, VT; H – s/o Gerald G. Strout and Elizabeth R. Wilmot, res. – Lyme; W – d/o Edwin G. Roberts and Stella M. Warren, res. – Thetford, VT

STRUCKHOFF,
Eugene Charles, III of Lyme m. Dolores Jean **Crate** of Enfield 5/29/1976 in W. Lebanon; H – b. 11/27/1944 in ME, s/o Eugene Struckhoff and Ruth N. Brewer; W – b. 1/16/1954 in NH, d/o Donald A. Crate and Evelyn J. Stanford

STRUE,
Willie D. of Lyme m. Cora H. **Lovejoy** of Lyme 12/28/1899 in Lyme; H - 23, laborer, b. Orford, s/o George E. Strue (Canada, laborer) and Alma E. Lamphere (Thetford, VT); W - 21, housework, b. Lyme, d/o Lewis P. Lovejoy (Orford, farmer) and Hattie Perkins (Canaan, housework)

SULLIVAN,
Brian of Madison, WI m. Katherine **Maddock** of Madison, WI 8/22/1992

SUNN,
George N., III m. Lorie S. **Hood** 2/11/1977 in Lyme

SUPER,
Kenneth George of Orford m. Elena Alexandrovna **Ainalovan** of

Orford 6/25/1999

SUTOR,
Scott of W. Fairlee, VT m. Mary Jane **Daly** of W. Fairlee, VT 7/10/1993

SWIFT,
Merlin K. of Thetford, VT m. Christine M. **Schuster** of Thetford, VT 8/19/1944 in Lyme; H – 21, farmer, b. N. Thetford, VT, s/o Kenneth J. Swift (Thetford, VT, mechanic) and Carrie I. Root (Strafford, VT, housewife); W – 19, housework, 2nd – D, b. Thetford, VT, d/o Luther Smith (Lyme, machinist) and Ellen Bailey (Strafford, VT, housewife)

TABBUTT,
Kenneth D. of Norwich, VT m. Rita V. **Malhotra** of Silver Spring, MD 10/21/1989 in Lyme

TANGERMAN,
John T. of Lyme m. Andree **Mitchell** of Hanover 5/15/1965 in Lyme; H – 33, geographer, 2nd, b. Brooklyn, NY, s/o Elmer Tangerman and Mary Christopher; W – 31, medical tech., b. Montreal, PQ, d/o John M. Mitchell and Jeanne Bertrand

TANNIN,
Benjamin H. of New York, NY m. Lisa Hope **Hirsch** of New York, NY 8/1/1993

TATTERSALL,
Al. E. of Lyme m. Dorothy **Eastman** of Lebanon 2/1/1947 in Benton; H – 29, carpenter, b. Lyme, s/o George Tattersall (Orford, retired) and Emily A. Mousley (N. Thetford, VT, housewife); W – 30, housework, b. Montpelier, VT, d/o Jerry Eastman (Randolph, VT, lumberman) and Bessie Cody (Granville, VT, household)
Ernest of Lyme m. Evelyn M. **Cox** of Concord 11/1/1929 in Lyme; H – 27, laborer, b. Lyme, s/o George E. Tattersall (Lyme, carpenter) and Hattie Merrill (Orford, housewife); W – 19, housework, b. Concord, d/o George H. Cox (Meredith, teamster) and Elizabeth Baker (Concord, housewife)
George E., Jr. of Lyme m. Hattie G. **Merrill** of Lyme 4/29/1901 in

Lyme; H - 24, laborer, b. Orford, s/o George E. Tattersall (England, farmer) and Mary H. Sweet (Plainfield, housewife); W - 18, housework, b. Orford, d/o Elijah N. Merrill (laborer) and Isabelle Greenough (housewife)

George E., Jr. of Lyme m. Emily A. **Mousley** of Lyme 3/19/1914 in Lyme; H - 36, carpenter, 2nd, b. Orford, s/o George E. Tattersall (Fairlee, VT, laborer) and Mary Sweet (Plainfield, housewife); W - 19, housework, b. Lyme, d/o Orton M. Mousley (Orford, buttermaker) and Hattie Fales (Lyme, housewife)

George E., Jr. of Lyme m. Bertha L. **Wells** of Dalton 3/29/1945 in Lyme; H – 20, sawmill emp., b. Lyme, s/o George E. Tattersall (Orford, carpenter) and Emily Mousley (Thetford, VT, housewife); W – 18, mill worker, b. Littleton, d/o Perley Wells (Whitefield, woodsman) and Alice Chellefoel (Canada, housewife)

Isaac of Lyme m. Malinda J. **Fitzgobbins** of Holyoke, MA 10/25/1900 in Lyme; H - 43, farmer, b. England, s/o Abraham Tattersall (England, laborer) and Hannah Eaton (England); W - 42, housework, 2nd, b. Canada, d/o ----- Cole (England, laborer)

TAYLOR,
Brian Allen of Lyme m. Holly Janette **Jenks** of Lyme 10/25/1997

TEMPLE,
Leslie J. of Lyme m. Amy L. **Pushee** of Lyme 8/7/1896 in Lyme; H - 25, laborer, b. Lowell, VT, s/o Joel Temple (Fletcher, VT, farmer) and ----- Stratton (Bakersfield, VT, housewife); W - 17, housework, b. Lyme, d/o Clarence S. Pushee (Lyme, farmer) and Fannie C. Post (Lyme, housewife)

TENSEN,
Arend R. of Lyme m. Paula R. **Balch** of Lyme 7/27/2002

TEWKSBURY,
M. B. of Winthrop, MA m. Helen E. **Fairfield** of Lyme 6/25/1908 in Lyme; H - 30, clerk, b. Winthrop, MA, s/o John Tewksbury (Winthrop, MA, farmer) and Caroline Banks (Winthrop, MA, housework); W - 28, teacher, b. Lyme, d/o Payson Fairfield (Lyme, clerk) and Caroline Churchill (Lyme, housework)

THOMAS,
Herbert G. of Lyme m. Lavina E. **Ormsby** of Springfield, VT 6/7/1917 in Lyme; H - 20, laborer, b. Lyme, s/o George W. Thomas (Lyme, carpenter) and Elizabeth V. George (Knowlton, Broome, PQ, housewife); W - 21, domestic, b. Peasleeville, NY, d/o J. Elisha Ormsby (Peru, NY, farming) and Julia Soulia (Essex, NY, housewife)

Jeffrey S. of Lyme m. Tessa **Vander Meijden** of Lyme 9/22/1985 in Lyme

William B. of Tilton m. Florence L. **Flint** of Lyme 9/22/1914 in Plymouth; H - 27, machinist, b. Lyme, s/o George W. Thomas (Lyme, carpenter) and Elizabeth V. George (Knowlton, PQ, dressmaker); W - 28, teacher, b. Boston, MA, d/o Moses L. Flint (Lyme, merchant) and Mary A. Richards (Boston, MA, housewife)

THOMPSON,
Allen J. of Lyme Ctr. m. Ellen F. **Yurek** of Lyme 7/10/1976 in Hanover; H – b. 4/15/1948 in NH, s/o Charles Thompson and Ruby Watson; W – b. 12/12/1950 in NJ, d/o William Yurek and Doris Gleason

Arthur W. of Lyme m. Rita Bell **Small** of Lyme 3/4/1956 in Thetford, VT; H – 19, US Army, s/o William H. Thompson and Della E. Bryant, res. – Lyme; W – 21, bookkeeper, d/o Harry A. Small and Daisy Melendy, res. – Lyme

Charles A. of Lyme m. Ruby A. **Watson** of Newbury, VT 12/31/1946 in Lyme; H – 20, laborer, b. Lyme, s/o Joseph Thompson (S. Ham, PQ, fireman) and Grace Archer (Colebrook, housewife); W – 19, at home, b. Newbury, VT, d/o Reginald Watson (Springfield, MA) and Grace Lund (Groton, VT, housewife)

Charles E. of Hanover m. Alice M. **Stark** of Lyme 8/12/1913 in Lyme; H - 19, teamster, b. Dudswell, PQ, s/o William W. Thompson (Dudswell, PQ, farmer) and Lillian F. Deavy (Danville, PQ, housewife); W - 19, teacher, b. Lyme, d/o George E. Stark (Lyme, farmer) and Alice M. Chaffin (Newport, housewife)

Frank P. of Lyme m. Effie **Cole** of Lyme 12/7/1898 in Lyme; H - 36, laborer, b. Glover, VT, s/o Z. L. Thompson and Alvira Fullington; W - 23, housekeeper, b. Lyme, d/o Albert C. Cole (Dorchester, farmer) and Alma Noyes (Manchester, housewife)

George of Lyme m. Marjorie **Brockway** of Lyme 6/3/1922 in Lyme;

H - 26, laborer, b. S. Ham, PQ, s/o Joseph G. Thompson (S. Ham, PQ, farmer) and Annie M. Devie (Danville, Canada, housewife); W - 18, tel. opr., b. Lyme, d/o G. A. Brockway (Lyme, laborer) and Nellie Dimick (Iron Hill, Canada, deceased)

George W. of Lyme m. Josephine M. **Smith** of Lyme 3/21/1935 in Piermont; H - 39, carpenter, 2nd - W, b. S. Ham, PQ, s/o Joseph G. Thompson (S. Ham, PQ, farmer) and Annie M. Devey (Danville, PQ, housewife); W - 22, domestic, 2nd - D, b. Lyme, d/o Albert B. Dennis (Stratford, farmer) and Maud A. Piper (Lyme, housewife)

Henry A. of Hanover m. Dorothy L. **Cunningham** of Lyme 2/25/1932 in Lyme; H - 22, laborer, b. Lyme, s/o William W. Thompson (S. Ham, PQ, farmer) and Lilly F. Devery (Danville, PQ, housewife); W - 21, housework, b. Big Timber, MT, d/o Lucius Cunningham (Freedom, ME, farmer) and Marie Paul (Spring Valley, ME, housewife)

Kenneth R. of Lyme m. Elisabeth **Brown** of Lyme 9/17/1988 in Lyme

Wayne J. of Lyme m. Ruth M. **Hook** of Orford 6/4/1971 in Orford; H – 23, b. NH, s/o Charles A. Thompson and Ruby Watson; W – 20, b. NH, d/o Lester E. Hook and Marian Lanefski

William H. of Lyme m. Della E. **Bryant** of Lyme 8/4/1924 in Lebanon; H - 36, laborer, b. Canada, s/o Joseph G. Thompson (Canada, laborer) and Mary A. Dewey (Canada, housewife); W - 16, at home, b. Lyme, d/o Fred J. Bryant (Lyme, farmer) and Florence Henry (Thetford, VT, housewife)

THOMS,
Frank R., III m. Margaret C. **Taylor** 9/29/1979 in Lyme

THORNTON,
Geoffrey G. of Lyme m. Nancy S. **Holland** of Norwich, VT 4/4/2001

THORP,
John Andersen, IV m. Janet Lee **Piper** 8/29/1981 in Strafford, VT

THURSTON,
Carlos H. of Lyme m. Marvel K. **Guyer** of Hanover 3/17/1951 in Lyme; H – 17, laborer, b. Lyme, s/o Lyle Thurston (Bradford, VT) and Sibyl Wilmott (Lyme); W – 19, housework, b. Vershire, VT, d/o Napoleon Guyer (Hanover) and Hazel Palmer (Chateaugay, NY)

Howard of Bradford, VT m. Alice M. **Smith** of Lyme 7/24/1937 in Fairlee, VT; H - 21, farmer, b. Brandon, VT, s/o C. F. Thurston (Bradford, VT) and Ethel Eaton (Landaff); W - 38, housework, 2nd - W, b. W. Fairlee, VT, d/o John F. Bixby (W. Fairlee, VT) and Lizzie Marion (W. Fairlee, VT)

TIBBETTS,
Karl E. of Lyme m. Delia M. **Bailey** of Lyme 4/26/1958 in Lyme; H – 21, s/o Carl Tibbetts and Elmira Chipogh, res. – Pike; W – 23, d/o Henry J. Bailey and Margaret Wilmot, res. – Lyme

TIBBITS,
Richard E. of NH m. Katherine A. **Bean** of NH 2/26/1972 in Hanover; H – 29, b. NH, s/o Forrest Tibbits and Ethel Stone; W – 24, b. NH, d/o Raymond Larocque, Sr. and Louise Adams

TILDEN,
Karl C., Jr. of E. Thetford, VT m. Janet B. **Clark** of Lyme 12/31/1960 in N. Thetford, VT; H – s/o Karl C. Tilden and Hester Rogers, res. – E. Thetford, VT; W – d/o William G. Clark and Ruth Callahan, res. – Lyme

TITCOMB,
Peter A. of Lyme m. Lisa B. **Morris** of N. Haven, CT 10/6/1968 in N. Haven, CT; H – 24, b. MA, s/o John Titcomb and Janet Foote; W – 21, b. Hartford, CT, d/o Irving Morris and Rita Shaw

TOMSEN,
Chris E. m. Vera **Molnar** 12/30/1981 in Lyme

TONER,
Thomas William of Lyme m. Rita Mae **Stearns** of Lyme 2/2/1974 in Hanover; H – b. 3/27/1951 in NJ, s/o Charles Toner and Beulah Willette; W – b. 8/12/1955 in NH, d/o Eli Stearns and Ramona LaDeau

TORRES,
Andres D. of Enfield m. Calysta J. **Reed** of Lyme 8/9/2003

TOYNBEE,
William M. of Ottawa, Canada m. Mary W. **Wright** of Lyme 7/1/1966

in Lebanon; H – 39, teacher, b. Canada, s/o Richard Toynbee and Jessie Mouat; W – 38, social worker, b. Yonkers, NY, d/o John K. Wright and Katherine W. McGiffert

TOZIER,
Everett C. of Boston, MA m. Edith E. **Kempton** of Lyme 4/28/1915 in Lyme; H - 21, laborer, b. Newport, RI, s/o Frank M. Tozier (Newport, RI, painter) and Mina Phillips (Canada, housewife); W - 26, housework, 2nd, b. Grantham, d/o Willard Kempton (Croydon, physician) and Elvira H. Johnston (W. Springfield, housewife)

TRAVIS,
Peter W. of Chicago, IL m. Valerie J. **Mooney** of Elgin, IL 6/17/1967 in Lyme; H – 28, student, b. Philadelphia, PA, s/o Walter W. Travis and Harriet D. Small; W – 25, teacher, b. Ireland, d/o Kenneth Mooney and Mary Simpson

TROTTIER,
Douglas R. of Lyme m. Corinne E. **Gamage** of Lyme 8/14/1955 in Lyme; H – 20, student, b. Lebanon, s/o Rodolphe Trottier (VT) and Olive D. Goodell (NH); W – 20, nurse, b. Litchfield, ME, d/o Russell W. Gamage (Litchfield, ME) and Irene Briggs (ME)
Richard P. of Lyme m. Carol J. **Sausville** of Hanover 4/12/1958 in Hanover; H – 21, s/o Rudolph J. Trottier and Olive D. Goodell, res. – Lyme; W – 20, d/o Victor J. Sausville and Edith M. LaBombard, res. – Hanover

TROUT,
Bruce David of Laurel, MD m. Heidi Brookes **Cornwell** of Lyme 10/20/1990 in Hanover

TRUSLOW,
David W., Jr. of Hollywood, CA m. Barbara L. **Begun** of Hollywood, CA --/--/1991

TRUSSELL,
Ronald Kenneth of Lyme m. Madelene Evelyn **Estes** of Lyme 8/22/1959 in Lyme; H – s/o Kenneth Trussell and Margaret McMillan, res. – Lyme; W – d/o Leonard R. Estes and Evelyn D. Powers, res. – Lyme

TULLAR,
Rendall C. of W. Fairlee, VT m. Katherine K. **Bryant** of Lyme 4/15/1967 in Lyme; H – 52, truck driver, b. Corinth, VT, s/o Charles E. Tullar and Alice Hastings; W – 52, secretary, b. Plymouth, d/o Everett Keniston and Martha Savage

TULLER,
Merlin A. of Corinth, VT m. Ivah A. A. **Bassett** of Lyme 11/29/1936 in Lyme; H - 20, farmer, b. Corinth, VT, s/o Arthur F. Tuller (Corinth, VT, farmer) and Anna M. Hooker (Corinth, VT, housewife); W - 19, at home, b. Canada, d/o Albert A. Bassett (Canada, mechanic) and Beatrice B. Bently (Canada, housewife)

TUPPER,
Ellsworth T. of Lyme m. Joanne E. **Thompson** of Hanover 3/2/1956 in Hanover; H – 22, bellman, s/o Charles E. Tupper of Sunapee and Alberta Uline of Lyme; W – 19, telephone operator, d/o Henry Thompson of Lyme and Dorothy Cunningham of MT

TURNER,
Hazen E. of Lyme m. Christine M. **Lake** of Keene 10/1/1916 in Saxtons River, VT; H - 22, machinist, b. S. Columbia, s/o Ambrose A. Turner (Hebron, ME, smith) and Susie Elliott (Cookshire, PQ, housewife); W - 21, at home, b. Keene, d/o Henry E. Lake (Rockingham, VT) and Virginia Wilkins (Weston, VT)

TUTTLE,
Freeman of Lowell, MA m. Blanche M. **Day** of Fairlee, VT 5/17/1937 in Lyme; H - 22, laborer, b. Dover, s/o Harry Tuttle (Dover, farmer) and Martha ----- (Newmarket, housewife); W - 18, domestic, b. Collins, OH, d/o Clair P. Day (Collins, OH, electrician) and Edith A. Waldron (Newbury, VT, housewife)
William M. of Lyme m. Donna L. **Gray** of Lyme 12/12/2003

TYLER,
Donald L. of Barnet, VT m. Marion C. **Bonnett** of Lyme 6/28/1940 in Fairlee, VT; H – 25, laborer, b. N. Haverhill, s/o Leon E. Tyler (Benton) and Arlene Dow (Meredith); W – 19, nurse, b. Ely, VT, d/o Frank Bonnett (Orford) and Rose Wilcox (Thetford, VT)

ULINE,

Hiram, Jr. of Lyme m. Grace M. **Gilbert** of Lyme 10/6/1903 in Lyme; H - 20, laborer, b. Lyme, s/o Hiram Uline (Canaan, barber) and Addie L. Lamphere (Lyme, housewife); W - 16, housework, b. Littleton, d/o George C. Gilbert (London, laborer) and Melvena B. Byron (Littleton, housework)

Kenneth H. of Lyme m. Marion R. **Bull** of Lyme 6/21/1947 in Hanover; H – 20, carpenter, b. Hanover, s/o Hiram Uline (Lyme, carpenter) and Grace Gilbert (Littleton, housewife); W – 25, nurse, b. Ashland, ME, d/o Wilbur I. Bull (Carlisle, MA, minister) and Anna Coffin (Ashland, ME, housewife)

Millard R. of Lyme m. Susie E. **Cadwell** of Thetford, VT 11/21/1928 in Thetford, VT; H - 21, laborer, b. Lyme, s/o Hiram Uline, Jr. (Lyme, laborer) and Grace M. Gilbert (Littleton, housewife); W - 23, dressmaker, b. Thetford, VT, d/o Louis M. Cadwell (Thetford, VT, farmer) and Eliza D. Eastman (Strafford, VT, housewife)

Ray A. of Lyme m. Lena F. **Brown** of Bradford, VT 3/11/1944 in Bradford, VT; H – 24, mechanic, b. Lyme, s/o Hiram Uline (Lyme, carpenter) and Grace Gilbert (Littleton, housewife); W – 21, bookkeeper, b. Newbury, VT, d/o Fred F. Brown (Strafford, VT, tel. const.) and Gladys Flanders (Newbury, VT, housewife)

VALENTA,

Stephen John of Lyme m. Deborah Jean **Olish** of Lyme 5/29/1999

VALLEY,

Clifton H., Jr. of Warren m. Marilyn A. **Balch** of Lyme 10/29/1960 in Orford; H – s/o Clifton H. Valley and Selma H. Litz, res. – Warren; W – d/o Raymond H. Balch and Esther E. Smith, res. – Lyme Ctr.

VANCE,

George H. of Campton m. Alice M. **Carr** of Lyme 2/14/1925 in Fairlee, VT; H - 21, foreman, b. Groton, VT, s/o Isaac R. Vance (Groton, VT) and Lillian Page (Groton, VT); W - 18, at home, b. Bristol, d/o Charles J. Carr (Albany, NY) and Daisy E. Day (Waits River, VT, housewife)

VAUGHAN,

George F., Jr. of Thetford, VT m. Daisy E. **Thompson** of Lyme

5/10/1953 in Lyme; H – 21, US Navy, b. Norwich, VT, s/o
George F. Vaughan, Sr. (MA) and Beatrice H. Emerson (VT); W
– 28, hairdresser, b. Lyme, d/o William H. Thompson (Quebec)
and Della Bryant (Lyme)

Richard W. of Thetford, VT m. Elizabeth **Thompson** of Lyme
6/28/1952 in Lyme; H – 21, US Army, b. Hanover, s/o George
Vaughan (MA) and Beatrice Emerson (VT); W – 21,
hairdresser, b. Lyme, d/o William Thompson (Canada) and
Della Bryant (Lyme)

Robert C. of Thetford, VT m. Lillian M. **Hill** of Lyme 6/21/1933 in
Lyme; H - 23, farmer, b. Thetford, VT, s/o Robert H. Vaughan
(Worcester, MA, carpenter) and Elizabeth Condoll (Worcester,
MA, housewife); W - 22, nurse, b. Quebec, d/o Talbert Hill
(Chateaugay, NY, farmer) and Lila M. Leet (Quebec,
housewife)

VEEDER,
Carlton L. of Cuttyhunk, MA m. Francis E. **Ackerman** of Lyme
5/10/1920 in Orford; H - 23, fisherman, b. New Bedford, MA, s/o
Frank B. Veeder (New Bedford, MA, fisherman) and Sadie
Keeney (New Bedford, MA, housewife); W - 17, at home, b.
Orford, d/o William J. Ackerman (St. Albans, VT, farmer) and
Esther E. Emery (St. Albans, VT, housewife)

VINSON,
Curtis M. m. Alison A. **Kelsey** 8/29/1981 in Hanover

VOGT,
Douglas of Lyme m. Mary Isabella **Arnold** of Lyme --/--/1991

WADE,
Richard of Lyme m. Hilda **Robichaud** of Lyme 12/31/1992

WAGNER,
Frederick F. of Lyme m. Creigh C. **Stern** of Lyme 7/31/1955 in
Lyme; H – 38, business, b. WI, s/o Edward R. Wagner (WI) and
Ellen C. Solberg (WI); W – 35, housewife, divorced, b. IL, d/o
John J. Collins (OH) and Harriet D. Oliphant (PA)

WALDRON,
Charles of Lyme m. Anna C. **Hurd** of Lyme 1/1/1906 in Lyme; H -

55, laborer, 2nd, b. Wentworth, s/o Nathaniel Waldron (farmer) and Betsy B. Davis (Wentworth, housework); W - 50, housework, 2nd, b. OH, d/o George Riggel (OH, farmer) and Hannah Mants (PA, housework)

WALKER,
Joseph F., Jr. of Fairlee, VT m. Beverly **Bailey** of Lyme 10/29/1950 in Lyme; H – 24, salesman, b. Highgate Ctr., VT, s/o Joseph Walker (Methuen, MA) and Catherine Cousins (Kennebunk, ME): W – 20, clerk, b. Hanover, d/o Henry A. Bailey (Lyme) and Ida Hall (NH)

WALLACE,
Tracy G. of Lyme m. Lisa A. **Jones** of Lyme 9/21/2002

WALN,
David A. of Fairbanks, AK m. Rachel A. **Hanchett** of Fairbanks, AK 12/20/1984 in Lyme

WALTERS,
John T. of MA m. Joan **Goldthwait** of NH 5/6/1972 in Lyme; H – 26, b. MA, s/o Edward Walters and Edith Leif; W – 29, b. NH, d/o Lawrence Goldthwait and Charlotte Sanders

WARD,
Perley G. of Lyme m. Rose M. **Bressett** of Orford 12/1/1909 in Lyme; H - 26, farmer, b. Bethlehem, s/o Caleb F. Ward (Pittsburg, farmer) and Ann L. Gordon (Lisbon, housework); W - 20, housework, b. Hanover, d/o William E. Bressett (farmer) and Hattie Bill (housewife)

WARE,
Edgar R. of Lyme m. Edith M. **Morrison** of Lyme 6/13/1906 in Lyme; H – 21, farmer, b. Thetford, VT, s/o Daniel A. Ware (Thetford, VT, farmer) and Luella F. Morsy (Manchester, housework); W - 22, housework, b. Somerville, MA, d/o Roland Morrison (Fairlee, VT, farmer) and Lizzie G. Chaffee (E. Providence, RI, housewife)

WARREN,
Arad J. of Lyme m. Harriet A. **Balch** of Lyme 10/6/1923 in Lyme; H -

67, ins. agent, 2nd - W, b. Lyme, s/o Asa Warren (Lyme, farmer) and Mary A. Derby (Lyme, housewife); W - 49, teacher, 2nd - W, b. Lyme, d/o Alfred W. Pushee (Lyme, farmer) and Edna E. Steele (Lyme, housewife)

Charles H. of Lyme m. Mary E. **Colby** of Lyme 11/27/1890 in Post Mills, VT; H - 29, farmer, b. Lyme, s/o John P. Warren and Eliza J. Colby; W - housekeeper, b. Lyme, d/o Alonzo P. Colby and Elizabeth Cook

Fred N. of Lyme m. Jennie M. **Camp** of Lebanon 12/22/1887 in Lyme; H - 29, farmer, b. Lyme, s/o Cyrus N. Warren (Lyme) and Miriam H. Lamphere (Thetford, VT); W - 21, housekeeper, b. Hanover, d/o George Camp (St. Johnsbury, VT) and Mary A. Runnels (Hanover)

WARSHAUER,
Lewis J. of Hanover m. Janet G. **Gierlatowicz** of Lyme 4/4/1976 in Hanover; H – b. 12/14/1951 in DC, s/o Martin Warshauer and Arline Meylach; W – b. 11/22/1948 in NH, d/o Walter Gierlatowicz and Donna Hover

WASKOW,
Andrew Vincent of NY m. Melinda Maxwell **Frank** of NY 8/5/2000

WATERBURY,
Calvin H. of Lyme m. Helen E. **Tingets** of Norwalk, CT 11/8/1958 in Lyme; H – 27, s/o Leon E. Waterbury and Elizabeth W. Litchfield, res. – Lyme; W – 20, d/o Lewis Tingets and Helene Kiba, res. – Norwalk, CT

WATERMAN,
Erni C. of Thetford, VT m. Ella B. **Wilder** of Lyme 4/3/1917 in Thetford, VT; H - 63, farming, 2nd, b. Thetford, VT, s/o David Waterman (Norwich, VT) and Roxana Newcomb (Thetford, VT); W - 58, 2nd, b. Lebanon, d/o George W. Berry (Alexandria) and Prudence Squires (Cornish)

WATERS,
Ralph of Littleton m. Ednor **Davis** of Lyme 1/9/1906 in Littleton; H - 23, laborer, b. Lyman, s/o Henry Waters (Bath, laborer) and Emma Williams (Lisbon, housewife); W - 21, housework, b. Canada, d/o William Davis (England, engineer) and Anna Lines

(England, housewife)

WATKINS,
William A. of Lyme m. Mary Ann **Alloway** of Lyme 10/31/1989 in Lyme

WATTS,
Donald E. of Lyme m. Mildred M. **Hazen** of Lyme 2/17/1937 in Lyme; H - 21, farmer, b. Canaan, s/o Ned E. Watts (Hanover, farmer) and Barbara Thompson (Canada, housewife); W - 27, domestic, 2nd - D, b. Strafford, VT, d/o John W. Hill (NH, farmer) and Mary Nawn (Canada, housewife)

WAUGH,
H. Bernard, Jr. of Lyme m. Mary A. **Grover** of Lyme 8/4/1984 in Woodstock

WEBB,
Charles B. of Lyme m. Rhoda E. **Smith** of Hanover 12/15/1892; H - 32, painter, b. Lyme, s/o Henry O. Webb (Lyme, farmer) and Mary M. Cline (Lyme, housewife); W - 25, housekeeper, b. Hanover, d/o Alonzo A. Smith (Hanover, farmer) and Julia A. Heath (Colebrook, housewife)

Charles B. of Lyme m. Lucy M. **Conant** of Lyme 1/27/1900 in Lyme; H - 39, painter, 2nd, b. Lyme, s/o Henry O. Webb (Lyme, farmer) and Mary M. Cline (Lyme, housewife); W - 20, housework, b. Lyme, d/o William H. Conant (Lyme) and Rhoda Clough (Canaan)

Charles D. of Lyme m. Nera M. **Bean** of Orford 9/27/1929 in Lyme; H - 23, laborer, b. Lyme, s/o Charles B. Webb (Lyme, painter) and Lucy R. Conant (Lyme, housewife); W - 20, at home, b. Orford, d/o Edwin F. Bean (Orford, farmer) and Alice M. Marsh (Orford, housewife)

Eddie G. of Lyme m. Clyde **Hanchett** of Lyme 7/3/1905 in Hanover; H - 21, farmer, b. Lyme, s/o Henry O. Webb (Lyme, farmer) and Mary Cline (Lyme, housewife); W - 23, housework, b. Lyme, d/o Dennis Hanchett (Hartland, VT, farmer) and Elizabeth Reed (Plainfield, housewife)

Frank O. of Lyme m. Maude L. **Thomas** of Lyme 12/16/1903 in Lyme; H - 23, laborer, b. Hanover, s/o Henry O. Webb (Lyme) and Mary M. Cline (Lyme); W - 19, housework, b. Lyme, d/o

George W. Thomas (Lyme, laborer) and Lizzie V. George (Knowlton, housewife)

Harold C. of Lyme m. Dorothy W. **George** of Fairlee, VT 9/16/1938 in E. Brookfield, VT; H - 23, clerk, b. Lyme, s/o Charles B. Webb (Lyme) and Lucy Conant (Thetford, VT); W - 18, b. Hanover, d/o Hawley George (Thetford, VT) and Marjorie Wheatley (Brookfield, VT)

WEBSTER,
Herbert E. of Lyme Ctr. m. Emily A. **Stevens** of Lebanon 7/6/1969 in Orford; H – 69, b. VT, s/o John H. Webster and Abbie Coates; W – 74, b. VT, d/o Orton Mousley and Hattie Fales

WEEDEN,
Stanley J. of Lyme m. Jean E. **Smith** of Hanover 7/14/1947 in Hanover; H – 19, clerk, b. Bridgewater, VT, s/o Royal E. Weeden (Bridgewater, VT, retired) and Mildred E. Jewett (Lebanon, housewife); W – 19, at home, b. Hanover, d/o Winslow W. Smith (Braintree, VT, caretaker) and Gladys Burnham (Belvidere, VT, housewife)

WELCH,
George H. of Lyme m. Lizzie M. **Morse** of Corinth, VT 4/26/1899 in Corinth, VT; H - 24, laborer, b. Lyme, s/o Joseph R. Welch (Lyme, carpenter) and Zilpha Cutting; W - 17, housework, b. Vershire, VT, d/o M. E. Morse (Middlesex, VT, farmer) and Arabel Young (Fayston, VT, housewife)

George H. of Lyme m. Abbie **Comstock** of Lyme 8/6/1912 in Lyme; H – 49, board sawyer, 2nd, b. Groton, VT, s/o Charles H. Jackson (carpenter) and Alma A. Welch (housework); W – 48, housework, b. Groton, VT, d/o Alfred Comstock (Canada, farmer) and Lucinda Drake (Chelsea, VT, housewife)

WELLS,
Alvin A. of Hastings, FL m. Fannie A. **Temple** of Lyme 9/2/1922 in Lyme; H – 22, laborer, b. Hastings, FL, s/o Alvin A. Wells (Moultrie, FL, carpenter) and May Simms (Moultrie, FL, deceased); W – 19, at home, b. Lyme, d/o Leslie J. Temple (Bakersfield, VT, farmer) and Amy L. Pushee (Lyme, housewife)

WENG,
I-Hsueh Hugo of Los Angeles, CA m. Sheila Anne **McDowell** of Los Angeles, CA 9/5/1993

WEST,
Frank E. of Piermont m. Jennie F. **Blood** of Lyme 4/17/1905 in Lyme; H - 28, merchant, b. Orford, s/o Edwin B. West (Orford, farmer) and Margaret L. Ames (Orford, housewife); W - 27, teacher, b. Orford, d/o Daniel A. Blood (Orford, builder) and Mercy Merrill (Groton, housewife)

WETHERELL,
Walter D. of Lyme m. Celeste M. **Tousignant** of Lyme 7/30/1983 in Lyme

WHITCHER,
Ivan of Lyme m. Thyressa M. **Tucker** of Bradford, VT 5/12/1940 in Lyme; H – 22, farming, b. Orford, s/o Howard Whitcher (Orfordville, mill hand) and Florence Gray (Lyme, housewife); W – 20, housework, b. W. Fairlee, VT, d/o Ernest Tucker (W. Fairlee, VT, laborer) and Lena M. Silloway (W. Fairlee, VT, housewife)

WHITE,
Clayton John of Lyme m. Gabriele **Panzer** of Lyme 8/25/1990 in Lyme

Levi O. of Lyme m. Edith M. **Dimick** of Lyme 9/12/1907 in Lyme; H - 34, farmer, b. Constable, NY, s/o Corliss White (farmer) and Elmira ----- (France, housewife); W - 37, housework, b. Lyme, d/o Charles H. Dimick (Lyme, farmer) and Viola Cook (Lyme, housework)

Richard S., Jr. of N. Dartmouth, MA m. Linda **Stevens** of S. Dartmouth, MA 6/21/1963 in Lyme; H – s/o Richard S. White of Somerset, MA amd ----- Davenport of N. Dartmouth, MA; W – d/o ----- Stevens and ----- Ashley, res. – S. Dartmouth, MA

Robert E. of Middlesex, VT m. Joyce I. **Buska** of Middlesex, VT 8/25/1952 in Lyme; H – 32, carpenter, b. Albany, VT, s/o Orra White (OH) and Grace Clark (VT); W – 25, at home, b. Burlington, VT, d/o John Buska (NY) and Ella Santamore (NY)

WHITESIDE,
Samuel of Waitsfield, VT m. Anna D. **DeLuca** of Warren, VT 6/7/1969 in Lyme; H – 27, b. MI, s/o Samuel Whiteside and Jean Winslow; W – 32, b. CT, d/o George DiScala and Antoinette Iacono

WHITTEMORE,
Albert of Lyme m. Marjorie **Morrison** of Lyme 8/29/1923 in Lyme; H - 21, laborer, b. Orford, s/o Luther Whittemore (Plymouth, farmer) and Carrie Washburn (Lyme, housewife); W - 27, teacher, b. Lyme, d/o Roland Morrison (Fairlee, VT, retired) and Lizzie G. Chaffee (Providence, RI, housewife)

WIGGIN,
Charles H. of Hanover m. Nellie E. **Holmes** of Hanover 4/17/1908 in Manchester; H - 46, laborer, 2nd, b. Amesbury, MA, s/o Benjamin Buzzell (Center Harbor, farmer) and Georgianna Wiggin (Waco, Texas, housework); W - 39, housework, 3rd, b. Haverhill, d/o J. M. Gannett (Haverhill, farmer) and Louise M. Blodgett (Waterford, VT, housework)

WILCOX,
Charles A. of Thetford, VT m. Leola **McEwan** of Lyme 12/15/1915 in Lyme; H - 23, farmer, b. Thetford, VT, s/o Henry F. Wilcox (Thetford, VT, farmer) and Abbie E. Skinner (Lyme, housewife); W - 23, housework, b. ON, d/o John L. McEwan (Matilda, ON, farmer) and Dyanthia Rattray (Wolf Island, ON, housewife)
Henry F. of Thetford, VT m. Abbie E. **Skinner** of Lyme 3/24/1891 in Lyme; H - 39, farmer, b. Thetford, VT, s/o Abner B. Wilcox (Thetford, VT, farmer) and Martha A. Wadleigh (Thetford, VT, housekeeper); W - 20, housekeeper, b. Lyme, d/o Cyrus B. Skinner (Lyme, farmer) and Calista P. Allen (Albany, VT, housekeeper)
Randy M. of Lyme m. Tina L. **Mason** of Lyme 4/14/2000
Robert T. of Fairlee, VT m. Pamela J. **Bacon** of Lyme 11/26/1967 in Lyme; H – 21, truck driver, b. Hanover, s/o Thomas H. Wilcox and Marion DeGoosh; W – 19, doctor's asst., b. Hanover, d/o George W. Bacon and Mina Hill

WILDER,
George E. of Lyme m. Ella A. **Burleigh** of Lyme 2/9/1887 in Lyme; H

- 42, laborer, 2nd, b. W. Wadsboro, VT; W - 34, housekeeper, 2nd, b. Concord, d/o George W. Berry (Alexandria) and Prudence Squires (Cornish)

WILKINSON,
Albert R. of Lyme m. Lottie L. **Holden** of E. Brookfield, MA 11/4/1932 in Lyme; H - 62, poultryman, 2nd - W, b. Dorchester, s/o Henry Wilkinson (England, lumberman) and Ellen Hyde (Barton Landing, VT, housewife); W - 70, pianist, 2nd - W, b. Providence, RI, d/o Charles Green (gas fitter) and Maria J. Brown (Nantucket, MA, housewife)
William J. of Lyme m. Marjorie L. **LaMott** of Lyme 6/5/1926 in Plainfield; H - 26, teacher, b. Portland, ME, s/o Albert Wilkinson (Dorchester, poultryman) and Dora A. Green (Nashua, housewife); W - 20, at home, b. Lyme, d/o James I. LaMott (Dorchester, carpenter) and Pearl M. Wing (Burke, NY, housewife)

WILLIAMS,
Steven of Piermont m. Tiffany **Cole** of Lyme 10/3/1992

WILLIAMSON,
Mark W. of Belmont, MA m. Kathy F. **Vinson** of Belmont, MA 5/5/1984 in Lyme

WILLIGAR,
Stephen Albert of Lyme m. Della H. **Dustin** of Lyme 11/12/1900 in Lyme; H - 27, laborer, 2nd, b. NS, s/o Thomas Willigar (NS, ship builder) and Elizabeth Vickoy (NS, housework); W - 23, teacher, b. Wentworth, d/o Cassens M. Dustin (Dorchester, farmer) and Dema B. Lary (Canaan, housewife)

WILLIS,
Clarence D. m. Marcia A. **MacEwan** 10/29/1979 in Orford

WILMOT,
Earl R. of Lyme m. Florence G. **Covell** of Thetford, VT 9/3/1932 in Thetford, VT; H - 20, laborer, b. Lyme, s/o Leo A. Wilmot (Lyme, farmer) and Fannie M. Chapin (S. Boston, MA, housewife); W - 16, at home, b. Charleston, VT, d/o Merton Covell (Pittsburg, VT) and Gertrude Davenport (Stanstead, PQ,

housewife)

Edwin N. of Lyme m. Sarah A. **Wolcott** of Enfield 6/20/1896 in Lyme; H - 24, farmer, b. Lyme, s/o Newton I. Wilmot (N. Thetford, VT, farmer) and Lizzie A. Ray (Bradford, VT, housewife); W - 19, housework, b. Enfield, d/o William Y. Wolcott (Barnard, VT, wheelwright) and Mary Culver (Pomfret, VT, housewife)

George of Lyme m. Fannie M. **Chapin** of Hanover 7/28/1908 in Lyme; H - 23, laborer, b., Lyme, s/o Eric F. Wilmot (Lyme, farmer) and Minnie Packard (Lyme, housewife); W - 20, housework, b. NS, d/o Charles Chapin (Ludlow, VT, laborer) and Fannie M. ----- (NS, housework)

Homer D. of Lyme m. Flora M. **Wing** of Lyme 9/18/1915 in Lyme; H - 23, farmer, b. Lyme, s/o Erni F. Wilmot (Thetford, VT, farmer) and Minnie E. Packard (Barnard, VT, housewife); W - 17, housework, b. Orford, d/o Milton L. Wing (Chateaugay, NY, farmer) and Nina H. Courtney (Rochester, VT, housewife)

Irvin, Jr. of Lyme m. Sandra **Antilla** of Concord 1/31/1964 in Hanover; H – s/o Irvin A. Wilmot and Lillian D. Sayre of Lyme; W – d/o Axel A. Antilla and Louise E. Guy, res. – Enfield

Irvin A. of Lyme m. Lillian D. **Sayre** of Thetford, VT 8/25/1917 in White River Jct.; H - 29, farming, b. Lyme, s/o Erni F. Wilmot (Thetford, VT, farming) and Minnie E. Packard (Barnard, VT, housewife); W - 21, b. Thetford, VT, d/o Henry Sayre (Thetford, VT, farming) and Rosa L. Dauphinee (NS, housewife)

Kenneth I. of Lyme m. Hannah M. **Camber** of Keene 5/7/1942 in Lyme; H – 29, farmer, b. Lyme, s/o Elber Wilmot (Lyme, farmer) and Myrtle Cummings (Lyme, housewife); W – 32, housewife, D, b. Westmore, VT, d/o Joseph Donna (Montgomery, VT, farmer) and Jennie Arel (Montgomery, VT, housewife)

Kenneth I. of Lyme Ctr. m. Ethel E. **Haskins** of Lyme 10/4/1963 in Charlestown; H – s/o Elber Wilmot and Merlie Cummings of Lyme Ctr.; W – d/o Dennis O'Brien of E. Weare and Florence Rogers

Kenneth I. of Lyme m. Ruth A. **Rapp** of Laconia 7/8/1967 in Hanover; H – 54, janitor, b. Lyme, s/o Albert E. Wilmot and Myrtle Cummings; W – 42, at home, b. Kingston, MA, d/o John Thompson and Cora Gildred

Leaman F. of Lyme m. Goldie **Oliver** of Lyme 12/4/1901 in Lyme; H - 21, farmer, b. Strafford, VT, s/o Erni F. Wilmot (E. Thetford, VT, farmer) and Minnie E. Packard (Tunbridge, VT, housewife);

W - 17, housework, b. Lyme, d/o Henry Oliver and Lillian Roberts (Lyme, housewife)

Leamon F. of Lyme m. Ida J. **Smith** of Lyme 12/31/1927 in N. Thetford, VT; H - 47, farmer, 2nd - W, b. Strafford, VT, s/o Erni F. Wilmot (Thetford, VT, farmer) and Minnie Packard (Tunbridge, VT, housewife); W - 19, domestic, b. Lyme, d/o Carlton A. Smith (Lyme, farmer) and Ida Brissett (Hanover, housewife)

Merle K. of Lyme Ctr. m. Linda L. **Horton** of Hanover 8/17/1963 in Hanover; H – s/o Kenneth Wilmot of Lyme Ctr. and ----- Donna; WE – d/o George E. Horton and ----- L. Gerue, res. – Hanover

Robert I. of Lyme m. Connie Sue **Trowbridge** of Lyme 5/27/1995

Tony Eric of Lyme m. Cammie Lyn **Goodrich** of Lyme 5/12/1990 in Hanover

WILMOTT,

A. Eug. of Stamford, CT m. Elsie **Mack** of Springdale, CT 8/12/1948 in Lyme; H – 28, factory main, b. Stamford, CT, s/o A. Eug. Wilmott (Darien, CT) and Mary C. Dooley (Stamford, CT, housewife); W – 27, bookkeeper, D, b. Springdale, CT, d/o August Mack (Mt. Vernon, NY, engineer) and Lou. Rothacker (Brooklyn, NY, housewife)

Archie F. of Lyme m. Dorothy M. **Brady** of Lyme 1/9/1947 in Union Village, VT; H – 22, laborer, b. Lyme, s/o Homer D. Wilmott (Lyme) and Flora M. Wing (Lyme); W – 16, at home, b. Newport, d/o John E. Brady (Cheyenne, WY) and Ethel M. Burr (Strafford, VT)

Chester of Lyme m. Margaret **Hastings** of Corinth, VT 11/14/1952 in Lyme; H – 26, refri. serviceman, b. Lyme, s/o Homer Wilmott (Lyme) and Flora Wing (Lyme); W – 22, teacher, b. Corinth, VT, d/o George Hastings (VT) and Bernice Huntley (VT)

Jess A. of Lyme m. Vera M. **Howe** of Lebanon 7/25/1958 in Lebanon; H – 25, s/o Homer D. Wilmott and Flora Wing, res. – Lyme; W – 18, d/o Edward C. Howe and Hazel A. Martin, res. – Plainfield

Lenwood of Lyme m. Viola B. **Merryfield** of Thetford, VT 12/12/1944 in Orford; H – 26, sawmill emp., b. Lyme, s/o Homer D. Wilmott (Lyme, farmer) and Flora Wing (Lyme, housework); W – 19, at home, b. Thetford, VT, d/o Norman Merryfield (Porterfield, ME) and Doris L. Gault (Sandwich, housework)

Lloyd E. of Lyme m. Margaret E. **Dunphy** of Claremont 2/25/1945 in

Claremont; H – 28, US Army, b. Lyme, s/o Homer D. Wilmot (Lyme, farmer) and Flora Wing (Lyme, housewife); W – 20, at home, b. N. Stratford, d/o James L. Dunphy (PEI) and Ivy E. Noble (Hastings, England, housewife)

Michael B. of Lyme m. Vanora K. **Taylor** of Fairlee, VT 9/17/1988 in Lyme

Wayne W. of Lyme m. Violet P. **Howe** of Plainfield 8/23/1957 in Plainfield; H – 27, s/o Homer D. Wilmott and Flora Wing, res. – Lyme; W – 19, d/o Edward Howe and Hazel Martin, res. – Plainfield

WILSON,

Cameron F. of Lyme m. Beverly C. **Adams** of Thetford, VT 8/15/1962 in Lyme; H – 38, s/o Albert Wilson of Enfield and Gladys Whittier; W – 33, d/o Harvey Cadwell and Nellie Harlow, res. – Thetford, VT

Henry F. of Lyme m. Sarah M. **Hall** of N. Attleboro, MA 12/5/1908 in N. Attleboro, MA; H - 23, board sawing, b. Lyme, s/o Henry Wilson and Georgie Flanders; W - 18, mill op., b. Fall River, MA, d/o William [Hall] and Mena Fontan

Louis M. of Lyme Ctr. m. Nancy E. **Holliday** of Lyme 2/12/1975 in W. Lebanon; H – b. 11/4/1938 in NY, s/o Darcy W. Wilson and Rosamonde Cyr; W – b. 4/17/1946 in MD, d/o Alfred Tucker and Lula Hammond

WING,

Albert L. of Lyme m. Esther M. **Small** of Lyme 10/15/1924 in Lyme; H - 25, laborer, b. Lyme, s/o Nathan L. Wing (Berkshire, VT, farmer) and Flora A. Hill (Chateaugay, NY, housewife); W - 18, tel. opr., b. Cornish, d/o Duane W. Small (Brownsville, VT, miller) and L. Minnie Lobdel (Pierrepont, NY, housewife)

David E. of Lyme m. Annie M. **Carter** of Hanover 11/29/1916 in Hanover; H - 35, carpenter, b. Burke, NY, s/o Nathan L. Wing (Berkshire, VT, farming) and Anna Hill (Chateaugay, NY, housewife); W - 32, teacher, b. Hanover, d/o Henry W. Carter (Newbury, VT, retired) and Ada Holt (Needham, MA, housewife)

Harold C. of Lyme m. Lillian A. **Thompson** of Hanover 12/23/1933 in Meriden; H - 21, farming, b. Lyme, s/o Milton L. Wing (Chateaugay, NY, laborer) and Nina H. Courtney (Rochester, VT, housewife); W - 18, at home, b. Orange, d/o Charles E.

Thompson (Canada, farmer) and Maude A. Stark (Lyme, housewife)

Henry N. of Lyme m. Delphine A. **Young** of Hanover 6/7/1943 in Lyme; H – 37, US Army, b. Thetford, VT, s/o Milton L. Wing (Chateaugay, NY, farmer) and Nina H. Courtney (Rochester, VT, housewife); W – 38, nurse, b. Easton, d/o Alfred T. Young (Easton, farmer) and Mary Louise Poor (Landaff, housewife)

John Henry, Jr. of Hartford, VT m. Lori Nell **Benson** of Sharon, VT 4/8/1995

Leonard T. of Lyme m. Florence **Rattray** of Lyme 12/7/1905 in Lebanon; H - 20, laborer, b. Chateaugay, NY, s/o Nathan L. Wing (Berkshire, VT, farmer) and Hannah F. Hill (Chateaugay, NY, housewife); W - 18, housework, b. Canada, d/o Edward Rattray (Canada, farmer) and Dora Horne (Canada, housewife)

Malcolm D. of Lyme m. Mary **DeGoosh** of Lyme 4/10/1949

Stanley K. of Magog, PQ m. Alfreda S. **Damon** of Lyme 10/2/1948 in Lyme; H – 23, clerk, b. Magog, PQ, s/o Raymond Wing (E. Bolton, Canada, farmer) and Ruth Patch (Brome, PQ, domestic); W – 23, reg. nurse, b. New London, CT, d/o Frederick Damon (New London, CT, mechanic) and Mae E. Stone (Brome, PQ, domestic)

WINGATE,

Walter Medley, Jr. of Cambridge, MA m. Gabriele Karin **Lieberg** of Cambridge, MA --/--/1991

WISTNER,

Floyd A. of Warren m. Evelyn R. **Lucius** of Lyme 1/24/1949

WOOD,

Ellis S. of Lyme m. Myrtle J. **Clark** of Corinth, VT 11/23/1930 in Lyme; H - 34, laborer, b. Strafford, VT, s/o John F. Wood (Strafford, VT, retired) and Bella C. Bacon (Arlington, MA, housewife); W - 32, housekeeper, 2nd - D, b. Peacham, VT, d/o Levi L. Cassaday (Kinsay Falls, PQ, farmer) and Mary J. Priest (Windsor, PQ, housewife)

Lewis M. of Lyme m. Lillian **Dimick** of Lyme 7/3/1888 in Lyme; H - 37, laborer, 2nd, b. Westmoreland, s/o Lewis Wood (Compton, PQ) and Mary Wood (Compton, PQ); W - 22, housekeeper, 2nd, b. Tunbridge, VT, d/o Harry Dike (Littleton) and Elizabeth Tucker (Williamstown, VT)

Stanley D. of Lyme m. Sandra L. **Denney** of Lyme 11/11/1975 in Lyme; H – b. 9/28/1939 in NH, s/o Philip Wood and Esther Puffer; W – b. 8/18/1941 in NY, d/o Edson Montague and Lucia Maguire

WOODBURY,
William D. of Rocky Mount, NC m. Janet E. **Balch** of Lyme 6/10/1957 in Hanover; H – 21, s/o Kenneth Woodbury of Rocky Mount, NC and Corinne E. Davis; W – 19, divorced, d/o John C. Balch and Marion L. Gerue, res. – Lyme

WOODWARD,
And. L. of Lyme m. Bertha E. **Lawson** of Lyme 6/22/1948 in Lyme; H – 26, plumber, b. W. Roxbury, MA, s/o Arthur Woodward (Bridgewater, VT, plumber) and Gert. M. Cobb (Provincetown, MA, housewife); W – 22, teacher, b. Barre, VT, d/o John Lawson (Barre, VT, janitor) and Mary E. Martin (Barre, VT, housewife)

B. N. of Enosburg, VT m. Belle **Coburn** of Lyme 9/15/1897 in Lyme; H - 25, farmer, b. Enosburg, VT, s/o Norman Woodward (Enosburg, VT, farmer) and Lucy Temple (Bakersfield, VT, housework); W - 25, housework, b. Berkshire, VT, d/o David Coburn (Berkshire, VT, farmer) and Lucy Smith (Berkshire, VT, housewife)

James M. of Lyme m. Jean M. **Delaney** of E. Thetford, VT 8/31/1985 in Orford

Melvin L. of Lyme m. Ethel F. **Gould** of Springfield, VT 1/25/1950 in Springfield, VT; H – 30, plumber, b. Roxbury, MA, s/o Arthur Woodward (Bridgewater, VT) and Gertrude Cobb (Provincetown, MA); W – 28, nurse, b. Rutland, VT, d/o Lewis Gould (Fair Haven, VT) and Louise Duel (Danby, VT)

Michael L. of Lyme m. Carol Lynn **Mackie** of Dover, NJ 2/6/1971 in Lyme; H – 20, b. NH, s/o Melvin Woodward and Ethel Gould; W – 19, b. NY, d/o Gordon Mackie and Sheila Hemingway

Michael Wayne of Concord m. Nicole Shannon **Perry** of Lyme 5/15/1993

Wendell L. of Orford m. Linda L. **Estes** of Lyme 2/12/1966 in Lyme; H – 22, student, b. Lebanon, s/o Norman Woodward and Grace Lear; W – 18, at home, b. Hanover, d/o Leonard Estes and Evelyn Powers

WORTHLEY,
George A. of Antrim m. Elsie A. **Stark** of Lyme 9/14/1893 in Lyme; H - 20, laborer, b. Hudson, s/o Edwin T. Worthley (Malden, MA, carpenter) and Lottie Ritchie (Peterboro); W - 20, domestic, b. Lyme, d/o David C. Stark (Lyme, farmer) and Mary Runnels (Lyme)

WRIGHT,
Thomas F. of Naples, FL m. Donna J. **Devins** of Naples, FL 6/27/1987 in Lyme

WYLIE,
Ralph L. of Norwich, VT m. Jean M. **Knapp** of Lyme 11/1/1986 in Lyme

WYMAN,
C. W. of Thetford, VT m. M. E. **Lovejoy** of Lyme 6/25/1919 in Bradford, VT; H - 49, fireman, 2nd - W, b. Cincinnati, OH, s/o F. O. Wyman (Dalton, tinsmith) and L. Suttle (Cleveland, OH, housewife); W - 37, b. Lyme, d/o L. P. Lovejoy (Orford, farming) and H. Perkins (Canaan, housewife)

YAGER,
James D. m. Joanne **Zurlo** 7/18/1981 in Hanover

YOUNG,
Harold C. of Thetford, VT m. Nellie M. **Brockway** of Lyme 4/22/1912 in Lyme; H - 26, farming, b. Chateaugay, NY, s/o Ira M. Young (Clarenceville, Canada, farmer) and Barbara W. Carr (Elgne, Canada, housewife); W - 23, housework, b. Lyme, d/o George A. Brockway (Waterbury, VT, laborer) and Nellie E. Dimick (Iron Hill, Canada, housewife)

Leon F. of Thetford, VT m. Louise M. **Columbia** of Lyme 5/9/1914 in Thetford, VT; H - 26, laborer, b. Chateaugay, NY, s/o Ira N. Young (Clarenceville, Canada, farmer) and Barbara W. Carr (Elgue, Canada, housewife); W - 21, housework, b. St. Albans, VT, d/o Edd B. Columbia (Lebanon) and Esther E. Emery (St. Albans, VT, housewife)

Leon F. of Lyme m. Winifred **Streeter** of Orford 1/25/1951 in Bradford, VT; H – 21, soldier, b. Orford, s/o Leon F. Young (Chateaqua, NY) and Louise Columbia (St. Albans, VT); W –

20, none, b. Orford, d/o Richard Bertman (Orford) and Dorothy Streeter (Orford)

Stanley C. of Lyme m. Alice L. **Moses** of W. Rumney 6/4/1939 in Plainfield; H - 23, laborer, b. Thetford, VT, s/o Leon F. Young (Malone, NY, laborer) and Louise M. Columbia (St. Albans, VT, housewife); W - 23, domestic, b. Dorchester, d/o William E. Moses (Malone, NY, mill man) and Lillian E. Goss (Dorchester, housewife)

YURCHENCO,
Peter D. m. Ingrid **Lafleur** 6/27/1977 in Lyme

ZAPPALA,
Christopher E. of Lyme m. Shannon Lee **McDermott** of Lyme 8/21/1993

ZERA,
Alfred John of Sharon, VT m. Denise Marie **Demers** of Sharon, VT 8/7/1993

Ackerman, Francis E. - Veeder, Carlton L.
Ackerman, Goldie - Hewes, Ralph W.
Ackerman, L. C. - Harrington, C. T.
Ackerman, Mary J. - Bailey, Frank H.
Adams, Beverly C. (Cadwell) – Wilson, Cameron F.
Adams, Martha Elizabeth – Brotman, Harvey Irvin
Ainalovan, Elena Alexandrovna – Super, Kenneth George
Alden, Anna A. - Camp, Frank L.
Alloway, Mary Ann – Watkins, William A.
Almon, Diane R. – Marsh, Peter C.
Alt, Nancy H. – Lester, Patrick S.
Ames, Luella P. - Alden, Ezra B.
Anable, Winnie J. - Smith, Earle M.
Andrews, Nora M. - Lamott, Owen B.
Andronova, Vera – Gaudette, Lawrence Bernard
Angel, I. Estella - Hewes, Fred C.
Antilla, Sandra – Wilmot, Irvin, Jr.
Antwiler, Eleanor - Crawford, Ward H.
Arachikavitz, Janet M. – Chesley, George J.
Archanbeault, Marilyn S. – Jarvis, Keith Gordon
Arffa, Lauren T. – Phillips, Jon F.
Armstrong, Orissa M. - Ross, John J.
Arnold, Mary Isabella – Vogt, Douglas
Ashley, Frances S. - Chesley, Harold M.
Ashley, Melinda D. - Metz, Donald A.
Ashton, Nancy Murray – Brandis, Durward Porter
Astles, Debra A. – Simonds, Spencer W.
Austin, Bettina L. – Bacon, Stuart B.
Avery, Lisa M. – Britch, Cecil Jay

Bacon, Janet J. – Maclay, Roderick J.
Bacon, Minnie A. - McEwan, Bertram
Bacon, Pamela J. – Wilcox, Robert T.
Bacon, Susan Marie – Ricker, Roger Frederick
Bacon, Vicki L. – Husband, Thomas C.
Bagley, Bernice A. – Brown, Fred F.
Bailey, Barbara J. – Stowe, Robert E.
Bailey, Beverly – Walker, Joseph F., Jr.
Bailey, Delia M. – Tibbetts, Karl E.
Bailey, Della S. (Biathrow) - Gilbert, Jessie G.
Bailey, Ellen M. - Smith, Luther F.

Bailey, Ida A. - Pike, Charles D.
Bailey, Jennie A. - Blanchard, Edwin L.
Bailey, Mary A. - Hazen, Robert D.
Bailey, Tammy – Pippin, Richard, Jr.
Balch, Anna M. (Webster) - Crocker, Clarence A.
Balch, Beverly M. – Piper, William C.
Balch, Charlotte H. – LaMott, Dean E.
Balch, Dora A. – Dix, Chester F.
Balch, Dora E. - Sanborn, Harry E.
Balch, Doris H. – Jenks, Thomas E.
Balch, Harriet A. (Pushee) - Warren, Arad J.
Balch, Hattie J. - Marshall, Bry
Balch, Janet E. – Lacoss, Paul R.
Balch, Janet E. – Woodbury, William C.
Balch, Julia M. – Elder, Don E.
Balch, Kathleen Piper – Boudreau, Raymond Alfred
Balch, Kendra J. – Glover, John Blandin
Balch, Marilyn A. – Valley, Clifton H., Jr.
Balch, Paula R. – Spaulding, Gary C.
Balch, Paula R. - Tensen, Arend R.
Balch, Penny M. – Patten, Dana D.
Balch, Priscilla A. – Power, Samuel D.
Balch, Ruth M. – Russell, David H.
Balch, Sharon D. – Greatorex, Alan R.
Balch, Sylvia F. – Morse, Robert E.
Balch, Wanita G. – Marsh, Henry G.
Banker, Jean C. – Buzzell, Max H.
Banks, Gail G. – Pinkus, Edward C.
Barber, Dianne – Lecuyer, Peter D.
Barker, Sharon – Reeves, Richard
Barnes, Emma L. - Holt, Herbert H.
Barnes, Sarah Swift - Freihofer, Daniel S.
Barrett, Evelyn G. - Savery, Wendell H.
Barry, Marjorie A. – Rice, John T.
Bartlett, Doris L. – Hanchett, Merlyn I.
Barton, Denise Lynn – Movelle, William Joseph, Jr.
Bassett, Ivah A. A. - Tuller, Merlin A.
Bassett, Julia A. (French) - Harwood, George G.
Batchelder, Etta - Braley, Charles L.
Bates, Alleen E. - Stone, Herman M.
Bates, Sarah E. (Pushee) – Gray, Clarence K.

Beach, Denise Eileen – Buckley, James E.
Beal, Marjorie E. – Morey, Robert C.
Bean, Caroline F. - Bradley, Ransom L.
Bean, Elizabeth J. (Thomas) - Bradley, Hiel
Bean, Katherine A. – Tibbits, Richard E.
Bean, Laurie E. – Carter, Dusty C.
Bean, Nera M. - Webb, Charles D.
Bean, Ruth A. - Clark, Charley W.
Beau, Arletta Lauraine – Martin, Harry Fred
Beauford, Susan M. – Pond, Richard C., Jr.
Beckett, Terry Lea – Eggleston, Eric David
Begun, Barbara L. – Truslow, David W., Jr.
Bellair, Nancy J. - Stark, George E.
Beloin, Anita - Ferry, Robert G.
Benson, Addie L. - Knoop, Jeshard W.
Benson, Lori Nell – Wing, John Henry, Jr.
Bentley, Diane L. – Markham, Burton L.
Benway, Joyce Marie – Packard, Mark A.
Berger, Cynthia – Spafford, Jason A.
Biathrow, Pearle N. - Follansbee, Perley A.
Bickford, Linda M. – Braley, Chester A.
Billingham, Julia (Perrin) - Braley, Charles L.
Billingham, Marguerite - Smith, Dennie C.
Bircher, Carole Agnes – Cushman, David Orin
Bircher, Cynthia – Odell, Brian K.
Blake, Alice E. – Perkins, Robert E.
Blake, Betany J. – Miller, John T.
Blake, Mattie - Stark, Robert A.
Bliss, Margaret L. - Stark, Chester A.
Bliss, Nancy Lynn – Byrd, Harry Flood, II
Blood, E. Addie - Hewes, Berton F.
Blood, Jennie F. - West, Frank E.
Bognolo, Anna Grace Roberts – Rajballie, Ramesh John
Bombard, Minnie A. - Pushee, Eugene C.
Bombard, Myrtle L. (Coates) - Pike, Earle H.
Bond, Helen - Hawthorne, James
Bonds, Thelma P. (Stickney) – Jenks, Arthur L.
Bong, Patricia Y. (Young) – Manhard, Warren B., II
Bonnett, Marion C. – Tyler, Donald L.
Borne, Alberta R. – Pacini, Augustine F.
Borovick, Frances A. – Johnston, Richard H.

Boutin, Michele – Estes, Timothy
Bowden, Barbara L. – Bellows, Eugene R.
Bowden, Jain – Himot, Peter
Bowden, Mary S. – Olmstead, Richard W.
Bowden, Nancy – Maynard, Michael L.
Bowen, Bertha L. - Hackett, Benjamin F.
Bowen, Mary L. - Emerson, Andrew
Bowker, Martha L. - Camp, Edward M.
Boyce, Bonnie L. – Ladeau, Alfred H., Sr.
Boyd, Margaret R. – Braman, Lawrence F.
Bradford, Paula C. – Kimball, Scott B.
Bradley, Janet – Pike, Earl F.
Brady, Dorothy M. – Wilmott, Archie F.
Brady, Joanne D. – Lawson, George M.
Braley, Gertrude - Slack, James P.
Braman, Ruth C. – LaBombard, Willis H.
Breck, Jane - Jewell, John
Breck, Mercy H. - Merrill, Stillman
Breed, Beverly A. – Balch, Jeffrey A.
Bressett, Ida M. - Smith, Carlton A.
Bressett, Rose M. - Ward, Perley G.
Brockway, E. B. - Bates, R. W.
Brockway, J. E. – Day, Jasper J.
Brockway, Margaret L. – Pixley, Wendell I.
Brockway, Marjorie - Thompson, George
Brockway, Nellie M. - Young, Harold C.
Broderick, Eileen M. – Coleburn, William C.
Bross, Avery Walker – Sargent, Steven King
Brown, Barbara P. – Hewitt, Charles W.
Brown, Elisabeth – Thompson, Kenneth R.
Brown, Lena F. – Uline, Ray A.
Brown, Linda P. – Gray, Bruce R.
Bryant, Annie (Burnham) - Sawyer, William F.
Bryant, Della E. - Thompson, William H.
Bryant, Ellen L. – Messer, Paul B., Jr.
Bryant, Esther C. – Heath, Norman E.
Bryant, Katherine K. (Keniston) – Tullar, Randall C.
Bryll, Doris M. - French, Ervin
Bull, Marion R. – Uline, Kenneth H.
Burgess, Barbara A. – Forward, Thomas C., III
Burleigh, Ella A. (Berry) - Wilder, George E.

Burnham, Marjorie M. – Perkins, Vernon J.
Burnor, Rosa D. - Kibbee, Edmund M.
Burns, Lavona J. K. – Lemere, James A., Jr.
Buska, Joyce I. – White, Robert E.
Butler, Madaleine L. – Raila, Paul M.
Butman, Carol J. (Campbell) – Slayton, Ray T.
Butman, Catherine – Eastburn, Jimmie J.
Butman, Genevieve M. – O'Donnell, Hugh B., III
Byrne, Maureen H. – Hughes, Thomas W.

Cadwell, Susie E. - Uline, Millard R.
Camber, Hannah M. (Donna) – Wilmot, Kenneth I.
Camire, Ann Marie – Joy, Gailon Arthur
Camp, Jennie M. - Warren, Fred N.
Camp, P. C. - Pike, C. D.
Campbell, Carol J. – Butman, Herbert C.
Campbell, Christie J. – Peavey, Larry M.
Campion, Kathleen H. – Lord, John C.
Carpenter, Cheryl Ann – Pushee, William Albert
Carpenter, Debra Marie – Ricker, Philip Jay
Carpenter, Rebecca Lee – Durkee, Gary James
Carr, Alice M. - Vance, George H.
Carr, Daisy E. (Day) - Jewell, John L.
Carr, Susan A. - Elliott, Harry A.
Carroll, Cynthia Ellen – Hoemann, Andrew Ramiro
Carter, Annie M. - Wing, David E.
Carter, Karen S. – Fillian, Richard M.
Carter, Roxanne J. – Bettis, Harley R.
Casey, Lynne Barbara – Chow, Timothy
Caswell, Deborah L. – Sanborn, Robert F.
Celley, Lena M. - Lamphere, Charles N.
Chaffee, Deborah – McPhail, Bruce G.
Chapin, Fannie M. - Wilmot, George
Chapley, Linda – Howe, Orin
Chase, Amy M. – George, Harry E.
Chase, Mary M. - Graham, Fred R.
Chase, Nancy J. – Davidson, Paul H.
Chase, Sally A. – Estes, Leo W.
Chatellier, Anne – Erwin, Wayne A.
Chertok, Maxine B. – Lerner, Elliot D.
Chesley, Alice C. - King, John Adams

Chesley, Carol Ann – Perry, Anthony W.
Chesley, Gladys C. - Emery, Fay S.
Chesley, Lena M. - Hewes, Fred C.
Chesley, Lena M. – Briggs, Hoyt A.
Chesley, Nellie M. - Gray, Lester E.
Chesley, Ruth L. - Cunningham, Lucius F.
Chicoine, Daune M. – Gray, Lawrence H.
Childs, Flora - Presby, Frank B.
Cioffredi, Teresa – Dunn, John M.
Claflin, Florance Dike – Stevens, Henry Wheeler
Claflin, Shelda L. – Ray, Michael D.
Clark, Alice E. - McEwan, Harry A.
Clark, Alice R. – Small, Duane W.
Clark, Ethel A. - Pellerin, Lewis
Clark, Inez A. - Pushee, Harris A.
Clark, Janet B. – Tilden, Karl C., Jr.
Clark, Myrtle J. - Wood, Ellis S.
Clark, Ruth – Colby, Howard
Clark, Ruth A. (Bean) – Elder, Kenneth E.
Clark, Vera E. – DeVaux, David M.
Clark, Verna M. – Roberts, Daniel W.
Cline, Emma B. - Pushee, George A.
Clunie, Barbara Carter – Kiviniemi, Jan A.
Coates, Carla A. – Hall, Glenn B.
Coates, Myrtle L. - Bombard, Charles W.
Coburn, Belle - Woodward, B. N.
Coburn, Mina - Lathrop, George A.
Cohen, Lisa B. – Mann, Richard K.
Colby, Dorothy M. (Brown) – Driscoll, Kenneth F.
Colby, Mary E. - Warren, Charles H.
Cole, Effie - Thompson, Frank P.
Cole, Elizabeth R. – Smallidge, Peter D.
Cole, Lulie K. - Flint, Herbert L.
Cole, Tiffany – Williams, Steven
Cole, Virginia L. – Frain, Richard F.
Collins, Alice S. (Sawyer) – Ansell, Ray H.
Colton, Keita – Metz, Donald A.
Columbia, Louise N. - Young, Leon F.
Comstock, Abbie - Welch, George H.
Conant, Lucy M. - Webb, Charles B.
Conant, Romona E. – Strange, William B.

Conley, Sheila M. – Perry, Ranson W.
Cook, Augusta E. - Downing, Everett H.
Cook, Blanche W. - Colton, Hial S.
Cook, Evelyn L. – Greenwood, Harry W.
Cook, Jessie M. - Bond, Otis D.
Cook, Ruth E. – Dwyer, John A.
Cooper, Laura Julie – Anderson, Glen David
Corliss, Vina G. – Sanborn, Norman R.
Cornell, Bonnie L. – Malcolm, William F.
Cornwell, Heidi Brookes – Trout, Bruce David
Corriveau, Paula J. – Bourassa, Christopher M.
Costello, Helen G. – Mason, Frank, Jr.
Courchesne, Alberta – Borne, Albert
Courtemanche, Margaret – Jenks, Stanley
Covell, Florence G. - Wilmot, Earl R.
Covey, Leomia O. – Stockman, Ralph R.
Cowle, Susan E. - Coates, Arthur M.
Cowles, Charlotte H. – Pond, Richard C.
Cox, Evelyn M. - Tattersall, Ernest
Cragg, Sheila Kay – Elkouh, Nabil Abdel-Fattah
Craig, Lorna M. – Stevens, James Casey
Crate, Dolores Jean – Struckhoff, Eugene Charles, III
Creighton, Karen Joy – Borgstrom, Keith Cornell
Crook, Marlene S. – Roy, Alan C.
Crookenden, Ann Mary – Steyn, Mark David Jenry
Crowley, Diana Rose – Hano, George David
Crump, Caryn May – Shepard, Curtis Jay
Cummings, Winifred Ida - Emery, Leroy W.
Cunningham, Dorothy L. - Thompson, Henry A.
Cunningham, Rebecca A. – Gaylor, Peter J.
Curran, Dorothy E. – Houston, Gregory R.
Currie, Joyce – Cheney, Alan V.
Currier, Kelly Ann – Hill, David Bradley
Curtis, Ingrid L. – Hill, Douglas P.
Cutler, Helen I. - Lamphere, Walter
Cutting, Annie B. - Shattuck, George F.
Cutting, Bertha L. - LaMott, Albert M.
Cutting, Elinor L. – Rollins, Leon C.
Cutting, Jean E. (Smith) – Bomhower, Harold W.
Cutting, Lena L. - Steele, Carl F.
Cutting, Louise A. – Hewes, Charles A.

Cutting, Mabel A. - McMann, Henry
Cutting, Rhonda L. – Fillian, Gary L.
Cutting, Viola M. - Pushee, Frank A.
Cutting, Virginia P. (Pushee) – LaCoss, Neal C.

D'Esopo, MaryAnn – Barrett, Charles Keith
Daley, Mary Jane Shannon – Buskey, Wilton L.
Daly, Mary Jane – Sutor, Scott
Damon, Alfreda S. – Wing, Stanley K.
Darbyson, Mildred J. – Lund, Burton G.
Daschbach, Mary E. - Assouramou, Eleuthere G.
Davidson, Sharon L. – Davis, Bruce H.
Davies, Josephine M. – Rich, Brian E.
Davis, Bertha H. - Perkins, Archie A.
Davis, Ednor - Waters, Ralph
Davis, Elsbeth S. (Schneyer) - Davis, Perry A.
Davis, Ervill A. – Mativia, Perry M.
Davis, Hattie K. - Davis, Gerald W.
Davis, Hazel B. – Pushee, Clarence L., Jr.
Davis, Mina E. (Clark) - Davis, Charles A.
Dawnorowitz, Debra Ann – Kilham, Benjamin
Day, Blanche M. - Tuttle, Freeman
Day, Brenda Marie – Lyster, Randy Michael
Day, Cindy May – Estes, Gary Lee
Day, Daisy E. - Carr, Charles J.
Dayton, Angela Claire – Kuhn, Scott D.
Dayton, Florence L. F. - Barnes, Earl F.
Decato, Amy Christiana – Nichols, Benjamin Jay
DeGoosh, Alice H. - Chapin, Orrin H.
DeGoosh, Anne – Carter, Roscoe F.
DeGoosh, Florence - Pushee, David J., Jr.
DeGoosh, Jane – Cramer, Reginald H.
DeGoosh, Mary – Wing, Malcolm D.
DeGoosh, Nancy – Doyle, Richard D.
DeGoosh, Nettie – Ackerman, Glen E.
Deland, Annie L. - Lord, Edward C.
Delaney, Jean M. – Woodward, James M.
Delmolino, Frances M. (Beliveau) – Hoag, Kenneth V.
DeLuca, Anna D. – Whiteside, Samuel
Demasse, Tamaura L. – Dowd, Jonathan O.
Demers, Denise Marie – Zera, Alfred John

Denney, Sandra L. (Montague) – Wood, Stanley D.
Dennis, Bessie M. - Hall, Frank W.
Dennis, Doris H. - Cross, Frank C.
Dennis, Josephine - Smith, Benjamin W.
Dennis, Mildred E. - Cutting, Elmer F.
Dennis, Ruth - Jackman, Charles R.
Dennis, Susan – Couture, Gerald A.
Derby, Jennie M. (Sloan) - Derby, Herbert F.
Detar, Patricia (Barnes) – Doherty, Edward J.
Devaux, Vera Ellen – Carter, Carl Richard
Devins, Donna J. – Wright, Thomas F.
Dickey, Carol Ann – Seace, Albert L.
Dickey, Tammy A. – Beane, Charles A.
Dike, Augusta F. - Stark, Loren G.
Dike, Edna - Hutchins, George
Dike, Florence E. - Claflin, Willis B.
Dike, Lizzie S. (Nash) - Morisette, Alfred J.
Dike, Martha - Roberts, Ed. O.
Dimick, Addie V. - Macklean, E. G.
Dimick, E. M. - Pratt, H. O.
Dimick, Edith M. - White, Levi O.
Dimick, Ethel I. - Bailey, Henry A.
Dimick, Lillian (Dike) - Wood, Lewis M.
Dimick, Ruth E. - Bryant, George H.
Dole, Carolyn – Balch, Alfred J.
Dolgin, Irene – Ruben, George J.
Donnelly, Mabel E. – Childs, Preston E.
Doscher, Margaret R. (Ruddle) – DeBaun, Roger W.
Downing, Kelly – Derego, Edward C.
Downs, Kandi K. – Balch, Stephen M.
Doyle, Patricia J. – Beede, Earl J., Jr.
Drew, Barbara I. – Blanchard, Charles A.
Drew, Carol Ann – Phelps, William C.
Drew, Emily G. – Orf, Walter Christian
Dube, Theresa L. – Guitar, Wilfred O.
Dubois, Susan Mary – Delong, John D.
Dudley, Doris A. – Buzzell, George L.
Dugdale, Gertrude - Cook, Homer
Dunbar, Anna M. - Noyes, Frank W.
Dunbar, Edith - Gilbert, Austin J.
Dunbar, Hattie M. - Dunbar, Frederick

Dunn, Lois A. – Morse, Emerson G.
Dunphy, Margaret E. – Wilmott, Lloyd E.
Durkee, Lori L. – Jenks, Richard F.
Durso, Maria Sue – McIntyre, Michael Edward
Dustin, Della H. - Williger, Stephen Albert
Dwyer, Ruth C. - Kent, Thomas W.
Dyke, Barbara Ann – Gray, Dale Edward
Dyke, Emma - Paige, Charles W.
Dyke, Jennie M. - Kibling, Charles A.
Dyke, Norine A. – Gray, Richard C.

Eastman, Dorothy – Tattersall, Al. E.
Eckert, Ginny – Jones, Matthew
Eddy, Bertha D. - Noble, Ralph E.
Elder, Esther V. - Demers, Alphonse E.
Elder, Gail M. – Breck, David L.
Elder, Joyce E. (Mack) – Stark, Thomas B.
Elder, Mildred E. (Underhill) – Clark, Charles W.
Elder, Nancy A. – Jackson, Leon D.
Elliott, Addie M. - Hewes, Frank S.
Elliott, Ethel R. - Hendrick, Shirley I.
Elliott, Jean L. – Grove, Murphy E.
Ellis, Ada D. (Stevens) - Gilbert, Charles A.
Emerson, Martha J. - Lamphere, Ralph A.
Emerson, Nancy C. - Kress, Brian T.
Emerson, Ruth M. – Bacon, Carlton G.
Emery, Eugenia - Hubbard, Charles H., Jr.
Emlen, Katherine P. – Chamberlin, Robert M.
Esterbrooke, Doris (Joslyn) – Russ, Daniel C., Jr.
Estes, Karen Jeane – Dennis, David Emerson, II
Estes, Linda L. – Woodward, Wendell L.
Estes, Madelene Evelyn – Trussell, Ronald Kenneth
Estes, Pauline M. – Gray, Samuel A.
Estes, Roberta A. – Pike, Allie W.
Evans, Barbara Jean – Balch, Ronald J. A.
Evans, Marjorie E. (Wilmot) – Hathaway, Ernest F.

Fairbanks, Jennie M. - Lamphere, Thomas A.
Fairfield, Anna C. - Claflin, Preston L.
Fairfield, Helen F. - Tewksbury, M. B.
Fanelli, Katherine A. – Gunn, Ghyler, Jr.

Farnham, Margo E. – DeRego, Edward C.
Farnham, Margo E. – Longacre, Joseph M.
Farnham, Patience B. – Rich, Aaron W.
Farrar, Julie L. – Alvarado, Francisco A.
Farrington, Jennie - Hutchins, Joseph D.
Fellows, Gladys J. - Claflin, Clayton H.
Fette, Petra Johanna – Bezara, Alfredo Enrique
Fey, Mildred - Chase, William F.
Fields, Joan F. – Durkee, Leonard
Fields, Mary Jane – Huntington, Harold L.
Fifield, Mary R. – Sargent, David B.
Fisher, Beverly K. – Gray, William A.
Fisher, Deborah F. – Shepherd, Evan J.
Fisher, Katherine – Britton, Douglas G.
Fisk, Elizabeth A. – Day, Michael W.
Fitchett, Sandra M. – Melendy, Arthur H.
Fitzgobbins, Malinda J. (Cole) - Tattersall, Isaac
Flanders, Georgia - Johnson, J. P. R.
Flanders, Nettie L. - Gilbert, David E.
Flint, Anna A. - Flinn, Frank L.
Flint, Bertha M. - Smith, Ezra M.
Flint, Cordelia H. (Smith) - Dimick, Charles H.
Flint, Florence L. - Thomas, William B.
Flomenhaft, Deborah S. – Papageorge, Tod
Fogg, Katherine M. – Bailey, Morton R.
Follansbee, Grace E. - Silloway, Mark
Fondry, Susan A. – LaMott, Nelson E.
Forward, Scarlett V. C. – Cockburn, Richard F.
Forward, Theresa – Cloud, Norman D., Jr.
Fowler, Donna J. – Cadwell, Benjamin T.
Fowler, Lunie B. - Rich, Ray B.
Francisco, Virginia – Lisa, Joseph
Frank, Melinda Maxwell – Waskow, Andrew Vincent
Franklin, Lisa Marie – Hayes, Kenneth Ronald
French, Vivian F. - Piper, Frank A.
French, Wendy Sue – Hathaway, Shaun Willard
Frost, Beverly Jean – Balch, Raymond John
Frost, Grace D. - Johnson, Haynes E.

Gallup, Noreen E. – Estes, Russell G.
Gamage, Corinne E. – Trottier, Douglas R.

Gamage, Rachel I. – Stocking, Steven S.
Gardner, Renee M. – Livingstone, Alfred, III
Garey, Ida E. (Kent) - Slack, Wilbur F.
Garrity, Elise A. – Hawthorne, Daryle L.
Garrity, Janice M. – Grant, Clyde F.
Gaughan, Kristen Colleen – Campion, Brian Walsh
Geisler, Katherine (Zartun) – Biscuti, Paul
Genereaux, Marguerite (Maskill) – Irving, John P.
George, Blanche C. (Matthews) - Pushee, George A.
George, Dorothy W. - Webb, Harold C.
George, Kathryn A. – Batchelder, Verne C.
George, Marilyn Kay – Shannon, William B.
George, Nadine E. – Hill, Lloyd D.
Gerue, Esther L. – Horton, George E.
Gerue, Hazel (Hall) - Lang, Roger
Gerue, Marion L. - Balch, John C.
Gibson, Myrtle I. – Dennis, Wendell L.
Giddings, Brooke - Hagerman, David S.
Gierlatowicz, Janet G. – Warshauer, Lewis J.
Gilbert, Agnes M. - Pushee, George A.
Gilbert, Bessie E. - Messer, Ernest M.
Gilbert, Grace M. - Uline, Hiram, Jr.
Gilbert, Hattie E. - Dimick, Edwin P.
Gilbert, Juliet Davenport – Pantel, Robert Craig
Gilbert, Lillian C. (Roberts) - Fowler, Charles E.
Gilbert, Lottie D. - House, Clinton E.
Gilbert, Mary M. - Pushee, David J.
Gilbert, Nellie L. - McMann, James
Gilbert, Rosa - McMann, John S.
Gile, Lorna C. – Gile, Amos W.
Gile, Pamela J. – Gamble, J. R. Peter
Gillen, Carol H. – Johnson, Arthur Herbert, II
Gladney, Sheila M. – Hayes, A. Reed
Glines, Jennie R. - Ellsworth, Joseph
Godfrey, Cynthia Lynn – Lawson, Terry George
Godfrey, June – Davidson, Harry
Godfrey, Ruth E. – Jenks, Roger C.
Goldthwait, Joan – Walters, John T.
Goodell, Katherine L. - Slack, Harold E.
Goodhue, Olive M. – Nunn, Paul R.
Goodman, Kim Eliza – Genzer, Scott Jacob

Goodrich, Bonnie M. – Harlow, Kenneth C.
Goodrich, Cammie Lyn – Wilmot, Tony Eric
Goodrich, Dianne M. – Raymond, Alan J.
Goodrich, Patricia A. – Beaupre, Peter L.
Goodwin, Dor. B. (Hart) – Bates, Zelma H.
Gordon, Katherine L. – Scoppettone, Peter N.
Gottschaldt, Helen B. – Christie, Kent F.
Gottschaldt, Mary L. – Pratt, Augustus K.
Gould, Ethel F. – Woodward, Melvin L.
Graham, Leslie H. – Henderson, James M.
Graham, Mary - Columbia, Charles
Grant, Andrea Lee – Cook, Duane Stanley
Grant, Ellen B. – Alfieri, Anthony V.
Grant, Jennifer – Prileson, Jeffrey A.
Grant, Patricia – Jenks, James
Gray, Beatrice H. – Movelle, James A.
Gray, Beverly K. – Gray, William A.
Gray, Donna L. – Merrill, Robert S., Jr.
Gray, Donna L. – Tuttle, William M.
Gray, Dorothy J. – Kidder, Stephen F.
Gray, Esther L. – Movelle, William J., Jr.
Gray, Julie Ann – Hill, Van Scott
Gray, Menta M. – Peavey, John P.
Green, Kathryn Lee – Perry, David William
Green, Mary B. (Mehan) - Louzer, Samuel
Greenwood, Abbie C. - French, Walter, Jr.
Greenwood, Elizabeth - Perry, Archie F.
Greenwood, Mil. G. – Bueddeman, N. L.
Greenwood, Olive L. - Fowler, David G.
Greer, Joyce E. – Gray, Harley, Jr.
Gregory, Dorothy M. - Sansbury, John W.
Gregory, Vivian M. - Piper, Walter J.
Grosjean, Joan D. (Davis) – Hill, Ransom D.
Grosjean, Susan – Dennis, David E., II
Grover, Mary A. – Waugh, H. Bernard, Jr.
Guerin, Darcy M. – Dowd, Leo B., III
Guerine, Wendy Mae – Stearns, Denzil Charles
Gunn, Nancy J. – Mativia, Darius R.
Gustin, Marjorie J. – Ryan, Anthony H.
Guthrie, Joanne M. – Coburn, Peter D.
Guyer, Marion E. – Fulton, Elmer E.

Guyer, Marvel K. – Thurston, Carlos H.

Hackett, Evelyn L. – Lamphere, Allen E.
Hackett, Velma L. - Bettis, Raymond H.
Hadlock, Flora B. - Stephens, James M. T.
Hadlock, Inese - Stickney, Charles L.
Hadlock, Mary E. – Day, Roy W.
Hadlock, Ruth A. - Morris, Fred W.
Haley, Marguerite J. – Smith, North Craig
Hall, H. H. - Gereau, A. C.
Hall, Ida M. - Bailey, Henry A.
Hall, Josephine - Hall, Frank H.
Hall, Sarah M. - Wilson, Henry F.
Hamm, Brenda L. – Conard, Nathaniel E.
Hanchett, Clyde - Webb, Eddie G.
Hanchett, Della - Rennie, Harold R.
Hanchett, Helen L. - Messier, Mylon I.
Hanchett, Marion - Jenks, Chester
Hanchett, Rachel A. – Wain, David A.
Hang, Phuong - Lee, Desmond
Hansen, Donna M. – Fitzgerald, Gary J.
Hanson, Emma M. (Drew) - Christiansen, Martin
Hanson, Mary E. – Cassidy, Bruce P.
Harden, Barbi-Jo – Danetra, Leonard Daniel
Hardtke, Elizabeth – Balch, James N.
Hardy, Ethel (Parker) - Johnson, Carl
Hardy, Martha E. - Perkins, Harry W.
Harriman, Elizabeth A. (Pike) – Hanchett, Merlyn I.
Harrington, Barbara C. – Schmidt, Kurt W.
Hart, Bertha - Balch, Mason
Hart, Frances - Brown, Everett A.
Hart, Nancy – Bishop, Myron
Hart, Sarah N. – Sanborn, Robert B., Jr.
Haskins, Ethel E. – Wilmot, Kenneth I.
Haskins, Priscilla M. – Hutchins, John Joseph, Jr.
Hastings, Claire - Nelson, Waino
Hastings, Margaret – Wilmott, Chester
Hatch, Diane Murray – Sector, Peter W.
Hawthorne, Dina D. – Cutting, Frank A., Jr.
Hayes, Jennifer Moore – Johns, Dirk Alexander
Hazen, Margaret A. - Perkins, Adna

Hazen, Mildred M. (Hill) - Watts, Donald E.
Heath, Marjorie M. – Pike, Allie C.
Henry, Annette Louise – Jenks, Robert Elbridge
Henry, Florence M. - Bryant, Fred J.
Hewes, Ethel M. - Aldrich, Almon F.
Hibbard, J. G. (Powers) - Claflin, E. L.
Hibbard, Sandra Jean – Elliott, Thomas Earl
Hickey, Beverly M. – Piper, Devey A.
Hilbert, Judith L. Shelnutt – Brotman, Harvey I.
Hill, Doris Hadley – Holford, Fred Dewitt
Hill, Frances F. - Jones, Maynard A.
Hill, Lillian M. - Vaughan, Robert C.
Hill, Mamie D. (Annis) - Murray, Dennis J.
Hilt, Dorothy C. – Stevens, Fred H.
Hinchcliffe, Priscilla Devitt – Freeman, Edward Bicknell
Hinckson, Angie C. (Smith) - Pike, Charles D.
Hirsch, Lisa Hope – Tannin, Benjamin H.
Hobart, Alice M. - Cutting, Lee W.
Hobart, Jennie M. - Roberts, Guy A.
Hobbs, Diane – Guyer, Richard M.
Hobbs, Jerene – Kennedy, John Willard
Holden, Lottie L. (Green) - Wilkinson, Albert R.
Holland, Nancy S. – Thornton, Geoffrey G.
Holliday, Nancy E. (Tucker) – Wilson, Louis M.
Holmes, Alta (Cushing) – Hutchins, John J., Sr.
Holmes, Jessie M. - Courser, Rodney C.
Holmes, Nellie E. (Gannett) - Wiggin, Charles H.
Holmes, Ruth A. – Dunkling, Paul R.
Holschuh, Nancy K. – Sailer, Eric A.
Holt, Augusta A. (Hall) - Berry, Solon K.
Hood, Jill C. – Stark, Gerry W.
Hood, Lorie S. – Sunn, George N., III
Hook, Ruth M. – Thompson, Wayne J.
Hopkins, Deborah – Kaufman, Michael
Horsfield, Betti Jo – Bohus, Robert W.
Horton, Ella L. - Flint, Berton M.
Horton, Linda H. – Wilmot, Merle K.
Hosmer, Patricia – Gould, Clarence F.
Hostettler, Verena E. – Putnam, Spencer C.
Houle, Jeanne C. – Palermo, Joseph R., Jr.
Houston, Margaret L. - Balch, Grant P.

Howard, Wenda M. (Sabre) – Knight, Raymond J.
Howe, Bernice A. – Bouchier, Lester J., Jr.
Howe, Vera M. – Wilmott, Jess A.
Howe, Violet P. – Wilmott, Wayne W.
Howland, Verla C. (Clogston) – Pushee, Albert W.
Huberth, Doris Marie (Rohmann) – Schriever, Jack Richard
Huckins, Laura B. (Webb) - Johnson, Fred H.
Hudson, Margaret F. - Roewer, George E., Jr.
Humphrey, Marie A. – Pike, Gary C.
Humphrey, Nell (Corey) - Lamphere, Abizio P.
Hurd, Anna C. (Riggel) - Waldron, Charles
Hutchings, Barbara J. – Lehet, John
Hutchins, Augusta F. (Pushee) - Fisher, Edmond C.
Hutchins, Edna L. (Dike) - Stark, John L.
Hutchins, Edna M. - Colby, Ambrose E.
Hutchins, Edna R. – Stearns, Fred O., Jr.
Hutchins, Hazel A. – Sanborn, Robert E.
Hutchins, Heather – Lazar, Robert, II
Hutchins, Inez K. – Cook, Samuel E.
Hutchins, Priscilla (Haskins) – Parkington, John K.
Hutchins, Rosemarie Ann – Labbie, Timothy Gerard
Hutchinson, Anabel (Gates) - Coburn, David
Hutchinson, Hazel - Rogers, George G.
Hutchinson, L. E. (Harlow) - Follansbee, E. J.

Jackman, Carolyn N. - Ragan, Laurence F.
Jackson, Suzanne L. – Crary, Jonathan K.
Jaquith, Dawna S. – Moultroup, Terry B.
Jenks, Beverly M. – Balch, Harvey R.
Jenks, Carol Ann – Audette, Paul, Jr.
Jenks, Holly Janette – Taylor, Brian Allen
Jenks, Linda – Gray, Edmund
Jenks, May L. - Bryan, Richard E.
Jenks, Melanie – Bacon, Stuart Bruce, II
Jenks, Patricia Lee - Jenks, Gregory Allen
Jenks, Ruth Marion – Cole, Allen Lee
Jesseman, Annie F. (Dodge) - Flint, Charles H.
Jewell, Addie V. - Dimick, Thomas E.
Jewell, Dora E. - Bombard, Frank J.
Jewell, Jane (Breck) - Mott, Edward
Jewell, Lucy E. - Pike, Lon C.

Jobling, Amelia V. - Mativia, Roswell L.
Johnson, Barbara – MacNamee, Duncan B.
Johnson, Doris - Pushee, Olyph
Johnson, Elsie E. – Chesley, Frank A.
Johnson, Emma A. (Cousineau) – Smith, S. Dean
Johnson, Emma A. (Cousineau) – Smith, Samuel D.
Johnson, Florence - Dyke, Leslie
Johnston, Dorothy - Cooper, Fred G.
Jones, Barbara F. – Mudge, Gilbert H.
Jones, C. G. - Horton, L. C.
Jones, Farrie L. - Blood, George G.
Jones, Lisa A. - Wallace, Tracy G.

Kane, Mable L. – Pushee, Bruce A.
Keller, Suzette – Ragan, Wallace E.
Kelsey, Alison A. – Vinson, Curtis M.
Kempton, Edith E. - Tozier, Everett C.
Kendall, Dorothy J. – DeGoosh, John S.
Kendall, Florence A. – Kingsbury, Dennis D.
Kendall, Mary T. – Hutchins, Joseph D., Jr.
Keniston, Elizabeth J. – Carter, Carl R.
Keniston, Katherine – Bryant, Fred J.
Kennedy, Jacqueline A. – Hewett, Charles E.
Kikals, Marit Kristin – Foster, Anthony, Jr.
Kimball, Elaine P. - Peavey, Albert M.
Kimball, Faith Carol – Pushee, Wayne Alan
King, Alice C. (Chesley) - Gray, Lester E.
King, Colleen Beth – Fifield, Gary Bernard
King, Elsie - Hutchins, Charles H.
King, Ida N. - Rich, John S.
King, Jill A. – Druhl, Michael D.
King, Judith A. – Johnson, Philip
King, Kathy L. – Hill, Richard H.
King, Nancy J. – Fellows, Thomas E.
King, Rosie B. - Rich, Preston W.
King, Sandra Gail – Simkulat, Michael W.
Kingsbury, Erma E. – King, Lloyd F.
Kinnett, Christina J. - Hall, Thord T., Jr.
Kitchell, Alice S. – McKeown, Stephan G.
Klyza, Leanne – Linck, Robert L.
Knapp, Catherine Ann – Aspinwall, Dwight Channing

Knapp, Jean M. – Wylie, Ralph L.
Knight, Jennifer Alyce – Brog, Timothy Edward
Kohnke, Stina L. – Rosen, Joseph M.
Kolo, Lucinda Marie – Caron, Joseph Albert
Kropp, Heide – Riess, Peter
Kuendel, Gwendolen Marie – Shamma, Shihab Ahmed
Kurgan, Gail S. – McKenna, Thomas S.

L'Esperance, Cherylann – Grady, John Richard, Sr.
LaBombard, Carol – Balch, Mason E., Jr.
LaBombard, Eleanor M. – Cutting, Frank A.
LaDeau, Ramona H. – Stearns, Eli Robert
LaFlam, Anita V. – Larocque, Raymond Arthur, Jr.
Lafleur, Ingrid – Yurchenco, Peter D.
LaFleur, Sharon C. – Nelson, David M.
LaFountaine, Nellie P. (Gage) - Gardner, Glen F.
Lahaye, Brenda J. – Barrows, Kenneth P.
Lake, Christine M. - Turner, Hazen E.
Lamott, Annie M. - Andrews, J. Earl
LaMott, Lela M. (Willis) - Pike, George W.
LaMott, Marjorie L. - Wilkinson, William J.
LaMott, Priscilla A. – Bacon, Talbert W.
Langmaid, Addie M. - Pushee, Walter S.
Lanphere, Dorotha E. - Messier, Roland M.
Lapine, Eva M. - Bailey, Morris A.
Larabee, Tracy Lee – Green, Thomas Daniel
Laufer, Susan B. – Bernstein, Charles K.
Lavasser, Roberta Bailey – Mathieu, William
Lavoie, Carole A. – Bowker, James F.
Lawson, Bertha E. – Woodward, And. L.
Lawson, Doris A. – King, Howard A.
Leavitt, Teresa Mavis – Barrett, Frank Joseph, Jr.
LeClair, Ruth E. - Dube, Ferdinand
LeDoux, Della Viola - Aldrich, George W.
Lefebvre, Vivian Lynn – Balch, Mason E., III
Leonard, Robin A. – Lornitzo, Steven F.
Letourneau, Tina M. – Drake, Francis G.
Lewis, Ashley – Officer, Thomas C.
Lewis, Mary E. - Johnson, Walter H.
Lewis, Minnie E. (Church) - Boynton, Fred A.
Lewis, Terri M. – Pare, Alan J.

Lieberg, Gabriele Karin – Wingate, Walter Medley, Jr.
Lieberman, Andrea Beth – Heitzman, Tom Craig
Lincoln, Hattie C. - Blood, Elmer A.
Lincoln, Ila M. - Converse, Sidney A.
Lincoln, Sarah F. (Sanborn) - Bryant, Horace M.
Lockwood, Barbara I. – Capron, Glenn C.
Long, Suzie H. - Blum, Steven G.
Longworth, Ann – Jenks, Sherwin A.
Lord, Lucy - Jenks, John E.
Lorenz, Suzanne Ellen – Brockett, Bruce Edward
Lorin, Jennifer Dewey – MacMillen, Robert Brooks
Loring, Cynthia – Aborjally, Richard V.
Loring, Tamara F. – Pellerin, Pierre
Lovejoy, Cora - Avery, William
Lovejoy, Cora H. - Strue, Willie D.
Lovejoy, M. E. - Wyman, C. W.
Lowell, Esther May - McGuire, Thomas H.
Luce, Ethel – Harriman, William B., Jr.
Lucius, Evelyn R. – Wistner, Floyd A.
Lull, Eleanor C. – Keefe, John Joseph
Lund, Emma A. (Cousineau) – Johnson, Curtis R.
Lund, Florence M. - Cummings, Harland
Lund, Mary E. - Brockway, Guy C.
Lutjen, Ann L. – Kearney, Patrick
Lyster, Regenna Ann (Day) – Kendall, Eugene Franklin

MacDonald, Katherine Eleanor – Sternbach, Yaron
MacDowell, Sheila Anna – Weng, I-Hsueh Hugo
Mace, Jane E. (John) – DeMasse, Raymond C., Jr.
Mack, Elsie – Wilmott, A. Eug.
Mack, Joyce Elaine – Elder, Philip Earl
Mackie, Carol Lynn – Woodward, Michael L.
Macomber, Evelyn V. – Hannett, Gordon E.
Maddock, Elizabeth Margot – Dillon, John Francis, Jr.
Maddock, Katherine – Sullivan, Brian
Malhotra, Rita V. – Tabbutt, Kenneth D.
Malmstrom, Ingrid E. – Saldibar, Stephen R.
Marden, Bessie E. (Page) - Briggs, Frank S.
Marez, Michelle Denise – Ogden, Fred Lee
Marsh, Deborah A. – Hadlock, Roger H.
Marsh, Evelyn V. - Grant, Alanson W.

Marsh, Janet E. (Balch) – Marsh, Elwin R.
Marshall, May L. - Gilbert, Charles A.
Martin, Louise M. - Dimick, Lawrence F.
Martinson, Lois Jean – Sargent, Lawrence Henry
Masiah, Annie - Kibbee, George W.
Mason, Barbara – Frasca, Salv.
Mason, Mattie M. (Vance) - Gregory, Frank T.
Mason, Tammy Etta – Bailey, James R.
Mason, Tina L. – Wilcox, Randy M.
Massicotte, Melissa J. – Ewell, Michael G.
Mativia, Edith M. - Judd, Carlos S.
Mativia, Erville D. (Davis) – Franklin, Harry P.
Mativia, Nellie J. - Pushee, Henry S.
Maurice, Karen – Gray, Richard
Mayberry, Florence - Ingalls, Nelson P.
Mayo, Maria Gema – Pushee, Steven Bruce
McAloney, Susan A. (Smith) - Rowe, George E.
McCoy, Lulu M. (Tattersall) – Clark, Forest E.
McDermott, Shannon Lee – Zappala, Christopher E.
McDowell, Constance B. – Blake, Charles H.
McElreath, Beth Ann – Schuirmann, Michael Lee
McEwan, Leola - Wilcox, Charles A.
McEwan, Marcia A. – Willis, Clarence D.
McIntyre, H. Minnie - Laird, Francis R.
McNamara, Rose Marie – Birch, Richard W.
Melendy, Daisy B. - Small, Harry R.
Melendy, Etta Mae (Pike) – Hudson, Edward J.
Melendy, Eva L. (Biathrow) - Dunbar, Frank H.
Melendy, Leona – Clogston, Gordon R.
Menard, Deborah Sue – Olsen, Timothy S.
Menge, Karen L. – Feick, Matthew F.
Merrick, Marion Woodward Atchley – Schillhammer, William Renold, III
Merrill, Alice M. - Ackerman, Joseph C.
Merrill, Hattie G. - Tattersall, George E., Jr.
Merrill, S. Louise - Bliss, Fred G.
Merrill, Stephanie A. – Child, Stephen T.
Merryfield, Viola B. – Wilmott, Lenwood
Messier, Edna B. (Gilbert) - Bushaw, Fred E.
Meyer, Melissa Usher – Rutstein, Michael Howard
Meyer, Tammy L. – Newton, Arthur L., Jr.

Miles, Louise A. – Pushee, Harris C.
Miller, Alicia Lind – Provost, David Alan
Miller, Imogene - Fisher, Floyd E.
Mintz, Amy Q. – Record, Walter L.
Mitchell, Andree – Tangerman, John T.
Mitchell, Vernone S. – Anthonisen, Niels L.
Molloy, Jean K. – Dalton, Norman T.
Molnar, Vera – Tomsen, Chris E.
Mongeur, Jenni Marie - Campbell, Paul Jason
Mooney, Reine K. - Stark, Walter E.
Mooney, Valerie J. – Travis, Peter W.
Morey, Alice M. - Soper, Ambrose A.
Morey, Lucie A. - Eaton, George B.
Morin, Marie L. – Haggard, Alfred K.
Morrill, Florence N. - Mayo, George S.
Morrill, Josie - Balch, Harvey H.
Morrill, Mary A. – Dumais, Thomas
Morrill, Mary L. – Roberts, Harry A.
Morris, Donna L. – Green, William E., III
Morris, Karen L. – Pullen, Michael C.
Morris, Lisa B. – Titcomb, Peter A.
Morrison, Edith M. - Ware, Edgar R.
Morrison, Marjorie - Whittemore, Albert
Morrissette, Tracy – Cutting, Donald
Morse, Leslie G. (Gibson) – Black, Harry A.
Morse, Lizzie M. - Welch, George H.
Morse, Sylvia F. (Balch) – Allen, Philip A., Jr.
Moses, Alice L. - Young, Stanley C.
Mosher, Blanche A. - Derby, Arthur E.
Mousley, Emily A. - Tattersall, George E., Jr.
Movelle, Gloria J. – LaBombard, William H.
Movelle, Mary Ann – Hambleton, James Thomas
Movelle, Mildred M. (Gilbert) – Smith, Chauncey
Movelle, Mildred M. – Bailey, Daniel R.
Movelle, Rose Marie – Glavickas, John L.
Mudge, Eleanor W. – Cares, Charles C.
Murdoch, Ann N. – Snelling, Michael A.
Murphy, Mary E. - Soper, Joseph H.
Muzzey, Etta - Gray, Andrew J. C.
Muzzy, Addie E. - Shattuck, Warren J.

Nadeau, Joan D. – Clark, Wilbur Gordon
Nakano, Nancy K. – Hart, Jeffrey
Nareau, Loretta M. – Elder, Roger B.
Nathans, Heather Shawn – Giltinan, Garvan Michael
Nelligan, Clara (Thurber) - Fowler, Charles E.
Nelson, Christina - Coates, Thomas D.
Newman, Bridie Christin – Napier, James Maurice
Newton, Lynne K. – Dickey, Thomas R.
Nichols, Elizabeth Ann – Morgan, Millett Granger, II
Nickerson, May E. (Cook) - Mousley, John H.
Nihei, Michelle Kei – Phillips, Charles David
North, Deborah Dressel – Cartisser, John James
Northrup, Marion Evelyn – Joyce, Roy Thomas

O'Donnell, Doris A. – Huntley, Thomas R.
O'Donnell, Linda Belle – Southworth, Howard E., Jr.
O'Donnell, Mabel C. – Pushee, Donald E.
O'Hara, Gail – Mayo, Lawrence R.
O'Keefe, Eleanor D. – Hill, Oscar B.
O'Mara, Barbara Anne – Hinsley, Michael Cagney
Olish, Deborah Jean – Valenta, Stephen John
Oliver, Goldie - Wilmot, Leaman F.
Oliver, Lillian (Roberts) - Gilbert, Senior P.
Oliver, Rose - Barton, Weston C.
Olsen, Carolyn – Pearl, Paul
Olsen, Diana S. – Samuels, Henry
Olsen, Patricia A. – Fields, James E.
Ordway, Betty J. (Huntley) – Fairbrother, Lawrence W.
Ormsby, Lavina E. - Thomas, Herbert G.
Osgood, Candie J. – Harlow, Robert D.
Owen, Linda J. – Hartt, Wayne P.
Owens, Ann Lee – Owens, Chester Raymond

Page, Eldora M. – Hill, Arnold R.
Page, Elizabeth – Brown, Matthew Whiting
Palmer, Vea M. – Jenks, Alan A.
Panzer, Gabriele – White, Clayton John
Papademas, Nancy A. – Odell, Timothy P.
Paquette, Rose E. - LaCount, Ralph T.
Parker, Flora M. - Still, George D.
Partridge, Elizabeth H. – Isenberg, William A.

Paskus, Katherine M. – Jenks, Steven R.
Pavljuk, Jelena – Malone, Keith
Pearson, Teresa W. – Jenks, Ronald Harvey
Pearsons, Mary L. (Goodwin) - Gibson, William M.
Pease, Janet Lee – Piper, William R.
Pellerin, Anna M. - Perkins, John J.
Pelton, Diane – LaFlam, Eddie
Pelton, Fannie M. - Ryan, Carlos
Pelton, M. Jennie - Piper, Walter G.
Penfield, Abbie G. – Cyr, Charles R.
Penfield, Laurie E. – Fichter, Joseph F.
Penfield, Tracy E. – Decker, Rand A.
Perkins, Juanita M. – Martin, Walter D.
Perkins, Shirley Y. – Reed, Allen G.
Perkins, Verla M. – Dimick, Kenneth C.
Perron, Emily J. (Farrell) - Grey, Gilbert
Perry, Christina Marie – Katz, Jason Stephen
Perry, Jennie - Dike, Charles E.
Perry, Nicole Shannon – Woodward, Michael Wayne
Peterson, Caroline J. – Lord, John D.
Phelps, Brenda J. – Jenks, Robert E.
Phelps, Nellie H. - Hobart, Albert
Phillips, Elizabeth S. – Bourne, Steven R.
Phillips, Katharine A. – Albertini, Ralph S.
Phillips, Pamela – Horton, Bradley
Piazza, Jeanne B. – Brownlow, Frank W.
Pickett, Elizabeth R. – Fieldman, Richard P.
Pierce, Louise E. (Hughes) – Preble, Arthur A.
Pierson, Lori Ann – Stearns, Brent Ernest
Pigott, Penelope E. – Schine, James D.
Pike, Carrie L. - Sanborn, Fred J.
Pike, Carrie L. – Cargill, Leland A.
Pike, Crystal Rene – Eastman, Brian Gene
Pike, Etta Mae – Melendy, Raymond A.
Pike, Ida J. – DeGoosh, E. J.
Pike, Janet (Bradley) – Baker, Ronald
Pike, Laura B. – DeGoosh, Richard
Pike, Marie A. (Humphrey) – Norton, Richard J.
Pike, Maxine (Heath) – Pike, Horace E.
Pike, Peggy E. – Gardner, Daren T.
Pike, Roberta K. – Hill, Alan H.

Pillsbury, Rhonda Y. – Green, Thomas D.
Piper, Clara F. - Franklin, Harry F.
Piper, Dorothy B. (Henry) – Flanders, Carl L.
Piper, Ellen E. – Brown, Charles H.
Piper, Janet Lee – Thorp, John Andersen, IV
Piper, Katherine M. – McTague, William D.
Piper, Katherine M. – Perkins, Calvin J.
Piper, Linda V. – Clark, Dean L.
Piper, Patty D. – Fillian, Douglas Steven
Piper, Patty D. – Dyke, John F.
Pippin, J. Marie – Finley, Gregory Scott
Place, Mary A. - Chase, William L.
Plaisted, Michelle D. – Balch, Kevin R.
Poisson, Margot E. – Perrone, Anthony Benedict
Pomeroy, Elizabeth Ann – Fracchia, John R.
Pommer, Lillian (Traynor) – Hosmer, Ralph
Poor, Carlie M. - Ladd, Horace F.
Porter, Sadie May - Gregory, Frank T.
Potter, Florence L. - Sanborn, Clifford O.
Poulin, Simone - Doyon, Davila
Powell, Elspeth - Eaton, Russell B.
Powell, Melissa J. – Pike, Earl F., Jr.
Powers, Breanna Comolli – Kirk, Christopher George
Prichard, Marion F. - Rich, Perley M.
Pruneau, Eleanor – Lackey, Douglas R.
Pruneau, Gerda E. (Rasmussen) - Aldrich, George W.
Pushee, Amy L. - Temple, Leslie J.
Pushee, Augusta F. - Hutchins, Lawrence
Pushee, Beth L. - Cole, Allen E.
Pushee, Blanche May - Pike, Carlton E.
Pushee, Donna L. – Laro, Arthur E.
Pushee, Donna L. – St. Peter, Lewis E.
Pushee, Ethel M. - Grant, George H.
Pushee, Harriet A.- Balch, Frank F.
Pushee, Irene D. – Gernhard, Frederick C.
Pushee, Jean – Ricker, John W.
Pushee, Joan – O'Donnell, Hugh B.
Pushee, Julia E. - Runnels, Arthur N.
Pushee, Julia F. - Balch, West S.
Pushee, Julie Anne – Pushee, William Albert
Pushee, Lois J. – Rondeau, David G.

Pushee, Mabel C. – Pushee, Albert William
Pushee, Mae E. – Borger, Richard F.
Pushee, Marion V. – Hobbs, George B.
Pushee, Mary A. - Coburn, David E.
Pushee, Nettie M. - DeGoosh, Howard E.
Pushee, Sarah E. - Bates, Zelma H.
Pushee, Suzanne – Butnam, Herbert C.
Pushee, Virginia L. – Cutting, Clyde A.
Putnam, Ruth E. - Abbott, Forrest L.

Quarti, Patricia – Smith, Clayton R.
Quint, Hattie F. - Strong, George F.
Quinton, Hebe Bate – Avery, David Leonard

Race, Anah M. – Stearns, David R.
Race, Thelma - Bix, Rendall
Rackow, Susan E. – Maddock, Stephen J.
Ragan, Brenda L. – Pushee, Timothy J.
Randall, Stella M. - Bacon, Frank A.
Randall, Valerie J. – Lee, Richard N.
Rapp, Ruth A. (Thompson) – Wilmot, Kenneth I.
Rathburn, Debra – Reeves, William R.
Rattray, Florence - Wing, Leonard T.
Rawnsley, Elizabeth S. – Ferguson, Paul D.
Record, Donna Estelle – Hadley, David Carroll, Jr.
Record, Edith M. – Jenks, Edward F.
Redman, Patricia Mary – Burelle, Timothy James
Reed, Calysta J. – Torres, Andres D.
Reed, Elinore L. (Allen) – Greenwood, Lionel J.
Reed, Gracie L. - Cutting, Edd M.
Reed, Inez M. – Ashline, Edward F., Jr.
Reed, Marsha M. – Harnish, Stephen N.
Reeve, Marie - Robinson, Frank E.
Reeves, Margaret L. – Miller, Caryl W.
Reynolds, Gladys B. - Bond, Alden W.
Reynolds, Paula Cowell – Bliven, David Christopher
Rice, Bonnie M. – Grady, John R.
Rich, Eunice M. - Norris, Frank D.
Richmond, Emily Ann - Carpenter, Seth Maxwell
Richter, Jaqueline A. – Menge, Richard B.
Rickard, Nettie M. - Morrill, Elmer F.

Ricker, Wendy D. – Pushee, Michael P.
Ricketts, Ola S. (Simpson) – Gray, Irving D.
Rieger, Ellen – Bryan, Jeffrey N.
Rines, Ouida N. (Nichols) – Jenks, Chester C.
Roberts, Anna B. - Pike, Fred L.
Roberts, Dorothy A. – Strout, Francis G.
Roberts, Florence M. – Lund, Arthur R.
Roberts, M. O. (Dyke) - Doty, F. E.
Roberts, Meda P. - Fields, John E.
Robichaud, Hilda – Wade, Richard
Robie, Sadie E. - Brooks, Wilbur E.
Robinson, Ann T. – Movelle, Gerald J.
Robinson, Minnie M. - Lamott, Charles W.
Rogers, Beverly J. – Sanders, Richard M.
Rogers, Doris M. (Morrison) – Barrell, Fred A.
Rogers, Emmerette E. - Pushee, Clarence L.
Rogers, Marion G. (Lyford) – Campbell, Willard L.
Rogers, Marion V. (Stark) – Camber, Harry E.
Rogers, Zippie L. - Johnson, Irving J.
Roliz, Heidi R. – Anderson, Carl E.
Rollins, Bonnie Sue – Reeves, Roger D.
Roman, Rose – Hutchins, Joseph D.
Root, Heidi Joan – Rose, Robert John
Ross, Sheila Mary – Pena, Geigel Cecil
Roth, Carolyn C. (Coultier) – Kegan, Robert C.
Rothney, Beatrice – Dix, George A.
Rousseau, Suzanne M. – Davis, Roger Martin, Jr.
Rowe, Grace L. - Jenks, Berton A.
Rowell, Della M. - Carr, Lewis F.
Rowell, Eva Jane - Carr, Charles J.
Rowley, Ruth C. - Gordon, Edwin R.
Runnels, Jennie W. - Cutting, Edd M.
Runnels, Minnie L. - Coburn, Lewis W.
Russ, Myrtle M. - Bailey, Morton B.
Russell, Georgia B. - LaMott, George J.
Ryan, Beatrice A. (Tobey) – Elder, Philip E.

Sample, Eltiena Johanna – Campbell, William Bruce
Sanborn, Esther C. (Crandall) – Hill, Parker S.
Sanborn, G. M. - Davis, P. A.
Sanborn, Georgia A. (Washburn) - Blake, Mark D.

Sanborn, Hannah W. (Willard) - Randlett, George W.
Sanborn, Michelle A. – Beane, David L.
Sanborn, Roberta J. – Rotz, John Joseph
Sanborn, Susan E. – Hart, Lawrence G.
Sanborn, Theda M. - Bryant, Arthur W.
Sanders, Dorothy E. – Roche, Harvey D.
Sanford, Gail – Bradley, William A.
Sansbury, Gail M. – Holman, Hugh F.
Sansbury, Jeanne R. – Bell, Robert C.
Sansbury, Sarah D. – Stevens, John T.
Santorelli, Carmella – Brown, Jeffery L.
Sapp, Karen Lee – Jackson, Christopher
Sargent, Edna H. (Hill) – Bond, Charles H.
Sargent, Elizabeth E. – Haggerty, Hugh C.
Sausville, Carol J. – Trottier, Richard P.
Sawyer, F. Gertrude - Alden, R. Seabury
Sawyer, Lindsay E. – Mather, David J.
Sawyer, Mary A. – Balch, Donald J.
Sawyer, Nettie M. - Badger, Charles H.
Sayre, Lillian D. - Wilmot, Irvin A.
Schager, Ilana – Maletz, Mark C.
Schaub, Marjorie – Ryan, Anthony H.
Scholl, Heather Jean – McCarthy, Ian Aquinas
Schurman, Margaret Ann – Fisher, Richard Kaye
Schuster, Christine M. (Smith) – Swift, Merlin K.
Schwotzer, Betty C. – Pike, Charles C.
Scott, Jodi L. – Graf, Kevin L.
Seace, Frances E. – Perkins, Robert E.
Seace, Paula R. – Berquist, Allen E.
Seaver, Glenna H. – Stearns, David R.
Seavey, Ella M. - Blood, Sidney A.
Seeley, Julia Ellen – Emlen, Robert P.
Seiter, Connie Lu – Roberts, Thomas M.
Seiter, Sherry L. – Scott, William E.
Seiter, Sherry Lynn – Merrick, Keith Russell
Sengstaken, Elizabeth Ann – Laughlin, Herbert L., Jr.
Senter, Marian J. – Pushee, Ronald H.
Shamos, Elaine F. – Gaylor, Michael F.
Shatavsky, Esther – Hodson, David Thomas
Shattuck, Dorothea C. – Kingsbury, Karlton K.
Shattuck, Flora B. - Cole, Fred A.

Shaw, Regan Vanessa – Shaw, Scott Michael
Shea, Florence C. (Twomey) - Gamins, Albert
Shepard, Bertha Virginia (Miller) – Maxfield, Leslie E.
Shores, Carolin A. - Colby, Ambrose
Silloway, Una G. – McKee, Lindsay L.
Simmons, Carrie E. - Mariner, Jessie L.
Simmons, Verna W. – Rich, Everett B.
Simonds, Arlene - Crawford, Maurice J.
Simpson, Edith M. - Dunbar, Robert A.
Sirois, Pamela J. – Bosworth, Hazen W.
Sithavady, Paphanh – Sengpanya, Khanty
Skinner, Abbie E. - Wilcox, Henry F.
Slack, Virginia A. – Southworth, Kenneth B.
Slayton, Carol (Campbell) – Patterson, Ronald F.
Small, Esther M. - Wing, Albert L.
Small, Evelyn M. – Hamel, Joseph T.
Small, Marion N. - Perkins, Earl C.
Small, Minnie A. – Pushee, Albert W.
Small, Rita Bell – Thompson, Arthur W.
Smalley, Mareta J. - Balch, Ralph W.
Smith, Alice M. (Bixby) - Thurston, Howard
Smith, Anna M. - Melvin, Story
Smith, Annie M. - Derby, Lewis S.
Smith, Bertha M. (Flint) - Johnson, Fred H.
Smith, Ella - Mack, Willie F.
Smith, Emma D. - Jenks, William F.
Smith, Ester E. – Balch, Raymond H.
Smith, Freda G. - Dennis, Alger E.
Smith, Ida J. - Wilmot, Leamon F.
Smith, Jean E. – Weeden, Stanley J.
Smith, Jennifer Sage – Schiffman, Mark Lawrence
Smith, Josephine M. (Dennis) - Thompson, George W.
Smith, Laura A. - Barnes, George W.
Smith, Lida A. (Roberts) - Aldrich, Lucian C.
Smith, Lottie (Preston) - Moses, Jonathan
Smith, Lottie M. - Columbia, Fred
Smith, Lydia C. – McAssey, Patrick M.
Smith, Lynne E. – Spitanly, Kenneth C.
Smith, Rebecca D. – Baer, Eric R.
Smith, Rhoda E. - Webb, Charles B.
Smith, Verna L. - Granger, Ira N.

Smith, Victoria L. – Peterson, Kevin A.
Smith, Violetta L. - Adams, Aldrich L.
Snelling, Beverly Ann – Balch, Alfred James
Snelling, Hope R. – Oathout, Douglas M.
Southworth, Gloria Jean – Melendy, Jon David
Southworth, Lizzie F. - Goodell, Charles N.
Southworth, Margaret – Eaton, Maurice
Spencer, Ethel - Hewes, Fred C.
Spoll, Zelda G. – Shepard, James W.
Spooner, Muriel I. - LaMott, Paul I.
Sprague, Saidee A. (Duckless) – Fellows, Harold A.
Squeo, Michele – Foster, Richard W.
Squires, Ina C. - Mativia, Roswell
Stanley, Barbara Jewette – Stanley, Keith Alan
Stark, Alice M. - Thompson, Charles E.
Stark, Elsie A. - Worthley, George A.
Stark, Ida A. - Mativia, Darius R.
Stark, Olivia M. - Camp, Willie E.
Starkey, Arlene B. – Rich, Roger K.
Staszewski, Robin L. – Gernhard, Jerry J.
Stearns, Bernita A. – May, Earl E.
Stearns, Doris L. – Stanhope, David C.
Stearns, Rita Mae – Toner, Thomas William
Stephenson, Katharine H. – Kirwan, Robert J.
Stern, Creigh C. (Collins) – Wagner, Frederick F.
Stevens, Emily A. (Mousley) – Webster, Herbert E.
Stevens, Linda – White, Richard S., Jr.
Stevens, Mary E. – Sansone, Paul
Stevens, Ruth M. - Allis, George W.
Stevenson, Jane Bancroft – Meyer, Robert Scott
Stevenson, Wendy – Blau, Christopher
Stone, Arlene Corina – Larocque, Richard A.
Stone, Elizabeth (Lovely) – Stebbins, Jesse A.
Storms, Jessie J. – Pike, Herbert E.
Straw, Emma F. (Stevens) - Kilburn, Gilbert G.
Streeter, Sylvia – Gray, Gerald
Streeter, Winifred – Young, Leon F.
Strohbehn, Marguerite A. – Bent, C. Colby
Strout, Evelyn – Northup, Gilbert P.
Strout, Karen M. – Lewis, Edwin M., IV
Strout, Katie M. (Hatch) - Bailey, Laurence F.

Strout, Rose L. – Rivera, Valentin
Strout, Tracy E. – Flickinger, Henry S., Jr.
Strue, Ina - Marsh, Frank D.
Strue, Minnie Bell - Roberts, Thomas W.
Sturtevant, Edna - Jenks, Charles C.
Sturtevant, Violet M. – Stone, Harold S.
Sullivan, Lucinda A. (Allen) - Stark, David C.
Sunn, Elizabeth G. – Stearns, Fred O., III
Sutula, Lauren Corinne – Bargmann, Brian Christopher
Swasey, Eleanor F. - Stevens, Ira H.
Sweeney, Sandra J. – Balch, Russell R.
Swift, Fiona – Olsen, Joel T.
Swift, Margaret - Hendrick, Robert N.
Swift, Patricia M. – Robinson, Harrie E.

Tarjan, Jan-Roberta – Brewster, Raymond W.
Tash, Evelyn S. (Sees) – McGranahan, Ivan M.
Tatro, Theresa D. – Morey, Frederick A.
Tattersall, Emma S. - Dike, Frederick V.
Tattersall, Evelyn T. - Pushee, Clarence L.
Taylor, Beth – Barnes, Russell Lee
Taylor, Bobbye B. – Donahue, Paul A.
Taylor, Daisy C. (Wilder) - Sanborn, Charles D.
Taylor, Dora D. - Pike, George W.
Taylor, Dora D. - Harriman, William B.
Taylor, Eunice M. (Smith) - Stevens, John A.
Taylor, Laura Ingrid – Gray, Michael Shawn
Taylor, Margaret C. – Thoms, Frank R., III
Taylor, Vanora K. – Wilmott, Michael B.
Temple, Fannie A. - Wells, Alvin A.
Thibodeau, Germaine H. – Pushee, Robert D.
Thomas, Kathryn Elizabeth – Garberson, James Whitney
Thomas, Maude L. - Webb, Frank O.
Thompson, Annie K. - Piper, Lee W.
Thompson, Arlene D. - Rose, Martin W.
Thompson, Barbara - Pelletier, Timothy
Thompson, Daisy E. – Vaughan, George F., Jr.
Thompson, Elizabeth – Vaughan, Richard W.
Thompson, Geraldine M. - Chesley, Arthur B.
Thompson, Joanne E. – Tupper, Ellsworth T.
Thompson, Josephine M. – Roberts, Jesse L.

Thompson, Lillian A. - Wing, Harold C.
Thompson, Nina I. - Burke, John F.
Thompson, Nora Esperanza - Shine, John Francis
Thompson, Olive A. – Gray, Richard H.
Thurston, Betty M. – Konya, John A.
Thurston, Roberta J. – Blanford, Franklin C.
Thurston, Shelly – Barnett, Wallace, Jr.
Tibbetts, Della M. (Bailey) – Bickford, Roland G.
Tillotson, Janet L. – Pike, Earl Francis, Jr.
Tingets, Helen E. – Waterbury, Calvin H.
Tippit, Susan K. – Krueger, Myron W., II
Toffoli, Corrie L. – Murphy, Norman C.
Toner, Marilyn – Drew, William
Torres, Alexandra C. - Rowlinson, Matthew C.
Tousignant, Celeste M. – Wetherell, Walter D.
Towle, Linda J. – Macomber, Richard H.
Townsend, Janet L. – Pageau, Mark G.
Tozier, Henrietta C. - Rathbon, John W.
Train, Patricia A. – Grant, James M.
Trask, Alberta P. (Perry) - Putnam, Ora D.
Trask, Maude M. - Noyes, Frank W.
Travis, Martha E. - Cook, Guy M.
Trottier, Donna M. – Nehei, Taiichi
Trottier, Luane C. – Cole, Albert A.
Trowbridge, Connie Sue – Wilmot, Robert I.
Truell, Terri L. – Ragan, Charles R.
Truman, Judith E. – Pushee, William J.
Trussell, Arlene W. - LaDeau, Kenneth J.
Tucker, Thyressa M. – Whitcher, Ivan
Turcotte, Gail P. – DeGoosh, Edward A.
Turgeon, Sandra L. – McNair, Peter H.
Turino, Christine Mary – Blair, Donald Robert
Turner, Nellie S. - Lamphere, Charles O.

Uline, Isabel S. – Pushee, Roger C.
Uline, Margaret L. – Menard, Girard J. L.
Uline, Mertie L. – Balch, Charles R.
Uline, Shirley I. – Hubbard, F. Alden
Ulman, Patricia I. - Parshley, Ronald C.
Underhill, Mildred - Elder, Kenneth E.

Vachon, Mildred - Balch, Ellery L.
Van Ells, Patricia L. – Fields, Dale R.
Van Zandt, Ruth Jane Brower – Dingman, Stanley L.
Vander Meijden, Tessa – Thomas, Jeffrey S.
Varney, June M. (Matthews) – Ashton, Norman W.
Vavreck, Lynn – Lewis, Jeffrey B.
Versyp, Nicole Yvette – Brumsted, John Robert
Veverka, Shirley T. (Tanzi) – Horton, Charles E.
Vincent, Anna L. (Longley) – Gray, Wallace R.
Vinson, Kathy F. – Williamson, Mark W.
Vredenburgh, Carol Ann – Alden, Stephen Bruce

Wagner, Ellen Creigh – Ryan, Richard Bret
Wakefield, Esther P. – Park, Donald I.
Waldron, Clara E. (Baily) - Ellsworth, Isaac N.
Walker, Anna M. - LaCoss, Dorrance R.
Walker, Barbara R. – Claflin, Willis B., Jr.
Walker, Carol A. – Fellers, Gregory E.
Wallis, Virginia Lee – Harel, Uni
Ware, Helena L. (Leete) - Godfrey, Roy B.
Ware, Viola E. - Grant, Fred W.
Warren, Vera M. - Davis, Alfred T.
Waterbury, Susan J. – Pike, Lon J.
Waterman, Rosa M. (Balch) - Rowe, George E.
Watson, Bernice V. - Hunt, Walter C.
Watson, Margaret M. - Little, Arthur M.
Watson, Ruby A. – Thompson, Charles A.
Watts, Frances J. H. - Fay, George H.
Webb, Bertha M. - Eaton, Ray B.
Webb, Charlotte - Perkins, Forest R.
Webb, Ida Anna - Goodell, John Wesly
Webb, Muriel Augusta – Frost, Robert Edward
Webster, Albin A. (Coates) - Beede, Gilman F.
Webster, Carlene J. – Shattuck, Amos E.
Webster, Mary E. (Fellows) - Quint, Orrison D.
Webster, Mary E. - Day, William W.
Weeden, Jean S. (Smith) – Cutting, Frank A.
Weingart, Joyce L. – Pike, Arthur D.
Welch, Alice M. - Smith, Fenton H.
Welch, Eliza E. - Sanborn, Newton F.
Wells, Bertha L. – Tattersall, George E., Jr.

Wells, Florence M. - Melvin, Leon O.
Werner, Tracey K. – Sherry, Thomas W.
West, Margie L. (Ames) - Newell, Benjamin C.
Wheeler, Rebecca A. – Carter, Lawrence, Jr.
Whipple, Gertrude M. - Straw, John F.
White, June D. (Davenport) – Foster, Anthony
White, Linda J. – Kobokovich, William J.
White, Priscilla – Small, Richard
White, Stephanie L. - Ferland, Scott M.
White, Toni L. – Evans, James E.
Wickware, Jane I. – Hillner, H. Randall
Wiggin, Faith Macleod – Bethel, Mark Leslie
Wilcox, Mina Beth – Smolinski, Christopher Patrick
Wilder, Ella B. (Berry) - Waterman, Erni C.
Wilder, Rosa E. - Jewell, Carrol
Willard, Lucia - Bombard, Leon C.
Willcock, Carol Lynn – Cook, Timothy R.
Willey, Barbara A. – Buska, Olan J.
Williams, Deborah Ann – Gessay, Richard Stephen
Williams, Drusilla - Paquin, Raymond Eugene
Williams, Susan M. – Carchia, Antonio
Wilmot, Florence E. – Jenks, Merton A.
Wilmot, Gladys M. - Kramer, George S.
Wilmot, Irene E. – Prior, Lyle W.
Wilmot, Joyce E. – Aldrich, George M.
Wilmot, Leila R. – Barrett, Selby
Wilmot, Marion E. – Greenwood, Paul F.
Wilmot, Marjorie E. – Evans, Robert W.
Wilmot, Sylvia - Humiston, Frank
Wilmot, Vivian H. - Coutermarsh, Lawrence
Wilmott, Lori Ann – Mack, Brian Lewis
Wilmott, Myrtle P. (Cummings) – Avery, Harry E.
Wilson, Cynthia A. - Gibson, Frederick L.
Wilson, Ella M. (Dodge) – Godfrey, Roy B.
Wilson, Sarah J. - Grant, John E.
Wing, Cassie May - Bailey, Forrest E.
Wing, Flora M. - Wilmot, Homer D.
Wing, Lorraine A. – Bryant, Sterle H.
Wing, Nettie E. - Buffum, Jabos Arthur
Wing, Nina Ruth - Piper, Allen E.
Wing, Pearl M. - LaMott, James I.

Wing, Pearle A. - Hall, Everett A.
Wing, Ramona J. – Dennis, Ralph E.
Wing, Shelbie N. – Pike, Earl Francis, Jr.
Winnett, Sarah Barrelett – McCarthy, Dean Allan
Winslow, Myra J. (Post) - Bailey, John T. B.
Winthrop, Jennifer – Navarro, Julio Fernando
Withington, Mildred V. – Bailey, Russell E.
Woerner, Pat. A. – Fersch, Emer. C.
Wolcott, Sarah A. - Wilmot, Edwin N.
Wolfe, Evelyn M. – Chivers, Roland W.
Wolfe, Helen H. – Sonthoff, Herbert G.
Wolosin, Corrie Sue – Martin, William Canavan
Woodward, Gertie - Skinner, Ephriam H.
Wright, Delia - Dimick, Edson L.
Wright, Mary W. – Toynbee, William M.
Wright, Suzanne L. – Melendy, Jon David
Wright, Thelma H. - Green, William M.
Wynkoop, Karen – Chase, Robin A.

Yarbrough, Gina Marie – Rogers, Kenneth Shantz
Young, Delphine A. – Wing, Henry N.
Young, Esther M. - Hart, Lawrence F.
Young, Hazel - LaMott, Irving
Young, Ida D. - Small, Ralph D.
Young, Patricia A. – Poitras, Everett B.
Yurek, Ellen F. – Thompson, Allen J.

Zachar, Pamela Ann – Jones, Benjamin Parker
Zurlo, Joanne – Yager, James D.

LYME DEATHS

ABBOTT,
Edwin C., d. 12/14/1935 at 80/10/11 in Lyme; farmer, blacksmith; married; b. Fairlee, VT; Leonard P. Abbott (Fairlee, VT) and Lydia P. Cutting (Lyme)
Hattie W., d. 3/23/1936 at 75/4/9 in Lyme; housewife; widow; b. Dorchester; Wells Robbins (Dorchester) and Emma B. Youngman (Lyme)
Henry W., d. 8/5/1939 at 86/0/2 in Lyme; farmer; married; b. Fairlee, VT; Leonard P. Abbott (Fairlee, VT) and Lydia P. Cutting (Lyme)
Lydia P., d. 10/25/1898 at 76/1/19 in Lyme; housework; Chauncey Cutting (Lyme) and ----- Philocsa (Lyme)
Mildred, d. 1/6/1968 at 62 in Hanover; housewife; married; b. NH; Guy Day and Minna Pike
Roy C., d. 1/2/1969 at 59 in Canaan; contractor; widower; b. NH; Charles Abbott and Eva Tyrell
Roy Watson, d. 5/3/1996 in Lyme; Roy Charles Abbott and Mildred Louise Day

ACKERMAN,
Esther F., d. 3/7/1928 at 54/9/5 in W. Lebanon; housewife; married; b. St. Albans, VT
Fred J., d. 12/19/1938 at 74/5/29 in Belmont, MA; farmer; divorced; b. Chelsea, VT; Samuel J. Ackerman (Farmington) and Eliza Verrill (Alexandria)
William J., d. 8/14/1957 at 86 in Farmington; farmer; widower; b. St. Albans, VT; John Ackerman

ADAMS,
John C., d. 5/16/1986 at 76; Clinton B. Adams and Julia Cascaden
John H., d. 6/19/1888 at 22/10/5 in Lyme; farmer; single; b. Enfield; Hiram Adams (Enfield) and Harriet F. Cook (Lyme)

ALDEN,
Amos B., d. 12/10/1890 at 71/8/28 in Lyme; farmer; married; b. Lyme; Ezra Alden (Lyme) and Clarissa Beal (Lyme)
Emma B., d. 4/8/1899 at 79/6/23 in Lyme; widow; b. Wilmot; Jaber Youngman and Emma Baldwin
Ezra B., d. 7/6/1931 at 76/6/25 in Lyme; hotel keeper; married; b. Lyme; Amos B. Alden (Lyme) and Lydia M. Hall (Newbury, VT)
F. Gertrude S., d. 7/29/1891 at 24/2/17 in Lyme; housekeeper;

married; b. Lyme; Albert E. Sawyer (Lyme) and Esther A. Carpenter (Strafford, VT)

Luella, d. 4/20/1948 at 79/4/8 in Hanover; none; widow; b. Orford; Asa Ames (Orford) and Mary Runnells (Piermont)

ALDRICH,

Mercie H., d. 6/21/1963 at 77 in Hanover; housewife; b. Norwich, VT; Amos Clough and Susie Dudley

Sarah Emma, d. 8/13/1947 at 79/5/26 in Woodsville; housewife; widow; b. Hanover; Marshall Woodward (Hanover) and Lydia Southard

Sarah G., d. 12/10/1909 at 71/2; housewife; married; William C. Rider (Orange) and Isabelle Hoyt

William C., d. 12/10/1909 at 77/7/14; farmer; married; b. Barnstead, PQ; Elicha D. Aldrich (Dorchester)

ALGER,

Emma F., d. 1/4/1918 at 62/8/16 in Lyme; housewife; married; b. Fairhaven, MA; Alexander A. Tripp (New Bedford, MA) and Mary Lancaster (England)

Sanford T., d. 3/12/1940 at 80/3/2 in Lyme; engineer; widower; b. New Bedford, MA; Charles B. Alger (CT) and Anne Toner (Ireland)

AMES,

Mary Runnels, d. 11/30/1910 at 69/6/6; housewife; widow; b. Piermont; Arthur Runnels (Haverhill) and Luella Hall (Newbury, VT)

Persis, d. 9/23/1890 at 81/4/24 in Lyme; housewife; widow; b. Lyme; Salmon Bixby (Tolland, CT) and Pattie Ketchum

AMSDEN,

George P., d. 9/2/1924 at 89/4/17 in Lyme; retired; widower; b. Lyme; William W. Amsden and Mary Pushee

Lucinda D., d. 5/29/1910 at 70/0/26; housewife; married; b. Lyme; Alfred Dimick (Lyme) and Lydia Davidson (Lyme)

Mary C., d. 8/26/1894 at 88/0/11; housewife; widow; b. Lyme; James Cook (CT) and Clarissa Gilbert (Lyme)

ANDREW,

Alberta C., d. 12/2/1931 at 55/11/8 in Binghamton, NY; housewife;

married; b. Hyde Park, VT; Myron P. Cheeney (Lowell, VT) and Abbie Watkins (Montgomery, VT)

ANDREWS,
Annie M., d. 9/29/1946 at 70/3/10 in Haverhill; housekeeper; married; b. Dorchester; James LaMott (Brompton, Canada) and Catherine McBain (Drinest'n, Canada)
J. Earl, d. 8/23/1969 at 90 in Manchester; retired; widower; b. NH; Nelson H. Andrews and Minnie L. Cook
John, d. 7/22/1899 at 79/9/14 in Lyme; farmer; married; b. Weare; John Andrews and Nancy Melvin (Weare)
Lee C., d. 8/1/1948 at 71/5/27 in M'r'y, NY; millworker; widower; b. Lyme; Nelson Andrews (VT) and Minnie -----
Martha D., d. 8/27/1913 at 86/8/17; housewife; widow; b. Weare; Aaron Dow (Sanbornton) and Marion Eaton
Minnie L., d. 6/9/1922 at 68/11/25 in Fairlee, VT; housewife; widow; b. Lyme; Sears Cook (Lyme) and Lavina W. Rand (Greensboro, VT)
Nelson H., d. 11/2/1910 at 62/4/12; farmer; married; b. Dorchester; John Andrews (Weare) and Martha Dow (Weare)

ANSELL,
son, d. 1/10/1921 at – in Lyme; b. Lyme; Ray Ansell (Manchester) and Margaret Gray (Bradford, VT)
Lula E., d. 2/28/1944 at 58/3/21 in Lyme; re. teacher; married; b. Whitefield; John H. Wilkins (Stockton, England) and ----- Quimby

ARCHER,
Olive, d. 6/5/1956 at 85 in Lyme; housewife; widow; b. Colebrook; Truman Barnet and Harriet Philbro

ARMSTRONG,
John D., d. 7/22/2003 in Rutland, VT; John H. Armstrong and Agnes Babe

ASH,
Kim L., d. 9/26/2002 in Lebanon; Neil Robertson and Aloha Mason

ASHLINE,
daughter, d. 9/15/1968 at 0/0/1 in Hanover; b. NH; Edward Ashline,

Jr. and Inez M. Reed

ASHTON,
Norman W., d. 6/24/1980 at 57; communications consultant; Carl Ashton and Clarie Milner

ATWELL,
Eliza E., d. 9/24/1904 at 74/6/12 in Lyme; housework; widow; b. Mt. Holly, VT; Isaac Roberts

AUBREY,
Vera C., d. 3/4/1958 at 73 in Keene; domestic; married; b. Conway; Herbert B. Colbath and Clara Whitney

AULIS,
Elizabeth C., d. 11/2/1996 in Lyme; John B. Clogston and Susie Preston

AUSTIN,
Chauncey G., d. 2/15/1917 at 37/5/16 in Lyme; farming; married; b. Fairlee, VT; Albert Austin (Fairlee, VT) and Addie Baker (Orford)

AVERY,
Cora Lovejoy, d. 12/30/1945 at 68/2/23 in W. Lebanon; housewife; widow; b. Lyme; Louis P. Lovejoy (Orford) and Harriet Perkins (Canaan)
Harry E., d. 4/28/1956 at 65 in Lyme; watchmaker; married; b. Canaan; Frederick F. Avery and Lizzie M. Warner
Myrtle Phoebe, d. 5/18/1974 at 83 in Lebanon; homemaker; b. NH; Carlo Cummings and Electra Burnham

BACON,
Carlton G., d. 3/21/2001 in Lyme; George Bacon and Mina Hill
George W., d. 11/8/1983 at 73; William Bacon and Katie Goulett
Mina H., d. 9/4/1983 at 69; Talbert W. Hill and Lila Leet

BADGER,
Clara P., d. 5/29/1921 at 69 in Hastings, FL; housewife; married; b. Lyme; Winthrop F. Post (Lyme) and Laura Wise (Hebron)
Elmer E., d. 12/30/1919 at 5/11/10 in Lyme; b. Lyme; C. E. Badger

(Lyme) and S. Pellicer (FL)
Henry M., d. 2/21/1929 at 82/7/17 in Hastings, FL; retired; widower;
b. Lowell, MA; Hugh Badger and Sarah Tallman (Orford)
Reginald T., d. 11/17/1965 at 56 in Hanover; clerk; single; b.
Hanover; William H. Badger and Margaret Densmore

BAILEY,
Amos, d. 8/29/1888 at -3/5/17 in Lyme; farmer; married; b. Bath;
Caleb Bailey (Bath) and Deborah Fitch (Lebanon)
Augusta A., d. 2/10/1913 at 65/8/6; housewife; married; b. Lyme;
Zadok Howard (Lyme) and Balinda Bishop (Lyme)
Clayton H., d. 6/21/1934 at 50 in Hanover; single; b. Lyme; Henry A.
Bailey (Lyme) and Augusta Howard (Lyme)
Ethel I., d. 5/24/1925 at 25/3/10 in Hanover; housewife; married; b.
Lyme; Charles P. Dimick (Lyme) and Florence Carpenter
(Littleton)
Ethelinda L., d. 5/27/1896 at 79/2/28; domestic; single; b. Lebanon;
Caleb Bailey (Bath) and Deborah Fitch (Windham, CT)
Flora I., d. 1/14/1921 at 67/4/4 in Lyme; housewife; widow; b. Cabot,
VT; William Ingalls (Walden, VT) and Sally Hancock (E.
Hardwick, VT)
Frank H., d. 1/13/1958 at 82 in Lyme; ret. farmer; married; b. Lyme;
Henry A. Bailey and Augusta Howard
Henry A., d. 10/26/1913 at 65/1/14; farmer; widower; b. Lyme; Amos
Bailey (Troy) and Mary Aiken (Hallowell, ME)
Henry A., d. 4/21/1967 at 73 in Hanover; farming; married; b. Lyme;
Henry A. Bailey and Augusta Howard
Henry J., d. 9/30/1968 at 52 in Lyme; orderly; married; b. VT;
Charles Bailey and Della Biathrow
Ida M., d. 9/14/1973 at 72 in Lebanon; Hiland Hall and Agnes
Dunham
John T. B., d. 5/2/1929 at 83/5/29 in Ayer, MA; retired; widower; b.
Lowell, MA; John T. Bailey (Andover, MA) and Orilla Norcross
(Woodbury, VT)
Margaret, d. 9/16/1992 in Lebanon; Elber Wilmot and Myrtle
Cummings
Mary, d. 7/19/1971 at 93 in Lyme; housewife; b. VT; Joseph
Ackerman and Elizabeth Currier
Mary A., d. 12/26/1902 at 81/2/10 in Lyme; housewife; widow; b.
Chesterfield; John Aiken (Boston, MA) and Temperance Joy
(Lyme)

Morton B., d. 1/20/2002 in Lebanon; Frank Bailey and Mary Ackerman
Myra J., d. 6/19/1921 at 62/11/27 in Lyme; housewife; married; b. Lyme; Winthrop F. Post (Lyme) and Laura Wise (Hebron)
Myrtle R., d. 9/25/2000 in Lyme; Daniel Russ and Harriet Boyd

BAILY,
Laura J., d. 2/20/1890 at 19/7/28 in Lyme; teacher; single; b. Acworth; George Baily (Acworth) and Sarah Whittemore (Litchfield)

BAKER,
Charles H., d. 1/30/1935 at 74/6/28 in Lyme; farmer; married; b. Canaan; James Baker (Bow) and Mary Flanders (Dorchester)
Frank W., d. 2/6/1894 at 73/0/28; farmer; married; b. Thetford, VT; David Baker (Lyme) and Irene Carpenter (Lyme)
Louise D., d. 1/30/1951 at 84 in Orford
Lucy Heaton, d. 10/1/1889 at 87/1/2 in Fairlee, VT; housekeeper; widow; b. Thetford, VT; King Heaton ("Cozuz") and Miriam Moore (Thetford, VT)
Ronald R., d. 9/15/2004 in Lyme Center; Maurice Baker and Hattie Streeter
Sarah F., d. 3/3/1916 at 88/6/5 in Lebanon; widow; b. Lyme; Sylvanus Hewes (Lyme) and Meriam Wright (Lyme)
Sarah J., d. 5/16/1897 at 77/10/16; housekeeper; single; b. Pembroke; Joseph Baker (Pembroke) and Susan Holt (Pembroke)

BALCH,
daughter, d. 5/29/1928 at 0/0/3 in Lyme; b. Lyme; Harvey H. Balch (Hartland, VT) and Josephine Morrow (Hartford, VT)
Anna L., d. 4/3/1893 at 12/8/3 in Lyme; Brights disease; b. Lyme; West S. Balch (Lyme, farmer) and Mary E. Grant (Lyme)
Barbara A., d. 7/16/1987 at 41; Clesson Moore and Mabel Currier
Bertha L., d. 7/16/1975 at 58 in Hanover; homemaker; b. NH; Frank Hart and Julia Buckley
Ellery, d. 8/5/1971 at 60 in Hanover; tree surgeon; b. NH; Harvey Balch and Lillian Morrill
George B., d. 6/12/1896 at 38/2/20; married; Robert Greenough (Atkinson) and Delilah Bradbury (Lyme)
Grant P., d. 11/24/1986 at 80; Frank Balch and Harriet Pushee

Harvey, d. 4/3/1975 at 39 in Lebanon; gasoline filling station operator; b. NH; Roy Balch and Olive Blanchard
Harvey H., d. 3/8/1954 at 87 in Hanover; retired; married; b. Taftsville, VT; Hiram Balch
J. P., d. 8/15/1948 at 84/1/13 in Lyme; housewife; widow; b. Lyme; Alfred W. Pushee (Lyme) and Edna E. Steele (Lyme)
James N., d. 8/31/1974 at 51 in Hanover; night watchman; b. NH; Harvey Balch and Lillian Morrill
John Carroll, d. 8/27/1889 at 51/1/21 in Lyme; timekeeper; married; b. Lyme; Theodore Balch (Lyme) and Sally Lovejoy (Hebron)
Lillian, d. 3/30/1954 at 67 in Hanover; none; married; b. Hartland, VT; William Morrill and Lillian Chamberlain
Mareta Smalley, d. 9/20/1961 at 70 in Haverhill; housewife; b. Easton; James A. Smalley and Martha Langmaid
Margaret L., d. 11/9/2001 in Lebanon; Alfred Houston and Florence Johnson
Mason E., Sr., d. 10/1/1987 at 73; Harry H. Balch and Josie Morrill
Mason Elwin, Jr., d. 10/5/1995 in Lebanon; Mason Balch, Sr. and Bertha Hart
Olive, d. 5/26/1997 in Lebanon; Raymond Blanchard and Mabel Cushion
Ralph W., d. 10/28/1987 at 93; West S. Balch and Julia Pushee
Ramona J., d. 3/8/1939 at – in Hanover; b. Hanover; Mason E. Balch (Lyme) and Bertha L. Hart (Canaan)
Raymond H., d. 2/9/1973 at 56 in Hanover; road agent; b. NH; Harvey Balch and Lillian Morrill
Roy, d. 9/17/1985 at 79; Harvey Balch and Lillian Morrill
Samuel West, d. 5/27/1889 at 85/11/12 in Lyme; tanner; widower; b. Lyme; Joshua Balch (Beverly, MA) and Nanny P. Shaw (Bridgewater, MA)
Sarah P., d. 2/24/1919 at 76/10 in Lyme; single; b. Lyme; S. W. Balch (Lyme) and J. E. Perkins (Hanover)
Theodore, d. 1/31/1892 at 87/3/27; farmer; widower; b. Lyme; Isaac Balch and Elizabeth Bell (Lyme)
Wealthy A., d. 12/8/1922 at 87/7/8 in Lyme; widow; b. Lyme; George Flint (Lyme) and Joanna Newell (Orford)
West S., d. 1/28/1934 at 85/8/12 in Lyme; farmer; married; b. Lyme; Samuel W. Balch (Lyme) and Joanna Perkins
William W., d. 3/1/1918 at 83/10/2 in Lyme; farming; married; b. Lyme; Theodore Balch (Lyme) and Sally Lovejoy (Hebron)

BALDWIN,
John, d. 7/19/1979 at 72 in Lyme; student; b. DE; Norman Baldwin and Martha Baldwin

BALL,
Laura A. G., d. 11/4/1909 at 72/4/22; housewife; married; b. Dorchester; Cyrus Gordon (Henniker) and Olive Jesseman (Dorchester)
Lydia Lestina, d. 1/30/1931 at 94/9/18 in Rutland, MA; retired; single; b. Thetford, VT; Elisha P. Ball (Vershire, VT) and Lydia Chamberlin (Charlestown, VT)
Samuel F., d. 5/6/1915 at 82/0/6 in Lyme; farmer; widower; b. Thetford, VT; Elisha P. Ball and Lydia Chamberlin (Charleston, VT)

BARKER,
John W., d. 6/13/1961 at 85 in Lyme; clergyman; b. England; John Barker and Annie Wilson

BARNES,
Esther G., d. 2/12/1909 at 78/10/8; housewife; widow; b. Thetford, VT; Joseph Gillette (Thetford, VT) and Eliza Pierce (Fairlee, VT)
George W., d. --/--/1955 at 89 in Lyme; bank president; widower; b. Lyme; Hiram Barnes and Esther Gillett
Herbert W., d. 7/10/1930 at 61/11/1 in Thetford, VT; farmer; divorced; William L. Barnes (Chelsea, VT) and Elizabeth Camp (Hanover)
Hiram, d. 10/27/1892 at 71/3; farmer; married; b. Lebanon; Josiah Barnes (Acton, MA) and Dorothy Gale (Amesbury, MA)
Laura S., d. 6/27/1935 at 66/6/16 in Lyme; housewife; married; b. Hanover; Chandler P. Smith (Hanover) and Sarah Camp (Lyme)

BARRETT,
Leila R., d. 10/26/2003 in Hanover; Leo Wilmot and Fannie Chapin

BARTLETT,
Aseneth, d. 4/14/1923 at 83/8/20 in Lyme; retired; widow; b. Berlin, MA; Daniel Barnes (Berlin, MA) and Betsy Langley (Boylston, MA)

Frank, d. 3/8/1925 at 34 in S. Fayette; married

BATCHELDER,
Elmer, d. 10/28/1941 at 70/11/14 in Lyme; laborer; married; b. Stanstead, PQ; Harvey Batchelder (Vershire, VT) and Sarah ----- (Hillsboro)

BATES,
Gertrude H., d. 10/18/1964 at 90 in Lebanon; housewife; b. Plainfield; Dennis Hanchett and Elizabeth Read
Sidney W., d. 8/12/1939 at 65/0/8 in Hanover; farmer; married; b. W. Fairlee, VT; Kimball Bates (Hartland, VT) and Ella Wallace (W. Fairlee, VT)
Zelma H., d. 4/15/1959 at 56 in Hanover; laborer; b. Lebanon; Sidney Bates and Gertrude Hanchett

BEAL,
Selah, d. 6/29/1889 at 84/0/25 in Lyme; farmer; married; b. Lyme; James Beal (Woodstock, CT) and Uranus Tucker (Woodstock, CT)
Thaddeus R., d. 5/2/1981 at 64; manager; Thaddeus R. Beal and Alice L. Dresel

BEAN,
Alice M., d. 2/13/1981 at 90; homemaker; David March and Delia Smith
Donald F., d. 12/16/1973 at 54 in Lyme; janitor; b. NH; Edwin G. Bean and Alice Marsh
George L., d. 9/5/1987 at 75; Edwin Bean and Alice Marsh
Ruth A., d. 3/26/2004 in Lebanon; William W. Day and Mary E. Webster

BEAUFORD,
Ralph E., d. 6/3/1981 at 61; receiving clerk; Wilfred Beauford and Blanche Roderick

BECKWITH,
Charles, d. 12/3/1901 at 69/9 in Lyme; farmer; married; b. Williamstown, VT; Rufus Beckwith (Williamstown, VT) and Rhoda Lyman (Norwich, VT)

BEDELL,
C. C., d. 12/19/1893 at 68/5/29 in Lyme; consumption, heart disease; farmer; married; b. Fayston, VT; Jacob Bedell (farmer) and Persis Carr
Caroline S., d. 4/29/1913 at 76/2/10; housewife; widow; b. Thetford, VT; Buckly Holton (Concord, VT) and Catherine Judevine
Malcolmb L., d. 9/10/1934 at 0/0/27 in Norwich, VT; b. Norwich, VT; Lloyd E. Bedell (Johnson, VT) and Gladys DeWitt (Lyme)

BEEDE,
Albin, d. 9/15/1918 at 45 in Hanover; housewife; married
Gilman F., d. 5/24/1937 at 75/5/2 in Haverhill; farmer; widower; b. Orange, VT; John Beede (Topsham, VT) and Melissa Thompson (Orange)

BEESLEY,
Jill, d. 1/31/2004 in Hanover; Frank Fidkin and Hilda Swift

BELFORD,
William H., d. 2/28/1901 at 42/7/24 in Lyme; laborer; b. Lyme; William H. Belford (Ireland) and Mary A. Lamphere (Hartland, VT)

BELKNAP,
Susan W. B., d. 5/11/1909 at 94/6/10; housewife; widow; b. Lyme; Reuben Bliss and Nancy Williams

BEMIS,
Lula E., d. 2/6/1973 at 94 in Lyme; housewife; b. MA; Henry W. Wakefield and Emma Allen

BENNETT,
Atwood, d. 9/16/1941 at 86/7/8 in Hanover; retired farmer; widower; b. Burke, NY
Emma L., d. 10/8/1934 at 79/8/3 in Lebanon; housewife; married

BERGERON,
Electa Edna, d. 10/20/1975 at 63 in Lebanon; homemaker; b. NH; Charles L. Hildreth and Electa M. Boynton
Reginald, d. 8/6/1968 at 63 in Enfield; vending stand op.; married; b. VT; Charles H. Bergeron and Mable Granger

BEUSMAN,
Augusta M., d. 4/18/1966 at 82 in Lyme; housewife; widow; b. New York, NY; August Zinbitz and Marie Dowding
Vera H., d. 9/29/1974 at 71 in Hanover; retired teacher; b. NY; John Beusman and Augusta Zauvitz

BICKFORD,
Della M., d. 10/22/2003 in Lebanon; Henry Bailey and Margaret Wilmot
Henry N., d. 8/30/1983 at 69; Newell Bickford and Mary Richards
Roland Gene, b. 6/19/1990 at 58; Harry Bickford, Sr. and Gertrude Tibbetts

BILLINGHAM,
son, d. 2/17/1917 at – in Lyme; b. Lyme; James Billingham (England) and Julia V. Perrin (Island Pond, VT)

BINGHAM,
Wallace A., d. 12/28/1893 at 68/0/10 in Lyme; asthma, la grippe; farmer; single; b. Lyme; Asa Bingham (farmer) and Lucy Cutting

BINKLEY,
Irene C., d. 7/8/1904 at 44/10/12 in Lyme; housework; married; b. Orange; Alvin H. Derby (Canaan) and Catherine E. May (Hanover)

BIRCHER,
Lillian M., d. 8/15/2004 in Hanover; Leo White and Evelyn Berube

BISHOP,
Charles F., d. 12/19/1944 at 70/0/8 in Lyme; plumber; married; b. Brownington, VT; Alanson J. Bishop (Island Pond, VT) and Mary Jondro (Holland, VT)

BLADER,
Rubin, d. 5/3/2000 in Lebanon; Julius Blader and Bessie Hubsmitt

BLAISDELL,
Charlotte K., d. 6/10/1917 at 79/7/7 in Amherst, MA; widow; b. Lyme; Chauncey Marshall (Lyme) and Elizabeth Kimball (Lyme)

BLAKE,
Fred M., d. 9/22/1904 at 23/9/25 in Lyme; farmer; single; b. Lyme Ctr.; Mark D. Blake (Dorchester) and M. Frances Brown (Lyme)
Georgia W., d. 11/18/1911 at 58/10/30; housewife; married; b. Canaan; Charles Washburn (Woodstock, VT) and Harriet Richardson (Canaan)
Mahala B., d. 9/27/1905 at 58/4/10 in Lyme; housewife; married; b. Lyme; Joseph Brown (Lyme) and Eliza Kimball (Lyme)
Mark D., d. 8/12/1916 at 67/2/10 in Lyme; farming; widower; b. Dorchester; Charles D. Blake (Dorchester) and Jerusha Elliott (Boscawen)

BLANCHARD,
Mildred, d. 10/6/1962 at 69 in Haverhill; b. MA; Edward Blanchard
Sarah B., d. 8/12/1889 at 74/1/27 in Lyme; housekeeper; single; b. Vershire, VT; Joseph Blanchard (Westmoreland) and Abigail Bartlett (Shutesbury, MA)

BLISS,
Charles A., d. 8/4/1957 at 86 in Lyme; retired; widower; b. Concord; Albert Bliss
Emma, d. 7/14/1956 at 47 in Hanover; divorced; b. NH; Herbert Horton and Frances Kempton
John W., d. 1/6/1908 at 84/5/13; farmer; widower; b. Lyme; Reuben Bliss and Nancy Williams
Nancy G., d. 10/14/1899 at 76/6/9 in Lyme; housewife; married; b. Lyme; John Goodell and Lucy Storrs

BLOOD,
Ada C., d. 8/16/1922 at 67/6/3 in Lyme; housewife; married; b. Lyme; Ezra F. Cutting (Lyme) and Fannie P. Meade (Benton)
Daniel A., d. 5/21/1915 at 71/7/1 in Hanover; butcher; widower; b. Orford; Samuel Blood and Nancy Chase
Dennis F., d. 12/26/1896 at 20/1/26; laborer; single; b. Lyme; Edwin Blood (Orford) and Louisa J. Jewell (Dorchester)
Elmer, d. 7/16/1953 at 78 in Hanover; gen. handyman; married; b. Orford; Daniel Blood and Mercy Merrill
Hattie C., d. 8/14/1973 at 96 in Hanover; teacher; b. NH; Gardner H. Lincoln and Sally F. Sanborn
Mercie A., d. 3/9/1893 at 46/5/29; housewife; married; b. Plymouth; Richard Merrill and Betsy Willy

BOARDMAN,
Horace A., d. 1/10/1896 at 70/9/20; mechanic; widower; b. Middlebury, VT; Horace Boardman (Middlebury, VT) and Harriet Addams (Plattsburg, NY)
Mary A., d. 8/25/1894 at 68/1/16; housewife; married; Jacob Randlett (Sanbornton) and Effie Wells (Bristol)

BODWARE,
Henry, d. 11/20/1932 at 65 in Hanover; laborer; single

BOGDANICH,
Judith L., d. 9/24/2003 in Lyme; Norman Lloyd and Doris MacLeod

BOMBARD,
Ellen M., d. 11/6/1929 at 75/2/18 in Lyme; housewife; widow; b. Northfield, MA; James Welch (Northfield, MA) and Ellen Howard (Northfield, MA)
Frank, d. 1/26/1929 at 49/6/7 in Norwich, VT; farmer; married; b. Northfield, VT; Philip Bombard (Burlington, VT) and Ellen Welch (S. Vernon, MA)
Mildred G., d. 12/29/1903 at 0/0/22 in Lyme; b. Lyme; Frank J. Bombard and Dora E. Jewell (S. Vernon, MA)
Philip, d. 3/12/1905 at 57/7/1 in Lyme; teamster; married; b. Burlington, VT; Joseph Bombard and Mary -----
Roy W., d. 11/28/1942 at 1/4/0 in Hanover; b. Hanover; Leon Bombard (Lyme) and Lucia Willard (Warham, MA)

BOND,
Clara F., d. 4/15/1935 at 66/2/26 in Lyme; housewife; married; b. New Haven, CT; Hiram C. Davison (Lyme) and Mary Jeffers (Bethel, VT)
Kenneth A., d. 9/3/1933 at – in W. Lebanon; b. W. Lebanon; Francis Bond (Berlin) and Katherine Quint
Louis S., d. 10/30/1935 at 69/3/4 in Lyme; retired; widower; b. Springfield, MA; John Bond (MA) and Eldora Smith (MA)
Otis D., d. 12/9/1936 at 51/8/2 in Lyme; post master; widower; b. Corinth, VT; Daniel M. Bond (Topsham, VT) and Julia E. Bailey (Corinth, VT)

BOODRY,
Leonard, d. 9/17/1892 at –; laborer; widower

BOUSHEHRI,
Djahangir, d. 12/31/1998 in Lebanon; Djavad Boushehri and
    Fatemeh Mahdavi

BOUTILLETTE,
Mary C., d. 7/1/1960 at 65 in Lyme; housewife; b. Newark, NJ; Albert
    Cooper and Catherine Heminger

BOWDEN,
Philip Price, d. 8/28/1974 at 34 in Lyme; sales clerk; b. NY; John
    Warren Bowden and Mary Sharples

BOWEN,
Clarence I., d. 9/24/1935 at 80/3/23 in Meredith; farmer; married; b.
    Corinth, VT; Guay Bowen and Mary Richardson
Ida Lillian, d. 1/22/1905 at 13/1/26 in Lyme; b. Lyme; Clarence S.
    Bowen (Corinth, VT) and Jennie Gammell (Barnet, VT)

BOYNTON,
Ruth A., d. 1/31/1933 at 60/9/17 in Lyme; housewife; married; b.
    Lyme; Charles P. Hadlock (Rock Island, PQ) and Drusilla
    Hoover (Springfield, OH)

BRADBURY,
David, d. 4/12/1887 at 85/2 in Lyme; farmer; married; b. Canaan;
    William Bradbury (Newburyport, MA) and Mary Meade
    (Canaan)
Enos W., d. 8/25/1908 at 87/9/30; farmer; widower; b. Canaan;
    Samuel Bradbury (Canaan) and Phebe Gould

BRADLEY,
Ann, d. 7/25/1968 at 96 in Lyme; housewife; widow; b. MA; Thomas
    Henessey and Sarah Skillings
Florence M., d. 9/15/1966 at 65 in Lyme; choir director; single; b.
    Rochester, NY; William Bradley and Kathleen McDermott
Leo, d. 9/7/1971 at 61 in Lyme; laborer; b. MA; John J. Bradley and
    Ann L. Hennesy

BRAMAN,
Clarence F., d. 10/14/1973 at 88 in Lyme; farmer; b. MA; James S.
    Braman and Fanny Knight

Eva, d. 12/27/1971 at 86 in Haverhill; housewife; b. MA; Austin Laurence and Mary J. Stebbins

BRIDGE,
Norman, d. 8/28/1968 at 61 in Lyme; clerk; widower; b. VT; Edwin Bridge and Kitty Smalley

BRINSON,
Helen Louise, d. 2/15/1996 in Lyme; Jesse R. Trull and Hattie Velma Wild
Russell T., Sr., d. 8/23/1995 in Lebanon; George Brinson and Kathrinka Tennyson

BROCKWAY,
Carl A., d. 7/26/1898 at 1/0/5 in Lyme; b. Lebanon; George A. Brockway (Waterbury, VT) and Nellie E. Dimick (Iron Hill, PQ)
Earl D., d. 3/23/1907 at 0/1/23 in Lyme; b. Lyme; George A. Brockway (Waterbury, VT) and Nellie E. Dimick (Iron Hill, PQ)
Florence M., d. 2/11/1963 at 75 in Claremont; housekeeper; b. Lyme; George A. Brockway and Nellie Dimick
George A., d. 3/17/1936 at 76/0/7 in Lyme; farmer; widower; b. Waterbury, VT; Charles Brockway (NY) and Margaret Hadley (NH)
Guy C., d. 10/21/1958 at 66 in Hartford, VT; farmer; married; b. Lyme; George A. Brockway and Nellie Dimick
Mary L., d. 9/8/1976 at 80 in Bradford, VT; housewife; b. VT; George Lund and Sarah Ricker
Nellie, d. 6/14/1922 at 56/11 in Hanover; housewife; married; b. Iron Hill, PQ; Ethan A. Dimick (Lyme) and Rachel Cutting (Craftsbury, VT)

BROOKS,
Charles, d. 2/19/1892 at 69/1/26; laborer; widower; George Brooks (Nicolett, PQ) and Mary Ann Pray (Nicolett, PQ)

BROWN,
Angeline E., d. 3/14/1914 at 78/7/12; tailoress; single; b. Orford; Joseph Brown (Lyme) and Eliza Kimball (Lyme)
Dorothy P., d. 3/17/1982 at 64; Isaac Park and Hazel Irvine
Edgar, d. 12/3/1921 at 80/10/6 in Lyme; retired; widower; b. Lyme; Joshua W. Brown (Lyme) and Martha T. Brown (Concord)

Eliza K., d. 2/5/1894 at 85/3/20; housewife; widow; b. Lyme; Eliphalet Kimball (Canterbury) and Betsey Colburn (Hollis)

Frances, d. 4/16/1932 at 19/2/2 in Lyme; housework; married; b. Canaan; Frank Hart (Lyme) and Julia Buckley (Ireland)

Frank H., d. 7/15/1890 at 32 in Lyme; engineer; single; b. Piermont; Richard Brown and Mary Pilsbury

Gerald, d. 8/28/1928 at 27/7/6 in Lyme; laborer; single; b. Walden, VT; Charles Brown (Coventry, VT) and Flora Allen

Joseph, d. 6/11/1891 at 84/8 in Lyme; married; farmer; b. Lyme; Joseph Brown

Ronald Michael, d. 5/21/1989 at 52; Milton F. Brown and Pauline Kroll

Silas P., d. 5/26/1908 at 66/7/26; farmer; widower; b. Wentworth; Charles Brown (Scotland) and Polly Heaton (CT)

BRYAN,

Helen Matilda, d. 2/13/1993 in Haverhill

Hugh, d. 9/29/1961 at 59 in Haverhill; farmer; b. Lyme; Richard Bryan and Mary E. Jenks

Mary L., d. 12/28/1935 at 61/6/15 in Hanover; housewife; married; b. Lyme; Marshall Jenks (Lyme) and Sarah A. Meader (Newbury, VT)

Neal R., d. 4/18/1956 at 45 in Lyme; house painter; married; b. Lyme; Richard E. Bryan and Mary L. Jenks

Richard, d. 9/11/1943 at 76/3/17 in Haverhill; none; widower; b. Canaan, VT; Edmund Bryan and Edith Walker

BRYANT,

daughter, d. 1/18/1901 at 0/0/1 in Lyme; b. Lyme; Fred J. Bryant (Lyme) and Florence M. Henry (N. Thetford, VT)

Arthur W., d. 1/9/1931 at 28/6/26 in Hanover; laborer; married; b. Lyme; Fred J. Bryant (Lyme) and Florence M. Henry (Thetford, VT)

Florence J., d. 4/9/1945 at 63/4/3 in Hanover; housewife; married; b. Thetford, VT; William Henry (Derby, VT) and Elizabeth Emery (Thetford, VT)

Fred J., d. --/--/1955 at 77 in Lyme; farmer; married; b. Lyme; Horace M. Bryant and Clara Chesley

George, d. 6/19/1980 at 76; farming; Fred Bryant and Florence Henry

Horace M., d. 5/8/1931 at 77/9/23 in Lyme; farmer; widower; John

Bryant (Hanover) and Sally Ellsworth (Wentworth)
Randy, d. 9/9/1986 at 21; Sterle Bryant and Lorraine Bryant
Ruth E., d. 3/16/1959 at 56 in Lyme; housewife; b. Lyme; Charles P. Dimick and Florence Carpenter
Sarah F., d. 4/26/1925 at 81/4/2 in Lyme; housewife; married; b. Topsham, VT; Ebenezer Sanborn (Warren) and Ruth Maynard (Topsham, VT)
Sterle H., d. 2/25/2001 in Lebanon; George Bryant and Ruth Dimick

BUGBEE,
Edwin, d. 1/4/1908 at 81/2/12; farmer; married; b. Pomfret, VT; Rufus Bugbee (Pomfret, VT) and Elizabeth Hunter (Canada)
Jane W., d. 4/29/1915 at 83/11/16 in Lyme; housewife; widow; b. Barnard, VT; Charles Walcott (E. Barnard, VT) and Sarah Ashley (E. Barnard, VT)

BURGESS,
George F., d. 8/16/1977 at 58 in Hanover; maintenance; b. Pittsburg; Albert N. Burgess and Nora Stevens
Geraldine Vera, d. 10/2/2000 in Lyme; Arthur B. Chesley and G. Monte Thompson

BURRILL,
Elisha H., d. 11/6/1902 at 76/4/0 in Lyme; carpenter; married; b. Stanstead, PQ; George W. Burrill and Mary Hall (Lisbon)

BUZZELL,
Lewis G., d. 6/9/1969 at – in Las Vegas, NV; U. S. Air Force; b. NH; Glen R. Buzzell and Marian Buzzell
Marion, d. 2/17/1999 in Woodsville; Herbert Harris and Bertha Davenport

BYRON,
Hyacinth L., d. 9/22/2002 in Hanover; Jacob Gardy and Cardy Bell
Oliver, d. 4/7/1947 at 89/5/18 in Lyme; laborer; single; b. Littleton; Oliver Byron (Canada) and Mary Ann Hall (France)

CADWELL,
Louis, d. 5/6/1954 at 87 in Lyme; farmer; married; b. Thetford, VT; Harvey Cadwell and Frances Coburn

CADY,
Lillian, d. 7/11/1929 at 8 in Hanover; Leon Cady and Bertha Rowe (Lyme)

CAMBRIDGE,
Anna B., d. 1/28/1946 at 94/2/18 in Lyme; housewife; married; b. Union Village, VT; Hiram Barrett and Almeda Wilmot
Elsie, d. 9/23/1978 at 85 in Lebanon; homemaker; b. Winnipeg, MT; Fernand Cambridge and Emily Elliott

CAMP,
Anna A., d. 5/1/1938 at 71/2/4 in Lyme; housewife; married; b. Lyme; Amos B. Alden (Dorchester) and Lydia M. Hall (NH)
Bushrod W., d. 1/21/1901 at 77/7/17 in Lyme; farmer; married; b. Elmore, VT; Philander Camp and ----- Stewart (Lowell, VT)
Edward M., d. 3/21/1936 at 73/7/6 in Haverhill; retired; single; b. Hyde Park, VT; Bushrod W. Camp (Morrisville, VT) and Ellen L. Spiller (Chelsea, VT)
Ellen L., d. 9/15/1904 at 71/3/11 in Lyme; housework; widow; b. Chelsea, VT; Joseph Spiller, Jr. (Chelsea, VT) and Lucy Dinsmore (Chelsea, VT)
Frank L., d. 5/28/1945 at 76/6/28 in Lyme; retired; widower; b. Lyme; Bushrod Camp (Elmore, VT) and Ellen L. Spiller (Chelsea, VT)
Goule Jason, d. 12/19/1936 at 43/2/14 in Lyme; farmer; single; b. Lyme; Frank L. Camp (Lyme) and Anna A. Alden (Lyme)
Jay Edward, d. 7/9/1894 at 0/0/2; b. Lyme; Edward M. Camp (Morristown, VT) and Martha L. Bowker (Bolton Center, PQ)
Martin, d. 3/27/1974 at 69 in Lyme Ctr.; retired farmer; b. NH; Frank Camp and Anna Arabella Alden
Olivia, d. 5/31/1937 at 79/5/15 in Calais, VT; widow; b. Calais, VT; David C. Stark (Lyme) and Mary Runnells (Lyme)
Willie E., d. 4/20/1932 at 65/5 in Haverhill; railroad man; married; b. Orford; Bushrod W. Camp (Morristown, VT) and Ellen L. Spiller (Chelsea, VT)

CANEY,
George M., d. 9/2/1987 at 68; Jeremiah Caney and Marjorie Cook

CANFIELD,
Joel S., d. 11/12/1898 at 88/3/4 in Lyme; blacksmith; widower; b. Orford; Joel S. Canfield (Orford)

Mary A., d. 12/2/1892 at 68/4/8; housewife; married; Jonathan Lougee (Hanover) and Eliza Bennett

CARPENTER,
Fannie M., d. 3/2/1893 at 74 in Lyme; cancer, pulmonary congestion; housewife; widow; b. Lyme; Gideon Morey (CT, farmer) and Ada Cutting (CT)

CARR,
daughter, d. 7/20/1902 at – in Lyme; b. Lyme; Charles J. Carr (Albany, NY) and Daisy E. Day (Waits River, VT)
son, d. 8/8/1906 at 0/0/5 in Lyme; b. Lyme; Charles J. Carr (Albany, NY) and Daisy E. Day (Waits River, VT)
Charles H., d. 3/25/1914 at 0/2; b. Lyme; Charles J. Carr (Albany, NY) and Eva J. Rowell (Strafford, VT)
Ellen J., d. 9/24/1897 at 64; housewife; married; b. Bethel, VT; Alvah Jeffers (Lyme) and Mary Hall (Lyme)
Fannie P., d. 2/24/1910 at 35; single; b.Orange, VT; Robert Carr (Corinth, VT) and Ella Lawrence (Fairlee, VT)
Horace F., d. 6/8/1916 at 83/7/7 in Hanover; retired; widower; b. Haverhill; Peter Carr
Peter, d. 10/21/1892 at 89/5; farmer; widower; Peter Carr

CARRIER,
Florence M., d. 7/8/1943 at 71/4/1 in Proctor, VT; housewife; divorced; b. Old Chatham, NY; Edgar Van A. Krum (Old Chatham, NY) and Emma J. Westfall (Nassau, NY)

CARTER,
Lawrence, Sr., d. 9/14/1990
Vivian H., d. 3/17/1974 at 62 in Hanover; at home; b. NH; Elber Wilmott and Myrtle Cummings

CHAFFEE,
Dorcas D., d. 5/22/1999 in Lebanon; James Dixon and Mary Russell

CHAMBERLIN,
Sardine, d. 5/12/1924 at 74/8/14 in Lyme; carpenter; married; b. Hartford, VT; Nelson Chamberlin (Pomfret, VT) and Josephine Howard (Cabot, VT)

CHANDLER,
Edwin, d. 3/9/1954 at 63 in Haverhill; farming; single; b. Hanover

CHASE,
[male], d. –/–/1896 at 92/6/11; farmer; married; b. Hanover; John Chase (Chester) and Prudence Stark (Lyme)
Adna, d. 3/7/1926 at 88/2/25 in Lyme; retired; married; b. Lyme; Moody Chase (Hanover) and Almina Kendrick (Lyme)
Caroline L., d. 4/29/1932 at 89/2/22 in Lyme; retired; widower; b. Lyme; Sidney S. Grant (Lyme) and Louisa Turner (Lyme)
Hannibal, d. 7/24/1903 at 71/2/10 in Lyme; farmer; married; b. Bristol; William L. Chase (Salisbury, MA) and Sallie Minot (Bristol)
Herbert E., d. 8/22/1979 at 71; executive; Herbert R. Chase and Grace Barbell
Irene M., d. 7/15/1890 at 0/7/11 in Lyme; b. Lyme; Edwin M. Chase (Piermont) and Emma F. Churchill (Lyme)
Marinda J., d. 1/22/1906 at 70/6/12 in Lyme; housewife; widow; b. Lyme; Alvah Jeffers and Mary Hall
Mary A., d. 5/19/1950 at 81 in Lyme; housewife; widow; b. Hygate, VT; George Place
Nancy A., d. 2/13/1901 at 89/4/22 in Lyme; widow; b. Chester; Joseph Chase (Chester) and Nancy Eaton (Candia)
Sallie M., d. 5/17/1893 at 83/1/28 in Lyme; influenza and old age; housewife; widow; b. Sutton; James Minot (merchant) and Sallie Wilson
William F., d. 11/28/1960 at 55 in Lyme; salesman; b. Lyme; William L. Chase and Mary Place
William L., d. 11/7/1924 at 64/1/15 in Lyme; farmer; married; b. New Haven, CT; Hannibal Chase (Bristol) and Marinda Jeffers (Lyme)

CHENEY,
Vincent, Jr., d. 4/27/1999 in Biddeford, ME; Vincent Cheney and Hazel Sleep

CHESLEY,
Arthur B., d. 12/12/1964 at 82 in Hanover; retired mail carrier; b. W. Fairlee, VT; Frank Chesley and Louisa Morey
Elsie E., d. 8/25/1987 at 77; Stuart Johnson and Alice Jenkins
Frances A., d. 4/30/1957 at 42 in Lyme; housewife; married; b.

Rumney; Gordon Ashley and Lillian French
Frank A., d. 8/7/1935 at 77/2/15 in Lyme; farmer; widower; b. W. Fairlee, VT; John E. Chesley and Hannah Moody
Frank A., d. 7/3/1988 at 78; Arthur B. Chesley and Geraldine M. Thompson
George J., d. --/--/1991 in Montana; Arthur V. Chesley and Monte Thompson
Guy O., d. 2/14/1951 at 19 in Korea; US Army; single; Arthur B. Chesley and Geraldine M. Thompson
Herman T., d. 4/23/1970 at 53 in Hartford, VT; carpenter; b. NH; Arthur B. Chesley and Monte Devey
Julia G., d. 5/23/1913 at 83/5/21; housewife; widow; b. Strafford, VT; Lewis Greene (Strafford, VT)
Louisa, d. 11/1/1933 at 75/1 in Lyme; housewife; married; b. W. Fairlee, VT; Benjamin Morey (Strafford, VT) and Nancy Rowell (NY)
Monte T., d. 12/15/1968 at 79 in Hanover; housewife; widow; b. Canada; Joseph G. Thompson and Annie Devey

CHILDS,
Abram A., d. 2/20/1901 at 87/9/28 in Lyme; cooper; widower; b. Springfield, MA; Aldrich Childs

CHOQUETTE,
Barbara Hope, d. 7/26/1999 in Windsor, VT; James Morris and Hazle Hallett

CHURCHILL,
David C., d. 5/25/1890 at 69/1/12 in Lyme; merchant; married; b. Lyme; David C. Churchill (Fairlee, VT) and Polly Franklin (Lyme)

CLAFLIN,
Clayton H., d. 5/26/1972 at 72 in Hanover; retired; b. NH; Preston Claflin and Eva Turner
Eva M., d. 4/19/1941 at 82/3/14 in Lyme; housewife; widow; b. Hebron, ME; Melzer A. Turner (Hebron, ME) and Samantha Jordan (Columbia)
Gladys F., d. 9/15/1977 at 75 in Hanover; housewife; b. Hanover; Fred Fellows and Nina Camp
Hannah S., d. 4/3/1889 at 82/7/9 in Lyme; housekeeper; married; b.

Moira, NY; Jotham Stevens (Grafton) and ----- Miller
Harriet L., d. 10/17/1910 at 63/7/17; housewife; widow; b. Canaan, VT; William Loomis and Harriet Thompson
Hazen S., d. 3/16/1951 at 57 in N. Reading, MA; banker; single; Preston Claflin and Eva Turner
John W., d. 6/15/1889 at 74/7/22 in Lyme; retired farmer; married; b. Lyme; Preston Claflin (Attleboro, MA) and Lydia Williams (Attleboro, MA)
Maria H., d. 5/14/1902 at 82/1/19 in Lyme; housewife; widow; b. Concord; James Culver (Strafford, CT) and Aurelia Hall (Hanover)
Preston, d. 4/30/1906 at 72/10/22 in Lyme; farmer; married; b. Lyme; Preston W. Claflin (Attleboro, MA) and Hannah H. Stevens (Moira, NY)
Preston H., d. 4/15/1910 at 53/10/18; postmaster; married; b. Auburn; Preston Claflin (Lyme) and Mary Ella Southard (Lyme)
Willis, d. 3/3/1979 at 73 in Hanover; mechanic; b. VT; Herbert Claflin and Emma Avery

CLARK,
Alexander G., d. 12/4/1964 at 85 in Lyme; farmer; b. Thetford, VT; Wilbur Clark and Mary Cameron
Bathia, d. 4/7/1887 at 79 in Lyme; housekeeper; widow; b. Lyme; Gideon Morey (Newton, MA) and Ada Cutting (Hebron, CT)
Benjamin, d. 6/19/1889 at 65/10 in Lyme; laborer; married; b. Thetford, VT; Solomon Clark and Rachel Sargent
Charles W., d. 10/25/1985 at 80; Alexander Clark and Harriett Houston
Eliza, d. 1/16/1925 at 69/0/8 in Lyme; housekeeper; single; b. Lyme; John Clark (Orange, VT) and Harriet Sloan (Lyme)
Eliza C., d. 1/22/1892 at 87; housewife; widow; b. Strafford, VT; Charles Fox (Strafford, VT)
Harlan P., d. 11/3/1926 at 73/9/2 in Lyme; farmer; single; b. Orange, VT; John Clark (Orange, VT) and Harriet Sloane (Lyme)
Harold F., d. 6/22/2002 in Lebanon; Gilman Clark and Harriet Houston
Harriet Sloan, b. 3/5/1911 at 93/10/5; housewife; widow; b. Lyme; William Spencer Sloan (Lyme) and Lydia Felshaw (Hebron, CT)
Isaac F., d. 11/22/1894 at 84/4/22; farmer; widower; b. Tewksbury, MA; Jonas Clark (Tewksbury, MA) and Dolly Hunt (Tewksbury, MA)

John, d. 10/21/1909 at 90/10/27; farmer; married; b. Orange, VT; David Clark (Lancaster, MA) and Lydia Wyman (Weston, MA)

Laura H., d. 2/15/1892 at 73/5/7; housewife; married; b. Hebron; Moody Pike (Hebron) and Laura Graves (Palmer, MA)

Phebe A. S., d. 10/24/1926 at 88/2/25 in Lyme; retired; widow; b. Lyme; David Steele (Lyme) and Harriet Southard (Lyme)

Susan L., d. 11/15/1939 at 79/7/24 in Lyme; housewife; widow; b. Greengarden, IL; Henry A. Pritchard (New Ipswich) and Emily M. Avery (Plainfield)

Wesley H., d. 12/9/1915 at 77/2/1 in Lyme; farmer; married; b. Lyme; Isaac F. Clark (Tewksbury, MA) and Laura H. Pike (Hebron)

CLEASBY,

Elvina Rowe, d. 7/10/1893 at 61 in Lyme; disease of heart; housewife; married; b. Concord; Ephraim Rowe (New Durham, farmer) and Elvina ----- (Bethel, ME)

CLEMENT,

David, d. 3/1/1887 at 89/10/11 in Lyme; farmer; widower; b. Corinth, VT; Job Clement (Warren) and Polly Currier (Warren)

Eliza Ann, d. 5/16/1902 at 78/8/0 in Lyme; housewife; married; b. Dorchester; Aaron Reed

Fred L., d. 5/2/1918 at 58/6 in Lyme; farming; married; b. Dorchester; Samuel W. Clement (Hillsboro) and Eliza A. Reed (Dorchester)

CLIFFORD,

George, d. 7/20/1928 at 68 in Lyme; laborer; divorced; b. Hanover; Harvey Clifford and Carrie Lowe

CLINE,

Benjamin, d. 5/5/1904 at 67/0/1 in Lyme; farmer; widower; b. Lyme; Benjamin Cline (Lyme) and Caroline Farwell (MA)

CLOUGH,

Anson, d. 10/2/1898 at 96/3/6 in Lyme; farmer; widower; b. Strafford, VT; Wadleigh Clough

Sarah E., d. 7/16/1898 at 95/1/11 in Lyme; housewife; married; b. Potsdam, NY; Isaac Campbell

COATES,
infant, d. 9/21/1960 at – in Lebanon; b. Lebanon; George B. Coates and Hazel Whitcher

COBURN,
Alvah W., d. 11/22/1934 at 28/1/14 in Hanover; farmer; single; b. Lyme; Lewis W. Coburn (E. Berkshire, VT) and Minnie A. Runnels (Wentworth)
Anna G., d. 7/27/1891 at 0/2/28 in Lyme; b. Lyme; Alvin S. Colburn (Enosburgh, VT) and Lulu F. Coburn (Berkshire, VT)
Annabelle, d. 3/2/1923 at 69 in Lyme; housewife; married; b. Corinth, VT; H. M. Gates (Hanover) and Susan Gates (Scotland)
Ellen D., d. 9/3/1911 at 65/3/15; housewife; married; b. Richford, VT; Knight Banister (Richford, VT)
George D., d. 10/12/1985 at 82; Lewis Coburn and Minnie Runnels
Helen L., d. 4/10/1932 at 27/3/7 in Hanover; teacher; single; b. Lyme; Lewis W. Coburn (E. Berkshire, VT) and Minnie A. Runnels (Wentworth)
Lewis, d. 4/23/1964 at 87 in Lyme; farmer; b. E. Berkshire, VT; David Coburn and Lucy Smith
Lucy R., d. 3/27/1906 at 69/3/0 in Lyme; housewife; married; b. Enosburgh; Elisha Smith and Lydia Wedge
Mary Pushee, d. 7/20/1960 at 81 in Lyme; housewife; b. Lyme; Albert Pushee and Sarah Jeffers

COLBY,
Alonzo P., d. 5/8/1891 at 56/4 in Lyme; farmer; married; b. Weare; David S. Colby (Weare) and Nancy M. Melvin (Weare)
Earl E., d. 6/23/1968 at 71 in Lyme; salesman; married; b. Canada; John A. Colby and Katherine Lewis
Elizabeth C., d. 12/6/1905 at 69/0/14 in Lyme; housewife; widow; b. Lyme; Thomas Cook (Lyme) and Betsey Flint (Lyme)
Emily F., d. 4/12/1905 at 75/2/26 in Lyme; widow; b. VT; Alex Decato (Canada) and Nancy Willey (Sharon, VT)
Guy A., d. 12/20/1897 at 22/7; farmer; single; b. Lyme; Alonzo P. Colby (Weare) and Elizabeth M. Cook (Lyme)

COLE,
Allen L., d. 6/1/1984 at 73; John Cole and Beatrice McVety
Beth, d. 2/28/1970 at 59 in Hanover; reg. nurse; b. NH; George A.

Pushee and Agnes Gilbert

Martha, d. 6/25/1901 at 81/10/14 in Lyme; housewife; widow; b. Ireland; Robert Maynes (Ireland) and Ann Corker (Ireland)

CONANT,

Asa, d. 12/30/1887 at 80/0/4 in Lyme; single; b. Lyme; Martin Conant (Bridgewater, MA) and Lucie McClevier (Bridgewater, MA)

Hannah, d. 1/12/1900 at 75/11/22 in Lyme; housework; single; b. Lyme; Martin Conant (Bridgewater, MA) and Lucy McHuron (Bridgewater, MA)

Mary C., d. 8/26/1942 at 70/1/21 in Lyme; physician; single; b. Thetford, VT; Jonathan Conant (Lyme) and Martha P. Howard (Thetford, VT)

Sarah H., d. 7/16/1937 at 73/4/27 in Lyme; retired; single; b. Thetford, VT; Jonathan J. Conant (Lyme) and Martha P. Howard (Thetford, VT)

William H., d. 9/21/1908 at 80/6/14; farmer; widower; b. Lyme; Martin Conant (Bridgewater, MA) and Lucy M. Huron (Bridgewater, MA)

CONLIN,

James E., d. 6/17/1960 at 73 in Lyme; machinist; b. Windsor, VT; James Conlin and Mary Mann

CONVERSE,

Alonzo T., d. 5/6/1891 at 56/1/6 in Lyme; farmer; married; b. Lyme; Marquis Converse (Lyme) and ----- (Vershire, VT)

Ella, d. 12/27/1930 at 82 in Boston, MA; at home; single; b. Lyme; Erastus Converse (Orford) and Rebecca Handley (S. Acton, MA)

Erastus, d. 9/10/1889 at 80/2/24 in Lyme; farmer; married; b. Orford; Lyman Converse (Thompson, CT) and Sally Kent (Orford)

Henry E., d. 5/24/1903 at 59/6/20 in Lyme; farmer; married; b. Newbury, VT; Erastus Converse (Lyme) and Rebecca E. Hadley (Acton, MA)

Ila M., d. 11/25/1940 at 70/2/10 in Lancaster; housewife; widow; b. Tunbridge, VT; Gardner A. Lincoln (Chelsea, VT) and Sarah F. Sanborn (VT)

Jennie Evelyn, d. 11/1/1964 at 79 in Goffstown; retired; b. Lyme; Alonzo Converse and Julia Clement

Julia, d. 2/29/1928 at 86/10/3 in Lyndeboro; domestic; widow; b. Corinth, VT; Obediah Clement (Corinth, VT) and Phebe Merrill

Marietta W., d. 12/2/1910 at 50/0/12; single; b. Lyme

Peter Mills, d. 4/1/1900 at 79/3/3 in Lyme; farming; married; b. Lyme; Marquis Converse (Lyme) and Electa White (Vershire, VT)

Rebecca H., d. 2/13/1902 at 85/10/1 in Lyme; housewife; widow; b. S. Acton, MA; Samuel Handley (S. Acton, MA) and Rebecca Ransom (Concord, MA)

Sarah D., d. 7/31/1935 at 97/0/26 in Piermont; retired; widow; b. Lyme; Reuben Waite (Lyme) and Pamelia Gilbert (Lyme)

Sarah J., d. 1/10/1898 at 52/8/29 in Lyme; housekeeper; single; b. Lyme; Benjamin Converse (Lyme) and Miranda Walker (Charlestown)

Sarah S., d. 3/19/1913 at 87/9; widow; b. Corinth, VT; David Clement (Corinth, VT)

Sidney A., d. 3/23/1929 at 70/8/18 in Lyme; farmer; married; b. Lyme; Benjamin P. Converse (Lyme) and Miranda Walker (Claremont)

William A. C., d. 3/1/1912 at 81/0/10; clergyman; married; b. Lyme; Joel Converse (Thompson, CT) and Abigail Coult (Lyme)

COOK,

Adaline B., d. 9/7/1908 at 75/4/16; housewife; married; b. Washington; Alonzo Barette (Brandon, VT) and Elizabeth Peacock

James M., d. 2/3/1907 at 87/2/4 in Lyme; gardener; widower; b. Orford; Paul G. Cook (Lyme) and Betsy Berry

John A., d. 7/14/1913 at 91/3/4; farmer; widower; b. Lyme; Lewis Cook (Lyme) and Rhoda Conant (Lyme)

Louise R., d. 10/28/1907 at 94/11/7 in Lyme; housewife; widow; b. Greensboro, VT; Ezekiel Rand (Rindge) and Polly Stone (Fitzwilliam)

CORY,

Carlton L., d. 3/4/1899 at 43/10/1 in Lyme; miller; married; b. Chelsea, VT; P. Cory (Derby, VT) and Elizabeth Maine (Hartland, VT)

Frank L., d. 10/16/1950 at 66 in Lebanon; print. prop.; married; b. Hanover; Carlton Cory and Dema Slack

COURTNEY,
Thomas, d. 12/31/1929 at 92/6/29 in Lyme; blacksmith; widower; b. Broom, PQ; Torrence Courtney (Dublin, Ireland) and ----- (Canada)

CRAIG,
John W., d. 3/21/1967 at 85 in Enfield; caretaker; married; b. NB

CRAVEN,
Dorothy M., d. --/--/1991 in Lyme; Edgar M. Cathro and Caroline Uhl
Gordon R., d. 10/13/1981 at 83; inn keeper

CRAWFORD,
Arlene E., d. 1/5/1985 at 70; Robert Simonds and Annie Ebson
Maurice J., d. 1/19/1980 at 71; painter & paper hanger; Ray S. Crawford and Sarah Pushee

CROSS,
child, d. 3/22/1929 at – in Hanover; b. Hanover; Frank G. Cross (Meredith Ctr.) and Doris G. Dennis (Lyme)
Joseph, d. 9/22/1904 at 84/6/10 in Lyme; farmer; married; b. Stanstead, PQ; Caleb Cross (Methuen, MA)
Norma L., d. 4/5/1933 at 0/0/6 in Farmington; Frank G. Cross (Meredith) and Doris G. Dennis (Lyme)

CROWLEY,
Agnes Belle, d. 12/16/1964 at 91 in Lyme; housewife; b. Quebec; Potter Hassard and Elizabeth Grimble

CULLENBERG,
Garrett, d. 5/17/1997 in Boston, MA; David Cullenberg and Christine Leavens

CUMMINGS,
Carlos, d. 6/23/1930 at 80/5/15 in Lyme; farmer; married; b. Thetford, VT; Abbott Cummings (Thetford, VT) and Phebe Waterman (Norwich, VT)
Electa A., d. 12/3/1940 at 90/7/29 in Lyme; housewife; widow; b. Windsor, VT; J. Burnham (US) and Ann ----- (US)

CUNNINGHAM,
Lucius, d. 6/20/1934 at 55/11/8 in Hanover; farmer; married; b. Belfast, ME; Al. W. Cunningham (Freedom, ME) and Marie G. Rose (Searsmont, ME)
Marie G., d. 12/23/1965 at 85 in Hanover (Etna); housewife; widow; b. Spring Valley, MN; Elisha Rose and Ella Cook
T. F., d. 7/18/1922 at 26/6/25 in Lyme; printer; single; b. New Bedford, MA; John Cunningham (England) and Annis Hoag (England)

CURRIE,
Sarah E., d. 3/10/1900 at 0/3/3 in Lyme; b. Lyme; James Currie and Hattie Dunbar (Canada)

CURRIER,
Carolyn G., d. 8/18/1988 at 41; Frank Currier and Harvie Stembridge
Chauncey H., d. 10/3/1944 at 68/5/9 in Lyme; dealer; widower; b. E. Topsham, VT; Garlan Currier and Betsey -----
Grace Warren, d. 2/28/1957 at 48 in Springfield, MA; machine operator; divorced; b. Lyme; Fred N. Warren and Jennie M. Camp

CUTTER,
Donald deJongh, Sr., d. 3/25/1997 in Lyme Ctr.; Victor Cutter and Florence deJongh

CUTTING,
Alice M., d. 3/3/1972 at 82 in Hanover; housewife; b. NH; Albert Hobart and Harriett Phelps
Bernice A., d. 3/12/1888 at 66/3/5 in Lyme; housekeeper; widow; b. Lyme; Benjamin Cline (Plymouth) and Caroline Farwell (MA)
Carolyn, d. 8/17/1924 at 26/8/2 in Lyme; domestic; single; b. Lyme; Frank W. Cutting (Broome, Canada) and Elizabeth Cole (Canaan)
Clyde A., d. 2/21/1990 at 61; Lee W. Cutting and Alice Hobart
E. Dimick, d. 6/4/1927 at 77/5/29 in Lyme; merchant; married; b. Broome, PQ; Hollis Cutting and Sarah Dimick (Broome, PQ)
Edd M., d. 8/9/1942 at 79/3/24 in Lyme; farmer; married; b. Lyme; Ezra F. Cutting (Lyme) and Fannie P. Mead (Benton)
Ella F., d. 5/20/1893 at 35/9/26 in Lyme; phthisis pulmonalis; housewife; married; b. Lyme; Preston Warren (Lyme, farmer)

and Eliza Colby (Lyme)
Elmer W., d. 2/26/1954 at 60 in Lyme; sawyer; married; b. Whitingham, VT; Lewis A. Cutting and Effie Reed
Ezra F., d. 9/26/1902 at 78/4/22 in Lyme; farmer; widower; b. Lyme; Horace Cutting (Lyme) and Sophronia Dimick (Lyme)
Fannie Mead, d. 12/3/1891 at 65/3/28 in Lyme; housewife; married; b. Benton; Moses Mead (CT) and Mary Mathews (England)
Frank, d. 4/7/1946 at 93/3/11 in Ashland; auctioneer; widower; b. Lyme Ctr.; Ezra F. Cutting and Fannie Mead
Frank W., d. 1/19/1920 at 64/1/20 in Lyme; wheelwright; widower; b. Broome, Canada; Hollis A. Cutting (Broome, Canada) and Sarah Dimick (Broome, Canada)
Grace Reed, d. 7/1/1968 at 89 in Lyme; seamstress; widow; b. NH; Henry Reed and Lenora Merrill
Henry P., d. 6/2/1915 at 64/4/7 in Lyme; farmer; single; b. Lyme; Ezra F. Cutting and Fannie P. Mead
Lee Wesley, d. 1/15/1967 at 76 in Lyme; laborer; married; b. Lyme; Frank W. Cutting and Elizabeth Cole
Lilla J., d. 10/29/1942 at 88/11/28 in Lyme; prac. nurse; widow; b. Bidgetown, NJ; Nathaniel Rugg (VT) and Elizabeth Phillips (Salem, MA)
Lizzie C., d. 2/13/1898 at 30/6/24 in Lyme; housewife; married; b. Stanstead, Canada; Elijah Cole and Caroline Bixby
Ray, d. 4/8/1893 at 1/1/13 in Lyme; whooping cough, convulsions; b. Lyme; Frank W. Cutting (Canada, mechanic) and Lizzie C. Cole (Canada)
Sarah M., d. 8/26/1897 at 71/11/28; housewife; married; b. Sutton, Canada; Adolphus Dimick (Lyme) and Priscilla Pelton (Lyme)
Viola E., d. 5/2/1929 at 0/3/24 in Haverhill; Elmer F. Cutting (Lyme) and Mildred E. Dennis (Piermont)

DALE,
Robert A., d. 7/24/1923 at 15/6/26 in Lyme; student; single; b. Springfield, MA; John A. Dale (Stillwater, MN) and Marilla L. Angell (Corinth, VT)

DALEY,
Jill A., d. 3/20/1968 at 3 in Pittsfield; b. NH; Ford A. Daley and Gloria J. Beaulieu

DALL,
Stewart M., d. 1/20/2004 in Claremont; Charles Dall and Emily Maurice

DARION,
Joseph, d. 6/16/2001 in Lebanon; Isak Darion and Rose Nadelle

DARLING,
Bertrand C., d. 1/9/1961 at 84 in Lyme; farming; b. Craftsbury, VT; Conroy Darling and Alma Hyde

DAUBENSPECK,
Mary E., d. 3/24/2001 in Lebanon; Benjamin Daubenspeck and Eleanor Smith

DAVIS,
Alfred, d. 6/29/1892 at 71/2/4; farmer; married; b. Londonderry; Samuel Davis and Hannah -----
Annie E., d. 4/10/1918 at 55/4/17 in Lyme; housewife; widow; b. England; George Lines (London, England) and Ann Chinn (London, England)
David E., d. 12/1/1937 at – in Lyme; b. Lyme; Perry A. Davis (Thetford, VT) and Elsbeth Schneyer (Danbury, CT)
Eileen W., d. 11/24/1917 at – in Lyme; b. Lyme; Alfred T. Davis (Stanstead, PQ) and Vera M. Warren (Thetford, VT)
William E., d. 6/23/1909 at 48/2/15; engineer; married; b. England; Samuel Davis (England) and Jane Summerton (England)

DAY,
Archie, d. 3/12/1919 at 35/6/14 in Lyme; farming; single; b. W. Topsham, VT; J. Day (Haverhill, MA) and E. Simpson (W. Topsham, VT)
Arlene May, d. 10/14/1934 at 7/4/7 in Hanover; student; b. Lyme; William W. Day (Bradford, VT) and Mary E. Webster (Lyme)
Frank C., d. 3/11/1959 at 72 in Lyme; laborer; b. Vershire, VT; Clarence Church
Mary Elizabeth, d. 2/22/1998 in Haverhill; John H. Webster and Albram Coates
William, d. 4/16/1968 at 78 in Hanover; retired; married; b. VT; Jasper Day and Alfretta Simpson

DEGOOSH,
Carroll A., d. 7/1/1914 at 0/4; b. Lyme; Elmer E. DeGoosh (W. Fairlee, VT) and Belle N. Keyes (Reading, VT)
Howard, d. 12/14/1966 at 74 in Haverhill
Nettie P., d. 3/19/1958 at 64 in Lyme; housewife; married; b. Lyme; David J. Pushee and Mary M. Gilbert

DEMAREST,
Charles S., d. 4/10/1969 at 82 in Lyme; elect. engineer; married; b. MI; Sidney B. Demarest and Georgia Reed
Ethel W., d. 4/17/1974 at 86 in Hanover; housewife; b. NY; Clarence West and Susie Luce

DENNIS,
Albert, d. 9/5/1965 at 83 in Lyme; farming; widower; b. Stratford; Fred A. Dennis and Mary A. Gamsby
Alger, d. 12/16/1966 at 69 in Lyme; hotel main.; married; b. Lyme; George Dennis and Carrie Church
Carrie F., d. 7/26/1923 at 54/8/26 in Lyme; housewife; married; b. Vershire, VT; George A. Church (Vershire, VT) and Sarah Aldrich (Corinth, VT)
Dewer L., d. 12/21/1940 at 83/11/21 in Hanover; farmer; married; b. Stratford; Damon Dennis (Stratford) and Belinda Young (Stratford)
Effie G., d. 1/16/1950 at 57 in Lyme; housewife; widow; b. Orford; Everett L. Gage and Nellie Pebbles
Freda G., d. 4/10/1982 at 77; Ezra Smith and Bertha Flint
George W., d. 3/5/1940 at 77/6/0 in Lyme; farmer; widower; b. Stratford; Emore Dennis (Stratford) and Mary Haynes (Warren)
Leroy E., d. 10/21/1945 at 58/7/15 in Lyme; farmer; married; b. Stratford; Dewer L. Dennis (Stratford) and Sarah A. Curtis (Stratford)
Loraine H., d. 10/8/1905 at 2/1/4 in Lyme; b. Lyme; Albert B. Dennis (Stratford) and Maude S. Piper (Lyme)
Maude A., d. 11/1/1934 at 49/8/22 in Hanover; housewife; married; b. Lyme; Walter C. Piper (Pembroke) and Hattie E. Estey
Myron A., d. 2/16/1922 at 60/4/20 in St. Johnsbury, VT; married; b. Stratford; William Dennis (Stratford) and Lucy Baker (Stratford)
Sarah A., d. 8/10/1942 at 76/3/27 in Lyme; housewife; widow; b. Stratford; James Curtis and Diana -----
Steven, d. 4/19/1954 at 0/5 in Hanover; b. Lebanon; Wendell Dennis

and Myrtle Gibson
Wendell, d. 3/13/1969 at 49 in Hanover; bus operator; married; b. NH; Roy Dennis and Effie Gage

DERBY,
Abbie D., d. 1/12/1898 at 67/2/4 in Lyme; housekeeper; married; James P. Dimick (Lyme) and Pamelia Blanchard (Vershire, VT)
Arthur Elmer, d. 4/15/1968 at 85 in Lyme; farmer; widower; b. NH; Jonathan Derby and Ruhanna Gordon
Blanche M., d. 3/5/1965 at 85 in Hanover; housewife; married; b. NS; William Mosher and Sophie Keddy
Charles H., d. 9/22/1960 at 64 in Lebanon; retired; b. Etna; Dana Derby and Mary Thatcher
Dana A., d. 4/5/1949 at 84 in Ashland
John H., d. 12/31/1922 at 90/9/3 in Lyme; farmer; married; b. Troy, VT; William H. Derby and Hannah Avery
Lewis S., d. 11/24/1920 at 84/1 in Concord; farmer; married; b. Lyme; William H. Derby (Lyme) and Hannah Avery (Orford)
Mary E. T., d. 7/2/1940 at 73/4/20 in Lyme; housewife; married; b. OH; John Thatcher (Canada)
Patricia M., d. 12/8/1940 at 82/11/9 in Lyme; schoolgirl; single; b. E. Weare; Walter Derby (OH) and Arlene Hayford (Goffstown)
Ruhama E., d. 9/17/1931 at 91/11/25 in Lyme; housewife; widow; b. Dorchester; Cyrus Gordon (Henniker) and Olive Jesseman (Dorchester)
Sarah L., d. 6/14/1932 at 64/11/26 in Lyme; housework; single; b. Lyme; John H. Derby (Troy, VT) and Ruhama E. Gordon (Dorchester)
Walter, d. 6/5/1962 at 70 in Plymouth; woodsman; b. Toledo, OH; Dana Derby and Mary -----

DESME,
Marcelle, d. 12/10/1994 in Washington
Robert G., d. 1/19/1979 at 80 in Lebanon; teacher; b. France; Andre Desme and Charlotte Janot

DEWITT,
son, d. 7/6/1907 at – in Lyme; b. Lyme; Melvin Dewitt (NB) and Melvina Byron (Littleton)
Mel. B., d. 2/19/1948 at 77/3/6 in Lyme; housewife; married; b. Littleton; Oliver Byron (Canada) and Mary Hall (France)

Melvin E., d. 2/5/1953 at 90 in Lyme; laborer; widower; b. NB; Daniel DeWitt and Emma Webb

DEXTER,
R., d. 1/4/1892 at 76/11/1; laborer; widower; b. Corinth, VT; Rufus A. Dexter (Corinth, VT) and Sophronia Magoon (Corinth, VT)

DICKINSON,
Abbie L., d. 5/23/1953 at 90 in Lyme; housewife; widow; b. Hopkinton, MA; Levi Haven and Sarah ----
Elizabeth, d. 6/22/1954 at 1 in Lyme; b. Lyme; Edwards Dickinson and Marjory Stocking

DICKSON,
Joyce E., d. 2/2/2001 in Lebanon; Richard Dickson and Mona Watkins

DIKE,
Addie F., d. 12/28/1923 at 70/1/1 in Lyme; housewife; married; b. Thetford, VT; Ira Wilmot and Eliza Roberts
David K., d. 1/13/1925 at 90/0/7 in Lyme; retired; widower; b. Lyme; Omri Dike and Hannah Kendrick (Lyme)
Florance L., d. 4/5/1970 at 77 in Lyme; housewife; b. NH; Wilson D. Johnson and Alice Woodward
Frederick, d. 2/18/1930 at 52/7/26 in Haverhill; widower; b. Lyme; Volney R. Dike (Lyme) and Lizzie Nash (Plainfield)
Henry N., d. 8/27/1925 at 79/6/18 in Lyme; laborer; widower; b. Dalton; William F. Dike (Dalton) and Charlotte Fisk
Herbert W., d. 12/13/1950 at 68 in Lyme; barber; single; b. Lyme; Henry Dike and Addie Wilmot
Leslie H., d. 2/13/1948 at 70/2/9 in Lyme; carpenter; married; b. Lyme; Henry N. Dike (Lyme) and Addie F. Wilmot (Thetford, VT)
Lucinda, d. 5/24/1915 at 65/1/27 in Hanover; housewife; married; b. Strafford, VT; Stephen Roberts and Alvira Fox
Volney R., d. 12/24/1911 at 74/9; laborer; married; b. Lyme; Omry Dike (Cavendish, VT) and Hannah Kendrick (Lyme)

DIMICK,
A. D., d. 11/7/1921 at 70/4/23 in Wakefield, MA; mechanic; married; b. Lyme; Daniel B. Dimick (Lyme) and Diadema Walker

Addie J., d. 1/31/1965 at 85 in Ludlow, VT; widow

Adolphus, d. 3/23/1887 at 78/6/6 in Lyme; stone mason; married; b. Lyme; Adolphus Dimick (Folland, VT) and Betsey Gilbert (Folland, CT)

Alfred B., d. 6/24/1897 at 85/4/16; farmer; widower; b. Lyme; Adolphus Dimick (Tolland, CT) and Betsey Gilbert (Hebron, CT)

Charles H., d. 1/21/1928 at 83/9/5 in Lyme; farmer; married; b. Lyme; James P. Dimick (Lyme) and Paulina Blanchard (Vershire, VT)

Charles P., d. 12/18/1946 at 81/10/4 in Lyme; farmer; widower; b. Lyme; Lewis S. Dimick (Canada) and Joan Welch

Cordelia H., d. 3/4/1933 at 88/2/26 in New Boston; retired; widow; b. Guilford; Edmond H. Smith and Hannah L. Field

Edwin P., d. 2/10/1950 at 86 in Lyme; farmer; widower; b. Lyme; William H. Dimick and Delia Ames

Florence J., d. 4/22/1946 at 70/4/15 in Concord; housewife; married; b. Littleton; George Carpenter and Mary Jane -----

Freddie, d. 8/22/1887 at 19/2/15 in Lyme; none; single; b. Lyme; Lewis C. Dimick (Canada) and Joannah Welch (Groton, VT)

Gertrude M., d. 1/4/1933 at 59/6/22 in Watertown, MA; single; b. Lyme; Carroll D. Dimick (Lyme) and Maria Woodward (Lyme)

Hattie C., d. 1/19/1929 at 66/8 in Lyme; housewife; married; b. Lyme; Israel Gilbert (Lyme) and Minerva Cutting (Lyme)

Jane B., d. 9/17/1910 at 68/2/7; housewife; married; b. Bradford, VT; Jonathan Smith and Maria Bartholomew

Joanna W., d. 7/17/1914 at 72/6/15; domestic; widow; b. Groton, VT; J. Welch

Kenneth C., d. --/--/1991 in Lyme; Charles Dimick and Florence Carpenter

Maria W., d. 3/16/1916 at 73/3/11 in Watertown, MA; housewife; widow; b. Lyme; R. C. Woodward (Lyme) and Adaline Clark (Tewksbury, MA)

Nancy F., d. 10/4/1904 at 85/7/0 in Lyme; housework; widow; b. Lyme; Lemuel Franklin (Lyme) and Philena Warren (Hardwick, MA)

Nellie M., d. 7/31/1931 at 75/9/14 in Melrose, MA; housewife; widow; b. Lyme; Isaac G. Stark (Lyme) and Rachel Goodell (Newbury, VT)

Pamelia M., d. 5/21/1887 at 81/9/2 in Lyme; housekeeper; widow; b. Vershire, VT; Joseph Blanchard (Walpole) and Abigail Bartlett (Shewsbury, MA)

Pearl May, d. 7/31/1995 in Lebanon; Edwin Dimick and Hattie Gilbert

Rachel D., d. 3/18/1899 at 73/2/18 in Lyme; housekeeper; widow; b. Craftsbury, VT; Isaac Cutting (Lyme) and Achsah Allen (Craftsbury, VT)

Sarah R., d. 5/20/1910 at 74/7/22; housewife; widow; b. Byer, OH; ----- Romaine (CT) and ----- (OH)

Shirley A., d. 10/10/1939 at 54/9/10 in Wakefield, MA; postal clerk; married; b. Wakefield, MA; Augustus D. Dimick (Lyme) and Nellie M. Stark (Lyme)

William H., d. 9/18/1918 at 80/9/23 in Lyme; farming; married; b. Lyme; Alfred B. Dimick (Lyme) and Lydia H. Davison (Lyme)

DIMOCK,
H. R., d. 10/10/1948 at 80/0/0 in Worcester, MA

DION,
Amy E., d. 8/8/1920 at 52/11/18 in Grantham; housewife; widow; b. Springfield; John Heath (Springfield) and Dalby Clark (Springfield)

DIXON,
James, d. 8/5/1951 at 67 in Concord; farmer; married; James P. Dixon and Mary Lord

Mary R., d. 8/1/1990 at 97; John Russell and Sarah Carvill

DODGE,
Ralph H., d. 2/10/1974 in 88 in Enfield Ctr.; business man; b. NH; Elmore Dodge and Hattie Brown

Russell A., d. 8/2/1935 at 25/6/4 in Lyme; laborer; single; b. Stockbridge, VT; F. F. Ed Mills (Stockbridge, VT) and Lela Thornton

DONALDSON,
Charles, d. 11/19/1954 at 81 in Concord; none; single; b. Lyme; Marcus Donaldson and Charlotte LeLeam

Charlotte S., d. 2/4/1887 at 58/0/4 in Lyme; housewife; married; b. Canada; ----- LaSime (Canada)

DONNELLY,
Nellie, d. 2/13/1999 in White River Jct.; Asa Cummings and Nellie

Randall
Robert Joseph, Sr., d. 6/26/1998 in Wilder, VT; Jay William Donnelly and Della Pease

DOW,
Cyrus, d. 6/20/1894 at –; farmer; single; Aaron Dow (Dover) and Miriam Eaton (Seabrook)

DOWNING,
Robert E., d. 7/12/1926 at 0/0/25 in Lyme; b. Lyme; Walter Downing (Campton) and Mabel G. Parker

DRAKE,
Mason K., d. 3/11/1978 at 68 in Lebanon; store manager; b. Lebanon; Charles Drake and Belinda Tappan
Sarah J., d. 12/30/1892 at 65/6/19; housekeeper; widow; Samuel Drake (Chichester) and Elizabeth Sherbern (Epsom)

DREW,
Irene B., d. 5/19/2003 in N. Haverhill; Henry Blake and Emily Field
Leslie P., d. 12/4/1965 at 80 in Lyme; farmer; married; b. Fair Haven, MA; Frank Drew

DRUGE,
Louise, d. 2/3/1956 at 65 in Lyme; housewife; divorced; b. Thetford, VT; Isaac Messier and Abbie Ricker

DUNBAR,
son, d. 4/4/1903 at 0/0/1 in Lyme; b. Lyme; Robert A. Dunbar (Canada) and Edith M. Simpson (Bradford, VT)
son, d. 11/16/1923 at – in Lyme; black; b. Lyme; Robert Dunbar (Canada) and Edith M. Simpson (Bradford, VT)
Emma J. D., d. 3/23/1891 at 21 in Lyme; single; b. Canada; George E. Dunbar and Sarah Clough
Ernest E., d. 4/29/1914 at 0/0/23; black; b. Lyme; Robert Dunbar (Canada) and Edith Simpson (Bradford, VT)
Frank, d. 9/13/1951 at 73 in Waterbury, VT; widower
Frederick E., d. 7/6/1977 at 79 in Lyme; b. Lyme; Martha Dunbar
George E., d. 3/31/1927 at – in Lyme; farmer; widower; colored; b. Guildhall, VT; ----- and Sarah E. Pelham
Nellie, d. 3/20/1900 at 0/0/10 in Lyme; b. Orford; Flora A. Dunbar

(Potter, Canada)
Robert H., d. 8/5/1927 at 0/0/3 in Corinth, VT; colored; b. Corinth, VT; Robert A. Dunbar (Canada) and Edith M. Simpson (Bradford, VT)
Sarah S., d. 9/16/1899 at 13 in Lyme; single; b. Lyme; George E. Dunbar (Guildhall, VT) and Sophia Clough
Sophia E., d. 3/1/1923 at 86 in Lyme; housewife; married; b. Washington, VT; Anson Clough (Strafford, VT) and Sarah Campbell (Potsdam, NY)

DUNLAP,
Fred A., d. 10/1/1958 at 85 in Lyme; mechanic; married; b. Salisbury; William Dunlap and Ellen Fellows

DUNN,
Charles, d. 4/23/1968 at 92 in Lyme; retired; widower; b. PA; Washington Dunn and Annie -----

DURANTY,
Raymond T., d. 6/6/1982 at 62; Thomas Duranty and Mary Harrigan

DUSTIN,
Cassius M., d. 1/2/1911 at 61/7/28; farmer; widower; b. Dorchester; Ebenezer Dustin and Elizabeth Clark
Lodema B., d. 5/12/1906 at 61/2/8 in Lyme; housewife; married; b. Canaan; Uriah F. Larey and Sallie Chase (Chester)

DYKE,
Elizabeth T., d. 10/1/1908 at 69/4/25; housewife; married; b. Strafford, VT; Ichabod Tucker (Strafford, VT) and Ora Barrett (Strafford, VT)
Emma S., d. 1/17/1905 at 24/7/4 in Lyme; housewife; married; b. Lyme; George E. Tattersall (England) and Mary H. Sweet (Plainfield)
Hannah K., d. 11/20/1897 at 89/9/3; housewife; widow; b. Lyme; Thomas Kendrick (Lyme) and Zepora Kendrick (Lyme)
Harry, d. 3/7/1918 at 81/8/20 in Lyme; cobbler; widower; b. Tunbridge, VT; Benjamin Dyke (Cavendish, VT) and Clovis Carpenter (Littleton)
Janet, d. 3/27/1920 at 34/6/7 in Hanover; housewife; married; b. PEI; Joseph Perry (PEI) and Mary Clare (PEI)

EASTMAN,
Anna B., d. 3/20/1929 at 66/10/8 in Lyme; housewife; widow; b. W. Fairlee, VT; Moses DeGoosh (Canada) and Anne Jones (England)
George W., d. 4/3/1931 at 79 in Lyme; retired; b. Corinth, VT; James Eastman (Corinth, VT) and Marinda Heath (Vershire, VT)
Isaac T., d. 6/24/1890 at 89/9/7 in Lyme; farmer; married; b. Boscawen; Parson Eastman
James C., d. 3/5/1925 at 69/3/4 in Lyme; farmer; married; Carlton Eastman (Hartland, VT) and Annie Henderson (Malone, NY)
Jane B., d. 2/26/1906 at 68/1/18 in Lyme; housewife; married; b. Lyme; Thomas Hall (Lyme) and Emily Brick (Lyme)
Marinda J., d. 3/23/1910 at 83/0/17; housework; widow; b. Corinth, VT; Jesse Eastman (Corinth, VT) and Marinda Tewksbury (Corinth, VT)

EATON,
Anna D., d. 12/16/1953 at 49 in Hanover; storekeeper; single; b. Irasburg, VT; Luke Eaton and Ina Bryant
Benjamin F., d. 10/5/1945 at 77/0/14 in Lyme; farmer; widower; b. Irasburg, VT; Solomon W. Eaton (Irasburg, VT) and Anna D. Kenny (Irasburg, VT)
Bertha M., d. 3/7/1987 at 93; Charles B. Webb and Rhoda Smith
George Brown, d. 1/23/1900 at 61/10/6 in Lyme; farmer; married; b. Plainfield; Jacob Eaton and Mehitabel Garland
Ray P., d. 7/19/1970 at 78 in Hanover; retired; b. VT; Henry Eaton and Eliza Brown

EHRLICH,
Paul, d. 2/18/2003 in Lyme; Jacob Ehrlich and Iram Hutter

ELDER,
son, d. 12/31/1916 at – in Lyme; b. Lyme; B. W. G. Elder (Nashua) and Clara L. Blackman (Huntington, CT)
daughter, d. 12/31/1916 at – in Lyme; b. Lyme; B. W. G. Elder (Nashua) and Clara L. Blackman (Huntington, CT)
child, d. 9/8/1926 at – in Bradford, VT; b. Bradford, VT; Bert Elder (Nashua) and Cora L. Blackman (Huntington, CT)
George Burton, b. 1/2/1962 at 73 in Lyme; farming; b. Canada; Gabriel B. Elder and Margaret Waller
Gordon Lee, b. 10/21/1952 at 0/0/4 in Lebanon; b. Lebanon;

Kenneth Elder and Ruth Bean
Rose L., d. 12/16/1965 at 70 in Hanover; housewife; widow; b. Lyme; Frank Camp and Anna Alden
Ruth A., d. 7/23/1989 at 72; Edwin Bean and Alice Marsh

ELLIOTT,
son, d. 7/16/1888 at 0/0/1 in Lyme; b. Lyme; John F. Elliott (Campton) and Kate Hewes (Lyme)
son, d. 4/12/1903 at 0/0/1 in Lyme; b. Lyme; Harry A. Elliott (Lyme) and Susan A. Carr (Orange, VT)
Allen C., d. 4/24/1929 at 0/0/26 in Lyme; b. Orford; Stanley C. Elliott (Lyme) and Lula Baker (Orford)
Charles B., d. 1/25/1939 at 65/9/20 in Haverhill; laborer; single; b. Lewiston, ME; Thomas Elliott and Susan French
Cora Francis, d. 7/12/1909 at 28/8/9; nurse; single; b. Lyme; John Frank Elliott (Campton) and Kate N. Hewes (Lyme)
Earl H., d. 1/11/1985 at 68; Samuel Elliott and Bernice Webb
Eliza M., d. 4/16/1899 at 75 in Lyme; housewife; married; b. Ireland; John McGay (Ireland)
Flora A., d. 1/24/1920 at 66/10/27 in Lyme; housekeeper; single; b. Campton; John Elliott (Richmond, Canada) and Julia Southmaid (Campton)
Fred H., d. 2/22/1925 at 48/2/11 in Haverhill, MA; divorced; b. Orford; John F. Elliott (Campton) and Kate Hewes (Lyme)
Harry, d. 4/28/1957 at 75 in Newport; store clerk; widower; b. Lyme; John F. Elliott and Kate Hewes
Henry C., d. 11/18/1918 at 58/9/24 in Lyme; farming; single; b. Campton; John Elliott (Richmond, PQ) and Lulia A. Southmay (Campton)
James, d. 1/16/1914 at 91/7/20; farmer; widower; b. Canada; Andrew Elliott (Ireland)
John F., d. 11/2/1925 at 75/2/10 in Lyme; farmer; married; b. Campton; John Elliott (Canada) and Julia Southmaid (Campton)
Kate H., d. 10/2/1932 at 76/0/26 in Lyme; retired; widow; b. Lyme; John R. Hewes (Lyme) and Dolly Stark (Lyme)
Margaret, d. 1/22/1935 at 64/8/23 in Berlin; housewife; widow; b. Westbury, PQ; James Elliott (Quebec City, PQ) and Eliza Magethy (Ireland)
Stanley C., d. 12/16/1943 at 41/5/18 in Laconia; auto mechanic; widower; b. Lyme; Harry A. Elliott (Lyme) and Susan Carr

(Orange, VT)
Susan C., d. 2/9/1919 at 37/7/11 in Lyme; housewife; married; b. Orange, VT; R. Carr and E. Lawrence (Fairlee, VT)
William, d. 11/1/1926 at 77/3/21 in Lyme; laborer; single; b. Mills Isle, Canada; James Elliott (Quebec) and Eliza Maghy (Ireland)

ELLIS,
Gage B., Jr., d. 8/12/1987 at 55; Gage B. Ellis and Elizabeth Kinder

EMERY,
Benjamin, d. 7/11/1943 at 87/8/24 in Haverhill; laborer; widower; b. Strafford, VT; Addison Emery (Thetford, VT) and Miranda Downer (Thetford, VT)
Elizabeth S., d. 3/29/1934 at 83/1/8 in Haverhill; housewife; married; b. Lyme; Ruel H. Warren (Lyme) and Fidelia Cutting (Lyme)
Leroy W., d. 9/1/1916 at 68/6/11 in Lyme; farming; single; b. Thetford, VT; Addison A. Emery and Miranda B. Downer (Thetford, VT)
Lydia Warren, d. 12/4/1909 at –; housewife; married; b. Lyme; Ruel A. Warren (Lyme) and Fidelia Cutting (Lyme)

EMMONS,
Marinda M., d. 3/22/1887 at 77/8/29 in Lyme; housekeeper; widow; b. Lyme; Benjamin Miller (CT) and Hannah Tyler (VT)

ENGLISH,
Andrew, d. 11/12/1897 at 85/9/23; farmer; widower; b. Orford; Andrew English (Lyme) and Mary Goodell (Lyme)
Celinda, d. 12/30/1891 at 75/11/21 in Lyme; married; Preston Claflin
David F., d. 7/7/1898 at 61/7 in Lyme; farmer; single; b. Orford; Andrew English and Celinda Claflin
Mary S., d. 6/20/1933 at 80/7/14 in Waltham, MA; retired; widow; b. Lyme; Zachariah Gardner (Lyme) and Mary A. Robinson (Groton)

ESTES,
Gail Lyn, d. 1/21/1963 at 0/0/7 in Hanover; b. Hanover; Leo W. Estes and Sally Ann Chase
Leonard R., d. 7/18/1966 at 48 in Hanover; equip. contr.; married; b. Norwich, VT; Silas T. Estes and May Waterman

ESTEY,
Caroline, d. 8/2/1906 at 79/2/8 in Lyme; weaver; single; b.
  Rockingham, VT; John D. Estey (Keene) and Betsey Howard
John D., d. 5/9/1921 at 81/3/11 in Lyme; harnessmaker; widower; b.
  Groton, VT; John Estey (Lyme) and Caroline Lamphere (Lyme)
Sarah W., d. 9/30/1920 at 72/7/3 in Lyme; housewife; married; b.
  Hardwick, VT; Charles Wilby (W. Danville, VT) and Betsey
  Taylor (W. Danville, VT)

EVERETT,
Arthur H., d. 1/15/1891 at 25 in Lyme; architect; single; b. Boston,
  MA; Mary S. Clement
Dexter W., d. 8/27/1941 at 63/6/22 in Lyme; farmer; married; b. Ft.
  Fairfield, ME; George Everett (England) and Annie Dorsey (ME)
Mary S., d. 6/24/1894 at 67/8/16; housewife; widow; b. Corinth, VT;
  David Clement (Corinth, VT) and Elvira Spear (Shutesbury,
  MA)

FAIRFIELD,
Ada M., d. 10/31/1904 at 52/4/26 in Lyme; single; b. Lyme; Calvin P.
  Fairfield (Lyme) and Sarah Harris (Canaan)
Caroline C., d. 12/1/1938 at 86/0/25 in Norwich, VT; housewife;
  widow; b. Lyme; David C. Churchill (Lyme) and Lydia A. Perry
  (Lyme)
Payson E., d. 5/27/1923 at 81/10/5 in Lyme; retired; married; b.
  Lyme; Calvin Fairfield (Lyme) and Sarah S. Harris (Canaan)

FALES,
David C., d. 12/3/1915 at 74/8/14 in Littleton; farmer; married; b.
  Lyme; David Fales (Canaan) and Sophia Hadley (Canaan)
Emily, d. 3/19/1919 at 77/4/13 in Littleton; housewife; widow

FANEUF,
A. Nesett, d. 2/15/1934 at 85/8/13 in Concord; farmer; married; b.
  Canada; Euzeb Faneuf and Modest Love
Mary, d. 2/13/1937 at 85/0/14 in Lyme; housewife; widow; b.
  Thetford, VT; Ira Wilmot (Thetford, VT) and Eliza E. Roberts
  (Mt. Holly, VT)

FARLEY,
Peter Dominic, d. 3/8/1977 at 20 in Lyme; operating room orderly; b.

Ireland; Hugh F. Fairley and Denyse Chappuis

FARRAR,
Louis Vollers, d. 8/30/1990 at 63; Holden Farrar and Myrtle Vollers

FARWELL,
Ida, d. 8/28/1922 at 59/3/17 in Hanover; teacher; divorced; b. Lyme; Fred B. Palmer (Orford) and Jennie Beal (Center Harbor)
Maurice L., d. 1/15/1887 at 0/3/2 in Lyme; b. Greenville; George M. Farwell (Nashua) and Ida M. Palmer (Lyme Ctr.)

FELDMAN,
Samuel, d. 2/8/1973 at 72 in Hanover; retired professor; b. NY; Louis Feldman and Celia Lowenthal

FELLOWS,
Nina Camp, d. 4/16/1958 at 79 in Lyme; housewife; widow; b. Hanover; Julius J. Camp and Sarah J. Rutan

FENNO,
Jesse Keller, d. 11/29/1962 at 67 in Lyme; pilot; b. Canton, MA; Herbert L. Fenno and Lucy Foster

FIELDS,
John E., d. 12/7/1982 at 69; Benjamin Fields and Fanny Crossin

FISHER,
Ralph E., d. 5/29/1967 at 59 in Hanover; salesman; married; b. Portland, OR; Ralph Fisher and Bertha Kaye

FISK,
John W., d. 3/9/1998 in TN; Donald Fisk and Abbie Grant

FITCH,
Henry L., d. 9/29/1888 at –/10/4 in Lyme; farmer; married; b. Thetford, VT; Lyman Fitch and Rhoda Crocker

FLINN,
Anna A., d. 10/18/1929 at 57/4/7 in Lyme; housewife; married; b. Lyme; Francis Flint (Lyme) and Cordelia Smith (Guilford, VT)
Edith C., d. 6/18/1922 at 72/4/5 in Lyme; housewife; married; b.

Concord, MA; Levi Sanborn and ----- Vance
Frank, d. 9/19/1954 at 82 in Lyme; furniture refinishing; widower; b. Guildhall, VT; Frank Flinn and Maria Willis

FLINT,
Caroline L., d. 12/15/1922 at 78/7/20 in Lyme; single; b. Lyme; George Flint (Lyme) and Joanna Newell (Orford)
Cora H., d. 1/31/1935 at 59/10/25 in Haverhill; retired; single; b. Lyme; Joseph N. Flint (Lyme) and Sarah E. Balch (Lyme)
Diantha, d. 9/3/1912 at 85/5/30; housekeeper; single; b. Jay, VT; John Flint (Lyme) and Elizabeth Balch (Lyme)
Fannie Goodell, d. 6/19/1887 at 85/7/28 in Lyme; housekeeper; married; b. Lyme; Luther Goodell (MA) and Martha Waterman (MA)
J. Newell, d. 8/2/1903 at 64/11/27 in Lyme; farmer; married; b. Lyme; George Flint (Lyme) and Johann Newell (Lyme)
Mary E., d. 10/28/1891 at 44/4/22 in Lyme; housekeeper; single; b. Lyme; Samuel Flint (Lyme) and Fannie Goodell (Lyme)
Moses L., d. 2/6/1913 at 71/11; salesman; married; b. Lyme; George Flint (Lyme) and Joan Newell (Lyme)
Olivia M., d. 12/15/1917 at 74/3/27 in Lyme; housewife; widow; b. Canaan; James M. Cook and Esther S. Richardson (Canaan)
Ralph M., d. 11/15/1967 at 66 in Lyme; janitor; single; b. Fairlee, VT; Burton Flint and Ella Horton
Samuel, d. 6/16/1891 at 89/5/4 in Lyme; farmer; single; b. Lyme; Samuel Flint
Sarah E. B., d. 7/29/1909 at 68/1/11; housewife; widow; b. Lyme; Theodore Balch (Lyme) and Sally Lovejoy (Hebron or Milford)

FOGG,
Alice M., d. 4/8/1888 at 1/11/28 in Lyme; b. Lyme; George Fogg (Hartford, VT) and Alice L. Fogg (Benson, VT)

FOLLANSBEE,
Elmer J., d. 5/11/1963 at 83 in Lyme; farmer; b. W. Fairlee, VT; John Follansbee and Ella DeGoosh
Grace M., d. 10/11/1965 at 72 in Lyme; housework; widow; b. Lebanon; William Carlisle and Emma Amer
John H., d. 11/4/1926 at 76/1/10 in Lyme; farmer; married; b. Vershire, VT; Sherburn Follansbee and Jane Blood (Vershire, VT)

Mary E., d. 1/3/1930 at 74/9/19 in Lyme; retired; widow; b. W.
  Fairlee, VT; Mason DeGoosh (Canada) and ----- (England)

FOOTE,
Caroline Libby, d. 9/26/1893 at 43/4/29 in Lyme; gangrene,
  Raynards disease; housewife; married; b. Warren; Ezra Libby
  (Warren, farmer) and Laura Swaine (Warren)
Sarah A., d. 7/3/1901 at 87/7/22 in Lyme; housework; widow; b.
  Thetford, VT; Timothy Burnham (Thetford, VT) and Hannah
  Thayer (Thetford, VT)
Timothy B., d. 12/2/1920 at 72 in Lyme; farmer; widower; b.
  Thetford, VT; Ezra B. Foote (Warren) and Sarah A. Burnham

FORTUNE,
Anna B., d. 3/19/1907 at 70/0/19 in Lyme; housewife; married; b. S.
  Kent, England; George Bates and Elizabeth Draper
Lummis, d. 2/24/1909 at –; farmer; widower

FOSTER,
Electa W., d. 12/16/1895 at 77/1/28; housewife; widow; b. Lyme;
  Marquis Converse (Lyme) and Electa White (Vershire, VT)
Thaxter, d. 5/17/1888 at 71/1/19 in Lyme; farmer; married; b.
  Hanover

FOWLER,
David G., d. 6/6/1968 at 66 in Lyme; laborer; married; Charles
  Fowler and Clara Thurber
David G., Jr., d. 1/9/1937 at 0/1/20 in Lyme; b. Lyme; David G.
  Fowler (Newport) and Ollie Greenwood (Norwich, VT)
Lillian C., d. 2/21/1929 at 59/10/9 in Lyme; housewife; married; b.
  Wentworth; Thomas F. Roberts (Raymond) and Caroline Smith
  (Wentworth)
Olive L., d. 10/24/2001 in Lebanon; John Greenwood and Evelyn
  McGill

FRANKLIN,
Betsy D., d. 10/20/1887 at 73/8 in Lyme; housewife; married; b.
  Lyme; Adolphus Dimick (Lyme) and Betsey Gilbert (Lyme)
Elizabeth S., d. 5/28/1932 at 85/11/13 in Lyme; housewife; married;
  b. Dorchester; Nathan G. Shattuck and Hannah P. Sanborn
  (Dorchester)

Erville A., d. 7/19/1986 at 83; Charles A. Davis and Ava Wheet
Harry F., d. 2/11/1960 at 82 in Manchester; retired; b. Lyme; Harry
   O. Franklin and Lizzie Shattuck
Harry O., d. 12/20/1932 at 90/11/11 in Lyme; farmer; widower; b.
   Lyme; Theo. M. Franklin (Lyme) and Betsey Dimick (Lyme)
Harry P., d. 12/27/1993 in Hanover; H. Foster Franklin and Clara
   Piper
Henrietta, d. 5/11/1931 at 77/4/26 in Boston, MA; retired; single; b.
   Lyme; Theodore Franklin (Lyme) and Betsey Dimick (Lyme)
Theodore M., d. 4/15/1901 at 91/9/16 in Lyme; farmer; widower; b.
   Lyme; Lemuel Franklin (Lyme) and Philana Warren (Lyme)
Viola L., d. 2/23/1968 at 60 in Lyme; housewife; married; b. NH;
   Charles A. Davis and Ava H. Wheet

FRENCH,
Nellie F. K., d. 1/26/1943 at 71/9/4 in Lyme; housewife; widow; b. N.
   Hartland, VT; Lorenzo M. Knight (Cornish) and Celestia L.
   Austin (Plainfield)
Walter H., d. 2/2/1933 at 70/1/15 in Lyme; sheriff; married; b. Orford;
   Henry French and Emeline Kenyon

FROST,
Cadis E., d. 3/16/1958 at 47 in Lyme; RR trackman; married; b.
   Topsham, VT; Charlie C. Frost and Rose Boyce
Charlie C., d. 3/28/1957 at 73 in Lyme; teamster; married; b. VT;
   Elija Frost and Mae Packard
Frank, d. 1/18/1928 at 74/4/18 in Lyme; farmer; married; b.
   Topsham, VT; John Frost and Finett Jones
Madelia, d. 7/6/1934 at 72/9 in Lancaster; housewife; widow; b.
   Corinth, VT; Lewis Mativia (France) and Marinda Eastman
   (Corinth, VT)
Maria P., d. 10/28/1910 at 80/1/27; housekeeper; widow; b. Canaan;
   J. L. Pressey (Washington, VT) and Sara Corser (Boscawen)

FULTON,
Bessie, d. 12/21/1969 at 86 in Haverhill; housewife; widow; b. MA;
   George Marston and Louisa Cushing
Elmer Bryant, d. 6/14/1997 in Lebanon; George Fulton and Bessie
   Marsten

GALLUP,
Harry M., d. 6/9/1961 at 73 in Haverhill; b. Plainfield, VT; Hoyt Gallup and Lizzie Glitton

GAMAGE,
Russell W., d. 12/21/1967 at 59 in Lyme; rural mail carrier; married; b. Greene, ME; Alfred Gamage and Bertha Works

GANIARD,
Martha A., d. 8/15/1957 at 83 in Brattleboro, VT; ret. housewife; widow; b. Mt. Pleasant, MI; Henry Heminger and Mary Murray

GARDNER,
Emaline F., d. 5/18/1916 at 79/11/18 in Orford; housewife; widow
Hannah, d. 2/17/1922 at 75/8/29 in Westboro, MA; single; b. Lyme; Zachariah Gardner (Lyme) and Mary Robinson
Lewis, d. 10/10/1918 at 55 in Fairlee, VT; single; b. Lyme; Zachariah Gardner (Lyme)
Mary Jeanette, d. 8/4/1964 at 79 in Lyme; housekeeper; b. NS; William Grant and Annie MacGregor

GAREY,
Julia A. C., d. 2/21/1919 at 69/7/1 in Lyme; housewife; widow; b. Chateaugay, NY; S. Cook and M. Powell
Maria W., d. 12/11/1927 at 68/11/13 in Lyme; housewife; married; b. Thetford, VT; William Slade (Brookfield, VT) and Helen Palmer (Cornwall, VT)

GAULIN,
Katherine, d. 2/22/1959 at 64 in Hanover; none; b. Lyme; Dana Derby and Mary Thatcher

GAULT,
Eva M., d. 5/21/1924 at 42/9 in Lyme; domestic; widow; b. Sandwich; Charles Bagley and Martha Mudgett

GEIGER,
Laura M., d. 6/7/1958 at 81 in Hanover; housewife; married; b. Quincy, IL; Peter H. Meyer and Hannah Menke

GELO,
Adeline, d. 10/11/1935 at 87/3/13 in Canaan; retired; widow; b. Leston, MA; John Camell
Moses, d. 9/16/1919 at 82/6/1 in Lyme; farming; married; b. Milton, Canada; M. Laporte

GENEREUX,
Harrison E., d. 1/29/1951 at 57 in Hanover; none; married; Joseph Genereux and Delia Breanso

GERRY,
Henry J., d. 2/10/1923 at 39/2/26 in Lyme; monotype opr.; married; b. Thetford, VT; John C. Gerry and Sophia H. Elmer (Hartland, VT)
Sophie, d. 11/13/1951 at 85 in Hanover; housewife; widow; Henry J. Elmer

GERSCH,
Clarence, d. 5/10/1979 at 72 in Lyme; police officer; b. IL; Andrew Gersch and Victoria Michaels
Pearl F., d. 4/16/1984 at 82; George Clemmons and Nora Chase

GERUE,
Louise R. T., d. 2/13/1946 at 81/5/28 in Lyme; housewife; widow; b. Chateaugay, NY; Charles Tourville (Canada) and Julia King (Canada)

GIBBS,
Franklin I., d. 11/8/1919 at 80/4/1 in Haverhill; widower
Rhoda S., d. 4/24/1916 at 77/9/10 in Lyme; housewife; married; b. Chelsea, VT; Joseph Spiller (Chelsea, VT) and Lucy Densmore (Chelsea, VT)

GIBERSON,
Floman G., d. 10/10/1965 at 67 in Hartford, VT; laborer; divorced; b. Norton Mills; George Giberson and Lucy Daniels

GIBSON,
Emmons L., d. 2/4/1942 at 61/5/13 in Lyme; painter; divorced; b. S. Wheelock, VT; James B. Gibson (Canada) and Lutheria Alexander (Canada)

GILBERT,
son, d. 3/31/1932 at – in Concord; b. Concord; Charles A. Gilbert (E. Barnet, VT) and Doris Pease (Orford)
Ann L., d. 6/4/1893 at 18/4 in Lyme; single; b. Lyme; Elam Gilbert (Seabrook, CT, laborer) and Rhoda Pelton (Seabrook, CT)
Ansel P., d. 11/6/1895 at 81/3/17; farmer; married; b. Lyme; Ahimaaz Gilbert (Brookfield, MA) and Rhoda Pelton (Saybrook, CT)
Augusta E., d. 6/19/1925 at 77/3/18 in Lyme; domestic; widow; b. Thetford, VT; ----- Chamberlain (Newbury, VT) and Mehitable Annis (Scotland)
Benjamin Franklin, d. 6/6/1900 at 74/11/1 in Lyme; farmer; married; b. Lyme; Jonathan F. Gilbert (Lyme) and Flavilla Grant (Lyme)
Charles A., d. 5/2/1957 at 87 in Haverhill; carpenter; divorced; b. Barnet, VT; Harris A. Gilbert and Agusta E. Gilbert
David, d. 5/–/1912 at 45; widower; b. Lyme; John Gilbert (Lyme) and Elizabeth Post
Elam, d. 11/18/1901 at 77/10/6 in Lyme; harness maker; widower; b. Lyme; Ahimaar Gilbert (Bromfield, MA) and Rhoda Pelton (Gaybrook, CT)
Frances E., d. 6/6/1918 at 77/7/26 in Boston; clerk; single; b. Lyme; Thomas L. Gilbert (Lyme) and Mary D. Fletcher (Thetford, VT)
Hannah M., d. 6/29/1890 at 45 in Lyme; housewife; married; b. Bradford, VT; Henry B. Kenedy (Bradford, VT) and Mary M. Cotton
Harris A., d. 5/16/1921 at 74/0/25 in Lyme; farmer; married; b. Orford; Israel H. Gilbert (Lyme) and Minerva Cutting (Lyme)
Henry L., d. 8/24/1914 at 56/3/16; farmer; married; b. Lyme; Ansel P. Gilbert (Lyme) and Louisa Smith
John A., d. 11/25/1892 at 74/4/25; laborer; married; b. Lyme; Ahimaaz Gilbert (Seabrook, CT) and Rhoda Pelton (Seabrook, CT)
Julia L., d. 5/3/1914 at 21/10/3; housework; single; b. Somerville, MA; Henry L. Gilbert (Lyme) and Mary Jordon (Scotland)
Laura P., d. 1/16/1891 at 67/0/13 in Lyme; housewife; married; b. Dorchester; Samuel Piper (Dorchester) and Clarisa Clark (Dorchester)
Louisa C., d. 11/27/1901 at 80/10/12 in Lyme; widow; b. Lyme; Joseph N. Smith (Hadley, MA) and Esther Bixby
Maria, d. 9/24/1958 at 89 in Concord; none; single; b. Lyme; Zadok Gilbert and Julia Gilbert

Mary, d. 1/2/1964 at 100 in Lyme; housewife; b. Edinburgh, Scotland; William Jordan and Mary Boyl

May L., d. 12/24/1913 at 46/3/22; housewife; married; b. Lyme; George C. Marshall (Lyme) and Sarah Blaisdell (Dorchester)

Minerva Jane, b. 6/11/1900 at 76/3/16 in Lyme; widow; b. Lyme; Dudley Cutting (Lyme) and Mary Bixby (Lyme)

Rosa, d. 4/1/1940 at 77/8/28 in Lebanon; housewife; widow; b. Orford; Eben Woodbury and Sarah Tillotson

Senior P., d. 1/3/1921 at 71/10/28 in Lyme; carpenter; married; b. Lyme; Israel H. Gilbert (Lyme) and Minerva Cutting (Lyme)

Will E., d. 3/7/1917 at 56/11/1 in Lyme; farming; married; b. Lyme; Israel H. Gilbert (Lyme) and Minerva Cutting (Lyme)

Zadok, d. 2/13/1903 at 76/9/1 in Lyme; farmer; widower; b. Lyme; Ahimaaz Gilbert (Bromfield, MA) and Rhoda Pelton (Gaybrook, CT)

GODFREY,
Della E., d. 10/29/1929 at 25/5/26 in Hanover; housewife; married; b. Orford; David Marsh (W. Fairlee, VT) and Delia Smith (Corinth, VT)

GOLDTHWAITE,
Dema D., d. 3/15/1946 at 67/2/17 in Boston, MA; housewife; married; b. Thetford, VT; Carroll Dimock (VT) and Maria Clark (VT)

GOLDWIRE,
Maxine G., d. 9/29/2000 in Lyme; Horace Gaither and Alice Gaither

GOODELL,
Alvin, d. 7/7/1932 at 80/7/27 in Norwich, VT; farmer; married; b. Lyme; Luthur Goodell (Lyme) and Sarah Brown

Anna C., d. 10/5/1915 at 75/9/20 in Lyme; housewife; widow; b. Lebanon, ME; Charles Carr

Charles N., d. 12/24/1935 at 63/2/25 in Lyme; farmer; married; b. Lyme; John S. Goodell (Lyme) and Anna L. Carr (ME)

Ida A., d. 5/8/1918 at 59/8/13 in Hanover; housewife; married; b. Hanover; Charles C. Webb (Newbury, VT) and Mahala Jackson (VT)

Jennie M., d. 7/7/1958 at 97 in Boscawen; housewife; widow

John S., d. 12/18/1897 at 72/8/29; farmer; married; b. Lyme; John

Goodell (Lyme) and Lucy Storrs (Lyme)

John W., d. 12/21/1918 at 52/9/3 in Hanover; painter; widower; b. Lyme; John S. Goodell (Lyme) and Anna S. Carr (Lebanon, ME)

Louise S., d. 6/24/1929 at 79/9/12 in Concord; housewife; single; b. Boston, MA; Luther Goodell (Lyme) and Sarah Brown

Oliver, d. 6/6/1907 at 72/0/22 in Lyme; farmer; married; b. Fairlee, VT

Rose, d. 10/15/1915 at 73/7/6 in W. Lebanon; housewife; widow

GOODRICH,

Hattie M., d. 6/14/1903 at 35/3/19 in Lyme; housewife; married; b. Lyme; Henry N. Tracy (Cornish) and Hannah E. Moore (Stillwater, ME)

Marion, d. 4/2/1987 at 62; Alger Dennis and Freda Johnson

Phillip, d. 8/14/1909 at 75/3/5; farmer; widower; b. Derby, VT; John Goodrich (Derby, VT) and Mary -----

Robert Lee, d. 10/28/1978 at 64 in Hartford, VT; painter; b. NH; Lee Goodrich and Nettie Leavitt

Steven, d. 1/20/1992 in Lebanon; Robert Goodrich and Marion Dennis

Wayne Robert, d. 2/24/1995 in Lebanon; Robert Goodrich and Marion Dennis

GOODWIN,

Fannie E., d. --/--/1955 at 84 in Hanover; none; widow; b. Hanover; George Hill and Mary Ann Waterman

GORDON,

Charlotte Cline, d. 8/20/1900 at 73/0/25 in Lyme; widow; b. Lyme; Benjamin Cline (NY) and Caroline Farwell (MA)

Cyrus, d. 1/21/1897 at 87/10/19; farmer; widower; David Gordon (Weare) and Polly Hoyt

George H., d. 10/1/1/906 at 71/0/0 in Lyme; farmer; married; b. Landaff; J. Gordon and Harriet Hardy

Olive, d. 3/10/1889 at 73/11/3 in Lyme; housekeeper; married; b. Dorchester; George Jesseman (Lisbon) and Phebe Jewell (Sandwich)

GOULD,

John N., d. 10/9/1963 at 16 in Lyme; student; b. Manchester;

Adelard Gould and Theresa Robichaud

GRAF,
Leonard H., d. 11/30/2002 in White River Jct.; Leonard H. Graf and Edith R. Reynolds

GRANDINE,
Joseph D., d. 8/12/2003 in Lyme; Lester Grandine and Amy Smith

GRANGER,
Charlotte, d. 3/2/2001 in Lebanon; Ira Granger and Verna Smith
Ira, d. 4/24/1962 at 67 in Lyme; retired; b. Elgin, Quebec; John Granger and Charlotte Carr
Verna, d. 12/11/1984 at 84; Charles Smith and Anna Foss

GRANT,
Bernice M., d. 11/4/1984 at 66; George Grant and Ethel Pushee
Clyde F., d. --/--/1991 in Hanover; Fred Grant and Viola Ware
David A., d. 4/21/1944 at 87/6/28 in Lyme; farmer; widower; b. Lyme; Sidney S. Grant (Lyme) and Louisa Turner (Lyme)
Elliott M., d. 2/11/1969 at 73 in Hartford, VT; professor; married; b. MA; Ernest B. Grant and Kate Mansfield
Evelyn, d. 9/16/1999 in Hanover; Frank Nay and Helen Lord
Fred W., d. 7/9/1964 at 83 in Lebanon; farmer; b. Lyme; David A. Grant and Phoebe Whipple
George P., d. 9/3/1936 at 50/9/20 in Lyme; foreman; divorced; b. Lyme; John H. Grant (Lyme) and Cina A. Pelton (Lyme)
George W., d. 10/19/1912 at 0/1/19; b. Lyme; George P. Grant (Lyme) and Ethel M. Pushee (Lyme)
Isabella L., d. 11/24/1943 at 87/5/6 in Wentworth; teacher; single; b. Oakland, CA; Justus Grant (Lyme) and Sabra Underwood (Jaffrey)
Janet, d. 10/8/1972 at 52 in Hanover; housewife; b. NH; Frank Piper and Vivian French
John Erastus, d. 3/22/1956 at 73 in Hanover; none; divorced; b. Lyme; John Grant and Cina Pelton
John H., d. 8/5/1907 at 60 in Lyme; farmer; married; b. Lyme; Erastus Grant and Samantha Jenks
John H., d. 4/10/1973 at 64 in Lyme; cook; b. NH; George Grant and Ethel M. Pushee
Louisa Turner, d. 2/14/1895 at 77/4/16; housewife; widow; b. Lyme;

David Turner (Lyme) and Lavina Jenks (Lyme)

Mildred M., d. 9/7/1980 at 95; milliner; David Grant and Phoebe Whipple

Phebe L., d. 1/18/1935 at 77/9/27 in Lyme; housewife; married; b. Lyme; Simeon R. Whipple (Lyme) and Lucy D. Rugg (Orford)

Sidney Smith, d. 2/28/1893 at 76/11/12 in Lyme; marasmus senilis; farmer; married; b. Lyme; Alanson Grant (Lyme, mechanic) and Polly Fairfield

Viola E., d. 11/12/1926 at 48/9/3 in Lyme; housewife; married; b. Thetford, VT; Daniel A. Ware (Thetford, VT) and Luella Morey (Manchester)

GRAY,

daughter, d. 8/30/1895 at 0/0/1; b. Lyme; Orren Gray (Sheffield, VT) and Effie E. Lazott (Nashua)

son, d. 12/2/1967 at 0 in Lebanon; b. Lebanon; Richard C. Gray and Norine Dyke

son, d. 7/13/1968 at 0/0/1 in Lebanon; b. NH; Richard C. Gray and Norine A. Dyke

Aaron H., d. 7/13/1910 at 73/5/15; farmer; married; b. Sheffield, VT; Alec Gray (Sheffield, VT) and Hannah Libbey

Andrew J. C., d. 12/12/1940 at 74/5/12 in Lyme; farmer; married; b. Sheffield, VT; Aaron Gray (VT) and Sarah Simpson (VT)

Beverly Ann, d. 8/18/1938 at – in Lyme; b. Lyme; Harley H. Gray (Lyme) and Hattie M. Pike (Lyme)

Clarence, d. 5/19/1950 at 75 in Lebanon; laborer; divorced; b. Barton, VT; Aaron Gray and Sarah Simpson

Edmund G., d. 8/28/1999 in Lyme; W. Raymond Gray and Irene Page

Emily P., d. 5/3/1913 at 35/0/6; housewife; married; b. Belfast, ME; John S. Farrell and Ellen Keith

George E., d. 12/15/1922 at 0/5/7 in Lyme; b. Lyme; Jesse G. Gray (Sheffield, VT) and Florence Larvey (Craftsbury, VT)

Harley, d. 5/18/2002 in Lebanon; Harley Gray and Hattie Pike

Harley H., Sr., d. 5/18/1975 at 79 in Hanover; laborer; b. NH; Jack Gray and Etta Muzzey

Harry N., d. 3/29/1942 at 49/0/22 in Hanover; laborer; married; b. Plymouth, ME; Dana Gray (ME) and Vinnie Maloon (ME)

Hattie May, d. 3/8/1993 in Haverhill; Henry M. D. Pike and Anna P. Gilbert

Hazel, d. 8/28/1958 at 57 in Hanover; housewife; widow; b. Athens,

ME; Noah Staples and Ida Bubir

Jesse A., d. 10/23/1910 at 0/2/23; b. Lyme; Jesse G. Gray (Sheffield, VT) and Sarah Simpson (Belfast, ME)

Laura Etta, d. 2/2/1947 at 76/5/27 in Lyme; housewife; widow; b. Bradford, VT; Melvin Muzzey and Lauslette Muzzey

Lavinia B., d. 4/12/1893 at 27/5/26 in Lyme; consumption; housewife; married; b. St. Giles, PQ; John Buchanan (Ireland, farmer) and Martha ----- (Ireland)

Lawrence H., d. 12/3/1964 at 44 in Fairlee, VT; logger; b. Lyme; Harlie Gray and Hattie Pike

Nellie C., d. 7/7/1929 at 36/9/28 in Hanover; housewife; married; b. Lyme; Frank A. Chesley (W. Fairlee, VT) and Louisa M. Morey (W. Fairlee, VT)

Richard H., d. 11/26/2004 in Lyme; Harley Gray and Hattie Pike

Samuel A., d. 12/8/1985 at 44; Richard Gray and Olive A. Thompson

Sarah, d. 6/2/1913 at 69/11/30; housewife; widow; b. Sheffield, VT; John Simpson (Ireland)

GREEN,

Clayton M., d. 10/29/1979 at 18 in Hanover; mechanic; William E. Green, III and Donna Morris

Lester T., d. 9/–/1912 at 0/0/6; b. Hanover; William T. Green (Hanover) and Mary Mehan (Littleton)

William, d. 5/12/2002 in White River Jct., VT; Theodoses Tsodakos and Starvioula Kostes

GREENOUGH,

Charles H., d. 5/25/1933 at 80/9/18 in Lyme; carpenter; single; b. Canaan; Robert Greenough (Bradford, MA) and Delina Bradbury (Lyme)

GREENWOOD,

George A., d. 8/4/1946 at 66/11/3 in Hanover; steam fitter; married; b. Walden, VT; Ulric Greenwood (Troy, VT) and Inez Hibbard (Walden, VT)

Harley M., d. 7/27/1985 at 84; George A. Greenwood and Maude Moore

Harry W., d. 4/30/1975 at 64 in Hanover; laborer; b. VT; John Greenwood and Eva McGill

John, d. 7/16/1963 at 82 in Haverhill; farmer; b. Canada

Maude I., d. 2/2/1966 at 83 in Lyme; postmaster; widow; b. Warren,

VT; Foster Moore and Ida Robinson

GREGORY,
Frank T., d. 12/16/1961 at 78 in Manchester; painter; b. Grantham; Louis Gregory
Mildred, d. 3/18/1992 in Lebanon; Frank Gregory and Sadie Mae Porter
Sadie M., d. 4/11/1929 at 43/8/18 in Lyme; housewife; married; b. S. Ham, PQ; Elisha Porter (S. Ham, PQ) and Margaret Thompson (S. Ham, PQ)

GRIFFITH,
William Albert, d. 11/27/1977 at 66 in Lyme; salesman; b. ME; Rufus D. Griffith and Lydia May Haigh

GUDAITES,
Alfred, d. 11/3/1940 at 20/10/2 in Lyme; forestry dept.; single; b. Nashua; John Gudaites (Lithuania) and Pauline Bonntovisch (Lithuania)

GUILD,
Sarah K., d. 12/15/1901 at 87/9/4 in Lyme; divorced; b. Lyme; Eliphalet Kimball (Canterbury) and Elizabeth Colburn (Hollis)

GUITAR,
child, d. 3/28/1925 at – in Lyme; b. Lyme; Harry E. Guitar (Frederickton, NB) and Margaret Gray (Bradford, VT)
son, d. --/--/1955 at – in Hanover; b. Hanover; Phineas Guitar and Kiyoko Ishigaki
Gale Brenda, d. 12/20/1952 at 0/0/5 in Hanover; b. Hanover; Phineas Guitar and Kiyoko -----
Harry C., d. 5/29/1937 at 8/5/2 in Hanover; Harry E. Guitar and Margaret Gray
Harry E., d. 9/1/1960 at 61 in Lyme; painter; b. Merryside, O.; Phineas Guitar and Emily Henry
Margaret, d. 5/17/1961 at 60 in Lyme; housewife; b. Bradford, VT; Andrew J. C. Gray and Etta Muzzey

GUTHRIE,
Robert W., d. 2/14/1981 at 64; salesman; John Guthrie and Agnes Crookston

GUTTERSON,
Dorothy, d. 7/22/1970 at 77 in Lyme; housewife; b. NY; James Taylor and Mary E. Coughlin

HADLOCK,
Charles P., d. 6/9/1925 at 81/0/9 in Lyme; carpenter; married; b. Rock Island, PQ; James Hadlock (Monroe) and Mary Fifield (Ryegate, VT)
Drusilla H., d. 3/2/1931 at 84/7/19 in Lyme; retired; widow; b. Springfield, OH; William Hoover and ----- Taplin
James, d. 5/5/1890 at 73/11/12 in Lyme; farmer; married; b. Bath; Benjamin Hadlock and Marion Blake (Calais, ME)
Mary, d. 12/7/1893 at 73/8/7 in Lyme; pneumonia; housewife; widow; b. Salisbury; Benjamin Fifield (Wilmot) and Polly ----- (Wilmot)

HAGGARD,
Muriel, d. 8/26/2000 in Lyme; Warren Hubbard and Miriam Folson

HALE,
Howard A., d. 11/16/1974 at 56 in Lyme; electrician & plumber; b. NH; Walter A. Hale and Eula Jones

HALL,
Agnes Dunham, d. 12/4/1946 at 84/0/7 in Lyme; housewife; widow; b. St. George, NB; William Dunham (ME) and Lucy Helms (NS)
Bessie, d. 6/18/1981 at 92; homemaker; George Dennis and Carrie Church
Everett A., d. 5/27/1965 at 71 in Hartford, VT; married
Frank W., d. 10/22/1940 at 50/10/28 in Lyme; farmer; married; b. Easton; William B. Hall (Allenstown) and Adria J. Kibble (Tunbridge, VT)
Perley, d. 6/19/1954 at 74 in Concord; laborer; married; b. NH; Henry K. Hall and Roystine Grant
Susan C., d. 6/8/1933 at 84/7/7 in Malden, MA; widow
Thomas, d. 1/15/1888 at 77 in Lyme; farmer; widower; b. Ellington, CT; John Hall (Ellington, CT) and Mary Culver (Hebron)
William B., d. 9/18/1967 at 15 in Canaan; student; single; b. Canaan; Richard Hall and Eugenia Blain

HAMMOND,
Eugene C., d. 1/25/1937 at 72/8/27 in Fairlee, VT; Lorenzo D. Hammond and Sarah Colby
Lorenzo D., d. 3/7/1916 at 78/11/7 in Fairlee, VT; carpenter; widower; b. Fairlee, VT

HANCHETT,
Bernice L., d. 12/27/1978 at 85 in Hanover; housewife; b. Lebanon; Charles Homan and Carrie Kinne
Dennis A., d. 6/24/1912 at 69/9/2; farmer; widower; b. Hartland, VT; Henry N. Hanchett (Hartland, VT) and Phoebe Ann Avery (England)
E. C., d. 2/5/1903 at 55/3/19 in Lyme; housewife; married; b. Plainfield; Albert K. Read (Plainfield) and Sophronia Palmer (Plainfield)
Florence P., d. 10/19/1968 at 89 in Lebanon; housewife; widow; b. NH; Bailey C. Clark and Persis Harvey
Ivan D., d. 6/22/1930 at 57/6 in Hanover; farmer; married; b. Plainfield; Dennis A. Hanchett (Hartland, VT) and Elizabeth C. Reed (Plainfield)
Marlyn, d. 2/8/1986 at 82; Ivan Hanchett and Florence Clark

HARDY,
Herbert W., d. 11/4/1915 at 0/0/1 in Lyme; b. Lyme; Solon B. Hardy (Enfield) and Eliza A. Johnson (Canada)

HARLOW,
Maria E., d. 6/21/1933 at 76/10/3 in Lyme; retired; widow; b. Barnard, VT; Joseph Gray (Barnet, VT) and Rachel Johnson (Canada)

HART,
Clifford F., d. 3/27/1972 at 73 in Lyme; engineer; b. NY; John Hart and Muriel O'Brien
Franklin, d. 4/11/1962 at 74 in Hanover; retired farmer; b. Lyme; Lyman Hart and Minnie Columbia
Gladys M., d. 7/25/1968 at 65 in Hanover; housewife; married; b. NY; Albert Reith and Bertha Ruff
Julia E., d. 2/28/1950 at 63 in Lebanon; housewife; married; b. Ireland; Lawrence Buckley and Nora Tunney
William F., d. 2/1/1965 at 84 in Enfield; hwy. engineer; widower; b.

Louisville, KY; William H. Hart and Julia Stoebling

HARTSON,
Sarah J. O., d. 7/4/1889 at 42/4/17 in Lyme; housekeeper; married; b. Stanstead, PQ; James Hadlock (Bath) and Mary Jane Fifield (Salisbury)

HARWOOD,
George G., d. 2/21/1915 at 53/9/4 in Lyme; farmer; married; b. England; Joseph Harwood (England) and Juliana Guy (England)
Julia F., d. 11/21/1916 at 53/7/9 in Lyme; housewife; widow; b. NY; Edson W. French (NY) and Katherine Bradley (New Haven, CT)

HASTINGS,
son, d. 2/19/1944 at 0/0/0 in Lyme; b. Lyme; Elwin C. Hastings (Corinth, VT) and Viola M. Tyler (E. Barnet, VT)

HATHAWAY,
Ernest F., Sr., d. 10/10/1984 at 67; William F. Hathaway and Blanche Braman

HEATON,
Amanda, d. 11/16/1922 at 81/5/11 in Wilmot; widow
Arthur, d. 4/13/1919 at 80/6/13 in Thetford, VT; farming; married; b. Lyme; J. Heaton

HELLER,
Morris L., d. 6/19/1989 at 75; David Heller and Rose Heller

HEMPTON,
Hollis B., d. 10/15/1977 at 26 in Hanover; dental assistant; b. CA; Gordon Hempton and Nancy Walker

HENRIQUES,
Horace F., Jr., d. 12/12/2003 in Lyme; Horace Henriques and Christine Corlett

HENRY,
Frances, d. 7/10/1930 at 15 in Hanover; student; single; b. CT; John Henry (NY) and Cassie Little (NY)

Lee Suttle, d. 3/20/1904 at 0/6/18 in Lyme; b. Lyme; Ora M. Henry (Thetford, VT) and Bessie M. Mayo (Cabot, VT)

HERMES,
Peter P., d. 7/23/1982 at 79; Peter Hermes and Ledewey DeBryen

HERWIG,
Frederick, d. 6/21/1969 at 76 in Hanover; retired; married; b. Germany; Ferdinand Herwig and Marie Rodenburgen
Trudy P., d. 2/24/1995 in Lyme; Albert Lief and Gertrude -----

HEWES,
Addie E., d. 1/13/1968 at 90 in Newport; housewife; widow; b. NH; John Elliott and Kate V. Hewes
Burton F., d. 1/14/1983 at 89; Burton Hewes and Minnie Pierce
Charles A., d. 11/29/1980 at 60; Burton F. Hewes and Lena Camp
Charles E., d. 12/1/1932 at 80/2/22 in Nashua; b. Lyme; Oliver Hewes (Lyme) and Sophia Bingham (Hanover)
Della C., d. 9/19/1887 at 16/2/24 in Lyme; single; b. Orford; John R. Hewes (Lyme) and Dolly R. Stark (Lyme)
Dolly S., d. 3/29/1899 at 60/3/24 in Lyme; housewife; married; b. Lyme; Albert Stark (Lyme) and Elsie Dodge (Lyme)
Eleazer W., d. 8/22/1911 at 79/2/15; farmer; married; b. Lyme; Ira Hewes (Lyme) and Sophia Jackson
Etta E., d. 5/10/1927 at 69 in Nashua; shoeworker; single; b. Lyme; Oliver Hewes (Lyme) and Sophia Burnham (Hanover)
Frank S., d. 2/23/1947 at 75/6/24 in Lyme; ret. farmer; married; b. Lyme; Nathan W. Hewes (Lyme) and Lucy Cobb (Hardwick, VT)
Gerald Francis, d. 12/31/1996 in Lyme; Berton F. Hewes and Lena Camp
Grace T., d. 11/18/1912 at 0/2/2; b. Lyme; Fred C. Hewes (Lyme) and Ethel G. Spencer (Hanover)
John R., d. 11/3/1912 at 84/7/14; farmer; widower; b. Lyme; John F. Hewes (Lyme) and Elizabeth Richardson (Canaan)
Lucy W., d. 6/4/1888 at 49/0/27 in Lyme; housekeeper; married; b. Hardwick, VT; Anson Cobb (Hardwick, VT) and Arabella Wright (Hanover)
Michael J., d. 3/19/1891 at 60/11/17 in Lyme; carpenter; married; b. Lyme; Ira Hewes (Lyme) and Sophia Jackson (Lyme)
Nancy, d. 5/6/1979 at 32; in Lyme; none; b. NH; Gerald F. Hewes

and Margaret Pierce
Nathan W., d. 1/22/1908 at 75/8/29; farmer; widower; b. Lyme; Sylvanus Hewes (Lyme) and Miriam Wright (Hanover)
Ralph W., d. 4/17/1929 at 23/6 in Lyme; laborer; married; b. Lyme; Frank S. Hewes (Lyme) and Addie Elliott (Lyme)
Ruth M., d. 3/7/1914 at 78/9/9; housewife; widow; b. Orford; James Learned
Sarah Alice, d. 2/12/1957 at 88 in Lyme; none; single; b. Lyme; Sewell Hewes and Minette Webb
Sarah M. W., d. 11/23/1905 at 72/2 in Lyme; housewife; married; b. Lyme; Charles C. Webb (Newbury) and Mahala Jackson (Lyme)
Sewell, d. 11/17/1924 at 90/3/20 in Lyme; farmer, painter; widower; b. Lyme; Cyrus Hewes (Lyme) and Sallie Dimick (Lyme)
Starlus J., d. 8/14/1902 at 25/6/21 in Lyme; farmer; single; Eleazer W. Hewes (Lyme) and Ruth M. Learned (Bath)

HIGGINS,
Arthur G., d. 2/24/1984 at 69; Arthur Higgins
Charles A., d. 1/10/1984 at 48; Harold Higgins and Myrtle Jordan

HILL,
Ernest, d. 6/23/1957 at 76 in Hanover; wood worker; divorced; b. St. Johnsbury, VT; Joseph Hill and Dimmia Stone
Newton, d. 7/18/1898 at 66 in Lyme; widower; b. Lyme

HILLIAR,
Benjamin H., d. 6/1/1985 at 75; Raymond H. Hilliar and Mary Lawson

HINCHCLIFFE,
George, d. 5/17/1970 at 81 in Hanover; retired; b. Canada; John Hinchcliffe and Ida Devitt

HOAG,
Ellen, d. 6/13/1932 at 73/8/28 in Lyme; widow; b. Forestdale, VT; John ----- and Lucinda McDowell (Brandon, VT)

HOBART,
Albert, d. 9/9/1918 at 73/5/2 in Hanover; farming; married
Hariett N., d. 2/8/1952 at 95 in Lyme; retired; widow; b. Lowell, MA;

Timothy Phelps and Hariett N. Dickey

HOBBS,
Carlos, d. 12/7/1913 at 67/1/19; farmer; married; b. Wentworth; Daniel Hobbs (Wentworth) and Abigail Whitman (Lyme)
Chester, d. 11/11/1966 at 85 in Lyme; farming; single; b. Wentworth; Carlos Hobbs and Mary Ellsworth
Daniel, d. 5/20/1893 at 85/1/26 in Lyme; old age, heart disease; farmer; widower; b. Wentworth; Joshua Hobbs
George B., d. 4/17/1972 at 49 in Hanover; salesman; b. NH; Hervey Hobbs and Jessie Waterman
Hervey H., d. 8/25/1941 at 61/5/10 in Lyme; coal dealer; married; b. Wentworth; Carlos Hobbs (Wentworth) and Mary Ellsworth (Wentworth)
Jessie D., d. 5/15/1947 at 60/2/8 in Lyme; housewife; widow; b. Thetford, VT; Erni Waterman (Thetford, VT) and Hattie Roberts (Lyme)
Larry B., d. 10/1/1951 at 1 in Hanover; George Hobbs and Marion Pushee
Mary A., d. 5/16/1916 at 54/11/7 in Lyme; housewife; widow; b. Wentworth; Benjamin Ellsworth (Wentworth) and Hannah Davis (Wentworth)
Maurice, d. 3/25/1953 at 42 in Lyme; clerk; single; b. Lyme; Hervey Hobbs and Jessie Waterman

HODGDON,
Kathleen, d. 6/12/1992 in Lebanon; Alfred Hill and Kate Stone

HOFHEINS,
Roger W., d. 6/26/1975 at 64 in Hartford, VT; consulting engineer; b. NY; Walter Hofheins

HOKANS,
Cory Barnes, d. 9/23/1969 at 21 in Lyme; student; married; b. MA; Corlyn B. Hokans and Ruth Weheldon

HOLDING,
William H., d. 6/3/1999 in Lyme; George Holding and May Porter

HOLT,
Clarence E., d. 5/7/1895 at 21/3/9; single; b. Lyme; Henry H. Holt

(Dorchester) and Martha A. Warren (Lyme)
Emily M., d. 8/3/1900 at 78/1/26 in Lyme; housework; widow; b. Hartland, VT; Esther B. Finley
Franklin, d. 1/29/1906 at 88/0/21 in Lyme; farmer; widower; b. Dorchester; Jedediah Holt (Pembroke) and Martha Noyes (Pembroke)
Freeman J., d. 6/23/1889 at 63/0/26 in Lyme; farmer; married; b. Lyme; Lester Holt and Lydia French (Rumney)
George H., d. 7/28/1926 at 68 in Keene; retired; married; b. Lyme; Isaac P. Holt (Lyme) and Esther Swan
Herbert H., d. 2/16/1922 at 64/4/19 in Lyme; farmer; married; b. Lyme; Isaac P. Holt (Lyme) and Emily Mallard
Henry H., d. 8/20/1902 at 59/5/20 in Lyme; merchant; married; b. Dorchester; Franklin Holt (Dorchester) and Eliza Sanborn (Dorchester)
Ida May, d. 6/14/1889 at 37/4/29 in Lyme; housekeeper; married; b. Lyme; Hiram Barnes (Lebanon) and Esther G. Gillett (Thetford, VT)
Isaac P., d. 4/6/1897 at 78/11/10; farmer; married; b. Lyme; Lester Holt (CT)
Martha W., d. 1/20/1929 at 83/10/14 in Lyme; housewife; widow; b. Lyme; Asa Warren (Lyme) and Mary Ann Derby (Lyme)
Sara, d. 7/31/1966 at 86 in Daytona Beach, FL; single

HOOD,
Nelson R., d. 1/11/1930 at 0/9/9 in Lyme; b. Lyme; Nelson A. Hood (Newbury, VT) and Ida Filbrick (Springfield)

HORTON,
Clark, d. 12/9/1966 at 66 in Lyme; professor; married; b. Crawford Co., OH; Willie Horton and Louisa Schurr
Ethel M., d. 3/5/1969 at 77 in Bradford, VT; housewife; married; b. NH; Clarence S. Pushee and Fanny Post
Frances B., d. 3/17/1928 at 48/4/27 in Lyme; housework; widow; b. Springfield; William C. Kempton (Croydon) and Alvirah H. Johnson (W. Springfield)
Gertrude E., d. 11/4/1984 at 79; William Crowley and Belle Hazzard
Herbert C., d. 11/10/1921 at 64/5/5 in Lyme; farmer; married; b. Enfield; Charles H. Horton (Enfield) and Daisy Purmort (Enfield)
Louisa H., d. 6/28/1889 at 63/11/11 in Lyme; housekeeper; widow; b. Lyme; Shubael Dimick (Lyme) and Mary Gardner (Lyme)

William, d. 4/5/1974 at 66 in Hanover; houseman; b. NH; Herbert
Horton and Frances Kempton

HOSFORD,
Clarence, d. 6/12/1956 at 80 in Lyme; lumberman; widower; b.
Thetford, VT; Joseph T. Hosford and Julia Kent

HOUGHTON,
Henry N., d. 2/22/1963 at 83 in Hanover; retired farmer; b.
Lunenburg, MA; Hiram R. Houghton and Flora L. Simonds

HOUSE,
Clinton E., d. 12/28/1933 at 70/3 in Troy, VT; laborer; widower; b.
Newport, VT; Timothy J. House (Stanstead, PQ) and Charlotte
C. Martin (Stanstead, PQ)
Lottie D., d. 8/30/1906 at 35/8/20 in Lyme; housewife; married; b.
Lyme; Elam Gilbert (Lyme) and Hannah M. Kennedy (Bradford,
VT)
Louisa M., d. 9/9/1896 at 0/4; b. Littleton; Clinton House (Newport,
VT) and Lottie Gilbert (Lyme)

HOWARD,
Anderson, d. 1/11/1927 at 82/3/2 in Rumney; farmer; married; b.
Lyme; Zadock Howard (Lyme) and Talbath Fifield (Lyme)
Blanche S., d. 1/4/1929 at 49 in Rumney; single; Anderson Howard
(Lyme) and Julia Cutting (Canada)
Emily Bailey, d. 5/29/1896 at 87/5/19; housewife; widow; b. Bath;
Caleb Bailey (Bath) and Deborah Fitch (Windham, CT)
Julia A., d. 4/21/1929 at 75/5/20 in Rumney; housewife; widow; b.
Canada; Hollis A. Cutting and Sarah A. Dimick
Rhoda, d. 12/24/1888 at 79/5/23 in Lyme; housekeeper; married; b.
Lyme; John Bishop (New York, NY) and Sally Kimball
(Sanbornton)
Zadok, d. 1/26/1890 at 85/8/12 in Lyme; mechanic; married; b.
Lyme; Zadok Howard (Lyme) and Deborah Clapp

HOWITT,
Blanch, d. 8/19/1888 at 1/2/2 in Lyme; b. New York, NY; Charles
Howitt (England) and Lucy Baswood (New York, NY)

HUBERTH,
Martin F., Jr., d. 1/3/1968 at 63 in Hanover; retired realtor; married; b. NY; Martin Huberth and Francis Hotze

HUGHES,
Maurice E., d. 3/23/1926 at 73/1/10 in Lyme; printer; widower; b. Narrows, NB; William M. Hughes (St. Johns, NB) and Anne M. Carey (Narrows, NB)

HUMISTON,
son, d. 4/13/1898 at 0/2/11 in Lyme; b. Lyme; John A. Humiston (Chateaugay, NY) and Mabel Small (Rockburn, PQ)
Frank, d. 1/12/1974 at 79 in Lyme Ctr.; laborer; b. NH; Frank Humiston and Carrie M. Tarbel
Kenneth J., d. 7/23/1979 at 44 in Lyme; laborer; Frank Humiston and Sylvia Wilmot
Sylvia J., d. 6/8/1966 at 57 in Lyme; housewife; married; b. Lyme; Elber Wilmot and Myrtle Cummings

HUMPHREY,
Hattie M., d. 4/9/1940 at 75/10/8 in Lyme; housewife; widow; b. Vershire, VT; Daniel Clark (Berwick, ME) and Lucy P. Brown (Enosburg, VT)

HUNTINGTON,
son, d. 4/27/1924 at – in Lyme; b. Lyme; John Huntington (Thetford, VT) and Eva L. Granger (Chateaugay, NY)

HURLBURT,
Matilda, d. 6/23/1908 at 70/3/16; housewife; widow; b. W. Rumney; David Emerton (Lyme) and Fannie Bowers (Hanover)

HURLBUTT,
Martha, d. 3/22/1969 at 82 in Haverhill; retired; widow; b. Canada; William Maguire and Ella Everett

HUTCHINS,
Charles H., d. 2/28/1937 at 63/6 in Lyme; farmer; married; b. Hanover; John W. Hutchins (Bolton, CT) and Lizzie Webb (Hanover)
George, d. 10/31/1933 at – in Haverhill; divorced; John W. Hutchins

(Boltonville, CT) and Eliza Webb (Hanover)
John, d. 3/15/1909 at 74/10/16; housewife (?); widower; b. CT
John, d. 5/17/1974 at 64 in Lyme; heavy equip. operator; b. NH; Joseph D. Hutchins and Kate Johnson
Lawrence, d. 1/30/1957 at 57 in Hanover; carpenter; divorced; b. NH; Charles Hutchins and Elsie King
Mary Eliza, d. 12/5/1900 at 54/10/5 in Lyme; housewife; married; b. Lyme; Charles Webb (Newbury, VT) and Mahala Jackson (Lyme)
Ruth Ann, d. 6/28/1972 at 62 in Hanover; housewife; b. NH; Wilbur Beard and Minnie George

HYMAN,
Trina Schart, d. 11/19/2004 in Lebanon; Albert Schart and Margaret Bruck

IMREDY,
Denis S., d. 11/8/1981 at 79; research; Stephen Imredy and Agnes Elder

INGALLS,
son, d. 12/5/1921 at – in Lyme; b. Lyme; Fred E. Ingalls (Chester, MA) and Ray Sherwood (NJ)
Ray S., d. 12/9/1921 at 40/10/21 in Lyme; housewife; married; b. NJ; Morgan Sherwood (MI) and Sarah K. Stout (NJ)

INGRAHAM,
David, d. 9/2/1978 at 60 in Lyme; lawyer; b. Brooklyn, NY; Henry Ingraham and Mary Shotwell

IRVINE,
Frances, d. 4/3/1954 at 89 in Hanover; none; single; b. Hackensack, NJ; William Irvine and Lucinda Yearance

ISBELL,
Margaret, d. 3/15/1971 at 72 in Bermuda; b. MA

JACKMAN,
Charles Ray, d. 1/9/1965 at 74 in Lyme; carpenter; married; b. Lyman; Charles Jackman and Netta Noyes
Mary W., d. 11/18/1919 at 70/11/5 in Mech., NY; housewife; widow;

b. Lyme; J. Whipple (Lyme) and E. Flint (Lyme)

Ruth, d. 4/19/1966 at 75 in Hanover; housewife; widow; b. Piermont; George Dennis and Carrie Church

JACKSON,
Eleanora A., d. 6/20/1902 at 46/1/26 in Lyme; divorced; b. Weare; John Andrews (Weare) and Martha A. Dow (Hill)

Maisie C., d. 9/13/1999 in Lyme; Christopher Cowper and Mary Waite

JAMESON,
Harold L., d. 6/21/1974 at 65 in Lyme; woodsman; b. NH; Howard C. Jameson and Alice L. Bellieviau

JEFFERS,
Mary Hall, d. 8/18/1889 at 83/3/13 in Lyme; widow; b. Lyme; John Hall and Mary Culver (CT)

JENKS,
Arthur Lewis, d. 12/4/1963 at 94 in Haverhill; farming; b. Ludlow, NH; Lucien Jenks and Almeda Bartlett

Benjamin B., d. 5/17/1915 at 60 in Boston, MA; meat cutter; married; b. Lyme; Elias Jenks (Lyme) and Matilda Lamphere (Lyme)

Chester C., d. 10/31/1974 at 67 in Hanover; retired const. worker; b. NH; Edward Jenks and Mae Lamont

Clara Mae, b. 5/16/1951 at 65 in Littleton; housewife; widow; David LaMotte and Lavina Jenks

Deborah M., d. 6/6/1980 at 21; pharmacy technician; Thomas E. Jenks and Doris Balch

Edith G., d. 10/19/1941 at 73/2/29 in Nor'd, MA; housewife; married; b. Granby, MA; Martin S. Arnold (Pelham, MA) and Lydia A. Warner (Belchertown, MA)

Edward B., d. 12/30/1917 at 0/0/3 in Lyme; b. Lyme; Andrew B. Jenks (Albany, VT) and Amy M. Guyer (Lebanon)

Edward E., d. 4/23/1925 at 51/7/14 in Lyme; laborer; married; b. Lyme; John E. Jenks (Lyme) and Kate DeCato

Edward L., d. 4/23/2000 in Lyme; Edward F. Jenks and Edith Record

Elbridge, d. 1/28/1982 at 72; Richard E. Jenks and May C. LaMott

Elias, d. 1/21/1888 at 65/0/14 in Lyme; mechanic; married; b. Lyme; Elias Jenks (Woodstock, CT) and Lavisa Jackson (Corinish)

Esther M., d. 1/13/1919 at 1/8/17 in Lyme; b. Lyme; E. E. Jenks

(Lyme) and M. C. LaMotte (Lyme)

Ethel C., d. 1/14/1978 at 72 in Hanover; housewife; b. Holyoke, MA; Florus Carrier and Florence Krum

Jonathan C., d. 11/25/1980 at 0/9; James L. Jenks and Patricia A. Grant

Leo A., d. 7/25/1956 at 55 in Hanover; lumber dealer; married; b. MA; Arthur Jenks and Edith Arnold

Lillian B., d. 2/18/2000 in Lebanon; Frank Gregory and Sadie Porter

Marion E., d. 9/23/1953 at 41 in Lyme; housewife; married; b. Lyme; Fred Hanchett and Bernice Homan

Marshall, d. 3/12/1888 at 65/1/2 in Lyme; laborer; married; b. Lyme; Elias Jenks (Woodstock, CT) and Lavisa Jackson (Corinish)

Richard F., d. 11/26/1978 at 45 in Hanover; construction worker; b. Hanover; Chester Jenks and Marion Hanchett

Sarah A., d. 6/26/1919 at 76/5/16 in Lyme; housewife; widow; b. Thetford, VT; N. Mealer and M. Lamphere

Steven Roy, d. 12/31/1976 at 23 in Reidsville, NC; serviceman, US Navy; b. NH; Thomas Edward Jenks and Doris Helen Balch

Thelma P., d. 6/30/1976 at 80 in Hanover; housewife; b. NH; Charles Stickney and Inez Hadlock

Thomas E., d. 4/23/1979 at 47 in Lyme; folder operator; b. NH; Elbridge Jenks and Lillian Gregory

JEWELL,

Caroline W., d. 5/8/1889 at 62/0/4 in Lyme; housekeeper; married; b. Wentworth; Henry Whitcher (Chester) and Betsey E. Sanders (Dunbarton)

Carroll C., d. 7/23/1919 at 53/5/1 in Lyme; farming; married; b. Lyme; J. Jewell and C. Whitcher (Wentworth)

Daisy E., d. 6/14/1940 at 55/11/23 in Hanover; housewife; married; b. VT; Jasper Day and Alferetta Simpson

Frank, d. 8/6/1932 at 83/1/6 in Lyme; farmer; widower; b. Dorchester; John Jewell (NY) and ----- Jesseman

John, d. 5/20/1894 at 77/2/7; farmer; married; b. Berlin, ME; Mark Jewell (Berlin, ME) and Mabel Hall

John L., d. 5/15/1956 at 69 in Hanover; widower; b. Canada; Frank Jewell

Otis Franklin, d. 10/24/1896 at 14/4/8; single; b. Barnston, PQ; Frank Jewell (Dorchester) and Eliza Jewell (VT)

JEWETT,
Maude J. S., d. 4/7/1941 at 72/3/26 in Lyme; housewife; widow; b. Randolph, VT; George Stearns (Lebanon) and Josephine Perley (Randolph, VT)

JOCELYN,
Maria R., d. 9/15/1892 at 59/6/28; widow; b. Lyme; Freeman Jocelyn (Lyme) and Abigail Bowman (Lyme)

JOHNSON,
child, d. 1/12/1888 at – in Lyme; b. Lyme; Wilson D. Johnson (Hanover) and Alice S. Woodward (Hanover)
son, d. 12/23/1894 at 0/0/3; b. Lyme; Wilson D. Johnson (Hanover) and Alice S. Woodward (Hanover)
Alice, d. 3/12/1935 at 73/9/10 in Concord; housewife; married; b. Hanover; John M. Woodward (NH) and Lydia Southard (VT)
Barbara C., d. 2/2/1959 at 43 in Laconia; b. Orange, MA; Ernest L. Johnson and Kathleen F. Cook
Bertha M., d. 6/15/1960 at 82 in Haverhill; housewife; b. Lyme; Francis Flint and Cordelia Smith
Fred H., d. --/--/1955 at 91 in Woodsville; retired; married; b. Norwich, VT; John J. Johnson and Harriet Fox
Frederick A., d. 10/27/1968 at 60 in Lyme; sales executive; married; b. NH; Hans Johnson and Elida Nelson
George Lawton, d. 4/2/1986 at 76; Clyde W. Johnson and Isabelle Woodward
Georgia A., d. 3/27/1930 at 72/1/4 in White River Jct.; housewife; b. Concord; Samuel H. Flanders and Jane Nelson (Lyme)
Grace D., d. 4/12/1931 at 51/3/24 in Lyme; housewife; married; b. Lyme; Frank Frost (Topsham, VT) and Delia Mativia (Hartland, VT)
Hanes E., d. 10/7/1958 at 79 in Hanover; janitor; widower; b. Bradford; Arthur F. Johnson and Ida Carlton
Harriet, d. 10/2/1927 at 89/5/18 in Lyme; housewife; widow; b. Hanover; Daniel Fox and Margaret Griffin
John H., d. 11/10/1923 at 91/11 in Lyme; farmer; married; b. Underhill, VT; Peter Johnson and Tryphoena Elmer
Leon H., d. 1/10/1890 at 0/5/4 in Lyme; b. Lyme; W. D. Johnson (Hanover) and Alice T. Woodward (Hanover)
Leon H., d. 8/13/1900 at 9/8/8 in Lyme; b. Lyme; Wilson D. Johnson (Hanover) and Alice E. Woodward (Hanover)

Wilson D., d. 10/22/1944 at 83/2/1 in Lyme; blacksmith; widower; b. Hanover; John H. Johnson (Underhill, VT) and Harriett K. Fox (Hanover)

JORDAN,
Jennie Sarah, d. 2/2/1905 at 26 in Lyme; married; b. NS; William Dale (NS) and Lizzie Foster (NS)

JUDD,
Lillian B., d. 7/29/1949 at 66 in Hanover

KEITH,
George, d. 3/8/1912 at –; farmer; married; b. Haverhill; George Keith

KELEMAN,
Barbara A., d. --/--/1991 in Hanover; Joseph D. Boushall and Alice Marvel

KEMP,
Alvah J., d. 2/3/1926 at 91/10/22 in Manchester; retired; married; b. Lyme; Lyman Kemp (Pomfret, VT) and Electa Brown (Lyme)
Charles H., d. 11/10/1907 at 67/5/10 in Lyme; farmer; married; b. Nashua; Charles Kemp (Orford) and Hannah Richards (Goffstown)
Doris, d. 7/17/1926 at 18/10/15 in Boston, MA; single; Charley Kemp
Helen M., d. 8/8/1891 at 46/9/28 in Lyme; housewife; widow; b. Lyme; Joseph Brown (Lyme) and Eliza Kimball (Lyme)
Henry J., d. 3/11/1931 at 64/4 in Lyme; clerk; married; b. Chelsea, MA; James B. Kemp (Lisbon) and Susan Thompson (E. Corinth, VT)
Martha, d. 4/7/1928 at 80/0/7 in Manchester; widow; b. Lyme; Abel W. Clough (Concord) and Betsy -----
Mary Farris, d. --/--/1955 at 85 in Lyme; housewife; widow; b. Zanesville, OH; John Calvin Farris and Elizabeth McKnight
Susan E., d. 10/3/1932 at 92/10 in Windsor Locks, CT; retired; widow; John Estey (Lyme) and Caroline Lamphere (Lyme)

KENDRICK,
Letitia C., d. 12/3/1902 at 60/2/0 in Lyme; housewife; married; b. Dorchester; Elijah Cole (Orange) and Lucinda Holt (Dorchester)
Willie, d. 3/7/1894 at 0/0/7; b. Lyme; William H. Kendrick (Newbury,

VT) and Nellie M. Bowen (Piermont)

KENNISTON,
Ida M., d. 12/16/1926 at 50/5/1 in Sanford, ME; housewife; married; b. Topsham, VT; Israel Smith (Topsham, VT) and Mary Sanborn (Ryegate, VT)

KENT,
Charles, d. 11/15/1890 at 75/1/8 in Lyme; farmer; married; b. Lyme; Stephen Kent (Hebron, CT) and Sally Hezelton (Hebron, CT)
Elmira, d. 2/2/1900 at 80/10/7 in Lyme; domestic; single; b. Lyme; Moses Kent (Newburyport, MA) and Mary Stark (Lyme)
Janet R., d. 7/30/2000 in Lebanon; John Reed and Sylvia Euwell
John S., d. 10/12/1895 at 82/5/25; farmer; widower; b. Lyme; Abel Kent (Lyme) and Joanna Shaw
Mary F., d. 9/21/1895 at 78/4/20; housekeeper; single; b. Lyme; Moses Kent (Newburyport) and Mary Stark (Lyme)
Sophronia D., d. 7/22/1888 at 63/9/8 in Lyme; housekeeper; married; b. Lyme; George Perkins (Lyme) and Polly Woodward (Hanover)

KIBBEE,
Marion E., d. 8/16/1899 at 57/4/26 in Lyme; housewife; married; b. Hawley, MA; Ethan Hitchcock (Hawley, MA) and ----- (Stephenstown, NY)

KIBLING,
Charles A., d. 3/3/1938 at 70/0/3 in Rye, NY; salesman; widower; b. Norwich, VT; George Kibling and ----- Huntley
Jennie, d. 7/15/1926 at 57 in Hanover; domestic; married; b. Lyme; David K. Dike (Lyme) and Lucinda Roberts (Strafford, VT)

KILHAM,
Jane, d. 1/31/1992 in Lyme; Frederick Kaufholz and Grace Wurst
Lawrence, d. 9/21/2000 in Lyme; Walter Kilham and Jane Houston

KILPACK,
Gilbert, d. 9/22/1999 in Lyme; John Kilpack and Helena Hawthorne

KIMBALL,
Almira O., d. 10/23/1897 at 84; housewife; widow; b. Lyme Ctr.;

Reuben Bliss and Nancy Bliss
Mildred Ruth, d. 9/26/1995 in Lebanon; Henry Souliske

KING,
daughter, d. 10/27/1887 at 0/0/10 in Lyme; b. Lyme; John King (Ephrah, NY) and Matilda Suitor (Canada)
Betsey, d. 9/3/1925 at 61 in Hanover; housewife; married; b. Lyme; Alfred Davis (Londonderry) and Clarinda Tinkham (Lyme)
Charles Henry, Sr., d. 7/8/1993 in N. Haverhill; Newton King and Exilia Audette
Everett R., d. 3/5/2003 in Lebanon; Clarence King and Flora Rogers
Ida N., d. 2/25/1922 at 63/9/15 in Hanover; housewife; widow; b. Dorchester; John Norris (Dorchester) and Phebe Jessiman (Dorchester)
John, d. 7/10/1919 at 65/8/28 in Lyme; farming; married; b. Euphrates, NY; J. King (Co. Tyrone) and M. Starr (Co. Tyrone, Ireland)
John A., d. 6/24/1928 at 47/6/19 in Hanover; farmer; married; b. Dorchester; Walter E. King (Groton) and Ida S. Norris (Dorchester)
Lucinda C., d. 7/16/1894 at 58/0/28; housewife; married; b. Chelsea, VT; Anson Clough (Tunbridge, VT) and Sarah Campbell (Potsdam, NY)
Lucy M., d. 12/31/1985 at 89; John King and Matilda Suitter
Matilda, d. 6/4/1935 at 78/10/2 in Lyme; housewife; widow; b. Broughton, PQ; David Suiter (Broughton, PQ) and Mary McKeage (Broughton, PQ)
Walter E., d. 3/22/1916 at 65/9/6 in Lyme; farming; married; b. Groton; Benjamin King (Groton) and Mahala Powers (Groton)
Walter W., d. 8/25/1891 at 0/7/15 in Lyme; b. Newport; Lorenzo E. King (Washington, VT) and Maggie Delias (Canada)

KINGSBURY,
Marie, d. 11/20/1925 at 77 in Lyme; retired; widow

KIRWAN,
Robert J., d. 4/17/1994 in Lyme; Aloysius Kirwan and Helen A. Monahan

KOBURGER,
Marga, d. 3/6/1985 at 81; Hans Quilitz and Vivic -----

KOELLER,
Ivy, d. 1/27/1957 at 67 in Hanover; housewife; married; b. England; Alexander Noble and Elizabeth Sherrir

KOVATSH,
Henry, d. 5/24/1907 at 38/1/14 in Lyme; farmer; married; b. Hungary; John Kovatsh (Hungary) and Nancy Alexander (Hungary)

LACOSS,
Virginia L., d. 7/9/2003 in St. Cloud, FL; Roger Pushee and Isabel Uline
William, d. 6/8/1935 at 67/7/20 in Lebanon; janitor; married

LACROSS,
Grace M., d. 7/20/1975 at 93 in Concord; ret. school teacher; b. VT; Rufus Wilson and Nancy Huntley

LADD,
Samuel M., d. 7/18/1899 at 70/7/10 in Lyme; lumber bus.; married; b. Sharon, VT; Alfred Ladd (CT) and Sarah Stratton (Woodstock, VT)

LAIGN,
Andrew D., d. 3/25/1923 at 33 in Lyme; steward; b. Scotland

LAILER,
William, d. 12/25/1956 at 74 in Hanover; retired; single; b. Boston, MA; Waldo B. Lailer and Louise Fessenden

LAMBERT,
Angie F., d. 1/25/1939 at 78/5/27 in Lyme; housewife; widow; b. Henniker; Micah C. Howe (Newbury) and Harriet C. Smith (Langdon)
George W., d. 11/23/1932 at 79/3/11 in Lyme; farmer; married; b. Lyme; Thomas Lambert (Newbury, VT) and Harriet Waite (Lyme)
Harriet W., d. 8/28/1897 at 79/4/3; housewife; widow; b. Lyme; Solomon Waite (Lyme) and Deborah Cooke (Lyme)
Roger N., d. 12/25/1938 at 92/5/20 in Lyme; farmer; single; b. Lyme; Thomas Lambert (Newbury, VT) and Harriet Waite (Lyme)

LAMONE,
Ellen L., d. 4/13/1921 at 26/3/8 in Haverhill; housewife; married; b. Lyme; Fred L. Pike (Lyme) and Anna P. Roberts (Lyme)

LAMOTT,
son, d. 1/30/1898 at – in Lyme; b. Lyme; David Lamott (Quebec, Canada) and Lavina S. Jenks (Lyme)
Albert M., d. 2/2/1953 at 81 in Lebanon; lumberman; married; b. Dorchester; James LaMott and Catherine McBain
Bertha N., d. 11/27/1959 at 81 in Haverhill; retired housewife; b. Lowell, MA; Ethan Dimick Cutting and Lilly J. Rugg
David L., d. 3/11/1938 at 85 in W. Rumney; laborer; widower; b. Quebec City, PQ
Dean, d. 2/17/1994 in Lyme; Elwyn A. LaMott and Lela M. Willis
George J., d. 9/3/1933 at 55/10/8 in Thetford, VT; laborer; married; b. Lyme; David LaMott (Canada) and Lavina Jenks (Lyme)
Irving E., d. 8/1/1926 at – in Lyme; b. Lyme; Irving E. LaMott (Lyme) and Hazel F. Young (Burke, VT)
Irving Earl, d. 5/6/1966 at 69 in Thetford, VT; married
James, d. 7/15/1922 at 84/1/6 in Fairlee, VT; retired; widower; b. Brompton, Canada; Adolphus LaMott (Frances) and Nancy Plant (Ireland)
James I., d. 10/4/1961 at 82 in Lyme; carpenter; b. Dorchester; James LaMott and Katherine McBain
Katherine, d. 8/22/1918 at 79/4/12 in Lyme; housewife; married; b. Ormstown, PQ; Malcolm McBain (Scotland) and Margaret Wood (Scotland)
Lavina E., d. 2/26/1913 at 1/3/14; b. Lyme; Owen LaMott (Lyme) and Nora Andrews (Wilksboro, NY)
Lavina J., d. 12/28/1906 at 50 in Lyme; housewife; married; b. Lyme; Dexter Jenks and Betsey Fox
Owen B., d. 7/17/1921 at 30/0/19 in France; soldier; married; b. Lyme; David Lamott (Canada) and Lavina Jenks (Lyme)
Pearl M., d. 5/26/1968 at 88 in Lyme; housewife; widow; b. NY; Nathan Wing and Flora Hill
Verde Elwin, d. 9/8/1906 at 0/6/15 in Lyme; b. Lyme; George J. Lamott (Lyme) and Georgia B. Russell (Wilton, ME)

LAMPHERE,
son, d. 3/9/1947 at 0/0/8 in Hanover; b. Hanover; Walter R. Lamphere (Lyme) and Helen Cutler (Wolcott, VT)

Abizer P., d. 12/2/1895 at 76/1/26; laborer; married; b. Hartland, VT; David Lamphere (Hartland, VT) and Sarah Lamphere (New Fairfield, CT)

Albert A., d. 4/28/1892 at 57/11/8; laborer; married; b. Thetford; Thomas Lamphere (Bridgewater) and Annie Baker (Thetford, VT)

Bular A., d. 7/24/1891 at 0/5/23 in Lyme; b. Lyme; Charles O. Lamphere (Lyme) and Nellie S. Turner (Thetford, VT)

Charles N., d. 11/4/1893 at 67/11/27 in Lyme; disease of heart; laborer; married; b. Hartland, VT; David Lamphere (Hartland, farmer) and Sally Lamphere (Hartland, VT)

Charles O., d. 2/28/1920 at 58/5/28 in Lyme; farmer; married; b. Lyme; Albert Lamphere (Thetford, VT) and Sarah Lamphrey (Rutland, VT)

Helen, d. 6/7/1968 at 61 in Lebanon; housewife; married; b. VT; Fred Cutler and Elsie Phillips

Martha E., d. 6/16/1956 at 64 in Hanover; housewife; married; b. Lancaster; Charles Emerson and Jennie Morse

Mattie, d. 6/2/1953 at 83 in Haverhill; widow; b. N. Littleton; Harry Dyke and Sarah Tucker

Nellie S., d. 4/25/1928 at 65/0/18 in Lyme; housework; widow; b. Thetford, VT; Allen O. Turner (Thetford, VT) and ----- Gove (Thetford, VT)

Ralph, d. 5/29/1972 at 79 in Enfield; retired; b. NH; Charles O. Lamphere and Nellie Turner

Stephen R., d. 2/4/1887 at 72 in Lyme; farmer; married; b. Lynn, MA; John Lamphere

Thomas A., d. 11/4/1941 at 76/11/5 in Lyme; road comm.; married; b. Lyme; Albert A. Lamphere and Sarah Lamphere

Walter, d. 3/25/1974 at 72 in Hanover; farmer; b. NH; Charles Lamphere and Turner Nellie Lamphere

LANCASTER,
Alice D., d. 9/27/1959 at 80 in Lyme; housewife; b. Bolton, England; John Davis and Marion Watson

LANGMAID,
son, d. 1/23/1910 at 0/0/2; b. Lyme; George V. Langmaid (Brockton, MA) and Josie Goodell (Worcester, VT)

Elmina M., d. 4/12/1903 at 1/3/0 in Lyme; b. Lyme; George B. Langmaid (Brockton, MA) and Josie M. Goodell (Hardwick, VT)

Florence, d. 1/11/1905 at – in Lyme; b. Lyme; George B. Langmaid
(Brockton, MA) and Josie M. Goodell (Calais, VT)
Frank F., d. 3/29/1905 at 1/9/27 in Lyme; George B. Langmaid
(Brockton, MA) and Josie M. Goodell (Duxbury, VT)
George B., d. 3/16/1920 at 52/0/23 in Hanover; peddler; widower; b.
Brockton, MA; Frank Langmaid (Brockton, MA)
Josephine G., d. 7/11/1912 at 41/3/25; housewife; married; b.
Hardwick, VT; Fernando Goodell (Worcester, VT)
William, d. 2/9/1910 at 0/0/19; b. Lyme; George V. Langmaid
(Brockton, MA) and Josie Goodell (Worcester, VT)

LANPHER,
Homer B., d. 2/6/1940 at 62/6/24 in Hanover; clerk; married; b. VT;
Arthur Lanpher and Maria Parmentier
Minnie May, d. 6/3/1976 at 88 in Hanover; housewife; b. USA;
Jessie Pellerin

LARAWAY,
Beatrice M., d. 4/29/1999 in Lebanon; Clinton Willey and Leda
Randall

LARO,
Lisa Marie, d. 10/13/1963 at 0/0/4 in Hanover; b. Hanover; Arthur E.
Laro and Donna L. Pushee

LARSON,
Jane, d. 7/12/2000 in Lebanon; H. Larson and Helen Benson

LARTY,
Carol R., d. 10/16/1997 in Lebanon; John E. Larty and Ruth F. Larty

LATHAM,
Mary, d. 4/3/1907 at 92/6/24 in Lyme; single; b. Lyme; Robert
Latham (Lyme) and Mary Wise (Hebron)

LATHROP,
Edith M., d. 3/12/1949 at 89 in Lebanon

LAWSON,
Emma, d. 1/22/1976 at 77 in Lyme; retired; b. VT; Thaddeus Martin
and Bertha Perkins

John W., d. 3/26/1958 at 65 in Hanover; janitor; married; b. Barre, VT; George W. Lawson and Eva Wheaton

LEONARD,
Charles, d. 12/19/1921 at 81/1/3 in Lyme; farmer; married; b. Burlington, VT; James Leoanrd

J. Hoag, d. 4/12/1948 at 91/10/29 in Lyme; dressmaker; widow; b. Lincoln, VT; Chase Hoag (Lincoln, VT) and Rosina Wright (Starksboro, VT)

LEVESQUE,
Darin S., d. 3/16/1989 at 23; Charles H. Levesque and Shirley Pratt

LEWIS,
George F., d. 5/2/1921 at 60/3/6 in Lyme; farmer; married; b. Binghamton, NY; Charles F. Lewis (Plainfield) and Mary Stickney (Plainfield)

LIBBY,
Susan, d. 11/5/1887 at 59/0/12 in Lyme; retired; widow; b. Lyme; Josiah Swain and Jane Eaton

LINCOLN,
Gardner H., d. 5/20/1895 at 57/0/7; farmer; married; b. Chelsea, VT; Elihu Lincoln (Chelsea, VT) and Cynthia Cowdry (Tunbridge, VT)

LIS,
Walter James, d. 12/29/1980 at 59; Alexander Lis and Mary Waskiewicz

LIVINGSTON,
Clara, d. 1/29/1992 in Lebanon; Alfred Livingston and Nellie Hallock

LOBDELL,
Nancy, d. 2/16/1914 at 79/11; widow; b. Pierrepont, NY; Lewis W. Daniels and Mary Chase

LOCKWOOD,
Charles E., d. 12/14/1938 at 54/8/15 in Haverhill; widower; b. Meriden; Ed Lockwood (Chester, VT) and Sarah Robinson

Ellen, d. 6/16/1924 at 38/2/3 in Hanover; housewife; married; b. Lyme; David Lamott (Canada) and Lavina Jenks (Lyme)

LORD,
Helen, d. 4/21/2003 in Lebanon; Joseph Wioneck and Helena Spernal
Jennie E. C., d. 8/13/1942 at 80/2/26 in Bradford, VT; housewife; widow; b. Norwich, VT; Joseph B. Cloud (Norwich, VT) and M. Emiraett Lyman (Norwich, VT)

LOUGEE,
Martha, d. 8/8/1964 at 84 in Hanover; none; b. Canada; George Dunbar and Sophie Clough

LOVEJOY,
Harriet P., d. 12/30/1931 at 73/2/13 in Lyme; housewife; widow; b. Canaan; Elbridge Perkins (Ipswich, MA) and Harriet Perkins (Canaan)
Lewis P., d. 5/22/1915 at 72/10/3 in Lyme; farmer; married; b. Orford; Enos Lovejoy and Mary Hale
Marion Fairfield, d. 10/1/1972 at 91 in Nashua; retired; b. NH; Payson Fairfield and Caroline Churchill
Mary H., d. 6/20/1899 at 91/3/6 in Lyme; housewife; widow; b. Orford; John Hale (Barrington) and Rhoda Davis (Concord)

LUND,
Daniel Lewis, d. 1/3/1963 at 79 in Lyme; farm laborer; b. VT; George R. Lund and Sarah Ricker

LYONS,
Jonathan P., d. 5/17/1968 at 0/9 in Hanover; b. NH; Dana Lyons and Marilyn J. Chappell
Ruth, d. 2/19/1972 at 78 in Hanover; b. MA; William Mitchell and Ann Harlow

MACBAIN,
Mabel G., d. 3/27/1938 at 62/1/24 in Lyme; housewife; married; b. Buffalo, NY; Edward E. Gyles (Ireland) and Mary Mansfield (Ireland)

MACKENZIE,
Eleanor, d. 4/28/1985 at 92; Henry W. Hobson and Katherine Thayer

MACLEAN,
Elwin G., d. 1/7/1906 at 27/8/16 in Lyme; farmer; married; b. Wentworth, NS; Thomas H. Maclean and Margaret Grant
Theodore, d. 2/25/1956 at 51 in FL; retired; single; b. Lyme; Elwin G. Maclean and Abbie Dimick

MAGUIRE,
Vinal L., d. 2/27/1970 at 62 in Hanover; retired; b. ME; Fred Maguire and Martha J. Hurlbutt

MALCOLM,
Miriam B., d. 4/16/1983 at 36; Hans Bauer and Eva Guggenheim

MARSH,
Alice J., d. 4/4/1922 at 56 in Boston; housewife; married; b. Lyme; Fred B. Palmer (Orford) and Jennie Beal (Center Harbor)
Lisa M., d. 10/10/2001 in Lyme; Henry Marsh and Wanita Balch

MARSHALL,
child, d. 10/16/1970 at 0/0/1 in Hanover; b. NH; Richard D. Marshall and Sharon Parvin
child, d. 10/16/1970 at 0/0/2 in Hanover; b. NH; Richard D. Marshall and Sharon Parvin
Dorothy A., d. 2/10/1890 at – in Lyme; housewife; widow; b. Stoddard; Nathaniel Evans
Eliza, d. 12/19/1893 at 86/4/2 in Lyme; old age; retired; widow; b. Lyme; Nathan Ross (Hollis, farmer) and Mary Howard (Thetford, VT)
George A., d. 4/10/1949 at 73 in Concord
Lulu N., d. 10/9/1892 at 3/1; b. Lyme; Bry Marshall (Auburn) and Hattie J. Balch (Orford)
Sarah J., d. 1/11/1911 at 72/2/10; housewife; widow; b. Dorchester; John Blaisdell and Sally Rollins

MARTIN,
Ezekiel, d. 1/14/1894 at 71; farmer; widower; b. Dorchester; Simeon Martin (Dorchester) and Mehitabel Sanborn (Dorchester)
Gertrude, d. 5/8/1953 at 73 in Hanover; none; single; b.

Williamstown, VT; Gurdon Martin and Mary Ella Burnham
Mary E., d. 3/19/1912 at 78/2/18; housewife; widow; b. Canaan; Phineas Dunham (Lyme) and Annie Martin (Grafton)
Nathaniel H., d. 6/29/1908 at 80/10/11; clergyman; widower; b. Dorchester; Simeon Martin (Dorchester) and Mehitable Sanborn (Dorchester)

MARTZ,
Lawrence Stannard, d. 7/8/1975 at 78 in Lyme; communications consultant; b. OH; Lawrence Michael Martz and Blanche Underhill

MASON,
Mabel, d. 1/13/1932 at 61/8/31 in Lyme; housewife; single; b. S. Hadley, MA; Lewellin Pike (Eastport, ME) and Jane McCurdy (Eastport, ME)

MASSEY,
Carley W., d. 12/9/1989 at 75; William Massey

MATIVIA,
daughter, d. 8/7/1887 at – in Lyme; b. Lyme; Henry Matina (sic) (Corinth, VT) and Hattie C. Stickney (Fairfax, VT)
Amelia J., d. 11/16/1924 at 28/2/18 in Lyme; housewife; married; b. W. Burke, VT; Joseph Joblin (England) and Jennie Bell (Canada)
Darius R., d. 3/19/1944 at 80/8/25 in Lyme; married; b. N. Hartland, VT; Lewis Mativia (France) and Miranda Eastman (Corinth, VT)
Hattie C., d. 1/14/1935 at 73/4/24 in Lyme; housewife; married; b. Fairfax, VT; Joseph M. Stickney (Jay, VT) and Caroline McClellan
Hattie May, d. 11/27/1964 at 78 in Lyme; practical nurse; b. Lyme; Henry Mativia and Hattie Stickney
Henry J., d. 9/7/1937 at 82/3/8 in Lyme; veterinary; single; b. Corinth, VT; Lewis Mativia (France) and Merinda Eastman (Corinth, VT)
Ida A., d. 7/6/1945 at 78/2/10 in Lyme; housewife; widow; b. Lyme; John L. Stark (Lyme)
Ina C., d. 11/15/1984 at 77; Lewis Squires and Florence Caswell
Lewis, d. 4/23/1907 at 89/0/16 in Lyme; farmer; married; Lewis Mativia (France)

Perry Mills, d. 1/22/1960 at 63 in Lyme; retired; b. Lyme; Henry J. Mativia and Hattie Stickney

Roswell L., d. 5/14/1977 at 82 in Hanover; carpenter; b. Lyme; Darius Mativia and Ida Starks

MAXFIELD,
Andrew C., d. 10/21/1965 at 72 in Lyme; laborer; married; b. Londonderry; Daniel Maxfield and Hattie Gould

Grace, d. 8/26/1959 at 76 in Lyme; housekeeper; b. New Hampton; Warren D. Moody and Mary E. Wallace

Lesle Ernest, d. 4/28/1994 in Lyme; Dan Maxfield and Hattie Gould

MAYBERRY,
Augusta, d. 9/22/1926 at 60 in Hanover; housewife; married; b. Haverhill; Amos Stearns (Haverhill) and Lucy Merrill (Woodstock, VT)

John H., d. 10/27/1930 at 87/7/7 in Worcester, MA; retired; widower; b. Cumberland, ME

MAYO,
Ada M., d. 7/3/1917 at 69/8/1 in Lyme; housewife; married; b. Manchester; William Morey (Lyme) and Elizabeth Langdon (Goffstown)

Alma M., d. 8/7/1899 at 50/6/20 in Lyme; housewife; married; b. Lyme; Benjamin P. Converse (Lyme) and Miranda Walker (Charlestown)

Bartlett, d. 10/14/1966 at 87 in Lyme; farming; married; b. Lyme; Nathan W. Mayo and Mary Bartlett

Carrie E., d. 9/20/1888 at –/10/4 in Lyme; single; b. Lyme; Joel W. Mayo (Lyme) and Ada M. Morey (Manchester)

Cora M., d. 4/27/1982 at 97; Ira Young and Barbara Carr

Florence M., d. 12/9/1940 at 82/11/9 in Lyme; housewife; widow; b. Landaff; Benjamin Morrill (Danville, VT) and Harriett S. Smith (Landaff)

George S., d. 10/5/1931 at 89/6/6 in Lyme; retired; married; b. Lyme; Hiram Mayo (Ludlow, VT) and Betsey Whipple (Lyme)

Hiram B., d. 3/2/1918 at 66/0/27 in Thetford, VT; farming; married; b. Lyme; Hiram Mayo (Ludlow, VT) and Betsey Whipple (Lyme)

Joel W., d. 7/9/1933 at 90/0/19 in Lyme; widower; b. Lyme; Hiram Mayo (Ludlow, VT) and Betsy Whipple (Lyme)

Mary B., d. 4/11/1915 at 74/11 in Lyme; housewife; married; b.

Thetford, VT; Hazen Bartlett and ----- Canfield
Wesley N., d. 5/7/1929 at 84/1/20 in Lyme; farmer; widower; b. Lyme; Hiram Mayo (Ludlow, VT) and Betsey Whipple

McALISTER,
Frank E., d. 11/30/1888 at –/3/26 in Lyme; laborer; single; b. Lyme; Isaac E. McAlister (Bedford, MA) and Angell M. Sawyer (Orford)
Ralph J., d. 10/25/1954 at 59 in Lyme; machinist; married; George McAlister

McCONNELL,
Doris Fay, d. 1/17/1941 at 0/0/14 in Lyme; b. Lyme; Forrest McConnell (Whitefield) and Althea Nelson (Haverhill)

McEWAN,
Aurlie, d. 1/19/1933 at 0/0/1 in Hanover; b. Hanover; Leslie McEwan (Lyme) and Marcia Simmons (Piermont)
Bertram, d. 7/19/1971 at 75 in Lyme; carpenter; b. Canada; John McEwan and Diantha Rattery
John Leslie, d. 10/11/1908 at 40/1/22; farmer; married; b. Aulisville, PQ; John McEwen (Canada) and Jane Make (Canada)
Minnie B., d. 2/7/1983 at 90; Gilman Bacon and Frances Green

McKENNEY,
C. Ross, d. 10/12/1971 at 81 in Lyme; retired teacher; b. ME; Winfield S. McKenney and Bertha Cromett

McMANN,
Henry, d. 12/17/1931 at 58/6/6 in Lyme; laborer; widower; b. Groveton; Michael McMann (Canada) and Margaret Sheridan (Canada)
Mabel A., d. 12/11/1917 at 34/1/11 in Lyme; housewife; married; b. Lyme; Frank Cutting (Lyme) and Ella Warren (Lyme)
Mary E. Moore, d. 6/18/1896 at 21/9/20; housewife; married; b. Lyme; William A. Moore (Bangor, ME) and Mary Perkins (Canaan)
Maurice, d. 6/8/1922 at 13/2/29 in Orford; b. Lyme; Henry McMann (Groveton) and Mabel Cutting (Lyme)

MEAD,
Alice Gertrude, d. 7/8/1975 at 92 in Haverhill; housewife; b. NH; George Hamlin and Emma Jane Von Dell

MEHAN,
Albert P., d. 11/22/1908 at 54/4/8; laborer; married; b. PQ; Charles Mehan (Canada) and Mary Welsh

MELENDY,
Albert, d. 1/10/1914 at 61; teamster; married
Robert H., d. 1/15/2003 in Hanover; Don Melendy and Phila Hazen

MELVIN,
Anna M., d. 10/24/1896 at 43/6/2; housewife; married; b. Haverhill; Charles G. Smith (Washington, VT) and Ruth Morse (Haverhill)
Betsy J., d. 7/14/1892 at 66/5/14; housekeeper; widow; b. Weare; William Marshall (Weare) and Martha Eaton (Sanbornton)
Florence W., d. 7/20/1943 at 63/0/16 in E. Ludlow, MA; widow; b. Lyme; Rollo Wells (Lyme) and ----- Hall (Lyme)
George, d. 10/25/1910 at 54/5/11; merchant; married; b. E. Weare; Oscar Melvin (Weare) and Betsey Jane Marshall (Weare)
Leon O., d. 8/16/1939 at 58/1/15 in Springfield, MA; engineer; married; b. Lyme; George Melvin (Lyme) and Mary D. Warren (Lyme)
Mary D., d. 8/30/1935 at 82/6/14 in Lyme; housewife; widow; b. Lyme; Asa Warren (Lyme) and Mary A. Derby (Lyme)
Story, d. 11/11/1932 at 73/4/9 in Lyme; janitor; married; b. Lyme; Oscar Melvin (Weare) and Betsey J. Marshall (Weare)
William H., d. 5/10/1912 at 58/7/18; laborer; single; b. Weare; Oscar Melvin (Weare) and Betsey J. Marshall (Weare)

MENGE,
John A., d. 2/18/2002 in Lebanon; Irving Menge and Lorraine Kraus

MERRIAM,
Jane C. S., d. 9/14/1940 at 82/10/12 in Lyme; housewife; widow; b. Allegheny, PA; Robert W. Stevenson (Allegheny, PA) and Jane Cooper (Allegheny, PA)

MERRILL,
Mercy H., d. 5/8/1918 at 71 in Concord; married; b. Lyme; Melvin C.

Breck (Lyme) and Matilda Andross (Dorchester, MA)
Stillman, d. 5/24/1913 at 82/3/10; wheelwright; married; b. Groton; Leonard M. Merrill (Hopkinton) and Susan Ray

MESSIER,
Dorothy, d. 5/20/1977 at 68 in Lyme; housewife; b. NH; Homer Lampher and Minnie Pellerin
Helen, d. 8/27/1978 at 87 in Hanover; housewife; b. Lyme; Dennis Hanchett and Lizzie Rood
Mylon I., d. 9/4/1960 at 75 in Orford; farming; b. Thetford, VT; Isaac H. Messier and Abbie Ricker
Roland Mylon, d. 8/9/1975 at 67 in Hanover; ret. hardware salesman; b. VT; Mylon Messier and Helen L. Hanchett

MILLER,
Elizabeth C., d. 6/12/1978 at 85 in Lyme; owner rooming house; b. Portage, WI; George Clemmons and Nora Chase
Rachel A., d. 8/15/1970 at 79 in Lyme; housewife; b. NY; Robert A. Miller and Louise Igoe

MIRKIL,
Hazleton, III, d. 3/--/1967 at 44 in Hanover; professor; married; b. Philadelphia, PA; Hazleton Mirkil, Jr. and Charlotte Morris

MOFFATT,
Earle C., d. 12/2/1957 at 74 in Hanover; ret. lawyer; widower; b. Berkshire, VT; Orrin S. Moffatt and Minnie Hadd
Edith M., d. 12/30/1956 at 72 in Lyme; housewife; married; b. Brattleboro, VT; William Stearns and Ella Rockwell

MONROE,
Celia B., d. 1/22/1931 at 50/2/7 in Haverhill; widow; b. Canaan; Friend Pressey and Hattie Elliott
Charles A., d. 5/30/1929 at 59/6 in Lyme; laborer; married; b. Boston, MA; Caleb Monroe and Agnes Ryan

MOORE,
Alonzo, d. 8/27/1904 at 88/4/26 in Lyme; farmer; married; b. Chelsea, VT; Samuel H. Moore (Chelsea, VT) and Eudotia Fuller (Vershire, VT)
Jane J., d. 10/2/1904 at 82/7/29 in Lyme; housework; widow; b.

Hartland, VT; William Jennings and Jane Billings
Mary P., d. 2/10/1915 at 70/5/19 in Norwich, VT; housewife; widow
William A., d. 3/11/1908 at 72/11/4; farmer; married; b. Bangor, ME; William G. Moore (England) and Margaret Fanning (St. Johns, NB)

MORAN,
D. James, d. 12/22/1922 at 37/9 in Lyme; laborer; married; b. New Haven, CT; Dennis Moran (Ireland) and Elizabeth O'Hara (Ireland)

MORANCY,
Kimberly D., d. 4/8/1978 at 6 in Hanover; student; b. Lebanon; Robert W. Morancy and Pamela Poire

MOREY,
Annie W., d. 3/21/1898 at 83/3/21 in Lyme; housework; widow; b. Lyme; John Hall (Lyme) and Mary C. Culver
Benjamin, d. 1/4/1887 at 75/9/16 in Lyme; farmer; widower; b. Lyme; Gideon Morey (Newton, MA) and Ada Cutting (Hebron, CT)
Benjamin D., d. 4/13/1910 at 82/1/19; farmer; widower; b. Strafford, VT; Roswell Morey (Strafford, VT) and Louisa Robinson (Strafford, VT)
Charles C., d. 4/1/1934 at 67/7/24 in Lebanon; laborer; single; b. W. Fairlee, VT; Benjamin Morey (VT) and Nancy Rowell (NY)
Susan (Mrs.), d. 11/15/1887 at 87 in Lyme; retired; widow; b. Lyme; Nathan Russ (Hollis) and Mary Howard (Thetford, VT)
William D., d. 11/13/1892 at 41/1/16; laborer; married; b. Manchester; William S. Morey (Lyme) and Elizabeth Langdon (Goffstown)

MORGAN,
Agnes, d. 2/19/1956 at 78 in Lyme; housewife; widow; b. Sunapee; George D. Young and Nellie T. -----

MORRILL,
Abbie E., d. 3/1/1906 at 49/8/20 in Lyme; housewife; married; b. Corinth, VT; Joseph H. Eastman (Corinth, VT) and Martha A. Thurber (Unity)
Elmer F., d. 2/13/1937 at 75/2/11 in Lyme; farmer; married; b. Boscawen; Enoch L. Morrill and Susannah Coffin

Lela M., d. 3/23/1935 at 65/3/25 in Lyme; housekeeper; single; b. Orford; Joseph M. Morrill (Danville, VT) and Lucy A. Peabody (Pepperill, MA)
Nettie, d. 6/11/1954 at 88 in Haverhill; housewife; widow; b. S. Woodbury, VT; Thomas Rickard and Sally Handcock

MORRIS,
Samuel T., d. 11/2/1989 at 84; David J. Morris and Mary Edwards

MORRISETTE,
Lizzie, d. 6/7/1925 at 64/4/12 in Hanover; housewife; married; b. Plainfield; ----- Nash (Plainfield) and Jane Westgate (Plainfield)

MORRISON,
Addie L., d. 6/2/1937 at 78/11/17 in Lyme; housewife; widow; John Fellows (Orford) and Mary Bean
E. C., d. 5/25/1903 at 65/6/18 in Lyme; housework; married; b. Dunbarton; Thomas Perkins (Dunbarton) and Clarissa Towne (Goffstown)
Edson L., d. 1/29/1937 at 76/4/14 in Lyme; farmer; married; b. Lyme; Parker I. Morrison (Fairlee, VT) and Martha P. Marshall (Lyme)
Lizzie G., d. 7/9/1925 at 62/10/24 in Lyme; housewife; married; b. E. Providence, RI; Oliver Chaffee (Seekonk, MA) and Maria Gray (Seekonk, MA)
Parker I., d. 1/31/1893 at 87/2/27 in Lyme; Brights and heart disease; farmer; widower; b. Fairlee, VT; James Morrison (Londonderry, carpenter) and Martha Pelton (Lyme)
Zadok H., d. 11/21/1917 at 75/1/12 in Lyme; retired; married; b. Lyme; Marquis C. Morrison and Mary C. Ball (Thetford, VT)

MORSE,
Eliza A., d. 11/1/1897 at 60; housework; single; b. Lyme; David Morse (Hebron) and D. Ladd (Alexandria)
Emerson G., d. 3/14/1965 at 70 in Hanover; dir. purchasing; married; b. W. Medford, MA; Elijah Morse and Molly Christopher
Leon J., d. 9/30/1958 at 77 in Lyme; minister; married; b. VT; Orlando Morse and Edna Towne
William S., d. 7/10/1913 at 80/6/10; peddler; widower; b. Hebron; David Morse (Hebron) and Dollie Ladd

MOTT,
Jane Matilda, d. 4/18/1909 at 64/9/27; housekeeper; married; b. Lyme; Melvin Brick (Lyme) and Matilda W. Andrews (Dorchester)

MOUSLEY,
Catherine J., d. 1/28/1911 at 70/10/11; housewife; widow; b. Orford; Thomas W. Quint (Orford) and Jane Archer (Orford)
George W., d. 9/15/1928 at 67/0/12 in Orford; farmer; married; b. Lyme; William Mousley (Canada) and Katherine Quint
John H., d. 8/24/1933 at 65 in Gerrish; farmer; widower; b. Lyme; William Mousley (Canada) and Katherine Quint (Orford)
Mary E., d. 10/21/1931 at 82/0/14 in Lyme; retired; married; b. Canaan; James Cook (Lyme) and Esther S. Richardson (Canaan)

MOVELLE,
Alfred, d. 7/31/1971 at 44 in Hanover; carpenter; b. NH; William Movelle and Mildred Gilbert
Esther, d. 4/26/1974 at 49 in Hanover; housewife; b. NH; Harley Gray, Sr. and Hattie Pike
William J., d. 1/21/1945 at 59/2/15 in Lyme; carpenter; divorced; b. New Bedford, MA; Patrick Movelle (NF) and Cecelia Burfi (NF)
William J., d. 9/13/1956 at 35 in Hartford, VT; carpenter; married; b. Lyme; William Movelle, Sr. and Mildred M. Gilbert

MUDGE,
Gilbert H., d. 10/28/1996 in Lyme; Alfred E. Mudge and Alice Horton

MUNN,
John Robert, d. 2/1/1907 at 1/6/27 in Lyme; b. Lyme; C. H. Munn (Canterbury) and Katherin Ordway (Northfield, MN)

MURPHY,
Daniel P., d. --/--/1955 at 84 in Lyme; retired; single; b. St. Albans, VT; Michael Murphy and Helen Sullivan
Gabrielle, d. 4/16/1970 at 0/0/9 in Hanover; b. NH; William Murphy and Karen Obermeyer

NELSON,
Clara, d. 10/16/1904 at 81/0/12 in Lyme; housework; married;

Charles Fox (Hanover) and Margaret Allen

Fred F., d. 5/3/1893 at 29/7/28 in Lyme; diabetes mellitus; laborer; single; b. Lyme; William C. Nelson (Lyme) and Nell Sawyer (Lyme)

George M., Jr., d. 8/26/1943 at 16/6/15 in Lyme; student; single; b. Barnet, VT; George M. Nelson (E. Barnet, VT) and Lessie M. Cobb (Westford, VT)

John, d. 10/18/1928 at 104/0/4 in Rehoboth, MA; retired; widower; William C. Nelson (Lyme) and Sarah Chapin (Milford, MA)

Sarah, d. 9/14/1906 at 84/5/12 in Lyme; tailoress; single; b. Lyme; William Nelson (Lyme) and Sarah Chapin (Milford, MA)

Susan S., d. 9/17/1904 at 64/2/11 in Lyme; housework; widow; b. Bath; John Simpson

NEUMANN,

Bertha, d. 10/7/1954 at 73 in Hanover; not given; widow; b. Germany; ----- Rappuhn

NEWCOMB,

Carrie B., d. 4/19/1902 at 66/0/14 in Lyme; housewife; married; b. Norwich, VT; Rhapal Curtis (Thetford, VT) and Cynthia Gould (Norwich, VT)

Daniel B., d. 9/7/1906 at 76/6/15 in Lyme; farmer; widower; b. Thetford, VT; ----- Newcomb (Thetford, VT) and Mary Winslow (Dorchester)

John M., d. 5/6/1908 at 64/0/6; farmer; widower; b. Lyme; D. Newcomb and Mary Winslow

Mary A., d. 4/15/1894 at 72/11; housewife; married; b. Orford; John R. Closson (Thetford, VT) and A. P. Gilson (Groton, MA)

NEWELL,

Alma H., d. 2/15/1914 at 78/1/5; housewife; widow; b. Chelsea, VT; Levi Thompson (VT) and Mary Sanborn (VT)

Benjamin C., d. 4/18/1902 at 74/10/3 in Lyme; farmer; married; b. Jaffrey; Jacob Newell (Jaffrey) and Mary Cummings (Cornish)

Hannah S., d. 1/31/1913 at 87/10/25; widow; b. Troy, VT; John Flint (Lyme) and Elizabeth Balch (Lyme)

Harry, d. 5/4/1893 at 83/5 in Lyme; farmer; married; b. Orford; Joseph Newell (Salem, MA, farmer)

Marguerite H., d. 12/30/1915 at 66/9/5 in Lyme; housewife; widow; b. Orford; Nathan Ames (Orford) and Pamela Homer (Orford)

Sarah Jane, d. 10/31/1891 at 65 in Lyme; housekeeper; married; b. Lyme; Asa P. Warren (Lyme)

NEWTON,
Henry, d. 1/18/1959 at 84 in Hanover; farmer; b. Quechee, VT; Charles Newton and Amelia Russ

NICHOLS,
Esther E., d. 2/18/2001 in Norwich, VT; Lloyd Chaffee and Ethel Ball
Guy Edgar, d. 1/5/1993 in Lebanon; George Nichols and Carla Woodard

NORRIS,
John L., d. 3/8/1913 at 75/9/5; farmer; married; b. Dorchester; Farley Norris (Dorchester) and Abigal Lawrence (Canaan)

NORTHAM,
Cecelia, d. 10/27/1976 at 69 in Hanover; housewife; b. CT; Gabriel Reff and Mary Ericson

NOVACK,
John Z., d. 1/25/1965 at 44 in Lyme; doorman; married; b. Scranton, PA; ----- Novack and Victoria -----

NOYES,
daughter, d. 3/19/1891 at 0/1 in Lyme; b. Lyme; Frank W. Noyes (Dorchester) and Anna M. Dunbar (Canada)
Charles, d. 4/27/1929 at – in Hanover; retired; Amos Noyes and Hannah Peasley
Frank B., d. 2/14/1942 at 73/11/21 in Lyme; widower; b. Dorchester; Amos Noyes (Landaff) and Hannah Peasley (Manchester)
Hannah, d. 10/21/1889 at 64/6/6 in Lyme; housekeeper; widow; b. Wilmot; Jonathan Peaslee and Marian Pierce
Mary E., d. 5/23/1947 at 79/1/29 in Haverhill; housewife; widow; b. Bradford, VT; Elmer Gilbert and Hannah Kennedy

O'DONNELL,
daughter, d. 2/19/1957 at – in Hanover; b. gx; Leo W. O'Donnell and Lila F. Corey
Hugh B., Sr., d. 3/11/1989 at 85; Alvah O'Donnell and Edith Chase

O'DOUGHERTY,
Randy B., d. 2/19/2003 in Lebanon; ----- and Kathy Clay

O'HARA,
Dwight, d. 7/26/1961 at 68 in Lyme; retired; b. Waltham, MA; Danial O'Hara and Mayfred Leonard
Elvie H., d. 2/27/1998 in Lyme; Alfred Hopton and Blanche Bracy

O'KEEFE,
James, Jr., d. 1/31/1960 at 79 in Claremont; laborer; b. Island Pond, VT; James O'Keefe, Sr. and Mary Baker

OAKLEY,
George Fuller, d. 1/16/1900 at 58/3/7 in Lyme; musician; single; b. Boston, MA; Jeremiah Oakley (Halifax, NS) and Mary Louise Crowe (Halifax, NS)

OKSA,
Flora G., d. 11/29/1982 at 73; ----- Gustafson and Hilja Klaavu
Toivo, d. 7/16/1984 at 81

OLSEN,
Douglas E., d. 11/6/1971 at 18 in Lyme; laborer; b. NH; Edward Olsen and Elizabeth Davis
Edward, Jr., d. 12/16/1950 at 0/3/1 in Lyme; b. Lyme; Edward T. Olsen and Elizabeth Davis
Edward Thomas, d. 12/25/1975 at 52 in Hartford, VT; carpenter; b. VT; Harry Olsen and Mary Gates

PAIGE,
Sarah Belle, d. 10/15/1908 at 20/0/29; domestic; single; b. Lyme; Charles W. Paige (Orford) and Emma J. Dyke (Lyme)

PALMER,
Dyantha May, d. 10/1/1964 at 93 in Hartford, VT
Fred B., d. 5/14/1895 at 68/3/15; lumber mfr.; married; b. Orford; Asa Palmer (Orford) and Pamelia Rugg (Sullivan)
Jennie, d. 11/23/1924 at 90/6/6 in Claremont; housewife; widow; b. Center Harbor; Selah Beal (Lyme)
Sallie M., d. 1/21/1906 at 35/10/13 in Lyme; housewife; married; b. Lyme; Hannibal Chase (Bristol) and Marinda Jeffers (Lyme)

PARK,
Isaac, d. 2/1/1945 at 58/8/4 in Lyme; merchant; married; b. S. Ronaldsay, Scotland; John Park (S. Ron., Scotland) and Elizabeth Swaney (S. Ron., Scotland)

PARKER,
Ella F. D., d. 10/17/1938 at 89/6/6 in Lyme; housewife; widow; b. Bellows Falls, VT; Marshall A. Davis (Rockingham, VT) and Rebecca Pulsifer (Windham, VT)
Warren, d. 12/23/1928 at 84/11/6 in Lyme; retired; single; b. Albany, NY; William C. Parker (Dalton, MA) and Adaline Ames (Orford)

PARSONS,
Marselis C., d. 9/22/2000 in Hanover; Marselis Parsons and Jesse Stott

PEARSON,
Keziah C., d. 3/16/1892 at 81/3/9; housekeeper; widow; b. Lyme; Isaac Cutting and Olive Hewes

PELLERIN,
Jules, d. 7/15/1918 at 80/9/17 in Hanover; farming; b. T. Rivers, Canada
Marie T., d. 11/19/1911 at 73/6/21; housewife; married; b. Canada; John McDannell (Canada) and Lucy Burke (Canada)

PELTON,
Josiah C., d. 10/8/1899 at 69/0/3 in Lyme; farmer; married; b. Plymouth; Josiah Pelton (Lyme, CT) and Percy Pelton (Lyme, CT)
Julia B., d. 10/10/1916 at 86/3/4 in Hinesburg, VT; b. New Haven, VT
Mary A., d. 12/28/1921 at 82/3/21 in Lyme; housewife; married; b. Manchester, England; Thomas Roycroft and Mary Brown (Scotland)
Samuel, d. 4/23/1938 at 82/1/16 in Haverhill; laborer; widower; b. Lyme; Church Pelton (Lyme) and Mary Rhycroft (England)

PENNOCK,
Lizzie D., d. 4/12/1918 at 66 in Lyme; housewife; married; b. Stratford; William Dennis (Stratford) and Luceba Curtis

(Stratford)

PERKINS,
Addie M., d. 9/28/1951 at 76 in Lyme; none; widow; Spellman Hazen and Phila Poulett
Adna, d. 10/15/1929 at 83/5/16 in Lyme; farmer; married; b. Lyme; Apollas Perkins (Lyme) and Demarias Converse (Lyme)
Anna M., d. 1/10/1917 at 65/9/5 in Fairlee, VT; housewife; widow; b. Constable, NY; Sherburn S. Ingalls (Constable, NY) and Mary J. Schoffe (Constable, NY)
Charlotte M., d. 3/21/1988 at 84; Benjamin Webb and Lucy Conant
Christie K., d. 1/19/2002 in Lyme; Adna Perkins and Margaret Hazen
Damaris W., d. 6/14/1902 at 79/6/20 in Lyme; housewife; widow; b. Lyme; Lyman Converse and Polly Kent
Earl C., d. --/--/1955 at 71 in Woodsville; painter; divorced; b. Lyme; Adna Perkins and Mary Clement
Edwin H., d. 11/24/1932 at 74/6/22 in Lyme; farmer; married; b. Lyme; Isaac N. Perkins (Lyme) and Lucina Bingham (Lyme)
Forrest Ryder, d. 1/1/1995 in Lyme; Adna Perkins and Margaret Hazen
Frank W., d. 4/26/1937 at 76/3/27 in Hanover; farmer; married; b. Quebec; Edward Perkins (Littleton) and Jeanette Hubbard (Quebec)
George A., d. 2/25/1958 at 64 in Lebanon; farmer; single; b. Lyme; Adna P. Perkins and Margaret Hazen
Harriet, d. 9/7/1903 at 81 in Lyme; housework; widow; b. Ipswich, MA; ----- Smith (Ipswich, MA)
Harry W., d. 4/15/1982 at 79; Adna Perkins and Margaret Hazen
Herbert I., d. 3/10/1982 at 77; Adna Perkins and Margaret Hazen
Isaac N., d. 3/31/1916 at 88/6/28 in Lyme; farming; married; b. Lyme; Cyrus Perkins and Lucy Densmore (Lyme)
Kate G., d. 12/13/1938 at 81/3/23 in Hanover; housewife; widow; b. Lyme; Apollos Perkins (Lyme) and Damirus Converse (Lyme)
Marion S., d. 12/19/1967 at 65 in Hanover; secretary; divorced; b. Cornish; Duane Small and Minnie Lobdell
Mary C., d. 10/29/1890 at 34/10/29 in Lyme; housewife; married; b. Dorchester; S. W. Clement (Hillsborough) and Eliza A. Reed (Dorchester)
Nellie M., d. 5/13/1917 at 29/3/25 in Lyme; nurse; single; b. Lyme; Adna Perkins (Lyme) and Mary C. Clement (Dorchester)
Robert, Sr., d. 10/29/1971 at 41 in Hanover; lumberman; b. CT;

Edmund Bass and Marjorie Perkins

PERRY,
Elizabeth, d. 3/–/1929 at 20 in Hanover; married; John Greenwood

PETERS,
Alice, d. 9/11/1962 at 88 in Lyme; housewife; b. Piermont; Joseph Lawrence and Ellen Chandler

PETTENGILL,
Jayne, d. 7/1/1992 in Lyme; Joseph Thompson and Annie Mary Dewey

PHELPS,
H. [female], d. –/–/1896 at 80/10/7; housewife; widow; b. Windham; James Dickey (Windham) and Mary Clark (Windham)

PIKE,
son, d. 6/11/1948 at – in Lyme; b. Lyme; Horace Pike (Lyme) and Maxine Heath (Littleton)
son, d. 6/11/1948 at – in Lyme; b. Lyme; Horace Pike (Lyme) and Maxine Heath (Littleton)
child, d. 4/9/1964 at – in Lebanon; b. Lebanon; Allie Wayne Pike and Roberta Estes
Angie S., d. 3/5/1926 at 69/2/6 in Lyme; housewife; married; b. Farmington, ME; William P. Smith (Livermore, ME) and Susan W. Dow (Livermore, ME)
Anna B., d. 11/28/1915 at 48/7/29 in Lyme; housewife; married; b. Lyme; Thomas F. Roberts (Raymond) and Caroline Smith (Lyme)
Archie Florence, d. 12/15/1887 at 14/2/21 in Lyme; single; b. Haverhill; Edwin B. Pike (Haverhill) and Addie A. Miner (Lowell, MA)
Beatrice A., d. 2/13/1925 at 0/0/14 in Lyme; b. Lyme; Earl H. Pike (Lyme) and Myrtle Coates (Corn Hill, NB)
Bertram E., d. 2/13/1925 at 0/0/14 in Lyme; b. Lyme; Earl H. Pike (Lyme) and Myrtle Coates (Corn Hill, NB)
Carleton, d. 12/31/1928 at 51/6/19 in Concord; teacher; married; b. Boston, MA; Elbridge Pike (MA) and Ella Fay (MA)
Charles Chester, d. 3/14/1997 in Hanover; Chester Pike and Polly Corinne Camp

Charles D., d. 6/18/1940 at 89/0/12 in Lyme; farming; widower; b. Hanover; Horace G. Pike (Hebron) and Eliza R. Tripp (New Bedford, MA)

Chester D., d. 6/8/1969 at 75 in Hanover; farmer; married; b. NH; Charles Pike and Ida Bailey

Earl Francis, II, d. 5/29/1969 at 37 in Lyme; laborer; married; b. NH; Earl H. Pike and Myrtle Coates

Eliza Rebecca, d. 6/3/1909 at 85/4/10; housewife; widow; b. New Bedford, MA

Forrest C., d. 2/1/1917 at 0/0/13 in Lyme; b. Lyme; Lon C. Pike (Lyme) and Lucy E. Jewell (Canada)

Foster M., d. 2/2/1917 at 0/0/14 in Lyme; b. Lyme; Lon C. Pike (Lyme) and Lucy E. Jewell (Canada)

Fred L., d. 8/15/1947 at 88/4/11 in Haverhill; widower; b. Lyme; Horace Pike (Hanover) and Lizzie Tripp (New Bedford, MA)

George Weymouth, d. 12/18/1964 at 68 in Lyme; highway patrolman; b. Lyme; Charles D. Pike and Ida Bailey

Gerald C., d. 12/27/1912 at 0/0/22; b. Lyme; Ella L. Pike (Lyme)

Henry M., d. 5/30/1927 at 62/10/12 in Lyme; laborer; b. Lyme; Horace Pike (Hebron) and Lizzie Tripp (New Bedford, MA)

Holly N., d. 8/7/1926 at – in Hanover; b. Hanover; Weymouth Pike (Lyme) and Dora Taylor (Thetford, VT)

Holly W., d. 2/5/1923 at – in Hanover; b. Hanover; G. Weymouth Pike (Lyme) and Dora D. Taylor (Thetford, VT)

Horace G., d. 9/1/1890 at 69/9/3 in Lyme; farmer; married; Moody Pike (Hebron) and Laura Graves (Sutton, MA)

Horace H., d. 4/28/1918 at 24/6/14 in Haverhill; farming; single; b. Hanover; Henry M. D. Pike (Lyme) and Anna P. Gilbert (Hanover)

Ida B., d. 2/25/1901 at 44/7/2 in Lyme; housewife; married; b. Lyme; Amos Bailey (Bath) and Mary Aiken (Chesterfield)

Jessie L., d. 3/5/1922 at 0/0/1 in Lyme; b. Lyme; Earl H. Pike (Lyme) and Myrtle L. Coates (Corn Hill, NB)

Lawrence F., d. 8/30/1969 at 25 in Strafford, VT; inspector; single; b. NH; Charles C. Pike and Betty C. Schwotzer

Lela M., d. 4/14/1984 at 86; Eugene Willis and Nellie Flanders

Lon C., d. 8/5/1950 at 59 in Hanover; unknown [occupation]; married; b. Lyme; Charles Pike and Ida Bailey

Lon J., d. 1/2/2002 in Lebanon; Lon Pike and Lucy Jewell

Lucy, d. 9/3/1968 at 84 in Haverhill; housewife; widow; b. Canada

Myrtle, d. 6/5/1970 at 81 in Concord; b. Canada; ----- Coates and

Lillian -----
Polly Corinne, d. 3/3/1971 at 78 in Enfield; housewife; b. NH; Frank
   Camp and Anna Alden
Ralph C., d. 7/27/1980 aat 38; practical nurse; Charles C. Pike and
   Betty C. Schwotzer
Susan, d. 5/7/1992 in Lebanon; Leon Waterbury and Elizabeth
   Litchfield
William C., d. 1/16/1937 at 0/0/2 in Lyme; b. Lyme; Verne Hobbs
   (Lyme) and Carrie Pike (Lyme)

PILLSBURY,
Louisa J., d. 2/28/1915 at 72/3/13 in Hanover; housewife; married; b.
   Dorchester; John Jewell

PINGREE,
Ella N., d. 12/8/1888 at 21/8/5 in Lyme; single; b. Orford; Irenus H.
   Pingree (Hanover) and Laura A. Currier (Thetford, VT)
Irenus H., d. 12/21/1895 at 66/3/13; farmer; widower; b. Hanover;
   Sylvanus Pingree (Hanover) and Sarah Woodward (Hanover)

PIPER,
Allen D., d. 3/20/1901 at 64/7/19 in Lyme; farmer; divorced; b.
   Dorchester; Samuel D. Piper and Clarissa Clark
Anna R., d. 6/1/1898 at 45/5/18 in Lyme; housewife; married; b.
   Stratford; John C. Robinson and Anna Dennis
Benjamin Carroll, d. 11/23/1903 at 23/0/28 in Lyme; hotel work;
   single; b. Hanover; Carroll G. Piper (Hanover) and Ara
   Fullington (Hanover)
Charles, d. 1/31/1899 at 42/11/13 in Lyme; farmer; widower; b.
   Fairlee, VT; Elijah P. Piper (Lyme) and Maria Fuller
Gerald W., d. 6/13/1889 at 1/11/20 in Barre, VT; b. Lyme; Walter G.
   Piper (Pembroke) and Hattie E. Esty (Hardwick, VT)
Harriet E., d. 10/28/1921 at 79/0/24 in Lyme; housewife; widow; b.
   Lyme; Jonathan Gilbert (Lyme) and Flavilla Grant (Lyme)
Hattie E., d. 12/3/1894 at 28/7/28; housewife; married; b. Troy, VT;
   John D. Esty (Haverhill) and Sarah Willey (Danville, VT)
Jennie M., d. 2/21/1945 at 83/7/17 in Lyme; housewife; widow; b.
   Lyme; Josiah C. Pelton (Plymouth, VT) and Mary A. Roycroft
   (Manchester, England)
John C., d. 3/15/1898 at 67/7/6 in Lyme; undertaker; married; b.
   Dorchester; Samuel Piper and Clarisa Clark

Katherine Annie, d. 1/22/1976 at 83 in Lyme Ctr.; housewife; b. Canada; Joseph Thompson and Annie Devey

Lee, d. 1/1/1977 at 86 in Hanover; retired; b. Lyme; Walter Piper and Hattie Esty

Ruth W., d. 4/6/1985 at 87; Nathan Wing and Anna Hill

Susan G., d. 8/27/1904 at 76/4/8 in Lyme; housework; widow; b. Pembroke; Joseph Baker and Susan Holt

Vivian F., d. 8/10/1980 at 86; housewife; Walter French and Nellie F. Knight

Vivian M., d. 11/15/2003 in Lyme; Frank Gregory and Sadie Porter

Walter G., d. 1/14/1913 at 51/8/14; carpenter; married; b. Pembroke; John C. Piper (Dorchester) and Susan G. Baker (Lempster)

Walter J., d. 9/18/1979 at 63 in Lyme; groundskeeper; Lee W. Piper and Katherine Thompson

Walter Joseph, d. 9/18/1979 at 63; grader operator; Lee W. Piper and Katherine Thompson (1980)

William C., d. 4/20/1937 at 41/10/6 in Haverhill; laborer; married; b. Chicago, IL; Herman Piper (Germany) and Mary Hoelbner

Willie, d. 2/6/1904 at 18/10/19 in Lyme; farming; single; Charles Piper (Orford) and Annie Robinson (Stratford)

PIXLEY,

Jennie W., d. 12/16/1921 at 72/9/19 in Lyme; housewife; widow; b. Pottsdam, NY; George Wells (Strafford, VT) and Almeda Gates (Pottsdam, NY)

Richard B., d. 9/30/1920 at 81/3/5 in Lyme; farmer; married; b. Sharon, VT; Horace Pixley and Charlotte Merrill (Plymouth)

PLUMMER,

Anna, d. 3/21/1980 at 87; ward clerk; Leander Plummer and Amelia Hawls

Marianne, d. 5/27/1982 at 82; Leander A. Plummer and Amelia H. Hawes

POMEROY,

Albert S., d. 2/1/2000 in Lyme; Charles Pomeroy and Mary Pitts

POOLE,

Florence B., d. 7/7/1993 in Wentworth; Elmer E. DeGoosh and Belle Keyes

POOLER,
Chester E., d. 1/10/1958 at 76 in Lyme; laborer; divorced; b. Highgate, VT; John Pooler and Ann Rood

PORTER,
Caroline L., d. 1/7/1915 at 94/5/20 in Lyme; housewife; widow; b. Randolph, VT; Augustus Hobart (Braintree, MA)
Eva J., d. 6/29/1913 at 29; single; b. Canada; Elisha Porter (Canada) and Margaret Thompson (Canada)
Francis, d. 10/16/1901 at 85/9/17 in Lyme; farmer; widower; b. Lyme Oliver K. Porter (Lyme) and Betsey Franklin (Lyme)
Frank A., d. 2/20/1932 at 83/2/18 in Lyme; mechanic; single; b. Thetford, VT; Hammond Porter (Thetford, VT) and Caroline Hobart (Randolph, VT)
Isaac N., d. 1/19/1893 at 75/2/18 in Lyme; apoplexy; farmer; single; b. Lyme; Oliver K. Porter (Lyme, farmer) and Betsey F. Porter (Lyme)
Julia K., d. 6/26/1899 at 81/3/22 in Lyme; housewife; married; b. Lyme; Stephen Kent (Newburyport) and Betsy Hazelton (Orford)

POST,
Ruth, d. 2/26/1901 at 69/9/23 in Lyme; single; b. Orange, VT; Aaron Post (Lyme) and Ruth Ashley (Vershire, VT)
Winthrop F., d. 9/28/1891 at 82/7/20 in Lyme; farmer; widower; b. Lyme; Aaron Post (Lyme)

PRATT,
Eliza Ann, d. 1/15/1889 at 65/0/8 in Lyme; housekeeper; married; b. Orange; Amos Hadley (Canaan) and Mehitable Briggs (Orange)
Frank B., d. 12/20/1926 at 77/5/9 in Boston, MA; drummer; married; b. Orange; Henry Pratt (Boston, MA) and Eliza A. Hadley (Canaan)
Henry, d. 11/12/1908 at 82/7/5; farmer; widower; b. Boston, MA; Thomas Pratt

PRESCOTT,
daughter, d. 5/23/1893 at 1 hr. in Lyme; asphyxia; b. Lyme; Joseph Prescott and Flora R. Eastman
Flora R. E., d. 5/23/1893 at --- in Lyme; post partum hemorrhage; housewife; married; b. Topsham, VT; William Eastman

(Topsham, VT, farmer) and Harriet White (Norwich, VT)

PRESSEY,
Harriet U., d. 7/22/1923 at 96/6/1 in Thetford, VT; retired; widow; b. Lyme; Jesse Stetson (Lyme) and Esther Heaton (Hanover)
Jennie L., d. 6/26/1925 at 64/2/7 in Derry; domestic; widow; b. Newbury, VT; Simeon Senter (Thetford, VT) and Sallie Clark (Andover)
Orrin T., d. 1/15/1918 at 63/3/16 in Thetford, VT; farmer; married; b. Hanover; Harrison Pressey

PRESTON,
Florence L., d. 12/22/1964 at 86 in Lyme; dormitory director; b. Jackson, MI; Arthur Lathrop and Alice Osborn

PUSHEE,
son, d. 6/15/1896 at –; b. Lyme; George A. Pushee (Lyme) and Emma B. Cline (Manchester)
daughter, d. 5/14/1898 at – in Lyme; b. Lyme; George A. Pushee (Lyme) and Emma B. Cline (Manchester)
daughter, d. 5/14/1898 at – in Lyme; b. Lyme; George A. Pushee (Lyme) and Emma B. Cline (Manchester)
Alfred W., d. 1/17/1900 at 66/3/28 in Lyme; farmer; married; b. Lyme; David Pushee (Fitzwilliam) and Amy Carpenter (Lyme)
Charles D., d. 1/6/1939 at 75/11/26 in Lyme; farmer; single; b. Lyme; Alfred W. Pushee (Lyme) and Edna E. Steel (Lyme)
Clarence, d. 3/17/1918 at 69/1/1 in Lyme; farming; widower; b. Lyme; Sylvester Pushee (Lyme) and Sarah Emerton (Lyme)
Clarence L., d. 3/7/1968 at 70 in Hartford, VT; carpentry; divorced; b. NH; Clarence Pushee and Fannie Post
Clarissa M., d. 2/4/1890 at 53/3/13 in Lyme; housewife; single; b. Lyme; Harvey Pushee (Lunenburgh, MA) and Nancy Pierce (Lunenburgh, MA)
David J., d. 12/10/1940 at 74/9/18 in Lyme; laborer; married; b. Lyme; Albert J. Pushee (Lyme) and Sarah F. Jeffers (New Haven, CT)
David J., Jr., d. 11/4/1959 at 54 in Lyme; farmer; b. Lyme; David J. Pushee and Mary Gilbert
Dean, d. 3/26/1985 at 64; Clarence Pushee and Emmerrette Rogers
Donald E., Sr., d. 5/20/1988 at 60; David J. Pushee and Florence B. DeGoosh

Edna S., d. 12/12/1916 at 75/5/1 in Lyme; housewife; widow; b. Lyme; David Steele (Lyme) and Harriet Southard (Lyme)

Emma C., d. 5/19/1898 at 25 in Lyme; housewife; married; b. Manchester; Benjamin Cline (Lyme) and Luthera B. Cook (Lyme)

Emmerette, d. 10/15/1953 at 55 in Hanover; none; divorced; b. Fairlee, VT; Charles S. Rogers and Minnie Morris

Eugene C., d. 10/28/1951 at 68 in Lyme; foreman; married; Clarence Pushee and Fannie Post

Eugene P., d. 1/12/1918 at 65/4/28 in Thetford, VT; single; b. Lyme; Sylvester Pushee (Lyme) and Sarah Emerton (Lyme)

Fannie C., d. 4/27/1913 at 52/4/27; housewife; married; b. Lyme; Winthrop Post (Lyme) and Sarah Wise (Groton)

Frances J., d. 1/6/1917 at 77/11/26 in Lyme; housewife; widow; b. Lyme; Alvah Jeffers (Bethel, VT) and Mary Hall (Lyme)

Frank A., d. 7/20/1928 at 52/10/26 in Lyme; farmer; married; b. Lyme; Albert J. Pushee (Lyme) and Sarah F. Jeffers (Lyme)

Frank H., d. 8/6/1889 at 57/11/20 in Lyme; single; b. Lyme; Harvey Pushee (Lyme) and Nancy Pierce (Lyme)

George A., d. 4/27/1947 at 71/2/14 in Lyme; farmer; married; b. Lyme; Alfred Pushee (Lyme) and Edna Steele (Lyme)

Harris A., d. 6/22/1978 at 86 in Hartford, VT; carpenter; b. NH; David Pushee and Mary Gilbert

Harris C., d. 5/16/2002 in Lebanon; Harris Pushee and Inez Clark

Henry S., d. 2/14/1954 at 75 in Lyme; farmer; widower; b. Lyme; Alfred W. Pushee and Edna Steele

Inez Clark, d. 1/23/1975 at 83 in Lyme; housewife; b. NH; Samuel W. Clark and Susan L. Pritchard

Isabel Shirley, d. 1/28/1998 in Lebanon; Hiram Uline and Grace Gilbert

M. Agnes, d. 8/15/1922 at 45/9/22 in Hanover; housewife; married; b. Lyme; Zodak Gilbert (Lyme) and Julia Gilbert (Lyme)

Minnie A., d. 9/14/1956 at 75 in Newport; at home; widow; b. Northfield, MA; Phillip Bombard and Ellen Welsh

Nellie, d. 10/24/1939 at 73/0/20 in Hanover; housewife; widow; b. Strafford, VT; Andrew J. Preston and Sarah -----

Nellie Jane, d. 1/23/1932 at 48/9/15 in Lyme; housewife; married; b. Lyme; Henry J. Mativia (Corinth, VT) and Hattie Stickney (Fairfax, VT)

Roger Clarence, d. 6/29/1975 at 57 in Hartford, VT; truck driver; b. NH; Clarence Pushee and Emeretta Rogers

Sarah, d. 1/8/1888 at 73/1/6 in Lyme; retired; widow; b. Lyme; Joseph Emerton (Dover) and Sarah Andross

Shirley B., d. 12/26/1929 at 0/4/21 in Lyme; b. Lyme; David J. Pushee, Jr. (Lyme) and Florence DeGoosh (Unity)

Sidney A., d. 6/30/1887 at 65/10 in Lyme; machinist; married; b. Lyme; David Pushee (Walpole) and Anna Carpenter (Bridgeport, CT)

Stanley D., d. 7/5/1982 at 46; David Pushee and Florence DeGoosh

Verla C., d. --/--/1991 in Hanover; John B. Clogston and Susie Preston

Walter S., d. 12/21/1941 at 55/6/1 in Los Angeles, CA; carpenter; married; b. Lyme; Clarence S. Pushee (Thetford, VT) and Fannie C. Post (Corinth, VT)

PUTNAM,
William F., d. 9/13/1988 at 77; George W. Putnam and Bertha Cole

RAFUSE,
Morris J., d. 6/3/1943 at 83/3/27 in Bellows Falls, VT; lumberman; married; b. NS; Nelson Rafuse and Sophia -----

RAGAN,
Barbara L., d. 4/30/1985 at 45; Thomas Scirocco and Mildred Esposito

Carolyn J., d. 7/10/2001 in Hanover; Charles Jackman and Ruth Dennis

Ida Mae, d. 1/20/1959 at 85 in Haverhill; housework; b. Yorktown, SD; John Brondle and Mirandy Sheppard

Laurence Edward, d. 12/17/1994 in Lebanon; George W. Ragan and Ida Bramble

Pamela, d. 12/27/1959 at 0/4 in Lyme; b. Hanover; Wallace Ragan and Barbara Scirocco

RANDLETT,
Fred A., d. 6/22/1934 at 72/5/14 in Lyme; merchant; single; Asa Randlett (Sanbornton) and Sophia Gardner (Troy, NY)

George W., d. 7/28/1895 at 60/7/18; hardware bus.; married; b. Plymouth; Jacob Randlett (Sanbornton) and Effie Wells (Bristol)

Hannah W., d. 3/6/1902 at 64/10/27 in Lyme; housewife; widow; b. Orford; Stedman Willard (Winchester, MA) and Meriel Wheeler (Orford)

RAY,
Alvina F., d. 7/26/1966 at 70 in Weymouth, MA; at home; married; b. New York, NY; John C. Fayen and Dorothea -----
John L., d. 9/11/1971 at 74 in Red Bank, NJ; retired

RAYMOND,
Edith G., d. 7/8/1978 at 88 in Lebanon; homemaker; b. Concord, MA; Carvosso Neily and Amelia Parker

RECORD,
Donald L., d. 5/30/1961 at 53 in Lyme; farmer; b. Hanover; Walter J. Record and Eva May Stander
Walter J., d. 8/27/1956 at 72 in Hanover; farmer; widower; b. Canaan; Edgar Record
Walter L., d. 8/18/1996 in Lebanon; Donald Record and Ada Olsen

REED,
Henry T., d. 8/20/1937 at 84/0/10 in Lyme; farmer; married; b. Dorchester; Joseph Reed (Dorchester) and Harriett Davis (Groton)
Irene H., d. 8/13/1997 in Lebanon; Andrew Hansen and Christine Jensen
Julia A., d. 4/27/1957 at 73 in Lebanon; housewife; widow; b. Landaff; Matthew Allbee and Ida Noyes
Leonora A., d. 5/24/1944 at 87/10/0 in Lyme; housewife; widow; b. Groton; Stillman Merrill (Groton) and Mary Ann Hall (Groton)

REEVES,
Otto Ralph, d. 11/24/1974 at 67 in Concord; construction foreman; b. ME; George Reeves and Lola Daggert
Rose R., d. 3/7/1979 at 72 in Lyme; housewife; b. ME; Herbert Raymond and Esta Whittier

RENNIE,
Kenneth R., d. 2/21/1966 at 56 in Hanover; store clerk; married; b. Hanover; Roy Rennier and Della Hanchett
Marion Regnier, d. 6/12/1962 at 56 in Lyme; housewife; b. Pittsfield; George Renier and Esme Banker
Roy, d. 11/14/1950 at 66 in Hanover; farmer; married; b. Canada; Alexander Rennie and Mary Glastow

RENNIS,
Della S., d. 6/18/1979 at 91 in Hanover; homemaker; b. NH; Dennis Hanchett and Elizabeth -----
Eileen M., d. 5/24/1980 at 57; Frank Lorraine and Inez Dickerson

REYNOLDS,
Helen M., d. 5/24/1998 in Lyme; Albert Franz and Pauline Stotz
Mary A., d. 5/6/1890 at 50 in Lyme; housewife; married; b. Hanover; Thomas Reynolds (Ireland) and Jerusha Hall (Hanover)

RHODES,
Cecil E., d. 10/3/1980 at 32; Stanley Rhoades and Viola Lewis

RICE,
Freda R., d. 7/15/1922 at 0/0/16 in Hanover; b. Lyme; Freda E. Rice (Winthrop, NY) and Laura S. Simmons (Lyme)
Laura Simmons, d. 5/23/1940 at 50/11/17 in Haverhill; housewife; married; b. Lyme; Lewis A. Simmons (Wentworth) and Mae Belle Clement (Warren)

RICH,
daughter, d. 9/28/1897 at 0/0/6; b. Lyme; Fred Rich (Northumberland) and Ada F. Swift (Strafford)
son, d. 5/11/1916 at – in Hanover; b. Hanover; Preston Rich (Stratford, VT) and Rosa B. King (Lyme)
Afton E., d. 12/16/1956 at 70 in Sanford, ME; carpenter; married; b. N. Stratford; Dwight Rich and Isabel Claflin
David A., d. 12/10/1988 at 46; Dwight S. Rich and Nellie A. Perkins
Dexter F., d. 5/3/1905 at 26/4/27 in Lyme; farmer; single; b. Stratford; Dwight Rich (Groveton) and Sarah I. Claflin (Auburn)
Dwight, d. 9/3/1921 at 67/10/7 in Lyme; farmer; married; b. Northumberland; Daniel Rich (Northumberland) and Eunice Bradbury (Dorchester)
Eunice, d. 2/28/1901 at 74/3/19 in Lyme; widow; b. Dorchester; Samuel Bradbury (Canaan) and Phobe Gould (Warner)
Everett B., d. 10/27/2000 in Lyme; John Rich and Ida King
John S., d. 2/5/1934 at 45/5/4 in Lyme; merchant; married; b. N. Stratford; Dwight Rich (Groton) and Sarah Claflin (Auburn)
Linda C., d. 12/10/1988 at 41; Horace E. Pike and Maxine L. Marsh
Marion F., d. 3/4/196 at 81 in Hanover; housewife; widow; b. MA; Charles Pritchard and Grace Fuller

Perley, d. 7/31/1957 at 73 in Hanover; ret. butcher; married; b. Strafford, VT; Dwight Rich and Isabel Claflin

Preston W., d. 5/13/1950 at 68 in Hanover; crossing ten.; married; b. Stratford; Dwight Rich and Sarah Claflin

Ray B., d. 1/20/1947 at 53/8/4 in Newport; meat cutter; married; b. Lyme; Dwight Rich (Northumberland) and Belle Claflin (Auburn)

Rosie B., d. 4/4/1960 at 75 in Lebanon; housewife; b. Lyme; Walter E. King and Ida L. Norris

Sarah I., d. 4/12/1937 at 77/9/18 in Hanover; retired; widow; b. Auburn; William P. Claflin (Lyme) and Mary E. Southard (Lyme)

RILEY,
Caroline M., d. 2/28/1922 at 70/11/18 in Haverhill; widow; Elbridge Perkins (Boston) and Harriet Perkins (Boston, MA)

RINEHART,
Roscoe S., d. 7/4/1961 at 66 in Concord; parole officer; b. Woodsville; Carroll Rinehart and Blanche Handeford

RIOS,
Pablo, d. 1/12/1945 at 0/0/2 in Lyme; b. Lyme; Anselmo Rios Baez (Dorado, PR) and Aleja M. Rivera (Dorado, PR)

ROBERTS,
Alphonso, d. 10/24/1898 at 2 in Lyme; b. Lyme; Thomas W. Roberts (Lyme) and Ella M. White (Orford)

Caroline, d. 5/19/1890 at 63/2/13 in Lyme; housewife; married; b. Wentworth; Jonathan Smith (Wentworth) and Amelia Brown (Orford)

Florence, d. 7/19/1928 at 42 in Hanover; single; b. Bradford, VT; Alphonso Roberts (Lyme)

Guy A., d. 11/23/1927 at 39/9/10 in Hanover; road foreman; married; b. Bradford, VT; Harris A. Roberts (Lyme) and Emma S. Wells (Bath)

Jennie, d. 10/3/1982 at 91; Albert Hobart and Nellie Phelps

Jessie L., d. 12/28/1972 at 54 in Hartford, VT; bridgeman; b. NH; Guy Roberts and Jennie Hobart

John K., d. 9/1/1937 at 4/9/1 in Hanover; b. Lyme; John P. Mara (Portsmouth) and Meda P. Roberts (Lyme)

Thomas W., d. 1/1/1930 at – in Dorchester; laborer; married; b. Lyme; Thomas F. Roberts (Raymond) and Caroline Smith

(Wentworth)

ROBINSON,
John C., d. 12/2/1894 at 74 in Lyme; cerebral hemorrhage; painter; widower
Ruth M., d. 9/12/1987 at 64; William Preston and Mable French

ROCK,
Lizzie, d. 7/27/1944 at 77/4/17 in Lebanon; widow; b. Haverhill, MA; Frank P. French (Deerfield) and Emily A. Richardson (Candia)
Napoleon, d. 7/30/1907 at 68/6/30 in Lyme; farmer; widower; b. Vershire, Canada; Xavier F. Rock and Margaret Young
Napolian B., d. 3/14/1942 at 74/1/15 in Lyme; farmer; married; b. Hanover; Napolian Rock (Vershire, Canada) and Arminne Bernell (Vershire, Canada)

RODGERS,
Cora A., d. 1/12/1898 at 0/0/10 in Lyme; b. Lyme; George R. Rodgers (Lone Valley, Canada) and Hattie M. McDonald (Peacham, VT)

ROGERS,
Ruth M., d. 10/9/1970 at 63 in Hanover; librarian; b. NH; Henry S. Pushee and Nellie Mativia

RONCA,
Anthony, d. 12/13/1968 at 59 in Hanover; janitor; married; b. PA; Albino Ronca and Theresa Tava

RONDEAU,
Irene, d. 9/5/2003 in Lebanon; Anargyros Capilos and Anastasia Gianacopoulos

ROUSSEAU,
Helen R., d. 9/26/2003 in Lebanon; Adlord Rousseau and Rosa Towns

ROWE,
George E., d. 10/3/1938 at 82/1/13 in Thetford, VT; laborer; widower; b. Auburn, ME; William Rowe (Stratford) and Elvira P. Madden (Lancaster)

Mary, d. 11/5/1905 at 41/6/27 in Lyme; housewife; married; b.
   Rockburn, PQ; John Mulhen (Ireland) and Margaret Steele
   (Canada)

ROWELL,
Leon, d. --/--/1955 at 57 in Concord; none; single; b. NH

ROWLEY,
Clara, d. 3/26/1939 at 72/6/14 in Hanover; teacher; single; b.
   Greenfield, MA; James Rowley (Sheffield, England) and Teresa
   Deakin (Sheffield, England)

RUHL,
George H., d. 10/4/1963 at 62 in Lyme; retired; b. Albany, NY;
   Frederick K. Ruhl

RUNNELS,
George W., d. 7/4/1900 at 68/1/20 in Lyme; farmer; widower; b.
   Hanover; Jeremiah Runnels (Hanover) and ----- (Corinth, VT)
Mary E., d. 4/1/1891 at 51/10 in Lyme; housewife; married; b. Lyme;
   J. Tyler (Lyme) and P. Hall (Lyme)

RUSS,
Harriet Boyd, d. 1/23/1946 at 57/8/5 in Lyme; housewife; widow; b.
   Chateaugay, NY; George A. Boyd (Canada) and Betsey Cook
   (Canada)

ST. PETER,
Lewis, d. 9/17/1990

SABINE,
Josephine, d. 1/29/1928 at 63 in Lyme; housewife; married; b.
   Perkins Cove, NS; Robert Hardwick

SAILER,
Nancy K., d. 6/18/1993 in Lebanon; William F. Kopp and A.
   Lemoyne (Betts)

SANBORN,
daughter, d. 6/10/1896 at –; b. Lyme; Newton F. Sanborn (Lyme)
   and Eliza Welch (Lyme)

Arthur E., d. 5/27/1953 at 75 in Lyme; farmer; single; b. Lyme; Freeman Sanborn and Mary Avis Moore

Charles D., d. 8/20/1937 at 76/6/28 in Hanover; farmer; widower; b. Lyme; Freeman P. Sanborn (Dorchester) and Mary A. Moore (Thetford, VT)

Charles F., d. 3/17/1910 at 75/2/20; farmer; widower; b. Dorchester; John Sanborn (Epping) and Lydia Piper (Dorchester)

Daisy C., d. 11/15/1922 at 51/9/16 in Lyme; married; b. Thetford, VT

Dora E., d. 3/25/2004 in Lebanon; Harvey Balch and Lillian Morrill

Eliza, d. 1/21/1964 at 92 in Saratoga Springs, NY; housewife; b. Lyme; Joseph R. Welch and Zilpha Cutting

Emma, d. 12/26/1938 at 75/4/19 in Lyme; housekeeper; single; b. Lyme; Freeman P. Sanborn (Dorchester) and Mary A. Moore (Thetford, VT)

Freeman P., d. 2/3/1905 at 74/2/27 in Lyme; lumberman; married; b. Dorchester; John Sanborn (Epping) and Lydia Piper (Dorchester)

George W., d. 1/11/1917 at 83/1/13 in Goffstown; widower

Gordon W., d. 9/6/1968 at 52 in Hartford, VT; laborer; single; b. NH; Gordon W. Sanborn and Grace Perkins

Harry E., d. 1/11/1996 in Lebanon; Otis Sanborn and Grace Perkins

John, d. 11/25/1889 at 67/8/5 in Lyme; farmer; married; b. Bradford, VT; John Sanborn

Jonathan P., d. 10/3/1887 at 72/2/15 in Lyme; retired; widower; b. Dorchester; John Sanborn (Dorchester) and Polly Palmer (Epping)

Margaret, d. 1/21/1958 at 91 in Hanover; none; widow; b. Somerville, MA; Dennis Tynan and Mary Hogan

Mary A., d. 6/26/1922 at 81/6/22 in Lyme; housewife; widow; b. Thetford, VT; William Moore

Newton F., d. 2/26/1927 at 57/1/7 in Lyme; millman; married; b. Lyme; Freeman P. Sanborn (Dorchester) and Mary Moore (Thetford, VT)

Rosetta A., d. 3/25/1910 at 37/3/22; housework; single; b. Lyme; Freeman Sanborn (Dorchester) and Mary A. Moore (Thetford, VT)

Sarah, d. 1/19/1896 at 79/9/19; housewife; married; b. England; ----- Simmes (England)

Sarah J., d. 8/31/1902 at 62/5/9 in Lyme; housewife; married; b. Varleboro, ME; Paul Hussey and Esther Newman

SANSBURY,
Dorothy C., d. 1/10/1986 at 70; Frank G. Gregory and Sadie Porter
John W., d. 9/7/1979 at 73; supervisor; Raymond Sansbury and Rosa Hall

SAWYER,
Albert E., d. 5/9/1893 at 70/9/9 in Lyme; disease of heart; farmer; married; b. Lyme; Benning Sawyer and Lydia Thompson
Arthur H., d. 10/12/1889 at 35/8/6 in Lyme; single; b. Lyme; Bela Sawyer (Orford) and Deborah Joselyn (Lyme)
Bela, d. 10/16/1904 at 79/2/6 in Lyme; merchant; married; b. Orford; Jared Sawyer and Cynthia Dewey
Deborah T., d. 2/8/1917 at 89/2 in Lyme; retired; widow; b. Lyme; Freeman Josselyn (Lyme) and Abigal Bowman (Henniker)
Esther Ann, d. 11/26/1912 at 83/0/27; domestic; widow; b. Strafford, VT; Nathan Carpenter (Strafford, VT) and Sarepta Chamberlain
John T., d. 10/25/1894 at 84/6/16; wheelwright; widower; b. Orford; Benning Sawyer and Lydia Thompson

SCHMECKEBIER,
Alexandra K., d. 3/10/1980 at 70; Emile Kluge and Olga deMoravsky
Laurence E., d. 7/5/1984 at 78; William F. Schmeckebier and Anna Lubben

SCHMITT,
Annette, d. 12/19/1994 in Lyme; James Paddock and Viola Quinn
Richard F., d. 10/21/1975 at 66 in Hanover; retired; b. WI; Nicholas Schmitt and Ida Powell

SCHRIEVER,
Edna, d. 6/2/1973 at 65 in Hanover; housewife; b. NY; Henry Neuman and Bertha Rappuhn
Jack R., d. 4/23/1982 at 75; John Schriever and Marie Rebenklau

SCHWEER,
Henry, d. 9/10/1932 at 72/11/2 in Lyme; farmer; widower; b. Brooklyn, NY; Henry Schweer (Germany)

SCRIBNER,
Olive A., d. 9/16/1927 at 74/5/6 in Lyme; housewife; widow; b. Ellsworth; Samuel Sanborn (Ellsworth) and Carolyn Sanborn

(W. Campton)

SEACE,
Henry, d. 6/9/1929 at 46 in Hanover; farmer; single; b. E. Concord, VT; Sylvester Seace (Quebec) and Lucinda Camer (Quebec)

SEARS,
Charles M., Jr., d. 5/15/1970 at 73 in Lyme; bus. adminis.; b. MA; Charles M. Sears and Lucy D. Kendall
Dorothy W., d. 5/3/1961 at 62 in Hanover; housewife; b. Lenox, MA; Alfred Wingett and Maude Loomis

SEAVER,
Caleb, d. 12/11/1893 at 79/11/26 in Lyme; bronchitis, dis. of heart; farmer; married; b. Enfield; Caleb Seaver (Enfield, farmer)
Sallie E., d. 4/1/1907 at 90/1/5 in Lyme; housewife; widow; b. Wentworth; Jerry Ellsworth (Wentworth)

SENTER,
Brenda, d. 12/2/1992 in Lyme; Kenneth Senter and Beatrice Campbell

SEPESSY,
Antonie, d. 9/18/1967 at 83 in Lyme; unknown; widow; b. Czechoslovakia; Antone Vasmusius

SHACKFORD,
Emma, d. 4/9/1921 at 26/3/8 in Lyme; housewife; widow; b. Antrim; Wells Robbins and Emma Youngman

SHARP,
John E., d. 2/13/1925 at 29/10/4 in Lyme; brick mason; single; b. Tilton; Alexander Sharp (Scotland) and Laura Hopkins (Alexandria)

SHATTUCK,
Addie, d. 3/11/1948 at 78/5/29 in Lyme; housewife; married; b. Orford; Jesse Muzzey (Topsham, VT)
George F., d. 6/11/1925 at 59/8 in Lynn, MA; married; Charles Shattuck (Bethlehem) and Lydia M. Bryant (Hanover)
George H., d. 9/5/1949 at 44 in Woodstock, VT

Hannah P., d. 4/27/1889 at 80/9/27 in Lyme; widow; b. Dorchester; John Sanborn (Hollis) and Polly Palmer
Warren J., d. 3/4/1949 at 85 in Lyme

SHAW,
Richard M., d. 8/1/1932 at 68/8/8 in Lyme; widower; b. Douglas, MA

SHEPARD,
Irene, d. 7/30/1952 att 36 in Hanover; housewife; married; b. Lebanon; Peter Ducharme and Alice Leware

SIEMONS,
Robert F., d. 9/29/1984 at 20; Frederick C. Siemons and Judith Feller

SIMMONS,
Alice G., d. 2/21/1959 at 73 in Lyme; housewife; b. Piermont; Harvey Smith and Eliza Corliss
Auburn L., d. 8/18/1931 at 71/3/3 in Fairlee, VT; married; b. Lyme; George A. Simmons (Lyme) and Abbie Piper (Piermont)
Farrie, d. 8/2/1929 at 34/10/14 in Hartford, CT; bookkeeper; single; b. Lyme; Auburn L. Simmons (Lyme) and Mary B. Clement (Benton)
Lewis A., d. 5/21/1961 at 77 in Lyme; farmer; b. Wentworth; Auburn L. Simmons and May Belle Grant

SIMPSON,
Flora, d. 11/18/1970 at 98 in Concord; retired; b. Canada; George Dunbar and Sophie Clough
Martin R., d. 2/23/2002 in Lyme; Arthur Simpson and Alice McIlory

SKINNER,
son, d. 11/7/1887 at – in Lyme; b. Lyme; Brewster Skinner (Lyme) and Carrie Farnham (Plymouth)
son, d. 7/24/1897 at –; b. Lyme; Brewster P. Skinner (Lyme) and Carrie P. Farnham (Plymouth)
Brewster, d. 2/9/1925 at 73/7 in St. Johnsbury, VT; married; b. Lyme; George Skinner
Carrie P., d. 10/7/1939 at 77/8/12 in St. Johnsbury, VT; housewife; widow
Joshua G., d. 7/16/1890 at 76 in Lyme; farmer; widower; b. Lyme;

Cyrus Skinner and Betsey English
Theda I., d. 10/20/1898 at 2/1/15 in Lyme; b. Lyme; Grant G. Skinner (Lowell, VT) and Jennie A. Corley (Craftsbury, VT)

SLACK,
Abbie G., d. 5/26/1905 at 80/0/26 in Lyme; housework; widow
Ida E., d. 2/24/1925 at 74/4/4 in Lyme; housewife; married; b. Akron, OH; John S. Kent (Lyme) and Sophronia Perkins (Lyme)
Wilber F., d. 11/11/1935 at 85/9/29 in Malden, MA; retired; widower; b. Wells River, VT; Fred S. Slack (Thetford, VT) and Angeline Goodman (Montpelier, VT)

SLOANE,
Henry C., d. 9/19/1891 at 78/3/22 in Thetford, VT; farmer; single; b. Lyme; William S. Sloan and Lydia Felshaw (Lyme)

SMALL,
son, d. 6/11/1935 at – in Lyme; b. Lyme; Harry Small (Lyme) and Daisy B. Melendy (W. Fairlee, VT)
Duane W., d. 5/12/1925 at 53/6/24 in Lyme; grain dealer; married; b. W. Windsor, VT; Ira C. Small (Goffstown) and Martha Walker (Cavendish, VT)
Lucy Minnietta, d. 12/3/1947 at 76/4/5 in Lyme; housewife; widow; b. Pierrepont, NY; George Lobdell and Nancy Daniels
Mary Jane, d. 1/24/1947 at 0/1/26 in Hanover; b. Lebanon; Harry Small (Lyme) and Daisy Melendy (W. Fairlee, VT)
Ralph Duane, d. 3/9/1975 at 74 in Lyme; carpenter; b. NH; Duane Walker Small and L. Minnie Lobdell

SMALLEY,
James A., d. 6/6/1942 at 74/8/2 in Hanover; blacksmith; widower; b. Littleton; James H. Smalley (NH) and Johanna Elkins (Littleton)
Martha H., d. 12/22/1935 at 67/2/1 in Lyme; housewife; married; b. S. Ryegate, VT; Albert Langmaid (ME) and Martha Carruth

SMITH,
son, d. 2/5/1897 at –; b. Lyme; Charles D. Smith (Corinth, VT) and Annie R. Flanders (W. Fairlee, VT)
son, d. 10/18/1898 at – in Lyme; b. Lyme; Bion Smith (Mount Vernon) and Esther M. Sanborn (Lyme)
Albert L., d. 4/21/1928 at 35/0/21 in Windsor, VT; Edgar Smith

Alice, d. 7/21/1961 at 83 in Lyme; housewife; b. Thetford, VT; Allen Turner and Edna Gove

Benjamin, d. 7/25/1910 at 75/2; laborer; widower; b. Wentworth; Jonathan Smith

Bertie E., d. 6/29/1912 at 32/8/4; farmer; married; b. Sullivan; George D. Smith (Sullivan) and Gertrude Thayer (Providence, RI)

Charles N., d. 9/21/1925 at 57/4/22 in Lyme; retired; widower; b. Hanover; Chandler P. Smith (Hanover) and Sarah F. Camp (Hanover)

Clayton, d. 6/12/1895 at 0/0/30; b. Lyme; W. Scott Smith (Holderness) and Minnie D. Delno (Montreal)

Deborah C., d. 1/27/1917 at 84/7/23 in Lyme; housekeeping; widow; b. Lyme; John Claflin (Lyme) and Lydia W. Tyler (Lyme)

Edgar, d. 12/10/1936 at 85/5/2 in Hartford, VT

Esther S., d. 7/3/1974 at 71 in Hanover; housewife; b. CT; Charles Starkweather and Lucy Williston

Eva May, d. 9/20/1900 at 25/0/9 in Lyme; single; b. Lyme; Benjamin Smith (Wentworth) and Angeline B. Worthen (Lyme)

Ezra M., d. 11/14/1914 at 42/11/9; laborer; married; b. Hanover; Alonzo Smith (Hanover) and Julia A. Heath (Colebrook)

Fenton H., d. 12/3/1922 at 56/7/15 in Lyme; farmer; married; b. Lyme; Rodney V. Smith and Deborah Claflin

Hannah E., d. 11/12/1913 at 84/0/17; single; b. Hanover; Ashbel Smith (Hanover) and Lucinda Tenney (Hanover)

Hannah K., d. 10/12/1911 at 87/7/9; housewife; widow; b. Chester, VT; Jonathan Kendall

Katie C., d. 8/31/1895 at 0/4; b. Lyme; Scott Smith (Holderness) and Minnie D. Delno (Canada)

Lelia E., d. 3/23/1907 at 45/11/24 in Lyme; housewife; married; b. W. Windsor, VT; Joel Burnham (Windsor, VT) and Lucia A. Marcey (Haverhill)

Rodney V., d. 5/3/1888 at 56/7/16 in Lyme; mechanic; married; b. Hadley, MA; John Smith

SNELLING,
Kenneth, d. 8/4/1970 at 29 in Berlin, VT; lumberman; b. NH; Kenneth Snelling and Vivian Jones

SNOW,
Mary Q., d. 12/16/1890 at 72/5 in Lyme; housewife; married; b. Calis

SOUDER,
Robert H., Jr., d. --/--/1955 at 23 in Lyme; single; Robert H. Souder and Hazel Kurtz

SOULE,
Byron, d. 3/28/1952 at 79 in Lebanon; retired; married; b. Providence, RI; Edward B. Soule and Sarah Gilson
Nora B., d. 3/8/1958 at 88 in Hanover; housewife; widow; b. Richmond, RI; Dyer Kingsley and Jane Cord

SPEAR,
Sarah Hall, d. 5/5/1895 at 78/9/17; housewife; widow; b. Lyme; John Hall and Mary Culver

SPRAGUE,
Harry R., Sr., d. 11/25/1987 at 74; John Sprague and Lizzie Thayer

SQUIRES,
Adeline M., d. 5/8/1901 at 64/0/20 in Lyme; housewife; widow; b. Alexandria; George W. Berry (Meredith) and Prudence M. Squires (Haverhill)

STAHNKE,
Carl A., d. 2/23/1949 at 63 in Lyme

STARK,
Alice, d. 10/1/1947 at 77/8/1 in Lebanon; housewife; widow; b. Newport; Alvaro Chaffee (Newport) and Isabelle Wheeler (Newport)
Alton G., d. 11/29/1906 at 15/1/10 in Lyme; single; b. Newport; George E. Stark (Lyme) and Alice M. Chaffee (Newport)
David C., d. 12/23/1905 at 66/5/2 in Lyme; farmer; married; b. Lyme; Anson Stark (Lyme) and Lydia Dodge
Edna L., d. 12/16/1929 at 64 in Hanover; widow; b. Lyme; David Dike (Lyme)
Edward J., d. 12/7/1929 at 77 in Westboro, MA; b. Lyme; Isaac G. Stark (Lyme) and Rachel Goodell (Newbury, VT)
George E., d. 5/7/1941 at 74/5/14 in Hanover; retired farmer; married; b. Lyme; Anson Stark and Lucinda Clough
Isaac Davis, d. 5/30/1889 at 84/7/2 in Lyme; tanner; widower; b. Lyme; Hezekiah Stark and Nancy Lacomb

Isaac G., d. 2/17/1894 at 64/8; laborer; widower; b. Lyme; Peavy D. Stark and Rhoda Fitts

Jennie F., d. 12/25/1916 at 61/3/10 in Lyme; housewife; b. Lyme; Francis Gordon (Bethlehem) and Charlotte Cline (Lyme)

John L., d. 6/3/1925 at 71/11/4 in Lyme; carpenter; married; b. Hanover; John Stark (Lyme) and Emeline Warren (Lyme)

Julius M., d. 6/3/1919 at 69/2/24 in MA; single; b. Lyme; Z. J. Stark (Lyme) and C. M. Converse (Lyme)

Mary Runnels, d. 8/31/1897 at 58/4/11; housewife; married; b. Hanover; Jeremiah Runnells (Farmington) and Sarah Colony (New Durham)

Rachel M., d. 9/26/1893 at 69/11/26 in Lyme; cerebral hemorrhage; housewife; married; b. Newbury, VT; E. Goodell (farmer) and Nancy Follett

STEARNS,
Fred O., Jr., d. 6/22/2003 in Lyme; Fred Stearns, Sr. and Doris Hazelton

Reginald E., d. 6/20/1988 at 47; Fred O. Stearns and Doris Hazelton

STEELE,
Carlos F., d. 7/17/1908 at 36/0/25; farmer; married; b. Lyme; David C. Steele (Lyme) and Matilda Pushee (Lyme)

Clarence S., d. 4/20/1931 at 61/6/23 in Lyme; farmer; single; b. Lyme; David C. Steele (Lyme) and Matilda Pushee (Lyme)

David Carlos, d. 3/31/1910 at 77/8/22; farmer; married; b. Lyme; David Steele (Tolland, CT) and Harriet Southard (Lyme)

Georgiana B., d. 4/15/1930 at 65/3/29 in Melrose, MA; housekeeper; widow; b. NS

Lena, d. 3/5/1948 at 70/1/2 in Norwich, VT; housekeeper; widow; b. Lyme; Frank Cutting

Matilda M., d. 4/21/1910 at 69/10/12; housewife; widow; b. Lyme; Sylvester Pushee (Lyme) and Sarah Emerton (Lyme)

STETSON,
Eugene R., d. 1/4/1912 at 48/1/16; married; b. Damariscotta, ME; Abner Stetson and Mary Hitchcock

George E., d. 5/2/1947 at 78/0/28 in Bridgeton, ME; laborer; married; b. Lyme; Otis W. Stetson and Mary L. -----

Harvey F., d. 12/15/1917 at 86/7/8 in Lyme; farming; widower; b. Lyme; Jessie Stetson (Lyme) and Esther Heaton (Hanover)

Horace, d. 4/24/1895 at 73/3/18; laborer; widower; b. Lyme; Jesse Stetson (Lyme) and Esther Eaton (Hanover)

Lizzie L., d. 9/23/1946 at 70/4/29 in Laconia; at home; widow; b. S. Ham, PQ; William Thompson (England) and ----- Mackie (England)

Maria L. E., d. 3/3/1896 at 57; housewife; married; b. Groton; Asa Elliot (Groton)

Myrtie May, d. 6/7/1891 at 14/0/23 in Lyme; b. Lyme; Otis W. Stetson (Grafton) and Myra L. Elliott (Hebron)

Sarah E., d. 6/22/1909 at 75/10/23; housewife; married; b. Candia; Emery Currier (Candia) and Mary Hibbard (Candia)

STEVENS,

Anna M., d. 8/10/1970 at 79 in Hartford, VT; housewife; b. VT; Edwin Cole and Nellie Phelps

Frank J., d. 2/17/1965 at 41 in Kissimee, FL; hospital empl.; married; b. Springfield; ----- Stevens and Sarah -----

Hattie P., d. 6/22/1946 at 66/9/0 in Lyme; housewife; married; b. Alstead; Jared Parker and Clara Leason

Warren S. L., d. 4/24/1891 at 24/4/25 in Lyme; laborer; single; b. Haverhill, MA; Alvah B. Stevens (Orford) and Abbie P. Lane (Manchester)

William M., d. 5/24/1954 at 78 in Lyme; machinist; married; b. Franklin; George Stevens and Ella Morrison

Winifred, d. 9/26/1960 at 90 in Concord; housewife; b. Lyme; Dennis Hanchett and Elizabeth Reed

STEWART,

Jennie, d. --/--/1955 at 79 in Haverhill; housewife; divorced; b. Stanstead, PQ; William Wardrobe and Martha Moulton

STICKNEY,

Joseph M., d. 2/18/1914 at 93/2/27; retired; widower; b. Jericho, VT; Joseph Stickney and Sarah Goodrich

STILL,

Horace E., d. 2/16/1907 at 0/5 in Lyme; b. Lyme; Charles E. Still (Newport) and Maggie Shea (Manchester)

STOCKING,

Adelia L., d. 2/5/1954 at 89 in Lyme; physician; widow; b. Macomb,

IL; Abram Stickle and Sarah Metcalf

STONE,
Chester Warren, d. 8/24/1993 in Myrtle Beach, SC; Charles Raswell Stone and Kathleen Brown

STORRS,
Almeda L., d. 1/28/1918 at 65 in Concord; retired; married; b. Lyme; Jonathan Whipple (Lyme) and Elizabeth Flint (Lyme) (1923)
Augustus C., d. 2/3/1938 at 71/4/10 in Trono, CA; single; b. Hanover; Augustus C. Storrs (Hanover) and Fannie D. Clark (Lyme)
Caroline H., d. 7/7/1889 at 77/5/2 in Lyme; housekeeper; widow; b. Weathersfield, CT; Perey Haskell and Hannah Baulding
Fannie D., d. 2/6/1920 at 83/4/22 in Lyme; housewife; widow; Isaar F. Clark (Lyme) and Laura H. Pike (Lyme)
Hinkley H., d. 11/1/1924 at 72/11/15 in Lyme; farmer; widower; b. Lyme; Dan Storrs (Hanover) and Caroline Haskell (Weathersfield, VT)
Mary, d. 4/24/1927 at 45/8/20 in Lyme; housekeeper; single; b. Lyme; Hinkley H. Storrs (Lyme) and Almeda E. Whipple (Lyme)
Royal, d. 3/21/1890 at 82/3/3 in Lyme; farmer; widower; b. Hanover; Augustus Storrs (Mansfield, CT) and Amy Fales (Mansfield, CT)

STOWELL,
William R., d. 12/26/1949 at 64 in Lyme

STRAW,
Charles L., d. 6/20/1901 at 41/0/11 in Lyme; farmer; married; b. Lyme; Daniel M. Straw (Lyme) and Hannah Weed (Lyme)
Daniel M., d. 3/30/1904 at 72/0/12 in Lyme; farmer; married; b. Lyme; Moses Straw (Gilmanton) and Sarah Curtis (Stewartstown)
Hannah W., d. 4/16/1904 at 68/11/28 in Lyme; housework; widow; b. Orford; Benjamin Weed (Unity) and ----- Ames (Strafford, VT)

STRONG,
Sarah Harriett, d. 7/10/1978 at 92 in Lebanon; homemaker; b. Niskayuna, NY; Levi Strong and Hannah Veder

STROUT,
Leslie J., d. 8/15/1975 at 30 in Hanover; laborer; b. NH; Gerald Strout and Elizabeth Wilmot

STRUE,
Alma L., d. 3/3/1892 at 42/5/3; housewife; married; b. Lyme; A. P. Lamphere (Hartland, VT) and Maria Lamphere (Thetford, VT)
George E., d. 5/18/1915 at 69/8/7 in Lyme; laborer; widower; b. Canada; Jacob Strue

SULLEY,
Cora, d. 9/9/1965 at 93 in Lyme; housewife; widow; b. Orleans, VT; Charles Gray and Augusta Gray

SWAN,
Esther B., d. 1/12/1895 at 92/4/2; housewife; widow; b. Hartland, VT; Ebenezer Billings and Patience Fisher

SWITZER,
Maria V. M., d. 4/6/1937 at 78/8/10 in Lyme; housekeeper; widow; b. Lebanon; Ira Mayette and Catherine -----

SYMONDS,
Dexter, d. 8/24/1887 at 69/4/7 in Lyme; farmer; married; b. Hancock; Charles Symonds (Hancock) and Sarah Symonds (Hancock)

TALLMAN,
David F., d. 2/14/1918 at 77/6/22 in Thetford, VT; carpenter; married; b. Lyme; David Tallman (Lyme) and Theodocia Smith (Hanover)
Hannah, d. 3/7/1891 at 92/4/3 in Lyme; housekeeper; single; b. Lyme; Thomas Tallman and Hannah Perkins (Lyme)

TANGERMAN,
John T., d. 5/23/1965 at 33 in Lyme; oceanographer; married; b. Pt. Washington, NY; Elmer Tangerman and Molly Christopher

TATTERSALL,
George, d. 7/19/1963 at 87 in Hanover; retired; b. Orford; George Tattersall and Hattie Swett
George E., d. 9/21/1924 at 77/11/21 in Lyme; laborer; married; b.

England; Abram Tattersall (England)
Hattie S., d. 4/4/1912 at 28; housewife; married; b. Orford; Elijah Merrill (Hebron) and Isabel Soper (MA)
Isaac, d. 4/12/1917 at 58/6 in Hanover; farming; married; Abraham Tattersall (England)
Leona L., d. 3/7/1906 at 0/3/18 in Lyme; b. Lyme; George E. Tattersall, Jr. (Orford) and Hattie G. Merrill (Orford)
Matilda, d. 9/7/1930 at 71 in Lyme; widow; b. Canada; Edward Cole (England) and Martha Wayne (England)

TAYLOR,
Aaron, d. 1/28/1891 at 87/0/17 in Lyme; farmer; widower; b. Hartford, VT; John Taylor and Betsey Dimick
Warren M., d. 12/28/1891 at 4 in Lyme; b. W. Concord, VT; J. C. Taylor (Wolcott, VT) and Abbie Fay (Danville, VT)

TENNEY,
Myra, d. 7/20/1953 at 84 in Haverhill; none; widow; b. Lyme; Nathan Hewes and Lucy Cobb

TERRY,
Galen, d. 1/16/1894 at 60/7/21; farmer; widower; b. Warwick, PQ; William Terry (England) and Lucy Degoosh (Warwick, PQ)
Milo J., d. 9/23/1949 at 93 in Lyme

THATCHER,
Harriett M., d. 3/10/1944 at 90/0/27 in Lyme; housewife; widow; b. Peacham, VT; Mark Donaldson (Scotland) and Charlotte -----

THAYER,
Alice W., d. 10/26/1956 at 74 in Hanover; housewife; married; b. Preakness, NJ; Benjamin Wyckoff and Fannie Drew

THOMAS,
son, d. 11/2/1889 at 0/0/1 in Lyme; b. Lyme; Schuyler W. Thomas (Lunenburg, VT) and Luvia Bugbee (Burke, VT)
Elizabeth, d. 4/10/1948 at 85/4/2 in Lebanon; housewife; widow; b. Quebec; James George (Knowlton, Canada) and Sarah Aldrich (Knowlton, Canada)
George W., d. 3/15/1938 at 88/2/9 in Lyme; carpenter; married; b. Lyme; William B. Thomas (England) and Nancy Cook (Lyme)

Nancy C., d. 9/22/1901 at 71/9/8 in Lyme; widow; b. Lyme; Thomas
    Cook (Lyme) and Betsey Flint (Lyme)
William, d. 5/19/1892 at 72/9/15; carpenter; married

THOMPSON,
Addie, d. 9/2/1925 at 64/10/27 in Lyme; housewife; married; b.
    Lisbon; Newell Dexter (Lisbon) and Julia Streeter (Franconia)
Amelia, d. 1/29/1925 at 82/5/5 in Haverhill
Annie M., d. 4/16/1905 at 43/6/14 in Lyme; housewife; married; b.
    Danville, PQ; Charles J. Devey (Havsworth, England) and Ann
    Tanks (England)
Arlene, d. 12/25/1924 at 0/1 in Hanover; b. Lyme; Joseph A.
    Thompson (S. Ham, Canada) and Grace M. Archer (Colebrook)
Barbara, d. 3/18/1930 at 88/11/20 in Lyme; housewife; widow; b. S.
    Ham, PQ; Joseph Mackay (S. Ham, PQ) and Rebecca Evans
    (S. Ham, PQ)
Bertha, d. 10/27/1922 at 0/0/30 in Hanover; b. Lyme; J. A.
    Thompson (Canada) and Grace Archer (Colebrook)
Daniel, d. 5/20/1924 at 19/1/15 in Laconia; single; b. Lyme; Joseph
    G. Thompson (S. Ham, PQ) and Annie E. Devey (Danville,
    Canada)
Daniel H., d. --/--/1955 at 87 in Hanover; farmer; single; b. South
    Ham, PQ; William Thompson and Barbara Mackay
Daniel Moses, d. 10/3/1971 at 45 in Lyme; farming; b. NH; William
    Thompson and Della E. Bryant
Elizabeth, d. 2/26/1914 at 73/10/2; housewife; married; b. St.
    Hyacinth, PQ; Edward Dagneau (St. Hyacinth) and Martha A.
    Moore (Salisbury, VT)
Frances M., d. 7/12/1935 at 0/5/26 in Hanover; b. Lebanon; Henry A.
    Thompson (Lyme) and Dorothy L. Cunningham (Big Timber,
    MT)
George D., d. 9/30/1915 at 23/3/23 in Lyme; blacksmith; single; b.
    St. Johnsbury, VT; Joseph Thompson (Medway, MA) and Ella
    A. Dexter (Lisbon)
George Washington, d. 4/8/1959 at 63 in Lyme; carpenter; b. South
    Ham, PQ; Joseph G. Thompson and Annie M. Devey
Grace A., d. 7/8/1965 at 74 in Norwich, VT; widow
Henry A., d. 12/27/1979 at 70 in Hanover; grader operator; William
    W. Thompson and Lilly Devey
John S., d. 1/30/1952 at 79 in Hanover; farmer; married; b. S. Ham,
    PQ; William Thompson and Barbara Mackay

Joseph A., d. 4/3/1953 at 62 in Hanover; fireman; married; b. Quebec; Joseph Thompson and Annie Devey

Joseph G., d. 4/19/1933 at 72/10/4 in Lyme; farmer; widower; b. S. Ham, PQ; Will. H. Thompson (Canada) and Barbara Mackey (Canada)

Joseph W., d. 11/3/1928 at 71/3/10 in Lyme; blacksmith; widower; b. Medway, ME

Marjorie, d. 9/27/1931 at 27/6 in Enfield, CT; housewife; married; b. Lyme; George A. Brockway (Waterbury, VT) and Nellie Dimick (Canada)

Patricia A., d. 4/18/1936 at 45 min. in Hanover; b. Lyme; George W. Thompson (Canada) and Josephene M. Dennis (Lyme)

William, d. 10/13/1910 at 76/6/26; farmer; married; b. Ireland; William Thompson (Glasgow, Scotland) and Marguerite Orr (Ireland)

William H., d. 10/10/1954 at 67 in Lyme; farming; married; b. PQ; Joseph Thompson and Annie Devey

THURSTON,
Alice M., d. 11/6/1952 at 50 in Hanover; housewife; married; b. Fairlee, VT; John F. Bixby and Lizzie Mannion

TITUS,
Cora C., d. 5/24/1940 at 57/0/12 in Lyme; housewife; married; b. Vershire, VT; George Church (Vershire, VT) and Sarah Aldrich (Vershire, VT)

TONER,
Beulah M., d. 12/27/2003 in N. Haverhill; Fred Willette and Mary McDermott

Charles S., d. 1/10/1983 at 69; Patrick H. Toner and Elizabeth Schrimger

TOUPIN,
Joseph E., d. 1/20/1933 at 58/2/24 in Lyme; retired barber; married; b. Champlain, PQ; Moses Toupin (Champlain, PQ) and Zoe Vizina (Champlain, PQ)

TOZIER,
Jared M., d. 4/28/1900 at 65/0/15 in Lyme; clergyman; married; b. Newcastle; Charles Tozier and Susan Rogers

TRACY,
William E., d. 8/23/1960 at 91 in Lyme; b. Toledo, OH

TRUELL,
Sarah, d. 8/13/1895 at 24/11/13; housewife; married; J. L. Pray (Effingham) and Annie Downs (Gilmanton)

TUPPER,
Alberta M., d. 9/17/1983 at 69; Hiram Uline and Grace Gilbert
Charles E., d. 3/20/1959 at 45 in Lyme; interior decorator; b. Newbury; Charles L. Tupper and Belle E. Thomas

TURNER,
Ambrose A., d. 3/28/1924 at 62 in Boston, MA; garage; widower; b. Hebron, ME; Melzer Turner (Hebron, ME) and Samantha Jordon (Columbia)
Frank S., d. 1/20/1938 at 69/6/1 in Thetford, VT; single; b. Richmond, VA; David Turner, Jr. (Lyme) and Marcy C. Perry (Lyme)
Gladys, d. 6/9/1965 at 73 in Burlington, VT; single
Marilyn E., d. 1/3/1928 at 0/0/1 in Lyme; b. Lyme; Hazen E. Turner (Lyme) and Christine M. Lake (Keene)
Samantha F., d. 1/18/1900 at 61/0/24 in Lyme; housework; widow; b. Columbia; Abel Jordan and ----- Hix
Susie J., d. 3/2/1918 at 51/7/1 in Concord; housewife; married; b. Canada; James Elliott (Canada) and Eliza McGay (Ireland)

TYLER,
Edward, Rev., d. 11/18/2004 in Lyme; Frederick Tyler and Anna Greene
Lydia Wilmott, d. 7/14/1889 at 78/4/19 in Lyme; housekeeper; single; b. Lyme; Jephthah Tyler (Corinth, VT) and Polly Wilmot (Attleboro, MA)

ULINE,
daughter, d. 2/1/1889 at 0/0/2 in Lyme; b. Lyme; Hiram Uline (Canaan) and Addie L. Lamphere (Lyme)
Addie, d. 1/10/1933 at 73/9/4 in Concord; retired; widow; b. Lyme; Albert A. Lamphere (Lyme) and Sarah Lamphere (Lyme)
Gerald G., d. 4/15/1917 at 13/4/15 in Hanover; student; b. Lyme; Hiram Uline, Jr. (Lyme) and Grace M. Gilbert (Littleton)

Grace Gilbert, d. 6/12/1959 at 72 in Lyme; housewife; b. Monroe; Malvina Byron

Harry M., d. 9/20/1919 at 24/9/28 in Lebanon; laborer; single; b. Lyme; H. Uline (Canaan) and A. L. Lamphere (Lyme)

Hiram, d. 1/28/1929 at 78/0/4 in Lyme; barber; married; b. Canaan; Hiram Uline (Greenbush, NY) and Mary Dunham (Canaan)

Hiram, d. 12/8/1945 at 62/2/2 in Lyme; carpenter; married; b. Lyme; Hiram Uline (Canaan) and Adelaide Lamphere (Lyme)

Mary E., d. 2/16/1916 at 25/4/29 in Lyme; housework; single; b. Lyme; Hiram Uline (Canaan) and Addie F. Lamphere (Lyme)

Millard R., d. 9/19/1972 at 65 in Haverhill; bld. contractor; b. NH; Hiram Uline and Grace Gilbert

Pauline, d. 11/1/2004 in Hanover; Millard R. Uline and Susie E. Cadwell

Ruth, d. 6/8/1992 in Lebanon; Wilbur Bull, Sr. and Anna Coffin

Susie E., d. 3/7/1996 in Lebanon; Louis Cadwell and Eliza Eastman

UNDERHILL,
stillborn son, d. 9/8/1899 at – in Lyme; b. Lyme; L. G. Underhill (Orange) and Augusta S. Welch (Lyme)

Lancelot G., d. 12/31/1946 at 71/5/27 in Lyme; ret. farmer; widower; b. Orange; Edgar S. Underhill (Orange) and Carrie E. Burnham (Hanover)

VALLEY,
Marilyn, d. 10/30/1993 in FL; Raymond Balch and Esther Smith

VAN ETTEN,
Edwin J., d. 10/7/1956 at 72 in Lincoln, MA; clergyman; single; b. Rhinebeck, NY; Cornelius Van Etten and Sarah C. Hill

VAUGHAN,
Oscar, d. 2/11/1968 at 85 in Lebanon; farming; single; b. NY; Adnarm Vaughan and Sarah Darling

VON METTENHEIM,
Nance M., d. 3/11/1981 at 58; interior designer; Henry McDuff and Ethel Fifield

WADE,
Elizabeth, d. 12/20/1918 at 89 in Lyme; housewife; married; b. OH;

William Suttle and Elizabeth Hoover (OH)

WADLEIGH,
George H., d. 1/1/1941 at 89/8/22 in Lyme; farmer; married; b. Lyme; Benjamin D. Wadleigh (Hanover) and Mary Cushman (Norwich, VT)
Mary C., d. 4/14/1903 at 95/4/15 in Lyme; housework; widow; b. Norwich, VT; Oliver Cushman (Strafford, CT) and Maria C. Thomas (Lebanon, CT)
Nancy P., d. 3/3/1901 at 65/8/19 in Lyme; nurse; single; b. Hanover; Benjamin D. Wadligh (Hanover) and Esther Webster

WAGNER,
Creigh C., d. 7/22/1994 in Lyme; John Collins and Harriet Oliphant
Earl G., Jr., d. 11/4/1988 at 59; Earl G. Wagner, Sr. and Dorothy S. Steel
Frederick E., d. 11/1/1981 at 64; management; Edward R. Wagner and Ellen Solberg
Judith, d. 6/7/2003 in Lebanon; Pierre Dover and Lucy Johnson

WAIN,
Carol Lee, d. 3/19/2004 in Lyme; Harold Wain and Frances Mason

WAITE,
Bertha J., d. 6/14/1993 in FL; Harvey H. Balch and Lillian J. Morrill
Frank E., d. 7/2/1986 at 81

WALDRON,
Charles, d. 11/21/1928 at 77/3/24 in New Boston; farmer; widower; b. Dorchester; Nathaniel Waldron and Betsy Davis
Martha, d. 9/9/1903 at 62/1/23 in Lyme; housework; married; b. Wentworth; Roswell Sawyer (Wentworth) and ----- Whitcher (Wentworth)

WALKER,
Arthur C., d. 9/21/1939 at 65/3/22 in Albany, NY; married
Augustus, d. 4/5/1918 at 84/9/27 in Cambridge, MA; physician; widower; b. Barnstead; Joseph A. Walker (Barnstead) and Abigail Murray (Barnstead)
Maria C., d. 8/17/1917 at 78/10/19 in Cambridge, MA; housewife; married; b. Lyme; Sidney S. Grant (Lyme) and Louisa Turner

(Lyme)
Robert T., d. 12/24/1931 at 64/2/8 in Boston, MA; architect; single; b. Lyme; Augustus C. Walker (Barnstead) and Maria C. Grant (Lyme)

WARD,
Ann L., d. 2/5/1916 at 68/10/14 in Lyme; housewife; married; b. Lisbon; Savory Gordon and Margaret Cobleigh (Lisbon)
Caleb F., d. 1/16/1926 at 79/1/19 in Lyme; farmer; widower; b. Pittsburg; Samuel F. Ward (Haverhill) and Emily Eastman (Haverhill)
James, d. 5/18/1918 at 55 in Lyme; lumberman; single
Samuel T., d. 12/17/1907 at 93/7/19 in Lyme; farmer; widower; b. Hanover; Samuel Ward (Enfield) and Chloe Thorp
Sheila, d. 4/6/1987 at 66; John R. Ward and Sylvia Whiting

WARE,
Daniel A., d. 7/10/1905 at 58/10/2 in Lyme; farmer; married; b. Thetford, VT; Daniel A. Ware (Thetford, VT) and Mary Marston (Fairlee, VT)
Luella A., d. 3/4/1932 at 77/11/13 in Lebanon; retired; widow; b. Manchester; William S. Morey (Lyme) and Elizabeth Langdon (Goffstown)
Roland W., d. 1/11/1908 at 0/0/5; b. Lyme; Edgar R. Ware (Lyme) and Edith M. Morrison (Somerville, MA)

WARNER,
Harry, d. 8/17/1894 at 14; single

WARREN,
son, d. 4/1/1887 at – in Lyme; b. Lyme; Charles H. Warren (Lyme) and Emma L. Gilbert (Lyme)
Arad J., d. 12/1/1944 at 88/11/18 in Lyme; insurance agt.; married; b. Lyme; Asa Warren (Lyme) and Mary Ann Derby (Lyme)
Asa, d. 9/29/1891 at 72/10/3 in Lyme; farmer; widower; b. Lyme; Ruel Warren (Lyme) and Martha Alden (Lyme)
Cyrus N., d. 10/2/1908 at 82/11/28; farmer; married; b. Lyme; Cyrus Warren (CT) and Azaba Alden
David A., d. 12/20/1891 at 68/4/19 in Lyme; farmer; married; b. Lyme; Ruel Warren (Lyme) and Martha Alden (Lyme)
Elizabeth, d. 3/2/1925 at 49/2/1 in Medford, MA; retired; single; b.

Lyme; Lewis W. Warren (Lyme) and Ella A. Webster (Lyme)
Ellen L., d. 4/2/1930 at 81/2/6 in Medford, MA; widow; b. Warren;
  Asa Thurston (Boscawen) and Eliza Hartwell (Haverhill)
Emma L., d. 4/9/1890 at 32/3/25 in Lyme; housewife; married; b.
  Hanover; David Gilbert (Lyme) and Mercy A. Gordon (Troy, VT)
Fidelia, d. 5/2/1887 at 57/11/2 in Lyme; housekeeper; married; b.
  Lyme; Manley Cutting (Lyme) and Mary Meade (Lyme)
Frank Gilbert, d. 8/2/1887 at 54/1/19 in Lyme; farmer; married; b.
  Lyme; Asa P. Warren and Lydia Gilbert (Lyme)
Fred N., d. 8/22/1923 at 65 in Hanover; farmer; married; b. Lyme;
  Cyrus Warren (Lyme) and Miriam Lamphere (Thetford, VT)
Harriet, d. 8/27/1961 at 87 in Lyme; housewife; b. Lyme; Alfred
  Pushee and Edna Steele
Jennie M., d. 8/18/1939 at 73/5/17 in Lyme; housewife; widow; b.
  Hanover; George Camp
John G., d. 11/24/1914 at 73/9/23; whipmaker; married; b. Lyme;
  Ruel Warren (Lyme) and Martha Alden (Lyme)
Lawrence P., d. 9/4/1888 at -/5/3 in Lyme; b. Lyme; Charles H.
  Warren (Lyme) and Emma L. Gilbert (Lyme)
Lewis J., d. --/--/1955 at 55 in Hanover; farmer; single; b. Lyme; Fred
  Warren and Jennie Camp
Lewis W., d. 7/20/1924 at 75/3/20 in Medford, MA; retired; married;
  b. Lyme; Asa Warren (Lyme) and Mary A. Derby (Lyme)
Lizzie, d. 7/4/1907 at 73/2/14 in Lyme; housewife; married; b.
  Coventry, VT; Calvin Church (Putney, VT) and Clementine
  Howard (Troy, VT)
Mary A., d. 2/2/1907 at 77/2/4 in Lyme; housewife; widow; ----- Burrill
  and Mary Hall
Myra L., d. 9/11/1921 at 62/3/18 in Lyme; housewife; married; b.
  Starksboro, VT; David L. Stearns (Hinesburg, VT) and Susan
  Nichols (Newbury)
Ruel Alden, d. 1/8/1898 at 67/6/12 in Lyme; laborer; widower; b.
  Lyme; Ruel Warren (Lyme) and Martha Alden (Lyme)
Wayne H., d. 4/27/1889 at 0/5/27 in Lyme; b. Lyme; Charles H.
  Warren (Lyme) and Emma L. Gilbert (Lyme)
William, d. 6/26/1910 at 79/7/29; laborer; widower; b. Lyme; Cyrus
  Warren (CT) and Azaba Alden

WASHBURN,
Alice L., d. 3/6/1961 at 95 in Lyme; companion; b. Lyme; Allen G.
  Washburn and Paulina Dimick

Allen G., d. 11/25/1910 at 86/0/6; farmer; widower; b. Lyme; Libeus Washburn (Lyme) and Mehitabel Gannett (Tamworth)

Benjamin, d. 6/11/1908 at 75/11/25; farmer; married; b. Lyme; John Washburn (Lyme) and Sarah Tucker (Lyme)

Carroll H., d. 12/21/1997 in Hanover; Henry S. Washburn and Alice Little

Katherine, d. 6/1/1922 at 84/11/10 in Hollis; retired; widow; Jeremiah Oakley (Halifax, NS) and Mary L. Crome (Halifax, NS)

Louise, d. 12/30/1948 at 81/5/5 in Hanover; at home; single; b. Lyme; Allen Washburn (Lyme) and Pauline Dimick (Vershire, VT)

Paulina D., d. 3/8/1957 at 84 in Lyme; practical nurse; single; b. Lyme; Allen Washburn and Paulina Dimick

Pauline, d. 2/24/1905 at 73/1/2 in Lyme; housewife; married; b. Vershire, VT; James P. Dimick (Lyme) and Pauline Blanchard (Vershire, VT)

Ruth E., d. 8/1/2004 in Wilder, VT; David S. Reed and Julia Allbee

WATERBURY,
Leon, d. 8/2/1980 at 76; farmer; Lewis H. Waterbury and Annie Cutbill

WATERMAN,
Almon, d. 2/7/1925 at 81/10/24 in Lyme; farmer; widower; b. Thetford, VT; Cyrus Waterman and Martha Howard

Ella A., d. 9/3/1925 at 72/6/25 in Thetford, VT; housewife; married; b. Lebanon; George W. Berry (Alexandria) and Prudence Squires (Cornish)

M. A., d. 3/3/1918 at 60/6/17 in Bradford, VT; married; b. Morrisville, VT; Austin Waterman (Norwich, VT) and Mary E. Clark (T'c'oga, NY)

Mabel H., d. 3/5/1904 at 0/7/22 in Lyme; b. Lyme; Charles H. Waterman (Springfield, MA) and Emma J. Baker (Springfield, MA)

Mary E., d. 6/14/1891 at 63/0/1 in Lyme; housewife; widow; Nathan S. Clark (Ticonderoga, NY) and Emeline Burroughs (Groton, CT)

Rosa M., d. 12/6/1937 at 81/3/6 in Lebanon; retired; married; b. Lincoln, VT; William W. Balch (Lyme) and Weltha Flint (Lyme)

WATKINS,
William A., d. --/--/1991 in ME

WATSON,
Edythe L., d. 2/11/1987 at 80; John R. Watson and Laura Hennigan
Laura A., d. 3/27/1907 at 36/1/27 in Lyme; housewife; married; b. Clinton Co., NY; David Hennigan (Huntington Co., PQ) and Barbara Arthur (Huntington Co., PQ)

WEBB,
Charles B., d. 1/23/1938 at 77/10/28 in Lyme; painter; married; b. Lyme; Henry O. Webb (Lyme) and Mary M. Cline (Lyme)
Charles D., d. 5/2/1916 at 75 in Hanover; farming; married; b. Lyme; Charles C. Webb (Lyme) and Mahala Jackson (Lyme)
Charles D., d. 9/9/1967 at 61 in Lebanon; millwright; divorced; b. Lyme; Charles B. Webb and Lucy Conant
Clyde, d. 4/25/1976 at 95 in Hanover; housewife; b. NH; Dennis Hanchett and Elizabeth Reed
Edward G., d. 8/19/1967 at 83 in Hanover; laborer; married; b. Lyme; Henry O. Webb and Mary Cline
Ella W., d. 11/26/1928 at 76/4/20 in Lebanon; housewife; widow; b. Lyme; William Warren (Lyme) and Sarah Archer
Frank O., d. 9/25/1965 at 85 in Lyme; carp. – painter; widower; b. Hanover; Henry O. Webb and Mary Cline
Fred H., d. 5/5/1959 at 77 in Lebanon; machine operator; b. Lebanon; Otis Webb and Mary Cline
Henry O., d. 2/18/1901 at 66/6/21 in Lyme; farmer; married; b. Lyme; Charles C. Webb (Newbury) and Mahalah Jackson (Lyme)
Lucy, d. 11/27/1961 at 81 in Hanover; housewife; b. Lyme; William Conant and Rhoda Clough
Maude, d. 12/15/1963 at 79 in Lyme; housewife; b. Lyme; George W. Thomas and Lizzie V. George
Mary C., d. 12/20/1905 at 66/4/13 in Lyme; housework; widow; b. Lyme; Benjamin Cline and Caroline Farwell (Lyme)
Rhoda E., d. 3/24/1898 at 30/5 in Lyme; housewife; married; b. Hanover; Alonzo Smith (Langdon) and Julia Heath (Colebrook)
Rhoda M., d. 9/8/1901 at 0/0/2 in Lyme; b. Lyme; Charles B. Webb (Lyme) and Lucy M. Conant (Lyme)

WEBSTER,
Anna, d. 2/11/1965 at 84 in Hanover; retired; single; b. Hanover;

Samuel H. Webster and Mary Fellows
Elizabeth C., d. 12/25/1890 at 67/9/17 in Lyme; housewife; widow; b. Lyme; Marquis Converse (Lyme) and Electa White (Vershire, VT)
Emily A., d. 10/31/1978 at 83 in Hanover; housekeeper; b. VT; Orton Mosley and Hattie Fales
Herbert E., d. 9/13/1983 at 82; John Webster and Elizabeth Abbie
Ida, d. 11/19/1960 at 65 in Hanover; housewife; b. Lyme; Walter E. King and Ida L. Norris
John C., d. 8/7/1901 at 68/5/14 in Lyme; trader; married; b. Pelham; John Webster (Pelham) and Hannah Cummings (Hudson)
John H., d. 1/28/1911 at 40/8/3; farmer; married; b. Lyme; Samuel H. Webster (Newport, VT) and Mary E. Fellows (Dorchester)
Katherine, d. 12/5/1968 at 82 in Hanover; housewife; married; b. VT; Jasper Day and Etta Simpson
Mary E., d. 9/21/1924 at 77/3/8 in Lyme; housewife; widow; b. Dorchester; Samuel Fellows (Ipswich, MA) and Sarah Niles (England)
Samuel H., d. 4/5/1910 at 62/11/17; farmer; married; b. Newport, VT; Samuel M. Webster (Roxbury, VT) and Sarah Flint (Braintree, VT)

WEEDEN,
Mildred Jewett, d. 11/23/1964 at 75in Hanover; housewife; b. Lebanon; Charles Hutchins and Edna Jewett

WELCH,
Abbie A., d. 2/3/1924 at 60/5/5 in Barre, VT; married; b. Groton, VT; Alfred Comstock (Orange, VT) and Lucinda Drake (Chelsea, VT)
Arthur J., d. 7/21/1942 at 64/2/2 in Lyme; laborer; single; b. Lyme; Joseph Welch (Canaan) and Zilpha Cutting (Broom, Canada)
Caroline D., d. 11/21/1908 at 72/6; housekeeper; widow; b. Stanstead, Canada
Edmund S., d. 8/2/1960 at 88 in Lyme; laborer; b. Lyme; Joseph R. Welch and Zilpha Cutting
Eliza, d. 1/8/1904 at 40/7/22 in Lyme; housewife; married; b. Orange, VT; Thomas Jenkins and Fannie Williams
Frederick C., d. 9/26/1942 at 76/1/6 in Lyme; carpenter; single; b. Canada; Joseph R. Welch (Canaan) and Zilpha Cutting (Canada)

George H., d. 11/27/1919 at 56/5/9 in Topsham, VT; board saw; married; C. H. Jackson and A. A. Welch
Hattie, d. 2/10/1965 at 94 in Hanover; retired; single; b. Lyme; Joseph Welch and Zilpha Cutting
Joseph R., d. 5/17/1905 at 74/8/2 in Lyme; farmer; widower; b. Canaan; Simeon Welch (Canaan) and Deborah Richardson (Canaan)
Lydia J., d. 9/9/1890 at 43 in Lyme; housewife; single; b. Hartland, VT; Francis Welch (Hartland, VT) and Abigail Colby (Sutton)
Rae, d. 6/3/1997 in Lyme; Homer Welch and Emma Garrison
Rob., d. 8/20/1948 at 0/4 in Lyme; b. Littleton; Robert Welch (Berlin) and Barbara Young (Arlington, MA)
William P., d. 6/19/1940 at 69/8/16 in Lyme; carpenter; single; b. Canaan; Joseph R. Welch (Canaan) and Zilpha Cutting (Canada)
Zilpha, d. 2/16/1887 at 41/0/4 in Lyme; housewife; married; b. Canada; Hollis Cutting (Craftsbury) and Sarah Dimick

WELLS,
Carroll S., d. 7/15/1936 at 75/10/27 in Lyme; farmer; married; b. Cambridge, VT; Rollin S. Wells (Waterville, VT) and Eliza Jane Hall (Lyme)
Eliza H., d. 9/11/1901 at 62/9/19 in Lyme; housewife; married; b. Lyme; Joseph Hall (Canada) and Lucy Pushee (Lyme)
Jane N., d. 2/8/1911 at 81/1; housewife; widow; b. Lyme; William C. Nelson (Lyme) and Sarah Chapin (Milford, MA)
Rollin S., d. 3/1/1909 at 77/1/11; laborer; widower; b. Underhill, VT; Simeon Wells and Juliette Chamberlain

WENG,
Virginia D., d. 2/27/2003 in Lyme; Kenyon Dzung and Nyui Dau

WEST,
Frank E., d. --/--/1955 in Cranston, RI; retired merchant; widower; b. Orford; Edwin B. West and Margaret L. Ames
Jennie B., d. 7/5/1950 at 72 in Lyme; housewife; married; b. Orford; Daniel Blood and Mercie Ann Merrill

WETTERHAHN,
Karen E., d. 6/8/1997 in Lebanon; Gustave Wetterhahn and Mary E. Thibault

WEYMOUTH,
Forrest, d. 12/26/1892 at 0/7/6; b. Lyme; George W. Weymouth (Andover) and Minnie T. Morgan (Sacramento, CA)
George W., d. 5/30/1934 at 77/9/6 in Hanover; physician; widower; b. Andover; Henry A. Weymouth and Louisa Young
Louise M., d. 1/31/1953 at 64 in Concord; housekeeper; single; b. Grafton; George Weymouth and Mary Morgan
Minnie T., d. 3/11/1934 at 72/0/7 in Concord; housewife; married; b. CA; Jerry Morgan (NH)

WHEELER,
Edward, d. 4/21/1922 at 64/0/17 in Lyme; farmer; married; b. Isle La Motte, VT; Edward Wheeler (Grand Isle, VT) and Albina Pike (Isle La Motte, VT)
Ernest, d. 9/12/1985 at 59; Lester Wheeler and Sadie Johnson
Ivan L., d. 11/29/1957 at 10 in Lyme; school; b. Lebanon; Ernest Wheeler and Hazel Campbell

WHEELOCK,
Dorman C., d. 8/16/1978 at 73 in Berlin; crane operator; b. E. Fairfield, VT; Marsellus Wheelock and Lillie Rich

WHIPPLE,
Asenath E., d. 7/3/1905 at 80/11/3 in Lyme; single; b. Lyme; Joel G. Whipple (Kirby, VT) and Asenath Goodell (Lyme)
Elizabeth B., d. 8/29/1897 at 79/7; housewife; married; b. Lyme; Samuel Flint (Jaffrey) and Mary Spaulding (Jaffrey)
Jonathan, d. 12/31/1898 at 84/3/21 in Lyme; farmer; widower; b. Lyme; Joel G. Whipple (Lyme) and Lois Goodell (Lyme)
Lucy D. R., d. 1/7/1909 at 89/11/1; housewife; widow; b. Orford; Nathan Rugg and Lavina Newcomb (Thetford, VT)
Mary L., d. 4/5/1892 at 38/10/12; dressmaker; single; b. Lyme; Simeon R. Whipple (Lyme) and Lucy D. Rugg (Orford)

WHITCHER,
Florence, d. 2/23/1920 at 26/1/17 in Lyme; housewife; married; b. Bradford, VT; A. J. C. Gray and Etta Muzzy (Bradford, VT)

WHITE,
Edith, d. 8/24/1938 at 69/4/7 in Lyme; housewife; married; b. Lyme; Charles H. Dimick (Lyme) and Viola Cook (Lyme)

Levi O., d. 8/4/1952 at – in Newbury, VT; widower

WHITMAN,
Breck, d. 4/21/1994 in California; Michael Whitman and Katherine Breck

WHITNEY,
Karl E., d. 1/26/1988 at 75; Ned L. Whitney and Jennie Harwood

WHITTEMORE,
Carrie W., d. 12/7/1938 at 67/6/2 in Lyme; housewife; widow; b. Lyme; Allen C. Washburn (Lyme) and Paulina Dimick (Vershire, VT)
Clara, d. 6/24/1923 at 72/2/21 in Haverhill; retired; single; Gilman Whittemore (Pembroke) and Lavina Cushman (Norwich, VT)
Fr'k G., d. 2/7/1914 at 66; farmer; married; b. Manchester; Gilman Whittemore (Manchester) and Lavina Cushhman (Manchester)
Lavina C., d. 10/18/1897 at 82/7/15; housewife; widow; b. Norwich, VT; Oliver Cushman and Maria C. Cushman
Luther L., d. 4/7/1935 at 60/8/30 in Lyme; salesman; married; b. Plymouth; Peter Whittemore (Bridgewater) and Elizabeth Woodworth (Hebron)
Pauline E., d. 3/26/1998 in Lyme; Luther Whittemore and Carrie Washburn

WICKWARE,
Robert K., d. 1/19/1997 in Lebanon; Morley C. Wickware and Margaret Miller

WILBER,
Ida A. V., d. 2/25/1919 at 29/7 in Lyme; housewife; married; b. Norwich, VT; H. Valley and J. J. Bowker (Vershire, VT)

WILDER,
Caroline, d. 1/27/1921 at 76/8/10 in Lyme; housewife; widow; b. Thetford, VT; Hiram Barrett (Thetford, VT) and Almeda Wilmot (Genesee Co., NY)
George E., d. 6/3/1916 at 71/8/15 in Lyme; farming; married; b. Rudsboro, VT; Juliette Streeter

WILKINSON,
Charlotte L., d. 1/13/1951 at 89 in Concord; housewife; married; Charles Green and Ann M. Gay
Dora G., d. 3/15/1931 at 64/7/15 in Lyme; housewife; married; b. Lebanon; Charles Greene (Nashua) and Helen Gile (VT)

WILLEY,
child, d. 5/8/1897 at –; b. Lyme; Bertram E. Willey (Hinsdale) and Mary A. Ramsey (Barton, VT)

WILLIGAR,
Della D., d. 8/5/1919 at 41/9/28 in Lyme; housewife; married; b. Wentworth; C. M. Dustin (Dorchester) and Lo D. Leary (Canaan)
Stephen, d. 9/9/1924 at 51/4/13 in Lyme; farmer; widower; b. NS; Thomas Willigar (NS) and Elizabeth Vickory (NS)

WILLIS,
Eugene F., d. 7/2/1911 at 41/11/11; carpenter; married; b. Warren; Daniel S. Willis (Mansfield, CT) and Maranda M. Hazelton (Orford)

WILMOT,
daughter, d. 7/15/1915 at 0/0/1 in Lyme; b. Lyme Elber E. Wilmot (Lyme) and Myrtle Cummings (Lyme)
daughter, d. 7/15/1915 at 0/0/1 in Lyme; b. Lyme Elber E. Wilmot (Lyme) and Myrtle Cummings (Lyme)
daughter, d. 9/18/1916 at – in Lyme; b. Lyme; Leo A. Wilmot (Lyme) and Fannie M. Chapin (Boston, MA)
son, d. 12/8/1917 at – in Lyme; b. Lyme; Leo A. Wilmot (Lyme) and Fannie M. Chapin (Boston, MA)
son, d. 12/14/1917 at 0/0/6 in Lyme; b. Lyme; Leo A. Wilmot (Lyme) and Fannie M. Chapin (Boston, MA)
son, d. 3/8/1918 at – in Lyme; b. Lyme; Irvin A. Wilmot (Lyme) and Lillian D. Sayre (Thetford, VT)
daughter, d. 10/25/1919 at – in Lyme; b. Lyme; L. F. Wilmot (Thetford, VT) and G. L. Oliver (Bradford, VT)
son, d. 12/14/1921 at – in Lyme; b. Lyme; Leo A. Wilmot (Lyme) and Fannie M. Chapin (Boston, MA)
daughter, d. 3/12/1923 at – in Lyme; b. Lyme; Leo A. Wilmot (Lyme) and Fannie M. Chapin (S. Boston)

Betty S., d. 4/23/1971 at 25 in Lyme; technician; b. NH; Kenneth Wilmot and Hanna Donna

Elber E., d. 4/9/1950 at 72 in Lyme; farmer; married; b. S. Strafford, VT; Erni Wilmot and Mynetta Packard

Erni F., d. 2/6/1935 at 79/4/10 in Lyme; farmer; widower; b. Thetford, VT; Ira Wilmot and Eliza E. Roberts (Mt. Holly, VT)

Fannie, d. 2/19/1969 at 79 in Hanover; housewife; married; b. MA; Charles Chapin and Mary Deveau

Fay A., d. 2/19/1921 at 0/1/26 in Lyme; b. Lyme; Homer D. Wilmot (Lyme) and Flora M. Wing (Lyme)

Goldia L., d. 1/26/1923 at 37/8/5 in Lyme; housewife; married; b. Bradford, VT; Henry Oliver (England) and Lillian Roberts (Lyme)

Hannah, d. 5/29/1962 at 52 in Hanover; housewife; b. W. Burke, VT; Joseph Donna and Jennie Myotte

Harold E., d. 2/23/1913 at 0/0/3; b. Lyme; Leo A. Wilmot (Lyme) and Fannie M. Chapin (S. Boston, MA)

Hope O., d. 4/15/1917 at 0/5/26 in Lyme; b. Lyme; Leaman F. Wilmot (Strafford, VT) and Goldia Oliver (Bradford, VT)

Irvin A., d. 5/3/1946 at 59/8/1 in Lyme; farmer; married; b. Lyme; Erni F. Wilmot (Thetford, VT) and Minnie Packard (S. Strafford, VT)

Irvin A., Jr., d. 10/17/2004 in Lyme; Irvin A. Wilmot and Lillian Sayer

Kenneth, d. 9/16/1992 in Lebanon; Elber Wilmot and Myrtle Cummings

Leamon F., d. 1/19/1940 at 59/6/0 in Thetford, VT; farmer; married; b. Strafford, VT; Erni Wilmot (Lyme) and Minnie Packard (Barnard, VT)

Leo, d. 5/3/1976 at 91 in Claremont; farmer; b. NH; Erni Wilmot and Minnie Packard

Lillian, d. 10/20/1969 at 74 in Hanover; housewife; widow; b. VT; Henry Sayre and Rose Dauphine

Margaret E., d. 2/13/1980 at 55; licensed practical nurse; James Lewis and Ivy Noble

Minetta E., d. 11/18/1932 at 81/7/7 in Lyme; housewife; married; b. Barnard, VT; Alanson E. Packard (Stockbridge, VT) and Marguerite A. Whitney (Boston, MA)

Robert I., d. 12/6/2004 in Lebanon; Irvin A. Wilmot, Jr. and Sandra Antella

Virginia R., d. 1/17/1930 at 0/0/2 in Lyme; b. Lyme; Leamon F. Wilmot (Strafford, VT) and Ida J. Smith (Lyme)

WILMOTT,
Alan S., d. 4/5/1986 at 20; Wayne W. Wilmott, Sr. and Violet Howe
Archie E., d. 12/29/1998 at 64; Homer Wilmott and Flora Wing
Dorothy M., d. 12/2/1999 in Lebanon; John Brady and Ethel Burr
Flora, d. --/--/1955 at 57 in Hanover; housewife; widow; b. Lyme;
 Milton Wing and Nina Courtney
Homer D., d. --/--/1955 at 62 in Lyme; farmer; married; b. Lyme; Erni
 Wilmott and Mynette Packard
Lloyd E., d. 1/30/1985 at 67; Homer Wilmott and Flora Wing

WILSON,
Cameron, d. 3/18/1989
Henry, d. 4/8/1905 at 58/1/17 in Lyme; farmer; married; b. Byer, OH;
 James Wilson (NY) and Cynthia Grey (Byer, OH)

WING,
son, d. 9/4/1963 at 0/0/1 in Keene; b. Keene; John D. Wing and
 Nancy Lu
Esther, d. 9/4/1992 in Lebanon; Malcolm Wing and Minnie Lobdell
Flora A., d. 8/12/1923 at 65/10/16 in Lyme; housewife; married; b.
 Chateaugay, NY; David Hill (Chateaugay, NY) and Sarah White
 (Chateaugay, NY)
Harold, d. 1/14/1999 in Lebanon; Milton Wing and Nina Courtney
Karl W, d. 4/7/1995 in Lebanon; Pearl Wing
Leonard F., d. 10/14/1913 at 27; married; b. Chateaugay, NY;
 Nathan L. Wing (Berkshire, VT) and Hannah F. Hill
 (Chateaugay, NY)
Lillian A., d. 9/30/1990 at 75; Charles Thompson and Maude Stark
Milton L., d. 11/23/1945 at 72/4/3 in Lyme; farmer; married; b.
 Chateaugay, NY; Nathan L. Wing (Berkshire, VT) and Flora
 Ann Hill (Chateaugay, NY)
Muriel G., d. 4/7/1995 in Lebanon; George Allen and Frances Colton
Nathan L., d. 3/3/1924 at 69/4/20 in Lyme; farmer; widower; Jared
 Wing and Harriet Green
Nina, d. 3/12/1960 at 81 in Enfield; housewife; b. Rochester, VT;
 Thomas Courtney and Ann Crosby
Walter, d. 10/1/1890 at 0/10/24 in Lyme; b. Burke, VT; Nathan L.
 Wing (Berkshire, VT) and Anna Hill (Chateaugay, NY)

WINN,
Helen, d. 11/24/1958 at 85 in Lyme; b. Woodstock, VT

WINSLOW,
Addie L., d. 2/24/1932 at 67/4/2 in Newbury, VT; housekeeper; widow; b. Thetford, VT; Samuel Ladd (Sharon, VT) and Ann Gilman (Chelsea, VT)
Alice M., d. 8/14/1915 at 25/0/17 in Lyme; housekeeping; single; b. Lyme; George Winslow (Lyme) and Maria J. Post (Lyme)
Alnette A., d. 1/19/1888 at 36/10/18 in Lyme; teacher; single; b. Lyme; Bela Winslow (Lyme) and Ester A. Carpenter (Strafford, VT)
Banks B., d. 11/14/1950 at 63 in Hanover; railway man; married; William Winslow and Ada Ladd
Elsie, d. 12/17/1955 at 66 in Thetford, VT; housewife; widow; b. Canada; Thomas Reeve and Isabella McKensie
George D., d. 9/23/1903 at 51/1/28 in Lyme; farmer; married; b. Lyme; Daniel Winslow (Dorchester) and Mary Clark (Strafford, VT)
Harvey N., d. 10/18/1901 at 51/1/18 in Lyme; expressman; married; b. Lyme; Daniel Winslow (Lyme) and Mary C. Clark (Strafford, VT)
Theda Blanche, d. 3/15/1896 at 1/8/23; b. Lyme; William B. Winslow (Lyme) and Addie Ladd (Post Mills, VT)
Theda Post, d. 3/26/1887 at 89/4/3 in Lyme; housekeeper; widow; b. Lyme; Joseph Otis Post (Lyme) and Patience Palmer (Orford)
William B., d. 3/14/1896 at 35/8/16; farmer; married; b. Lyme; Bela B. Winslow (Lyme) and Esther A. Carpenter (Strafford, VT)

WISE,
George G., d. 6/20/1921 at 72/7/26 in Lyme; farmer; married; b. Lyme; George W. Wise (Fairlee, VT) and Harriet Gardner (Lyme)
George W., d. 10/19/1890 at 72/1/24 in Lyme; farmer; widower; b. Groton; Jonathan Wise and Mary Blanchard
George W., d. 6/3/1956 at 59 in Hartford, VT; car salesman; married; b. Lyme; Willie Wise and Helen Goulett
Hattie May, d. 10/8/1962 at 73 in Lyme; nurse; b. Lyme; Theodore Wise and Mary Bragg
Ida H., d. 3/25/1919 at 17/6/18 in Thetford, VT; student; single; b. Lyme; W. F. Wise (Thetford, VT) and H. S. Goulette (Norwich)
Luther Jackman, d. 12/21/1888 at 73 in Lyme; laborer; widower; b. Hebron; Jonathan Wise (Hebron) and Mary Blanchard (Plymouth)

Mary L. B., d. 1/3/1930 at 63/7/4 in Lyme; housewife; widow; b. Fairlee, VT; William Bragg (Fairlee, VT) and Irena Putnam

Theodore W., d. 2/5/1926 at 71/7 in Lyme; farmer; married; b. Lyme; George W. Wise (Groton) and Harriet Gardner (Lyme)

Willie F., d. 5/20/1933 at 66/6/7 in Thetford, VT; farmer; married; b. Thetford, VT; George W. Wise (Groton) and Harriet Gardner (Lyme)

WITHINGTON,
Harriet M., d. 1/5/1899 at 67/7/1 in Lyme; housework; widow; b. Lyme; Dudley Cutting (Lyme) and Polly Bixby (Lyme)

WOLFE,
Ruth, d. 11/5/1962 at 72 in Hanover; housewife; b. Rochester, NY; William Hubbard and Helen Vosburgh

WOOD,
Esther P., d. 1/9/1990 at 77; Stanley B. Puffer

James Albert, Jr., d. 9/24/1975 at 70 in Hanover; ret. professor; b. DE; James Wood and Anna Wood

Louise M., d. 7/18/1979 at 72 in Hanover; weaver; b. OH; Allen Morse and Edith McCord

WOODBURY,
Harriet M., d. 4/16/1958 at 89 in Hanover; widow; b. NH

Sarah S., d. 12/6/1905 at 84/6/4 in Lyme; housework; widow; b. Orford; Obadiah Tillotson (Orford) and Betsey Marshall (Northumberland)

WOODS,
Jennie, d. 9/14/1964 at 91 in Lyme; housewife; b. Bradford, VT; Charles Sawyer and Lucy DeGoosh

WOODWARD,
Andrew L., d. 10/25/2002 in Hanover; Arthur Woodward and Gertrude Cobb

Arthur L., d. 4/1/1966 at 83 in White River Jct.; plumber; married; b. Bridgewater, VT; Henry Woodward and Laura Dutton

Bertha L., d. 12/1/2003 in Hanover; John Lawson and Emma Martin

Ethel G., d. 9/22/2000 in Lyme; Lewis Gould and Louise Duel

Gertrude, d. 12/27/1980 at 94; Abbott Cobb and Etta Sparrow

Mary S., d. 2/2/1903 in Lyme; housewife; married; b. Lyme; George Skinner (Lyme) and Paulina Plummer (Lyme)

Melvin L., d. 7/2/1999 in Lebanon; Arthur Woodward and Gertrude Cobb

Reginald Mark, d. 11/12/1990 at 30; Emerson Woodward and Ruth Gray

WOODWELL,

Alice F., d. 12/29/1925 at 63/3/28 in Lyme; housewife; married; b. Waterford, ME; Leander Stone (Waterford, ME) and Hannah Pride (Waterford, ME)

George M., d. 4/19/1927 at 69/11/6 in Lyme; clergyman; widower; b. Norwalk, OH; Jacob A. Woodwell and Caroline Masters

WOOLGAR,

William J., d. 5/29/1942 at 78/2/17 in Lyme; physician; widower; b. Isle of Wight, England; Edward Woolgar (England) and Anne Webster (England)

WRIGHT,

John K., d. 3/24/1969 at 77 in Hanover; retired; married; b. MA; John H. Wright and Mary Tappan

WYMAN,

Maude E., d. 12/3/1951 at 60 in Lebanon; housewife; widow; Lewis Lovejoy and Harriet Perkins

YOUNG,

Gideon S., d. 12/20/1899 at 76 in Lyme; laborer; widower; b. Lyme; George Young and Rebecca Smith

Harold C., d. 3/7/1942 at 55/11/27 in Hanover; laborer; widower; b. Chateaugay, NY; Ira N. Young (Canada) and Barbara Carr (Canada)

Laurence, d. 8/11/1924 at 1/7/21 in Lyme; b. Lyme; Leon F. Young (Chateaugay, NY) and Louisa Columbia (St. Albans, VT)

Leon F., d. 11/27/1933 at 46/0/24 in Lyme; laborer; married; b. Chateaugay, NY; Ira Young (Clarenceville, NY) and Barbara Carr (PQ)

Louise M., d. 12/20/1978 at 86 in Hanover; chambermaid; b. VT; William Ackerman and Esther -----

Lucinda, d. 6/28/1890 at 55 in Lyme; housewife; married; b. Lyme;

Zedediah Davison (Lyme) and Anna A. Rood (Lyme)
Nellie B., d. 5/31/1928 at 38/10/9 in Lyme; housework; married; b. Lyme; George A. Brockway (Waterbury, VT) and Nellie E. Dimick (Iron Hill, PQ)
Ralph C., d. 4/25/1917 at – in Lyme; Harold C. Young (Burke, NY) and Nellie Brockway (Lyme)
Robert C., d. 8/6/1934 at 17/3/12 in Hanover; CCC camp; single; b. Lyme; Harold C. Young (Burke, NY) and Nellie M. Brockway (Lyme)
Robert J., d. 9/18/1973 at 67 in Lyme; janitor; b. NH; Frank W. Young and Nellie M. Pease

YUREK,
Doris, d. 1/9/2004 in Hanover; William Gleason and Helen Willans

ZACK,
Ethel M., d. 5/27/1997 in Lyme; Lawrence Melvin

UNKNOWN,
man, d. probably June or July, 1913

DORCHESTER BIRTHS

AHEARN,
son, b. 8/11/1892 in Dorchester; William Ahearn (laborer, Blackbrook) and Berthie Youngman (Dorchester)

ASHLEY,
son, b. 4/20/1905 in Dorchester; sixth; Alfred W. Ashley (farmer, 37, PEI) and Minnie O. Malley (Colton, NY)
daughter, b. 12/3/1905 in Dorchester; eighth; Herbert H. Ashley (farmer, 36, PEI) and Annie Pollard (35, PEI)
daughter, b. 5/19/1907 in Dorchester; ninth; Herbert H. Ashley (farmer, 38, PEI) and Annie G. Pollard (38, PEI)
Alice Bell, b. 3/8/1902 in Dorchester; fifth; Alfred W. Ashley (farmer, PEI) and Minnie O. Malley (PEI)
Bert, b. 11/22/1899 in Dorchester; fourth; Alfred W. Ashley (farmer, PEI) and Minnie O. Malley (Colton, NY)
Blanche Annie, b. 9/29/1934; third; Herbert A. Ashley (mail carrier, Dorchester) and Phyllis A. Bean (Orford)
Charles C., b. 12/3/1902 in Dorchester; sixth; Herbert H. Ashley (farmer, PEI) and Annie Pollard (PEI)
Gertrude, b. 9/11/1898; fourth; Herbert H. Ashley (farmer, PEI) and Annie G. Ashley (PEI)
Gladys E., b. 9/6/1904 in Dorchester; seventh; Herbert H. Ashley (farmer, PEI) and Annie G. Pollard (PEI)
Herbert A., b. 5/9/1900 in Dorchester; fifth; Herbert H. Ashley (farmer, PEI) and Annie G. Pollard (PEI)
Janith Louise, b. 9/22/1935; second; Albert E. Ashley (laborer, Dorchester) and Esther A. Holland (Mitchfield)
Jean Ellen, b. 3/14/1932; first; Herbert A. Ashley (mail carrier, Dorchester) and Phyllis Arlene Ashley (Orford)
Mary Josephine, b. 9/16/1937; third; Alfred E. Ashley (laborer, Dorchester) and Esther Holland (Litchfield)
Myrtle Blanche, b. 5/27/1898; eighth; George M. Ashley (farmer, PEI) and Annie B. White (PEI)
Nancy Caroyn, b. 8/8/1933; second; Herbert A. Ashley (mail carrier, Dorchester) and Phyllis A. Bean (Orford)

AYRES,
Levon Graham, b. 12/23/1983 in Dorchester; George Little Ayres (MA) and Margaret Rose Knipfer (OH)
Sarah Jane, b. 3/10/1978 in Rumney; George L. Ayres (MA) and Margaret H. Knipfer (OH)

Silas Little, b. 12/23/1981 in Hanover; George Little Ayres (MA) and Margaret Rose Knipfer (OH)

BABB,
Jacob James, b. 8/10/1990 in Hanover; James Victor Babb (PA) and Bonny Lynn Harrison (PA)

BAILY,
Elizabeth H., b. 1/25/1897; Abel Baily (farmer, 52, Groton) and Josie M. Fellows (27, Dorchester)

BEAN,
Barbara Ann, b. 11/17/1938; first; Bertram P. Bean (farmer, Orford) and Agnes A. Guilmette (St. Johnsbury, VT)
Jessica Rachel, b. 8/20/1979 in Plymouth; Kenneth Cedric Bean (OH) and Cathleen Anne Rennert (NY)
Maurice Fay, b. 12/21/1914 in Dorchester; first; Fay C. Bean (farmer, Orford) and Bessie A. Burnham (Dorchester)

BENNETT,
Edna, b. 3/13/1899 in Dorchester; seventh; John Bennett (farmer, Mason) and Denarge Douville (St. Casmer)

BENSON,
daughter, b. 7/19/1901 in Dorchester; second; Eugene E. Benson (laborer, Jay, VT) and Bell K. Noyes (Dorchester)

BICKFORD,
son, b. 4/16/1895 in Dorchester; first; Arthur J. Bickford (farmer, Dorchester) and Mary Dubuque (North Hero)
son, b. 6/26/1896 in Dorchester; Arthur J. Bickford (farmer, Dorchester) and Mary Dubuque (North Hero, VT)
daughter, b. 8/12/1920 in Dorchester; first; Preston Bickford (farmer, Dorchester) and Mary Broadley (Tilton)

BILL,
Tyler James, b. 12/23/1999 in Lebanon; Clifton Bill and Lisa Bill

BISHOP,
Leon K., b. 1/21/1899 in Dorchester; fifth; George L. Bishop (farmer, Morgan, VT) and Annie V. Dow (Brooklyn)

BLACK,
Angus Cecil, b. 2/20/1892 in Dorchester; first; Charles A. Black (farmer, Pasley, Scotland) and Maggie J. Black (Scotland)
Estella R., b. 9/17/1895 in Dorchester; second; Charles A. Black (farmer, Pasley, Scotland) and Maggie Kennedy (Glasgow, Scotland)

BLAIN,
daughter, b. 12/9/1908 in Dorchester; third; Ralph P. Blain (farmer, 26, Canada) and Alice Simard (27, Canada)
Florence M., b. 11/8/1925 in Dorchester; first; Wilfred Blain (farmer, Albion, RI) and Yvonne Dupris (Canaan)
Irene M., b. 5/26/1907 in Dorchester; second; Ralph P. Blain (farmer, 24, Canada) and Alice Simard (25, Canada)
Stella, b. 1/11/1910; fourth; Ralph Blain (farmer, 28, Canada) and Alice Simard (28, Canada)

BLUM,
Robert Edward, b. 4/15/1995; Michael Thomas Blum (Germany) and Katherine B. Comey (CT)

BRALEY,
son, b. 3/13/1891 in Dorchester; Ormand J. Braley (laborer, Danbury) and Luella M. Taylor (Orange)

BURNHAM,
son, b. 10/10/1895 in Dorchester; first; F. Y. Burnham (farmer, Concord) and Alta M. Brown (Wentworth)
daughter, b. 7/8/1897; F. Y. Burnham (farmer, 46, Concord) and Alta M. Brown (30, Wentworth)
son, b. 5/10/1903 in Dorchester; third; Frank Y. Burnham (farmer, Concord) and Altie M. Brown (Wentworth)
daughter, b. 2/6/1908 in Dorchester; fourth; Frank Y. Burnham (farmer, 57, Concord) and Alta M. Brown (40, Wentworth)
stillborn son, b. 3/3/1914 in Dorchester; first; Frank W. Burnham (farmer, Dorchester) and Bertha M. Tilton (Alexandria)
daughter, b. 4/15/1921 in Dorchester; fifth; Frank W. Burnham (farmer, Dorchester) and Bertha Tilton (Alexandria)
Evelyn May, b. 9/21/1937; first; Kirk Burnham (lumberman, Dorchester) and Muriel M. Ryea (Sheldon, VT)
Frances Ann, b. 3/31/1930 in Dorchester; first; Kirk N. Burnham

(farmer, Dorchester) and Susie I. Chase (Wentworth)
Isaac Hazen, b. 5/17/1915 in Dorchester; second; George N.
    Burnham (farmer, Dorchester) and Jennie J. Hazen (N. Hero, VT)
Kirk N. Y., b. 7/23/1907 in Dorchester; first; George N. Burnham
    (farmer, 26, Dorchester) and Jennie Hazen (23, N. Hero, VT)
Marion Lila, b. 2/4/1916 in Dorchester; second; Frank W. Burnham
    (farmer, 30, Dorchester) and Bertha M. Tilton (26, Alexandria)
Mildred Lela, b. 2/4/1916 in Dorchester; third; Frank W. Burnham
    (farmer, 30, Dorchester) and Bertha M. Tilton (26, Alexandria)
Ruby Velma, b. 10/5/1917 in Dorchester; fourth; Frank W. Burnham
    (farmer, Dorchester) and Bertha M. Tilton (Alexandria)

BURT,
son, b. 7/29/1913 in Dorchester; second; Frank A. Burt (lumber mfg.,
    33, Northport, NY) and Mabel Lefferte (35, Centreport, NY)
daughter, b. 10/28/1914 in Dorchester; third; Alden Burt (lumber
    mfg., North Port, LI) and Flora B. Hall (Groton)

BYERS,
Samantha Jean, b. 10/2/1988 in Hanover; Dennis Charles Byers
    (NH) and Deborah Jean Kennedy (MA)

CAMPBELL,
daughter, b. 12/12/1892 in Dorchester; first; William J. Campbell
    (laborer) and Susan Nelson
Forrest A., b. 4/14/1897; William Campbell (laborer, 23, Boston) and
    Mabel Wescott (23, Canaan)

CARTER,
stillborn son, b. 4/26/1907 in Dorchester; sixth; Carlyle A. C. Carter
    (farmer, 37, Yorkshire, England) and Jane A. Fairburn (34,
    Colchester, England)
Albert Barnett, b. 4/20/1935; fourth; Ernest Carter (laborer, Methuen,
    MA) and Arlene Barrett (S. Waldron, VT)
Barbara Anne, b. 1/19/1949 in Plymouth; second; James Carter
    (woodsman, Methuen, MA) and Nettie May Salls (Hardwick,
    VT)
Candy Lyn, b. 12/25/1959 in Plymouth; Albert B. Carter and Peggy
    Mae Hammel
Cindy Lou, b. 1/31/1960 in Plymouth; Richard P. Carter and Marjorie

P. Martel
David James, b. 1/21/1944 in Plymouth; first; James Carter (laborer, Methuen, MA) and Nettie Mae Sals (Hardwick, VT)
Lisa Ann, b. 11/3/1966 in Plymouth; Richard P. Carter (Plymouth) and Marjorie P. Martel (Plymouth)
Michael Albert, b. 6/3/1957 in Plymouth; Albert B. Carter (Dorchester) and Peggy M. Hammel (Plymouth)
Richard Paul, b. 3/24/1932; third; Ernest Carter (laborer, Methuen, MA) and Arline Barnard (Methuen, MA)
Sharon Ann, b. 3/21/1956 in Plymouth; Albert B. Carter (Plymouth) and Peggy M. Hammel (Plymouth)

CELLEY,
Martha B., b. 5/25/1893 in Dorchester; second; J. Edward Celley (laborer, Kingston) and Lucy C. Celley (Beverly, MA)

CHASE,
Winona Mae, b. 6/16/1926 in Dorchester; third; George Chase (chauffeur, Orford) and Mary Bosence (St. Johns, NB)

CILLEY,
son, b. 1/5/1917 in Dorchester; second; Ester Cilley (Colraine, MA)

CLARK,
daughter, b. 7/3/1897; Leonard Clark (farmer, 35, Germany) and Emma J. Hagan (35, Germany)
son, b. 8/3/1899 in Dorchester; fourth; Conrad Clark (farmer, Germany) and Emma J. Hazen (VT)
son, b. 5/9/1901 in Dorchester; fifth; Conrad Clark (farmer, Germany) and Emma Hazen (N. Hero, VT)
daughter, b. 12/6/1902 in Dorchester; sixth; Conrad Clark (farmer, Germany) and Emma J. Hazen (No. Hero, VT)
daughter, b. 11/22/1904 in Dorchester; seventh; Conrad Clark (farmer, Germany) and Emma J. Hazen (N. Hero, VT)

CLOGSTON,
Albert W., b. 6/25/1926 in Dorchester; first; Walter Lee Clogston (laborer, Lyme) and Barbara Pearl Willey (Groton)
Gerald A., b. 5/14/1928 in Dorchester; second; Walter L. Clogston (mill laborer, Lyme) and Barbara Pearl Willey (Groton)

CLOUGH,
son, b. 1/1/1892 in Dorchester; third; Charles A. Clough (farmer, Dorchester) and Sarah E. Burnham (Wentworth)
son, b. 1/6/1892 in Dorchester; first; Orrin O. Clough (teamster, Wentworth) and Dora M. Richardson (Manchester)

COFFIN,
Robert Grant, b. 5/27/1934; first; Lester W. Coffin (farmer, Campton) and Mildred A. Camp (Boston, MA)

COLBURN,
son, b. 9/27/1887 in Dorchester; James L. Colburn (laborer, Dorchester) and Emma Brooks (Dorchester)
daughter, b. 9/27/1891 in Dorchester; James L. Colburn (farmer, Dorchester) and Sarah E. Brooks (Dorchester)
stillborn daughter, b. 1/4/1895 in Dorchester; James L. Colburn (farmer, Dorchester) and Sarah Brooks (Dorchester)
daughter, b. 5/29/1898; fifth; James M. Colburn (farmer, Dorchester) and Emma S. Brooks (Dorchester)

COLE,
daughter, b. 8/8/1892 in Dorchester; first; Fred A. Cole (laborer, Dorchester) and Flora B. Shattuck (Canaan)

COLEMAN,
Devin Charles, b. 7/27/1991; Charles Henry Coleman (CT) and Sherrie Lee Young (NH)
Morgan Pearl, b. 7/6/1995; Charles H. Coleman (CT) and Sherrie Lee Young (NH)

CONKEY,
Craig Wayne, b. 9/5/1966 in Plymouth; Raymond Conkey (Campton) and Pauline M. Landon (Plymouth)
Daniel Lee, b. 7/14/1974 in Plymouth; George Chester Conkey (NH) and Nadine Althea Barrows (CT)
Emaline Sylvia, b. 8/26/1998 in Lebanon; George C. Conkey, II and Jeanne M. Conkey
George Chester, b. 11/3/1966; George C. Conkey (Ellsworth) and Nadine A. Barrows (Stafford Springs, CT)
Matthew Dillon, b. 6/11/1996; Daniel L. Conkey (NH) and Dawn Curran (MA)

Michael Gene, b. 9/23/1968 in Plymouth; George Chester Conkey (NH) and Nadine Althea Barrows (CT)

Nadine Irene, b. 2/20/1964 in Plymouth; George Conkey (Ellsworth) and Nadine A. Barrows (Stafford Springs, CT)

COTE,
John Paul, b. 1/7/1970 in Plymouth; John A. Cote (NH) and Nancy A. Duval (NH)

Katy Lorraine, b. 12/30/1980 in Laconia; William Gene Cote (NH) and Cathy Lorraine Delaney (WV)

Sara Jane, b. 4/28/1971; John Allen Cote (NH) and Nancy Ann Duval Cote (NH)

CRANSTON,
Herbert, b. 11/8/1895 in Dorchester; second; Henry L. Cranston and Maria B. Clifford (Alexandria)

DANNER,
Annabelle Petra, b. 7/14/2003 in Lebanon; Aaron Danner and Tina Danner

DAVIS,
Ethel I., b. 9/18/1898; first; Frank A. Davis (farmer, Wentworth) and Izetta A. Davis (Dorchester)

Henry Walter, b. 9/4/1899 in Dorchester; seventh; Weston H. Davis (farmer, Haverhill, MA) and Frances A. Petit (Woodstock, ON)

Joseph E., b. 4/26/1896 in Dorchester; Walter L. Davis (farmer, Wentworth) and Rebecca Whicher (Dorchester)

Weston A., b. 8/20/1901 in Dorchester; fifth; Nestor H. Davis (farmer, Haverhill, MA) and Francis A. Pettit (Woodstock, Can.)

DAY,
James Thomas, II, b. 11/24/1974 in Plymouth; James Thomas Day (NH) and Cynthia Geanne Cummings (ME)

Stephanie Anne, b. 10/5/1976 in Plymouth; James Thomas Day (NH) and Cynthia Jeanne Cummings (NH)

DELILE,
child, b. 12/19/1904 in Dorchester; sixth; Nelson Delile (laborer, Canada) and Thabiola LaCroix (Canada)

DELSART,
Amanda Jean, b. 1/19/1980 in Plymouth; Louis Adolph Delsart (NH) and Eleanor Grace Dow (NH)
Andrea Marie, b. 4/23/1981 in Plymouth; Louis Adolph Delsart (NH) and Eleanor Grace Dow (NH)
Hazel May, b. 8/7/1936; second; Adolf W. Delsart (laborer, Lakewood, NJ) and Marion E. McKinley (Warren)
Heather Elise, d. 5/4/1977; Louis Adolph Delsart (NH) and Eleanor Grace Dow (NH)
Justine Carol, b. 12/14/1943 in Dorchester; fourth; Adolph W. Delsart (farmer, Lakewood, NJ) and Marion E. McKinley (Warren)
Louis A., b. 5/30/1941 in Dorchester; third; Adolph W. Delsart (laborer, Lakewood, NJ) and Marion E. McKinley (Warren)
Patricia Ann, b. 8/22/1938; third; Adolph Delsart (laborer, NJ) and Marian McKinley (Warren)

DODGE,
Henry Leroy, b. 1/3/1908 in Dorchester; first; Clarence L. Dodge (laborer, 20, Littleton) and Grace Way (19, Pittsfield); residence – Plymouth

DOE,
Phillis E., b. 7/5/1925 in Dorchester; first; Claude Doe (laborer, Canaan) and Ruby M. Marshall (Wilmot); residence - Canaan

DOW,
Bria Louise, b. 5/13/2000 in Lebanon; Matthew Dow and Rebecca Dow

DUFORD,
Francis Leo, b. 10/12/1932; first; Leo N. Duford (laborer, Suncook) and Estell A. Durocher (Holyoke, MA)

DUGOE,
Eva M., b. 8/9/1893 in Dorchester; sixth; Ben Dugoe (NS) and Maggie Dugoe (NS)

DUQUETTE,
Courtney Yvonne, b. 4/24/1992; Rene M. Duquette (NH) and Stephanie Dalton (NH)

EDGECOMB,
Danny John, b. 11/7/1981 in Laconia; Dennis Paul Edgecomb (MA) and Glenda Alice Toomey (MA)

EVANS,
Dale Harold, b. 12/4/1953 in Dorchester; second; Benjamin I. Evans (woodsman, NH) and Ruth May Meekins (NH)

FAIRBORNE,
Mary Louisa, b. 6/3/1939; eighth; mulatto; Stewart L. Fairborne (farmer, b. West Indies, black, residence - Dorchester) and Mabel Faintaine (b. Warren, white, residence – Wentworth)

FAIRBURN,
Agnes, b. 2/13/1904 in Dorchester; fourth; William Fairburn (farmer, Howe, England) and Mary Fleming (Manchester, England)
George, b. 8/25/1900 in Dorchester; third; Frederick W. Fairburn (farmer, England) and Mary Fleming (England)
John Wilson, b. 12/2/1898; second; William F. Fairburn (farmer, London, England) and Mary Flemming (Manchester, England)

FALLON,
Amanda Louise, b. 1/4/1989 in Laconia; Brian Scott Fallon (MA) and Marion Irene Wright (MA)

FARRELL,
Andrew Cole, b. 1/2/1998 in Lebanon; Donald Farrell and Sherri Farrell
Samantha Jo, b. 8/29/1999 in Lebanon; Donald Farrell and Sherri Farrell

FELLOWS,
Mark Sawyer, b. 2/20/1898; first; Joseph E. Fellows (farmer, Dorchester) and Nellie E. Henderson (NY)
Oscar S., b. 8/29/1896 in Dorchester; Charles O. Fellows (carpenter, Dorchester) and Ina B. Simpson (Piermont)

FORD,
daughter, b. 6/26/1899 in Dorchester; twelfth; Israel Ford (laborer, Canada) and Mary Grover (Canada)

FORTIN,
son, b. 8/26/1898; fourth; Wilfred Fortin (farmer, Canada) and Sophia Gagnon (Canada)

FOSTER,
Gary Lee, b. 12/3/1951 in Plymouth; third; Laurence B. Foster (farmer, NH) and Laura B. Davis (NH)
John Ben, b. 4/16/1950 in Plymouth; second; Laurence B. Foster (farmer, Wentworth) and Laura B. Davis (Clarksville)

FRANZ,
Albert John, b. 5/12/1980 in Hanover; Albert John Franz (PA) and Patricia Ann Evans (PA)
Katrina Elizabeth, b. 3/4/1984 in Hanover; Albert John Franz (PA) and Patricia Ann Evans (PA)

GAGNON,
daughter, b. 8/6/1897; Adolph Gagnon (farmer, 33, Canada) and Eliza Daigle (27, Canada)
Joseph Amey, b. 9/7/1898; eighth; Adolph Gagnon (farmer, Canada) and Elise Daigle (Canada)

GOODE,
Joshua Aaron, b. 8/13/1993 in Lebanon; James Robert Goode (MA) and Suzanne C. Campbell (MA)
Wyatt Nathan, b. 11/16/1998 in Lebanon; James Goode and Suzanne Goode

GOODFELLOW,
son, b. 3/8/1904 in Dorchester; second; Joseph Goodfellow (farmer, Glasgow, Scotland) and Esther J. McRoberts (Bowmanville, ON)
Arthur R., b. 4/17/1906; third; Joseph Goodfellow (farmer, Glasgow, Scotland) and Estha McRobers (Bomansville, ON)

GOSS,
daughter, b. 6/1/1899 in Dorchester; fifth; Ezra J. Goss (farmer, Clinton Co., NY) and Maggie M. Martin (Ireland)
Adeline M., b. 5/19/1905 in Dorchester; fifth; Lester J. Goss (carpenter, 37, Andover, MA) and Katie Ackroyd (32, Undercliff, England)

Ezra Gilbert, b. 8/26/1908 in Dorchester; sixth; Lester J. Goss (carpenter, 40, Andover, MA) and Kate Ackroyd (35, Undercliff, England)

Frederick L., b. 7/29/1896 in Dorchester; Lester J. Goss (carpenter, Andover, MA) and Katie Ackroyd (Bradford, England)

Maggie Alice, b. 2/13/1899 in Dorchester; third; Lester J. Goss (carpenter, Andover, MA) and Katie Acknoyd (Undercliff, England)

Raymond W., b. 7/7/1924 in Dorchester; first; Ulysses A. Goss (painter, Dorchester) and Addie A. Hill (Canaan)

Ulysses S. A., b. 6/28/1901 in Dorchester; fourth; Lester J. Goss (carpenter, Andover, MA) and Kate Ackroyd (Bradford, England)

GOVE,
Trevor Lawrence, b. 3/26/1981 in Lebanon; Ralph Lawrence Gove (NH) and Linda Marion Merrill (NH)

GRAY,
Mackenzie Lin, b. 3/21/2001 in Lebanon; Eric Gray and Lacy Gray

GRIGAS,
Theresa Christine, b. 10/4/1978 in Plymouth; Robert Steven Grigas (NH) and Stephanie Ann Dickerson (ME)

GROCHOCKI,
Frederick Wayne, b. 7/23/1949 in Plymouth; first; Joseph Grochocki (mink farmer, Bronx, NY) and Katherine Cinkouski (Brooklyn, NY)

HALL,
Crystal Starr, b. 1/9/1977; Henry L. Hall (NH) and Paula M. Comeau (MA)

HANLEY,
son, b. 4/16/1899 in Dorchester; second; John T. Hanley (farmer, Calais, ME) and Mary E. Brooks (NB)

son, b. 12/5/1900 in Dorchester; third; John T. Hanley (farmer, Princeton, ME) and Mary Brooks (NB)

daughter, b. 12/23/1902 in Dorchester; fourth; John T. Hanley (farmer, Princeton, ME) and Mary E. Brooks (Bristol, NB)

Brad Loren, b. 12/24/1958 in Plymouth; Ernest Hanley, Jr. and
  Priscilla R. Downing
Dorothy M., b. 7/17/1929 in Dorchester; second; Ernest J. Hanley
  (farmer, Dorchester) and Edith R. Crosby (Malden, MA)
Ernest J., Jr., b. 9/16/1927 in Dorchester; first; Ernest J. Hanley
  (farmer, Dorchester) and Edith R. Crosby (Malden, MA)
Pamela Lee, b. 7/9/1960 in Plymouth; Ernest J. Hanley and Priscilla
  Downing

HARRIS,
daughter, b. 10/8/1904 in Dorchester; second; Frank Harris (farmer,
  Canaan) and Annie Sleeper (Suncook)
daughter, b. 1/4/1908 in Dorchester; fourth; Frank E. Harris (laborer,
  27, Canaan) and Annie Sleeper (28, Suncook)
Wendell, b. 4/14/1910; fifth; George R. Harris (farmer, 60,
  Hopkinton, MA) and Bertha I. Hinxman (39, Bear River, NS)

HAZELTON,
Daniel Malcolm, b. 7/13/1959 in Hanover; Walter Hazelton, Jr. and
  Frances A. Burnham
Walter Francis, b. 7/19/1950 in Hanover; first; Walter Hazelton, Jr.
  (laborer, Orange) and Frances A. Burnham (Dorchester)

HENDERSON,
daughter, b. 8/12/1887 in Dorchester; C. H. Henderson (farmer) and
  Ann -----

HENLEY,
daughter, b. 4/27/1910; fourth; Zenas R. Henley (farmer, 30, NS)
  and Mary Berry (32, Ireland)

HILL,
son, b. 8/1/1897; James Hill (farmer, 34, Canada) and Aurelie
  Camire (27, Canada)
son, b. 4/26/1910; sixth; Walter H. Hill (laborer, 31, Grafton) and
  Laura J. Rollins (31, Enfield)
Alan John, b. 1/3/1954 in Lebanon; fourth; Carl J. Hill, Jr. (Hanover)
  and Marjorie L. Burley (Sutton)
Joshua Benjamin, b. 11/7/1988 in Laconia; Oscar Hill (NH) and
  Veronica Lynn Piascik (NH)
Thomas W., b. 5/5/1904 in Dorchester; first; John A. Hill (farmer,

Canada) and Abbie M. Ford (Barton, VT)

HOLMES,
son, b. 1/23/1914 in Dorchester; fifth; Fred E. Holmes (engineer, Portsmouth) and E. M. Holmes (Portsmouth)
Michaela Faith, b. 3/21/2001 in Lebanon; Robert Holmes and Donna Holmes

HOLT,
Chester, b. 3/14/1917 in Dorchester; sixth; Ernest Holt (teamster, Hancock) and Grace M. Sinchols (Messina, NY); residence - Hillsboro

HORTON,
Albert, b. 4/22/1901 in Dorchester; first; Albert W. Horton (teamster, Andover) and Olive M. Melanson (Dorchester)

HOUGHTON,
Gregory Andrew, b. 5/29/1999 in Lebanon; Andrew Houghton and Elizabeth Houghton
Justin Daniel, d. 1/10/2001 in Lebanon; Andrew Houghton and Elizabeth Houghton

HOWE,
Matthew Kenneth, b. 12/18/1985 in Hanover; Brian Alan Howe (NH) and Brenda Alice DeLong (MA)

HOWES,
Amanda Jane, b. 5/10/1977; David Hermon Howes (MA) and Patrica Ellen Sheridan (NY)

HOWLAND,
Guy Ai, b. 5/15/1908 in Dorchester; third; Harry J. Howland (laborer, 25, Franconia) and Altie J. Bickford (25, N. Dorchester); residence – N. Dorchester
Ila J., b. 10/29/1903 in Dorchester; first; Harry J. Howland (laborer, Franconia) and Altie J. Bickford (Dorchester)

HUNTINGTON,
Chelsea Scott, b. 7/21/1988 in Laconia; Eric Scott Huntington (NH) and Catherine Louise Terrill (VT)

JACKSON,
Kyle Stephen, b. 9/17/1994; Daniel Stephen Jackson (MA) and Doris Ann Young (NH)

JENKS,
Freeda May, b. 3/27/1919 in Dorchester; fourth; Andrew B. Jenks (lumberman, Albany, VT) and Amy M. Geryer (Lebanon)

JEWELL,
daughter, b. 4/21/1897; Alice M. Jewell (19, Groton)
daughter, b. 2/14/1899; second; Alice M. Jewell (Groton)

JOHNSON,
Eva Doris, b. 10/25/1911 in Dorchester; fourth; Elmer J. Johnson (farmer, 43, Newport) and Ella Peterson (33, Plainfield)

JOYCE,
Diana Lynn, b. 10/31/1955 in Plymouth; George H. Joyce, Jr. and Muriel A. Willey
Sharon Ann, b. 4/12/1953 in Plymouth; first; George Joyce, Jr. (US Army, NH) and Muriel A. Willey (NH)
Walter George, b. 7/19/1954 in Plymouth; second; George H. Joyce, Jr. (NH) and Muriel A. Willey (NH)

JUTRAS,
William, b. 4/24/1897; Louis Jutras (farmer, 43, Canada) and Philman Saucete (42, Canada)

KEEZER,
Pearl R., b. 12/12/1905 in Dorchester; third; George W. Keezer (farmer, 25, Haverhill, MA) and Mary York (20, Pittsfield)
Rose G., b. 11/6/1904 in Dorchester; second; George W. Keezer (farmer, Haverhill, MA) and Mary York (Pittsfield)

KIMBALL,
daughter, b. 1/25/1923 in Dorchester; twelfth; Charles Kimball (farmer, W. Berwick, ME) and Rosie LaRoe (White River Jct., VT)

LAMOTT,
Raymond M., b. 5/15/1903 in Dorchester; first; James I. LaMott

(lumberman, Dorchester) and Pearl M. Wing (Burke, NY)

LAVOY,
daughter, b. 4/29/1896 in Dorchester; Edward Lavoy (farmer, Canada) and Jennie Gote (Canada)

LEGG,
John Graydon, b. 8/6/1991; John Graydon Legg, III (VA) and Cheryl Ann Legg (RI)
Rachel Alexandra, b. 2/27/1995; John G. Legg (VA) and Cheryl Ann Toro (RI)

LEONHARDT,
daughter, b. 7/18/1907 in Dorchester; fifth; John Leonhardt (laborer, 32, New York City) and Ella Gill (32, New York City)

LEVASSEUR,
Robert, b. 2/20/1899 in Dorchester; fourth; Joseph V. Levasseur (teamster, Canada) and Sarah E. McCarron (Boston, MA)

LITTLEFIELD,
Donna Aurora, b. 11/20/1949 in Plymouth; second; Edwin L. Littlefield (mining, Rumney) and June A. Tremblay (Newton, MA)

MARK,
Michala Ann, b. 5/16/1995; Philip William Mark (CT) and Melanie Jase Mason (CT)

MARSH,
Kelly Louise, b. 1/24/1975 in Concord; Ernest E. Marsh, Jr. (NH) and Georgianna Mary Roberts (VT)

MARTIN,
Louis Oswald, b. 8/4/1899 in Dorchester; first; Frank Martin (farmer, Danbury) and Maggie J. Kennedy (Ireland)

MATAVA,
Reginald I., b. 6/21/1920 in Dorchester; first; Charles Matava (teamster, N. Andover, MA) and Lillian V. Kidder (N. Groton, MA)

McCARTHY,
Myles Joseph, b. 10/30/1991; Timothy Joseph McCarthy (MA) and Theresa Adele McCarthy (MA)

McKEE,
daughter, b. 11/10/1913 in Dorchester; third; William J. McKee (farmer, 28, Melburn, ON) and Ethel M. Armstrong (27, S. Dedham, ON)
son, b. 8/5/1916 in Dorchester; fourth; William J. McKee (farmer, 30, Melbourne, ON) and Ethel Armstrong (30, S. Durham, ON)

MERRILL,
son, b. 5/9/1892 in Dorchester; first; Velorous O. Merrill (farmer, Dorchester) and Velma E. Follansbee (Orford)
daughter, b. 1/2/1895 in Dorchester; second; Bernard L. Merrill (farmer, Dorchester) and Lilly B. Nichols (Wentworth)
Blanche, b. 7/13/1899 in Dorchester; first; Henry M. Merrill (farmer, Dorchester) and Helen M. Jewell (Lyme)
Frank, b. 4/29/1895 in Dorchester; second; Henry M. Merrill (farmer, Dorchester) and Blanche C. Kidder (Groton)
Frank Henry, b. 4/21/1893 in Dorchester; first; Bernard L. Merrill (machinist, Dorchester) and Lilly B. Nichols (Wentworth)
Leon Henry, b. 8/24/1893 in Dorchester; first; Henry M. Merrill (farmer, Dorchester) and Blanche C. Kidder (Groton)
Lillian I., b. 11/11/1905 in Dorchester; third; Henry M. Merrill (farmer, 36, Dorchester) and Helen M. Jewell (26, Lyme)
Linda Marion, b. 12/12/1949 in Hanover; third; Malcolm D. Merrill (carpenter, Grantham) and Frances E. Willey (Meredith)
Malcolm Dunbar, b. 2/17/1945 in Dorchester; first; Malcolm D. Merrill (carpenter, Grantham) and Frances E. Willey (Meredith)
Sidney J., b. 11/11/1903 in Dorchester; second; Henry M. Merrill (farmer, Dorchester) and Helen M. Jewell (Lyme)

MOCK,
Cole Michael, b. 11/8/1990 in Littleton; Michael Joseph Mock (VT) and Heidi Sue Golden (NH)

MONAST,
son, b. 7/3/1906; eighth; Henry Monast (laborer, Chicopee Falls, MA) and Eva Blaine (Montreal, Canada)
Marie J. S., b. 7/22/1902 in Dorchester; sixth; Henry Monast (farmer,

Chicopee, MA) and Eva Blain (Montreal, PQ)
Theadou, b. 11/3/1907 in Dorchester; ninth; Henry Monast (farmer, 35, Chicopee, MA) and Eva A. Blain (34, Montreal, Canada)

MOORE,
Llewellyn F., b. 2/9/1938; second; Elmer L. Moore (lumberman, Mt. Chase, ME) and Vera M. Parker (Oakfield, ME)

MORRILL,
Stephen David, b. 3/5/1987 in Plymouth; David Allen Morrill (NH) and Martha Jean Osgood (NH)
Thomas Edward, b. 7/17/1984 in Plymouth; David Allen Morrill (NH) and Martha Jean Osgood (NH)

MOSES,
Alice Lillian, b. 3/11/1916 in Dorchester; fourth; William E. Moses (laborer, 27, Malone, NY) and Lillian E. Goss (21, Dorchester)
Laforest, b. 8/6/1930 in Dorchester; eighth; William E. Moses (truck driver, Malone, NY) and Lillian E. Moses (Dorchester)
Linda Lee, b. 2/11/1950 in Dorchester; second; Forest M. Moses (lumberman, Dorchester) and Ida M. Ewens (Bristol)
Morton M., b. 6/6/1923 in Dorchester; sixth; William Moses (laborer, Malone, NY) and Lillian Goss (Dorchester)
Royal Edward, b. 4/16/1919 in Dorchester; fifth; William Edward Moses (farmer, Malone, NY) and Lillian E. Goss (Dorchester)
Sheldon M., b. 10/2/1925 in Dorchester; seventh; William E. Moses (mechanic, Malone, NY) and Lillian E. Goss (Dorchester)

MOSHER,
Ray Otis, b. 3/11/1890 in Dorchester; fifth; Ira C. Mosher (farmer, Barnston, Quebec) and Mary Phelps (Groton)
Sadie Ethel, b. 4/10/1892 in Dorchester; sixth; Ira C. Mosher (farmer, Barnston, PQ) and Mary F. Mosher (Groton)

MURDOCK,
John Richard, Jr., b. 3/4/1993 in Plymouth; John Richard Murdock, Jr. (NH) and Tammy Marie Ward (NH)

MUTCH,
daughter, b. 6/5/1903 in Dorchester; first; David Mutch (mill hand, Woodstock, NB) and Hannah Perkins (Coventry, England);

residence – Lowell, MA

MUZZEY,
Florence, b. 1/7/1893 in Dorchester; first; Lauretta Muzzey (Bradford, VT)

NELSON,
daughter, b. 10/17/1891 in Dorchester; William B. Nelson (laborer, Scotland) and Margie Campbell (Canada)
daughter, b. 7/--/1893 in Dorchester; fourth; William B. Nelson (farmer, Scotland) and Margery Campbell (Canada)
daughter, b. 10/22/1896 in Dorchester; William B. Nelson (farmer, Glas., Scotland) and Margery Campbell (Canada)

NOLAND,
daughter, b. 5/18/1904 in Dorchester; fourth; William E. Noland (farmer, Jordon, IN) and Susan Burr (Lebanon, MO)

NORRIS,
Faith Anne, b. 3/29/1979 in Nashua; Donald William Norris (NJ) and Donna Marie Lelis (MA)

NOYES,
daughter, b. 12/20/1919 in Dorchester; fifth; Harrison H. Noyes (farmer, Lowell, MA) and Iola M. Stevens (Rumney)
Harrison H., Jr., b. 3/27/1922 in Dorchester; sixth; Harrison H. Noyes (lumber operator, Lowell, MA) and Iola M. Stevens (Rumney)
Iola Ruth, b. 5/24/1913 in Dorchester; fourth; Harrison H. Noyes (farmer, 28, Lowell, MA) and Maud Stevens (27, Rumney)

O'BRIEN,
Margarie Ethel, b. 7/22/1914 in Dorchester; third; Alexander T. O'Brien (farmer, Amherst, NS) and Hattie Gates (N. Reading, MA)

OSBORNE,
William C., b. 11/9/1906; third; Fred S. Osborne (laborer, Lindboro) and Florence E. Rogers (Larchwood, IA)

OVIATT,
Sharon Lynn, b. 7/20/1950 in Hanover; Alfred E. Oviatt (architect,

Bridgeport, CT) and Harriet B. Bean (Orford)

PALMER,
Joan Barbara, b. 9/17/1934; first; Donald Scott Palmer (salesman, Groveland, MA) and Madeline O. Merrill (Glencliff)

PAREAULT,
daughter, b. 5/23/1908 in Dorchester; fourth; James Pareault (farmer, 33, Somersworth) and Leona Colzene (32)

PARKER,
daughter, b. 5/24/1887 in Dorchester; John C. Parker (farmer, Sutton) and Sarah A. Wescott (Bedford)

PEASLEE,
son, b. 3/26/1895 in Dorchester; fourth; George B. Peaslee (laborer, Canaan) and Carrie M. Titus (Newton, OH)

PERAULT,
daughter, b. 8/18/1905 in Dorchester; third; James Perault (farmer, 30, Somersworth) and Leonie Tousegnant (30, Canada)

PERREAULT,
stillborn son, b. 1/5/1915 in Dorchester; sixth; James A. Perreault (farmer, Somersworth) and Leonie Tousignant (Canada)
Nikolas Alan, b. 10/23/2002 in Plymouth; Bruce Perreault and Monique Perreault
Oreuse, b. 3/11/1911 in Dorchester; stillborn; fifth; James Perreault (farmer, 36, Somersworth) and Leonie Tousignant (36, Canada)

PILLSBURY,
I. M. [daughter], b. 5/15/1887 in Dorchester; B. Q. Pillsbury (farmer, Piermont) and Mary E. Bickford (Dorchester)
Sarah Adda, b. 5/6/1890 in Dorchester; third; Byron Q. Pillsbury (farmer, Piermont) and Ella M. Bickford (Dorchester)

POQUETT,
daughter, b. 5/23/1892 in Dorchester; second; Herman L. Poquett (farmer, North Hero) and Emma Giggs (North Hero)
son, b. 7/22/1901 in Dorchester; third; Emery M. Poquett (farmer, N. Hero, VT) and Delia L. Burley (N. Hero, VT)

PRATT,
Kayla Marie, b. 9/13/1991; Kevin Gene Pratt (NY) and Charlene Marie Pratt (NH)
Kyle Gene, b. 2/26/1990 in Laconia; Kevin Pratt (NY) and Charlene Marie Cobin (NH)

PUTNEY,
Norris S., b. 9/16/1905 in Dorchester; second; Bert C. Putney (farmer, 30, Bolton, NY) and Lena B. Dickinson (27, Caldwell, NY)

QUILTY,
Clifford J., b. 1/11/1900 in Dorchester; second; John W. Quilty (laborer, Newfoundland) and Ida A. Garland (NB)

QUIMBY,
daughter, b. 10/4/1910; first; Custer Quimby (farmer, 30, Dorchester) and Bertha B. Parker (23, Dorchester)
Pamela Lucille, b. 11/23/1952 in Plymouth; third; Stanley A. Quimby (NH) and Margaret E. Colburn (NH)
Roger, b. 8/2/1920 in Dorchester; third; Custer Quimby (lumberman, Dorchester) and Bertha Parker (Dorchester)
Stanley Amos, b. 1/8/1919 in Dorchester; second; Custer Quimby (farmer, Dorchester) and Bertha B. Packer (Dorchester)

QUIRK,
Amanda Lynn, b. 4/11/1993 in Lebanon; James Vincent Quirk (CT) and Lisa Marie Ceravone (CT)

RAY,
Maxwell Tyler, b. 10/5/1990 in Laconia; Matthew Everett Ray (NH) and Debra Dorothy Anderson (MA)

RAYNOR,
Rose Elizabeth, b. 8/31/1937; first; Albert F. Raynor (farm laborer, Canaan) and Rose Geeb (New York City)

REED,
Leland C., b. 10/11/1899 in Dorchester; fourth; Caddie C. Reed (farmer, Dorchester) and Annie S. Wescott (Manchester)

REYNOLDS,
Daneilya Cassandra, b. 1/29/1982; David William Reynolds (NH) and Dianne May Kennedy (VT)
Tina Louise, b. 8/4/1964 in Hanover; Elwyn K. Reynolds (Stafford, VT) and Patricia A. Delsart (Dorchester)

ROBB,
Wendy Ann, b. 4/18/1970 in Plymouth; Edward M. Robb (NH) and Judy A. Cote (NH)

ROLLINS,
Abbigail Faith, b. 3/9/1994; Daniel Wayne Rollins (NH) and Gertrude Edith Lapre (NH)
Jeremiah Stephen, b. 12/12/1989 in Laconia; Daniel Wayne Rollins (NH) and Gertrude Edith Lapre (NH)

ROUSSEAU,
Joyce Maxine, b. 11/5/1933; first; Clarence W. Rousseau (laborer, Grafton) and Vera M. Clough (Wentworth)

ROWE,
Cody Adams, b. 4/24/1996; Joseph Poitras (NH) and Monica Rowe (NH)

RUSSEAU,
Jeffrey Alan, b. 7/11/1980 in Hanover; Larry Gene Russeau (MI) and Jacqueline Lois Gramolini (MA)

RUSSELL,
daughter, b. 5/30/1912 in Dorchester; fourteenth; Fred Russell (farmer, 46, Turner, ME) and Eva Ellingwood (37, Hereford, ON)
daughter, b. 5/30/1912 in Dorchester; fifteenth; Fred Russell (farmer, 46, Turner, ME) and Eva Ellingwood (37, Hereford, ON)

SANBORN,
Heather Ann, b. 2/26/1987 in Hanover; Gene Sanborn (NH) and Cheryl Lynn Carter (NH)
Michelle Ann, b. 1/12/1981 in Plymouth; Gene Craig Sanborn (NH) and Cheryl Lynn Carter (NH)

SEWELL,
son, b. 3/17/1904 in Dorchester; third; William S. Sewell (farmer, Elmore, VT) and Philomene Dionne (Campton, PQ)
son, b. 8/22/1908 in Dorchester; fifth; William S. Sewell (farmer, 44, Elmer, VT) and Philomene Dionne (39, Campton, Canada)
Albert E., b. 5/18/1905 in Dorchester; fourth; William S. Sewell (farmer, 40, Elmore, VT) and Philomene Dionne (36, Campton, Canada)

SKIPPER,
Paige Elizabeth, b. 12/2/1991; Paul Edward Skipper (MA) and Janet Mary Kummer (CT)

SLEEPER,
Brittany Nicole, b. 5/19/1993 in Lebanon; Tony Lee Sleeper (NH) and Cindy Lou Carter (NH)

SMITH,
son, b. 3/5/1897; W. Scott Smith (lumberman, Holderness) and Minnie Deline (Canada)
Eva Bell Bertha, b. 6/1/1914 in Dorchester; first; Osmon L. Smith (lineman, Springfield, MA) and Bertha Miller (Russia)

SNOW,
Joshua Victor, b. 8/24/1983 in Plymouth; Roger Alan Snow (Germany) and Charlotte Jean Coy (MA)

STEVENS,
Alice May, b. 3/8/1928 in Dorchester; first; Joseph O. Stevens (laborer, Groton) and Yevonne R. Rosseau (Fitchburg, MA)

STRATTON,
Charles P., b. 7/15/1892 in Dorchester; first; Charles E. Stratton (farmer, Marblehead, MA) and Carrie E. Stratton (Boxford, MA)

SYLVESTER,
Rachael Marie, b. 12/28/1989 in Laconia; Steve Alan Sylvester (NH) and Holly Lisa Gelinas (NH)

TAYLOR,
John Z., b. 10/12/1899 in Dorchester; first; Zackary G. Taylor

(farmer, Orange) and Grace McLucy (Boston, MA)

TENNEY,
son, b. 3/27/1893 in Dorchester; second; Oscar W. Tenney (sawyer, Alexandria) and Kate Welch (Manchester)

THOMAS,
Emily Ann, b. 6/24/1985 in Hanover; Kenneth Wesley Thomas (MA) and Cynthia Ann Bertrand (NY)
Megan Victor, b. 5/26/1983 in Hanover; Kenneth Wesley Thomas (MA) and Cynthia Ann Bertrand (NH)

TILTON,
daughter, b. 10/16/1892 in Dorchester; first; Henry A. Tilton (farmer, Andover) and Mabel L. Rowan (W. Rumney)

TURLEY,
Johanna Laessle, b. 5/29/1981 in Hanover; Paul John Turley (CT) and Joan Roberts Laessle (NJ)

WALDRON,
daughter, b. 8/10/1901 in Dorchester; fifth; Clarence P. Waldron (carpenter, Hebron) and Nettie Lee (Andover, VT)
daughter, b. 4/13/1924 in Dorchester; third; Fred Waldron (farmer, Wentworth) and Georgie Braley (Groton)

WALKER,
Charles I., b. 6/24/1926 in Dorchester; first; Harold Walker (farmer, Lawrence, MA) and Elsie L. Krahenbuhl (New York City)
Gary Allen, b. 10/23/1965 in Plymouth; Larry H. Walker (Plymouth) and Martha L. Phinney (Plymouth)
Hugh Dyson, b. 2/21/1934; second; Hubert Walker (sawyer, Lawrence, MA) and Lena M. Bosence (St. Johns, NB)
Kate Laura, b. 6/9/1911 in Dorchester; fifth; Isaac D. Walker (farmer, 39, Lowell, MA) and Margaret S. Fairburn (35, Hull, England)
Larry Harold, b. 8/5/1938; first; Harold Walker (laborer, Lawrence, MA) and Nella M. Higgins (Glover, VT)
Larry Harold, b. 1/12/1963 in Plymouth; Larry Walker and Martha L. Phinney (Plymouth)
Mary Josephine, b. 11/27/1916 in Dorchester; seventh; Isaac D. Walker (farmer, 44, Lowell, MA) and Margaret S. Fairburn (40,

Holland, England)
Winona Beatrice, b. 8/1/1908 in Dorchester; fifth; Isaac D. Walker (farmer, 37, Lowell, MA) and Margaret S. Fairburn (32, Hull, England)

WEBSTER,
Chelsea Noel, b. 7/9/1990 in Hanover; Phillip Robert Webster (MA) and Shelley Anne Newhall (MA)

WEIGEL,
Jeremy Stanley, b. 4/13/1980 in Lebanon; Daniel Albert Weigel (NH) and Pamela Lucille Quimby (NH)

WELD,
Bennie, b. 11/30/1902 in Dorchester; first; Bert C. Weld (laborer, Canaan) and Carrie D. Pressey (Canaan)

WHEELER,
Helen E., b. 6/3/1901 in Dorchester; fourth; Delmont I. Wheeler (farmer, Starksboro, VT) and Mary L. Howard (Ripton, VT)

WHICHER,
daughter, b. 6/5/1890 in Dorchester; seventh; Joseph A. Whicher (farmer, Wentworth) and Celesta Jefferson (Lisbon)
son, b. 11/24/1895 in Dorchester; first; Frank L. Whicher (farmer, Wentworth) and Nora Stephens (Rumney)
daughter, b. 9/10/1900 in Dorchester; tenth; Emri S. Whicher (carpenter, Dorchester) and Lydia A. Willoughby (Groton)
Elvira M., b. 8/31/1895 in Dorchester; tenth; Joseph Whicher (farmer, Wentworth) and Celestia Jepperson (Lisbon)
Francis Ethel, b. 5/25/1899 in Dorchester; tenth; Joseph A. Whicher (farmer, Wentworth) and Celestia Jepperson (Lisbon)
James S., b. 5/15/1893 in Dorchester; ninth; Joseph A. Whicher (farmer, Wentworth) and Celesta E. Jefferson (Lisbon)
Roy E., b. 3/5/1895 in Dorchester; ninth; Emri C. Whicher (farmer, Dorchester) and Lydia Willoughby (Groton)

WHITCOMB,
daughter, b. 1/25/1908 in Dorchester; first; Nellie E. Whitcomb (17, Fitchburg, MA)

WILLEY,
Anna Pearl, b. 8/24/1939; seventh; Edgar C. Willey (laborer, Farmington) and Mildred M. Clogston (Bradford)
Barbara Pearl, b. 8/20/1953 in Plymouth; third; Leroy E. Willey (laborer, NH) and Barbara M. Sweeney (MA)
Lawrence Almon, b. 5/21/1937; fourth; Edgar C. Willey (laborer, Farmington) and Mildred M. Clogston (Bradford, VT)
Leroy Edgar, b. 7/16/1935; fifth; Edgar Willey (laborer, Farmington) and Mildred Clogston (Bradford, VT)
Muriel Aleta, b. 6/10/1933; second; Edgar C. Willey (laborer, Farmington) and Mildred M. Clogston (Bradford, VT)
Winona Mildred, b. 5/22/1931; second; Edgar C. Willey (farmer, Farmington) and Mildred M. Clogston (Bradford, VT)

WILLIAMS,
Aaron Allan, b. 9/11/1993 in Plymouth; Donald Allan Williams (ME) and Jaye Ellen Blanchette (ME)
Isaac George, b. 11/4/1997 in Plymouth; Donald Allan Williams and Jaye Ellen Blanchette
Kerrie Elizabeth, b. 12/26/1970; Gordon Clark Williams, Jr. (MA) and Kathleen Lennox Williams (NH)

WILSON,
son, b. 2/6/1898; fourth; Norman Wilson (farmer, Chazy, NY) and Gertrude Wilson (Chazy, NY)
son, b. 8/27/1899 in Dorchester; seventh; Chittendon Wilson (farmer, Chazy, NY) and Jessie Weeks (Rouses Pt., NY)
Pauline A., b. 4/14/1908 in Dorchester; fourth; Albert G. Wilson (engineer, 32, Lyndeboro) and Elsie M. Bryant (23, Northwood Narrows)

YETMAN,
Yvonne Marie, b. 7/10/1984 in Hanover; David Michael Yetman (RI) and Karen Marie Roland (ME)

YORK,
Harry Francis, b. 10/25/1898; sixth; William F. York (farmer, Wentworth) and Sarah J. Beard (Reading, MA)

YOUNG,
Alexander Colby, b. 9/16/1993 in Concord; Richard Melvin Young,

Sr. (NH) and Pearl Dorothy Cameau (NH)

Anthony James, b. 3/16/1974 in Plymouth; Ira Morris Young (MA) and Evelyn Priscilla Watkins (NH)

Candida May, b. 6/21/1972 in Plymouth; Ira Morris Young (MA) and Evelyn Priscilla Watkins (NH)

Christopher Glenn, b. 11/5/1976 in Laconia; Richard Melvin Young, Sr. (NH) and Pearl Dorothy Comeau (NH)

Corima Leigh, b. 3/11/1974 in Plymouth; Ralph Young (NH) and Elaine Alice Roy (NH)

Doris Ann, b. 12/8/1977; Richard Melvin Young, Sr. (NH) and Pearl Dorothy Comeau (NH)

Marnie Lynn, b. 3/12/1969 in Plymouth; Ralph Leon Young (NH) and Elaine Alice Roy (NH)

Richard Melvin, b. 10/24/1947 in Dorchester; sixth; Stanley C. Young (laborer, Thetford, VT) and Alice L. Moses (Dorchester)

Scott Leon, b. 5/19/1977; Ralph Leon Young (NH) and Elaine Alice Roy (NH)

Sherry Lee, b. 9/30/1970 in Plymouth; Richard M. Young (NH) and Pearl Dorothy Comeau (NH)

DORCHESTER MARRIAGES

ANDREWS,
Clarence H. of Dorchester m. Thelma M. **Ryea** of Dorchester 2/22/1941 in Plymouth; H – 26, truck driver, b. Laconia, s/o C. H. Andrews (farmer, Sutton) and E. L. Hildret (housewife, Orfordville); W – 25, at home, b. E. Berkshire, VT, d/o M. C. Ryea (farmer, Enosburg, VT) and V. M. Prine (housewife, E. Highgate, VT)

ANNIS,
Edwin W. of Dorchester m. Agnes D. **Clark** of Groton 10/5/1897; H - 52, farmer, b. Groton, s/o John B. Annis (VT) and Sophronia Buell (Groton); W – 34, housewife, b. Groton, d/o Augustus Remick (Groton, carpenter) and Eliza A. Prior (MA, housewife)

ARANO,
Francis Dominic of Boston, MA m. Jean Ellen **Ashley** of Dorchester 9/5/1959 in Dorchester; H – 23, elevator const.; W – 27, nurse

ARCHIBALD,
Charles Alan of Dorchester m. Rhonda Yvonne **Towne** of Dorchester 1/8/1994 in Plymouth; H – s/o John Lyle Archibald and Margaret Ann Jacobson; W – d/o Howard Stacy Towne and Carol Yvonne Thisell

ASHLEY,
George S. of Dorchester m. Glia Muriel **Wheat** of Keene 6/11/1916 in Keene; H – 23, locomotive fireman, b. Lawrence, MA, s/o Alfred W. Ashley (farmer, PEI) and Minnie O'Mallie (housewife, Dorchester); W – 19, musician, b. Woodsville, d/o George Wheat (RR employee, Barre, VT) and Jennie M. Wheat (housekeeper, Braintree, VT)
Herbert A. of Dorchester m. Phyllis A. **Bean** of Orford 12/14/1931 in Rumney; H – 31, RFD carrier, b. Dorchester, s/o Herbert H. Ashley (farmer, PEI) and Annie G. Philpot (housewife, PEI); W – 22, stenographer, b. Orford, d/o Phillip L. Bean (farmer, Orford) and Blanch H. Burnham (housewife, Dorchester)

AYRES,
George Little of Dorchester m. Margaret Rose **Knipfer** of Dorchester 10/12/1975 in Dorchester; H – s/o George L. Ayres and Joanne Spellenburge; W – d/o Richard L. Knipfer and Monica Schesky

BAILEY,
Charles G. of Dorchester m. Sarah L. **Wheet** of Groton 4/13/1895 in Groton; H – 21, farmer, b. Groton, s/o Abel Bailey (farmer, Groton) and Mar. Willoughby (housewife, Groton); W – 16, housewife, b. Groton, d/o Lafayette Wheet (farmer, Groton) and Emma Colburn (housewife, Groton)

BAKER,
Hilton F. of Dorchester m. Gertrude O. **Mason** of Dorchester 12/25/1926 in Canaan; H – 36, mill man, 2nd, b. Huntington, VT, s/o William Baker (farmer, Huntington, VT) and Lucinda Small (housewife); W – 25, housekeeper, 2nd, b. Piermont, d/o Byron H. Demus (farmer, Bradford, VT) and Eva May Spencer (housewife, Norwich, VT)

BARTON,
Michael John of Dorchester m. Veronica Lynn **Hill** of Dorchester 2/29/1996 in Dorchester; H – s/o Wayne H. Barton and Carol J. Sturtevant; W – d/o James A. Piascik and Clara L. Landon

BEAN,
Roger B. of Dorchester m. Olga T. **Aguirre** of Dorchester 6/15/1985 in Dorchester; H – s/o Bertram Bean and Agnes Gillmette; W – d/o Joe I. Valencia and Mary S. Salcido

BELAIR,
James Ross of Dorchester m. Renee Frances **Bood** of Plymouth 2/24/1995 in Plymouth; H – s/o Jean R. Belair, Sr. and Marima J. Straley; W – d/o Robert F. Bood and Ruth F. Rich

BENNETT,
Clarence P. of Somerville, NJ m. Janith L. **Adams** of Warren Twp., NJ 7/15/1961 in Dorchester; H – 31, engineer; W – 25, bookkeeper

BERRY,
Lawrence D. of Dorchester m. Elaine A. **Young** of Dorchester 4/30/1983 in Ashland; H – s/o Lawrence E. Berry and Aura Harriet Drake; W – d/o George S. Roy and Mamie M. Hilliard

BICKFORD,
Arthur J. of Dorchester m. Alice **Matava** of Dorchester 10/23/1900 in Dorchester; H – 28, farmer, b. Dorchester, s/o Albert F. Bickford (farmer, Dorchester) and Emma Norris (housewife, Dorchester); W – 20, domestic, b. Hamstead, d/o Isaac Matava (laborer) and Nellie Matava (housewife, England)

Chester A. of Dorchester m. Louise A. **Howland** of Boston, MA 12/24/1904 in Rumney; H – 19, farmer, b. Dorchester, s/o Albert F. Bickford (farmer, Dorchester) and Emma J. Norris (housewife, Dorchester); W – 18, school teacher, b. Boston, MA, d/o Charles W. Howland (bookkeeper, Boston, MA) and Caro W. Lewis (housewife, Boston, MA)

Clarence E. of Center Harbor m. Elizabeth P. **Ashley** of Dorchester 6/25/1938 in Cheever; H – 30, laborer, b. Center Harbor, s/o Minot W. Bickford (painter, Moultonboro) and Etta M. Dow (housewife, Moultonboro); W – 33, teacher, b. Dorchester, d/o Herbert H. Ashley (carpenter, PEI) and Annie G. Pollard (housewife, PEI)

BLAIN,
Wilfred F. of Dorchester m. Yvonne S. **Dupuis** of Canaan 10/23/1922 in Enfield; H - 31, farmer, b. Albion, RI, s/o Francois Blain (Canada, farmer) and Agnes Robert (Canada); W - 20, housewife, b. Canaan, d/o Samuel Dupuis (Canada, farmer) and Jennie Patrie (Manchester, housewife)

BOYAJIAN,
Harold Hrant of Providence, RI m. Mary Josephine **Ashley** of Dorchester 3/24/1956 in Dorchester; H – 28, shop foreman, s/o Samuel Boyajian and Margaret H. Arslanian; W – 18, student, d/o Alfred E. Ashley and Esther R. Holland

BRECK,
John L. of Dorchester m. Clara A. **Taylor** of Dorchester 6/20/1906 in Dorchester; H - 67, farmer, 2nd, b. Wentworth, s/o Marshall H. H. Breck (Lyme, farmer) and Martha Coolidge (Sherban, MA, housewife); W - 52, domestic, b. Orange, d/o John Taylor (England, farmer) and Clarissa D. Taylor (Orange, housewife)

BROOKS,
John A. of Dorchester m. Martha J. **Ward** of Campton 9/6/1897; H -

35, farmer, b. Dorchester, s/o John W. Brooks (Canada, farmer) and Sarah Sampier (VT, housewife); W - 16, housewife, b. Campton, d/o George M. Ward (Plymouth, farmer) and Nellie Elliott (housewife)

BROWN,
Carl Russell of Dorchester m. Paula Glen **Stone** of Dorchester 10/7/1989; H – s/o George Herbert Brown and Olga Christine Muhr; W – d/o Alfred Augustus Stone and Anna Rita McLean

Walter H., Jr., of Dorchester m. Billie June **DeWeese** of Wentworth 9/23/1950 in Plymouth; H – 24, weaver, b. NH, s/o Walter H. Brown and Ruth M. Currier; W – 18, at home, b. CA, d/o John E. DeWeese and Wilda W. Willis

BRYNE,
Harry Thomas of Hartford, CT m. Nancy Carolyn **Ashley** of Dorchester 6/15/1957 in Dorchester; H – 27, insurance; W – 23, buyer

BURKE,
Ryan L. of Fenton, MO m. Amanda J. **Delsart** of Dorchester 9/8/2001

BURNHAM,
Frank W. of Dorchester m. Bertha M. **Tilton** of Alexandria 3/9/1913 in Alexandria; H – 27, farmer, b. Dorchester, s/o Frank Y. Burnham (farmer, Dorchester) and Josiphene C. Colburn (Wentworth); W – 32, school teacher, b. Alexandria, d/o Horace F. Tilton (farmer, Alexandria) and Flora Noyes (Alexandria)

George N. of Dorchester m. Jennie J. **Hazen** of Hanover 6/30/1903 in Dorchester; H – 22, farmer, b. Dorchester, s/o N. K. Burnham (farmer, Dorchester) and Eliza Kimball (housewife, Wentworth); W – 19, domestic, b. No. Hero, VT, d/o Emma J. Hazen (housewife, No. Hero, VT)

Isaac Hazen of Dorchester m. Barbara Charlotte **Wheeler** of N. Haverhill 7/9/1943 in Warren; H – 28, Army, b. Dorchester, s/o George N. Burnham (farmer, Dorchester) and Jennie J. Hazen (housewife, N. Hero, VT); W – 30, at home, 2nd, b. Pike, d/o Harry O. Wheeler (salesman, Orange, VT) and Rachel C. Heath (housewife, Whitefield)

Isaac Hazen of Dorchester m. Antoinette **O'Haire** of Dorchester

7/20/1952 in Hebron; H – 37, farmer, 2nd, b. Dorchester, s/o George N. Burnham (farmer, Dorchester) and Jennie J. Hazen (at home, N. Hero, VT); W – 39, housewife, 2nd, b. Lowell, MA, d/o Marietta Doris (housewife, Lawrence, MA)

Isaac M. of Dorchester m. Clara E. **Ellsworth** of Wentworth 8/31/1890 in Wentworth; H – 30, farmer, b. Wentworth, s/o N. Burnham (farmer, Antram) and Hattie Youngman (Wilmot); W – 32, b. Wentworth, d/o J. L. Ellsworth (farmer, Wentworth) and Emily Ellsworth (Wentworth)

Kirk N. of Dorchester m. Muriel M. **Ryea** of Wentworth 6/27/1933 in Plymouth; H – 26, farmer, 2nd, widower, b. Dorchester, s/o George N. Burnham (farmer, Dorchester) and Jennie J. Hazen (housewife, N. Hero, VT); W – 19, houskeeper, b. Franklin, d/o Marshall Ryea (farmer, Enosburg, VT) and Violet Ryea (housewife, S. Ryegate, VT)

Kirk N. Y. of Dorchester m. Susie Irene **Chase** of Dorchester 6/12/1927 in Fairlee, VT; H – 19, farmer, b. Dorchester, s/o George Burnham (farmer, Dorchester) and Jennie J. Hazen (housewife, N. Hero, VT); W – 25, teacher, b. Wentworth, d/o Walter E. Chase (Wentworth) and Mary B. Smith (Orford)

CAMPBELL,
William C. of Dorchester m. Mabel **Wescott** of Canaan 3/11/1897; H - 23, farmer, b. Boston, s/o ----- Campbell; W - 23, housekeeper, b. Canaan, d/o Edwin Wescott and ----- Wallace

CARR,
Deane C. of Dorchester m. Murial I. **Ray** of Rumney 10/24/1930 in Rumney; H - 21, laborer, b. Sugar Hill, s/o Frank J. Carr (farmer, NB) and Stella Aldrich (housewife, Easton); W - 18, at home, b. Dorchester, MA, d/o Edward E. Ray (farmer, W. Rumney) and Sadie E. Stock (housewife, Boston, MA)

Frank J. of Dorchester m. Roberta **Burnett** of Dorchester 10/10/1937 in Rumney; H – 59, farmer, 2nd, divorced, b. NB, s/o William A. Carr (farmer, NB) and Mary Cahill (at home, NB); W – 37, at home, b. Boston, MA, d/o Edward Burnett (merchant, Boston, MA) and Mary Clifford (at home, Boston, MA)

Larry P. of Lebanon m. Audrey A. **Butcher** of Dorchester 10/16/1982 in Lebanon; H – s/o Charlie L. Carr and Guila Moodie; W – d/o Frederick A. Butcher and Theresa R. Dufault

CARSSON,
Bjron O. of Sweden m. Kathleen J. **Melanson** of Dorchester 3/23/2002

CARTER,
Albert Barnett of Dorchester m. Peggy May **Hammel** of Plymouth 7/2/1955 in Plymouth; H – 20, mining, b. Plymouth, s/o Ernest Carter and Arlene Barnett; W – 18, at home, b. Plymouth, d/o Leonard D. Hammel and Gertrude Smith

Charles of Dorchester m. Ethel F. **Short** of Dorchester 6/4/1948 in Rumney; H – 51, woodsman, 2nd, b. Methuen, MA, s/o Caryle Carter (Hull, England) and Jane Fairburn (housewife, Hull, England); W – 38, nurse, 3rd, b. Ellsworth, d/o Melvin Allard (factory laborer, Whitefield) and Mary Morton (Lyman)

James of Dorchester m. Nettie M. **Barnett** of Dorchester 10/18/1941 in Canaan; H – 39, laborer, b. Methuen, MA, s/o C. A. C. Carter (farmer, England) and J. A. Fairborne (housewife, England); W – 24, homemaker, 2nd, b. E. Harwich, VT, d/o M. E. Salls (farmer, Canada) and M. J. Allen (housewife, Canada)

Richard P. of Dorchester m. Marjorie Priscilla **Martel** of Bridgewater 9/19/1959 in Hebron; H – 27, dozer operator; W – 20, at home

CAYES,
Reginald M. of Plymouth m. Katie Laura **Walker** of Dorchester 6/25/1930 in Dorchester; H - 24, carpenter, b. Plymouth, s/o Edmund E. Cayes (carpenter, Plymouth) and Harriet E. Dexter (housewife, Plymouth); W - 19, at home, b. Dorchester, d/o Isaac D. Walker (farmer, Lowell, MA) and Margaret S. Fairburn (housewife, Yorkshire, England)

CERAVANE,
Joseph Dominic of Dorchester m. Tracy Anne **Radowski** of Dorchester 5/9/1993 in Dorchester; H – s/o William Joseph Ceravone and Nora Ferris; W – d/o Stanislaw Radowski, Jr. and Laura Ann Bebon

CHAMBERLAIN,
Henry H. of Dorchester m. Martha A. **Motts** of Lowell, MA 5/4/1919 in Dorchester; H – 77, farmer, 2nd, b. Augusta, ME, s/o William Chamberlain (farmer, Sidney, ME) and Esther Leighton (school teacher, Mt. Vernon, ME); W – 58, shoe operator, 2nd, b.

Hemingford, Canada, d/o John O. Cornell (farmer, Burlington, VT) and Mary Lavoie (school teacher, St. Edwards, Canada)

CHURCHILL,
Fred A. of Dorchester m. Ester U. **Willey** of Dorchester 10/2/1922 in Fairlee, VT; H - 47, farmer, b. Rowe, MA, s/o Anson Churchill (Kingston) and Anna Cilley (Charlemont, MA); W - 38, housewife, 2nd, b. Colrain, MA, d/o Daniel Cilley and Ida Hathaway

CLARK,
Roy A. of Bridgewater m. Heather E. **Delsart** of Dorchester 4/11/1998

CLOGSTON,
Albert Walter of Dorchester m. Marjorie Violet **Rowley** of Dorchester 7/18/1955 in Rumney; H – 29, trucking, 2nd, b. NH, s/o Walter Lee Clogston and Barbara Pearl Willey; W – 30, housewife, 2nd, b. NH, d/o Lucien Marcel Parris and Violet Goldie Parris

Gerald A. of Dorchester m. Priscilla R. **Downing** of Ashland 8/19/1950 in Wentworth; H – 22, truck driver, b. NH, s/o Walter L. Clogston and Pearl B. Willey; W – 23, teacher, b. NH, d/o Walter A. Downing and Ethel M. Brown

CLOUGH,
Hazen H. of Dorchester m. Louise K. **Wagner** of New York City 1/10/1915 in Dorchester; H – 53, farmer, 2nd, b. Dorchester, s/o Joseph M. Clough (farmer, Gilmanton) and Harriett A. Bickford (housekeeper, Dorchester); W – 45, nurse, 2nd, b. Triest, Austria, d/o George N. Kafga (Schadalt, Hungary) and Hellene M. Wirtz (Loorin, Hungary)

COFFIN,
Daniel C. of Rumney m. Lisa A. **MacDonald** of Dorchester 9/26/1981 in Dorchester; H – s/o Charles Coffin and Marguerite Latulippe; W – d/o Irving MacDonald and Blanche Ashley

Lester W. of Quincy m. Mildred A. **Camp** of Dorchester 5/27/1934 in Canaan; H – 21, farmer, b. Campton, s/o Nathan Coffin (farmer, Quincy) and Mertie E. Wallace (housewife, Quincy); W – 18, at home, b. Boston, MA, d/o Guy E. Camp (farmer, Elmore, VT) and Flossie Camp (housewife, Salem, MA)

COLBURN,

John G. of Dorchester m. Razola P. **Cluff** of Reading, MA 9/25/1918 in Reading, MA; H – 48, farmer, 2nd, b. Hartford, VT, s/o Horace Colburn (farmer, Hartford, VT) and Lucy A. Raymond (housewife, Hartford, VT); W – 34, nurse, b. Lynn, MA, d/o John Parker (boxmaker, Kennebunk, ME) and Henrietta Raddin (housewife, Groton, MA)

COLE,

Arthur M. of Dorchester m. Ila Z. **Quimby** of Dorchester 12/17/1900 in Dorchester; H – 18, farmer, b. Raymond, s/o Albert S. Cole (painter, Wentworth) and F. Eva Prescott (housewife, Epping); W – 18, domestic, b. Dorchester, d/o John Quimby (farmer) and Agnes F. Quimby

COLEMAN,

Charles Henry of Dorchester m. Sherrie Lee **Young** of Dorchester 9/25/1991 in Wentworth; H – s/o Ray Edwin Coleman and Catherine Ruth Smith; W – d/o Richard Melvin Young, Sr. and Pearl Dorothy Comeau

CONKEY,

Albert R. of Dorchester m. Margaret E. **Quimby** of Dorchester 4/15/1967 in Dorchester; H – 50, state employee, s/o Albert S. Conkey and Olive M. Heth; W – 47, at home, d/o Clyde H. Colburn and Florence E. White

Allen J. of Dorchester m. Sharon W. **Zwicker** of Campton 3/27/1986 in Dorchester; H – s/o Raymond Conkey and Pauline Parris; W – d/o Charles Bishop and Marjorie Smith

Daniel Lee of Dorchester m. Dawn Marie **Curran** of Dorchester 4/19/1997

George Chester, II of Dorchester m. Jeanne Marie **Jalbert** of Dorchester 5/3/1990 in Dorchester; H – s/o George Chester Conkey I and Nadine Barrows; W – d/o Ovila G. Jalbert and Cecile Desjarais

COOPER,

Joseph A. of Dorchester m. Eunice C. **Coombs** of Dorchester 5/27/1986 in Dorchester; H – s/o Clarence Cooper and Nina Crocket; W – d/o William Walker and Gladys Powell

COTE,
John Allan of Dorchester m. Nancy Ann **Duval** of Plymouth 3/17/1969 in Plymouth; H – s/o David L. Cote and Ethel P. Joyce; W – d/o Paul Duval and Gladys Reta Marsh

COUTU,
Roger W. of Dorchester m. Catherine L. **Bailey** of Dorchester 8/17/1985 in Dorchester; H – s/o Richard A. Coutu and Sally Bruce; W – d/o Thomas G. Bailey and Lucille Noddin

CUMMINGS,
George William of Warren m. Gloria **Landon** of Dorchester 9/28/1968; H – 50, s/o George Wm. Cummings and Ada Beatrice Davis; W – 41, d/o Lucien M. Parris and Violet G. Parris

CYNOSKI,
Chester Francis of Hartford, CT m. Anne Carole **Hebert** of Hartford, CT 3/14/1964 in Dorchester; H – 20, lab. technician, s/o Leo Francis Cynoski and Josephine Jones Dziedic; W – 18, at home, d/o Paul G. Hebert and Luciel Anna Tardif

DANIELS,
Sargent B. of White River Jct., VT m. Lori A. **Parent** of White River Jct., VT 4/29/1995 in Dorchester; H – s/o Sargent H. Daniels and Marion Blair; W – d/o Raymond P. Parent and Betty Davis

DAVIES,
Henry H. of Dorchester m. Anna L. **Morris** of Dorchester 6/11/1966 in Enfield; H – 76, retired, s/o John H. Davies and Isabelle Matherson; W – 66, retired, d/o George Lintaman and Anna Geary

DAY,
John H. of Bristol m. Cathy L. **Cote** of Dorchester 8/16/1997

deBLOIS,
Romeo R. of Laconia m. Mary J. **Walker** of Dorchester 6/30/1939 in Laconia; H – 28, clerk, b. Laconia, s/o Alphonse J. deBlois (forestry proj't, Canada) and Alice Gelinas (at home, Canada); W – 23, at home, b. Dorchester, d/o Isaac Walker (farmer,

Lawrence, MA) and Margaret Fairborne (at home, Hull, England)

DECATO,
William J. of Dorchester m. Delia B. **Rock** of St. Johnsbury, VT 11/1/1915 in Danville, VT; H – 33, farmer, 2nd, b. Canaan, s/o Joseph J. Decato (farmer, Canaan) and Agnes A. Hill (housewife, Canaan); W – 32, domestic, 2nd, b. St. Johnsbury, VT, d/o Joseph Burnett (farmer, St. Johnsbury, VT) and Exezlia V. Burnett (housewife, St. Johnsbury, VT)

DELSART,
Adolph W. of Dorchester m. Marion E. **McKinley** of Dorchester 11/1/1933 in Warren; H – 38, farmer, b. Lakewood, NJ, s/o Louis A. Delsart (barber, NY) and Elise Wagerman (cook, Germany); W – 25, housewife, b. Warren, d/o Ralph McKinley (laborer, NS) and Susie Whitney (housewife, Groveton)

DENNY,
Clyde Allen of DeFuniak Springs, FL m. Kathleen **Strickland** of Dorchester 8/11/1990 in Dorchester; H – s/o Clyde Allen Denny and Ellara Ingram Denny; W – d/o Robert I. Goode and Jean C. Bagley

DENONCOUR,
Maurice P. of Dorchester m. Valerie G. **Landon** of Dorchester 10/1/1977 in Dorchester; H – s/o Maurice P. Denoncour and Theresa M. Lemire; W – d/o Frederick Landon and Gloria Parris

DINSMORE,
Thomas Walter of Dorchester m. Janice Carol **Clayton** of Dorchester 9/18/1994 in Dorchester; H – s/o Earl T. Dinsmore and Jeanette Maiacjk; W – d/o Milton Boyd Rainey and Julia Carol Chester

DO,
Lam K. of Dorchester m. Susanne M. **Scotti** of Manchester 1/19/2000

DOWNING,
Richard L. of Wentworth m. Elsie K. **Walker** of Dorchester 4/2/1938

in Franklin; H – 28, truck driver, b. Wentworth, s/o Eugene C. Downing (lumberman, Wentworth) and Alice A. Wells (housewife, Wentworth); W – 32, at home, 2nd, b. New York City, d/o Charles A. Krahenbuhl (farmer, Switzerland) and Elizabeth Toth (housewife, Hungary)

DUFORD,
Leo N. of Dorchester m. Estell A. **Durocher** of Dorchester 8/15/1931 in Canaan; H – 26, laborer, b. Suncook, s/o Manual Duford (farmer, Suncook) and Cora Parent (housewife, Suncook); W – 16, at home, b. Holyoke, MA, d/o Alfred Durocher (salesman, Pawtucket, RI) and Clara D. Hill (housewife, Fall River, MA)

EASTMAN,
Clayton Herbert of Dorchester m. Winona Beatrice **Walker** of Alexandria 11/18/1943 in Laconia; H – 40, Army, b. N. Groton, s/o Herbert J. Eastman (lumberman, N. Groton) and Elizabeth Diamond (at home, N. Groton); W – 34, school teacher, d/o Isaac D. Walker (farmer, Lowell, MA) and Margaret Fairburn (at home, Hull, England)

EVANS,
David of Wentworth m. Sharon **Carter** of Dorchester 10/26/1974 in Wentworth; H – s/o Hugh A. Evans and Lillian DeLory; W – d/o Albert Carter and Peggy Hammell

FARNSWORTH,
Shawn P. of Canaan m. Yarrow A. **Jones** of Dorchester 8/3/1996 in Dorchester; H – s/o Henry Farnsworth and Carla Colburn; W – d/o Bruce Jones and Sharon Webb

FARR,
Charles T. of Dalton m. Mary L. **Morse** of Dorchester 4/20/1897; H - 37, cook, b. Dalton, s/o Norman N. Farr (Littleton) and Mary L. Hunter (Littleton); W - 17, housewife, b. Peterboro, d/o George M. Morse (MA) and Sarah J. York (MA, housewife)

FELLOWS,
Joseph E. of Dorchester m. Nellie E. **Handerson** of Dorchester 9/12/1897; H - 22, farmer, b. Dorchester, s/o Leonard S.

Fellows (Dorchester, farmer) and Sarah Bowden (ME, housewife); W - 17, housewife, b. NY, d/o C. H. Handerson (jeweler) and Anna M. Deaton (NY)

FILTEAU,
Donald E. of Dorchester m. Kelley A. **Rourke** of Dorchester 11/21/1998

FINKEL,
Joseph P. of Dorchester m. Anna H. **Feinen** of Dorchester 10/12/1923 in Woodsville; H – 27, machinist, b. Homestead, NJ, s/o Joseph Finkel (painter, Union Hill, NJ) and Christina W'gmann (housewife, Union Hill, NJ); W – 18, housewife, b. Union Hill, NJ, d/o Micheal Feinen (farmer, Hoboken, NJ) and Anna Lantz (housewife, Germany)

FITTS,
John M. of Dorchester m. Etta M. **Martin** of Somerville, MA 5/13/1890 in Somerville; H – 47, merchant, 2nd, b. Dorchester; Thomas J. Fitts (decensual, S. Hampton) and Thankful Moore (Dorchester); W – 22, housework, b. Chelsea, d/o George W. Martin (inventor, NY) and Kate S. Smith (housework, Bath, ME)

FRASER,
Thomas M. of Wentworth m. Grace E. **Morth** of Wentworth 9/3/1977 in Dorchester; H – s/o Thomas M. Fraser and Margaret L. Winnfield; W – d/o Ludwig J. Morth and Leota A. Jonsa

GOLDEN,
Martin of Dorchester m. Delfen **Ford** of Canaan 4/30/1899 in Canaan; H – 32, millman, b. Ireland, s/o John Golden (Ireland) and Margaret Golden (Ireland); W – 18, housework, b. Ashland, d/o Israel Ford (laborer, Dorchester) and Mary Grover (housewife, Dorchester)

GOOD,
Thomas of Dorchester m. Eva J. **Whicher** of Dorchester 10/1/1899 in Dorchester; H – 24, stone cutter, b. Canada, s/o M. J. Good (farmer, Ireland) and Kath. McNally (housewife, Ireland); W – 16, housework, b. Dorchester, d/o Emri S. Whicher (carpenter, Dorchester) and L. A. Willoughby (housewife, Groton)

GOODE,
James Robert of Dorchester m. Suzanne Christine **Campbell** of Dorchester 9/6/1992 in Dorchester; H – s/o Robert I. Goode and Jean C. Bagley; W – d/o Donald F. Campbell and Patricia Ann Wilkins

GOVE,
Ralph Lawrence of Dorchester m. Linda Marion **Kimball** of Dorchester 7/21/1979 in Dorchester; H – s/o Charles L. Gove and Leona Davis; W – d/o Malcolm D. Merrill and Frances E. Willey

Ralph Lawrence of Dorchester m. JoEllen Mary **DiRusso** of Dorchester 4/29/1990 in Dorchester; H – s/o Charles Lawrence Gove and Leona Perley Davis; W – d/o Anthony Joseph Guidi and Norma Lorraine Matarazzo

GRAY,
Bigby L. of Dorchester m. Emma **Tattersall** of Lyme 6/10/1899 in Lyme; H – 37, cook, b. Derby Centre, VT, s/o John Gray (carpenter, Derby Ctr., VT) and Emily Cook (housewife, Derby Ctr., VT); W – 22, housework, b. Lyme, d/o George Tattersall (farmer, Lyme) and Mary Tattersall (housewife, Lyme)

Eric W. of Dorchester m. Lacy G. **Barrow** of Dorchester 7/28/2001

GREENLEAF,
Harold R. of Holderness m. Ruth E. **Hanley** of Dorchester 10/24/1925 in Laconia; H - 28, mechanic, b. Holderness, s/o Horace Greenleaf (farmer, Holderness) and Gertrude Mudget (housewife, Holderness); W - 27, school teacher, b. Lowell, MA, d/o John T. Hanley (farmer, Calais, ME) and Mary Brooks (housewife, Florenceville, NB)

GRIGAS,
Albert P., Jr. of Rumney m. Betty Lou **Latuch** of Dorchester 11/23/1975 in Rumney; H – s/o Albert P. Grigas and Elaine Bouley; W – d/o Joseph Phinney and Sylvia Conkey

HALL,
Henry Lorenzo of Dorchester m. Paula Margaret **Comeau** of Rumney 4/20/1974 in Alexandria; H – s/o Kenneth L. Hall, Sr. and Rosalie Fischer; W – d/o Oliver Comeau and Agnes

Robicheau

HANLEY,
Brad Loren of Dorchester m. Dawn Lee **Higgins** of Dorchester 9/9/1995 in Dorchester; H – s/o Ernest J. Hanley and Priscilla Downing; W – d/o Gary L. Culbertson and Karen A. Leeming

Ernest J. of Dorchester m. Edith R. **Crosby** of Hyde Park, MA 7/22/1926 in Rumney; H – 25, miner, b. Dorchester, s/o John T. Hanley (farmer, Calais, ME) and Mary Brooks (housewife, Florenceville, NB); W – 20, at home, b. Maplewood, MA, d/o John C. Crosby (naval photographer, London, England) and Maud Ethel Cook (housewife, Malden, MA)

Ernest John, Jr. of Dorchester m. Priscilla Reed **Clogston** of Dorchester 12/14/1957 in Wentworth; H – 30, divorced, truck driver; W – 30, divorced, secretary

Frank B. of Dorchester m. Mildred E. **Percey** of Plymouth 5/24/1928 in Plymouth; H – 29, mechanic, b. Dorchester, s/o John T. Hanley (Calais, ME) and Mary E. Brooks (Florenceville, NB); W – 30, clerk, 2nd, b. Ashland, d/o Edward C. Brogan (Ashland) and Mabel J. Jewell (Belmont)

HAZELTON,
Walter of Dorchester m. Frances E. **Willey** of Dorchester 8/30/1930 in Dorchester; H - 23, laborer, b. Dorset, VT, s/o Ralza Hazelton (laborer, Dorset, VT) and Sadie Place (housewife, Chepachet, RI); W - 20, housekeeper, b. Meredith, d/o Joseph Willey (teamster, Hebron) and Eda M. Sanborn (housewife, Cambridge, MA)

Walter, Jr. of Dorchester m. Frances A. **Burnham** of Plymouth 11/20/1948 in White River Jct., VT; H – 17, laborer, b. Orange, s/o Walter Hazelton (Dorset) and Frances E. Willey (Meredith); W – 18, bookkeeper, b. Dorchester, d/o Kirk N. Burnham (Dorchester) and Susie I. Chase (Wentworth)

Walter, Jr. of Dorchester m. Ethel M. **Valia** of Dorchester 12/2/1966 in Hebron; H – 35, lumberman, s/o Walter Hazelton and Frances E. Willey; W – 31, seamstress, d/o Elwin S. Black and Pauline M. Eastman

Walter Francis of Dorchester m. Deborah Ann **Phillips** of Grafton 4/24/1971 in Canaan; H – s/o Walter Hazelton, Jr. and Frances Ann Burnham; W – d/o Stanley W. Phillips and Ruth H. Gleason

HEATH,
Jere J. of Dorchester m. Edith Goldy **Hull** of Dorchester 4/23/1997

HEMEON,
John Ernest m. Lorna Ann **Durgin** 3/29/1958 in Franklin; H – 21, Navy; W – 18, secretary

HESSION,
John W. of Hebron m. Valerie J. **Michaud** of Dorchester 8/4/2001

HIGGINS,
Robert of Stoneham, MA m. M. Magdalene **Yetman** of Stoneham, MA 11/21/1982 in Dorchester; H – s/o James P. Higgins and Ruby Frost; W – d/o David Hall and ----- Kennedy

HINKSON,
Forrest L. of Rumney m. Cheryl A. **Conkey** of Dorchester 10/29/1981 in Campton; H – s/o Forrest Hinkson and Elizabeth Elliot; W – d/o Raymond Conkey and Pauline Landon

HORN,
Kevin Joseph of Laconia m. Melissa Winthrop **Sawyer** of Dorchester 2/29/1992 in Plymouth; H – s/o Georard J. Horn and Yvonne T. Tardif; W – d/o Albion T. Sawyer and Maria Angelica Wulff

HOWLAND,
Harry J. of Dorchester m. Altie J. **Bickford** of Dorchester 1/1/1903 in Dorchester; H – 19, laborer, b. Franconia, s/o Israel Howland (farmer, Bethlehem) and Celestia Howard (housewife, Bethlehem); W – 19, domestic, b. Dorchester, d/o Albert F. Bickford (farmer, Dorchester) and Emma J. Norris (housewife, Dorchester)

HOWLETT,
Orrin D. of Cambridge, MA m. Addie M. **Elliott** of Dorchester 1/16/1890 in Rumney; H – 30, piano reg'r, s/o Enoch J. Howlet (treasurer, Boston, MA) and Ang'le S. Howlet (housework, Greene, ME); W – 22, housework, b. Ellensburgh, NY, d/o J. P. Elliott (farmer, Dorchester) and Malissa M. Sax (housework, Chazy, NY)

JENNINGS,
Rixford Owens of Dorchester m. Jean Barbara **Viglione** of Dorchester 11/23/1974 in Hanover; H – s/o Rixford V. Jennings and Sydney Owens; W – d/o Gaetano Viglione and Camille Gaskins

JESSEMAN,
Walter C. of Dorchester m. Luna A. **Merrill** of Dorchester 5/23/1892 in Dorchester; H – 28, laborer, b. Franconia, s/o James Jesseman (Franconia) and Martha Young (Franconia); W – 16, housemaid, b. Dorchester, d/o John S. Merrill (farmer, Andover) and Emma S. Streeter (Dorchester, housewife)

JOHNSON,
F. M. of Bridgewater m. Elsie M. **Rowen** of Dorchester 3/22/1891 in Campton; H - 28, farmer, b. Grafton, s/o M. H. Johnson (farmer, Campton) and H. M. Elliott (housewife, Rumney); W - 27, housekeeper, b. Springfield, d/o Joshua Rowen (farmer, Wentworth) and Helen Walker (housewife, Scotland)

JONES,
Seth Allen of Dorchester m. Buffi Ann **Santolucito** of Dorchester 10/15/1989; H – s/o Steven Allen Jones and Mary Emily Goodwin; W – d/o Robert Paul Santolucito and Mary Ann Pond

JOSLYN,
Brandon E. of Dorchester m. Sabrina S. **Stone** of Dorchester 6/21/2003

Robert Dale of Dorchester m. Ruth Etta **Moses** of Orford 6/20/1952 in Piermont; H – 23, farming, b. Orient, ME, s/o Bordman L. Joslyn (deceased, Canada) and Ida May Dwyer (housekeeper, Orient, ME; W – 16, at home, b. Haverhill, d/o Perley Moses (laborer, Tunbridge, VT) and Eva May Morey (housekeeper, Bradford, VT)

KEEZER,
George W. of Dorchester m. Mary **York** of Dorchester 9/27/1902 in Dorchester; H – 22, carpenter, b. Haverhill, MA, s/o Daniel H. Keezer (farmer, Kingston) and Luella Keezer (housewife, Saco, ME); W – 17, domestic, b. Pittsfield, d/o Wells G. York (Gilmanton) and Lizzie Harnden

KENNEDY,
Dale David of Dorchester m. Amanda Marie **Kennett** of Dorchester 8/12/1989 in Dorchester; H – s/o Donald T. Kennedy and Thelma S. Therrien; W – d/o Andrew William Kennett and Anne Beverly Crane

KIMBALL,
Clyde C. of Dorchester m. Linda M. **Merrill** of Dorchester 3/14/1970 in Newmarket; H – s/o Walter E. Kimball, Jr. and Mary E. Bean; W – d/o Malcolm D. Merrill and Frances E. Willey

KRAFT,
Timothy of Canaan m. Nadine I. **Conkey** of Dorchester 9/21/1996 in Dorchester; W – d/o George C. Conkey and Nadine A. Conkey

KRAMER,
William C. of Dorchester m. Marion A. **Plant** of Dorchester 7/13/2003
William C., Jr. of Dorchester m. Melanie F. **Smith** of Dorchester 10/15/1987 in Dorchester; H – s/o William C. Kramer, Sr. and Joyce R. Cutting; W – d/o Harold B. Smith and Edith E. Roy

LACHANCE,
Edgar A., Jr. of Dorchester m. Mary A. **Duval** of Windsor, VT 8/26/1961 in Plymouth; H – 26, student; W – 24, secretary

LAHUE,
Dominic S. of Warren m. Annie B. **Moses** of Dorchester 8/17/1895 in Wentworth; H – 44, job work, b. Canada, s/o D. Lahue (trader, California) and Julia Smith (housework, Canada); W – 29, housework, b. WI, d/o John S. Merrill (farmer, Andover) and Emma Streeter (housewife, Dorchester)

LAMBERT,
Tod W. of Dorchester m. Kathleen M. **Williams** of Dorchester 8/21/1982 in Dorchester; H – s/o Fred C. Lambert and Marilyn Brunings; W – d/o Alexander Lennox and Margaret M. Sime

LAMPHERE,
Russell J. of Dorchester m. Brenda L. **Wanamaker** of Dorchester 10/12/2002

LAMY,
Richard P. of Dorchester m. Alice M. **Gallagher** of Dorchester 7/11/1998

LANCASTER,
Mark Allen of Hanover m. Beverly Sue **Butcher** of Dorchester 8/12/1978 in Hanover; H – s/o William Lancaster and ----- Dufault; W – d/o Frederick A. Butcher and Rita Dulac

LANDRY,
Michael Anthony of Dorchester m. Linda Marion **Gove** of Dorchester 11/22/1991; H – s/o Joseph Aquila Landry and Georgia Lillian Johnson; W – d/o Malcolm D. Merrill and Frances E. Willey

LAPHAM,
Thomas W., Jr. of NY m. Rita Kouffman **Johnson** of RI 6/27/1981 in Dorchester; H – s/o Thomas W. Lapham and Grace W. Chapman; W – d/o Abraham Kouffman and Hilda Priest

LATUCH,
Joseph Andrew of Hill m. Sylvia Margaret **Conkey** of Hill 12/16/1967 in Dorchester; H – 32, pressman, s/o Roy Latuch and Verona Greenleaf; W – 27, at home, d/o Albert R. Conkey and Irene L. Avery

LEGG,
John Jay Graydon of Dorchester m. Cheryl Ann **Toro** of Dorchester 9/9/1989; H – s/o John Graydon Legg and Joan Smith; W – d/o Emanuel F. Toro and Helen A. Denoncour

LINN,
Robert Aylward of S. Strafford, VT m. Justine Carol **Delsart** of Dorchester 5/21/1964 in Dorchester; H – US Navy, s/o John Murry Linn and Abbie Irene Aylward; W – 20, at home, d/o Adolph W. Delsart and Marion E. McKinley

LIZOTTE,
David B. of Concord m. Candy L. **Carter** of Concord 9/3/1983 in Dorchester; H – s/o Camille Lizotte and Marion Corliss; W – d/o Albert Carter and Peggy Hammel

LOUNGE,
Wayne F. of Brockton, MA m. Rita M. **McCarthy** of Weymouth, MA 4/23/1967 in Dorchester; H – 21, electrician, s/o David F. Lounge and Claire N. Dale; W – 18, clerk, d/o Joseph A. McCarthy and Martha B. Bicknell

MACDONALD,
Irving A. m. Blanche A. **Ashley** 1/18/1958 in Dorchester; H – 24, civil engineer; W – 23, registered nurse

MACKENZIE,
Daniel A. of Dorchester m. Hazel P. **Galoway** of Warwick, RI 4/17/1965 in Dorchester; H – 61, stock man, s/o Daniel MacKenzie and Sarah MacKenzie; W – 60, housewife, d/o Guy Andrews and Eva Allen

MAHONEY,
Edward D. of Dorchester m. Valira D. **Noel** of Dorchester 3/17/2000

MALTAIS,
Joseph W. of Laconia m. Eunice C. **Hill** of Dorchester 6/21/1941 in Meredith; H – 26, sanding skiis, b. Concord, s/o J. G. Maltais (farmer) and Annie Mahaire (at home, Suncook); W – 18, housework, b. Charleston, VT, d/o James E. Hill (farmer, Canada) and Clara Beaudeauett (at home, Holyoke, MA)

MARTIN,
Everett E. of Providence, RI m. Margaret M. C. **Bourdon** of Providence, RI 11/22/1919 in Enfield; H – 33, mechanic, b. Providence, RI, s/o Frederick S. Martin (machinist, Derby Line, VT) and Lou Hill (housewife, Bellemere, KY); W – 18, elevator operator, b. Providence, RI, d/o Alfred Bourbon (joiner, Quebec, Canada) and Margaret Harrigan (housewife, Providence, RI)
Frank of Dorchester m. Maggie J. **Black** of Dorchester 9/12/1906 in Dorchester; H - 56, farmer, 2nd, b. Danbury, s/o Richard F. Martin (Grafton, farmer) and Maria Kimball (Grafton, housewife); W - 51, housewife, 3rd, b. North Ireland, d/o Christopher Kenedy (loom-fixer)and Mary J. Kenedy (Ireland, housewife)

MEARNS,
    James of Dorchester m. Madeline R. **Dickey** of Manchester 4/29/1918 in Plymouth; H – 34, farmer, b. Omerbeane, Ireland, s/o James Mearns (farmer, Ohoghil, Ireland) and Ann Casey (housewife, Ohoghil, Ireland); W – 32, housewife, b. Lawrence, MA, d/o Herbert C. Dickey (weaver, W. Topsham, VT) and Ellen W. Parker (weaver, Clarkesville)

MERRILL,
    Bernard L. of Dorchester m. Lily B. **Nichols** of Anoka, MN 3/10/1892 in Dorchester; H – 23, machinist, b. Dorchester, s/o John S. Merrill (farmer, Andover) and Emma Streeter (housewife, Dorchester); W – 20, housemaid, b. Wentworth, d/o Samuel Nichols (wheelwright, Concord) and Maud A. Mason (housewife, Lyme)
    Henry M. of Dorchester m. Blanche C. **Kidder** of Groton 3/8/1893 in Rumney; H – 24, farmer, b. Dorchester, s/o Hiram Merrill (farmer, Groton) and Louisa Follansbee (housewife, Danbury); W – 16, housework, b. Groton, d/o Mark B. Kidder (farmer, Groton) and Belinda Staples (housewife, Exeter)
    Henry M. of Dorchester m. Helen M. **Jewell** of Lyme 12/14/1898; H – 30, farmer, b. Dorchester, s/o Hiram Merrill (farmer, Groton) and S. L. Follansbee (housewife, Danbury); W – 20, housewife, b. Lyme, d/o John A. Jewell (farmer, Hebron) and Inda E. Welch (housewife, Woodstock, VT)
    Leon H. of Dorchester m. Irene K. **Chamberlain** of W. Bridgewater, MA 1/6/1915 in W. Bridgewater, MA; H – 21, farmer, b. Dorchester, s/o Henry M. Merrill (farmer, Dorchester) and Blanchie Kidder (housewife, Groton); W – 21, clerk, b. Brockton, MA, d/o Ernest Chamberlin (Augusta, ME) and Sarah M. George (nurse, Frederickt'n, MS)
    Malcolm D. of Dorchester m. Frances **Hazelton** of Dorchester 6/29/1935 in White River Jct., VT; H – 26, carpenter, b. Grantham, s/o Wilbur Merrill (NB) and Helen Dunbar (Grantham); W – 25, 2nd, divorced, b. Meredith, d/o Joseph Willey (Meredith) and Eda Sanborn (Cambridge, MA)
    Wilbur of Dorchester m. Phebe T. **Stevens** of Orange 10/8/1915 in Plymouth; H – 44, farmer, 3rd, b. NB, s/o William Merrill (ship carpenter, NB) and Rebecca Malcolm (housewife, NB); W – 43, nurse, 2nd, b. NS, d/o William Redding (teacher, NS) and Mary M. Caldwell (housewife, NS)

MINER,
James M. m. Elizabeth F. **Kendrick** of Dorchester 7/5/1887 in Dorchester; H - 69, farmer, b. Canaan, s/o Elijah Miner; W - 63, housework

MONROE,
Beryl C. of Plymouth m. Hazel L. **Allen** of Plymouth 12/6/1941 in Rumney; H – 22, truck driver, b. W. Canaan, s/o E. R. Monroe (blacksmith, Canaan) and A. O. Farrington (housewife, Canaan); W – 18, millhand, b. Fairlee, VT, d/o M. E. Allen (clerk, Fairlee, VT) and M. O. Short (millhand, Warren)

MORRISON,
Michael of Dorchester m. Jennie **Melanson** of Dorchester 6/4/1908 in Enfield; H – 26, laborer, b. S. Boston, MA, s/o Roderick Morrison (laborer, NS) and Emphenia McJecasa (domestic, Canada); W – 18, domestic, b. Wentworth, d/o Joseph Melanson (laborer, Canada) and Delia Grover (domestic, Canada)

MOSES,
Morton Maurice of Dorchester m. Ella Vera **Ewens** of New Hampton 9/19/1948 in New Hampton; H – 25, lumberman, b. Dorchester, s/o William E. Moses (lumberman, Malone, NY) and Edith L. Goss (housewife, Dorchester); W – 15, at home, b. New Hampton, d/o Henry A. Ewens (farmer, Orford, PQ) and Margaret M. Hughes (housekeeper, Liverpool, England)

MURDOCK,
John Richard of Dorchester m. Tammy Mari **Smith** of Dorchester 9/28/1991 in Wentworth; H – s/o Richard William Murdock and Beverly Louise Richardson; W – d/o Jane Ann Jantti

NGANGA,
Paul K. of Everett, MA m. Joevana L. **Gilbert** of Dorchester 8/4/2001

NICKERSON,
Richard of Sunapee m. Alice W. **Ashley** of Dorchester 6/15/1935 in Dorchester; H – 21, barber, b. Sunapee, s/o Orrin Nickerson (laborer, Bangor, ME) and Rose Hamel (housewife, Sunapee); W – 28, school teacher, b. Dorchester, d/o Herbert H. Ashley

(farmer, PEI) and Annie G. Pollard (housewife, PEI)

NICOL,
William B. of Dorchester m. Mary A. **Libby** of Warren 6/17/1899 in Laconia; H – 31, blacksmith, b. NB, s/o John Nicol (farmer, NB) and Bertha Beck (housewife, Germany); W – 19, domestic, b. Warren, d/o Ira N. Libby (carpenter, Warren) and Lucia Whiteman (housewife, Warren)

NILES,
Howard C. of Dorchester m. Emeline M. **Conkey** of Dorchester 4/15/1967 in Dorchester; H – 30, supervisor, s/o Lawton A. Niles and Dorothy L. Hackett; W – 21, machine operator, d/o Albert R. Conkey and Irene L. Avery

O'KEEFE,
James of Dorchester m. Elizabeth H. **Murray** of Dorchester, MA 9/18/1906 in Woodsville; H - 25, farmer, b. Boston, MA, s/o John O'Keefe (Cork, Ireland, tailor) and Katherine Flaherty (Cork, Ireland, housewife); W - 28, domestic, b. Beverly, MA, d/o True W. Murray (Woburn, MA, farmer) and Mary A. Shea (Ireland, housewife)

PARKER,
Amos G. of Dorchester m. Sylvania M. **Cheney** of Bristol 8/1/1908 in Lisbon; H – 17, spinner, b. Dorchester, s/o John C. Parker (farmer, Sutton) and Annie S. Wescott (domestic, Dorchester); W – 23, weaver, b. Bristol, d/o Henry D. Cheney (miller, Bristol) and Sarah Cheney (housewife, Meredith)
Christopher Martin of Dorchester m. Beth Joan **McGilvray** of Sea Cliff, NY 8/6/1994 in Dorchester; H – s/o Valentine F. Parker and Judith Ann Rasmussen; W – d/o James McGilvray and Joan Norma Hess
Stev Y. of Huntington, NY m. Cindy Lee **Turke** of Traverse City, MI 4/15/1983 in Dorchester; H – s/o Valentine F. Parker and Judith Rasmussen; W – d/o Walter Turke, MD and Rosemarie Longsfeld

PARRIS,
Brian Fletcher of Groton m. Marjorie Ann **Spead** of Dorchester 9/19/1959 in Dorchester; H – 24, truck driver; W – 19, at home

PAYNE,
Adrian J. of Somerville, MA m. Anne M. **Melanson** of Dorchester 7/21/1984 in Dorchester; H – s/o George Payne and Margaret Fairhurst; W – d/o Henry L. Melanson and Alice E. Krim

POITRAS,
Clarence L., Jr. of Dorchester m. Mernie M. **Lemay** of Dorchester 4/5/1987 in Dorchester; H – s/o Clarence L. Poitras, Sr. and Maxine I. Conkey; W – d/o Donald Newhall and Mabel Chadwick

PRATT,
George H. of Wakefield, MA m. Paula A. **Belair** of Wakefield, MA 10/24/1986 in Dorchester; H – s/o George H. Pratt, Jr. and Alice McCarty; W – d/o Jean R. Belair and Marima J. Straley

QUIMBY,
Custer of Dorchester m. Bertha B. **Parker** of W. Rumney 5/1/1907 in Dorchester; H – 26, farmer, b. Dorchester, s/o John Quimby (farmer) and Frank Kenson (Bedford); W – 20, domestic, b. Dorchester, d/o John C. Parker (farmer) and Annie Wescott (housewife, NY)
John of Dorchester m. Marion J. **Mortensen** of Groton 9/12/1942 in Plymouth; H – 64, farmer, b. Dorchester, s/o John Quimby (farmer, Manchester) and Agnes F. Kinsen (housewife, Manchester); W – 45, cook, divorced, b. W. Campton, d/o Joseph M. Willey (retired, W. Thornton) and Eda M. Sanborn (housewife, Cambridge, MA)
Roger Custer of Dorchester m. June Caroline **Weeks** of Warren 2/27/1938 in Warren; H – 20, laborer, b. Dorchester, s/o Custer Quimby (lumberman, Dorchester) and Bertha Parker (housewife, Dorchester); W – 18, servant, b. Rumney, d/o Vallie J. Weeks (lumberman, Warren) and Lillian M. Dennis (housewife, Boscawen)
Ronald Stanley of Dorchester m. Marjorie Frances **Cronin** of Plymouth 11/18/1960 in Rumney; H – 20, doctor's aid; W – 18, at home

RAYMOND,
Guy T. of Merrimack m. Linda L. **Nadeau** of Merrimack 3/6/1982 in Dorchester; H – s/o Tracy Raymond and Hilda French; W – d/o

Robert Fryer and Carolyn Barker

RAYNOR,
Albert F. of Canaan m. Rose Geeb **Jerfie** of Dorchester 10/17/1936 in Enfield; H – 29, farmer, b. Canaan, s/o Robert Raynor (farmer, England) and Susan Chase (housewife, ME); W – 28, at home, 2nd, divorced, b. NY, d/o Joseph Geeb (machinist, Hungary) and Sarah Geeb (housewife, Hungary)

REED,
Caddie C. of Dorchester m. Annie C. **Parker** of Dorchester 2/7/1898; H – 24, farmer, b. Dorchester, s/o Joseph Reed (farmer, Dorchester) and Liza M. Merrill (housewife, Groton); W – 27, housewife, b. NY, d/o Edwin Wescott (laborer) and ----- Wallace (housewife, unknown)
Robin E. of Rumney m. Lori A. **Mayer** of Dorchester 12/19/1981 in Plymouth; H – s/o Raymond Reed and Josephine White; W – d/o Laurent Mayer and Mildred Greenia

REYNOLDS,
David William of Dorchester m. Dianne M. **Henry** of Dorchester 8/12/1989 in Dorchester; H – s/o Kenneth William Reynolds and Ruth May Morse; W – d/o Donald T. Kennedy and Thelma S. Therrien
Elwyn Kenneth of Lebanon m. Patricia Ann **Delsart** of Dorchester 8/5/1962 in Dorchester; H – 19, Marine Corps; W – 23, typist

RICHARDSON,
Chris. of Canaan m. Annie M. **Greenwood** of Dorchester 6/21/1921 in Canaan; H – 30, lumberman, b. Mineville, NY, s/o Chris. Richardson (farmer, Mineville, NY) and Louise Miller (Mineville, NY); W – 16, b. Manchester, d/o Antoine Greenwood (lumber, Sherbrooke, PQ) and Tebe Carrier (Ham Sud, Canada)

ROBINSON,
Earl J. of Dorchester m. Viola B. **Downing** of W. Rumney 11/7/1904 in Dorchester; H – 25, farmer, b. Dorchester, s/o Nellie J. Robinson (domestic, Ashland); W – 19, school teacher, b. W. Rumney, d/o Charles F. Downing (farmer, Meredith) and Bell D. Wells (housewife, Canaan)

ROLLINS,
Stuart K. of Dorchester m. Nadine I. **Conkey** of Dorchester 2/24/2001

ROUSSEAU,
Clarence W. of Dorchester m. Vera M. **Clough** of Wentworth 8/12/1933 in Wentworth; H – 21, laborer, b. Grafton, s/o Arthur D. Rousseau (farmer, Canada) and Eliza Busson (housekeeper, Fitchburg, MA); W – 19, housekeeper, b. Wentworth, d/o Omar Clough (mechanic, VT) and Ada True (housewife, Orange)

ROWEN,
George W. of Dorchester m. Maud M. **Buck** of Dorchester 3/1/1887 in Dorchester; H - 20, farmer, b. Dorchester, s/o W. W. Rowen (farmer, Wentworth); W - 17, housework, b. PQ, d/o William Buck (PQ)
George W. of Dorchester m. Leona M. **Quimby** of Dorchester 5/21/1898; H – 31, farmer, b. Dorchester, s/o Warren W. Rowen (farmer, Wentworth) and Elvira S. Wicher (housewife, Wentworth); W – 22, housewife, b. Dorchester, d/o John Quimby (farmer) and Agnes F. Quimby (housewife)

RYEA,
Carl C. of Dorchester m. Georgianna G. **Loupis** of Enfield 4/28/1941 in Enfield; H – 22, mill employee, b. Sheldon Springs, VT, s/o M. C. Ryea (farmer, Ryegate, VT) and V. M. Prine (at home, E. Highgate, VT); W – 17, at home, b. Enfield, d/o G. G. Loupis (restaurant m., Greece) and B. E. Follansbee (housewife, Enfield)

ST. GEORGE,
Arthur F. of Dorchester m. Jeanette E. **Wellman** of Dorchester 7/16/1988 in Dorchester; H – s/o Arthur N. St. George and Mary Pleasure; W – d/o Alfred M. Wallace and Beatrice E. Wood

ST. PIERRE,
Andre of Hanover m. Laura **Vigneault** of Somersworth 7/26/1903 in Somersworth; H – 28, farmer, b. Ossipee Ctr., s/o Andre St. Pierre (farmer, Canada) and Eleocadie Gaudette (housewife, Canada); W – 21, dressmaker, b. Ossipee Ctr., d/o Norbert

Vigneault (shoemaker, Canada) and Rosie Marchand (housewife, Canada)

SANBORN,
Gene of Dorchester m. Cheryl Lynn **Carter** of Dorchester 12/9/1980 in Salisbury; H – s/o Eugene Sanborn and Elsie Barrell; W – d/o Richard P. Carter and Marjorie Martell

SCHMIDL,
Joseph of Hollis m. Maryann **Oakley** of Dorchester 6/20/1999

SEARS,
Raymond L. of Dorchester m. Abbie E. **Stewart** of Dorchester 11/14/1936 in Dorchester; H – 28, truck driver, b. W. Moreland, s/o William L. Sears (mill hand, Ludlow, VT) and Bernice E. Graves (housewife, Mt. Holly, VT); W – 16, at home, b. Newry, ME, d/o Daniel T. Stewart (lumberjack, Bath, ME) and Izeeta M. Ferrin (housewife, Errol)

SKIPPER,
Paul E. of Dorchester m. Janet M. **Kummer** of Dorchester 2/14/1997

SOMERS,
Patrick J. of Dorchester m. Susan A. **Moreau** of Dorchester 12/14/2002

SOUCY,
Louis of Canaan m. Alice **Rousseau** of Dorchester 3/26/1936 in Dorchester; H – 25, cook, b. Canada, s/o David Soucy (deceased, Canada) and Mary Maillouix (housewife, Canada); W – 28, at home, b. Fitchburg, MA, d/o Arthur Rousseau (farmer, Canada) and Eliza Brissin (housewife, Fitchburg, MA)

SPEAD,
Irving James m. Virginia Alice **Stone** 10/11/1958 in Plymouth; H – 21, Air Force; W – 22, Air Force
James A. of Dorchester m. Virginia D. **Harriman** of Rumney 3/14/1970 in Conway; H – s/o James V. Spead and Rose Champagne; W – d/o Asa Harriman and Laura E. Hardy

STEVENS,
Joseph O. of Dorchester m. Yevonne R. **Rosseau** of Dorchester 2/13/1928 in Canaan; H – 18, laborer, b. Groton, s/o Samuel D. Stevens (carpenter, Dorchester) and Ellie M. Braley (housewife, Groton); W – 17, at home, b. Fitchburg, MA, d/o Arthur D. Rosseau (farmer, Canada) and Eliza Brisson (housewife, Fitchburg, MA)

STEWART,
James S. of Dorchester m. Lena D. **Morin** of Enfield 1/2/1937 in White River Jct., VT; H – 19, laborer, b. Errol, s/o Daniel Stewart (lumberjack, Bath, ME) and Izetta Ferrin (housewife, Errol); W – 16, at home, b. Lawrence, MA, d/o Peter Morin (mill hand, E. Jaffrey) and Celia Bernard (housewife, Enfield)

TARR,
Herbert W. of Dorchester m. Marion B. **Ryea** of Dorchester 6/15/1939 in Plymouth; H – 22, farmer, b. Richmond, ME, s/o Wilbur S. Tarr (farmer, Richfield, ME) and Haddie M. Morrison (housewife, Webster, ME); W – 18, at home, b. Plymouth, d/o Marshall C. Ryea (farmer, E. Highgate, VT) and Violet M. Prisne (housewife, Enosburg, ME)

TAYLOR,
Frank Gilbert of Penacook m. Lillian Aletta **Ward** of Penacook 10/11/1946 in Canaan; H – 34, mechanic, b. Concord, s/o H. Oscar Taylor (machinist, Concord) and Annie Pearl Colby (housewife, Concord); W – 18, housekeeper, b. Concord, d/o George Ward (mechanic, Saratoga Springs, NY) and Alice Delia Rousseau (housekeeper, Fitchburg, MA)
Zachary G. of Dorchester m. Grace M. **Sanborn** of Wentworth 8/1/1891 in Wentworth; H - 27, farmer, b. Orange, s/o John Taylor (farmer, England) and Clarisa Stevens (housekeeper, Grafton); W - 19, housekeeper, b. Boston, MA

TENNEY,
Harry Douglas of Dracut, MA m. Linda Jean **Kincade** of Dracut, MA 4/9/1978 in Dorchester; H – s/o Donald Tenney and Eleanor Hayes; W – d/o Raymond Kryzak and Jean McLain

THAYER,
William F., Jr. of Dorchester m. Suzanne **Blydenstien** of Dorchester 7/23/1969 in Dorchester; H – s/o William F. Thayer and Allene Okmstrand; W – d/o William L. Baughium and Henriette Bonner

THIBODEAU,
Brian C. of Dorchester m. Wendy J. **Dubreuil** of Dorchester 7/1/2000

Donald Charles of Rumney m. Geri Lynn **Landon** of Dorchester 4/25/1974 in Rumney; H – s/o Donald E. Thibodeau and Marie Picknell; W – d/o Fred Landon and Gloria Parris

TIBBETTS,
Harold Dana of Dorchester m. Carrie Josephine **O'Sullivan** of Dorchester 10/11/1946 in Orford; H – 49, laborer, b. Bridgewater, MA, s/o Dana Tibbetts (farmer, Palermo, ME) and Caroline Allen (nurse, NS); W – 39, teacher, b. Orford, d/o Phillip L. Bean (farmer, Orford) and Blanche Burnham (housewife, Dorchester)

TOUTAINT,
Armand W. of Belmont m. Ann S. **Havenhill** of Dorchester 2/29/2000

TUTTLE,
Griffin Lawton of Wentworth m. Hazel Mae **Delsart** of Dorchester 6/29/1957 in Dorchester; H – 24, divorced, woodworker; W – 20, secretary

VALETTE,
Pierre Alexis of Newton, MA m. Hilary Selden **Illick** of Dorchester 9/2/1990 in Dorchester; H – s/o Jean-Paul Valette and Rebecca Marie Loose; W – d/o Christopher David Illick and Susan Selden Dunbar

WALDRON,
C. P. of Dorchester m. Nettie A. **Lee** of Wentworth 11/4/1899 in Wentworth; H – 32, carpenter, b. Hebron, s/o Orren H. Waldron (farmer, Orford) and Maria C. Clark (housewife, Dorchester); W – 32, domestic, b. Andover, d/o Herbert B. Lee (farmer, Fitchburg, MA) and Esther H. Smith (housewife, Fitchburg, MA)

Clarence P. of Dorchester m. Eva G. **Wilkins** of Boston, MA 11/20/1913 in Ashland; H – 46, carpenter, 2nd, b. Hebron, s/o Orrin H. Waldron (farmer, Orford) and Maria C. Clark (housewife, Dorchester); W – 45, b. Boston, MA, d/o George B. Wilkins (iron moulder, Peterboro) and Christina R. Hinkson (housewife, Brunswick, ME)

Fred G. of Dorchester m. Georgie **Brayley** of Groton 11/9/1921 in Rumney; H – 44, farmer, b. Wentworth, s/o Orrin Waldron (Dorchester) and Maria Clark (Dorchester); W – 19, b. Groton, d/o Ormond Brayley (Danbury) and Ella Taylor (Orange)

WALKER,
Harold of Dorchester m. Elsie L. **Krahenbuhl** of Dorchester 6/28/1925 in Dorchester; H - 24, farmer, b. Lawrence, MA, s/o Isaac Walker (farmer, Lowell, MA) and Margrett Fairburn (housewife, Hull, England); W - 20, housewife, b. New York City, d/o Charles Krahenbuhl (baker, Switzerland) and Elizabeth Toth (housewife, Hungary)

Harold of Dorchester m. Nella M. **Higgins** of Wentworth 3/12/1938 in Plymouth; H – 37, lumberman, 2nd, b. Lawrence, MA, s/o Isaac D. Walker (farmer, Lowell, MA) and Margaret Fairburn (at home, Hull, England); W – 21, at home, 2nd, b. Glover, VT, d/o Harold F. Higgins (farmer, Kingman, ME) and Melinda A. Willey (at home, Greensboro, VT)

Larry Harold m. Martha Lorraine **Phinney** 6/25/1958 in Hebron; H – 20, press operator; W – 20, at home

WARDWELL,
Ernest E. of Dorchester m. Marion V. **Richardson** of Dorchester 11/18/1928 in Rumney; H – 40, farmer, 3rd, b. Woburn, MA, s/o Clarence J. Wardwell (shoe maker, Lewiston, ME) and Hariett Chase (housewife); W – 22, housekeeper, 2nd, b. Woonsocket, RI, d/o George L. Dowry (electrician, Woonsocket, RI) and Emma F. Holbrook (housewife, Woonsocket, RI)

WEBSTER,
Phillip Robert of Dorchester m. Shelley Anne **Newhall** of Dorchester 4/28/1990 in Bridgewater; H – s/o Phillip A. Webster and Phillis Davies; W – d/o Frederick D. Newhall and Vivian C. Newhall

WHITCHER,
Lester A. of Dorchester m. Florence E. **Thibodeau** of Plymouth 10/23/1909 in Dorchester; H - 19, peg mill employee, b. Dorchester, s/o Emri S. Whitcher (Dorchester, carpenter) and Lydia A. Willoughby (Groton, housewife); W - 18, peg mill employee, b. Plymouth, d/o Solon Thibodeau (Canada, brick maker) and Eva G. Bacon (Canada, housewife)

WICHER,
Samuel H. of Dorchester m. Clara J. **Bushway** of Dorchester 5/15/1898; H – 45, farmer, b. Wentworth, s/o Reuben Wicher (farmer, Wentworth) and Rebecca Foster (housewife, Wentworth); W – 25, housewife, b. Rumney, d/o Moody Blake (farmer, Rumney) and Lydia Elliott (housewife, Rumney)

WILLEY,
Edgar C. of Dorchester m. Mildred **Clogston** of Dorchester 7/15/1929 in Wentworth; H – 25, garage man, b. Farmington, MA, s/o Almond Willey (shoe maker, New Durham) and Ester Cilley (housewife, Colerain, MA); W – 16, housekeeper, b. Bradford, VT, d/o William Clogston (mill man) and Ada Patch (housewife, Lyme)

WILLIAMS,
Gordon C., Jr. of Amesbury, MA m. Kathleen M. **Lennox** of Key West, FL 7/1/1967 in Plymouth; H – 25, student, s/o Gordon C. Williams and Ruby L. Lees; W – 22, student, d/o Alexander Lennox, Jr. and Margaret M. Sime

WILSON,
Fred G. of Dorchester m. Ella **Dodge** of Canaan 12/22/1905 in Canaan; H – 27, farmer, b. Lowell, MA, s/o C. H. Wilson (farmer, Chazy, NY) and Jessie A. Weeks (housewife, Rouses Point, NY); W – 18, domestic, b. Canaan, d/o Elmore Dodge (farmer, Francestown) and Hattie Brown (housewife, Lawrence, MA)

WOOD,
Jamie Scott of Francestown m. Jessica Mae **Andrews** of Dorchester 7/19/1997

WRIGHT,
Ernest C. of Dana, IL m. Jennie **Campbell** of Dorchester 10/24/1898; H – 28, farmer, b. Dana, IL, s/o George W. Wright (farmer, OH) and Mary C. Wright (housewife, OH); W – 23, housewife, b. Scotland, d/o unknown (Scotland)

YETMAN,
David M. of Dorchester m. Karen Marie **Roland** of Dorchester 4/3/1988 in Dorchester; H – s/o William F. Yetman and Mary M. Hall; W – d/o Paul J. Roland and Claire Quinn

YOUNG,
Ira Morris of Dorchester m. Evelyn Priscilla **Watkins** of Dorchester 11/21/1971 in Thetford, VT; H – s/o Stanley C. Young and Abie L. Moses; W – d/o Richard W. Watkins and Priscilla E. Ordway
Ralph L. of Dorchester m. Elaine A. **Roy** of Wentworth 6/28/1968 in Wentworth; H – 25, s/o Stanley Young and Alice Moses; W – 20, d/o George Roy and Mamie Hillard

YOUNGMAN,
Burgess M. of Dorchester m. Marrinette **Hall** of Rumney 1/22/1901 in Rumney; H – 29, farmer, b. Dorchester, s/o Wells C. Youngman (farmer, Rumney) and Mary McManes (housewife, Ireland); W – 28, domestic, b. Rumney, d/o Burgess A. Hall (farmer, Rumney) and Marrinett Hardy (housewife, Manchester)

Adams, Janith L. – Bennett, Clarence P.
Aguirre, Olga T. (Valencia) – Bean, Roger B.
Allen, Hazel L. – Monroe, Beryl C.
Andrews, Jessica Mae – Wood, Jamie Scott
Ashley, Alice W. – Nickerson, Richard
Ashley, Blanche A. – MacDonald, Irving A.
Ashley, Elizabeth P. – Bickford, Clarence E.
Ashley, Jean Ellen – Arano, Francis Dominic
Ashley, Mary Josephine – Boyajian, Harold Hrant
Ashley, Nancy Carolyn – Bryne, Harry Thomas

Bailey, Catherine L. – Coutu, Robert W.
Barrow, Lacy G. – Gray, Eric W.
Bean, Phyllis A. – Ashley, Herbert A.
Belair, Paula A. – Pratt, George H.
Bickford, Altie J. – Howland, Harry J.
Black, Maggie J. (Kenedy) - Martin, Frank
Blydenstien, Suzanne (Baughium) – Thayer, William F., Jr.
Bood, Renee Frances – Belair, James Ross
Bourdon, Margaret M. C. – Martin, Everett E.
Braylety, Georgie – Waldron, Fred G.
Buck, Maud M. - Rowen, George W.
Burnett, Nettie M. (Salls) – Carter, James
Burnett, Roberta – Carr, Frank J.
Burnham, Frances A. – Hazelton, Walter, Jr.
Bushway, Carrie C. (Blake) – Wicher, Samuel H.
Butcher, Audrey A. – Carr, Larry P.
Butcher, Beverly Sue – Lancaster, Mark Allen

Camp, Mildred A. – Coffin, Lester W.
Campbell, Jennie – Wright, Ernest C.
Campbell, Suzanne Christine – Goode, James Robert
Carter, Candy L. – Lizotte, David B.
Carter, Cheryl Lynn – Sanborn, Gene
Carter, Sharon – Evans, David
Chamberlain, Irene K. – Merrill, Leon H.
Chase, Susie Irene – Burnham, Kirk N. Y.
Cheney, Sylvania M. – Parker, Amos G.
Clark, Agnes D. (Remick) - Annis, Edwin W.
Clayton, Janice Carol (Rainey) – Dinsmore, Thomas Walter
Clogston, Mildred – Willey, Edgar C.

Clogston, Priscilla Reed – Hanley, Ernest John, Jr.
Clough, Vera M. – Rousseau, Clarence W.
Cluff, Razola P. (Parker) – Colburn, John G.
Comeau, Paula Margaret – Hall, Henry Lorenzo
Conkey, Cheryl A. – Hinkson, Forrest L.
Conkey, Emeline M. – Niles, Howard C.
Conkey, Nadine I. – Kraft, Timothy
Conkey, Nadine I. – Rollins, Stuart K.
Conkey, Sylvia Margaret – Latuch, Joseph Andrew
Coombs, Eunice C. (Walker) – Cooper, Joseph A.
Cote, Cathy L. – Day, John H.
Cronin, Marjorie Frances – Quimby, Ronald Stanley
Crosby, Edith R. – Hanley, Ernest J.
Curran, Dawn Marie – Conkey, Daniel Lee

Delsart, Amanda J. – Burke, Ryan L.
Delsart, Hazel Mae – Tuttle, Griffin Lawton
Delsart, Heather E. – Clark, Roy A.
Delsart, Justine Carol – Linn, Robert Aylward
Delsart, Patricia Ann – Reynolds, Elwyn Kenneth
DeWeese, Billie June – Brown, Walter H., Jr.
Dickey, Madeline R. – Mearns, James
DiRusso, JoEllen Mary (Guidi) – Gove, Ralph Lawrence
Dodge, Ella – Wilson, Fred G.
Downing, Priscilla R. – Clogston, Gerald A.
Downing, Viola B. – Robinson, Earl J.
Dubreuil, Wendy J. – Thibodeau, Brian C.
Dupuis, Yvonne S. - Blain, Wilfred F.
Durgin, Lorna Ann – Hemeon, John Ernest
Durocher, Estell A. – Duford, Leo N.
Duval, Mary A. – Lachance, Edgar A., Jr.
Duval, Nancy Ann – Cote, John Allan

Elliott, Addie M. – Howlett, Orrin D.
Ellsworth, Clara E. – Burnham, Isaac M.
Ewens, Ella Vera – Moses, Morton Maurice

Feinen, Anna H. – Finkel, Joseph P.
Ford, Delfen – Golden, Martin

Gallagher, Alice M. – Lamy, Richard P.

Galoway, Hazel P. (Andrews) – MacKenzie, Daniel A.
Gilbert, Joevana L. – Nganga, Paul K.
Gove, Linda Marion (Merrill) – Landry, Michael Anthony
Greenwood, Annie M. – Richardson, Chris.

Hall, Marrinette – Youngman, Burgess M.
Hammel, Peggy May – Carter, Albert Barnett
Handerson, Nellie E. - Fellows, Joseph E.
Hanley, Ruth E. - Greenleaf, Harold R.
Harriman, Virginia D. – Spead, James A.
Havenhill, Ann S. – Toutaint, Armand W.
Hazelton, Frances (Willey) – Merrill, Malcolm D.
Hazen, Jennie J. – Burnham, George N.
Hebert, Anne Carole – Cynoski, Chester Francis
Henry, Dianne M. (Kennedy) – Reynolds, David William
Higgins, Dawn Lee (Culbertson) – Hanley, Brad Loren
Higgins, Nella M. – Walker, Harold
Hill, Eunice C. – Maltais, Joseph W.
Hill, Veronica Lynn (Piascik) – Barton, Michael John
Howland, Louise A. – Bickford, Chester A.
Hull, Edith Goldy – Heath, Jere J.

Illick, Hilary Selden – Valette, Pierre Alexis

Jalbert, Jeanne Marie – Conkey, George Chester, II
Jerfie, Rose (Geeb) – Raynor, Albert F.
Jewell, Helen M. – Merrill, Henry M.
Johnson, Rita (Kouffman) – Lapham, Thomas W., Jr.
Jones, Yarrow A. – Farnsworth, Shawn P.

Kendrick, Elizabeth F. - Miner, James M.
Kennett, Amanda Marie – Kennedy, Dale David
Kidder, Blanche C. – Merrill, Henry M.
Kimball, Linda Marion (Merrill) – Gove, Ralph Lawrence
Kincade, Linda Jean (Kryzak) – Tenney, Harry Douglas
Knipfer, Margaret Rose – Ayres, George Little
Krahenbuhl, Elsie L. - Walker, Harold
Kummer, Janet M. – Skipper, Paul E.

Landon, Geri Lynn – Thibodeau, Donald Charles
Landon, Gloria (Parris) – Cummings, George William

Landon, Valerie G. – Denoncour, Maurice P.
Latuch, Betty Lou (Phinney) – Grigas, Albert P., Jr.
Lee, Nettie A. – Waldron, C. P.
Lemay, Mernie M. (Newhall) – Poitras, Clarence L., Jr.
Lennox, Kathleen M. – Williams, Gordon C., Jr.
Libby, Mark A. – Nicol, William B.
Loupis, Georgianna G. – Ryea, Carl C.

MacDonald, Lisa A. – Coffin, Daniel C.
Martel, Marjorie Priscilla – Carter, Richard P.
Martin, Etta M. – Fitts, John M.
Mason, Gertrude O. (Demus) – Baker, Hilton F.
Matava, Alice – Bickford, Arthur J.
Mayer, Lori A. – Reed, Robin E.
McCarthy, Rita M. – Lounge, Wayne F.
McGilvray, Beth Joan – Parker, Christopher Martin
McKinley, Marion E. – Delsart, Adolph W.
Melanson, Anne M. – Payne, Adrian J.
Melanson, Jennie – Morrison, Michael
Melanson, Kathleen J. – Carsson, Bjorn O.
Merrill, Linda M. – Kimball, Clyde C.
Merrill, Luna A. – Jesseman, Walter C.
Michaud, Valerie J. – Hession, John W.
Moreau, Susan A. – Somers, Patrick J.
Morin, Lena D. – Stewart, James S.
Morris, Anna L. (Lintaman) – Davies, Henry H.
Morse, Mary L. - Farr, Charles T.
Mortensen, Marion J. (Willey) – Quimby, John
Morth, Grace E. – Fraser, Thomas M.
Moses, Annie B. (Merrill) – Lahue, Dominic S.
Moses, Ruth Etta – Joslyn, Robert Dale
Motts, Martha A. (Cornell) – Chamberlain, Henry H.
Murray, Elizabeth H. - O'Keefe, James

Nadeau, Linda L. (Fryer) – Raymond, Guy T.
Newhall, Shelley Anne – Webster, Phillip Robert
Nichols, Lily B. – Merrill, Bernard L.
Noel, Valira D. – Mahoney, Edward D.

O'Haire, Antoinette (Doria) – Burnham, Isaac Hazen
O'Sullivan, Carrie Josephine (Bean) – Tibbetts, Harold Dana

Oakley, Maryann – Schmidl, Joseph

Parent, Lori A. – Daniels, Sargent B.
Parker, Annie C. (Wescott) – Reed, Caddie C.
Parker, Bertha B. – Quimby, Custer
Percey, Mildred E. (Brogan) – Hanley, Frank B.
Phillips, Deborah Ann – Hazelton, Walter Francis
Phinney, Martha Lorraine – Walker, Larry Harold
Plant, Marion A. – Kramer, William C.

Quimby, Ila Z. – Cole, Arthur M.
Quimby, Leona M. – Rowen, George W.
Quimby, Margaret E. (Colburn) – Conkey, Albert R.

Radowski, Tracy Anne – Ceravane, Joseph Dominic
Ray, Murial L. - Carr, Deane C.
Richardson, Marion V. (Dowry) – Wardwell, Ernest E.
Rock, Delia B. (Burnett) – Decato, William J.
Roland, Karen Marie – Yetman, David M.
Rosseau, Yevonne R. – Stevens, Joseph O.
Rourke, Kelley A. – Filteau, Donald E.
Rousseau, Alice – Soucy, Louis
Rowen, Elsie M. - Johnson, F. M.
Rowley, Majorie Violet (Parris) – Clogston, Albert Walter
Roy, Elaine A. – Young, Ralph L.
Ryea, Marion B. – Tarr, Herbert W.
Ryea, Muriel M. – Burnham, Kirk N.
Ryea, Thelma M. – Andrews, Clarence H.

Sanborn, Grace M. - Taylor, Zachary G.
Santolucito, Buffi Ann – Jones, Seth Allen
Sawyer, Melissa Winthrop – Horn, Kevin Joseph
Scotti, Susanne M. – Do, Lam K.
Short, Ethel F. (Allard) – Carter, Charles
Smith, Melanie F. – Kramer, William C., Jr.
Smith, Tammy Mari (Jantti) – Murdock, John Richard
Spead, Marjorie Ann – Parris, Brian Fletcher
Stevens, Phebe T. (Redding) – Merrill, Wilbur
Stewart, Abbie E. – Sears, Raymond L.
Stone, Paula Glen – Brown, Carl Russell
Stone, Sabrina S. – Joslyn, Brandon E.

Stone, Virginia Alice – Spead, Irving James
Strickland, Kathleen (Goode) – Denny, Clyde Allen

Tattersall, Emma – Gray, Bigby L.
Taylor, Clara A. - Breck, John L.
Thibodeau, Florence E. - Whitcher, Lester A.
Tilton, Bertha M. – Burnham, Frank W.
Toro, Cheryl Ann – Legg, John Jay Graydon
Towne, Rhonda Yvonne – Archibald, Charles Alan
Turke, Cindy Lee – Parker, Stev Y.

Valia, Ethel M. (Black) – Hazelton, Walter, Jr.
Viglione, Jean Barbara – Jennings, Rixford Owens
Vigneault, Laura – St. Pierre, Andre

Wagner, Louise K. (Kafga) – Clough, Hazen H.
Walker, Elsie K. (Krahenbuhl) – Downing, Richard L.
Walker, Katie Laura - Cayes, Reginald M.
Walker, Mary J. – deBlois, Romeo R.
Walker, Winona Beatrice – Eastman, Clayton Herbert
Wanamaker, Brenda L. – Lamphere, Russell J.
Ward, Lillian Aleta – Taylor, Frank Gilbert
Ward, Martha J. - Brooks, John A.
Watkins, Evelyn Priscilla – Young, Ira Morris
Weeks, June Caroline – Quimby, Roger Custer
Wellman, Jeanette E. (Wallace) – St. George, Arthur F.
Wescott, Mabel - Campbell, William C.
Wheat, Glia Muriel – Ashley, George S.
Wheeler, Barbara Charlotte – Burnham, Isaac Hazen
Wheet, Sarah L. – Bailey, Charles G.
Whicher, Eva J. – Good, Thomas
Wilkins, Eva G. – Waldron, Clarence P.
Willey, Ester U. (Cilley) - Churchill, Fred A.
Willey, Frances E. - Hazelton, Walter
Williams, Kathleen M. (Lennox) – Lambert, Tod W.

Yetman, M. Magdalene (Hall) – Higgins, Robert
York, Mary – Keezer, George W.
Young, Elaine A. (Roy) – Berry, Lawrence D.
Young, Sherrie Lee – Coleman, Charles Henry
Zwicker, Sharon M. (Bishop) – Conkey, Allen J.

DORCHESTER DEATHS

ACKER,
Marion Taylor, d. 11/7/1976 at 84 in Plymouth; b. Nashua; Elmer E. Roundy and Minnie L. Taylor

ALLEN,
Jeremiah B., d. 11/29/1910 at 72/5/13; kidney and heart disease; blacksmith; married; b. NB; William B. Allen (NB) and Alice Bronell (NB)

ANNIS,
Addie E., d. 2/5/1893 at 39/6/20 in Dorchester; housewife; married; b. Sharon, VT; Ira Joyce (Trenton, NJ) and Mary Waterman (Royalton, VT)

ARCHAMBEAULT,
J. J., d. 2/22/1923 at 63/8 in Dorchester; farmer; married; b. N. Slutey, Canada; J. Archambeault (Canada) and Lucy Coultire (Canada)

ASHLEY,
Alfred A., d. 12/19/1995 at 90 in Hanover; Alfred W. Ashley and Minnie O'Malley
Alfred W., d. 1/26/1959 at 91 in Plymouth; b. Alberton, Canada
Annie G., d. 7/19/1947 at 76/11/12 in Dorchester; at home; married; b. PEI; Benjamin Pollard and Elizabeth Mayhew (England)
Gertrude E., d. 5/28/1924 at 25/8/17 in Dorchester; nurse; single; b. Dorchester; Herbert Ashley (PEI) and Annie G. Pollard (PEI)
Herbert A., d. 7/18/1966 at 66 in Dorchester; retired; b. Dorchester; Herbert H. Ashley and Annie G. Pollard
Mary, d. 3/13/1958 at – in Plymouth; housewife; married; b. Colton, NH; James O'Malley and Catherine Brennan
Nella H., d. 4/24/1999 in Plymouth
Percy, d. 5/23/1916 at 22/7/27 in Ft. Slocum, NY; plural pneumonia; U.S. Navy; single; b. Wetask'n, Canada; Herbert H. Ashley (PEI) and Annie G. Pollard (PEI)

ATKINSON,
Thomas, d. 10/7/1891 at 2 in Dorchester; b. Manchester

AUTHIER,
Albert D., d. 2/7/1952 at 66 in Dorchester; carpenter; b. St. Hilaire,

Canada; Alfred Authier

AYERS,
Anna P., d. 6/19/1924 at 68/10/26 in Dorchester; housekeeper; divorced; b. Kingston; Joseph Cilley and Jane Davis (Kingston)

AYRES,
George Little, d. 6/13/1994 at 42 in Dorchester; George Little Ayres, Sr. and Joanne E. Spellenberg

BAGLEY,
Lillian, d. 2/26/1981 at 82 in Plymouth; Sigral Swensen and Jensiona Gustfsen

BARRY,
Edith, d. 6/22/1907 at 27 in Dorchester; tuberculosis; saleslady; divorced; b. Revere, MA; John Barry (Ireland) and Ellen McCarthy (Ireland)

BARTLETT,
Frederick B., d. 9/21/1971 at 37 on Smart's Mountain; b. NH; Richard L. Bartlett and Alta Haubrich

BEAN,
Bernard, d. 6/30/1946 at 22/2/8 in Dorchester; laborer; single; b. Orford; Philliph Bean (Orford) and Blanche Burnham (Dorchester)
Philliph, Jr., d. 6/30/1946 at 19/8/23 in Dorchester; laborer; single; b. Orford; Philliph Bean (Orford) and Blanche Burnham (Dorchester)

BELAIR,
Jean R., Sr., d. 11/1/1997 in Plymouth; Leonidius Belair and Reosealda Brosseau

BENNETT,
Jeanne K., d. 9/20/1971 at 47 on Smart's Mountain; b. DC; Harry T. Krummes and Elizabeth Dickey

BERGSTROM,
Helen, d. 8/30/1988 – noted by town clerk

BERRY,
Lancon D., d. 2/26/1901 at 44/5 in Dorchester; horse dealer; married; b. MI; Joseph Berry (N.E. States) and Sophia Brown (N.E. States)

BICKFORD,
Alice L., d. 1/14/1904 at 23/4/19 in Dorchester; housewife; married; b. N. Andover, MA; Isaac Martava (Danville, VT) and Nellie Woodhouse (Hardwick, England)
Charles A., d. 11/14/1895 at 0/6/29 in Dorchester; b. Dorchester; A. J. Bickford (Dorchester) and Mary Dubuque (North Hero)
Fred, d. 12/7/1900 at 23/4 in Dorchester; single; b. Dorchester; Albert F. Bickford (Dorchester) and Emma Norris (Dorchester)

BIGUE,
Philomen, d. 2/12/1895 at 58/11 in Dorchester; housework; b. St. Anne; Isidor Bigue and Agatt Lessier

BISHOP,
Alfred Joseph, d. 4/11/1975 at 63 in Dorchester; b. Ansonia, CT; George Bishop and Julia Hanna
Helena, d. 10/15/1977 at 71 in Hanover; b. CT; Herman Schelkowski and Bessie Bauer

BLACK,
Charles A., d. 12/26/1895 at 60 in Dorchester; farmer; married; b. Paisley, Scotland

BLAIN,
Francois, d. 7/3/1922 at 81/4/18 in Dorchester; retired; b. St. Michiel, PQ; John Blain (St. Constant) and Jovite Girouse (St. Constant)

BLAISDELL,
Eliza L., d. 2/5/1890 at 65/7/24 in Dorchester; married; b. Dorchester
Petengill S., d. 6/17/1891 at 39 in Dorchester; farmer; married; b. Dorchester; Pet. Blaisdell (Dorchester) and Laurett Lillis (Dorchester)
Pettengill, d. 5/23/1899 at 75/4/26 in Dorchester; farmer; widower; b. Dorchester; Sanborn Blaisdell and Mehitabel Sanborn

BLODGETT,
Sallie C., d. 10/2/1887 at 72/5/18 in Dorchester; housewife; widow; b. Henniker; David Clough and Abagail Davis

BRAILEY,
Clinton O., d. 2/27/1892 at 0/11 in Dorchester; b. Dorchester; Ormond Brailey and Ella Taylor

BRISSON,
Mary R., d. 2/1/1922 at 61/1/15 in Dorchester; housewife; married; b. Canada; Admir Bamfield (Canada) and Margarette ----- (Canada)

BROOKS,
David Edward, d. 7/25/1991 at 80 in White River Jct., VT; Frank A. Brooks and Liddia Lockhard
John W., d. 9/28/1898 at 54/9/10; farmer; married; b. Canada; John Brooks (Canada) and Angeline Cote (Canada)
William S., d. 11/1/1891 at 24/4/27 in Dorchester; laborer; single; b. Dorchester; John W. Brooks (Canada) and Sarah Z'mpear (Peachmont, VT)

BROWN,
J. S., d. 2/27/1911 at 53 in Dorchester; mitral endocarditis; married

BRYAR,
Iola M., d. 1/30/1964 at 79 in Haverhill; housewife; widow; b. Dorchester; buried – Riverside, Plymouth

BURLEIGH,
Scott David, d. 10/14/1938 at 75/3/14 in Dorchester; farmer; single; b. Dorchester; Gilman D. Burleigh (Dorchester) and Sarah N. Foster (Haverhill)

BURNHAM,
stillborn son, d. 3/3/1914 at – in Dorchester; stillborn; b. Dorchester; Frank W. Burnham (Dorchester) and Bertha M. Tilton (Alexandria)
Eliza A., d. 12/31/1922 at 71/10/15 in Dorchester; retired; widow; b. Wentworth; W. H. Kimball (Wentworth) and Mary Swain (Wentworth)

Frank W., d. 10/1/1926 at 42/0/18 in Dorchester; farmer; married; b. Dorchester; Frank Y. Burnham (Concord) and Josephine Colburn (Wentworth)

Frank Y., d. 4/19/1911 at 60/5/11 in Dorchester; appendicits; farmer; married; b. Concord; Nathaniel Burnham (Antrim) and Hattie B. Youngman (Wilmot)

George, d. 6/15/1956 at 74 in Haverhill; farmer; widower; b. Dorchester

Harriet B., d. 3/2/1908 at 81/10/17 in Dorchester; acute gastritis; widow; b. Wilmot; Jabez Youngman (Amherst) and Emma Baldwin (Hollis)

Isaac M., d. 7/5/1942 at 82/4/7 in Haverhill; laborer; widower; b. Wentworth; Isaac Burnham and Harriet Baldwin

Jennie J., d. 4/4/1954 at 69 in Dorchester; housewife; married; b. N. Hero, VT

Josephine, d. 12/18/1892 at 40/3/24 in Dorchester; housewife; married; b. Wentworth; Uriah Colburn and Betsey Smart

Nathaniel, d. 12/5/1906 at 87/0/23; chr. endocarditis; farmer; married; b. Antrim; Epps Burnham (Greenfield) and Sarah Cavendar (Greenfield)

Susie I., d. 4/4/1930 at 28/2/27 in Dorchester; housewife; married; b. Wentworth; Walter E. Chase (Wentworth) and Mary B. Smith (Orford)

BURPEE,
Gilbert W., d. 6/26/1890 at 28/6/23 in Dorchester; farmer; single; b. Dorchester; Marshall Burpee and Sophia Kidder

BURROWS,
Anna L., d. 6/8/1980 at 85 in Plymouth; Edward Fisher and Rhoda Johnson

Arthur N., d. 11/2/1974 at 79 in Jackson Hts., Queens, NY; b. Bronx, NY; Thomas Burrows and Debra Ryan

CAMP,
Guy Ellsworth, d. 11/26/1941 at 76/4/10 in Rumney; farmer; married; b. Ellsworth, VT; Harley W. Camp (Ellsworth, VT) and Mary E. Guyer (VT)

CANEDY,
Sherrill Allan (Buck), d. 10/2/1993 at 49 in Lebanon; Albert William

Canedy and Mary Helena Dolan

CARTER,
Arlene M., d. 12/30/1988 at 82 in Hanover; Arch Barnett and Melina Lamorey
Ernest, d. 4/15/1982 at 81 in Hanover; Caryle Carter and Arlene Barnett
James, d. 11/12/1956 at 54 in Dorchester; carpenter; married; b. Methuen, MA
Margaret, d. 12/2/1997 in Hanover; Onis J. Martel and Mildred Blood

CARY,
Joyce B., d. on or about 6/12/1982 at 55 in Dorchester; Ernest Boyce and Laura Wrisley

CHAMPAGNE,
Rose, d. 8/31/1943 at 50/3/16 in Dorchester; housewife; widow; b. Canada
Rudolph E., d. 7/16/1943 at 53/11/28 in Dorchester; highway patrolman; married; b. Pembroke; Alexander Champagne (Canada) and Clerine Provencher (Canada)

CHURCHILL,
Fred A., d. 5/20/1939 at 68/9/12 in Dorchester; farmer; married; b. Rone, MA; A. J. Churchill (Rone, MA) and Anna Cilley (Kingston)

CILLEY,
David F., d. 1/8/1933 at 75/3/12 in N. Dorchester; shoemaker; widower; b. Bridgewater, VT; Joseph C. Cilley (Dunbarton) and Katherine Jane Davis (Kingston)

CLARK,
daughter, d. 12/23/1902 at 0/0/17 in Dorchester; b. Dorchester; Conrad Clark (Germany) and Emma J. Hazen (N. Hero, VT)
Alice E., d. 2/4/1900 at 14/4/3 in Dorchester; b. Groton; Cyrus G. Clark (Groton) and Agnes D. Remick (Groton)
Ethel A., d. 4/13/1899 at 11/6/16 in Dorchester; b. Groton; Cyrus G. Clark (Groton) and Agnes D. Remick (Groton)
Mary, d. 1/15/1890 at 84/7/5 in Dorchester; housewife; widow; b. Dorchester; Benjamin Dow and Alice Burleigh

CLOGSTON,
Walter Lee, d. 1/30/1952 at 45 in Plymouth; mechanic; b. Lyme; Will Clogston and Ada Patch

CLOUGH,
Charles, d. 3/31/1913 at 86/6/6 in Dorchester; pneumonia; retired; married; b. Wentworth; Joseph Clough (Gilmanton) and Betsey Thompson (Gilmanton)
Elwin O., d. 1/25/1952 at 59 in Hartford, VT; lumber worker; b. Dorchester; Orrin O. Clough (Wentworth) and Dora Richardson (Goffstown)
Hazen H., d. 5/1/1935 at 73/4/11 in Dorchester; farmer; b. Dorchester; Joseph M. Clough (Gilmanton) and Harriett A. Bickford (Dorchester)
Jeremiah, d. –/–/1887 at – in Dorchester; farmer; married
Martha Pollard, d. 5/28/1891 at 74/0/14 in Dorchester; housekeeper; widow; b. Goffstown; David Pollard (Old Haverhill, MA) and Sarah G. Pollard (Goffstown)
Mary V., d. 6/10/1914 at 52/4/16 in Hanover; housewife; married
Myra M., d. 2/3/1912 at 33/2/6 in Dorchester; tuberculosis; single; b. Dorchester; Charles A. Clough (Dorchester) and Sarah Burnham (Dorchester)
Sarah E., d. 5/27/1900 at 42/11/7 in Dorchester; housewife; married; b. Wentworth; Nathaniel Burnham (Antrim) and Harriet Youngman (Wilmot)
Susan A., d. 9/29/1917 at 89/8/27 in Dorchester; retired; widow; b. Wentworth; Joshua Foster and Judith Nevans

COLBURN,
daughter, d. 1/4/1895 at – in Dorchester; b. Dorchester; James L. Colburn (Dorchester) and Sarah E. Brooks (Wentworth)
Margaret J., d. 1/7/1916 at 44/8/5 in Dorchester; valvular disease of heart; housekeeper; married; b. Lynn, MA; Hector Fraser (Montreal, Canada) and Nellie Munroe (Lynn, MA)
Mrs. George F., d. 5/31/1899 at 81/9/20 in Dorchester; housewife; married; b. Piermont; Daniel Mead and Mary Drew

COLMAN,
Carrie Gill, d. 3/3/1959 at 67 in Dorchester; b. Charlestown; residence – S. Wardsboro, VT

COMEAU,
Pearl D., d. 6/25/1994 at 77 in Dorchester; Chester Hinkson and Dorcas H. Gay

CONKEY,
Albert, Sr., d. 4/30/1988 – noted by Town Clerk
George C., Sr., d. 10/6/1997 in Dorchester; Albert R. Conkey and Irene Avery

CRAFTS,
Sam, d. 9/23/1930 at 68/11/11 in Dorchester; mail carrier; married; Ephriam Crafts and Charlotte Allen

CUMBERLAND,
Thomas, d. 8/11/1895 at 35 in Dorchester; cook; single

DAVENPORT,
Agnes, d. 3/3/1988 – noted by Town Clerk
John Charles, d. 10/6/1974 at 60 in Dorchester; b. Ayer, MA; Harry Davenport and Mary -----

DAVIES,
Henry Hiller, d. 8/28/1980 at 90 in Dorchester; buried – Mt. Calvary, Dorchester, MA

DAVIS,
Herbert H., d. 5/27/1902 at 33/9 in Dorchester; shoe cutter; single; b. Newmarket; John O. Davis (Greenland) and Hattie A. Davis (Exeter)
Nestor A., d. 9/12/1901 at 0/0/23 in Dorchester; b. Dorchester; Nestor H. Davis (Haverhill, MA) and Francis A. Pettit (Woodstock, Canada)
Rebecca, d. 5/27/1896 at 19/11/1 in Dorchester; housewife; married; b. Dorchester; Joseph A. Whicher (Wentworth) and Celesta Jefferson (Lisbon)

DECATO,
Bertha B., d. 1/28/1975 at 53 in Dorchester; b. NH; Dallas Decato and Exzelie Rameor
Joseph A., d. 8/16/1919 at 69/11/4 in Dorchester; farmer; single; b. Canaan; Charles Decato (Three Rivers, Canada) and Forties

Bushway (Three Rivers, Canada)

DELSART,
Adolph, d. 9/1/1974 at 79 in Hanover; b. NJ; Louis A. Delsart and Elsie Wagermann
Elsie, d. 3/13/1946 at 82/7/7 in Dorchester; housewife; widow; b. Germany; Fritz Wageman (Germany) and Maria Helington (Germany)
Henry, d. 3/12/1943 at 49/1 in White River Jct., VT; lumberman; single; b. Lakewood, NJ; Louis Delsarte (NY) and Elise Wagerman (Germany)
Louis A., d. 5/28/1916 at 74/8/18 in Dorchester; chronic Bright's disease; barber; married; b. New York City; Lewis T. Delsart (NY) and Marie Augustine
Marion, d. 4/8/1988 – noted by Town Clerk

DICEY,
Paul C., d. 5/21/1948 at 25/8/13 in Hartford, VT; farmer; single; b. Landeboro; George C. Dicey

DION,
Michael L., d. 3/4/1989 at 31 in Dorchester; Roland Dion and Edith Trudeau

DOLLOFF,
Frederick A., d. 6/15/1898 at 73/2/15; farmer; married; b. New Hampton; Asa Dolloff and Elmira Swan

DOW,
Frank W., d. 8/25/1903 at 50/11/3 in Dorchester; ex. messenger; married; b. Boston, MA; John R. Dow (Boston, MA) and Vilena Lore (ME)
John R., d. 3/30/1903 at 77/6/6 in Dorchester; cooper; single; b. Boston, MA; Simeon A. Dow and Lucy Young

DUNKERTON,
George Edward, d. 10/28/1989 at 73 in Dorchester; George Dunkerton and Sarah Bayberry

DUSTIN,
Ella H., d. 8/14/1988 at 87 in Ocala, FL; Alden L. Hall and Eliza J.

Bridgette

Harry Plumley, d. 9/28/1975 at 78 in Laconia; b. Canada; Adelbert Dustin and Cora Turner

ELLIOTT,
James P., d. 6/15/1915 at 77/10/17 in Dorchester; Bright's disease; retired farmer; married; b. Dorchester; James Elliott (Warner) and Theodate Waldron (Warner)
Lulu S., d. 4/11/1954 at 77 in Holderness; housewife; widow; b. Alexandria

ERNST,
Matilda Joanna, d. 9/19/1996 at 81 in Dorchester; Ernest Rogalski and Antonia Rowalski

FAIRBORNE,
Joan, d. 2/23/1940 at 0/8 in Manchester; black; b. N. Haverhill; Stewart Fairbourne (West Indies) and Mabel Gosselin (Canada)

FAIRBOURNE,
Stewart, d. 2/23/1940 at 44 in Manchester; farmer; married; black; b. Antigua, BWI; James Fairbourne (West Indies) and Sarah Jeffery (West Indies)

FAIRBURN,
Harriet, d. 1/7/1921 at 71/4/29 in Dorchester; housekeeper; widow; b. England; George Brown (England) and Elizabeth Penney (England)
John H., d. 2/17/1954 at 76 in Plymouth; lumberman; b. Hull, England
Winona M., d. 9/20/1936 at 59/1/14 in Dorchester; housewife; married; b. Lowell, MA; Harrison H. Noyes (Tunbridge, VT) and Euphemia Flanders (Tunbridge, VT)

FITZSIMMONS,
James F., d. 7/21/1919 at 47/9/25 in Dorchester; farmer; widower; b. Pinchney, MI; P. Fitzsimmons (Ireland) and Rose McGuire (Ireland)

FOLLANSBEE,
Herbert E., d. 7/28/1901 at 30/5/28 in Dorchester; school teacher;

married; b. Dorchester; Perley R. Follansbee (Danbury) and Mary A. McGrath

FORD,
Nellie, d. 4/6/1897 at 26/4/11; consumption; housewife; married; b. Groton; Abel Baily (Groton) and Jennie Willoughby
Stephen, d. 11/21/1904 at 14 in Dorchester; school boy; b. Wentworth; Israel Ford (Canada) and Mary Grover (Canada)

FORTIER,
Alfred, d. 1/15/1914 at 1/8 in Dorchester; whooping cough; b. Brentwood; Frank Fortier (Canada) and Margaret Murray (Hillsboro)
Delena, d. 2/6/1896 at 0/7 in Dorchester; b. Laconia; Joseph Fortier (Canada) and Leatine Chuping (Canada)

FOSTER,
Joshua, d. 4/7/1897 at 78/9/12; pneumonia; laborer; single; b. Wentworth; John Foster and Hannah Piper

FRENCH,
Barbara H., d. 1/25/2003 in Dorchester; Alfred Welch and Harriett Hoxie

FRYE,
Julius N., d. 8/23/1924 at 42/9/23 in Dorchester; salesman; single; b. Boston, MA; Morris Frye (Poland) and Hannah Soloman (Philadelphia)

GEEB,
Joseph, d. 4/30/1948 at 65/10/12 in Dorchester; machinist; married; b. Budapest, Hungary; Martin Geeb (Hungary) and Barbara Matizeka (Hungary)

GEORGE,
Fred B., d. 1/17/1895 at 36 in Dorchester; laborer; Asa K. George and A. A. Mansfield

GOODFELLOW,
Joseph, d. 9/6/1908 at – in Dorchester; old age

GOODSPEED,
Terry, d. 11/14/1997 in Wentworth; Edward Goodspeed and Evonne Caron

GOSS,
Adalina M., d. 10/3/1905 at 0/4/15 in Dorchester; spinal convulsions; b. Dorchester; Lester J. Goss (Andover, MA) and Kate Ackroyd (Undercliff, England)
Frederick L., d. 3/10/1972 at 75 in Plymouth; b. Dorchester; Lester Goss and Kate Ackroyd
Kate A., d. 6/29/1920 at 47/4/18 in Dorchester; housewife; married; b. Undercliff, England; Simeon Ackroyd (England) and Elizibeth Waltham (England)
Maggie Alice, d. 7/21/1900 at 1/5/8 in Dorchester; b. Dorchester; Lester J. Goss (Andover, MA) and Kate Ackroyd (England)
Ulysses S., d. 1/2/1990 at 88 in Meredith; Lester J. Goss and Kate Acriod

GRAY,
Delbert B., d. 6/23/1989 at 82 in Hanover; Delbert B. Gray and Maude Mudgett
Edith T., d. 11/15/2003 in Dorchester; William Trought and Ada Ainscough

GREGOIRE,
Joseph, d. 5/28/1909 at 44/10/17; consumption; single

GROCHOCKI,
Joseph, d. 9/1/1972 at 57 in Dorchester; b. Bronx, NY; Adam Grochocki and Mary Bukowski

GROVER,
George W., d. 6/12/1929 at 58 in Dorchester; lumberman; widower; b. Alexander, ME

HALL,
Alden L., d. 6/18/1951 at 76 in Dorchester; farmer; married; b. Canada; John N. Hall and Martha Blodgett
Walter R., d. 4/29/1887 at 90/5/20 in Dorchester; farmer; widower; b. Dorchester

HALLOWELL,
Morris L., d. 7/30/1963 at 75 in Plymouth; retired; married; b. Minneapolis, MN; buried – Mt. Auburn Crematory, Cambridge, MA
Nancy S., d. 3/30/1989 at 61 in Franklin; Lyman E. Snow and Ruth L. Briggs

HAMMOND,
Georgianna Isabel, d. 12/31/1994 at 77 in Dorchester; John Peter Cabral and Mary Gladys Frazier

HANLEY,
Ernest J., d. 7/2/1964 at 63 in Plymouth; lumberman; divorced; b. Dorchester; buried – Pleasant View, W. Rumney
Ernest J., d. 1/13/1996 at 69 in White River Jct., VT; Ernest Hanley and Edith Crosby
Gladys, d. 8/21/1992 at 89 in Texas
John Thomas, d. 9/4/1953 at 84 in Holderness; lumbering; widower; b. Princeton, ME; George Hanley and Anna Hill
Mary Elizabeth, d. 2/28/1952 at 80 in Dorchester; housewife; b. Greenfield, NB; Amos Brooks and Ann Mevelin

HANNON,
Doris R., d. 1/12/1981 at 52 in Hanover; Francis Jandro and Harriet Palmer

HAZEN,
Charles E., d. 6/15/1936 at 61/6/22 in Dorchester; farmer; divorced; b. Manchester; James Hazen (Goffstown) and Grace B. Rowen (Wentworth)

HILL,
Harold, d. 6/4/1922 at 25/6/20 in Dorchester; laborer; b. Norton Mills, VT; J. Hill (Coventry, VT) and Emma Brunnell (Newport, VT)

HOADLEY,
Elizabeth, d. 7/2/1988 – noted by town clerk

HODGE,
William Edward, d. 2/15/1960 at 54 in Dorchester; b. Corinth, VT; residence – W. Fairlee, VT

HOLMES,
Ella, d. 7/1/1914 at 36/2/7 in Dorchester; pernicious anaemia; housewife; married; b. Portsmouth; Charles Stover (Portsmouth) and Nellie Spinney (Portsmouth)
Lucina, d. 10/24/1921 at 81 in Dorchester; widow

HUMISTON,
George D., d. 7/15/1899 at 14 in Dorchester; b. NY; George Humiston (Chateaugay, NY) and Matilda Hero (Howache, PQ)

HUOT,
Bridget, d. 7/26/1905 at 70/11/20 in Dorchester; endocarditis; housewife; married; b. Canada; Stanislauss Camires (Canada) and Bridget Plante (Canada)

JENNINGS,
Edward, Jr., d. 10/15/1993 at 56 in Dorchester; Edward I. Jennings, Sr. and Margaret Borkowski

JESSEMAN,
George W., d. 3/11/1890 at 79/5 in Campton; clergyman; widower; b. Dorchester
Kate A., d. 3/26/1929 at 67/9/20 in Dorchester; housekeeper; widow; b. Orange; John Taylor (England) and Clarissa Stevens (Grafton)
William, d. 2/16/1928 at 78/3/14 in Dorchester; farmer; married; b. Dorchester; Gilman Jesseman (Dorchester) and Emeline Clock (Dorchester)

JOHNSTON,
Lucinda, d. 1/22/1916 at 60/6/11 in Dorchester; carcinoma liver; housewife; widow; b. Melbourne; Mathew Fleming (Belfast, Ireland) and Elizabeth Baxter (Belfast, Ireland)
Thomas, d. 9/21/1914 at 72/3 in Dorchester; arteriosclerosis; farmer; married; b. England; Thomas Johnston

JOYCE,
Annie Mae, d. 3/7/1961 at 58 in Dorchester; b. Clarksville
Charles W., d. 3/4/1976 at 83 in Plymouth; b. Canada; Herbert G. Joyce and Sarah Goodacre
George H., d. 3/20/1966 at 70 in Plymouth; retired; b. Holib, ME;

Herbert Joyce and Sarah Goodacre

Gretta E., d. 5/24/1986 at 87 in Dorchester; James Coleman and Percis Ord

KEARONS,
William M., d. 8/13/1948 at 70/5/22 in Dorchester; minister; married; b. England; George Kearons (Ireland) and Ann Maybresk (England)

KEEZER,
Daniel H., d. 7/12/1907 at 66/7/12 in Dorchester; shock; farmer; married; b. Hamstead; Jonathan Keezer and Louis Williams

Inez May, d. 8/4/1910 at 6/11/17; struck by lightning; b. Haverhill, MA; George W. Keezer (Haverhill, MA) and Mary York (Pittsfield)

KIDDER,
Laura, d. 10/29/1898 at 79/7/20; housewife; married; b. Hebron; Joseph Whipple and Lydia Blaisdell (Dorchester)

Laura M., d. 1/9/1931 at 75/6/8 in Dorchester; at home; single; b. Groton; Luther C. Kidder (Groton) and Laura Whipple (Hebron)

Luther, d. 4/23/1899 at 82/2/14 in Dorchester; farmer; widower; b. Groton; Jonathan Kidder (Amherst) and Susan Hall

Susan F., d. 6/8/1928 at 74/7/6 in Cheever; postmistress; single; b. Groton; Luther Kidder (Hebron) and Laura Whipple (Hebron)

KINSLEY,
Nathan B., d. 1/26/1902 at 78/5/12 in Dorchester; farmer; divorced; b. Grantham; Z. Kinsley (Easton, MA) and Johana Blodgett (Hudson)

KRAHENBUHL,
Charles Arthur, d. 12/28/1957 at 73 in Wentworth; baker; married; b. Switzerland

KRYZAK,
Jean M., d. 3/31/1998 in Lebanon; Ralph McLain and Evelyn Copeland

LACHANCE,
Edgar, Sr., d. 9/25/1971 at 72 in Dorchester; b. St. Samuel, PQ;

Andre LaChance and Mary Beaudoin

LAMOTTE,
Adolphus, d. 2/16/1890 at 75/9/23 in Dorchester; farmer

LANGMAID,
Alice M., d. 3/1/1901 at – in Dorchester; b. Lyme; George B. Langmaid (Brockton, MA) and Jessie Goodell (Hardwich, VT)

LEARNED,
John A., d. 1/16/1890 at 81 in Dorchester; farmer; married

LEAVITT,
Albert, d. 5/2/1893 at 64/10/23 in Dorchester; farmer; married; b. Canterbury; Joseph Leavitt (Northfield) and Mary Austin (Northfield)
Betsey M., d. 3/16/1898 at 80/4; housewife; married; b. Sutton, VT; Elisha Veasie (New Hampton) and Alice Dolloff (Meredith)

LINN,
Theodore F., Sr., d. 11/12/1981 at 85 in Dorchester; Max. C. Linn and Isabelle Carson

LITTLEFIELD,
Edwin, d. 11/15/1990 at 72 in White River Jct., VT; Edwin Littlefield and Annie Brown
Hiram, d. 2/10/1893 at 54/8 in Dorchester; hotel manager; married; b. Newburyport; Solo. Littlefield (Sanford, ME) and Sarah E. Welch (Shapley, ME)

LOTHROP,
Elizabeth, d. 6/25/1929 at 56/3/3 in Concord; housewife; married; b. Stoneham, MA; Lorenzo French (VT)

LYNDS,
David, d. 4/12/1910 at 52/7; Brights disease; farmer; widower

MACDONALD,
Blanche A., d. 9/29/2001 in Plymouth; Herbert Ashley and Phyllis Bean

MACKENZIE,
Edith M., d. 5/22/1964 at 61 in Hanover; housewife; married; b. Lynn, MA; buried – Pleasant View, W. Rumney

MANLEY,
George D., d. 12/29/1995 at 74 in Plymouth; James Manley and Ella Holmes

MARTEL,
Onis, d. 12/4/1974 at 73 in Haverhill; b. Canada; Thomas Martel and Mandy Tanpan

MATHEWS,
Thomas, d. 7/16/1905 at 30/7/24 in Dorchester; phthisis; clerk; single; b. Woburn, MA; Peter Mathews (Ireland) and Mary Morris (Ireland)

McGRATH,
Charlie E., d. 1/21/1890 at 11 in Dorchester; b. Dorchester; John McGrath and Ag'sta Wesc't
Ernest, d. 6/6/1887 at 1/9/1 in Dorchester; b. Dorchester; John McGrath (Dorchester) and Augusta Wescott (Dorchester)

MERRILL,
daughter, d. 1/2/1895 at – in Dorchester; b. Dorchester; Ber. L. Merrill (Dorchester) and Lilly B. Nichols (Wentworth)
Blanche C., d. 1/1/1896 at 19/0/2 in Dorchester; housewife; married; b. Groton; Mark B. Kidder (Groton) and Belinda Staples (Exeter)
Emma S., d. 1/5/1895 at 57/6/17 in Dorchester; housewife; married; b. Dorchester; Nel. F. Streeter and Ann Minard
Frank, d. 4/30/1895 at – in Dorchester; b. Dorchester; Henry M. Merrill (Dorchester) and B. C. Kidder (Groton)
Helen F., d. 2/9/1914 at 31/7/22 in Dorchester; pneumonia; housewife; married; b. Grantham; George W. Dunbar (Grantham) and Aurora Hemphill (New London)
Henry M., d. 11/18/1916 at 48/11/20 in Dorchester; valvular disease of heart; laborer; b. Dorchester; Louisa Follansbee (Danbury)
John S., d. 2/15/1919 at 81/8/24 in Warren; retired; b. Andover; John Merrill
Malcolm, d. 9/28/1985 at 76 in Hanover; Wilbur Merrill and Helen

Dunbar
Malcolm, 2nd, d. 7/11/1946 at 1/4/24 in Dorchester; b. Dorchester; Malcolm Merrill (Grantham) and Frances Willey (Meredith)

MERRITT,
Helen Josephine (Gert), d. 5/30/1993 at 75 in Lebanon; Gus Laware and Lucy Ammel

MILAY,
Jennie C., d. 7/4/1913 at 65 in Dorchester; Bright's disease; housewife; married; b. Ireland; Patrick Coleman (Ireland)

MITCHELL,
Ernest F., Jr., d. 12/2/1990 at – in Plymouth

MOODY,
Frank A., d. 3/24/1928 at 70/0/8 in Dorchester; farmer; single; John L. Moody

MORGAN,
Walter H., d. 9/13/2003 in Plymouth; R. Morgan and Rose Hamel

MORRISSEY,
Mary M., d. 7/1/2000 in Dorchester; James Lawnsby and Mary McDougall

MOSHER,
Ray Otis, d. 7/16/1890 at 0/4/5 in Dorchester; b. Dorchester; Ira C. Mosher and Mary Phelps

MUTCH,
Hannah, d. 6/15/1907 at 32/3/7 in Dorchester; rheumatism; housewife; married; b. Coventry, England; Thomas Perkins (England) and Ann Perkins (England)

MUZZEY,
Ossa Ann, d. 7/5/1906 at 52/9/20; heart disease; housewife; widow; b. Washington, VT; George W. Colby (Bradford, VT) and Roxanna Marks (Topsham, VT)

NELSON,
Henry, d. 6/17/1958 at – in Dorchester; molder; widower; b. Sweden; Nels Nelson and Anna Carter

NIMS,
Oscar B., d. 10/19/1942 at 50/8/4 in Dorchester; salesman; divorced; b. Keene; Louis A. Nims (Keene) and Martha Cutler (Keene)

NOEL,
Herbert C., d. 3/13/2002 in Dorchester; Franklin Noel and Beatrice Jermyn

NOYES,
daughter, d. 12/22/1919 at 0/0/2 in Dorchester; b. Dorchester; Harrison H. Noyes (Lowell, MA) and Iola M. Stevens (Rumney)
Euphemia M., d. 10/5/1914 at 69/4/23 in Dorchester; housewife; widow; b. Tunbridge, VT; George W. Flanders (Malone, NY) and Mary Cilley (Candia)
George B., d. 4/30/1904 at 54 in Dorchester; engineer; divorced; b. Woodford, VT; Hiram P. Noyes and Releafa Quimby

OSBORNE,
Mary J., d. 10/28/1906 at 1/0/11; cholera infantum; b. Franklin; Fred S. Osborne (Lindboro) and Florence Rogers

PARADIS,
Lesime, d. 8/26/1969 at 75 in White River Jct., VT; b. ME; Joseph Paradis and Adell Shorett

PARK,
William Humphrey, d. 10/31/1898 at 0/10/18; b. Plymouth; William R. Park, Jr. (Haverhill) and Elizabeth Dodge (Plymouth)
William R., d. 10/28/1920 at 65 in Dorchester; lumberman; widower; b. Haverhill; William Park and Lucy Ayers

PARKER,
John C., d. 10/7/1904 at 43/0/15 in Dorchester; farmer; divorced; Amos Parker
Valentine Fraser, d. 9/21/1992 at 60 in Lebanon; Cola Godden Parker and Martha Fraser

PARMALEAU,
Elise, d. 4/7/1941 at 85/0/27 in Dorchester; housewife; widow; b. Canada; ----- (Canada) and Bellon Jaubeau (Canada)

PERREAULT,
son, d. 1/5/1915 at – in Dorchester; stillborn; b. Dorchester; J. A. Perreault (Somersworth) and Leonie Tousignant (Canada)
Oreuse, d. 3/11/1911 at – in Dorchester; stillborn; b. Dorchester; James Perreault (Somersworth) and Leonie Tousignant (Canada)

PERRO,
Peter, d. 12/22/1890 at 29/4 in Dorchester; teamster; single; b. Canada

PETERSON,
Turner M., d. 4/1/1913 at 79/4 in Dorchester; general paresis; carpenter; widower

PITCHER,
David W., Jr., d. 9/9/1969 at 63 in Dorchester; b. Lebanon, CT; David W. Pitcher, Sr. and Edna Pitcher

POLLARD,
Elizibeth, d. 6/27/1920 at 82/3/24 in Dorchester; retired; widow; b. England; Thomas Mayhew (England) and Harriet Mayhew (England)

PORTER,
Robert A., d. 12/14/1941 at – in Dorchester; farmer; single; b. St. John, NB; Ford Fitch Porter (Halifax, NS) and Mary E. Rodeman (St. John, NB)

PROCTOR,
Arlene R., d. 2/2/2002 in Dorchester; Jesse Pye and Ruth Broderick

QUANCE,
Annie, d. 1/17/1970 at 84 in Lebanon; b. England; William N. Hinchliff and Martha Norman
Harry, d. 2/7/1955 at 64 in Plymouth; married; b. Lawrence, MA

QUIMBY,
Agnes F., d. 5/1/1925 at 73/11/13 in Dorchester; housewife; widow;
   b. Bedford; John Kenniston
Bertha, d. 12/2/1945 at 57/6/6 in Plymouth; housewife; married; b.
   Dorchester; John Parker (Dorchester) and Annie Wescott (New
   Britain, CT)
Clyde, d. 12/23/1973 at 89 in Canaan; b. Dorchester; John Quimby
   and Francena Kinson
Custer Burnell, d. 10/12/1962 at 83 in Dorchester; b. Dorchester;
   buried – Foster Cem., Wentworth
Daisy May, d. 12/31/1947 at 60/5 in Dorchester; at home; single; b.
   Dorchester; John Quimby (Manchester) and Francis Kennison
   (Bedford)
John, d. 11/21/1968 at 90 in Dorchester; retired; b. Dorchester; John
   Quimby and Agnes Francina Kinson
John, Sr., d. 3/4/1915 at 70/5/5 in Dorchester; cancer of face;
   mason; married; b. Manchester; John Quimby and Louisa Fish
Louisa, d. 2/2/1887 at 75/6/25 in Groton; housewife; widow; Joseph
   Fish and Clarrisa Shattuck
Stanley A., d. 6/25/1966 at 47 in Hanover; b. Dorchester; Custer
   Quimby and Bertha Parker

RAND,
Charlotte, d. 3/22/1893 at 65/7 in Dorchester; housewife; widow;
   James Elliott (Warner) and Theodate Walden (Warner)
John S., d. 2/7/1898 at 79/9/28; farmer; married; Moses Rand
   (Barnstead) and Sarah Calkins (England)

REBER,
Elizabeth A., d. 1987 – noted by Town Clerk

REED,
Aaron, d. 10/31/1892 at 84 in Dorchester; farmer; widower
Hiram, d. 9/1/1893 at 71/8/17 in Dorchester; farmer; widower; b.
   Dorchester; Aaron K. Reed (Westford) and Lydia Clifford
   (Wentworth)
Jesse B., d. 10/21/1928 at 78/0/15 in Dorchester; farmer; single; b.
   Dorchester; Jesse T. Reed (Dorchester) and Lucy Butterfield
   (Groton)
Joseph, d. 5/21/1893 at 77 in Dorchester; farmer; married; b.
   Dorchester; Aaron K. Reed (Westford) and Lydia Clifford

(Wentworth)
Silas F., d. 1/22/1914 at 58/5/12 in Dorchester; acute diarrhoea; farmer; single; b. Dorchester; Jesse F. Reed (Dorchester) and Laura Butterfield (Groton)

RING,
Ella G., d. 8/24/1895 at 20/4/6 in Dorchester; housewife; single; b. E. Farnham, PQ; James N. Ring (E. Farnham) and Emma Wilbur (E. Farnham)

ROBERTS,
Thomas W., d. 1/1/1930 at 72/0/6 in Dorchester; farmer; married; b. Dorchester

ROBY,
James M., d. 1/17/1892 at 77/0/13 in Dorchester; farmer; married; b. Hopkinton; Ellen Roby

ROUSSEAU,
Arthur D., d. 9/9/1943 at 60/11/26 in Dorchester; cook's helper; married; b. Canada; Didier Rousseau (Canada) and Rose Bounville (Canada)

ROWEN,
Elvira S., d. 8/23/1909 at 65/10/25; carcinoma; housewife; married; b. Wentworth; Rueben Whitcher (Wentworth) and Rebecca Foster (Wentworth)
George W., d. 12/14/1954 at 87 in Holderness; farmer; married; b. Dorchester
Helen W., d. 12/26/1890 at 65 in Dorchester; housework; married; b. Scotland
Leona Quimby, d. 1/2/19672 at 87 in Dorchester; b. Dorchester; buried – Pleasant View, W. Rumney
Mark W., d. 8/5/1895 at 5/9/11 in Dorchester; b. Dorchester; George W. Rowen (Dorchester) and Maud M. Buck (Canada)
Warren W., d. 9/26/1909 at 72/3/5; shock; farmer; widower; b. Wentworth; Jacob Rowen (Northfield) and Mary Copp (Sanbornton)

RUSSELL,
daughter, d. 6/1/1912 at 0/0/2 in Dorchester; lack of vitality; b.

Dorchester; Fred Russell (Turner, ME) and Eva Ellingwood (Hereford, ON)

Bryce, d. 11/10/1996 in MA

Ruth, d. 6/12/1912 at 0/0/13 in Dorchester; marasmus; b. Dorchester; Fred Russell (Turner, ME) and Eva Ellingwood (Hereford, ON)

RYEA,
Violet M., d. 11/15/1981 at 86 in Haverhill; William Prime and Alice Austin

ST. JEAN,
Eva R., d. 1/14/1925 at 15/4/15 in Dorchester; student; b. Gardner, MA; Moses St. Jean (Canada) and Ernestine L'fbrose (Canada)

ST. PIERRE,
Andre, d. 1/23/1903 at 60/0/12 in Dorchester; farmer; married; b. PQ; Pievoe St. Piere (PQ)

SALLS,
George M., d. 6/13/1943 at 67/0/1 in Dorchester; laborer; divorced; Melvin Salls and Lizzie Allen (NY)

SANTORO,
Anthony, d. 11/12/1992 at 64 in Plymouth; Stephen Santoro and Filomena Eligio

SAWYER,
Albion T., d. 4/19/1974 at 73 in White River Jct., VT; b. MA; Charles Sawyer and Mabel Warren

Mary B., d. 1987 – noted by Town Clerk

SCHOOLCRAFT,
Lydia, d. 9/23/1928 at 71/1 in Dorchester; housewife; married; b. Sycamore, IL; Ezera Keyes and Pauline Allen

SHACKFORD,
Emma R., d. 4/9/1921 at 77/3/30 in Lyme; housewife; widow; b. Antrim; Wells Robins and Emma Youngman

SMITH,

son, d. 3/5/1897 at –; debility; b,. Dorchester; W. S. Smith (Holderness) and Winnie Delms (Canada)

Emelius, d. 5/2/1893 at 88 in Dorchester; laborer; widow; b. Denmark

Paul Devens, d. 10/21/1961 at 74 in Lebanon; b. New York City, NY

STEVENS,

Lester Brydon, d. 11/9/1953 at 60 in Dorchester; lumbering; married; b. Orford; Warren Stevens and Phobe Reading

Samuel, d. 4/11/1892 at – in Dorchester; farmer; widower

Sarah, d. 10/22/1891 at 71/5 in Dorchester; single; b. Hudson; David Kendrick (Haverhill, MA) and Clarissa Blodgett (Hudson)

STONE,

A. R., d. 11/29/2001 in Lebanon; Hector McLean and Anna -----

STOORS,

Elizabeth, d. 7/31/1897 at 80/7/11; peritonitis; housewife; widow; b. Dorchester; James Dow and Sarah Noble

STORES,

Porter, d. 1/21/1892 at 75/8 in Dorchester; farmer; married; b. Lebanon; Constant Stores and Abagail

TAYLOR,

Mary E., d. 3/23/1913 at 62/11/14 in Dorchester; pneumonia; single; b. Grafton; John Taylor (Hecheam, England) and Charity Page (Grafton)

Zachary G., d. 1/28/1959 at 96 in Plymouth; b. Grafton

THAYER,

Allene Ohnstrand, d. 11/7/1982 at 89 in W. Palm Beach, FL; Eroch Ohnstrand and Hannah Johnson

Anne Nelson, d. 8/16/1992 at 89 in Dorchester; William B. Olmsted and Anne Starkweather

Robert W., Sr., d. 12/23/1998 in Plymouth; George A. Thayer, Jr. and Elizabeth Hicks Cox

William F., d. 1/28/1973 at 73 in Dorchester; b. Pt. Washington, NY; George A. Thayer and Elizabeth Hicks Cocks

THOMAS,
Addie E., d. 9/22/1904 at 51/6/17 in Dorchester; housewife; married; b. Leominster, MA; Carlton Buffum (Richmond) and Adaline Boardman (Cambridge, MA)

TIBBETTS,
Jeanette D., d. 5/22/1912 at 18/2/18; pneumonia; single; b. Lynn, MA; Dana Tibbetts (Palermo, ME) and Caroline Allen (N. River, NB)

TIBBITTS,
Dana, d. 6/1/1927 at 60/3/13 in Dorchester; farmer; married; b. ME; Benjamin Tibbitts (Liberty, ME) and Effie J. Turner (Palermo, ME)

TOTH,
Martha, d. 5/7/1955 at 94 in Dorchester; widow; b. Hungary

VERBECK,
Marie, d. 9/5/1906 at 64/6/16; Brights disease; housewife; widow; b. Paris, France; Jean M. LaPlat and Catharine Blais

WALDRON,
Maria C., d. 1/16/1902 at 66 in Dorchester; housewife; married; b. Dorchester; Samuel Clark and Betsey Rollins
Orrin H., d. 11/30/1904 at 62/11/19 in Dorchester; farmer; b. Dorchester; Nathaniel Waldron and Betsey Davis

WALKER,
Harold, d. 7/5/1958 at − in NY; construction; divorced; b. Lawrence, MA; Isaac Walker and Margaret Fairborn
Isaac D., d. 10/1/1927 at 59/9/5 in Dorchester; farmer; married; b. Lowell, MA; Edward Walker (England) and Mary Lynch
Margaret, d. 2/16/1946 at 70/0/27 in Bristol; housewife; widow; b. Hull, England; Francis Fairburn (England) and Harriett Brown (England)

WALLACE,
Alton E., d. 8/29/1887 at 28/2/16 in Dorchester; farmer; single; b. Dorchester; J. W. Wallace and E. J. Wescott

WEDEN,
Helen Augusta, d. 9/7/1975 at 70 in Laconia; b. NY; Albert ----- and Elizabeth -----

WESCOTT,
Elmira, d. 8/12/1905 at 90/13/1 (sic) in Dorchester; old age; housewife; widow; b. Springfield; Ebenezer Clough (Alexandria) and ----- Swett

WHEELOCK,
Robert C., d. 11/30/1916 at 77/9/5 in Dorchester; cerebral hemorrhage; retired; b. NS; Charles Wheelock and Hannah Baker (NS)

WHICHER,
Ada, d. 9/14/1891 at 1/3/9 in Dorchester; b. Dorchester; Joseph Whicher (Wentworth) and Celesta Jefferson (Lisbon)
Fannie E., d. 10/3/1899 at 0/0/4 in Dorchester; b. rx; Joseph A. Whicher (Wentworth) and Celeste Jepson (Lisbon)
Hattie B., d. 9/18/1896 at 34/1/21 in Dorchester; housewife; married; b. E. Haverhill; John W. Brooks (Canada) and Sarah Sampler (Peacham, VT)
Lydia A., d. 4/22/1914 at 52/0/6 in Dorchester; diabetes; housewife; married; b. Groton; George Willoughby and Jane Colburn
Samuel H., d. 6/11/1903 at 50/2/20 in Dorchester; farmer; married; b. Wentworth; Re[u]ben Whicher (Wentworth) and Rebecca Foster (Wentworth)

WHIPPLE,
Curtis Walter, d. 4/4/1957 at 75 in Hanover; none [occupation]; married; b. Florida, MA

WHITEHURST,
Frances Adair, d. 7/27/1996 at 75 in Lebanon; Bertram Whitehurst and Beatrice Hutchinson

WILLEY,
Eda May, d. 12/29/1930 at 53/0/29 in Dorchester; housewife; married; b. Campton; Daniel Sanborn (Highgate, VT) and Henrietta Eaton (Bethlehem)
Joseph M., d. 4/7/1949 at 76/10/17 in Concord; lumberman;

widower; b. Thornton; William Willey (Thornton) and Jane Drew (Thornton)

Winona M., d. 12/26/1936 at 5/7/4 in Dorchester; b. Dorchester; Edgar C. Willey (Farmington) and Mildred M. Clogston (Bradford, VT)

WOOSTER,
Lou L., d. 1/3/1892 at 25/11/16 in Manchester; housewife; married; Gardner Sibley and Ellen Sibley

WRIGHT,
Helen D., d. 8/12/2000 in Dorchester; James Gilchrist and Helen Burnhardt

YOUNG,
Alice L., d. 6/21/1987 at 71 in Plymouth; William E. Moses and Lillian S. Goss

Ralph L., d. 8/20/1978 at 34 in Orford; Stanley C. Young and Alice L. Moses

ZARR,
Randy R., d. 11/26/2002 in Plymouth; Paul Zarr and Lillian Plisko

Other books by the author:
Alton, New Hampshire Vital Records, 1890-1997
Barnstead, New Hampshire Vital Records, 1887-2000
Barrington, New Hampshire Vital Records
Dover, New Hampshire Death Records, 1887-1937
Gilmanton, New Hampshire Vital Records, 1887-2001
Marriage Records of Dover, New Hampshire, 1835-1909
Marriage Records of Dover, New Hampshire, 1910-1937
Milton, New Hampshire Vital Records, 1888-1999
Moultonborough, New Hampshire Vital Records
New Castle, New Hampshire Vital Records, 1891-1997
New Hampshire Name Changes, 1768-1923
New Hampshire Name Changes, 1923-1947
Ossipee, New Hampshire Vital Records, 1887-2001
Rochester, New Hampshire Death Records, 1887-1951
Vital Records of Durham, New Hampshire, 1887-2002
Vital Records of Effingham and Freedom, New Hampshire, 1888-2001
Vital Records of Farmington, New Hampshire, 1887-1938
Vital Records of New Durham and Middleton, New Hampshire, 1887-1998
Vital Records of North Berwick, Maine, 1892-2002
Vital Records of Orford and Piermont, New Hampshire, 1887-2004
Vital Records of Tamworth and Albany, New Hampshire, 1887-2003
Vital Records of Wakefield, New Hampshire, 1887-1998
Wolfeboro, New Hampshire Vital Records, 1887-1999

www.ingramcontent.com/pod-product-compliance
Lightning Source LLC
Chambersburg PA
CBHW060906300426
44112CB00011B/1369